Labor Arbitrator Development
A Handbook

Labor Arbitrator Development
A Handbook

Editors

Christopher A. Barreca
Labor and Employment Law Counsel
General Electric Company

Anne Harmon Miller
Arbitrator

Max Zimny
General Counsel
International Ladies' Garment
Workers' Union (AFL-CIO)

Associate Editor

Mary L. Fisher
Law Librarian
General Electric Company

American Bar Association
Section of Labor and Employment Law

The Bureau of National Affairs, Inc., Washington, D.C.

ACKNOWLEDGEMENTS:

"Judges and Arbitrators," by Lewis B. Kaden reprinted with permission of Columbia University.

Selections from *Dispute Resolution Training*, *Labor Arbitration Rules*, and *Expedited Labor Arbitration Rules* reprinted with permission of the American Arbitration Association.

LIBRARY OF CONGRESS CATALOGING IN PUBLICATION DATA

Main entry under title:
Labor arbitrator development.
    "Section of Labor and Employment Law, American Bar Association."
    Bibliography: p.
    Includes index.
    1. Arbitration, Industrial—Study and teaching.
    2. Arbitration, Industrial—United States—Handbooks, manuals, etc. I. Barreca, Christopher
A. II. Miller, Anne Harmon. III. Zimny, Max. IV. American Bar Association. Section of Labor and
Employment Law.
HD5481.L24   1983   331.89′143′07073   83-10129
ISBN 0-87179-413-6
ISBN 0-87179-430-6(pbk)

Printed in the United States of America
International Standard Book Number: 0-87179-413-6 (regular edition)
0-87179-430-6 (student edition)

Foreword

As the practice of labor and employment law has continued to grow, one of the increasing needs of the profession has remained unfulfilled: the development of additional arbitrators acceptable to the parties. This problem is particularly acute since selection of an arbitrator to resolve disputes is performed by the parties to the disputes largely on an ad hoc basis. We are therefore pleased that the Committee on Labor Arbitration and the Law of Collective Bargaining Agreements of the American Bar Association's Section of Labor and Employment Law recognized the need and took major steps toward meeting that need by conceiving, constructing, and executing a pilot arbitrator development program.

We are grateful to former Section chairman Jay S. Siegel for stimulating the program, and we wish to commend the efforts of the former co-chairmen of the Section's Committee on Labor Arbitration and the Law of Collective Bargaining Agreements: Christopher A. Barreca, Anne Harmon Miller, and Max Zimny. They carried the program through to completion and capped that effort with publication of this book. We wish to commend also the members of the subcommittees of the Arbitration Committee, whose good work contributed to the success of the undertaking.

Charles G. Bakaly, Jr.
1981–82 Chairman
Bernard F. Ashe
Chairman
Eugene L. Hartwig
Chairman-Elect
ABA Section of Labor and
Employment Law

June 1983

Preface

*Nothing is impossible, we only
haven't discovered how to do it.*

Emerson

In 1960, as a newly appointed member, I attended a meeting in New York City of the American Bar Association's Labor Law Section's Committee on Labor Arbitration. Practically the entire session was devoted to the problem of developing new arbitrators to replace the rapidly depleting ranks of the War Labor Board-experienced arbitrators. In the fifteen years which followed, Section members commiserated about the situation as giants such as David Cole, Aaron Horvitz, and Saul Wallen died and others aged. There were glimpses of up-and-coming professional arbitrators, but they were few in number and unable to cope with the ever-increasing tide of cases using the unique and valued process of grievance arbitration to dispose of disputes during the life of collective bargaining agreements.

A few national companies and the unions that regularly utilized arbitration embarked on their own training programs, as did some of the specialized industrial relations groups at various universities and the National Academy of Arbitrators, but these were efforts in isolation. What was really needed was the development of a basic program that could be used by any group in the country interested in trying to assist neophyte arbitrators to gain that initial reservoir of knowledge that would safely guide them past the dangerous shoals encountered in the early cases of their careers. It was this need which led me to propose the Pilot Arbitrator Development Program when I became Section Chairman in 1977.

It did not easily find support in either labor or management circles. The Council of the Section took the initial step of voting $5,000 as seed money. The major impetus, however, came from the Ford Foundation's agreement to contribute $25,000 of funding, if matched by contributions from business and labor. Credit for providing the equivalent capital came from these organized labor groups: United Steelworkers of America, the United Auto Workers Union, and the International Brotherhood of Teamsters. On the management side, U.S. Steel Corporation, Colt Industries, Inc., General Motors Foundation, Inc., International Telephone & Telegraph Corporation, ACF Industries, the FMC Foundation, and the Torrington Company were equally generous in their donations.

The chairpersons of the Section's Labor Arbitration and the Law of Collective Bargaining Agreements Committee, Anne Harmon Miller, Christopher Barreca, and Max Zimny then took over the task. The details of their efforts and the way the overall program was first structured and then implemented are related in the Introduction that follows. The Introduction is essential to understanding how the program works. I earnestly commend reading it before going on to the actual details for starting up a development project in your own area.

The Program was conducted on an experimental basis to avoid overcommitment to a fixed approach and to identify unworkable procedures. This how-to-do-it manual describes a model developmental structure that is highly mobile, sturdily constructed, and tested under actual conditions in the arbitration field. It is there to be used by all parties to the process of arbitration.

I want to express my personal appreciation to the many Section members who lent their support in a variety of ways to this important project. Their efforts serve to reinforce Emerson's comment. It is hoped that the success of the pilot program will become evident during the 1980s as groups throughout the country use it to develop a new cadre of knowledgeable persons entering labor arbitration as a career. In this way, the Section of Labor and Employment law will have made a lasting professional contribution of which all its members can be proud.

Jay S. Siegel

Hartford, Connecticut
December 1, 1981

Sponsors of ABA Pilot Program

ACF Industries
American Arbitration Association
Colt Industries
Columbia University
Federal Mediation and Conciliation Service
FMC Foundation
Ford Foundation
General Electric Company
General Motors Foundation
International Brotherhood of Teamsters, Chauffeurs, Warehousemen and
    Helpers of America
International Ladies' Garment Workers' Union
International Telephone and Telegraph Corporation
International Union, United Automobile, Aerospace and Agricultural
    Implement Workers of America
The Torrington Company
United States Steel Corporation
United Steelworkers of America

Contributors

C. Christopher Alberti
Debevoise, Plimpton, Lyons
    & Gates
New York, N.Y.

Arvid Anderson
Office of Collective Bargaining
New York, N.Y.

Richard I. Bloch
Arbitrator
Washington, D.C.

John L. Bonner
U.S. Dept. of Labor
Washington, D.C.

Marc H. Cahn
Cornell University
Ithaca, N.Y.

John Canestraight
formerly Federal Mediation
    and Conciliation Service
St. Louis, Mo.

Thomas T. Colosi
American Arbitration Association
Washington, D.C.

James K. Cook
Schuchat, Cook & Werner
St. Louis, Mo.

Joseph K. Costello
Siegel, O'Connor & Kainen, P.C.
Hartford, Conn.

Robert Coulson
American Arbitration Association
New York, N.Y.

David E. Feller
University of California
Berkeley, Cal.

Lewis T. Gardiner
Meserve, Mumper & Hughes
Los Angeles, Cal.

Joseph F. Gentile
Arbitrator
Los Angeles, Cal.

Raymond Goetz
University of Kansas
Lawrence, Kan.

Margery F. Gootnick
Arbitrator
Rochester, N.Y.

Alice B. Grant
N.Y. State School of Industrial
    and Labor Relations
Rochester, N.Y.

C. Brian Harris
Federal Labor Relations Authority
Washington, D.C.

Michael F. Hoellering
American Arbitration Association
New York, N.Y.

Robert G. Howlett
Arbitrator
Grand Rapids, Mich.

Joseph Jacobs
Jacobs & Langford
Atlanta, Ga.

Lewis B. Kaden
Columbia University
New York, N.Y.

Burton Kainen
Siegel, O'Connor & Kainen
Hartford, Conn.

Theodore W. Kheel
Battle, Fowler, Jaffin,
    Pierce & Kheel
New York, N.Y.

Arthur D. Kelso, Jr.
Bureau of National Affairs
Washington, D.C.

Jean T. McKelvey
Cornell University
Ithaca, N.Y.

Robert E. Meade
American Arbitration Association
New York, N.Y.

Bernard D. Meltzer
University of Chicago
Chicago, Ill.

Paul Prasow
University of California
Los Angeles, Cal.

William E. Roberts
Roberts, Ryder, Rogers
    & Neighbours
Indianapolis, Ind.

Eric Schmertz
Hofstra University
Hempstead, N.Y.

L. Lawrence Schultz
formerly Federal Mediation
    and Conciliation Service
Washington, D.C.

Ralph T. Seward
Arbitrator
Washington, D.C.

Jay S. Siegel
Siegel, O'Connor & Kainen
Hartford, Conn.

Michael I. Sovern
Columbia University
New York, N.Y.

Janet M. Spencer
St. John's University
New York, N.Y.

Steven H. Spencer
Morgan, Lewis & Bockius
Philadelphia, Pa.

Theodore J. St. Antoine
University of Michigan
Ann Arbor, Mich.

Jeffrey B. Tener
Rutgers University
New Brunswick, N.J.

Edwin R. Teple
Arbitrator
Willoughby, Ohio

Dennis H. Vaughn
Paul, Hastings, Janofsky
    & Walker
Los Angeles, Cal.

Judith P. Vladeck
Vladeck, Elias, Vladeck,
    & Engelhard
New York, N.Y.

Arnold M. Zack
Arbitrator
Boston, Mass.

Introduction

> *Of the various executive abilities, no one*
> *excited more anxious concern than that of*
> *placing the interests of our fellow-citizens*
> *in the hands of honest men, with*
> *understanding sufficient for their stations.*
>
> *Thomas Jefferson*

    This book provides a manual for training acceptable labor arbitrators. It can be used with local variations by groups and individuals concerned with the increasing need for acceptable neutrals in the private and public sectors. The editors believe the book provides a substantive as well as a procedural model for developing competent neutrals. In addition, the book creates a reference source for would-be arbitrators, practitioners, and experienced arbitrators generally, as well as for those who participate in internship or other arbitral training programs. The book can also serve as a text for university academic seminars in labor or industrial relations courses.

    Lectures delivered at the residential portion of the pilot program by several respected members of the arbitration community include the inspirational words of Ralph Seward, the scholarly historical presentation of Bernard Meltzer, the practical advice of Theodore St. Antoine, the insightful ruminations about arbitrator lifestyle of Richard Bloch, the thoughtful exposition of public sector issues by Arvid Anderson, the incisive evidentiary discussion of Eric Schmertz, the expository flow of Arnold Zack, and the crisp explanation of David Feller. These selections are valuable as a substantive portion of a learning program and should prove of great interest to anyone familiar, or hoping to become familiar, with the field of arbitration. Completing the Primer section is Lewis Kaden's piece on the impact of the judiciary on the arbitral process, a topic he addressed at a mid-winter meeting of the ABA Committee on

Arbitration and the Law of Collective Bargaining Agreements and later developed into the article reproduced here.

As editors we have summarized the history of arbitrator training and development antecedent and subsequent to the program. We have included the comments of some of the principal architects of labor arbitrator development programs in the excerpts reprinted from the Selected Proceedings of the Second Wingspread Conference. We have drawn from experience gained in operating the pilot program and reflect those experiences in Part IV, A Manual for Training, which is addressed to program sponsors and individuals hoping to develop an arbitration practice on their own. Part VI brings together valuable source material for arbitrator training. Informal discussions concerning the life and logistical practices of arbitrators as well as the expectations of the parties will be helpful to the aspiring arbitrator and also may answer some of the questions parties may have hesitated to put to those arbitrators to whom they submit their cases.

The arbitration cases included in Part V were chosen to reflect variety of writing styles of well accepted arbitrators responding to diverse arbitral issues. We have designed the questions which follow each decision to induce an appreciative as well as analytical consideration of the decision.

For ease of reading, the pronoun and the possessive form for arbitrator are uniformly masculine and should be read to cover both masculine and feminine.

We wish to thank Angela Weir, who painstakingly typed the many drafts which were synthesized into the final manuscript.

Contents

Part III— A Review of Arbitrator Development and Training

Part IV— A Manual for Training

Part V— Selected Decisions

Part VI— Selected Training Materials

Part I

A Primer for Arbitrators

The schoolmaster is abroad, and I trust to him, armed with his primer, against the soldier in full military array.

Henry Peter,
Lord Brougham

The Special Role of an Arbitrator

Ralph Seward

It occurred to me while I was sitting in the Nantucket Airport one morning that Nantucket was very much like the typical arbitration case. I was sitting in the middle of two very large centers of high pressure which were circulating varying degrees of cold logic or hot air, with the result being endless mountains of fog. Those of you who have arbitrated or will arbitrate cases will go through the experience of sitting in the fog for a long time wondering when, if ever, you are going to come out of it. Eventually you will have the feeling of rising above the fog, looking back, and seeing the territory below for which you have been searching and waiting so long.

Later chapters deal with what an arbitrator ought to know to meet present-day problems of procedure, precedent, and past practice, and present-day factors involving impingement of outside law on the function of an arbitrator. It may help to understand what is going on today if I review what went on yesterday and how the area of arbitration got to where it is now.

Genesis of Arbitration

I can go back only to World War II and the War Labor Board, but arbitration did not begin in this country with the War Labor Board. Earlier, the railroad industry devised its form of arbitration. The coal industry had a permanent umpire system in which the arbitrator never handled hearings and based his decisions on transcripts taken in the field. Hart, Schaffner and Marx had a permanent umpire system. A single arbitrator did a marvelous job for many years in the laundry industry in New York City. There were many systems, and in those days arbitration was something very special, unusual, and unknown to most people.

3

Arbitration was something not understood by most of American industry. It was new, wanted by some people, feared and objected to by others, and forced on them on a mass basis. There was the great pressure of quick mass organization under the combined impetus of the Wagner Act and the push by the exigencies of World War II. It was realized very soon that with a labor contract, disputes followed over its meaning. Much as one side or the other might want to, one could not strike over all disputes. There had to be some way to deal with them, and this curious thing called arbitration seemed a way. Turning over to someone else the settlement of things which seem so important that the parties cannot settle them themselves is indeed a paradoxical kind of solution.

In spite of past experience with arbitration which had worked, there was still a basic suspicion and fear of arbitrators. How could they not try to ingratiate themselves by throwing one decision one way and the next decision the other way, or not try to keep themselves in business by making friends of the parties and winning the parties' gratitude? I remember one of my early cases in 1943, when I was arbitrating in the milk industry on a permanent basis. One of the first ad hoc cases I undertook was with a little machine shop in Connecticut against which twelve grievances had been filed by the local machinists. I went up to a small Connecticut town and heard the cases in the basement of the plant. I thought that the union was groping and fumbling around, and did not have a leg to stand on contractually except for one case. In that one instance I felt they had a very good argument although technically there might have been some questions in some areas. Basically I felt the union was right. I came out with eleven decisions for the company and one for the union. About six months later, I encountered the company attorney in an elevator in New York. He told me how much he appreciated those decisions, and added that with respect to the last decision, he understood why I felt I had to give at least something to the union. That was the attitude. It was apparently impossible for anybody to believe that an arbitrator could call all the cases in a group as he saw them. Many companies, even though they had a large number of grievances, would insist on having only one case heard at a time because they were afraid that if the arbitrator decided one case for the company, he would be likely to decide the next one for the union. They would get another arbitrator to hear the next case.

It used to be very rare for a company or union to allow an arbitrator, if there was a jurisdictional question, to decide the question of jurisdiction and then proceed, if he held he had jurisdiction, to decide the merits. I remember an associate of mine, Rolf Valtin, having a very difficult jurisdictional issue involving a small company which insisted on hearing the jurisdictional issue separately. He was quite convinced that the company was right on the merits but was wrong on jurisdiction, so he decided the jurisdictional issue for the union whereupon the company, convinced that if it brought him the question on the merits he would also decide for the union, settled the case, although it was, he thought, an open and shut case for the company on the merits.

Three-Man Boards

Fear had an impact on the early formation of arbitration structures, and that impact persists. Some of the structures are hangovers in many respects from those early days. I suggest that the frequency with which arbitrators serve as the impartial member of a three-man board on grievances and contractual interpretation issues goes back to those days. It reflects the desire of the parties to protect themselves against the unknown and to be involved in the decision-making process, even though the tendency of a three-man board is simply to reargue the case *in camera*. If the partisan members of a board are trying to separate themselves and not present the case all over again, which is rare, the arbitrator may find himself asked to mediate the meaning of words and the interpretation of language of the agreement, which can sometimes be a strange process indeed. However, the three-man board had, and often still has, a second and most valuable function: that of helping to educate the arbitrator. How can an arbitrator who has never worked at a machine, does not know the language, and has never met a payroll really understand the case? Conveying this knowledge, particularly when having to work through lawyers and the sieve of procedural protections and objections to evidence in a formal arbitration procedure, is sometimes still a problem. The parties felt that when their own representatives could be part of the three-man board to help the arbitrator in the decision-making process, they could be of help in this educative process. It certainly is possible for the partisan board members to fill in the gaps in the arbitrator's knowledge of technical processes, local practices, and understandings not contained in the record. However, it can put the arbitrator serving on a three-man board on very shaky ground when, for example, partisan members expand *in camera* on what they know about the case. Should they be stopped and the arbitrator be confined to the record, or when should he ask what was behind the argument in the record when he does not understand it? Should he ask what it meant, encouraging the parties to give him a clear idea of the real facts?

Suppose the partisan members want to agree to agree to settle the case. The arbitrators obviously cannot settle the case themselves. They are not the company and the union and do not have authority to settle. It is always possible at any time for the company and the union, having agreed to settle, to interrupt the proceeding and take the case away from the arbitration board. I am sure that this has happened, that when the partisan members of a tripartite board listen to the impartial member and realize what kind of award he may issue, both sides get together and settle. If they want to, they can, of course, go back and tell their parties to settle the thing. The parties can adopt a joint company-union position on the resolution of a grievance, following which the impartial member has to make up his mind. He may be in the position of having a decision come out signed by the company and the union members of the board with himself dissenting. This happened only once to me.

Realistically, it puts the arbitrator in a very difficult position. It is very easy to say that the arbitrator has to make up his mind and stand his ground and not let the parties dictate his decision. That is right. Remember that the two other members of the board always know more about the union, company, and the problem than the neutral arbitrator ever will. They may not be as expert on some of the technical aspects, but as far as the problem is concerned and as to what makes sense, an arbitrator who defies or disregards the joint opinion of his fellow board members must act with great caution and hesitation. It is not an easy decision to act otherwise. If an arbitrator is sensitive to this position, nine times out of ten it can and should result in a unanimous decision of the board.

Permanent Arbitrators

Another approach in meeting the problem of educating the arbitrator was the development of permanent arbitration, that is, hiring an arbitrator not for an individual case, but for all the cases that arose during the life of the contract, for two or three years, or until one side or the other, or both parties, fired him. This, of course, was a bold leap into the dark in those early years, and a drastic move away from basic distrust of an arbitrator. It was also a bold step towards solving the knowledge problem, because it did not take an arbitrator very long to become familiar with the language, practices, and people in the industry on both sides and learn the background which makes otherwise unintelligible cases highly intelligible in realistic terms. There was widespread confusion and end-less argument in those days over the basic objective of arbitration. What was the purpose of this institution, and what was an arbitrator supposed to try to do?

In a typical hearing room, there might have been on one side, expert experienced trial lawyers hired from a large law firm, and on the

other side, members of a grievance committee who had never been in
an arbitration case or a legal procedure before. Each side expected very
different things from the arbitration process. The lawyer expected a
decision on the basis of the narrow and sometimes legalistic interpretation
of language. The union men expected the arbitrator to do justice: their
attitude was that to settle problems with the company they looked to get
a fair-minded man to arbitrate and hand down a decision as to what was
fair and right.

Broad Jurisdiction

Because everybody admitted that arbitration was an adjunct to
collective bargaining and the grievance procedure, sometimes both parties considered arbitration as a continuation of the settlement procedure.
A good arbitrator would find himself mediating the cases more often than
deciding them. Some parties regarded arbitrators as mediators or judges,
sometimes as the person to give the answer at the end of an informal
conversation. I remember in the early days going to Ohio to arbitrate a
case and being ushered into a lounge outside the office of the vice-
president for industrial relations. Some union grievance committee men,
company officials, and foremen were sitting together, informally discussing the weather and baseball scores. Then somebody on the company
side said to somebody on the union side, "Well, Bill, why don't you tell
Mr. Seward what this is all about." Bill began, "We've got a problem
down in such and such department. The other day this happened. The
foreman, Joe, did this, and we didn't think he was right. Isn't this the
question, Joe?" Joe would say, "Well, it didn't come up quite that way."
A discussion followed. And finally somebody who knew a little bit more
about it was sent for, and at the end they said, "Mr. Seward, what is
the answer?" That was arbitration as they knew it then. It was the form
of arbitration the parties wanted, and I gave them the best answer I
could off the cuff.

At about the same period, on an ad hoc basis, I went to arbitrate
a case and was ushered into a federal courtroom which happened to be
vacant, the federal court being on vacation at the time. I found myself
sitting up on the judge's bench with three law firms before me, swearing
witnesses and having motions for dismissal and summary judgment and
all of that sort of thing. Again this was arbitration, in the form these
parties expected and wanted.

In 1942, I was hired as impartial chairman of the milk industry in
Metropolitan New York. The milk industry had a contract with five locals
of the Teamsters and many different groups of employers. The companies

were competing with each other. All the milk drivers who worked on a commission basis were competing with each other. Everybody was suspicious of everybody else, and they could not agree to much. Adopting a word from the newspapers, they agreed to hire a czar. They asked the War Labor Board to appoint one. I was appointed as impartial chairman of the milk industry. In their contract they gave me authority to decide all questions of the language of the agreement and all disputes between the parties on other matters not covered by the agreement. I had power to decide how much milk should be put on any truck in New York, what hours they should leave the plant and come back, and so forth. This was an example of a complete abdication by management and labor in favor of an arbitrator because they had to do something to settle their disputes and stay in business. This was a complete problem-solving approach to arbitration; interpreting the contract was an adjunct. It was not an approach that I would recommend, but it was arbitration.

At the same time I got a request from a large steel company and the steelworkers union to arbitrate a dispute which was unique in my experience, concerning a department of a tin mill which sorted sheets for defects, a job done largely by women employees. The question was about overtime for the women and application of the overtime language of the agreement to certain situations in this department. Along with the request that I arbitrate, the parties sent me copies of their agreement, an agreed-upon statement of facts and the issues involving interpretation of this language, two argumentative briefs, and two draft decisions. They asked me to read the documents and briefs, and sign one of the two decisions. They did not want an arbitrator going all over the lot solving problems; they wanted to know what the language meant.

This variety in approach, this groping and experimenting, was typical of arbitration in those days. For a time, as the institution developed, a number of companies and unions deliberately adopted the problem-solving approach. I remember George Taylor telling about his experience as a permanent arbitrator in a Philadelphia textile company. When he took the job, they gave him one rule, that in deciding a case he was not to pay any attention to any decision he had ever made before. They wanted him to decide each case on its own merits, solving the problem presented as best he could.

Interpreting the Contract

Most companies and unions now have adopted the approach, with some variations, that the task of the arbitrator is not to develop his own solutions to plant problems but to apply to those problems the language of the agreement without adding, subtracting, or altering that language. That leads to the basic question which concerns arbitrators: how is the contract language to be interpreted and given practical meaning? The parties soon discovered that it was not enough simply to say that it was the arbitrator's task to interpret the language of the agreement, but to solve problems. They realized that the language of the agreement did not meet their problems the way they wanted and that the real question was not just to interpret the language cold but to interpret the language as it applied to the problem. What did the parties mean by those words, not necessarily in accordance with the dictionary, but as those words applied to the situation in Department 105 where they are annealing steel?

I suggest that although arbitrators operate between management and union and feel a tension between making one side happy and one side mad, the tension in case after case is really between the language and the problem. An arbitrator mediates between words and reality, how in a given case to make sense of language which does not by itself make sense. To what extent should the arbitrator follow the grammar and syntax, and to what extent is he free to depart from grammar to meet realities? To what extent is he free to interpret the meaning of the *absence* of applicable language in the agreement? What implications can he draw from the fact that the parties did not think it necessary to say certain things in the agreement? Could it be that the absence of a stated rule means that the rule was so much a part of their lives and understandings that they did not think it necessary to state it?

What is the meaning of the term job? It is a good word, defined in the dictionary. That one word is used in many different ways in different provisions of the contract, meaning a specific operation of a machine, a kind of work or product, something that the industrial engineers classify, or a position that one gets by seniority. These meanings are not the same. The arbitrator cannot tell what meaning the parties intended to give the word, unless he looks at the potential problem they had in mind when they were drafting the specific provision of the agreement that is involved in the case before him.

Developing Procedures

Other problems arose as the institution of arbitration developed. What kind of procedure should be used? Should it be a formal courtroom type of procedure or informal discussions? Should there be briefs and a transcript? I had an early case in which the union opposed transcripts and the idea of recording what was said at a hearing so violently that I had to spend a whole day on the question of whether or not a company could have a secretary taking notes in the back row for the convenience of its attorney.

People were groping in those days. I remember hearing one of R. H. Donnelly Company's first arbitration cases. It was a discipline case. In those days the idea that the company should proceed first in a discipline case was by no means generally accepted. Neither side was willing to start. The first two hours of the hearing were spent arguing about who was going to start, both sides threatening to leave the room and not proceed unless the other side started. Finally, not knowing what else to do, I started myself and began calling witnesses and asking questions of them and the attorneys. Soon they became so interested in the argument that they forgot about the procedure, and we got going on the case.

Such matters of procedure which are now second nature were uncertainties then. This was true of many principles applicable to the merits of grievance cases, which are now generally accepted assumptions in arbitration but were by no means accepted then. Now many unions would not take a case to arbitration which involved an employee who thinks the foreman is wrong under the agreement and refuses to obey the foreman's order. The idea that you obey and file a grievance is now second nature in arbitration as is the idea that there is an exception. If the order affects an employee's safety there may, and usually will, be a right to refuse, although sometimes special procedures exist to establish that right.

For a time there was an idea that a job description not only described a job but froze it, and that when the parties agreed to a sound description of what an employee normally did on the job, they were agreeing that these duties could not be changed without the union's consent. It took a lot of heated argument and dispute before that idea was abandoned and a job description was accepted as a description and not a limitation on managerial action.

As all these developments were taking place, the parties learned gradually the extent of their control over the arbitration procedure and how they could create the kind of arbitration procedure they wanted. They learned also to protect themselves somewhat against the ignorance of an arbitrator, by procedural devices, giving him experience through permanent arbitration, using him repeatedly, or abandoning normal procedure in a case and forgetting, for example, about the order of presentation and relevance of evidence or being willing to abandon argument for the first half hour while somebody who knows describes the process that was involved. Gradually ideas on the merits, not as binding precedents but as conclusions which arbitrators all over the country were coming to on the same kinds of issues, were becoming generally accepted by both the advocates and the arbitrators. With that development, some of the fear of arbitration was dispelled. Control came in.

Maturity of Process

Other things happened concurrently. Arbitration became more and more routine. In the old days a union district director might have sat in on a grievance to see what this curious procedure was. A company manager, the vice president of labor relations, or topflight people in the legal staffs might have sat in the back seat to see what was going on. This high-level participation is lessening in many cases to staff people, specialists to whom arbitration is routine.

As the process grew, the FMCS and AAA came forward with their lists of arbitrators to help the parties find people in whom they could have confidence. The parties developed services corresponding in function to court reporting. Commercial publishers began making available decisions to parties and arbitrators all over the country. Arbitration became accepted everywhere, until there arose a great undercurrent of protest and criticism centering upon the increasing formality of the process. Employees who had gone to get justice in arbitration found arbitrators talking in terms of briefs and decisions, citing decisions in their awards, and using language that could not be understood very well by a man at the machine. The protest that arbitration was being taken over by the lawyers and becoming too legalistic began to swell. Cases became more complicated. Arbitration became a more expensive process, and protests against expense rose. Arbitrators began charging for their time and were very busy because there were not enough of them. Many heard more cases than they should and wrote too much and took too long to get their decisions out. There was a feeling that delay and costs had gotten out of hand. Why did the parties find themselves in what looked like a court? How could this come back down to earth?

Expedited Arbitration

There is now the procedure called expedited arbitration, which started in the steel industry, I believe, in an effort to separate out from the bulk of the grievances those decisions which should not form a precedent. These cases are fact situations which can be decided one way or the other without threatening the future of the company or the union. Both sides can live with a decision regardless of which way it goes. Not taking those cases all the way through the grievance procedure, not letting them get in the hands of the lawyers, but getting a quick procedure for them with special arbitrators who will hand down quick and inexpensive decisions became popular. However, it is a very dangerous thing unless it is well handled, because even though it provides a quick and inexpensive way of arbitrating, it is easy to want to get on the bandwagon and arbitrate cases which should never go to expedited arbitration.

Public-Sector Interest Arbitration

Arbitration expanded into the public sector, which immediately got into interest arbitration. I will mention here only that two things which are typical of public-sector arbitration are tending to enter into industrial grievance arbitration. One is the introduction of multiple parties in the arbitration process. The other is interest arbitration.

One of the few securities an arbitrator has had, and still has for the most part, is knowing with whom he is dealing. He has been hired by the parties and, in trying to interpret and apply their agreement, he is supposed to be their servant. In the public sphere that is by no means clear. When dealing with a school board and teachers, for example, is the arbitrator dealing also with the mayor's office or a comptroller, or in some situation does the governor have a hand in it, if it is a prolonged case? When dealing with the union, is it only with that particular union, or also with other government unions or unorganized groups in the unit that are affected and whose presence becomes clear in the hearing?

This problem of multiple parties in interest is beginning to beset grievance arbitration. In minority grievance disputes the union is not the acknowledged representative of all the employees involved, and the unions operate in difficult situations because they are, on the one hand, not always able to represent effectively everybody they are supposed to represent, and, on the other hand, are in danger of actions for failure to represent adequately.

Interest arbitration is expanding in the public sector. Because of this expansion, I think it is beginning to be used more often in the private sector. In the steel industry, for two successive contract periods, the steelworkers union and the companies agreed to arbitrate the terms of their agreement rather than strike. Industry now is searching for new structural and procedural answers to the problems of interest arbitration which arbitrators were trying to solve twenty or thirty years ago in grievance arbitration. Med-arb is a term that is being bantered about. The med-arb procedure is a reflection of the idea that the terms of an agreement in an arbitration hearing are not litigated, just as statutes are not drafted effectively in a courtroom.

I was in Bermuda recently setting wages and contract terms for hotels there. The parties seemed to believe at first that this should be handled entirely as a trial, on an arm's length advocacy basis as though there were a right and wrong answer to the drafting of twenty or more different contract provisions covering everything from wages and seniority to grievance procedure. This was obviously absolute nonsense. The steel industry did that a few years ago when arbitrating incentive problems, an interest arbitration. They started by trying to go through the motions of litigation about the formation and setting of incentive wage principles for the steel industry. Because there were a lot of sensible people in both the steel companies and union, as well as on the panels, we were able to get the parties to appoint committees to sit in with the arbitrators during the decision-making process so that we could do the legislative job which had to be done with the assistance of the parties themselves. This was one form of med-arb, I suppose.

New Challenges

There are new challenges for arbitrators to face today. I am envious of those who enter routine procedures with a lot of background, some of which I just sketched. Many arbitration cases will be dull, detailed, microcosmic, and not world-shaking after the initial excitement wears off. However, latent in all of these situations are new problems and new developments. Arbitration is a very important procedure. Even a little case involving a three-day layoff for smoking in a prohibited area can be an important case because it represents an instance in which, on a free basis, people are trying to develop their own ways of applying reason and persuasion to a problem. As arbitrators you will love some of your work and hate some of it. You will be scared, insecure, and sometimes bored, but when you are arbitrating you will always be in the forefront of one of the sound, fine, human efforts.

Introduction to Grievance Arbitration

Bernard D. Meltzer

So-called students, according to reliable hearsay, are as diverse as their backgrounds are impressive. It is likely that my presentation will bore some and puzzle others. All readers have been students long enough to know how to cope with boredom and puzzlement. My topic is broad and involves problems that are important elements of background for arbitrators but that are at the periphery rather than at the center of an arbitrator's day-by-day work. There is an overlap between my assignment and Mr. Feller's. I propose to leave to him the principal discussion of external law and labor arbitration, although I will deal with aspects of that topic.

Indeed, the inclusion of external law reflects a significant change in the relationship between law and labor arbitration. Formerly, arbitration was essentially an autonomous and private system of industrial self-government with few direct links to the formal legal system. Courts now enforce the promise to arbitrate as well as the resulting awards. External laws such as the Sherman Act, National Labor Relations Act, Title VII of the Civil Rights Act of 1964, and Occupational Safety and Health Act impinge increasingly on employment relationships. Such laws directly influence the content of a collective bargaining agreement. *Gardner-Denver*'s footnote 21[1] illustrates the impact of external law on the procedures used in arbitration. In addition, external law is invoked sometimes to help interpret a collective agreement and sometimes to invalidate some of its provisions.

A bit of history may help to appreciate the transformation in the role of law. In the early nineteenth century, arbitration meant what we now call negotiation, that is, an essentially bipartite mechanism for setting the terms of employment. It was a substitute for the unilateral

---

[1] *Alexander v. Gardner-Denver Co.*, 415 U.S. 36, 7 FEP Cases 81 (1974).

promulgation of terms and conditions of employment by employers and occasionally by unions. The musicians' union, with respect to so-called club dates, still promulgates the terms and conditions of employment.

In its second phase, beginning about the turn of the century, arbitration by a third and neutral party became a substitute for strikes and economic pressure as a means of resolving bargaining deadlocks. We now call such arbitration economic or interest arbitration as distinguished from rights or grievance arbitration. In interest arbitration, a third party neutral resolves a bargaining impasse by making all or part of an agreement for the parties. Interest arbitration performs a legislative function whereas grievance arbitration is essentially judicial, with perhaps an occasional bit of interstitial judicial legislation. Grievance arbitration purports to apply or interpret the agreement reached by the parties.

This discussion is limited to the part of the private sector covered by the Wagner Act, as amended. Grievance arbitration got a big boost from several developments in the 1930s and 1940s. The Wagner Act called for recognition of unions that had majority support in an appropriate unit. The Act stimulated a sharp increase in unionization and collective agreements as well as in the use of grievance arbitration. The year before the passage of the Wagner Act, the Railway Labor Act, enacted in 1934, had endorsed arbitration in a specialized context by effectively compelling its use for the resolution of so-called minor railway disputes. World War II, with its obvious pressures for minimizing stoppages, also contributed to the wider use of the arbitral machinery. The War Labor Board not only called for the inclusion of grievance-arbitration and no-strike clauses in collective agreements, but also served as a training ground for a new crop of arbitrators.

Approximately 96 percent of current collective agreements provide that at least some disputes arising under an agreement should be handled by the grievance-arbitration process. The spread of this machinery reflects the contribution that it typically makes to industrial peace, justice, and order. Grievance arbitration provides the worker and the union with a vehicle for protest against employer actions perceived as incompatible with the expectancies arising from the provisions of the agreement and the common law of the shop. When coupled with the no-strike clause, as it typically is, grievance arbitration is designed not only as a vehicle for orderly protest against managerial action but also as an alternative to strikes and other forms of disruption. As Professor Feller[2] and the

---

[2]*See* Feller, *The Coming End of Arbitration's Golden Age*, in ARBITRATION-1976 (Proceedings of the 29th Annual Meeting, National Academy of Arbitrators) 97, 100–01 (BNA Books, 1976).

Supreme Court[3] have emphasized, grievance arbitration evolved as a substitute not so much for litigation as for self-help.

Finally, since grievance arbitration is largely a creature of contract, it can be and is shaped by particular parties so as to respond to their distinctive needs and relationships. While I discuss grievance arbitration as abstraction, it is well to remember that it is a custom-made rather than a mass-produced instrument. It is primarily because the underlying labor-management relationships vary that in a substantial number of cases arbitration and no-strike clauses fail to achieve their purposes. No-strike clauses fail to avoid stoppages, and I need refer only to the literature regarding wildcat strikes in the coal mining industry and elsewhere as a reminder that we have not yet reached an industrial paradise.

Despite such failures, grievance arbitration in general has met the parties' felt needs. It grew without much help from courts or Congress prior to the enactment of the Taft-Hartley Act in 1947. At common law agreements to arbitrate future disputes, the kind of agreements that are considered standard now, were revocable by either party. In addition, state statutes on the whole did not provide effective relief. When they existed at all, they usually granted specific enforcement only to an agreement to submit a preexisting dispute.

If a contract contained a future disputes clause and yet the parties did not want to arbitrate a particular dispute that rose after that clause had been agreed to, they could refuse to do so, and the courts would not specifically enforce the agreement.

Judicial Support for Arbitration

Section 301 of the Taft-Hartley Act was the basis for replacing this judicial laissez-faire with comprehensive judicial support for the arbitration system. The legislative history of that section focused on common law obstacles to recovery of damages against unions for breach of collective agreements, particularly no-strike clauses. The Supreme Court, however, used Section 301 as a basis for specifically enforcing both the promise to arbitrate and the resultant award. In a somewhat high-flown phrase, I once said that the Supreme Court's creative application of Section 301 transformed arbitration from the waif of the common law into the darling of the national labor policy.

Lincoln Mills[4] was a seminal case in which the Supreme Court summarily overrode the employer's constitutional and statutory objec-

---

[3]*See United Steelworkers v. Warrior & Gulf Navigation Co.*, 363 U.S. 574, 578, 46 LRRM 2416 (1960).
[4]*Textile Workers v. Lincoln Mills*, 353 U.S. 448, 40 LRRM 2113 (1957).

tions to being ordered to submit a grievance to arbitration in accordance with his collective agreement. The Court held that Section 301 was more than an effort to confer jurisdiction on federal courts, it authorized those courts to fashion a body of federal law for the enforcement of these collective bargaining agreements, and it included within that federal law specific performance of promises to arbitrate grievances. Under the Court's view, federal courts were entitled to borrow from state law. State law had been the basis for enforcing collective agreements, insofar as they had been enforced at all, but the Supreme Court made it clear that the law regarding enforcement was to reflect the policy of the national labor laws and was to be federal law. That characterization has had some important technical consequences including removal of actions brought in state courts to federal courts.

The Court in *Lincoln Mills* went on to deal with the problem before it, the specific enforcement of the arbitration clause. Conceding that such enforcement would be barred by a literal reading of the Norris-LaGuardia Act, the Court, speaking through Justice Douglas, held that Act inapplicable, finding, among other things, that such enforcement was "not part and parcel of the abuses against which Norris-LaGuardia had been aimed."

The Court, having authorized specific enforcement of the arbitration promise, sought in the celebrated Steelworkers Trilogy[5] to protect the arbitration process against what it deemed would be heavy-handed judicial intrusion before and after the award. In providing and justifying such protection, the Court eulogized arbitration and arbitrators so fulsomely as to pose a hazard, some people have said a redundant hazard, to arbitral humility. The Court said that the arbitrator is supposed to bring to his task knowledge of the common law of the shop, although typically he is, in fact, an ad hoc arbitrator, innocent of the particular shop. He is entitled to bring this knowledge that he may not have to bear insofar as the collective agreement permits. He is also supposed to have concern for productivity and morale. The ablest judge, Justice Douglas added, cannot be expected to bring the same experience and competence to bear upon the determination of a grievance because he cannot be similarly informed. Furthermore, the Court recognized that the processing of even frivolous grievances might have a therapeutic effect. Therapy might result from blowing off steam to a neutral, requiring coherent explanations of competing positions, showing a grievance committee or other supervisors that a genuine problem was involved, or

---

[5]*United Steelworkers v. American Manufacturing Co.*, 363 U.S. 564, 46 LRRM 2414 (1960); *United Steelworkers v. Warrior & Gulf Navigation Co.*, 363 U.S. 574, 46 LRRM 2416 (1960); *United Steelworkers v. Enterprise Wheel & Car Corp.*, 363 U.S. 593, 46 LRRM 2423 (1960).

taking union or management officials off the hook. Therapy is a couch of many colors.

There is a problem of possible overuse of the industrial couch. Furthermore, whether or not there is therapy depends a good deal on how the parties comport themselves in the arbitration hearing, how the arbitrator comports him or herself during the hearing, and, of course, the impact of the award.

After reviewing in the Steelworkers Trilogy what it deemed to be the potential contribution of arbitration to healthy industrial relations, the Supreme Court concluded that it was important that the merits of a contractual claim be resolved by an arbitrator and that courts should not poach on his turf. The Court called for such judicial limitation at least when a so-called standard arbitration clause—that is, one channeling to an arbitrator all disputes involving the interpretation or application of an agreement—was combined with a broad no-strike clause. The Court accordingly rejected a well-known New York rule, the *Cutler-Hammer*[6] doctrine, under which a court would not compel arbitration if it found that the meaning of a contract was beyond dispute, or, as it was said, if the grievance involved was plainly frivolous. The Supreme Court said even as to such grievances the arbitrator was to decide the case. His right to decide was, moreover, the right to decide wrongly, and, indeed, the right occasionally to be quite silly.

Even under the Trilogy, disputes over the arbitrability of a grievance—that is, over the arbitrator's jurisdiction or over the scope of the arbitration clause—were to be distinguished from disputes over the merits of the claim, and the courts were to determine issues of arbitrability unless the agreement clearly committed that question to the arbitrator. The difficulty is that questions regarding the merits of a claim often coalesce with questions regarding arbitral jurisdiction. Hence, the Supreme Court sought to block explicitly back-door judicial entanglement with the merits via the arbitrability question, which the Supreme Court said was generally for the courts. The Court said, "An order to arbitrate the particular grievance should not be denied unless it may be said with positive assurance that the arbitration clause is not susceptible of an interpretation that covers the asserted dispute. Doubt should be resolved in favor of coverage."[7]

The Court, moreover, also seemed to require that exclusion from the coverage of the arbitration clause be clear from the face of the agreement without reliance on bargaining history, past practice, or other

---

[6]*IAM, Local 402 v. Cutler-Hammer Inc.*, 271 App. Div. 917, 67 N.Y.S.2d 317, *aff'd*, 297 N.Y. 519 (1947).

[7]*United Steelworkers v. Warrior & Gulf Navigation Co.*, 363 U.S. 574, 582, 46 LRRM 2416 (1960).

matters that would enmesh courts with the merits of the claim. As the concurring opinion in the Trilogy indicated, this implied exclusion of bargaining history and past practice was somewhat puzzling, not to say ironic, in an opinion that emphasized the common law of the plant. Hence, it was understandable that lower courts were later to disagree on the propriety of their going beyond the four corners of the agreement and considering extrinsic evidence in determining arbitrability.

The Trilogy provoked an immediate reaction from lawyers, resulting in some quite complex clauses seeking to restrict arbitration. Occasionally such clauses provoked unfriendly and chilling judicial comment about their resemblance to Wall Street bond indentures.[8] Incidentally, such comments involve some tension with the national policy in favor of privately determined bargains. Under that policy there is no obligation to agree to any arbitration clause at all. Hence, it was surprising that the United States Court of Appeals for the Second Circuit raised a question as to whether it would be compatible with public policy to enter into an agreement that rejected the presumption of arbitrability embodied in the Trilogy cases.[9]

The curtailed judicial inquiry with respect to substantive arbitrability sharpens a question that arbitrators may face. After a court has decided that a claim is arbitrable, does the arbitrator get a second crack at the issue of arbitrability? Arguably, if that question is one for the court, the court's answer should be binding on the arbitrator. On the other hand, the arbitrator's frame of relevance is usually much broader than the court's. He looks at, among other things, past practice and bargaining history. In the *Warrior*[10] case itself, the second case in the Trilogy, despite the Supreme Court's finding of arbitrability, when the case came back, the arbitrator appeared to make an independent determination of arbitrability.

The question of whether or not the arbitrator should take a second crack at the arbitrability question may seem to be formal rather than practical, for ordinarily an arbitrator who disagrees with a judicial determination of substantive arbitrability does not have to rely on nonarbitrability in order to dismiss the grievance. He could base dismissal on the merits, but if early in an arbitration proceeding he says that it is nonarbitrable, he would shorten the hearing. In a subcontracting case, for example, such a finding would make it unnecessary to introduce evidence about economic justification or past practice, among other time-

---

[8]*See IUE v. General Electric Co.*, 407 F.2d 253, 258 (2d Cir.), 70 LRRM 2082 (1968), *cert. denied*, 395 U.S. 904, 71 LRRM 2254 (1969).

[9]*Id.* at 259.

[10]363 U.S. 574.

consuming topics. But if in the teeth of a contrary judicial determination, the arbitrator says this is not arbitrable, he may make waves in and out of court. The parties may be mystified or outraged by what appears to be the arbitrator's lack of deference to a prior judicial decision on a question within the court's jurisdiction. Perhaps in this context arbitrators should subordinate expedition to therapy or, indeed, prudence.

Strike Over Arbitrable Grievance

The second-crack question might get particularly acute in a *Boys Markets*[11] situation. The Supreme Court held in *Boys Markets* that the Norris-LaGuardia Act does not bar an injunction against a strike in breach of a no-strike clause, provided that the strike was prompted by an arbitrable grievance.

Suppose in a *Boys Markets* proceeding the court rules that the grievance that caused the strike is arbitrable, and issues an injunction against the strike. The parties go to the arbitrator who, getting a second crack, decides the court was wrong, the issue is not arbitrable. The underlying basis for the injunction disappears; the arbitrator is finished. Of course, it depends upon the case. I will not now pinpoint the relevant case-to-case differences.

I mention just one more problem in connection with *Boys Markets*. Under that case, a condition for an injunction is that the underlying dispute should be arbitrable. Should the same strong presumption in favor of arbitrability that is reflected in the Trilogy apply in an action for a *Boys Markets* injunction? In this context there is a strong countervailing policy reflected in the Norris-LaGuardia Act and indeed in American labor history, a strong distaste for government by the judiciary through injunctions against strikes. In enforcing anti-strike injunctions there are, moreover, substantial problems that are not present in enforcing a promise to arbitrate. These considerations sharpen the question of whether or not the presumption of arbitrability should apply in a *Boys Markets* situation. That presumption, coupled with a flimsy consensual basis for arbitration, is likely to increase the problems of getting compliance with an injunction on the part of the union.

The courts, as you might expect, have disagreed as to whether or not the Trilogy presumption should be folded into the *Boys Markets* situation. In *Standard Food Products v. Brandenburg*,[12] the Second Circuit, through Judge Hays, indicated that the answer was no. He

---

[11]*Boys Markets, Inc. v. Retail Clerks Local 770*, 398 U.S. 235, 74 LRRM 2257 (1970).
[12]436 F.2d 964, 76 LRRM 2367 (2d Cir. 1970).

suggested that a claim arguably nonarbitrable should, in that situation, be viewed as nonarbitrable. He turned the Trilogy presumption on its head. In *Southwestern Bell Tel. Co. v. CWA*,[13] the Fifth Circuit indicated that the Trilogy presumption applies even in the *Boys Markets* situation, and that arguably arbitrable was to be viewed as actually arbitrable.

Procedural Arbitrability

Procedural arbitrability may arise from provisions that a grievant is entitled to arbitration only if all the grievance steps have been followed and certain time limits have been met. Such time limits are specified in order to avoid stale claims, memories growing dim, and back pay piling up. Just as we have a statute of limitations in the external law system, we have limitation periods in provisions establishing grievance machinery. The question of whether or not such procedural prerequisites have been satisfied would appear on the surface to be as jurisdictional as the question of whether or not the claim that the agreement has been violated falls within the scope of the arbitration clause. Specifically, if an agreement provides that an arbitrator shall not hear a grievance unless it is filed within ten days of such and such an event, there is a bootstrap quality in letting the arbitrator resolve the claim that the ten-day requirement should be suspended in a particular case. Assume the claim is that the employer is estopped from invoking the limitations clause because he told the union not to worry about time limits.

Nevertheless, arbitrators may be more adept than courts in determining whether compliance with such time limits, for example, should be excused in a given case. The Supreme Court in the *John Wiley*[14] case and even more stunningly, I think, in *Flair Builders*[15] committed such questions of procedural arbitrability to the arbitrator, at least in the absence of contractual language clearly calling for a judicial determination of such questions. An arbitrator may be faced with questions of whether or not a given situation warrants excusing compliance with such time limits.

Successor Employer

The *John Wiley* case dealt with arbitration and the successorship problem. I do not intend to discuss the complicated aspects of that

---

[13]454 F.2d 1333, 78 LRRM 2833 (5th Cir. 1971).
[14]*John Wiley & Sons, Inc. v. Livingston*, 376 U.S. 543, 55 LRRM 2769 (1964).
[15]*IUOE, Local 150 v. Flair Builders, Inc.*, 406 U.S. 487 (1972).

problem. *John Wiley* deserves mention because it reflected and extended the Court's hospitality to arbitration. In the Trilogy, that hospitality purported to be based on the parties' intent or the parties' bargain viewed in the light of the national labor policy. In *John Wiley* the Court appeared to have abandoned, or at least seriously qualified, even a fictional reliance on an agreement by the party reluctant to arbitrate. A company called Interscience merged into John Wiley, a bigger company. The union, while the contract was still in effect, asked John Wiley to arbitrate claims purportedly based on the union's contract with Interscience. After the contract expired, the union went to court and said that John Wiley as a successor, which is a term of art, should arbitrate the union's claim based on the union's agreement with Interscience, even though John Wiley had never agreed to be bound by that contract. The Supreme Court upheld that claim, and required John Wiley to arbitrate on the basis of its predecessor's agreement read in the light of the national policy reflected in the Trilogy. The Court, after finding that the agreement survived, left it to the arbitrator to decide which of the substantive provisions of the old agreement bound the successor company. Under that approach, the arbitrator's authority came close to his authority under interest arbitration. He was restricted by the old agreement, to be sure, but he was given power to say which of these old provisions survived in the new situation.

John Wiley arose under Section 301 of the Taft-Hartley Act. A later case, *William J. Burns International Detective Agency*,[16] which arose under Section 8(a)(5) of the National Labor Relations Act, created obvious tensions with *John Wiley*. In *Burns*, the National Labor Relations Board held that a new company, which the Board treated as if it were a successor, had to assume the entire collective bargaining agreement of a predecessor company. But the Supreme Court said that is not true under Section 8(a)(5), which defines an unfair labor practice and which reflects the idea of freedom of contract. For the purpose of Section 8(a)(5), a successor was not to be bound by the substantive provisions of a predecessor's agreement.

The Court distinguished *John Wiley* on the ground that it arose under Section 301. That distinction is a little troublesome because under Section 301 you are supposed to look at the national policy, including Section 8(a)(5). Nevertheless, said the Court, *John Wiley* arose under Section 301, and Section 8(a)(5) is a different compartment. I think I

---

[16]182 NLRB 348 (1970), *Burns Int'l Detective Agency, Inc. v. NLRB*, 441 F.2d 911, 77 LRRM 2081 (1971); *NLRB v. Burns International Security Services Inc.*, 406 U.S. 272, 80 LRRM 2225 (1972).

have added enough confusion, or the Supreme Court has, to this particular corner of the law.

Arbitration After Expiration of Contract

The Court went even further in subordinating notions of consensus in the *Nolde*[17] case. The union and the company could not agree to a new collective bargaining agreement, and the union thereupon terminated the agreement by giving the required notice. The employer thereupon closed the plant and went out of business. There was no suggestion that the plant closure was an unfair labor practice. The union demanded vacation and severance pay—*after* the agreement was terminated. The employer said it would give vacation but not severance pay. The union sought to invoke arbitration, which the employer opposed on the grounds that the agreement, including its arbitration clause, had expired. The Supreme Court held that arbitration was required. Notice that in *Nolde* there was no continuing relationship to be protected by arbitral therapy. Furthermore, if, as seemed to be the case, the union was free from a no-strike obligation, the quid pro quo argument was not applicable. The general question is which terms of this expired agreement survive into the new period, a question which the Court in *Nolde* says is for the arbitrator.

Nolde involves something like deferred pay. An employee gets severance pay, and during the years worked he builds up little increments of credit. It may be that the employees should not be squeezed out; they have very strong equities. The question is, who should make that decision. The Supreme Court said that the arbitrator should make it even though the National Labor Relations Board in the same kind of situation had said that, once the agreement has expired, there is no obligation on the part of the parties to arbitrate. Again there is a tension going from one approach under Section 301 to a different approach by the Board under Section 8(a)(5). Now in view of *Nolde*, it is quite possible that the Board will change its position regarding the duty to arbitrate after the expiration of the agreement, and that the survival of arbitration will also mean the survival of the related no-strike clause. It is complications of this kind that lie behind my suggestion that arbitrators should not worry about all the gyrations in the decisions of the Board and the courts.

---

[17]*Nolde Bros., Inc. v. Local 358, Bakery & Confectionery Workers*, 430 U.S. 243, 94 LRRM 2753 (1977).

Enforcement of Awards

In *Enterprise Wheel*,[18] which dealt with the scope of judicial review of arbitration awards under Section 301, the Supreme Court again stressed that courts were not to intrude on the merits of an arbitration claim and stressed particularly the need for according arbitrators broad leeway in devising remedies. There are, of course, limits to that leeway, for the Court said:

> Nevertheless, an arbitrator is confined to interpretation and application of the collective bargaining agreement; he does not sit to dispense his own brand of industrial justice. He may of course look for guidance from many sources, yet his award is legitimate only so long as it draws its essence from the collective bargaining agreement. When the arbitrator's words manifest an infidelity to this obligation, courts have no choice but to refuse enforcement of the award.[19]

The Court had to apply that general language to an award of reinstatement and back pay that extended beyond the date of the agreement's expiration. There the arbitration proceeding involved a discharge that occurred before expiration of the agreement. The employer, after all sorts of delaying tactics, was directed to arbitrate by a court. By the time the arbitral award was issued, the contract with the arbitration clause had expired, but the arbitrator awarded back pay beyond the period of the expiration date, up to the time of reinstatement. The union had not entered into a renewal contract, and the company's argument went like this: they could have fired the grievant after the expiration date, they should not be required to give any back pay beyond the period of the expiration date, and they should not be required to reinstate the discharged grievant. The Supreme Court acknowledged that the arbitrator's award was somewhat ambiguous and said:

> It may be read as based solely upon the arbitrator's view of the requirements of enacted legislation, which would mean that he exceeded the scope of the submission. Or it may be read as embodying a construction of the agreement itself, perhaps with the arbitrator looking to "the law" for help in determining the sense of the agreement. A mere ambiguity in the opinion accompanying an award which permits the inference that the arbitrator may have exceeded his authority, is not a reason for refusing to enforce the award.[20]

The last sentence may be found comforting. The Court says that one may look to external law as an aid to interpretation of a bargain, but that an arbitrator is the proctor of the bargain and not the enforcer

---

[18]*United Steelworkers v. Enterprise Wheel & Car Corp.*, 363 U.S. 593, 46 LRRM 2423 (1960).
[19]*Id.* at 597.
[20]*Id.* at 597–98.

for the state. He may implement private purposes, not public purposes, as such. David Feller focuses on this language in considering the role of external law in arbitration.

I want to offer a word or two about the total impact of the Trilogy. The Trilogy imposed extraordinary limitations on judges, who were to enforce arbitration awards even if not rationally based on the collective agreement. It seemed as if arbitrators—or really the parties, on the basis of an arbitral award—were given almost a blank check to enlist the coercive power of the courts. In no other area of adjudication are courts asked to exercise their powers while they are denied any responsibility for the results that they are to enforce. This shrivelled judicial responsibility runs against the grain of the judicial tradition, and so commentators and courts suggested that when an award lacked *any* rational basis it should be not judicially enforced. In the *Torrington* case, the Court of Appeals for the Second Circuit quoted the following statement by Paul R. Hays, a long-time arbitrator and a member of that court: "No great harm is done by applying a liberal rule as to arbitrability, if the court carefully scrutinizes what the arbitrator later decides."[21]

I think that Professor St. Antoine has suggested that a truly preposterous award could be said to violate an implied limitation in the agreement. In other words, the parties say to an arbitrator that his award is to be final and conclusive, subject, however, to the implied condition that he is not going to be a lunatic. I think there is something more important than consensus here, and that is an attitude on the part of the courts that they should not be required to support what appears to them to be a manifestly capricious and arbitrary exercise of power. It is very rare that courts would be confronted with that kind of a situation, but if courts refuse to enforce awards because they are irrational, they are going to have a problem. An award that one may think is quite rational or has some rational element may be viewed by some court as irrational. We may thus get back to the old *Cutler-Hammer* days *after* the arbitration award, rather than before. That risk is troublesome, but I think that with the educative impact of the Trilogy, the new sensitivity of the courts and their reluctance to get into the merits, the intellectual climate is so different that *Cutler-Hammer* risks have substantially diminished.

Past Practice

Past practice is another problem area. Some past practices, but not all, may fairly be viewed as creating obligations. The line between these

---

[21]*Torrington Co. v. Metal Prods. Workers Local 1645*, 362 F.2d 677, 680, 62 LRRM 2495, 2497 (2d Cir. 1966).

two types is a fuzzy one. For example, suppose it is claimed a contract is wholly silent on whether or not wash-up time is paid for. Employees have had fifteen minutes for wash-up and have been paid for that time for five years. There has never been any bargaining or any provision about wash-up time, but the whole wage scale presumably reflected that payment. The company gets a new manager who directs that there be no more payment for wash-up time. A grievance is filed protesting the stopping of those payments. One way of dealing with a grievance about this change would be to say the wage provision includes this practice. There is no addition to the terms of the agreement; it is interpretation of a particular provision in the light of past practice.

There is a similar problem with respect to an agreement that is silent on subcontracts. Some arbitrators have been quite fancy in interpreting provisions of the agreement to impose limitations on subcontracts. Consider a case in which a company has not subcontracted for twenty years; that is the past practice. In addition, there may be reliance on the recognition and seniority clauses, or the combination of recognition, seniority, and discharge clauses, indicating an attempt to protect the employees' expectancy. Although there are great difficulties in knowing where to draw the line, it is doubtful that any one would say that the parties' expectation (unless they say so in so many words) is that no past practices are considered as obligatory by the arbitrator or as relevant in construing (rather than adding to) an agreement. However, there are past practices and there are past practices: there is a problem of innovation by an employer; the problem of when to suspend the rules because they might operate harshly in a particular case, without establishing a past practice; the past practice that may be viewed as a source of obligation; and the past practice that is simply an exercise of discretion, with full freedom in the future.

Let me turn now to settled and relatively noncontroversial grounds for denying judicial enforcement of an award. These grounds include corruption, fraud, or bias of the arbitrator; improper exclusion of material evidence; the denial of a fair hearing; an incomplete or ambiguous award, so the court doesn't know what it is being asked to enforce; and the incompatibility of an award with a federal statute or state law or policy that has not been preempted by national legislation.

Duty of Fair Representation

A more difficult and controversial ground for overturning an award was involved in *Hines v. Anchor Motor Freight, Inc.*[22] which raised the

---

[22]424 U.S. 554, 91 LRRM 2481 (1976).

question of whether an award that purports to be a final award should be overturned, not because of the arbitrator's dishonesty or incompetence, but because of a serious flaw in the union's representation of the individual grievant amounting to a breach of the union's duty of fair representation.

In that case two truck drivers were fired for allegedly padding expenses in connection with their motel bill. The drivers suggested that the motel be investigated, but the union told them to relax and that they need not hire their own lawyer. A joint area committee upheld the discharges. What seems to have happened was that the motel clerk padded the bills, while putting the true charges on the hotel records. Apparently, the clerk and not the drivers pocketed the difference between the drivers' padded bills and the statement on the motel register. That fact did not come out in the arbitration. The union did not investigate, for whatever reason.

In *Hines v. Anchor Motor Freight* the proceeding in which the discharges had been held was not exactly arbitration. The grievances had gone from the individual employer to a bipartite committee composed of employer and union representatives. One could view this as a step in the grievance procedure rather than a determination by an outside neutral, but the United States Supreme Court treated that committee as if it were the functional equivalent of arbitration. I will, for immediate purposes, do as did the Court.

Let us pretend that in the *Anchor Motor Freight* case the grievance actually had gone to an arbitrator, but that the union had not been very resourceful in investigating. The arbitrator found just cause for discharge. Then the individual grievants discovered the information about the motel clerk, and their lawyer sued for relief against the union and the employer. After all, only the employer can reinstate wrongfully discharged employees. The Supreme Court indicated that an award under such circumstances was not to be final and binding.

The Court's approach is reminiscent of a claim by a defendant found guilty of a crime that his conviction should be reversed on appeal, or in habeas corpus, on the ground that the incompetency of his lawyer deprived him of his constitutional rights. Are we going to import an analogue of that doctrine into the arbitration process? If so, even though we have a neutral arbitrator and what appears to have been a pretty good hearing, the individual may say after the award that the union did not effectively represent him and that the adverse award should not be final.

One might say that *Anchor Motor Freight* is a warning to unions that they must be careful in the investigative stages, and to employers that serious lapses by the union will undermine finality of awards. The justification will be that individual *rights* are involved. The answer may be that the agreement, the arbitration clause, typically seems to be a bipartite arrangement between the employer and the union and that the substantive rights are connected closely to the mode of enforcement. Hence if the grievance or arbitration process—at least if there was no corruption—upholds a discharge, under the agreement that discharge was for just cause. On the other hand, it is arguable that the real parties in interest under the agreement include individual employees. If they were in fact fired without just cause, their contractual rights were violated by the employer, and the employees should not be wholly deprived of entitlements on the basis of seriously flawed union representation. Perhaps the employer, if he was not a party to the union's breach, should at least be protected against back pay liability for the period after the award that resulted from the union's breach of duty.

Such protection of employees against inadequate representation involves problems at the hearing state and whether or not an arbitrator should risk intervention in order to insure effective representation. There is still considerable uncertainty about the implications of *Anchor Motor Freight.* The Court could easily retreat by emphasizing that the bipartite machinery in that case was not the equivalent of arbitration.

Statutory Standards

I have been asked to deal with related questions involving the impact of external law and its coordination with arbitration and the National Labor Relations Board or Title VII. I am going to focus on situations in which the external law does not conflict with the agreement but rather incorporates standards that coincide with contractual standards. For example, suppose that the grievant alleges that a discharge lacked just cause in that it would not have occurred but for activities protected under the National Labor Relations Act. Such a discharge would violate the National Labor Relations Act as well as the agreement. Similarly, both the agreement and Title VII would be implicated by a claim that a discharge would not have occurred but for the race or sex of the person discharged. Even though those allegations charge a violation of both the external law and the collective bargaining agreement, the arbitrator does not enforce, or does not have to enforce, external law as such. The arbitrator is enforcing only a contractual standard—just cause—which is loose enough and pliable enough to absorb the values reflected in the culture generally, including that element of the culture that we call law. Indeed, such general values might be poured into a just-cause provision without the benefit of a particular statute. A statute merely makes it easier for the arbitrator to recognize the relevance of a given value in the standards applicable to the plant.

In this situation, which I like to call the coincidence situation, the interesting question is not what the arbitrator should do with the law, but rather the converse, what should the law do with the arbitrator and his award. The answer to this question depends in part on the official body and the external law involved.

The NLRB, with respect to arbitration awards that have already been rendered, has adopted a policy of *deferring* to awards that meet the criteria set forth in the *Spielberg*[23] case. The arbitration proceedings have to be fair and regular, all parties involved have to agree to be bound by the award, and finally the arbitral decision is "not clearly repugnant to the purposes and policies of the Act." That is to say, the arbitral decision, given the facts found, is consistent with the Board's law. Under *Spielberg* the Board is not supposed to reexamine the evidence before the arbitrator and second-guess him, saying it would have decided this differently so it declines to defer to the award. Rather, the Board is to see whether the standards, the approach, and the procedure in the arbitration involved were generally consistent with the procedures and standards that the Board would have used had the claim been litigated before the Board instead of the arbitrator.

The Board from time to time has made an addition to the three *Spielberg* requirements that the arbitrator, if his award is to get deference under *Spielberg*, must have specifically considered the statutory issue that would confront the Board. If that requirement operated in our hypothetical discharge case, the Board would defer to an award dismissing the grievance only if the arbitrator had specifically found not only that there had been just cause for firing, but also that activity protected by the NLRA had not been an element in the discharge. Plainly, the latter question would have been the factual question or the mixed question of fact and law before the Board if the issue underlying the grievance had come to the Board.

This additional requirement may seem somewhat pedantic because, with all due respect, it would seem that if today you find just cause for a discharge, that finding presupposes that union activities did not play any part in the discharge. Indeed, unless the union was lying back and trying to preserve a second crack in another forum, the first thing the union would say to the arbitrator would be that Joe was not fired for the specific alleged infraction, that the company's claim is a pretext, and that the company was out to get Joe because he was filing more grievances

---

[23]*Spielberg Manufacturing Co.*, 117 NLRB 1080, 36 LRRM 1152 (1955).

than the company wanted. To be sure, in some cases an arbitrator might find just cause without having to resolve this thorny question of reprisal for protected activity, but this possibility seems too rare to warrant this addition to the *Spielberg* requirements.

I will not describe the Board's gyrations regarding that additional requirement. The important point, especially for the parties if they want to avoid two bites at the same apple, is to see to it that a statutory issue that coincides with the contractual issue is specifically addressed, preferably in the language of the NLRA, both in the arbitral proceeding and in the award. At a minimum, the arbitrator should specifically rule on those factual issues on which the statutory issue turns.

In *Collyer*[24] there had not been an arbitration award, and the question was should the Board defer to the arbitration process and give the arbitrator the first crack at the dispute, and then look at his award under the *Spielberg* requirements when requested to do so by an aggrieved party. The Board is in flux and so am I on *Collyer* and its variations. It does not have as much direct impact on our work as arbitrators as *Spielberg*, but it is part of the general culture.

Turning to Title VII, consider a contractual claim that coincides with a claim of a violation of the statutory proscription of employment discrimination on the basis of race or sex. *Alexander v. Gardner-Denver*[25] is the controlling case in which the Supreme Court, to the anguish of a good many employers, declined to apply an analogue of *Spielberg* to actions brought under Title VII. The Court rejected a rule of formal deference to arbitration awards, even though the claim of improper discharge had been rejected by an arbitrator under a contract that, like Title VII, banned racial discrimination, and even though racial discrimination had been urged in the grievance procedure. The Court ruled that the alleged victim of racial discrimination whose claim had been rejected in arbitration was entitled to a trial de novo on a statutory claim. In simpler language, the grievant could go to court and challenge his discharge again, even though the arbitrator had upheld the discharge on the ground that the grievant's rate of spoilage had been excessive and that race had had nothing to do with his discharge. In court the grievant would get another chance to prove that race, and not merely spoilage, entered into his discharge. The Court, in its famous footnote 21 and text, ruled that the arbitration award, even though not entitled to formal deference, was admissible into evidence in a later Title VII action on the same claim. In the note the Court also elaborated on the factors that would affect the weight to be given to the award.

---

[24]*Collyer Insulated Wire Co.*, 192 NLRB 837, 77 LRRM 1931 (1971).
[25]415 U.S. at 60.

I have argued elsewhere that *Gardner-Denver*'s rejection of the formal analogue to *Spielberg* is defensible on at least two interrelated grounds. First, grievance arbitration is, or at least was in an earlier period, a suspect forum for the resolution of Title VII claims. Second, concern for the appearance of justice in this sensitive context warranted the rejection of *Spielberg*. Although many unions and employers had been in the forefront of efforts to wipe out invidious discrimination, other employers and other unions had jointly or severally been responsible for a considerable amount of discrimination in the past. Hence, individuals who were to be protected by the statute might have doubts about the fitness of the arbitral machinery controlled by parties who had victimized them in the past. In this sensitive area, the old saw about the importance of the appearance of justice had a special force. Accordingly, it was understandable that the Court sought to mitigate both the appearance and possibly the reality of imperfections in the arbitral tribunal by preserving the plenary authority of the federal courts.

What the Court finally did was perhaps more important symbolically than operationally, for under footnote 21, if the case is properly tried before a competent arbitrator and properly handled by the arbitrator, the award is in fact likely to have as much effect as it would have had if the Court had transplanted the entire *Spielberg* rule. In short, the Court, by concluding that arbitral awards may be admitted into evidence, softened its rejection of an analogue of the *Spielberg* doctrine. To repeat, the results under the Court's approach may not in practice be significantly different from those that would have obtained under a *Spielberg* analogue. It is not clear, however, how the EEOC, in its administrative processing of a charge of a Title VII violation, treats an arbitration award that rejects that claim. Whatever may be the situation at the EEOC, it seems likely that the evidentiary guidelines set forth in *Gardner-Denver* will affect the conduct of arbitrations that in effect involve claims of Title VII violations. In such arbitrations there may well be increased pressures for transcripts, comprehensive opinions, and the general trappings of a trial. I do not know whether footnote 21 has brought about such consequences, but *Gardner-Denver* certainly involves a serious risk of more formality and expense, together with less finality. One can make that risk more tolerable by getting a clear idea about the content of footnote 21. If the arbitrator and the parties want to avoid the second bite, they should directly address the statutory issue.

A more interesting and tougher question is how interventionist should the arbitrator be. That depends on many variables, his relationships with the parties, their experience and sophistication, among others. Generally, I do not think that it is difficult to see to it that the statutory question is addressed. Frequently, for example, a union may charge that race or union activities brought about a discharge and that the company's explanation is a sham. If that point is not made explicitly, a question or two could flush out the basis for the grievance. If the arbitrator finds that race (or protected activities) did not enter into the discharge and he sees no basis for a claim under Title VII or the NLRA, he has taken care of the statutory issue. I think that it is perfectly sound for the arbitrator to show he has addressed such issues. The whole notion of finality, simplicity, and economy should lead us to help avoid relitigation unless in some special case there are good reasons not to do so That would be applicable in a Title VII context also. After all. *Alexander v. Gardner-Denver*, footnote 21, invites us and the parties to take action in order to give more weight to an award.

Future for Arbitration

I have talked about these direct linkages with external law and the overarching influence of the law on arbitration. Professor Feller is some-thing of a Cassandra in this respect in thinking that legal proliferation presents great threats both to autonomy and finality, the classic values of the grievance arbitration mechanism. Professor St. Antoine does not share those misgivings. I give both of those prophets their just desserts; I allow the future to take care of them and tell us whether we still have a golden age for arbitration before us. Despite all these perplexities I have been exploring, these two prophets do agree, as I do, that no matter what happens to the arbitration system because of the impact of external law, labor arbitrators face a bright and productive future. I hope that all arbitrators will deservedly remain or become acceptable and will flourish as readers of agreements or as adjuncts to the NLRB and the EEOC despite what Mr. Justice Holmes called "the brooding omnipres-ence of the law."

Relationship of the Agreement to External Law

David E. Feller

I distinguish external law from what I regard as the law the arbitrator enforces, the internal law of the collective bargaining agreement. External law is the law that is imposed by statute. Obvious examples are grievances of an employer's failure to promote because of racial discrimination in violation of Title VII of the Civil Rights Act or an employer's failure to grant overtime in violation of the Fair Labor Standards Act.

An arbitrator's job under a typical arbitration clause in the private sector is to interpret and apply the agreement. Whether or not the clause includes a variant of the standard language, the phrase, "should neither add to nor detract from," makes no difference. In the normal arbitration case, the grievance is one which claims that the employer has violated the agreement in some way. A grievance that alleges an employer has violated some statute has no place in the procedure. An arbitrator has no jurisdiction to decide a case claiming violation of a statute and ought not to hear it. Most arbitrators do not have to deal with public law unless there is something in the agreement which incorporates external law. That is a source of the problem.

Board Deferral to Arbitration

This is particularly true if the case comes to arbitration as a result of the National Labor Relation Board's *Collyer*[1] policy. I think the Board has a very foolish notion that if a labor dispute arises where there is a collective bargaining agreement which may involve some question under the collective bargaining, the Board should refer the matter to an ar-

---

[1] *Collyer Insulated Wire*, 192 NLRB 837, 77 LRRM 1931 (1971).

bitrator. I do not think that is particularly exceptional if the Board defers to an arbitrator to decide what the contract means, that is, to use that arbitration decision as a datum for the purpose of then deciding whether or not there is an unfair labor practice. However, the Board's position, at least up until fairly recently, was that when a dispute is taken to arbitration, the party that is claiming a violation of the National Labor Relations Act must make that claim before the arbitrator, and if that party fails to do so, he has waived his opportunity, and the Board will not decide whether or not there has been a violation of the Act.

The Board's current position is unknown. The Board has said[2] it will not defer in Section 8(a)(3) cases but that it will in 8(a)(5) cases. That is an impossible position to maintain and in my view is exactly wrong.

This question was raised in particularly sharp focus in *Western Massachusetts Electric.*[3] The company, having regularly given discounts on appliances to its employees, unilaterally discontinued that practice during the term of a contract. This was arguably an unfair labor practice inasmuch as it was a change in the terms and conditions of employment without first bargaining with the employees and a failure to maintain the terms and conditions of employment in violation of Section 8(d). I will not discuss the technicalities of the Act, but it certainly was an arguable unfair practice in that the company had not bargained with the union before it changed its practice on a matter not dealt with in the contract. Although there was no past practice clause, the union filed a grievance claiming that the company's action violated past practice and that past practices were automatically incorporated into the agreement on matters not spoken to by the agreement. The employer said the grievance was not arbitrable because there was nothing in the agreement about it.

The union then filed a Section 8(a)(5) charge with the National Labor Relations Board claiming the company's action constituted a refusal to bargain, to which the employer responded that it would arbitrate the question of arbitrability. The regional office of the Board deferred the case to arbitration. The case was tried before Arbitrator Summers. The union said that it had two possible claims: the company had violated the agreement because the past practice should be deemed incorporated in the agreement, and the practice was not in the agreement and therefore the employer had a duty to bargain under the Act before changing it.

---

[2]*See also Electronic Reproduction Service Corp.*, 213 NLRB 758, 87 LRRM 1211 (1974); *Roy Robinson Chevrolet*, 228 NLRB 828, 94 LRRM 1474 (1977); *General Am. Transp. Corp.*, 228 NLRB 808, 94 LRRM 1483 (1977).

[3]65 LA 816 (1975) (Summers, Arb.).

The union decided that the second claim was the stronger one. I read the union's reason into the decision; it is not spelled out.

Before Summers, the union claimed that the recognition clause of the agreement incorporated the duty to bargain and that the company violated the recognition clause by eliminating this practice without first bargaining with the union. The company responded that that question was clearly not arbitrable, and it had never agreed to arbitrate it. However, it was then prepared to arbitrate the question of whether or not it had violated some implied obligation to preserve past practices. Each party had said that one issue or the other was not arbitrable. The question is, what should the arbitrator do with two substantive questions before him. First, did the company violate the contract on the theory that it impliedly covered the question of whether or not the company had a right to discontinue the discounts on purchases of electrical appliances? The arbitrator may have felt that if he decided either of those contractual questions, the Board would say that his decision disposed of the controversy as to whether there had been a violation of the Act. He said neither question was arbitrable—because some party at one point had so contended—and refused to decide any of it. This appears to be an astonishing result, although the follow-up is that the union then proceeded with its Section 8(a)(5) charge, and the Board found there was a violation of the statutory duty to bargain. However, if the arbitrator had decided that the contract did not provide a duty to bargain—as I think he should have—the Board would probably have said that he had disposed of the statutory issue and would not have taken it up.

If I had been the arbitrator I would have said no to the question: does the recognition clause of the agreement include a duty to bargain about a change in a matter not dealt with in the agreement, a duty to bargain that is imposed by Section 8(a)(5) of the National Labor Relations Act. There is no evidence that the parties in a recognition clause meant to incorporate the whole National Labor Relations Act. Therefore, I would have rejected the grievance on that ground. I would have turned next to the past-practice question, and I do not know how I would have come out. It would have depended on the evidence, but I would have disposed of it because I clearly had jurisdiction to decide any question with respect to the interpretation and application of the agreement. If one party says a provision of the agreement incorporates the federal statute, I think I have an obligation to decide whether it does or not, because I am then interpreting what the agreement provides.

Mine would have been strictly a contract interpretation and application decision. The arbitrator of record was smarter because he knew that if he said that the agreement did not incorporate the National Labor

Relations Act, the Board would say the Act has nothing more to do with the case, which probably should have happened. The opposite happened, and the Board found a violation of the Act.

Incorporation of External Law

There are some agreements which specifically incorporate the outside law, and in those instances an arbitrator has no option. If both parties submitted the external law issue to the arbitrator, even if the parties intend to litigate the external law issue later in another forum, he must decide.

A classic case involved the U.S. Steel agreement provision that returning veterans shall have such rights as are guaranteed by the applicable Selective Service Act.[4] An employee was drafted during his probationary period. The selective service law then in effect gave reemployment rights to permanent but not temporary employees. Whether a probationary employee was a permanent or a temporary employee was a question of the proper interpretation of the words permanent and temporary in the statute. When that question came before the arbitrator, he had no option but to interpret the statute. He looked at the district court decisions which had analyzed the law, decided which court decisions he thought were right, and came to a conclusion as to what the federal statute meant.

There is a Fifth Circuit case[5] involving an agreement which said that the company agreed to abide by the provisions of Title VII of the Civil Rights Act of 1964. The parties incorporated the statute into their agreement. If the parties are very clear that they want the arbitrator to interpret and apply external law, and they do that either by the words in the agreement or in the arbitration, the arbitrator has no option but to do so.

Generally, I would avoid doing so whenever possible because it brings the remedy problem squarely to the fore. Under Title VII, if a seniority system is shown to be in violation, the remedy is not to apply back pay but to restructure jobs, change the job progression, order local unions integrated, and red-circle rates. In effect, it involves a whole new seniority system. That is the kind of remedy the courts give. If the parties authorize an arbitrator to apply Title VII, he becomes a kind of interest arbitrator because he has to restructure the relationship between

---

[4]*United Steelworkers Local 1104*, 51 LA 1253 (1968) (Garrett, Arb.).
[5]*Southbridge Plastics v. Local 759, Int'l. Union of United Rubber Workers*, 565 F.2d 913 (5th Cir. 1978).

the parties if he finds that a seniority system is in violation of Title VII. I think an arbitrator should be reluctant to do that in any case. Certainly a newer arbitrator should be reluctant to do it, because one is venturing out into very, very difficult terrain.

I would leave statutory interpretation to the courts unless the parties tell me in fairly explicit terms that they want me to decide it. Earlier I urged the parties not to tell arbitrators to apply external law because I thought it would undercut the effective performance of the function that arbitrators can perform better than courts. I now have a somewhat different view on that position in recognition of the fact that there is a real virtue in taking all problems arising out of the employment relationship to a single forum. Although it does open the arbitrator to review in the courts, it may be that the parties think that is a small price to pay. After all, if an employee gets a fair shake before a fair arbitrator, even though the decision ultimately may not be the one that a court would make, he may be satisfied with it and will not take it further. It is perfectly permissible for the parties to consider that the advantage to their relationship in putting all problems before the arbitrator is greater than the risk that the employee, after the arbitration decision, might say he is not satisfied, that it is a violation of Title VII, and go to court, as the Supreme Court says he is entitled to. I think it is not worth it for the arbitration profession, but the profession does not exist to serve itself. It exists to serve the parties, and if the parties think it is better to have arbitrators act as court masters, subservient to the courts and subject to review by them, arbitrators do not have any choice but to act as court masters.

When the parties specifically state that a violation of the law will be deemed to be a violation of this agreement, an arbitrator must decide what the law means. However, my general stricture is to avoid doing so unless it is quite clear that both parties intend that I do so. If a grievance is based on the law and the law is not specifically incorporated in the agreement, unless the parties say otherwise, I assume that what they said in the contract is what they want me to interpret and apply, even if the words in the contract may be the same as those in a federal statute. The parties have made a specific contractual commitment which the arbitrator is to interpret and apply. What a court may decide those same words mean in a statute may be entirely different.

Let me give an example in a no-discrimination context. Assume that the parties have a no-discrimination clause in the identical words of Title VII of the Civil Rights Act as well as a seniority provision which, for one reason or another, is alleged to violate Title VII of the Civil Rights Act because it constitutes discrimination. Let us push back the clock and assume that the seniority provision segregates jobs so that all jobs involving lifting and carrying more than fifty pounds are reserved exclusively for men. Women are not allowed to bid into seniority lines in which there are jobs that regularly involve lifting and carrying more than fifty pounds. For a time it was thought that such provisions did not violate Title VII of the Civil Rights Act, particularly when state statutes prohibited women from doing such jobs. It is now firmly decided by the courts that all such statutes are invalid, and any such limitation based on sex is discrimination in violation of Title VII. An arbitrator must make an individual judgment that a particular woman cannot safely lift and carry fifty pounds before disqualifying her.

If the parties have a no discrimination clause identical to the Civil Rights Act and have simultaneously negotiated a provision that women shall not be put on jobs that require lifting and carrying more than fifty pounds, they have clearly indicated that, as far as they are concerned, that is not discrimination. If a woman claims a job because, except for the fifty-pound limitation, she would be entitled to it, and asks the arbitrator to revise the seniority provision because it violates the no-discrimination clause, I think the arbitrator must say that he is interpreting this agreement. Although the courts and the EEOC may say that this provision constitutes discrimination, it is perfectly clear that within the four corners of this agreement, these parties did not think so because they simultaneously negotiated a no-discrimination clause and this seniority provision. He is interpreting and applying the agreement; that is his only job.

I think that decision is the path of wisdom. On this particular issue many arbitrators had to decide cases before the law was clear. A substantial number of them held that because there was a no-discrimination clause they had to decide whether or not these weight limitation provisions were valid. They looked at the court decisions then existing and decided that the limitation provisions were valid. They all subsequently turned out to be wrong. One takes a great risk in this area.

When parties use language identical to a statute or regulation, it is of some help for an arbitrator to use the interpretation of that statute or regulation as an interpretive aid in ascertaining the parties' intent, just as other arbitrators' decisions may be used, but it is not binding. An arbitrator should use whatever aids are available in interpreting the contract language. How identical language has been construed is obviously of some influence, but not if it contradicts other language in the agreement.

Contract Provisions in Violation of External Law

Many adventurous arbitrators like to say that every contract is deemed to embody the law, and since the arbitrator interprets and applies the agreement, he must embody all the law. I think that view is wrong. There is a more modified view based on the presence of a savings clause. A typical savings clause might read, "If any part of this agreement shall be held invalid, the rest shall remain in force and effect." Sometimes a clause reads a little more strongly such as, "Any provision in this agreement that is a violation of any law shall be of no further effect, but it will not affect the balance of the agreement." Some arbitrators interpret this as meaning that the arbitrator must decide which provisions of the agreement are in violation of an outside law. My view is that it does not. All the parties have done is say that they want to save whatever parts of the agreement are good, if any part of it should be found to be invalid, but that they do not intend by such a clause to give the arbitrator the jurisdiction to decide whether any part is valid or invalid.

Most of those clauses were introduced at the time of the Taft-Hartley Act with its restrictions on the union shop. Those clauses became quite popular at that time because no one was sure whether or not the union shop provisions would continue to be valid, and the Board held[6] that if the union shop provision in an agreement was invalid the whole agreement was invalid. There was a similar problem because of Section 14(b). If there is a national agreement, some parts of the agreement are valid in some states and not valid in other states. The clause was designed to preserve those things. Unless the parties exhibit an intention that they want the arbitrator to act as a judge and decide what the state or federal law means, I do not think the arbitrator has authority to do that. I would treat such a clause in the same way. If both parties agree that this is the question they want the arbitrator to decide, there is no problem. When one party wants the arbitrator to decide a question of law and the other party disagrees, I do not think the arbitrator has the authority. If he preempts that authority, I think he may find himself in a situation which he is not competent to handle. If an arbitrator decides what the law means and a party goes to court, all the nonreviewability of arbitrators' decisions theory is moot.

The public sector is different. In the public sector, employment is very often governed by civil service laws which are not superseded by a collective bargaining statute. There are two sets of laws governing the

---

[6]*Rockaway News Supply Co.*, 94 NLRB 1056, 28 LRRM 1133 (1951).

employment relationship. How that is to be integrated in the public sector I do not know and have not thought about it enough to make any generalization. I do not know if any generalization can be made, because the result depends on the particular state's statutes and the particular kind of public service employees involved.

Suppose the employer responds to a woman's seniority grievance by saying that while it may be what the agreement provides, it violates the law. The employer says that he will not give that woman that job because it would require lifting and carrying more than fifty pounds, and that would be a violation of a state statute; or, this woman would be entitled to this job but state law says one cannot employ a woman on a job which does not have a lunch period, and this job does not have a lunch period; or, this job requires working at night alone and the statute forbids a woman working alone at night. All these limitations reflect state statutes which have existed. The employer's position is that under the agreement the grievant would be entitled to the job under seniority provisions, but public law prevents him from giving her the job.

How does the arbitrator respond? If he entertains that defense, he has to decide first what the public law does or does not permit, and very often secondly, whether that law is valid or invalid under the supremacy clause of the United States Constitution. Lawyers might, by inclination, want to decide that question. Nonlawyers might be even more inclined to decide it. I feel strongly that an arbitrator should not decide it unless both parties agree that he should.

I use a case, modified, that I had involving this problem in particularly egregious form to illustrate. Under the contract assume, to simplify it for the moment, that the grievant is entitled to a job of off-loading lumber in a saw mill. The company refuses to give it to him because he is seventeen years old, and regulations under the Fair Labor Standards Act say that an employer cannot put any person under the age of eighteen at a job that requires cleaning a saw. The company contends it would be a violation of the Fair Labor Standards Act to put the employee on this job. The union files a grievance saying that under the agreement the company must put him on the job.

The possible issues between the parties are first, is the regulation valid; second, does this job require cleaning a saw, and if so, is it the kind of cleaning that the federal regulation is intended to cover.

The union argues first that the job does not require the employee to clean a saw at all. Secondly, if on occasion the employee does clean the saw, he does not get into the saw, and the regulation is really talking about getting into a saw. The only cleaning required of the employee is to stand with a hose five feet away and squirt it on the saw, and that should be construed as not cleaning the saw under the regulation. Therefore, he is entitled to the job.

If both parties want an arbitrator to decide whether giving the seventeen-year-old the job would be a violation of the regulation, the arbitrator has an obligation to do so even if technically he is only supposed to interpret and apply the contract. In my case the union said it was not within the arbitrator's scope to do more than decide if the grievant was entitled to the job under the contract. When the union presented its case, it established the grievant's contractual right, which was not contested, and rested in five minutes. The employer wanted a man from the Department of Labor to testify about the regulation, but the union objected.

Since I did not have agreement, I said that under the contract I have authority only to interpret and apply the contract. Under the collective bargaining agreement, the grievant is entitled to the job. If following the contract causes the company to violate the Fair Labor Standards Act, that problem should be solved in another forum. I made it quite clear that my award would be subject to nullification by a court. I was not trying to bind a court to the conclusion that the grievant was entitled to the job. The court should decide whether or not it would be a violation of the Fair Labor Standards Act, unless the parties agreed that I should do it.

I have simplified the case; there was another element. The person involved was an applicant for employment, not an employee. The contract provided that there should be no discrimination against any employee or applicant for employment on the basis of age, and the claim made was that this no-discrimination provision had been violated. The union's case was very simple. The company did not hire him because he was seventeen. What clearer case of discrimination on the basis of age could there be? He was disqualified solely because of his age. The company said that this was not a violation of the agreement because the agreement language is exactly the same as the language of the Age Discrimination in Employment Act, and that Act applies only to persons between ages forty and sixty-five. The person does not come within the Age Discrimination in Employment Act and, therefore, is not covered by the agreement.

In my decision I said there could have been an argument in the union's insistence of no discrimination based upon age, that meaning that there should be no discrimination if the man was capable of performing the job. For example, if an employer will not hire a five-year-old child, it would be very difficult to file a grievance on the basis of the age discrimination provision. The employer could legitimately say that a five-year-old cannot do the work. Therefore, it could be argued that because of the federal law, the seventeen-year-old is not capable of doing the work. That would have presented an interesting question, but unfortunately or fortunately—fortunately for me—the employer made no such argument. The employer said that the clause was only meant to apply the Age Discrimination in Employment Act to things covered by that Act. There was no evidence of that intent, and I saw no basis for doing that since a nineteen-year-old or a twenty-five-year-old would not be covered by that Act either. The other contention was that the Fair Labor Standards Act makes it impossible to comply with this provision if one construes it that way, and I declined to decide that question. That made the case relatively easy to decide.

Incidentally, because the parties had invested money in having me, I offered to make findings of fact as to what the job involved, and what the cleaning was, if any, if the parties agreed that I should. I had had no testimony, only an allegation in the opening statement that there was cleaning. The union accepted my offer but the employer refused. Because both parties did not agree, I did not make those findings.

The case could have been handled another way. Another arbitrator might have taken the stance that if there was a reasonable dispute about an issue, he would not decide it, but if it was perfectly clear that the action requested would violate the law, he would not entertain it because it was frivolous. Therefore he would assume the law was perfectly clear. That is a very risky stance because what is perfectly clear to A sometimes is very doubtful to B, but it would have been much more difficult in the case of the seventeen-year-old if the employer had gone to the Department of Labor and obtained a ruling that employment of the person violated the Fair Labor Standards Act. Of course if that were the case, I do not think the union would have filed a grievance, or if it did not file a grievance, it would have sought review of that ruling under the Fair Labor Standards Act.

I decided that the union was not claiming under the statute but rather under the no-discrimination clause. The no-discrimination clause said no discrimination on the basis of age, and clearly the company did make a distinction based on age, and I was only interpreting the agreement. I made it clear in the opinion that I expected the award to be subject to review on the question of external law, although not on the question of what the contract said. The union went to court to enforce the award. The employer refused to comply with the award contending that it violated the Fair Labor Standards Act.

In the case involving the seventeen-year-old for instance, the court should be free to take testimony as to what kind of cleaning was involved, whether or not the regulation was intended to cover that kind of cleaning, and conclude that under the regulation the company cannot employ the person and, therefore, cannot comply with the award. An arbitrator does not decide a question of federal law, and the court should not be prejudiced by his failure to do so. One must be very careful in this kind of problem to be quite explicit about what is and what is not being decided. The general lesson is that unless the parties agree either in the arbitration proceeding or in contractual terms that the arbitrator should apply the external law, he should not.

I had a case in which I was asked to interpret and find applicable a provision in an agreement which had been previously the subject of litigation before the Board and the Second Circuit and which had been held to be a violation of Section 8(e) of the National Labor Relations Act. The agreement required the employer, a shipping company, if it sold its ships, to provide in the contract of sale that the purchaser would man the ships with the people who were present occupants of the positions on the ships. The union contended the employer violated the agreement. The company argued that the agreement was invalid because the Board had declared it violative of Section 8(e) of the National Labor Relations Act as well as of the antitrust and maritime laws. The company argued that it would be a felony to enforce this provision because to do so would be to implement a violation of a criminal statute, which is what the antitrust laws are.

I felt that my job was to interpret and apply the agreement and determine what remedy seemed appropriate. I ordered the sale not to be completed unless a provision for the continued employment of the affected employees was taken care of in the sale. This was contrary to the terms of the sale. The company had already agreed to sell millions of dollars worth of vessels without any complement of the employees at issue. Of course I knew that the legal question would be decided elsewhere, and it was. Five days after my award the union asked the court to enforce the award by enjoining the sale unless the award was complied with, and the court refused to do so on the ground it was probably a violation of the antitrust laws. On appeal the Second Circuit said it was not sure whether there was a violation of the antitrust laws but, given the equities, it did not think it was an abuse of discretion for the lower court to deny the preliminary injunction.[7] The award was reversed and the people were forced off the job. I would not become involved in the antitrust allegation, a very murky area of the law, and I would not get

---

[7]*National Maritime Union*, 196 NLRB 1100, 80 LRRM 1198 (1972), 486 F.2d 907, 84 LRRM 2491 (2d Cir. 1973).

into the Section 8(e) question because I think the Second Circuit was wrong in its 8(e) decision.

Effect of Other Decisions

It is standard learning in the field of arbitration that each collective bargaining agreement is a fundamental law or constitution unto itself. No decision by another arbitrator under another collective bargaining agreement, even if the words are identical to different agreements, is precedent in the lawyer's sense. That is so legally. A prior arbitration decision by one arbitrator construing the precise provision of the same contract which is involved in current dispute being heard by another arbitrator is problematic. Another circumstance is one or the other party contending before the same arbitrator that he has erroneously construed an agreement in a particular way previously, in which instance I do not think any of the usual statements about the use of precedent apply. Ralph Seward addresses this last circumstance in a case reversing an earlier interpretation he had made of a particular provision of the Beth- lehem Steel contract.[8] He states that technically no prior decision is binding on an arbitrator. The arbitrator's responsibility is to decide an issue as fairly and wisely as possible, to interpret and apply the agree- ment, and not alter or depart from it; and at the same time to avoid perpetuating past errors merely because they have been embodied in prior decisions of another arbitrator or his own.

On the other hand, one of the primary purposes of the procedure is to aid the parties in reaching a clear understanding of the meaning of their agreement as applied in practice in the plant. Relitigation of decided issues generally defeats this purpose. In the last analysis the parties must decide how to treat their umpire machinery. They decide which cases shall be brought to arbitration and what effect shall be given to umpire decisions in their grievance meetings. The umpire is respon- sible for clear and consistent contractual interpretation, and in working toward that end, he must place a burden of proof and persuasion on the party that claims that prior decisions on a question of contractual inter- pretation were erroneous and should be reversed.

Some lawyers will argue res judicata, which technically is not applicable to a different grievance. It could be collateral estoppel, a somewhat different doctrine. I am very impatient with lawyers who use such words. An arbitrator is called to perform a function under the agreement, and the question is to what extent should he pay attention

---

[8]Steelworkers Handbook and Arbitration Decisions xxvii (1960).

to what other people have decided and, indeed, to what he has decided. He should pay considerable attention. I find reading other arbitrators' decisions on particular issues to be enormously illuminating in helping me to decide what I think is the proper resolution of a particular case, and I will very frequently cite them as illustrative of the way in which other arbitrators handled this kind of problem. I do not cite them as precedents which have to be followed, because they are not.

All an award settles is that grievance. It does not manifest an intention on the part of the parties that the arbitration award in a contract interpretation case is final and binding on that question for the term of the contract, but as a practical matter, one should not reverse a ruling once a contract has been construed. If it is one's own award, one must be fully persuaded that an egregious error has been made in the prior instance. If it can be shown that one has seriously erred, one should reverse. A particular case always involves a large conglomeration of facts. In deciding a case, an arbitrator thinks he sees the principle governing it and sets forth that principle. He may not quite see that a change in the fact pattern would make a decision come out the other way and that the principle expressed is broader than the facts and the principle expressed earlier is thereby wrong. This is the traditional way the common law has developed. The possibility of having to admit error in stating the broad principle may arise. The only thing that is final and binding is the award, not the reasons stated in the opinion.

I suppose there could be a different answer, if the parties specifically requested a broader decision. I have never had a case like that. Usually the question is what relief shall be granted the grievant. For example, in a case of a grievant claiming more overtime pay because he thinks it ought to be calculated one way and the company argues that it ought to be calculated another way, the only thing that is final and binding is that the grievance is granted and the employee is awarded the overtime pay.

If one arbitrator decides the company did not violate the contract by assigning overtime in a particular way, that determination could be, in fact, res judicata, because the arbitrator has answered a particular question asked by the parties, but that would be a rare situation. In most cases the issue is, did the company in this particular case violate the collective bargaining agreement, and that is all an arbitrator can decide. The arbitrator has a rationale as to why it did or did not violate the contract, but I do not think the parties are bound by the rationale.

It would be very unusual to have to decide that a prior interpretation of a contract was wrong. There was such a case involving the interpretation of language identical to the Bethlehem Steel language which Arbitrator Seward had interpreted in a previous opinion. The case was a very complicated one involving overtime, and Arbitrator Valtin said, with all due respect, that Seward was wrong. Valtin came out with the opposite result. Seward, in a subsequent Bethlehem case, said Valtin was right. In that case there was identical language in the same industry with the same negotiating background.

I caution that one should be very reluctant to reverse in that kind of a case. Arbitration awards exist not only to handle a particular grievance but to guide the parties as to how to conduct themselves in the light of the agreement as the arbitrator has interpreted it for them. Therefore, it should take the most extraordinary persuasion to reverse a standing interpretation.

In dealing with other arbitrators under other agreements, even though the language may be the same, the parties have not tailored their operation to a prior award. Other cases can be very helpful. For example in a discharge case, the question may be, is the conduct *just cause* for discharge? Does just cause mean what the arbitrator personally thinks is just, or is the question could the employer reasonably say it was just, and in either case what are the standards? Certain standards developed in the industrial community are reflected in arbitrators' decisions. I find it very helpful to read what arbitrators have written in similar kinds of situations, recognizing that I am simply informing myself about what other arbitrators have done when faced with similar kinds of problems, and ascertaining the mores of the industrial community.

I had a discharge case that involved marijuana. Just cause for discharge differs for possession and smoking. The mores of the community are changing on that subject, as are arbitrators' decisions. Earlier decisions held that an ounce found in an employee's pocket was reason to fire him. Under external law, possession is usually a felony. In my case, the grievant, a waiter at a Las Vegas hotel, was found smoking a marijuana cigarette and was fired on grounds that smoking marijuana is a felony in Nevada. The waiter said that he may have had possession of this cigarette but someone else had handed it to him, he had not brought it to the lot, and he never smoked marijuana. I concluded that he was not telling the truth. Obviously, if smoking marijuana is a felony, it is a ground for discharge.

Nevertheless, I was curious about how other arbitrators handled marijuana cases. In reviewing other decisions, I found many involving collective bargaining agreements in which a contract provision said that the possession of narcotic drugs on the premises was a ground for discharge. There are many decisions as to whether or not marijuana is a narcotic drug. As to use of marijuana without such a prohibiting contract provision, there was one case that possibly upheld discipline, and I thought it was wrong. I find it very useful in disciplinary cases to read what other arbitrators have done, not because they are binding or because they are precedent, but because they are just useful ways to help me come up with a reasonable application of the agreement in my case.

There was clearly cause for discipline. However, the second question involved consideration of just cause for discharge. I was very curious to find out whether, if I looked through the cases, I could find arbitrable jurisprudence to support the thesis that where there is refusal to obey a direct order, discipline is appropriate but discharge is too much if there was a reasonable basis for the employee to believe that the rule was in error or violated the contract.

I researched cases on discharge for refusal to obey a direct order and found that whenever there was a legitimate reason for the refusal, almost all arbitrators said discipline was proper but discharge was excessive, which had been my conclusion. The research reassured me that discharge was an excessive disciplinary response. I thought the company was wrong in discharging the grievant. I thought the union officials were absolutely outrageous in using this method of carrying out the protest about the cancellation of the bonus arrangement and jeopardizing the jobs of nine men. I thought the discharged drivers should be reinstated after a lengthy period of disciplinary suspension.

However, it is a great mistake to look at the published awards and, if ten decisions go one way and one decision another way, to say there is authority one way or the other. A decision to publish is an arbitrary selection process. Authority depends on who wrote the cited decision.

I recall another discharge case which involved this same insubordination principle, with a permanent arbitrator who was also a distinguished law professor. The company had small trucks used to haul tin plate to the head of a can line. Employee X drove such a truck whenever he had an opportunity, even though it was not his job. However, employee X was not a good driver, and he often got in trouble when he drove a truck. The plant manager told him that truck driving was not his job and that the next time he was caught driving a truck, he would be fired. Subsequently, when the assigned truck driver was not there, the foreman told employee X to drive the truck. Employee X refused, and the foreman ordered him to drive. When employee X requested permission to talk to his union steward, the foreman told employee X that he could talk to his union steward after he drove the truck on the specific assignment. The employee refused again, and the foreman fired him. The arbitrator sustained the discharge.

That was insubordination of a direct order three times repeated. Employee X had a legitimate reason why he thought he should not have driven the truck. I think he should have driven the truck, since he was specifically ordered to do so, and then filed his grievance. The company lost considerable production as the result of employee X's refusal, but employee X should not have been fired.

I want to emphasize that one thing an arbitrator cannot do is balance his award in relation to the parties. He may feel uncomfortable in denying fifteen successive grievances, but he must decide each case without regard to how many are decided one way or the other. Generally speaking, an employer is almost as unhappy in winning cases that he should not have won as he is in losing cases that he thinks he ought not to have lost. The employer may lose confidence in the arbitrator and want to be rid of him. An arbitrator should seek to create in both employer and union a feeling of understanding of their problems and fair, responsive judgments. That is what makes an arbitrator employable. Continued employability depends upon one's reputation, and when an arbitrator decides a case against a party fairly, it may even increase his employability by that party. Sometimes unions take a case to arbitration that they know they ought to lose, but there is internal pressure for the union to take it. Sometimes management, rather than settle, takes a case to arbitration although they think they should lose it, because of other factors. Both parties are as unhappy when they win a case they should not have won as they are in the opposite situation.

Past Practice

Past practice arises more than any other subject in arbitrations. It is a critical issue.[9] Obviously if an agreement is genuinely ambiguous, the way the parties have acted under that or previous agreements is very helpful and usually binding in interpreting the agreement. In an agreement which dictates that a grievance must be processed from one step to another within fifteen days, does it mean fifteen calendar days or fifteen working days? If the parties have always treated as timely an appeal taken within fifteen working days, then that is what *days* means. On the other hand, if the company has always refused to deal with a

---

[9]For a fuller discussion of the issue, *see* Aaron, *The Uses of the Past in Arbitration*, in ARBITRATION TODAY (Proceedings of the 8th Annual Meeting, National Academy of Arbitrators) 1 (BNA Books, 1955); Mittenthal, *Past Practice and the Administration of Collective Bargaining Agreements*, in ARBITRATION AND PUBLIC POLICY (Proceedings of the 14th Annual Meeting, National Academy of Arbitrators) 30 (BNA Books, 1961); and Waller, *The Silent Contract vs. Express Provisions*, in COLLECTIVE BARGAINING AND THE ARBITRATOR'S ROLE (Proceedings of the 15th Annual Meeting, National Academy of Arbitrators) 117 (BNA Books, 1962).

grievance filed more than fifteen calendar days afterward, then *days* means fifteen calendar days. The difficulty arises when the parties have not construed the provision consistently, and the arbitrator cannot get any other light on the subject. The arbitrator must then determine which interpretation he thinks is right in light of his experience.

Consider a contract interpretation case in which the company decided that it wanted to adhere to the contract, rather than to past practice that is contrary to what the contract says. For example, the contract seniority provision says that seniority shall be considered only for promotions, layoffs, recalls from layoff, demotions, and transfers, and yet the company has consistently allocated overtime on a seniority basis.

Note the definition of practice. It is not only that things have been done in a certain way, it is a practice only when it has become the accepted and understood way of dealing with a given set of facts. What does the arbitrator do when the company gives overtime to the junior man and says that the grievant has no grievance under this contract. If there is an established practice which has been uniform for a long period of time, acknowledged and known to both employees and employer, that a seniority provision should apply to overtime in accordance with the practice, despite the language in the contract, most arbitrators will concur in that kind of a situation. To those who would say it is unjudicious and unlawyerlike, I refer to *Markham v. Cabell*.[10] Construing a World War I statute in which the Supreme Court sustained a decision of the Second Circuit by Learned Hand, who said, "make a fortress out of the dictionary," the Court simply read 1917 to mean 1941.

A collective bargaining agreement is unlike a contract for the sale of real estate or a commercial contract drawn up by lawyers in great detail and usually expressing all the obligations and understanding of the parties who meet for one transaction and have no other relationship. The collective bargaining agreement is meant to govern the day-to-day relations of employer and employee, a very complex matter. One cannot possibly spell out in detail in the contract all the relationships which exist. Indeed if one were to try to spell them out, one would encounter problems in trying to negotiate such an agreement, particularly in a large enterprise. Generally speaking, the parties attempt to deal with the problem areas. Where there are no problems and no dispute, they do not attempt to write down the way things are. Sometimes, when the parties to a collective bargaining agreement cannot agree about an issue in dispute, they use ambiguous language in their contract, and that is when past practice becomes important. Sometimes, there are issues the

---

[10]148 F.2d 737 (2d Cir. 1945), 326 U.S. 404 (1945).

parties do not think about. It is surprising how many things one might naturally expect would be dealt with in a collective bargaining agreement that are not.

American Manufacturing,[11] one of the Steelworkers Trilogy cases, is a classic case where something was not dealt with in the collective bargaining agreement. An employee who was out on a compensable disability applied for compensation for permanent partial disability, and the claim was settled. Armed with a doctor's certificate, the employee sought to return to work. Based upon the compensable disability settlement, the company refused reemployment. A grievance was filed, and the company refused to arbitrate. To determine the right of the employee to return to work, the Court of Appeals looked to the seniority provisions of the contract which said seniority shall govern where abilities are relatively equal. The court concluded that an employee with a permanent partial disability cannot be relatively equal to other employees. That was a very interesting decision because the relative ability seniority standard had not been applied by the parties to return from illness situations before. The collective bargaining agreement at American Manufacturing was silent on this question. By practice, it was understood that if an employee were able to return to work from a disability, he got his own job back.

That is a classic case of a past practice which is not dealt with in the collective bargaining agreement but which everybody understands. If the company had changed its practice to invoke the relative ability seniority provision for an employee who was off on a compensable disability, an arbitrator should have enforced the constant past practice of entitling an employee to his own job when he is well enough to return. The Court of Appeals erred because it looked to the four corners of the agreement and had no knowledge of what the standard practice was with respect to disability. Sometimes an agreement will specify that seniority terminates when an employee is out sick after a certain period of time, but if it is a compensable disability it is a longer period of time. The assumption is that when an employee comes back within that time, he comes back to his old job, but the agreements usually do not say so because everybody understands that to be the case.

In the first case discussed, the parties never thought about overtime distribution. It had always been done on a seniority basis and so was not written into the contract. It would be quite a different matter if the contract said that seniority shall not be used in allocating overtime.

---

[11]*United Steelworkers v. American Manufacturing. Co.*, 264 F.2d 624, 43 LRRM 2757 (6th Cir. 1959), 363 U.S. 564, 46 LRRM 2414 (1960).

The distinction as to when the arbitrator should look to past practice is whether or not the parties have really addressed this problem in their agreement. Sometimes it is quite clear. The parties say there shall be no seniority rights to overtime. The parties have addressed this question and have decided what the rule is. Where they have so decided, and somebody says but the company has ignored the rule in practice, there, the parties have made an agreement and the arbitrator has an obligation to abide by the agreement. On the other hand, when the parties omit dealing with an issue in negotiating their collective bargaining agreement, an arbitrator can enforce their practice. He need not give the practice the exclusive force which would be given to a specific address of the problem in the contract and the setting out of a rule.

If there was any specific negotiating history that demonstrated that the parties had thought about a particular problem, that history would be relevant. I have mixed feelings about negotiating history. It is always very helpful for the adjudicator to have access to negotiating history. The problem is he often gets two versions of what the history was. Even if he does not, there is a policy question for the arbitrator if one party objects. Some of the steel contracts specifically forbid the use of negotiating history on the theory that it is necessary to free up the parties to say what they really think in negotiations. There is always the fear that when one party wants a provision that it really thinks is implied somewhere else but wants to secure, the other party will counter with negotiating history in arbitration and claim that this very thing was requested in negotiations and turned down.

It would be impossible for the party to establish a practice that I would use to override an agreement which said seniority shall not be considered in the allocation of overtime. Where the contract is silent and has no past-practice clause, a practice has to be there for a period of time. It is not just a one- or two-time reaction to a given situation. It has to be the understood way of doing things in that particular context by both parties. If that is the understood way of doing things, the arbitrator should enforce it.

The difficulty in that formulation is that when the subject is not mentioned in the collective bargaining agreement, the arbitrator can become enmeshed in all sorts of problems and has to be precise as to what a practice is. For example, I am quite clear how I would decide the right of the employee to get back his job upon return from illness, if it were shown that every time an employee was off for illness he went back. If the grievant was able to do the job, he would get it back.

A paid lunch period is a classic example where there is often no provision in the agreement. Assume that an employer has always allowed employees to go out to eat lunch, never docked their pay when they went out, and there is nothing in the agreement about it. Arbitrators will normally sustain a grievance based on that kind of an established past practice. Suppose workers established a pattern of a half-hour lunch following which someone took forty minutes and was reprimanded by the foreman for the additional ten minutes and thereafter the company took the position that there should be no paid lunch period. Perhaps if the agreement had specifically disallowed a paid lunch period, it would be a difficult case. However, if the company's only defense is a claim of eight hours work for eight hours pay, arbitrators will enforce the practice.

There are also washup-time cases, where employees clock in when they get to their work stations, but the practice at the end of the shift is to let employees leave their work stations and clock out after washing up. If the employer then says he does not want employees to do that anymore because he is paying for that time, employees must clock out when they leave their work stations. If the union can show continuous practice, arbitrators will enforce the practice.

Managerial Prerogatives

Distinguish the washup case from the crew-size case. Arbitration decisions generally do not limit an employer's right to determine crew sizes in the absence of a past practice clause. If there have been five people on a crew from time immemorial and the company decides that only four people should be assigned to a crew henceforth, most arbitrators will not say past practice requires that the fifth man be retained.

There is a past-practice clause in the steel industry which says that past customs or practices providing employee benefits which are within the scope of wages, hours, and working conditions or the application of the agreement in the area of working conditions shall be retained; there is also a provision for getting rid of the past practice if the basis on which the past practice existed is changed. Arbitrators in the steel industry have said that this clause covered crew size, as long as there was no change in the technology which led to the crew size. If in a job unit with an established crew of five, a company becomes aware that one person is always idle and seeks to cut the crew to four, arbitrators have held that the custom of a five-man unit is preserved by the agreement. The biggest strike in the country's history occurred over the attempt to change such a clause. On the other hand, if a company installs a new machine, it can reduce crew size. The classic instance involved a cab on a hot metal crane. Because the operator's job is a hot, miserable one, the practice was to have two people working the job alternately. When the company air-conditioned the cab, it was clear that the spell man could be withdrawn because the underlying conditions changed.

The company was claiming a management prerogative. To illustrate, assume that hypothetically a contract is silent on starting time. After twenty years of starting at 7 A.M., the company posts a new 8 A.M. schedule, and the union points to past practice. Most arbitrators will say that the fact that the employer did not exercise his right to change schedules does not mean that he gave up that right, and arbitrators will sustain his right to change schedules.

I cannot articulate a theory to differentiate this case from the earlier one. Of the various theories presented, none satisfy me. Some say that the washup time and the paid lunch period relate to employment emoluments, not to managerial prerogatives. Other arbitrators talk about management rights clauses. I suppose the distinction is really between specific employee benefits, such as lunch time or washup time, and restrictions which impede management's ability to manage the working forces. When a practice exists on the latter side of that line, an arbitrator does not rely on a past practice on the theory that management has the right to set the starting time. The fact that management had not exercised that right over a period of time does not mean it has lost it. In the case involving the lunch period, one could say equally well that management had the right to require work all during the eight hours paid for by the company, and they had not lost the right to do it just because they have not exercised that right, but arbitrators have come out the other way. I think one approach is regarded as a greater impingement on management's ability to run the enterprise than the provision of specific benefits, whether or not there is a management rights clause. The usual management rights clause is totally irrelevant, because I would come up with the same answer in every case, with or without the crutch of the management rights provisions. The grievant claims that management violated the agreement. The fact that management reserves the right to direct the working force, providing it observes the provisions of the agreement, does not mean anything.

When I was negotiating on behalf of unions, employers regularly added more pieces to the management rights clause. The union was concerned because these additions spelled out such factors as the right to direct the working force provided they observed the provisions of the agreement. My reaction was that the more the employer adds, the better for the union, because the one item the employer does not mention is the one that will cause trouble to management. Unless the contract does not have the express or implied proviso that management does these things subject to the provisions of the agreement, if the clause reads, "provided none of these management rights shall be subject to the grievance and arbitration provision," it really does make a difference. The standard no-discrimination clause does not make a difference either, because to discriminate in the application of the terms of the agreement is to violate the agreement whether or not there is a no-discrimination clause.

The existence of management rights clauses may make a difference to the National Labor Relations Board in deciding a *Collyer*-type case. If the arbitrator in the *Western Massachusetts Electric*[12] case had found nothing in the agreement providing for discounts and denied the grievance, the Board would have found this a subject not covered in the collective bargaining agreement and therefore a duty to bargain and a violation of Section 8(a)(5). If the arbitrator had said that he found nothing in the agreement providing for discounts and, in addition, there is a management rights clause which governs, the Board would have concluded that the management rights clause made the difference, and there would be no violation of Section 8(a)(5). Whether the arbitrator refers to the management rights clause or not is immaterial, but the use of the words will make a difference in what happens before the Board.

In writing any decision in which I deny a grievance, I say, "I find that the employer did not violate the agreement." I can add, "and therefore since the management is given the right to manage the plant and direct the working force, I deny the grievance," or I can omit that phrase. Some companies feel strongly that they do not want any management rights clause. I know of no difference in the outcome from two agreements which are otherwise the same except for the presence or absence of that clause.

A disciplinary case is different. Assuming that the contract gives the employer the right to change a rule, there must be fair notice given prior to disciplinary action. For example, a furniture factory employer has the right to forbid smoking, but if there is an area which he feels has become a fire hazard and which was not previously so designated, he cannot discipline employees for violating the changed no-smoking rule unless he tells them.

The arbitrator's job is to interpret and apply the agreement, and if there is a disagreement about what was actually said, to look at the whole agreement and ask what would be reasonable.

---

[12]*See supra* note 3.

Arbitration Procedures

Theodore J. St. Antoine

I am in the uncomfortable position of being the primary expositor on a subject that I think is very much a matter of discretion in most cases, that is, how an arbitrator handles a hearing. One of the common characteristics I have detected among arbitrators is their apparent certitude on a disputed issue, even though they may disagree violently with other experienced arbitrators. Some of them will say that whatever internal anguish or difficulty an arbitrator has in coming to a decision, he should never display that to the parties. I myself cannot accept that advice simply because I am a perennial worrier and never quite sure about anything; it would be pure fakery for me to exhibit any other attitude. I think that the surest way to get along with the parties is to be oneself and not try to emulate others.

Method of Designation

The way an arbitrator responds in dealing with the parties will depend to some extent upon the method of his designation. There are several different ways in which designation of an arbitrator can come about. Formal appointing agencies, the American Arbitration Association (AAA) or the Federal Mediation and Conciliation Service (FMCS), may make the designation. This means an arbitrator has gone through a sifting process, has been appointed to one of the panels, and the agency has offered a select number of names to parties requesting a list. That procedure involves discarding unacceptable arbitrators and listing preferences for others. If appointed by AAA, an arbitrator deals with the parties only through the Association; he has no direct contact with them by letter or telephone, only at the hearing itself. The setting of the time and place for the hearing and similar arrangements are made by AAA. If appointed by FMCS or contacted by a party or parties acting on their own, arrangements are handled by the arbitrator. If the parties have gotten together and selected an arbitrator, he must be careful to maintain equality and deal with the parties jointly.

I prefer to deal with the parties in writing because conference calls are inconvenient, and if I call one party or the other, there can be some uneasiness. Occasionally the parties' appointing letter will indicate that the arbitrator may use Mr. X or Ms. Y as contact. In that case, of course, the arbitrator is entitled to deal with that person individually. Usually the parties have not thought about these things. Therefore I think a letter sent to both parties indicating two or three available dates and asking them to list their preferences is the best way to proceed.

In writing to the parties (or talking to AAA) to suggest hearing dates available to you, do not give too many dates; I do not give more than two or three. Set a deadline by which the parties must respond, so as not to leave indefinite open dates and thus be unable to schedule anything else for them.

An arbitrator wants to avoid calling the parties individually. By sending a joint letter with both names and the addresses of both parties, the arbitrator accords equal treatment to the parties and has a written record of the communications. Some arbitrators have found it preferable to make a conference telephone call. In such cases it ought to be made clear that this telephone call is not for a discussion of the issues, because one or the other may try to discuss the merits of the case. The only topic for discussion is the date and place of the hearing.

Arbitrators differ with respect to a cutoff date for cancellations after which the parties are charged for the scheduled date. Full-time arbitrators invariably have a penalty clause, some of which are very elaborate. The usual format requires notification of cancellation within a certain number of days prior to the scheduled hearing or a certain percentage of the regular per diem charge is assessed. The majority of arbitrators do not charge a full rate. A full-time arbitrator can ordinarily put that day to use writing an opinion and award in another case. As a moonlighting arbitrator, I usually am so happy to find I have a free date that it does not occur to me to charge. Certainly a full-time professional should charge; that is only fair to him. If an arbitrator has been approached by parties on their own, there ought to be a statement in his first letter to them.

Need for Impartiality

The need for equality of treatment starts when an arbitrator is appointed and continues throughout the proceeding. It ought to be symbolized by a whole set of little gestures which may not seem terribly important in and of themselves, but all of which together create the notion that the arbitrator is not a friend of either party in the handling of this case. I usually make a point not to come early to the hearing room. I like to have both parties there first so I am not found chatting amiably with one side when the other arrives. When I do arrive, I introduce myself and shake hands with all the principals around the room. If there is an audience, I do not circulate through the audience.

If, as it often happens at the outset of one's career, there are friends present, I try to say hello first to a person who is not a friend. Needless to say, once the hearing starts, the counsel are addressed as Mr. or Ms.; do not use first names. I feel this is most necessary for somebody who on other occasions, as one of my closet friends, would be called by his first name. I think these little touches are important.

When the meal recess comes, I do not join a party for lunch or dinner, even though it means a lonely session at the table instead of a convivial get-together with an old chum. I express my regrets and go off by myself; that is the safest route. Very rarely, the two parties will say that they are not planning any caucuses at the lunch hour, are going to eat together, and ask the arbitrator to join them. There is no problem then, if nothing about the case is said to one or the other of the two groups. Surprisingly, even good friends sometimes try to take advantage in these situations.

It is extremely uncomfortable to walk into the hearing room and find only one party there, strenuously insisting that his witnesses are present and he is ready to begin. The case may have been scheduled three months ago and the other party called five minutes ago to say he cannot make it and wants a postponement. The party in attendance doesn't want a postponement and is ready to go forward with the evidence.

Ex Parte Hearings

American Arbitration Association rules provide that the arbitrator can, in appropriate circumstances, hold an ex parte hearing. I strongly advise, if possible, not to do that. Try to persuade the moving party not to push on the request, and find some good reason the motion should not be granted. It would be troublesome to proceed and is likely to lead to a court suit. To proceed would be to negate one of the most significant functions of arbitration, which is to heal whatever wounds the grievance has caused and to maintain the relationship between the parties. Often the latter is far more important, and you have heard said again and again that it is not important who wins or loses the particular case anyway. All of the differences between the parties will be exacerbated if an ex parte hearing occurs. Only under unusual circumstances in which, for example, the person present would be under the most serious inconvenience, or there is an extremely pressing time element, should an ex parte hearing be held. Make sure the evidence is placed on the record; do not accept some kind of motion for a default judgment. Make the party present enough evidence so as to get a sense of the facts, even if it is only coming from one side.

Although arbitrators ordinarily do not like to ask questions, at an ex parte hearing I think arbitrators must do so, to ensure that any obvious points that might have been made by the other side are at least reflected factually in the record in order not to wind up with a record that will lead to an easy subsequent court reversal. In a modest way, ask a few questions.

Ground Rules

I revert now to the usual two-party hearing. At the very outset I like to go over ground rules with the parties, if I have not dealt with them before. I discuss my notion of conducting a hearing but emphasize that the parties are ultimately the ones to be served. If they have any particular desires about procedure, I want to conform to them insofar as I find nothing unseemly or otherwise inappropriate about doing so.

I make known my feelings about how we should proceed. I like an orderly hearing, but also a relatively relaxed and informal one. I do not generally favor technical objections, including hearsay objections; in almost any situation I will accept the evidence and later weigh it on credibility grounds. Ordinarily I will not rule it inadmissible. I want everyone to feel he has had his say. I hope that the participants will not be unduly repetitious, and I will entertain objections if a party seems to be piling up too much cumulative evidence. I will try to keep the parties from getting into personalities unnecessarily, and I will sustain objections to the harassment of witnesses. This simply gives a sense of the kind of proceeding that I expect to have.

I pass appearance lists down each side of the room, asking the parties, their counsel, and witnesses to give their names, titles, and addresses, and at the same time I ask them to designate who is to receive copies of the award and how many copies they wish to receive. I then ask whether or not the parties want to have their witnesses sworn. Parties vary, although employers tend to favor testimony under oath, especially in disciplinary cases. If they defer to me, I will have the witnesses sworn, if it is at all likely there will be disputed questions of fact.

If the witnesses are to be sworn, I take it very seriously. I stand and face a standing witness, ask him to raise his right hand, and intone the oath. I do not run through it simply as chatter; I think it is important to treat it seriously. I do it individually. This reminder has greater impact on the testimony if each witness is sworn individually just before testifying, rather than as a group. I am willing to leave up in the air the issue of whether the swearing in of witnesses is done at all, but once the decision is made to do it, I do not want to cheapen it. Taking an oath is an important piece of business, and if it is going to be done, I want it done well.

Part of my philosophy is that I am at the parties' disposal. They are the ones who are setting the ground rules, as long as the rules are not offensive to me. Arbitrators differ on this. There are some who, while they may say they seek to follow the parties' wishes, take over the whole show after they are appointed and tell the parties how the hearing is to be conducted. Stylistically, I like to be a bit more deferential. I find I usually make most of the decisions anyway.

I tell the parties that I am going to maintain three strings of exhibits: a series of joint exhibits (J) which the parties agree upon, a union series (U), and an employer series (R). I try to collect the joint exhibits which the parties have agreed or can agree on before the record commences. If it is a hearing with a transcript, as soon as the hearing formally opens, I will repeat all the joint exhibits that have been introduced so they may be noted and numbered in the record.

I require nothing in advance of the hearing itself. The current tendency is not to ask for an advance stipulation of the issue and not to get it. Ordinarily the arbitrator will not even know the nature of the dispute. Sometimes because of the way the parties opt for a special expedited procedure there will be an indication that it is a disciplinary case. Very rarely does someone send the arbitrator a copy of a contract. Practically never is anything other than that sent ahead of time. I am naturally a procrastinating person, and I am not troubled by this. After all, 30 to 40 percent of the cases are not heard, and I hate to think of having read a contract and then not having the case go forward.

Official Record

Certain formalities of a hearing are often overdone; one is the matter of transcripts. In an ordinary discipline or discharge case in which there is no complex legal theory involved, I think that transcripts are super-fluous. They do not really add to what the arbitrator takes into account. They are unduly expensive not only because of the reporter's time in preparing the transcript but also because of the time that the parties and the arbitrator are going to spend going over that transcript, if in fact it is produced. In talking with people at conferences and elsewhere, I make this plea and try to alert the parties to what the vast majority of fellow arbitrators that I have talked with assure me is correct, that in the ordinary discipline or discharge case, the transcript is usually of little help and is simply an expensive luxury.

That is not true in complicated cases involving contract interpre-tation or complex job classification issues. In those cases a transcript can be extremely useful. In almost all cases the parties could arrange for a tape recording which is just about as helpful as a transcript and costs next to nothing. The quality of inexpensive cassette recorders has now been so improved that there is little trouble in a fairly sizable room in capturing all the testimony for forty-five minutes a side. It takes only ten seconds to flip the cassette over or replace it. This seems to me an excellent compromise solution to the problem of transcripts. I ask the parties in nearly all cases where there is not a transcript if I may use my own tape recorder, whether or not they are using one, and I find this extremely helpful. It means that I need not interrupt the witness to ask for matters to be repeated.

I take copious notes, and, incidentally, the notes are the official records of the proceeding, unless the parties have agreed on the prep-aration of an official transcript. However, the tape is available if nec-essary to refresh my recollection or to take care of a mass of figures. Occasionally it provides an exact comparison of the testimony of wit-nesses when they are clashing on crucial points, and often the signifi-cance of certain details in one piece of testimony does not become evident until the second witness has testified. I keep a running tally of the number of each tape side together with my notes so that it takes no more than a minute to locate an exact passage to recheck. I do not spend a whole day listening to tapes from beginning to end. That would be an unnecessary drain on the parties' time and my own. I use them simply for confirmation or amplification of what my notes said or clarification of a conflict in testimony. A number of arbitrators are now using this device. Naturally, if a party objects, I do not proceed. It is not required, however, for an arbitrator to give advance notice to the parties of his desire to use a recorder.

When the arbitrator does not know whether it is an ordinary dis-cipline case or a very involved contract interpretation case, and therefore cannot determine in advance whether a transcript would be helpful or not, the parties make that decision. I am always willing to express my view in a conference or to the parties in an informal setting that transcripts in simple cases are not very helpful and not worth the cost in time or trouble, but I would not do so in a given hearing. There I am the parties' servant. If I walk in and a reporter is present, I say nothing, leave my tape recorder in its holder, and go on about my business. In the absence of an official reporter, the parties actually tell me if I can use my own tape recorder.

The parties usually do not have a conflict about whether or not there should be a transcript. If either party wants a transcript, there is a transcript, and if only one party wants a transcript, then that party pays. The AAA rules so provide. The parties frequently dispute over whether or not a recording should be made. My position is that if either party objects, there will not be any recording, including mine. I sometimes feel I am pandering to a silly superstition in treating recordings this way, because it is quite clear that under accepted arbitration procedures either party has a right to a transcript if it insists upon it and is willing to pay for it.

If only one party is willing to pay for a transcript, I take the position that my notes are the official record of that proceeding. If only the employer gets the transcript (which means the union does not agree to pay for it as well) and would like the transcript to be the official record, an arbitrator may respond by saying that he will get a copy of the transcript and make it available to the union, because if it is going to be the official record they have to have access to it. There is one other way that it is sometimes done, and that is for the company to let their copy be made available for the union's examination and use in the company's offices. That is a convenient way to work it out. My position is if the company merely wants the transcript for its own purposes, however, that is not the official record of the proceeding, but my notes are. My position is that the employer can make the transcript the official record if he is willing to make it available to the union and to me, but not if it is for his exclusive use and benefit. That is the distinction. AAA Rule 21 seems in accord.

I have never had a party ask to see my notes. I would have no objection to making them available. Other arbitrators might disagree. In speaking of the official record, I refer only to its use in the arbitration itself for briefing and decisional purposes.

My view that the arbitrator's notes are the official record is shared by other arbitrators. The essence of my position is that nothing else can be the offical record of an arbitral proceeding unless it is available to me and all the parties. Once the employer gives me a copy, I am prepared, if the union wants, to let the union see it and use it in preparing a brief. If the employer wants a record either in tape or transcript form for his own purposes only, I do not regard that as the official record. We are probably exaggerating this as a practical point, because I have never had an employer ask for a transcript and not want me to have a copy.

In those situations where the union does not have practical, as distinguished from theoretical, access, I would insist that the transcript was not the official record of those proceedings. AAA Rule 21 states the arbitrator is to determine when and where the other party may inspect the transcript, if it is the official record. With regard to recordings, I am adamant that the official record is my notes. Tape recordings are simply too fallible and easily doctored.

In cases of enforcement or vacation of an award, parties may seek to get the arbitrator's notes. Often an arbitrator does not just take down what a person said, but also makes notes alongside, including credibility determinations and judgments of what he considers important. He would not want the parties to have access to these notes.

Setting aside the question of how arrangements could be made for transcribing an arbitrator's notes with appropriate deletions of extraneous material, I find it hard to see how those notes would not be subject to subpoena if one of the parties wanted to subpoena the official record of that proceeding. Any party that wants either to enforce or resist the award would be entitled to the whole official record. I do not know that it has ever come up. I have seen no cases on this question.

Most arbitrators would say that if no statement is made by the arbitrator as to his policy with regard to his notes being the official record, and no other statement is made by the parties, there is sound precedent to believe that the record is the arbitrator's notes. However, it is not the making of the statement, it is the recording of the notes that makes them the official record. I want to repeat that whenever arbitrators have said their notes were the official record, as far as I know they have been thinking of the disposition of the arbitration case. They have not been thinking of whether or not it is the kind of public document that would be subject to subpoena in a subsequent court or agency proceeding. Perhaps better policy calls for preventing anyone from going behind the arbitrator's decision to look at his notes and the scratchings he might have made along the margin. If the arbitrator's notes were subject to subpoena, they should certainly pass through some kind of excising or laundering process. I do not know of a single arbitrator who has been confronted with this problem. I do not think this is a matter of general concern.

Sequestration of Witnesses

One of the parties may ask for sequestration of witnesses. I always wince when that occurs because it suggests that arbitration is not going to serve one of its worthwhile therapeutic functions. Everybody in that room, most of whom have an intense interest in the case, is not now going to have a chance to hear the whole story come forth, to get a sense of what actually occurred, and maybe have his or her recollection jarred. Nonetheless, my inclination is to grant the request with any reasonable basis presented for the making of it. This is especially true in cases of discharge when there is likely to be eyewitness testimony, and there may be contradictions.

The issue will come up much less frequently in contract interpretation, job classification, or technical grievance. It arises when there is the possibility of conflicting eyewitness testimony, and I realize in those situations why a party may legitimately not want any witness aware of what others are saying or be influenced by their comments, so I grant that motion. If one party requests sequestration and the other party vigorously objects, I would ordinarily grant the request, with regrets.

There is a qualification which should be noted. The parties themselves are entitled to be present, including the individual grievant. The testimony of the individual grievant, perhaps the person discharged, obviously may be affected by what other witnesses say. Nonetheless, there is an overriding interest in the party grievant being present and being able to hear everything. Therefore, the grievant is an exception to the sequestration rule.

Framing the Issue

In the best prepared cases there will be a written submission agreed upon by the parties beforehand stating exactly what the issues are. It will be one or more short paragraphs presenting concisely the issue and in effect defining the arbitrator's authority. That is the question the arbitrator must answer, and that is all.

In many cases the parties come to the hearing without having defined the issue. Some experienced, competent arbitrators would stop the proceedings until the parties had written out and agreed upon a statement of the issues. Perhaps I am less demanding or naturally procrastinating and willing to let things develop, but I do not say anything about issues. I am prepared to let the proceedings unfold and listen to how the parties frame the issue. Each party may frame it a little differently or ultimately leave it to me to help articulate the issue.

At some point in the proceeding I like to make a brief statement of my own as to what I understand to be the real question between the parties and have their agreement. Sometimes I phrase it in terms of opposing arguments: I understand the parties' position; the union essentially is saying this; the company is saying essentially that; am I essentially right on this? That is my way of phrasing the issue and handling this troublesome problem, which some fine arbitrators say they simply will not allow to occur. Until they have the parties' written, signed submission, they feel that they do not have the authority as an arbitrator to dispose of it. I have never felt at the end of the hearing that I did not know the problem which was at the heart of the case.

Opening Statements

When an arbitrator receives notification of selection from an appointing agency, the matter at issue is not stated. I like opening statements. If there is anything that would be really helpful ahead of time, although I do not ask for it, it would be a prehearing statement or memorandum. I am not thinking of anything elaborate, but there is nothing that is more helpful, especially if we are dealing with something of any complexity, than to have a good statement in advance of the reception of any evidence as to just what the position of each party is. Ordinarily this is not hard to secure. Most people want to express their concerns. The only difficulty I have encountered is after the moving party makes the opening statement, the other party may ask to reserve its statement until the presentation of his side of the case. If I think there is some reason for that, I accept it, especially in discharge or disciplinary cases.

In a disciplinary case it is ordinarily assumed that the employer has the burden of proof and goes forward first. The union wants to find out exactly what the employer will set forth as the basis for the discipline or the discharge, and what the evidence is. The union then wants to deal with that in its opening statement. I am prepared to follow that procedure.

In other types of cases, such as a contract interpretation case, I want to hear both sides at the outset if at all possible because it aids me immensely in following the reasons and ruling upon any objections that may come up in the course of the hearing. I like to get the two juxtaposed. I have as good a notion at that point as if they were to argue for hours about a written stipulation of just what the difference of position is and what the issue is in this case. I have it without forcing the parties to play games and try to reach a written submission that for whatever reason they have not done voluntarily on their own. That is my solution, and I really think in most cases it works well.

Assuming I do know the nature of the case, I have no established rule as to which party I ask to speak first. The hearing is not a highly stylized, structured setting. It is very important to understand that the arbitrator is simply formulating the issue that the parties have presented, even though they cannot agree on the wording of it. The arbitrator is not formulating his own issue between the parties; he is simply characterizing in his language the issue they have brought him. In the vast majority of cases I find this no problem whatsoever. However, there are competent, experienced arbitrators who insist that they have a written issue submitted to them, agreed upon by the parties, or else they will not go forward.

In the Northeast and the Midwest, where I tend to arbitrate, I have had only a few cases in which the parties have presented me with a stipulation of specific issues at the outset of the hearing. At most the stipulated issue may be whether the employer has violated article X of the labor agreement. In other parts of the country this may vary.

Ordinarily the applicable contract provision comes up in the stipulated issue or in the opening statement. Remember this is a telescoped process. It is also a free-floating process in which the arbitrator may ask the question, what does this case generally involve, to which the parties will probably answer that it is a disciplinary or job promotion case. If it is a discipline case, I ordinarily make some comment to the effect that I assume the company is ready to proceed first, and the company invariably says yes. If it is not a disciplinary case I ask if the union is prepared to open.

In most cases which do not involve discipline, the union will go first. On the basis of who is to lead off, I ask if that party wishes to present an opening statement. A concise statement of what the problem is as one party sees it and then as the other party sees it follows.

In most discharge cases, the formulation of the issue is not important, and I do not mind waiting until the end of the company's case before hearing what the union has to say. The issue is usually simple, that is, was there just cause for the discipline.

If it is a more complicated case, however, there can be a battle over precisely what that issue is, or at least how it should be worded.

That is where I prefer not to sharpen the question too much if I feel that by letting each party state the issue I can get a sense of what it is and reformulate it, thus stating the issue as I see it. Almost invariably there is a quiet assent that that is the situation. I am then ready to proceed.

Stipulation of Facts

In an effort to shorten the hearing, I often give the parties a chance to enter into some factual stipulations to which both parties agree in order to save time used in putting people on to testify. Depending upon what I hear in that opening statement, I may say that there appears no dispute between the parties as to A, B, and C and ask if they are prepared to stipulate that. Ordinarily there will be no disagreement about certain facts such as dates and places, or the number of years an employee has worked. Often there will be no dispute about the time an employee was employed but considerable dispute as to precisely what that employee's seniority is. The arbitrator can easily avoid unnecessary and repetitious testimony by clearing the desk of undisputed facts at the outset.

I have never received anything argumentative directly from a party in advance of a hearing. Presumably any sort of prehearing brief would go through AAA, if it is one of their cases. My position is that before the arbitrator receives anything from anybody, the other party should be given the chance to respond. In terms of time, that might not be possible. I would be quite prepared to receive at the hearing a copy of the opening statement or a more elaborate version of it, on condition, of course, that the other side receive a copy too. I would not read beyond the line where I recognized a unilateral communication without notifying the other party and eliciting their response. I said at the outset that it is important to maintain always a posture of neutrality and impartiality and avoid anything that would give one side the feeling that the other was getting some undeserved benefit in the handling of the case.

Burden of Proof

There are some things that are important to keep in mind both as theoretical propositions and very practical points. Arbitrators will say again and again that the burden of proof does not mean much in arbitration, that all the arbitrator really wants to do is find out which side has the stronger case, what are the real facts, and what is the meaning of the contract. He is not interested in who has the burden of proof or what the quantity of that burden is, if that further issue comes up. In the vast majority of cases, for all practical purposes, that is a sound statement. It does not make much difference about burden of proof if you are satisfied one way or the other way how the case should come out.

One of the things I have discovered to my chagrin and occasional anguish, however, is that there are cases in which I simply cannot decide which side has prevailed when I am finished. As long as I can avoid reaching that mental state, I do not need to go on to the next question that I now raise. I have not been able to avoid it, and I do not know many other arbitrators who will not confess to the same predicament from time to time. In such a situation the arbitrator has to rule one way or the other, and I do not know how one can deny that it depends upon who has the burden of persuasion. In the usual case it is the grieving party, who is moving for relief of remedy under the contract. It is that party which has the burden of prevailing by a preponderance of the evidence.

There is a well-accepted exception to this rule, that being cases of discipline and discharge in which it is usually felt that the employer has the burden of proof, on the theory the employer has within his knowledge a greater sense of the facts as to why he acted in disciplining the employee. I am not sure that is the only explanation for placing the burden of proof upon the employer in discipline cases. There are other situations in which the employer probably has a better sense of the facts. For example, whether a particular employee is qualified for a job and thus was entitled to get it on the basis of seniority is also a question on which the employer may well have readier access to the critical data. However, the classic arbitrator's position is that the union has the burden of proof of persuading the arbitrator that the employer made a mistake in promoting someone else. Whatever the precise reasoning—it may be in part a feeling that the disciplined employee is subject to a serious hurt, especially in a discharge case—the traditional view is that the company ought to carry the burden of proof.

Moreover, while in the usual case the burden of proof must be sustained only by a preponderance of the evidence, that is, one finding is more likely than not 51–49, in the discipline or discharge case most arbitrators use a slightly different formulation. In cases where the reason for the discharge is the sort of reprehensible, immoral conduct that would amount to a criminal offense if tried in the courts, some arbitrators go so far as to say, and unions invariably argue for it, that there must be proof beyond a reasonable doubt, using the old criminal law standard.

After handling a number of these cases, I have come to the conclusion that I am prepared to uphold a discharge where I would not be prepared to send the grievant to prison. This is a very pragmatic reaction, but it satisfies me that I am not using the beyond a reasonable doubt standard. On the other hand, I want something more than 51–49 before I uphold a discharge. I want something that I can call clear and convincing, if that is any help at all in defining a standard in between preponderance and beyond reasonable doubt.

I want to emphasize that arbitrators take different positions on this. One groups says beyond reasonable doubt, relying on the criminal law analogy; others are prepared to accept a preponderance of the evidence, emphasizing that these are civil cases. My hunch is that a majority of arbitrators want more than a preponderance in a discharge case at least, and maybe in any discipline case as well.

I do not think that all this is embroidery. I have tried enough cases in which I have concluded to myself that the company has satisfied me that probably the employee did this thing, but there was a lot of conflict. It was very, very close, so close that even though I thought it was probable, I did not think it was clear and convincing, and I did sustain the discharge. On the other hand, I have had cases in which I would not have sent the man to prison, where I would not have been able as a member of a jury to find him guilty; nonetheless I was prepared to sustain the discharge. At least it was clear and convincing.

There is another distinction to be made. A significant number of arbitrators only apply the stiffer standard of beyond a reasonable doubt when the conduct is morally reprehensible, when there is criminal-like activity alleged by reason that even though the man is not being sent to prison by a criminal court, the stain on his record in the employment field is going to be of exactly the same nature. His future chances of getting a job with a theft discharge sustained will be seriously impaired, and thus that stiffer standard is considered appropriate.

Rules of Evidence

The strict rules of evidence do not apply to arbitration. However, I find an increasing tendency for proceedings to become formalized. I am not sure that this is because of the presence of lawyers. Certainly lay people can be just as formalistic, sometimes even pettifoggingly so. I am inclined to think that it is in the nature of almost any kind of process whose initial flexibility may depend upon the fact that there are not any rules—if there are not any rules, there is no precedent. As time goes by, people get used to doing things in a more structured way. Many things that we have talked about today are fairly well accepted. There are big battles about what precisely is the official record of the proceedings, because we do not have a precedent. As we set the precedent, people accept it and want to follow the rules. A process that began by having a good deal of play in the joints becomes a bit more rigid.

I am not unhappy about some of the movements in this direction, but I am unhappy about others. For example, it is still very hard for an arbitrator to convince a pair of representatives, if they are lawyers, not to heap hearsay objections even though I have indicated that there is almost no kind of hearsay objection that I am going to sustain unless a witness is right there, available to testify, and they try to give me his or her affidavit. I find that objectionable; why should not the witness testify? I am generally prepared to accept hearsay for the most part, even hearsay that is in the form of an affidavit. I may give it insignificant weight, and I am certainly not going to give it as much weight as I would a person who has testified and who is subject to cross-examination, but I will not rule it as inadmissible. I will sustain objections when testimony becomes unnecessarily repetitious or if there is unnecessary personal vilification or harassment of a witness. I try to avoid being any more definite or legalistic than I have to in rulings on objections. I tend to allow the parties to proceed a bit further. Then finally enough has been heard on that particular point. I try to maintain an informal air, even about rulings.

There is one troublesome area, and that is an attempt to introduce evidence that raises a serious question of relevancy. The threshold question is, does the proffered evidence have anything to do with the issue in the case. This is not evidence that is incompetent or to which objections may be raised that it be inadmissible because it is hearsay; the question is purely relevancy. One might say that to admit it is part of the general process of purging feelings, and that putting everything out on the table is one of the hallmarks of arbitration. Supposedly, there is a great therapeutic value in that process. It places the other side in a dilemma. Should the party take the time and trouble to refute the new evidence, which hypothetically has nothing to do with the case, or should he ignore it and run the risk the arbitrator will later consider it relevant? If I am completely satisfied that the evidence that is being offered does not bear in any way on the issue presented by this case, I shall not accept it.

Let me illustrate a troublesome, specific evidentiary problem. An employee has been fired. At the time of the firing, the employee was supplied with a written statement to the effect that he was discharged because of insubordination to Foreman X. The contract might have said that at the time of discharge there must be a written statement of reasons supplied to the employee with a copy to the union, or there might not have been such a provision in the contract. At the hearing the employer tries to show that the employee had a very bad work record, habitual absenteeism and tardiness, and that these were the reasons discharge was thought to be the appropriate penalty.

Ordinarily one may think that the past record of an employee should always be pertinent in a decision dealing with the type of discipline imposed, but on the other hand, at the time the discharge was made— and let us assume also in subsequent grievance steps—the only thing that was talked about was the insubordination. The past record was never mentioned.

The union, of course, stoutly insists—and a good deal of arbitration precedent supports this position, at least when the contract says there must be a reason supplied at the time of discharge—that the only reasons that can be used at the arbitration hearing to justify discharge are those presented to the employee at the time of discharge. What happened in the past to buttress the penalty imposed cannot be introduced, otherwise the preceding grievance procedure would be undercut, and the union would be caught by surprise at arbitration. When it is quite clear that only one reason was assigned and especially when the contract requires that the reasons be supplied, I will not accept evidence with regard to the employee's bad past record.

Needless to say, if the employee had a good record during twenty years of service with an unblemished disciplinary record and is now discharged, the union proffers that record of past performance to try to demonstrate that the discharge penalty is too stiff. At that point I take the position that the union can bring in the past record to contest the discharge, although I say that once the employee's past record is raised by the union as a basis for knocking out the discharge, it opens up the past record; anything that was negative (and not subject to a contractual exclusion) can be used by the employer to try to offset the good portions of it. Usually a union makes a shrewd judgment in advance on whether or not to bring up the past record.

It is sensible for an employer to look at the total record of the employee. Arbitrators do not want to become enmeshed in a situation tying arbitration up with all the niceties of common-law pleading. The principal and final incident that really provoked the company was insubordination. It may well be that it is implicit in the employment relationship that every discipline imposed really reflects—in what is regarded as very good industrial relations philosophy—a kind of progressive discipline, which is based on the entire past record.

If I find there was an oral discussion at the time of discharge whereby the employee knew the company was considering all the past incidents, even though the only thing marked on the official notification was insubordination, I let the employer use those past incidents, giving such weight as I feel is appropriate, depending upon their seriousness, their similarity to the type of incident now involved, and the time when they occurred. Obviously something that occurred twenty years ago is going to be given little if any weight. I try to be a little flexible in this, but if I am convinced that right up until the hearing the union had no reason to know that anything was going to be relied upon except that one incident, I will regard other evidence as irrelevant and inadmissible.

In a very tightly written contract limiting me to the written statement, I do not want to tie myself up too much with common-law pleading technicalities. I try to see ultimately that the case is handled in a commonsense fashion to the best of my ability, that the outcome is one that the parties can understand, and that it neither suprises nor offends them. If the union and the employee were quite aware from the whole tenor of the discussion that this employee had had a whole series of things go wrong, and that this was part of the reason for the discharge, even though insubordination was the only thing written, my inclination is to ask to hear all the facts to see what I think of it.

Another qualification that most arbitrators will apply is not to allow anything in from the past record to help sustain the penalty unless it was made known at the time to the employee that this was a matter that management considered improper, and the employee would then have had a chance to grieve. I offended a company attorney and a union attorney within the space of two weeks with dissimilar rulings based on the distinction between an established system of progressive discipline and an on-the-spot discharge later buttressed with evidence of oral warnings. In a case where no notion of progressive discipline had ever been communicated because it had never been part of the policy between union and employer, I refused to admit a past record and confined the employer to the written reasons furnished to the employee. On the other hand, in another case in which an employee was marked one point for the first incident, two points for the second, and in geometric progression leading to discharge after a certain accumulation within a specified time despite the fact that the only thing that was fastened upon at the time of the discharge was the final culminating incident, I did accept evidence with regard to incidents in the past about which the employee had been warned orally and in writing and for which points had been imposed, because I regarded this as so much an accepted practice within the company and well known and accepted by the union that it was an implied part of the final step.

In the first case, in which I said I would not accept the past record, the company went considerably further than the written statement. It went all the way through the grievance procedure on the basis of the final incident alone, as a matter of fact. In the opening statement, company counsel said that the only thing they needed to determine was whether or not the employee acted reasonably under the circumstances, and then to the surprise and outrage of the union, the employer tried to introduce evidence of past misdeeds toward the close of its case.

I have every reason to think that those past misdeeds, if the ground had been properly laid for them, would have been supportive of the discipline. I got a sense of what they were in passing upon the objection. I think they were matters that the employee was aware of, that he had had a chance to grieve, and that he was probably guilty. I know, if admitted, that they would have affected my thinking, but I was deeply troubled that at no point in the grievance procedure was this prior record mentioned. The union had no reason to take it into account in deciding on, or preparing for, arbitration. If one thinks about this, there *is* a question about the extent to which an arbitrator ought to help preserve the functioning of the informal process for the resolution of grievances, the grievance procedure itself. To the extent an arbitrator allows it to be bypassed, he is to that extent undermining it.

I take a much more relaxed attitude toward most new evidence, as long as I am satisfied that the other party is not being unfairly surprised and that it has a reasonable chance to respond. Unfortunately—and this undoubtedly undermines the grievance procedure a bit—I think it is beyond the realm of human nature to engage in quite as systematic an examination of the facts, giving a thorough thinking-through of the theory of the case, during the informal grievance sessions as when the case has been labeled for arbitration. It may indeed be only after the decision to go to arbitration has been made that a lawyer is ever involved.

It may be inconsistent with my theory of relevance, but I would permit the union to introduce evidence about the employee's age, marital status, unemployment, number of children, and other personal factors that are typically used in a discharge case after ruling the employee's past record inadmissible. As a practical matter, it has been so long accepted that the nature of a good employment record is automatically relevant to a disciplinary proceeding that I always let a union introduce it.

To anyone who wishes to pursue further the issues of procedural regularity, I commend R. W. Fleming's *The Labor Arbitration Process.*[1] He addresses this question of when to admit past misconduct, first in justifying the penalty (he is largely favorable toward that), second on the issue of the witness's credibility, and third on the question of guilt itself—whether it is more probable than not that since he has done this kind of thing in the past he has probably done it on this occasion. Consider a closely related situation of a man who has stolen goods every Friday night for the past two months and is charged with another Friday night theft, but he denies it. I would admit that evidence, but I do not know how much weight I would give it. If the man had been arrested for theft on the outside in an entirely different situation, I would not admit it. Arbitrators rely heavily on the particular facts of particular cases; they do not like sweeping rules.

Intervention by Arbitrator

I add a few words about the arbitrator's role in the handling of witnesses to show the sensitivities of the parties on this. Lawyers become incensed when an arbitrator intervenes in a case in a substantial way. The lawyer who gives a client a botched bit of representation, making the arbitrator feel he must intervene in the name of justice, is being shown up in front of his client, and the lawyer does not like that one whit. The opposing lawyer who grinned as he saw his adversary botch up his client's case is incensed that the arbitrator becomes an advocate for the other side. It is a terrible dilemma in some cases. The arbitrator should rely on his conscience and common sense, be as discreet as he can, and neither embarrass the parties nor inject himself to the point of dealing with issues that the parties have not raised. He should not open doors where there may be skeletons that both parties feel should be kept safely locked in. Especially when dealing with good lawyers, an arbitrator should not blunder into matters he thinks are obviously relevant but that the lawyers are not dealing with. They have their reasons, if they are good lawyers. Naturally, judgments have to be made about this.

If there is something that I think is truly important that is not being dealt with, I occasionally, during a recess, take the two lawyers aside and say that I do not understand why a certain contract provision does not have some bearing on this case and could they explain it to me. Sometimes they can do so, and it becomes perfectly understandable.

---

[1]Champaign, University of Illinois (1965).

Sometimes one lawyer becomes angry for my having pointed it out and the other one pounces, emphasizing its significance and believing it will win the case for him. Unfortunately it does sometimes, so that is dangerous. The arbitrator has made an enemy. There is a constant tension between having them play the game as a sporting event and trying to do justice. On occasion I find that rather traumatic.

I urge strongly in writing an award, especially if modifying any kind of penalty in a discharge or discipline case, that the arbitrator read the contract concerning his authority, particularly with respect to remedies. For example, in a disciplinary case he should determine whether he is entitled to modify the employer's sanction, required to sustain it, or may set it aside in toto. At the close he should try to get both parties to give a brief oral summation of just what their points are, if there is any doubt at all. Alternatively, the arbitrator may sum up his understanding of the parties' positions, and ask them if it is correct. At least they will go away content, happy that they got their arguments across.

Although it is very difficult to generalize, I think I would take a more activist role if I think the grievant's union counsel is not doing a good job than in a contract interpretation case wherein it is not an individual who may be hurt. There is a device that may permit an arbitrator diplomatically to do a little more than otherwise could be done without causing offense. While trying to convey the notion that I am not raising a new issue or reaching into new areas but simply making sure that I understand what is testified to, I sometimes ask for clarification that I understand properly a certain point. I then ask a question that carries beyond the question that has previously been asked, but not so much so that it appears I am taking over the questioning. I do not want to do that for more than about two questions at a time. However, occasionally I am concerned there is going to be a serious miscarriage of justice. Employers and unions are often upset at this, but the arbitrator owes a responsibility to himself as well as to the process and the parties, and I do not want to be a collaborator in an injustice.

Obviously it affects the arbitrator if there is a great disparity in the quality of counsel or if a lawyer opposes a lay person. Needless to say, one party, usually the employer, is incensed that the money spent in order to have superior representation is being counterbalanced in any way by the arbitrator who is hired not to represent the other side but to serve as the impartial arbiter. Quite certainly, professional representatives will take umbrage at any public intervention, even when it is helpful.

The contract is usually introduced as an exhibit and becomes part of the record. For example, there is a grievance that something is contrary

to that contract. Frequently the sections allegedly violated will be specified, but it is generally accepted that unless there is a square stipulation
to the contrary, the entire contract may be examined to shed light on
the meaning of the cited sections. The problem I have is really more a
matter of diplomacy than authority. Am I a bull in a china shop who is
opening up matters that should have been kept in the closet? Am I
embarrassing one of the parties to no good end? Those are matters of
diplomacy and they must be worked out by feeling one's way.

It is very easy to say that theoretically the arbitrator is a passive
spectator who, at the end of the match, decides who wins. When an
arbitrator sees something that he thinks can be corrected, there is a
terrible itch to prevent injustice. It does not just concern the union and
the company, for there is another party involved, the grievant. There is
a much stronger case for intervention when there is an individual grievant
than when there is a big contract problem that is more abstract.

Role of Counsel

Fortunately, I have never personally been involved in a case where
there was any clash between the union and a grievant's separate outside
counsel. It has come up more in recent times, especially in minority
cases with unfair representation claims in the background. That the
union represents the grievant would be the classical response of the
parties to collective bargaining agreements, and I believe that most
arbitrators would agree. I like to think that some of the racial suspicions
of a few years ago have been receding in industrial relations, and that
there is not as much antagonism between minority members and their
unions. Some of the steam behind the move for third-party representation
has dissipated, but there was a time when academic commentators, not
the parties in the field, were indeed trying to devise theories that would
permit minorities to be represented by counsel of their own choosing at
arbitrations.

I find most post-hearing briefs in the simpler, standard discipline
cases a waste of effort. They extend the time and cost, and they do not
affect the decision that I probably reached driving home following the
hearing. Do remember to set dates for briefs and tell the parties when
the award will be. Make sure both sides understand that, and end
graciously. Thank them both for their help and professional presentations.

When an arbitrator is satisfied that union counsel has done a good
job in representing a losing grievant, especially in a case that for any
reason might later prove troublesome, he might specifically point out

that a fine presentation was made on behalf of the grievant, but not before the case is decided; that would be misread. If the discharge is sustained, it should be included in the opinion and award. If that sort of commendation is fair, it can be extremely helpful to counsel in mollifying the client, perhaps even preventing an unfair representation suit.

Consent Awards

Initially, I felt very strongly about the question of consent awards in which the parties jointly request the arbitrator to make a certain decision, but I have become a little more troubled about some of the practicalities of these situations. The toughest case of all is in dealing with an individual employee. The union can handle this in a variety of ways. It can go forward and say not one word to the arbitrator and simply present the case in such a way as to make clear to the arbitrator that it agrees with the company that the employee is guilty, that he ought to be discharged, but that for some political reason the union has to go to arbitration. Any clever counsel can manage the affair.

I have never had company and union approach me and simply say that they had to go through with the charade, at the same time making me aware of their feelings, and that they have no objection to the discharge being sustained. I have been approached by union and company in situations where they wanted an interpretation of the contract and there were political problems on both sides. They have asked me to write the interpretation per their suggestion on grounds that I can bear the brunt of criticism, that is what I am paid for, and that is how I would decide the case anyway.

At least in the last instance, I am now satisfied that if it is a totally honest and fair solution that they have agreed upon—the kind that I might have worked toward on my own—there is nothing to cause me not to make my award to conform. Remember: this is something that is not wrong, it is something I might have come to on my own. It is probably better, as a practical matter, than the decision I would have arrived at on my own because they worked it out themselves. The problem, of course, is that the parties are deceiving their stockholders and their members. What is the arbitrator's function, ultimately: to keep trouble stirred up or to resolve it?

I return to that basic question of what role should the arbitrator play. I am quite prepared to have persons argue that as a matter of personal honor and personal integrity—not a matter of the integrity of the arbitration process, but personal integrity—an arbitrator is not going to put his name on an award he did not work out in his own mind, but I am now much more content with the notion of the agreed award under proper conditions.

Let me pose this question just a little differently. Suppose at the end of a case, after all the evidence is in, the arbitrator asks the two parties how the case should be decided and what should be the remedy. They both come up with the same answer. One might ask why the parties do not sign the contract and forget about an award. It sometimes happens, however, that while they both finally concluded what was the right answer, they do not want to carry that back to their constituencies. If one thinks this through and can justify their proposal, one can support it with reasons that make perfectly good sense. What exactly has the arbitrator done that is not a furtherance of the practicalities of the situation? He has ended a dispute and shaped a fair and sensible solution. Possibly he has caused problems for the chap who wants to run for president of the union or president of the company. Maybe he has done them an injustice.

The arbitrator's Code of Professional Responsibility justifies the consent award, with appropriate safeguards. It may be analogous to the tripartite hearing. In such a hearing, the two parties say they are really in accord and recommend that the arbitrator, as the deciding vote, go a certain way. They will then formally dissent from the portions of the award that go contrary to their interests. The arbitrator may think this is sound advice. It is exactly what he ought to do, but to the public you are the decisive vote.

There are no easy answers to these and some other procedural questions. For a new arbitrator, it is important to understand the issues involved so that conscious decisions may be made as these procedural questions arise.

Evidentiary Considerations

Eric Schmertz

What modifications of the rules of evidence are necessary to make them viable in the arbitration hearing, given the fact that arbitration is a special kind of adversary proceeding? Should arbitrators, at the same time, maintain a strong defense against creeping legalisms, a euphemism for keeping lawyers out?

In the Philippines, an attempt was made to legislate against having lawyers involved in collective bargaining and arbitration on the premise that they would distort the processes with protracted technicalities and would charge large fees. The assumption was erroneous, because the parties were unable to make the kinds of presentations they wanted in the absence of persons trained to present cases. Lawyers entered under guises of corporate or union business agents. There were lengthy recesses during the course of arbitration hearings to permit the untrained tryers of the case to call counsel who are standing by for advice on the next line or series of questions. The attempt to exclude lawyers was futile. It would also be futile in this country; the presence of lawyers will probably increase.

What is wanted is reasonable machinery for informal fact-finding in an adversary proceeding in which both parties exert great pressure to win, whether they believe the case is justified or not. I have collected here some procedural and evidentiary problems that I have encountered, which illustrate the need for balance between informality and formal rules.

Discovery

There are no pretrial procedures enforceable on demand in arbitration, with some exceptions governed by statute. By and large, they are unnecessary. Unlike a civil or criminal suit, it is presumed that all pretrial discovery interrogation has been done by the parties in the course of the grievance proceeding, and the case comes to the arbitrator after it has gone through the grievance procedure. Each side ought to know what the issue is before it gets to the arbitrator, since the arbitration process really does not start *ab initio* with the arbitration hearing. An arbitration begins with the first step of the grievance procedure.

Arbitration proceedings—unlike litigation in which without proper pleading or timely response, the right to raise a defense or an issue might be lost—are not that technical. For example, under AAA rules, failure to respond or standing silent is deemed to be a denial, whereas in most courtroom procedures, failure to answer the complaint is deemed to be an admission of the adverse claim. Without this difference, legalisms would ensnare the process before the hearing room stage.

Official Record

There is not a well-settled rule on the use of stenographic records and electronic devices. One practice regarding stenographic records is that if the company buys copies of the transcript for itself and the arbitrator and the union does not buy a copy, the arbitrator will make his copy available to the union if briefs are to be written. The same formula is applied if the affluent party is reversed. I do not follow that practice. I do not like the idea of a stenographic record which was paid for by one side being supplied to the other side by the arbitrator. However, one side should not get the advantage of a stenographic record simply because it can afford it. If there is a dispute about who gets the record and who pays for it, I take the position that it is not an official transcript of the arbitration hearing, and I do not want a copy. I am not put in a position where I have to decide whether or not my copy is to be made available to the other side. I take my own notes. I have yet to have a case where I had to have a stenographic record.

I have a strong aversion to an electronic tape recorder. Other people have different practices. I think that it does not provide an accurate record. I do not know who is talking. Furthermore, the tape can be tampered with, and it has its technical frailties. I am absolutely opposed to its use, and if there is an objection by one party I will not admit the device in the hearing room. In a case before me, the union wanted to have microphones available at the table in a fact-finding proceeding so that several hundred union members sitting in the back of the room could hear everything. Although there may have been a good reason for wanting that, I objected. People tend to make speeches into microphones or electronic devices. I think the devices are intrusions into the hearing.

Subpoenas

I dislike receiving in the mail before a hearing begins and before I know anything about the case a letter asking that the enclosed subpoenas be signed so they can be served and the people presented with the documents duces tecum. For an arbitrator to sign such subpoenas ex parte borders on an act of partisanship. I do not know whether or not the subpoenas are proper or if the people ought to be subpoenaed until I am convinced in an adversary setting that a subpoena ought to issue. I do not know whether or not the party requesting the subpoena has made a demand on the other side for the production of documents. The issuance of a subpoena after the proceedings begin is another matter. The arbitrator knows its relevance and can hear opposition to it, if there is opposition from the other side. It is an appropriate request at the hearing and appropriate and necessary for an arbitrator to rule on, under those circumstances. More than half the time, the person will appear voluntarily. Usually a voluntary production of the person and the documents is forthcoming. In the absence of that, if a person and his documents are essential or relevant to one party's case and that person is not immediately available, another hearing may be required to which that person may come voluntarily. If he does not come voluntarily, he will be served with a subpoena. The subpoena can be served that day, if the person is there. He may be present and for political or other reasons not willing to testify, but he will testify if subpoenaed. If the parties really want to arbitrate and dispose of the case, they will be willing to proceed without the witness unless the issue at hand ties in with what that witness has to say, or unless that witness' presence is necessary in sequence to make some sense out of what is to follow.

I have issued a subpoena prior to the hearing, but I do not like to do so, and in New York I do not have to. Under New York law, a party may issue the subpoena himself. If an arbitrator signs a subpoena before having even taken the oath of office in states where it is required, it may lead to some serious question about whether or not he has authority to sign a subpoena. In a jurisdiction where only an arbitrator can issue the subpoena, I believe that he ought to make known the request for a subpoena to the other side and ask if there is an objection.

I do not want to overburden a hearing with technicalities, but sometimes even a pre-hearing conference or a preliminary hearing on the question of the subpoena is a good approach. It may be the advisable thing for relatively new arbitrators to do in order to demonstrate their care, prudence, and impartiality.

Framing the Issue

Framing the issue may or may not be considered an evidentiary matter. The issue limits the arbitrator's authority and lacking the issue, the arbitrator's authority might not be quite so clear. Therefore, an arbitrator should make an effort to get the issue framed at the outset of the hearing. Was there just cause for the discharge, if not, what shall the remedy be? Did the company violate the contract when it did such and such? Does Section X of the contract bar the employer from doing this? There is no mystique about framing the issue. The arbitrator asks the parties if they have framed an issue, and if not, can he do so.

Do not spend much time framing the issue. It is nice to have the issue framed, but it is not necessary. Some parties try to argue that if the issue is not framed, the hearing cannot continue. That is untrue. The arbitrator can frame it himself from the presentations or can circumvent the whole thing by presenting the issue as, for example, "what shall be the disposition of the union's grievance number 796?" In a case I heard, the issue was so controversial and deemed so important by the parties, that they spent several hours trying to frame the issue, but they were ultimately unable to do so. With some degree of immodesty they then turned to me for help. I was able to frame an issue fairly quickly because the parties had exhausted themselves.

Oaths

The arbitrator should be familiar with the jurisdictional statute as to whether an arbitrator must take an oath, or if it can be waived by the parties. In a Connecticut case,[1] the court held that an arbitrator must take an oath, and the parties may not waive the arbitrator's oath. Usually in other jurisdictions where, for example, there is no convenient notary public to give the oath, the parties are asked if the arbitrator's oath can be waived. I make a notation in the record of an affirmative answer, and when I write my opinion, I always say that the parties expressly waived the arbitrator's oath. The fact that the arbitrator's oath cannot be waived in writing or that it cannot be waived at all is illustrative of creeping legalism.

Some jurisdictions do not require the arbitrator's oath at all, nor do they require that the arbitrator's signature on his award and opinion be acknowledged before a notary public. Pennsylvania and Connecticut do not require it; New York and New Jersey do.

---

[1] *Reinke v. Greenwich Hospital Ass'n.*, 175 Conn. 24, 392 A.2d 966 (1978).

In a jurisdiction where the arbitrator's signature must be acknowledged before a notary public and he fails to have it acknowledged, there is technical ground to set the award aside. As long as courts apply the technical rules to the enforceability and validity of the award, the arbitrator must comply. If a losing party is angry about the loss and the relationship between the parties is bad and perhaps the objecting party is unsophisticated and does not realize that to set an award aside on these grounds will be counterproductive to that relationship, the losing party can have an award vacated on these technicalities.

If a case appears to be one in which credibility issues will be raised, I swear the witnesses without asking the parties' permission. In discharge and discipline cases, I always swear the witnesses. In contract interpretation cases, I ask the parties if they want the witnesses sworn. If there is divided opinion, I swear them. What is needed otherwise is agreement on the waiver of the swearing of witnesses. What impact the oath has on a witness I do not know; that applies to court proceedings as well as arbitration.

Applicability of Rules

It has been said that the rules of evidence do not apply in arbitration. More accurately, it seems to me that the rules of evidence *need* not apply in arbitration. I refer to the proper questioning of witnesses in proper form, proper introduction of documentary evidence, best evidence rule, hearsay rules, scope rule, and privileges. It may be overly simplistic to say that the question of how strict an arbitration case will be with regard to the application of traditional rules of evidence rests more often with the parties than with the arbitrator. I hear some cases as if they were informal round-table discussions, each party in turn speaking what is on his mind and presenting exhibits. Technical objections might not be made at all, because the grievance and arbitration relationship between the parties is such that they find it unnecessary, or because they are very sophisticated and know each other well. Even the most sophisticated parties can present a case without a single invocation of the rules of evidence, because they know what they want the arbitrator to have.

The arbitrator should be able to separate probative from nonprobative evidence. When parties complain about the absence of the rules of evidence, I feel that they should not use the arbitration process. One of the things that they must accept is the absence of strict courtroom protections. They have to accept the fact that the arbitrator will not always rule favorably on objections strictly on the ground of rules of evidence. That is part of the arbitral process. In the end, the same amount of substantial justice comes out of arbitration as comes out of the courtroom, and that is true of commercial as well as labor arbitration.

On the other hand, an arbitrator would not be well-trained if he were unfamiliar with the rules of evidence, uniformly disregarded them, or ruled against counsel who raised certain objections based upon them. There are cases and there are times within cases when I think that an arbitrator does a better job, creates a better image, or instills more confidence in the process and in his own ability to handle the problem, if he demonstrates that he knows what the rules of evidence are, and in certain critical areas, is prepared to apply them.

There are times when the arbitrator has to make rulings. When there is a strong objection in a critical area, the arbitrator has to sustain or overrule that objection. Sometimes a successful approach is to make no ruling at all, but to simply assume an attitude of pained acceptance of the rhetoric and play-acting for the client's benefit until the advocate himself moves on to new matter. Arbitrators should be trained to respond in certain critical areas, at least to the degree that they demonstrate their understanding of the appropriate application of the rules of evidence.

I give no guidelines at the beginning of a hearing, because often I do not know to whom I am talking. If the arbitrator is a permanent umpire who knows the parties well, he could set forth certain parameters, but he does not have to give them guidelines. If an ad hoc arbitrator does not know the parties, it would be presumptuous to tell them what he is going to do, because he does not really know. He cannot anticipate the kind of objections the parties may raise or how formally the parties are going to present their evidence.

There are times when an arbitrator might stop the proceeding and remind the parties about the kind of a proceeding that arbitration is. If one side objects too much, the case will be totally bogged down unless the arbitrator assumes firmer control and makes appropriate rulings. On the rare occasions when I am dealing with an unsophisticated party, I will characterize the arbitration process as being informal, explaining that the arbitrator has long experience, understands the difference between what is probative and what is not, knows where the burdens are, and the objections are unnecessary. If the party persists, I will rule on the objection. If objections are raised in critical areas, they will be sustained. If the parties are there in good faith, the arbitrator should have no problem. If they are not acting in good faith but obstructing, there is little an arbitrator can do except to sit through it and make appropriate rulings. In most instances, parties do act in good faith, but sometimes they carry their courtroom training into arbitration. My experience is that the lawyers who try arbitration cases regularly are lawyers who do not invoke the rules of evidence except where it is necessary.

In critical areas the rules should be applied. For instance, an objection ought to be sustained against leading a witness on direct examination or matters of substance. Arbitrators who know the rules should not discard them entirely, and those who do not know them should learn them, because the arbitrators are asked to act upon them.

In a case I heard, the City of New York invoked the parol evidence rule, contending that I could not hear any testimony by former Mayor Beame or others on negotiating history, and that I should decide the case only on what was reduced to writing. Under the parol evidence rule, if the writing is clear, unambiguous, and complete, evidence of oral agreements made at the same time, which if admitted into evidence would change the terms of the agreement, may not be introduced. This fundamental rule of evidence is applicable in arbitration.

Hearsay

When I say rules of evidence are not necessarily binding, I mean that if I do not think the evidence is in a critical adversary area, if credibility is not involved, or if the issue is not sharply drawn at that point, I do not care whether the rules of evidence are followed or not, and I often waive an objection by saying that is not a critical area. However, when the objection comes up in a critical area, I will sustain the objection. If, for example, a party were to state that he knows that the grievant hit the foreman over the head with a monkey wrench, and to my question of how does he know that, he answers that he saw the foreman's gashed head the next day, to which an objection is made, I would not overrule the objection.

An arbitrator should advise the parties that such evidence has little probative value. The arbitrator may say that he recognizes that a certain statement is hearsay and that is a valid objection and the burden is then on the employer to show that the employee committed this offense. The mere fact that the foreman had a hole in his head and was seen the next day does not mean that the grievant did it.

Self-Incrimination

If, in a discharge case, the company calls the grievant as the first witness, the union representative objects on grounds that the grievant might make a self-incriminating statement, and the union has not yet decided if they would call the grievant to testify, can the employer call the grievant? The objection should not be sustained. Either side can call anybody in the room. Arbitration is not a criminal proceeding. The union lawyer may not reasonably assert that if the company calls the grievant, he becomes the company's witness and the company is bound by whatever grievant says, and therefore the case is over because he will deny the employer's claims. That is not the result in arbitration.

If an employee, accused of insubordination, refuses to testify on the grounds that his testimony might incriminate him with regard to the charge of insubordination, he has improperly invoked the Fifth Amendment because that relates only to criminal matters. However, hypothetically if an employee strikes his foreman and is charged with criminal assault pending in court, he is not invoking his Fifth Amendment rights with regard to the discipline that is being imposed by arbitration, but against the possibility that his testimony in arbitration might be used against him in the criminal proceeding. On that basis he probably has grounds for refusing to testify. Although the Fifth Amendment is not applicable in an arbitration because it is not a criminal case, if there is a showing that the issue involving the grievant has, or could have, a companion criminal proceeding, implications against which the grievant is attempting to protect himself and is advised by counsel to do so, an arbitrator must uphold the employee's refusal to answer.

If an employee, or counsel on his behalf, objects on grounds that the statute of limitations has not run and there is reason to believe the company or the assaultee will file a criminal complaint, the grievant should not be compelled to testify in that area. I think that is a proper objection and an arbitrator must honor it. An employee who may have committed an offense which is also subject to criminal sanctions exposes himself to two separate punishments.

Although I have advocated very strongly that the records in administrative disciplinary actions ought not to be made available in a criminal proceeding, they are made available for purposes of impeaching testimony and establishing credibility. My own view is that what happens in a disciplinary proceeding ought to be sealed from what is happening in criminal court, but my view is not supported by law. Because it is not supported by law, the arbitrator must proceed differently when that question comes up.

Once a grievant testifies on direct examination, he is subject to cross-examination. He may have said something on direct examination which he ought not to have said because it is the kind of testimony which would, if used elsewhere, constitute probative evidence towards incrimination. However, the witness has said it, and *it* is opened up on direct examination. If counsel pursues the point on cross-examination and there is an objection based upon criminal jeopardy, the objection must be overruled under the rules of evidence, because the issue was opened up on direct examination. The grievant, then, cannot slam the door on cross-examination.

The arbitrator cannot compel the grievant to testify. The arbitrator should not draw an inference during the hearing or announce that he has drawn or will draw an inference during the course of the hearing. One may use a self-serving prefatory statement asking that no inferences be drawn and that only some information is being sought.

Burden of Proof

There is a burden of proof on the grieving party, except in discharge cases when it is on the party charging the offense. On arbitrability issues, the burden is on the party asserting nonarbitrability. What does the burden of proof mean? It does not mean beyond a reasonable doubt, although there are arbitration cases in which arbitrators have said that the standard of proof in such matters is the criminal standard of beyond a reasonable doubt. Beyond a reasonable doubt is not a standard of proof in arbitration cases; that is the criminal standard, except in a theft case when both parties stipulate that the standard of proof to be used is beyond a reasonable doubt.

If the parties want to raise the standard of proof by joint agreement, that is fine. I advise to avoid spelling out the standard of proof. I avoid saying in a particular instance that the standard of proof is clear and convincing or is a fair preponderance of the credible evidence. I do not know the difference between substantial evidence, which is the administrative law rule, and a fair preponderance of the evidence, which is applicable in civil law. I prefer the term, clear and convincing evidence.

The arbitrator must be persuaded based upon the evidence submitted in a discipline case, for example, that the employee committed the offense charged and the penalty imposed is appropriate for that offense. I do not know what the standard is; it may shift. It means that the arbitrator thinks that the credible evidence submitted is in favor of the employer or the credible evidence is not enough to hold that the employee committed a certain offense. Rather than become entangled in the terminology of the standard of proof, the arbitrator should provide for the parties a careful analysis of the evidence and a fair and sincere conclusion based upon what has been presented.

However, one of the more controversial issues is whether the standard of proof, whatever it may be, is heightened somewhat closer to the criminal standard if the offense charged parallels a crime. Should an arbitrator uphold discipline to an employee who is frequently tardy, absent, insubordinate, or turns out poor work, on a standard of proof which is less than that applied to an employee caught stealing, engaged in a gambling ring inside the plant, found with a marijuana cigarette in his possession or smoking it during the break period, or willful aggravated assault on the vice president for labor relations? I am more demanding in a charge of a serious offense which parallels a crime. This is not to say that I am invoking beyond-a-reasonable-doubt criterion. I do not know if that is more demanding than a clear and convincing standard, although I sometimes think that the latter is more demanding than the former. I am prepared to accord a grievant a little more latitude or presumption of innocence in a case which involves a potential crime than I am in charges of insubordination, absenteeism, tardiness, or poor work. If there is any justification for my action at all, it is probably my own view of a stricter allegiance to due process. I do believe in due process, be it in an arbitration or administrative hearing.

Stare Decisis

Technically, one arbitrator is not bound by what another does, but there are circumstances where an arbitrator is bound by what a prior arbitrator has done not because of a technical requirement but because to do otherwise would be too disturbing to the collective bargaining relationship. If a prior arbitrator has interpreted a clause which is at issue with respect to a later grievant, in some instances it would be more troublesome, disturbing, and counterproductive to impose a ruling different from the prior arbitrator's view, thereby leaving the parties with two inconsistent rulings.

Illustrative is an instance in which a prior arbitrator found that a delay of over 100 days in filing a case for arbitration after the last step of the grievance procedure did not bar the case from arbitration; there was no filing time limit in the contract and the usual circumstances on which the principle of laches applied—a witness disappearing, evidence disappearing, or prejudice—were not present. He found that the grievance was properly arbitrable.

In a subsequent case involving a request for arbitration more than 100 days following the last grievance step with the same attendant argument and circumstances where invocation of laches were not applicable, supposing that a different arbitrator felt that there was no real explanation for the delay, he ought to imply into the contract a reasonable amount of time when no time limit is set, and that 160 days might have been unreasonable. Yet to come down with a decision holding that the latter case was not arbitrable whereas the former case was found to be arbitrable would obviously be very disturbing to the relationship. Rather than clarify anything, it would only muddy the waters for the parties on that question. Consequently, I think it is fair to say that although there is no rigid rule of stare decisis and no legal requirement that arbitrators follow what prior arbitrators have said, the tendency is not to disturb a prior decision when the prior decision is arguably sound or at least in judgment not palpably wrong. If the ruling is ridiculous, absurd, and palpably wrong in an arbitrator's judgment, he should not hesitate to overturn it; but if it makes good sense, although not the good sense that a second arbitrator would make, one should be cautious about disturbing an earlier ruling. If that is so in arbitration, there does exist a kind of stare decisis.

When an arbitrator is faced with an existing decision between the parties in a similar case by another arbitrator, I think it is appropriate to say that if he were considering this question for the first time he might not reach the same conclusion, but given the previous decision will now render the same decision.

Is there not also a kind of stare decisis in some substantive issues in arbitration? Every arbitrator follows the progressive discipline rule, the rule on insubordination, and the accrual theory. Certain well-settled rules are developing which arbitrators generally accept and which all parties ought to expect arbitrators to follow and uphold even though they are not absolutely bound by precedent. A kind of common law precedent is developing, even though it has not the finality of stare decisis in court proceedings.

Suppose an arbitrator has decided a previous case which could be dispositive of the case at hand. It may be the same set of circumstances, in which event it might come right down to the same decision, or it may be different. Sophisticated parties ought to know that the mere fact that an arbitrator has decided a case in a particular way does not necessarily mean that this is the way another arbitrator would have decided the case if it came to him as first impression. There may be different evidence which is more persuasive, testimony which is more or less credible, or, despite the similar appearance of the contract clauses, the intent at negotiations may have been different. It may have been an agreed-upon decision between the parties, which the arbitrator did not find unconscionable, neither representing an injustice to an employee nor constituting collusion by the parties to an employee's detriment. An arbitrator accepts an agreed-upon arrangement, such as a consent order and consent awards, and renders it as his award. It would not necessarily have been his award had it been strictly on the merits.

Res Judicata

Res judicata is a principle which is applicable in arbitration. The problem is that a second grievant is entitled to a day in court or a day in arbitration over the same contract clause and perhaps even with respect to the same facts. Therefore, one cannot say absolutely that the prior decision is res judicata to the subsequent one where applicable to different grievants. The question is whether the subsequent arbitration on the basis of a theory of stare decisis would follow what the prior arbitrator did.

Affidavits

I accept the affidavits of unavailable witnesses if it is proven to me that the witness is not available. How much weight I give to them I cannot measure, but not as much as if the witness were present. An affidavit has its frailty; how much depends upon the rest of the case.

An arbitrator should not say that he will unconditionally accept an affidavit. An arbitrator may admit the evidence, but he should advise the parties that he recognizes that there is no opportunity to cross-examine. How much weight, if any, to attach to such evidence should be decided within the context of the entire record. As an arbitrator gains experience, he should not hesitate to reject something which has inherent frailties and which is of little or no value. An arbitrator might reasonably ask why the witness was not called instead of submitting a statement.

Consider a case in which an employee with a serious physical disability was hired and initially worked adequately. Later, problems arose attendant to the disability which appeared chronic in nature. The employee was dismissed because of overriding disabilities beyond his control. The employer has shown a grossly unsatisfactory attendance record, which is ground for dismissal irrespective of the reasons. The grievant's defense is that he was no more disabled at the time of his dismissal than when he was hired and his work found satisfactory. The only evidence presented on the grievant's behalf is an unsubstantiated doctor's statement without testimony. The employer has presented an uncontestable, unsatisfactory attendance record.

In this instance, I think the burden is on the grievant to show that the new condition is not chronic. If the new condition is chronic, the company has the right to sever the employee from the payroll. The issue before the arbitrator is the chronic or temporary nature of the new problems. The grievant claims they are temporary, and the company claims they are chronic. Medical evidence on that question is necessary.

I would not be prepared to accept a bare written statement from the doctor to establish the temporary nature of the problem. There is a greater burden on the employee to show that he is now at least as healthy as he was before the new medical problems became apparent. The arbitrator ought to be available to schedule a hearing, at an awkward hour if necessary, to get the right person to testify. I would make it clear that I have serious reservations as to the sufficiency of just a written affidavit for this case. The reservation will be expressed in the written opinion.

If there is no objection, there is no need to express a reservation. Whether or not an arbitrator has the duty to point up the frailty of a party's case is a controversial question. In this example I do not think the arbitrator has a duty to tell the party that he has to bring the doctor in to present medical testimony as better evidence. However, I am not prepared to say that an arbitrator has made a mistake if he does that. One must assess the situation pragmatically. Sometimes it may be appropriate to warn the parties. As a general rule, however, it is not the arbitrator's role to shore up the case of either side. There may be other occasions when an injustice is done by the inadequacy of presentation, and an arbitrator has to feel his way. There is no hard and fast rule.

In this medical qualification case, perhaps counsel for grievant should have presented a substantial medical case showing that his new physical difficulties were in fact temporary, that he is now cured of them, and at least he has been restored to his prior physical condition and is ready to attend to his job at his previously satisfactory level of work. The grievant certainly has the burden of producing persuasive evidence, but once over the hearsay problem, it does not necessarily follow that a medical report that is quite comprehensive should not be accepted for what it says. The report may be so comprehensive and professionally sound that even in the absence of testimony, an arbitrator might accord it more weight than some scribble on a prescription pad to the effect that the employee was suffering from various ailments but is now well. It is the arbitrator's job to weigh what is given to him and to accord it the kind of weight to which he thinks it is entitled. There have been occasions when, because I thought that justice required it, I have asked if a certain witness was available, and if not why not. I have asked that he be brought in to testify. An arbitrator has the right to do that, and I have done it. However, this is precarious ground. It may be that the party does not want him to appear.

Acting on the premise that it is up to the parties to present a case, particularly if they are represented by counsel, an arbitrator takes what is given with its probative and inadequate aspects and decides on that record. The arbitrator is a hearing officer, not a board of investigation or a board of inquiry. On the other hand, there are occasions when good judgment and sense of fairness dictate, and due process demands, that the person talked about be present. If the parties do not call that person, they ought to give a satisfactory explanation. When an arbitrator thinks that it is essential to his decision-making for a witness to be called, he can and should do so.

Consent Awards

If the parties have reached their own agreement and asked me to make their settlement my award, it is a stipulated award. If the parties reach a private agreement, but they do not want to reveal that it is theirs, it is an agreed or consent award. I am willing to make an agreed or consent award if I am satisfied that there is good reason to believe that I would have reached that decision had I decided on the merits and that there is nothing about it that constitutes any injustice to any employee.

Most of these decisions are more favorable than unfavorable to the employees. They are usually compromise arrangements by which the employees get something they probably would not have gotten, but I want to be sure that the effect is not to do an injustice, and that it is not collusive in that regard. I use the word collusive only when the end result is an unsavory one.

All consent awards in which I have participated have met those criteria under which nobody has been hurt, and usually somebody has benefited. The relationship between the parties has been improved, and the arbitrator has played a salutary role. However, I must have been satisfied that the consent decision would be the decision that I reasonably could have reached if I had heard the case on the merits. If those conditions are met, there is nothing unethical about consent awards, because arbitrators are part of the collective bargaining process. One role of an arbitrator is to assume, in the interest of sound and sensible labor relationships, responsibilities that the parties have not the courage to take on themselves.

My criteria probably cannot be met in a disciplinary case when the agreed-upon award is dismissal because of the criteria regarding fairness to an employee. Assuming that I am approached by both parties who want the grievant fired, I would insist that the case be tried. Based upon the evidence, I would decide whether or not the case squares with what the parties want. That is the risk the parties must take if the case is put before me.

On rare occasions—for example, when the parties had agreed on dismissal and the case did not warrant it but I felt that my mind was so clouded by what had happened and what I was told—I have resigned and explained that for a variety of reasons I did not want to continue with the case. In a discharge case the parties must prove that the dismissal is warranted on the merits in order to support their joint agreement. I will not rubber stamp an agreed-upon dismissal. However, I do not feel prejudiced by the mere approach of both parties requesting a consent award. They can say virtually anything they want; I do not listen to them. No experienced arbitrator will be influenced by ploys or asides. Only that which is put forth at the hearing is germane. If the arbitrator is alerted to an overt request for dismissal and insists that a good case be submitted, he must be persuaded by the case that there are grounds for dismissal. Perhaps the employee thereby gets a little more protection than he might otherwise have received. It is easy for parties to say nothing to the arbitrator and arrange a case presentation where the outcome is inescapable. When an arbitrator is alerted and decides to go ahead with a consent award, the parties must present a persuasive case. Knowing that there may be a tendency by one party to present an inadequate case, and that he is then in a position to demand a full and persuasive presentation, the arbitrator may be able to provide greater protection for the employee.

Arbitration is a profession with high prestige and esteem; it has never been tarnished by scandal or corruption. An arbitrator's career is based upon acceptability, honesty, and integrity. His success turns on deciding the case on the merits. The parties must rely upon an arbitrator to decide a case based upon the record presented and he must be immune from any other influences.

Public Sector Arbitration

Arvid Anderson

I want to first describe briefly the differences between public sector grievance arbitration and private sector grievance (rights) arbitration, and then discuss the growing field of interest arbitration. The world in which I work is different from the private sector. Those who will work in the area of public sector dispute settlement will see that difference.

Grievance Arbitration

You perhaps have the impression that there is a world of arbitration and there is a world of law, and that it is better if the two do not mingle. In dealing with the subject of grievance arbitration in the public sector, however, one is concerned not solely with the law of the contract but also with the law of that jurisdiction. One is dealing with external law. The concerns are not solely with those of the private sector, such as the intrusion of *Alexander v. Gardner-Denver Co.*,[1] Title VII, OSHA, and ERISA requirements, all of which limit the authority and discretion of an arbitrator by forcing him to consider and comply with external public policy. In all likelihood, the sole source of authority to act as an arbitrator, the scope of arbitration, the procedure of arbitration, and the standards for judicial review in the public sector is external law.

One cannot assume that being familiar with and understanding the law of grievance arbitration in the private sector, one can comfortably move from New York to Wisconsin, Pennsylvania, or Connecticut and not be concerned with what is the education law, the law governing the employment of policemen and firemen, or what might be the state civil service procedures. For example, is the forum an exclusive one? It may be that the arbitrator is entering no more than an advisory opinion, which is not final and binding. The employee may have options. The issue of

---

[1]415 U.S. 36, 7 FEP Cases 81 (1974).

duty of fair representation, the scope of arbitrability, or the arbitrator's authority to fashion a remedy may be different. Consideration must be given to what is occurring in the jurisdiction involved.

This is not just my opinion. The message from the courts is loud and clear. There is a great deal of public sector litigation. The courts are establishing or enforcing standards that limit the scope of grievance and interest arbitration. This is particularly true with respect to fields such as education, police, and fire, and issues such as civil service and pension requirements.

The parties may be unfamiliar with the grievance arbitration process. To some extent this is a problem of education for the arbitrator. Not neccessarily will there be experienced counsel from the private sector on either side of the table. To illustrate my point, there is in the private sector a presumption favoring arbitrability that varies from government jurisdiction to jurisdiction. One does not have in the public sector grievance arbitration process the blessings of the highest court of the land, the Steelworkers Trilogy. In 1977 the New York Court of Appeals went out of its way to disown the concept of the Trilogy by asserting that there is no presumption favoring public sector grievance arbitration as such. In the *Liverpool Central School District* case,[2] the court found that the collective bargaining agreement did not compel arbitration. The decision added that unless the court can determine that the agreement to arbitrate expressly, directly, and unequivocally covers the specific issues or disputes that ought to be submitted to arbitration, it will not enforce the agreement to arbitrate. The case involved a school teacher who refused to submit to a male physician's examination as a condition of her return to the school. Since disciplinary matters were excluded from arbitration but health and safety matters were not, the court said that it was reasonable to interpret the clause as not intending to cover this arguably disciplinary subject. I think this is a very narrow ruling. Nevertheless, it is a clear indication that the highest court of New York State, and I suspect the courts of other states, construe narrowly the scope of arbitration in the public sector.

I am glad to report there have been some indications that the court is backing away from this view. Although *Liverpool* still stands, the New York Court of Appeals has taken a more favorable approach towards arbitration. In *Lakeland Central School District*[3] the court concluded

---

[2]*Acting Superintendent of Schools Of Liverpool Cent. School Dist. v. United Liverpool Facility Ass'n*, 42 N.Y.2d 509, 399 N.Y.S.2d 189 (1977).

[3]*Board of Education, Lakeland Cent. School Dist. of Shrub Oak v. Lakeland Fed'n of Teachers Local 1760*, 395 N.Y.S.2d 875 (Sup. Ct. 1975), aff'd mem., 42 N.Y.2d 854, 397 N.Y.S.2d 630 (1977).

that as long as the agreement to arbitrate is clear and unequivocal, there can be some ambiguity as to coverage of the applicable substantive provision of the contract. The New York City Collective Bargaining Law,[4] which is substantially equivalent but not identical to the state law, has a provision which specifically favors and encourages the settlement of grievances by arbitration.

The Office of Collective Bargaining (OCB) prevailed in a challenge brought by the City as to the arbitrability of a grievance concerning the applicability of a mayoral Executive Order to a personnel decision involving a promotion. The City took the narrow position that since only rules and regulations of an agency in addition to the terms of a contract itself were subject to arbitration, an executive order issued by the mayor, although applicable to all agencies, was not technically within the scope of arbitration. The court, however, affirmed OCB's finding of arbitrability, asserting that in this case,[5] there was an express policy of New York City favoring arbitration.

I cite this not as an extreme case—although I think it is, in that sense—but to emphasize that care must be taken in listening to the pleas and arguments of the parties, and that questions of arbitrability cannot be overridden if the award is to stick.

Mediation Requirement

Some statutes mandate, as New York City's does, that the impasse panel or the arbitrator shall attempt to mediate, and they really try. For example, a Wisconsin law[6] recognizes the role of the mediation-arbitration process, called med-arb, and requires that the effort be made.

In a circumstance in which the parties bring not just a few tough issues but a laundry list of a hundred or more issues, the appointing authority has in most instances made a gross mistake. The matter should not have been referred to arbitration in that context because the parties have obviously failed to bargain. Given any opportunity to return the dispute to them, the arbitrator ought to do so until such time as they make a serious effort to reduce the number of issues. Lacking that option, the arbitrator must winnow and sift as best he can; but when confronted with a laundry list, it is difficult to deal with.

One is also likely to encounter surprises. Issues which were resolved before they got to the arbitration stage while the parties thought they

---

[4]N.Y.C. Coll. Barg. Law § 1173–7.0C (1972).
[5]*City of New York v. Anderson*, No. 40532/78, slip op. (N.Y. Sup. Ct. July 17, 1978).
[6]Wis. Stat. Ann. § 111.70(4)(cm)6.

were going to have a settlement suddenly are back on the table. There are two different problems to be dealt with: the scope and the arbitrator's authority. The arbitrator must look at the law of the jurisdiction. What works for fact-finding, final offer arbitration, or interest arbitration may be quite different from jurisdiction to jurisdiction. The scope, authority, possibility of judicial review, and standards to be applied may also vary. Look carefully or find a large educational problem for the parties as well as oneself. For whatever reason, all too many of my colleagues are unwilling to do the "heavy lifting" that is required, feeling somehow that interest arbitration is endangering their economic health. They find that it is much harder work than the greener and friendlier pastures of grievance arbitration. Too few of the people who are held in high regard in the profession have been willing to take on major disputes. As a result, there has been much criticism of awards issued by arbitrators who thought they were confirming the agreement of the parties.

Interest Arbitration

There is a rather fine line between interest arbitration and mediation, although other people perceive this quite differently. An interest arbitrator is called to serve when mediation and fact-finding have failed, and his role is to adjudicate. This is particularly true in a final offer situation. The parties may feel that they would like to do something different, but the rules of the game do not allow it. Therefore the arbitrator pursues this at arm's length. The parties may insist that it be pursued at arm's length, in which case the arbitrator must do the best possible job within the applicable standards.

The arbitrator might ask the parties at the beginning of the hearing what they expect in terms of mediation on some issues, arbitration on others. The appointing authority should know something about the dispute and describe, for example, how many issues remain and what difficulties are likely to arise. Presumably the appointing authority is something more than just a designating agency; if not, the arbitrator should proceed on his own. There is no problem in including in the award an agreement by the parties in a stipulation on particular issues and also making a decision on other controverted issues.

I put my general view on the subject of grievance arbitration and its distinction from interest arbitration in terms of a mathematical formula. I regard grievance arbitration as a question of two plus two equaling four. Sometimes one gets there the hard way, but it should come out. In interest arbitration or contract making, two plus two equals three or five or seven or nine; it might equal four, but it is unlikely. Those who are worried about the right answers will have a very difficult time, because who is wise, sure, and competent enough to know that he has accurately determined what an employer can pay, what an employee should receive in terms of wages, or what the conditions of employment must be? The right answer to the problem is a difficult one. If the process is viewed primarily as one of adjustment or accommodation—a question of compromise rather than of adjudication—one will be able to function effectively as an interest arbitrator. If approached from the stance of having been annointed to be an itinerant philosopher and to pronounce one's version of justice, the arbitrator will be short-lived in the process. That is a fundamental precept. There are people who disagree with me. I can only repeat what Mr. Bloch stated in a different way. I refer to the slogan I saw on a theologian's wall: those of you who think you know everything are very disturbing to those of us who do.

It is very difficult to come in with positive convictions about what the proper answer should be. If one has that philosophy and has to look at the problem as one of adjustment, accommodation, and compromise in order to determine what the contract ought to be rather than what it means, then obviously the name of the game is mediation or some form of conciliation.

Interest arbitration concerns the making of the terms of a contract as contrasted with the problem of interpreting the terms of a contract. Interest arbitration is a substitute for the strike as a means of inducing bargaining and negotiations. It is a mechanism for making the contract. By contrast, such questions as, was Sally Jones discharged for just cause, did she properly earn her incentive rate, or was she insubordinate are the traditional subjects for grievance arbitration. It is interpreting what a contract means.

Interest arbitration is also different from fact-finding with recommendations, which usually is not binding. Provisions for interest arbitration are binding upon the parties, albeit with qualifications for judicial review.

Statutory Alternatives to Strike

With a few exceptions, there is in this country a ban on the right to strike in public employment. It is not always observed, but a ban exists. Some twenty jurisdictions, including the federal government, have statutory provisions that are alternatives to the right to strike if the parties cannot settle their contract by direct negotiations, namely the right to resort to arbitration to determine what the terms of that contract will be. These statutory provisions vary greatly from jurisdiction to jurisdiction. These different interest arbitration procedures include:

conventional arbitration of all unsettled claims

selection of the last offer of the employer or of the union on an issue-by-issue basis

selection of the last offer of the employer or of the union or the fact-finder's report on a single package

selection of the last offer of the employer or of the union or the fact-finder's report on an issue-by-issue basis

separation of the dispute into economic and non-economic issues and employing one of the selection procedures outlined above.

In New York there has been a rather remarkable experience with interest arbitration, but I ought to focus on how interest arbitration affects the people who have to play the role of itinerant philosopher and how to do that in an constructive fashion. How does an arbitrator get some satisfaction when he walks away? Has he done the right thing? When I was very new as a mediator, I became disturbed when I saw a great deal of power being exercised either by a large employer against a small union or by my Teamster friends who were deciding that the days of a small milk or cement company were numbered and they could no longer afford to subsidize the wages of certain small businessmen.

If I had the ability to fix the terms of employment, things would be all right, I thought. However, it then occurred to me that the day might come when there would be a mediator or an arbitrator who was not as wise or as fair as I am. He might make a mistake, and that would be bad. Obviously I am being facetious; no one is that wise. There are limits to what any one mediator or arbitrator can do, yet the arbitrator does have a unique kind of responsibility in many jurisdictions because the alternative is considered to be worse. The strike is bad compared to what? Arbitration is bad compared to what?

If an arbitrator believes in collective bargaining (and certainly he must because he makes his living from it), if collective bargaining is the soundest procedure for matching employers' needs and employees' desires, and if it helps to create a productive, fair society, if the extension of the right to bargain to the public sector is accepted and it is still denied the right to strike, there must be a fair system of dispute settlement. Arbitration is one of the ways of doing it.

As a philosopher once declared, there is nothing as likely to focus a man's attention as the certainty that he is to be hanged in the morning. The decision by employees to strike or by employers to take a strike by a certain deadline is not as critical a prospect as the hangman's noose. Nevertheless, the strike weapon, the notion of trial by economic combat, is a powerful inducement to decision-making and a great stimulus to private sector collective bargaining. Though illegal in most public jurisdictions, the strike has been very effective in settling some public sector disputes. It is widely accepted that one of the things government does best is nothing, which is not always bad. However, the strike or the threat of a strike is a means of forcing a government, in the absence of other bargaining deadlines, to make decisions. Similarly, it induces government employees and unions, who are also known to postpone decisions, to take a stand.

There are no absolute guarantees against strikes in a free society; the problem of how to deal with public employee labor relations remains. However, I do not accept the premise that the right to strike is the sine qua non of collective bargaining in the public sector. Although I am persuaded that either the strike or interest arbitration is needed to stimulate the collective bargaining process, I prefer arbitration. Strikes induce contract negotiations, but the possibility that an arbitrator is going to come down with something that the parties have to live with whether they like it or not is also a very powerful incentive to settlement, not only in grievance arbitration but particularly in interest arbitration.

To a considerable extent, there is a willingness of the parties in responsible jurisdictions to try to arrive at settlements short of invoking the interest arbitration process. I am happy to say that New York City has had this process for 6½ years, during which the City has had only one 5½ hour fire strike and some wildcats. Has there been a rush to arbitration? Only a little over 7 percent of all the contracts negotiated by the City have been concluded by this arbitration process. There have been many problems arising out of New York City's financial crises, including the role of arbitration in resolving them. The record is rather remarkable. Parties have not rushed to submit all their disputes to arbitration. Of the some thirty or forty cases that have come to interest arbitration, almost three-fourths of them resulted in a confirmation of the bargaining of the parties. What that means literally is that the arbitrator is "laying his hands" on the agreement of the parties.

The arbitrator has not written every line. However, he does have to have some understanding of what result is going to be acceptable. With good faith by both parties, there is belief that there has been good faith bargaining and there really isn't any hanky-panky or the desire to do somebody in. The narcotic effect, by which I mean repeated use of arbitration rather than direct negotiations, exists in some places, but it is regarded as a significant problem in only one reporting state, Pennsylvania.

Experimental Negotiating Agreement

Up to now my comments have concerned the public sector, but I want to point out a significant and ongoing experiment with interest arbitration in the private sector. This is the Experimental Negotiating Agreement (ENA) between the steel companies and the United Steel Workers of America. This agreement was executed in 1974 and renewed and renegotiated in accordance with procedures which call for interest arbitration in the event that the parties cannot resolve their disputes by direct negotiations. The ENA came into being because steel companies and unions recognized not only the cost of the strike to both the industry and employees but, more significantly, the cost to both of the practice of stockpiling and purchasing large amounts of imported steel before every negotiating period. Both the industry and the union came to realize that the costs of a strike were too devastating for either to bear. This was, by the way, not the first time an employer and a union discovered that the strike or threat of a strike had as its primary beneficiary a competitor, foreign or domestic. Time does not permit a more extensive description of the ENA, but it is a significant enough development to suggest that if it continues to be successful, other private sector employers and unions are likely to follow the steel industry example. However, this form of dispute settlement is usually regarded as anathema by the private sector in the firm belief that arbitration would chill collective bargaining, destroy the incentive of the parties to reach their own agreement, and result in gross distortions of the public treasury.

Political Decisions

Trouble arises in interest arbitration when there is a failure to disclose the full ramifications of an award or the arbitrator is inexperienced. An example is an arbitration award in Nassau County[7] which increased the salary of policemen by 24.5 percent over three years. This is not so outlandish in itself, but since Nassau policemen are already the highest paid policemen by far in the land, and this award placed

---

[7]*Nassau County Policeman's Benevolent Ass'n* (February 1978).

their salary substantially ahead of that of New York City policemen—
and New York City police and most City residents believe that there is
no comparison between the difficulty of the jobs—there has been a great
deal of controversy.

This occurred under the New York State Taylor Law.[8] In order to
alleviate this kind of problem, the governor submitted proposals to the
state legislature for the imposition of standards for arbitrators including
a requirement that arbitrators consider the financial ability of the public
employer to pay. Further, even if the arbitrator finds that the employer
is able to finance the award, he would also be required to consider
whether the award required an increase in taxes. This was a very political
question.

Part of the reason for the difficulty in the Nassau case was that the
arbitrator who was selected was really not an experienced labor arbitrator.
He was a management person on the staff of the telephone company,
and not involved in labor or personnel relationships. Subsequently, the
New York State Investigation Commission examined the conduct of the
arbitrator and found insufficient evidence of wrongdoing to take remedial
action.[9] The Commission noted that the arbitrator was unwilling to appear
voluntarily and that a subpoena was quashed in the absence of allegations
of criminal behavior. In reaching its conclusion, the Commission pointedly stated, "The Commission makes no findings as to questions concerning the amount of the award, the qualifications of Mr. French, the
competency of Nassau County's arbitration team, and the wisdom of
Nassau County in not appealing the arbitrator's award."

There has been indications that the County executive consented to
the award because he needed the political support of the Policeman's
Benevolent Association in an election. This is a problem, although I do
not want to exaggerate it. We are not talking about the same world as
the private sector. This is political decision-making.

I am sure the man involved believed he was confirming a deal
reached in good faith, but that is not the way it was perceived by the
public. There is a very thin line between confirming good faith negotiations which can be perceived to be in the public interest and which
are supported by the statutory standards, and confirming something that
is clearly not in the public interest because there has not been either a
full disclosure of what impact the award will have on the immediate
parties or any support in the record for the conclusions reached. I am

---

[8]N.Y. Civ. Serv. Law § 200 (McKinney).
[9]State Commission of Investigation Issues. REPORT ON NASSAU PBA ARBITRATION, March 16,
1980.

describing a different world; it is not an easy world. That is where the "heavy lifting" comes in.

Interest Arbitration Procedures

It should be pointed out that interest arbitration procedures in New York City are different from procedures in other jurisdictions. I describe the City's procedure because it is unique. It is an umpire system in a sense. A precondition to getting on the arbitration panel in New York City is the unanimous approval of City and labor members of the Board of Collective Bargaining. They each pay half of the arbitrator's fee. Then an arbitrator must be selected by both for a particular case. There is a statutory duty with responsibility of mediation. Under such circumstances, why is an award needed? The answer may be very straightforward: there is a local union which represents about ten different units, the City has settled with units A, B, C, D, E, and F, but unit G wants something more. We understand the City's situation. We bargained hard or we even had an arbitration with them; we think their demand is legitimate. The parties think they can present to the arbitrator the kind of case which will establish clearly that against both the City and State standards of comparability, this is what the arbitrator ought to do in this context. The City may have no problem recruiting lawyers, accountants, or teachers, but is unable to recruit or retain engineers, nurses, and doctors. However, all of these titles may be in the same professional bargaining unit, and it might be difficult for the City to voluntarily agree to differentials for the titles which are difficult to recruit or retain. An arbitrator could readily award the differentials agreed to by the parties, provided the record fully supported such a conclusion. I am not troubled with that, assuming it is an open-ended thing, although some of my colleagues are. It is a sensitive question, but I want to describe to you a world that exists.

In a grievance arbitration the parties and the reasons are set out. In an interest arbitration award it is very difficult to give reasons, with the exception of the comparability statistics which set forth the limits of the award. Following that, the arbitrator addresses other basic issues such as, do employees receive a uniform allowance or do they not. The answer may be no, because the money may be given somewhere else in the contract. Interest arbitration is a skill; the decisions are very difficult.

New York has a unique review procedure, which I think has some merit as I see what is happening around the country. I am always skittish about proposing solutions for other jurisdictions, based upon New York.

Particularly as a midwesterner, I am perfectly aware of the attitude of the outlanders (as city residents would say) toward events in the city. However, this procedure does make sense. It provides for the right of an appeal from an impasse award to a tripartite Board of Collective Bargaining, which is a unique structure consisting of two representatives each from labor and New York City and three neutrals who are chosen and paid by the partial members. The tripartite board has the authority to review the panel's award. That has been done about ten times in the past eleven years, and all of those decisions were unanimous. In two cases the awards were reduced, once because of the fiscal crisis when the arbitrator gave a 58 percent award over a five-year period as against a wage guideline of 8.6 percent per year.

In interest arbitration, I think that the possibility of modifying an award on appeal is significant. In order for an award to be confirmed, the arbitrator must ensure it meets the statutory standards. It is not good enough for the negotiators—even if they present what their understanding is and the results they would like to reach—to go on the record for the moment and say, "our heart is pure, our cause is just, do right," which is typical of a pleading in either a grievance or an interest arbitration case.

Occasionally the arbitrator may want to be presented with some facts or law or be given some reason why he should do what the parties are asking. It is essential that there be an adequate record which is not so selective, particularly if it deals with wage patterns, that it refer only to the highest level of settlements, unless there is a history which demonstrates that these particular benchmarks have always been used and found more persuasive. The award must be applicable, because I am convinced that the courts will exericse their right of judicial review. As with rights arbitration, judicial review is governed by tougher standards in the public sector than in the private sector.

Judicial review will exist in the interest field, and I am not unhappy with that. I do not want trials de novo, but the power of the arbitrator to adjudicate without review would be awesome. Society will require review if the arbitration process is to survive. Again let me caution that an arbitrator cannot simply sign a piece of paper: he has the burden of saying it is not good enough to put his imprimatur on it. He may say that he is quite willing to cooperate, that the statute mandates mediation, and that his first duty is to find a solution in the dispute. If the arbitrator helps to do that by adding his imprimatur, he must be sure that the award can apply against these standards and whatever else has not been disclosed.

New York City is different in another respect. There are only neutrals who serve either singly or as one of a three-member panel. On the other hand, the overall administrative structure is tripartite. For the most part, the members of the Board of Collective Bargaining are neutrals or advocates of such standing that they are not willing to be rubber stamps for the parties. I will tell you who they are that you might understand.

Virgil Day, a former Vice-President of General Electric, who is not just a yes-man for every management position the City takes, is one of the City representatives. Edward Silver is a senior partner in one of the largest and most prestigious law firms in New York, whose clients include major corporations. These two people, as well as the labor members, sit on our Board *pro bono*, and the cases are not easy. On the union side, there is Edward Gray, the regional director of the UAW, a remarkable fellow who has more seniority in the UAW than Woodcock had. He is not about to peddle his name. Harry Van Arsdale, Jr., the other union member, is president of the Central Labor Council. These people have not acted as strict partisans.

Tripartite structures elsewhere may be strictly partisan. Employer and union representatives may see themselves purely as advocates, which creates a problem. In New York City, however, the partisan members have always been very helpful in critical disputes, probing the possibility of accommodation and, where necessary, voting against the interest of the side they represent. As I mentioned earlier, all of the appeals in interest cases were decided unanimously by the tripartite board.

It may not be possible to decide all issues unanimously. There may be some real arm's-length issues involved. There may also be a circumstance in which there is a kind of political dissent, and that is not comfortable to deal with, depending upon how vigorous the dissent is. If the dissent is vigorous, as it was in Nassau County where the award was denounced even after the parties had apparently consented to it and the result was a fight to change the law, the arbitrator has a very difficult role. I understand why some of my colleagues do not want to take on these difficult assignments. I do not suggest that there is an easy role to play.

Standards for Decisions

An interest arbitrator has to look for guidance not just from the parties but also from the appointing agencies which may or may not know about the circumstances of a particular case, whether the agency is the American Arbitration Association, the Federal Mediation and

Conciliation Service in some jurisdictions, or a state agency. The arbitrator's imprimatur is going to be on a document that will be cited in other cases and bargaining, bringing forth such questions as, this is what was done for the police, why isn't it good enough for the firemen, what is the impact upon the sanitation workers or hospital workers, or what will be the impact on a similar jurisdiction where I might be called on to serve again?

One must probe a bit to make sure that the parties have presented the facts fully. It is not good enough to just sign off on what is presented; the arbitrator must be cautious and assume he is walking on a mine field.

The negotiating process requires skill. Our labor relations colleagues have experience in mediation and labor relations, even if it is only academic experience. They understand something about the collective bargaining process, rather than merely possessing a sense of doing right or doing good, for which intelligent but inexperienced people may be faulted.

New York City has had a problem of a wage freeze followed by a set wage guideline. I gave an illustration of how the Office of Collective Bargaining reduced an award to conform to that guideline because it would not be consistent with the statutorily mandated procedures which require a consideration of the public interest and welfare before confirmation of an award. The agency had a procedure to knock down that particular award with the agency acting as arbitrator.

During the time of the wage controls which were applicable to both the public and private sectors, the arbitrator had to make a best guess as to whether or not a determination would be within the controls. Assuming that the arbitrator wanted to stretch wage settlements beyond 5.5 or 7.6 percent, then he had to try his best shot, realizing that it might not be final, that it might be subject to change by someone else.

Except to the extent that the arbitrator might be persuaded that he sees no reason why a particular group—the uniformed forces or others— should be breaking a pattern, he may see no special inequity.

Arguments will be made about inequity and cost of living. While cost of living is a standard in most jurisdictions, one may have to recognize that the award is still subject to judicial review or definite wage guidelines. One has to look at all standards and decide which are applicable. If confronted with the question of ability to pay, it may be preclusive. One cannot assume that if asked to decide a question, and if as a consequence to that decision, park or sanitation employees are to be laid off, that it is solely the parties' problem. That luxury may not exist in some jurisdictions. The arbitrator has to look at the situation; he has not been accorded the full responsibility to determine priorities.

This is why I think the collective bargaining process is fascinating. It involves certain hazards, particularly to newer arbitrators. It is a professional responsibility to see that difficult cases are handled by professionals. If cases are handled by amateurs, there will be more of the type of fallout which I described in Nassau County, and a demand for legislative change. That kind of aberration discredits an otherwise honorable profession.

Criteria for Decisions

For the most part the statutes will provide criteria for interest arbitration decisions. The New York State statute[10] is quite similar to the Michigan statute[11] on which it is based. The standard requires a comparison of wages, hours, and conditions of employment of the employees involved in the arbitration proceeding with the wages, hours, and conditions of employment of other employees performing similar services or requiring similar skills under similar working conditions with other employees generally in public and private employment in comparable communities.

The first criterion in most jurisdictions is comparability. The thrust of public sector collective bargaining is to seek rights and benefits comparable to what has been achieved in the private sector. I think such statistical criteria have some bearing. I do not suggest that by punching computer buttons the answer will come out. However, whether it is expressed or not, there is some basis for the decision as to what pay should be given to sanitationmen or policemen. In this regard, I wish the Bureau of Labor Statistics would do in the public sector the job which it has done in the private sector of reporting this kind of data, so that arbitrators can make intelligent evaluations. Some of the necessary data exists, but not nearly enough.

The standards also provide that the arbitrator must consider the interests and welfare of the public; the financial ability of the public employer to pay (certainly we know this to be relevant in the City of New York); comparisons of peculiarities of employment to other trades or professions, including hazards of employment (this is designed for police and firefighters); physical, educational, and mental qualifications; job training skills; the terms of collective bargaining previously nego-

---

[10]N.Y. Civ. S. § 200 *et seq.* (McKinney).
[11]Mich. Comp. Laws Ann. § 423.201 *et seq.*

tiated between the parties providing for compensation and fringe benefits, including but not limited to the provisions for salary, insurance, retirement, medical, and hospitalization benefits; and the paid time off from the job. Total compensation must be considered.

However, New York City—and perhaps other jurisdictions—now mandate that other factors cannot be looked at until the threshold question of ability to pay has been considered. Does the public employer have the ability to pay anything? The arbitrator may have to look at that. In certain jurisdictions, one may find too that there has been such a long history of giving cost-of-living increments—maybe even predating collective bargaining—that this must be looked at first. On the other hand, this may not be the case, and cost-of-living will be factored in with all the other criteria.

I do not think there is a simplistic answer to the question of which fact is dominant, although I am inclined to think comparability is most important because it is a symbol of acceptability.

Data for Decisions

Since the arbitrator's imprimatur has to go on the interest award—either with the help and consultation of the parties or alone—he has to be certain that sufficient data has been entered to support the result. Assuming the existence of statutes or rules of government, the arbitrator has considerable responsibility as an arm of government. If he is not satisfied that he has been given the full story, he should ask for more data, e.g., from the Bureau of Labor Statistics. He may have been told only about base rates, not about longevity. He may not have been told about the value of the pension system. He may have been told only that wages in New York are that much less than elsewhere. The parties may not have evaluated what the fringe benefits are worth. In a hospital situation, he might have been told that city workers are getting less than voluntary hospital workers, without a comparison of the value of their pension benefits. The arbitrator has the duty under my standards to look at the total compensation.

If the parties have not presented the data, the arbitrator has the duty to ask for it, but I do not think he has the license to do his own economic research. If he wants to introduce additional evidence or subjects, he has a right to ask the parties about these areas and get their joint views. I do not believe in separate consultation. To the extent that he goes outside what the parties have presented or feels a compulsion to do so, he must not only disclose that fact but afford the fullest opportunity for comment about his actions.

I have greater difficulty with the consultation with colleagues. If the parties are dealing in good faith, I do not feel I have the right to bring others onto the scene, certainly not without the parties' full knowledge and consent. This kind of consultation, because it tends to produce surprise results, will have the parties asking, where did you get that kind of a ringer?

Sunshine Laws

I turn now to the very sensitive question of sunshine laws, questions dealing with public business and the public's right to know. We are experiencing in this country, and not just in the public sector, a circumstance where some media are much more interested in making the news than reporting it. During the ratification of a major coal settlement, there was a highly selective campaign to provide a national television audience for the dissidents before either side had the opportunity to sell or explain the contract. I do not believe such action was in the public interest. I do not mean dissidence should be disguised; that would be wrong also. I am not suggesting that I have any answers to the problem other than that the media should use discretion and watch where the emphasis is placed. I know the counter-argument will be secrecy in government, but that is my attitude.

The same media treatment occurred with respect to the negotiations with the Transport Workers Union in New York City. Ratification squeaked by with the aid of a federal court. There was a daily effort by the mass media to emphasize what was wrong with the settlement. The other extreme occurred when the polcie threatened to shut down *The Daily News* because they were unhappy with its editorial policy. They did in fact prevent publication for one day and delayed it on another.

How to properly balance the public's right to know, the public's business, and responsible reporting of the issues is a problem. The hearings themselves are a matter of public record. This in itself presents problems because of the temptation to perform for the benefit of the camera, microphone, and notebook rather than to seek a solution to the problem.

It is difficult for an arbitrator to maintain decorum in highly publicized situations, but not every case is dramatic. There are many low-key disputes involving peripheral issues which are not destined for the headlines. The press will not be interested in every interest arbitration. Interest is more likely to be engendered if the dispute involves police or firefighters in the community than, for example, clerical workers, doctors, or engineers.

Florida law[12] does permit going off the record for mediation purposes, but there is no binding arbitration in police and fire disputes in Florida. Instead, there is a fact-finding procedure called a special master procedure.[13] It is not quite the same thing.

The arbitrator also must play a guarded role, but in some cases the parties may want to confer on the arbitrator the responsibility of making statements to the media. Sometimes an inflammatory situation can be avoided by doing that. This strategy is especially useful if the arbitrator is an expert at making it sound like he has said a great deal when he has, in fact, not revealed much at all. In such a situation, this kind of tactic is very sound. There should not be premature disclosure, but a description of how difficult the problem is. Sensitivity and experience are required on the part of the arbitrator.

Career Opportunity

The task of an interest arbitrator is interesting and exciting. It is in the public interest that it be done by skilled people. By describing some of the problems, I hope to interest you in doing this kind of work rather than running exclusively to what may seem to be the greener and friendlier pastures of grievance arbitration. I am not downgrading grievance arbitration at all: I too am interested in doing some of it, and it is terribly important work. However, the interest arbitration process affects the whole profession. The public doesn't readily distinguish between grievance arbitration and interest arbitration; they just know the result. If they think somebody has gone awry with an award, they tend to denigrate the whole profession. Therefore, we all have a responsibility to make sure that the process works in the public interest.

When a statute requiring collective bargaining for public employees contains particular standards and criteria to guide the parties and defines the scope of arbitration, a settlement or award that meets those standards is in conformity with the public interest. If public interest means that in the hypothetical issue I should have given 8 percent rather than 4 percent, I cannot answer. Either answer may be right in a particular situation because it involves making a subjective judgment about the worth of services and the ability to pay.

An arbitrator is paid to assist the parties to reach a settlement in the fairest way possible. He may not arrive at the right answer, but the

---

[12]Fla. Stat. Ann. § 447.605 (West).
[13]*Id.* § 447.403.

parties will have another opportunity to correct the award either by direct negotiations or by selecting a different arbitrator the next time around.

Looking at different jurisdictions and different techniques, an arbitrator may want to keep in mind the story describing differences among European laws. In England everything is permitted except that which is prohibited. In Germany everything is prohibited except that which is permitted. In Russia everything is prohibited including that which is permitted, and in France everything is permitted including that which is prohibited.

Decision-Making

Arnold Zack

I shall explore that unseen world of how an arbitrator gets from the hearing, which everybody sees, to the decision, which everybody reads. Making an arbitration decision is little different from making any other decision, such as what kind of toothpaste to buy or when to do things in one's daily calendar. One has impressions and responds to those impressions and gives in to them or rejects them and tries others. My way of deciding a case may be totally different from the way anybody else decides a case. I shall review the procedures which I follow and discuss the question of arbitrability if that is raised, substantive issues, problems of ambiguity, role of the contract, precedents, and external law. Finally, I shall discuss the act of writing and the question of remedy. As a basis for discussion, I shall use a case which I heard.

An arbitrator enters a hearing and is confronted with two spokesmen. The arbitrator may or may not know the lawyers for the parties. Although it is irrelevant, I wonder why the parties selected me for a particular case. One advocate told me that he uses me only when he has a winning case. Since that time, when he is trying a case before me, I ask myself if he has selected me because he has a weak case and hopes that statement will influence my attitude in his favor. It creates a mind-set when I face the issue. I have ruled against him since that time. He is a very good lawyer, and he settles weak cases. He also told me that when he has cases about which he is uncertain, he tries to get a specific arbitrator, because that arbitrator is so unpredictable that the advocate has a good chance of winning what would be otherwise a losing case. This is one way advocates select arbitrators.

Framing the Issue

When entering a hearing I ask first what the issue is. The parties confer and try to get agreement on the issue, and in that process they

111

affect my view of the case. It may be a straightforward issue such as, was the termination of John Jones for just cause, if not, what shall be the remedy. That is a uniform way of stating a discharge grievance issue in which the parties are businesslike and want to establish the facts of the case. In contrast, phrasing the issue, was the termination of John Jones for theft, assumes agreement on the fact that he was stealing and leaves the issue of whether or not the termination was for just cause for *that fact* in dispute. *That fact* is probably the real issue. If a party tries to get the case prejudged by such a statement of the issue, I am on guard and make a mental note to watch carefully what that party does throughout the hearing. I ask myself if he recognizes that he has a very weak case and would like to have the decision predetermined in the statement of the issue. It creates a ripple of prejudice on my part. If the other side agrees with the statement, I become suspicious that the union representative is selling out his client by agreeing to the issue.

In a contract interpretation question, the same sort of suspicion may arise. The way an issue is phrased may depend upon the sophistication of the parties. Consider a contract interpretation case concerning a very clean issue such as, did the company violate the contract by subcontracting the building of a warehouse. The parties could try to prejudge that question as well by asking, did the company violate the agreement when, because of a shortage of personnel, unavailability of equipment, and shortage of time, it built a warehouse that was fourteen times the size of the original plan. That is a prejudicial statement of the issue. I want a clear statement of what seems to be the issue that is in dispute between the parties.

By carefully phrasing a case of termination due to alcoholism, a party may hope that the arbitrator will think that alcoholism is a disease and should be treated as such and that termination for alcoholism is therefore wrong. Other arbitrators may have concluded that termination for alcoholism, even though the employee may be sick, is justified as a way of preserving the enterprise.

Whatever the arbitrator's feelings, a slanted statement of the issue can influence his decision. One knows that the case is alcoholism and the discipline is termination, and that is prejudicing the arbitrator somehow. In this illustrative case, the dispute involves a termination for alcoholism. The issue is whether termination was for just cause. If the arbitrator finds that it is justified, he needs to decide nothing further. If the arbitrator finds that the termination was not for just cause, he may find that some quantum of discipline was in order but not discharge. If the issue was phrased in terms of, was the *discipline* of John Jones for just cause, the arbitrator may still have a problem if he thinks the discipline was for just cause but the penalty should be reduced. The arbitrator may not get to that second question of remedy.

An arbitrator should encourage the parties to specify what type of penalty was imposed. The term *discipline* should not be used because an arbitrator may find that some discipline was justified, but desires to impose a lesser penalty. If the second question in a submission to arbitration is, if not, what whall be the remedy, the arbitrator has no right to get to the remedy question if discipline was found justified. An arbitrator must be very careful about how the issue is phrased.

If an employer masks the issue in stating it and the other side does not challenge such a proposed submission, should the arbitrator serve as advocate to the other side? It is the arbitrator's responsibility to make sure that the issue is clean. Although I may be accused of taking the position of the other side, I question a slanted submission. If the employer asks whether the discipline of John Jones was for just cause, I would ask the parties—if I decide the discipline was justified but it should have been a lesser penalty—whether this statement of the issue will permit the arbitrator to order a lesser penalty. If the parties agree, I will suggest phrasing the issue accordingly. If the company says the submission does not permit a lesser penalty, the union is on notice and can change the issue if it wants to.

If the company insists upon a biased statement of the issue, I follow Saul Wallen's advice that an arbitrator should decide every case as if it is his last one. I do not care what the employer's or the union's counsel thinks about the way I handle a case. I run a hearing in the way I think will bring justice to both sides and protect the contractual rights of the individual to the extent that they may be relevant. The parties welcome and respect that measure of discipline. If they have selected an arbitrator because they believe he will be more lenient than another with respect to a given issue, they should be made to realize the fallacy of that reasoning. If an arbitrator is concerned about the parties' reactions to his rulings, he will not survive. An arbitrator must adhere to his own reasoning and judgment and establish his reputation on that.

If the arbitrator accepts a framing of the issue as was discipline for just cause, and he finds that the discipline was for just cause, he cannot get to the second question, what shall be the remedy. An arbitrator has a charge to decide only a given issue. If the parties have agreed upon that issue, the arbitrator is limited to a decision within the framework of that issue; he can change it only if both sides agree.

Parties often spend ten or fifteen minutes on framing the issue, but it may take longer. In complicated cases the issue may be debated for a long time. I will not proceed in a case unless it is clear to me that the parties have agreed upon the issue or have agreed to a procedure for resolving the issue. It is preferable that they agree on the issue themselves; if they cannot agree, I will pose as an alternative, what should be the resolution of the grievance. The union may contend that it cannot agree to that alternative because the grievance was not drafted by a lawyer and may not accurately or fully cover the issue in dispute. If it is an AAA or FMCS case, the arbitrator may be able to suggest as an issue, what should the disposition of the demand for arbitration be. If that does not bring about agreement, then I would ask the parties to authorize me to decide the statement of the issue.

I will not allow the parties to defer discussion of the issue until the end of the hearing, particularly in a contract dispute, because the parties may try and slant an issue in their favor based upon the evidence which has been presented. The concept of two distinct questions as the submission to arbitration would apply also in contract interpretation cases. Did the company violate the contract by subcontracting the building of a warehouse, and what shall be the remedy, if any? If the arbitrator does not get agreement on the remedy issue, he does not have the authority to decide a remedy. The parties will usually assume that the arbitrator will take jurisdiction over the remedy.

Opening Statements

The second procedure involves the opening statements. The union in a contract interpretation case or the employer in a discipline case usually makes the first opening statement. Assume a discipline case, in which the employer cites a litany of negative facts about the employee. The grievant had a poor attendance record. In an attempt to help the employee correct his problem, management was forced into ever harsher disciplinary penalties, which were not effective. The grievant was repeatedly absent and given first a two-week and later a one-month suspension. Subsequently, he was absent without any advance notification to or permission from the employer. He came back, provided no excuse to the employer, and was removed from his position. Because his attendance record was poor, the employer said he had no choice but to seek grievant's removal.

One may think that the company obviously will win in a situation in which the employee has such a bad record. It appears equally certain that the union will win after hearing the opening statement of a contract interpretation case. It always seems very logical when the first opening statement is presented. The other side restructures that imbalance in its response, and the arbitrator discovers that the facts presented in the first opening statement are not always complete.

In an illustrative case, the union described the grievant as a loyal employee of eight years. The company labeled him as an alcoholic, the union contended, and regardless of reasons for the employee's absence, the company accused him of being absent for alcoholism. He was hospitalized for five days for a back injury, the union claimed, during which time the company terminated him. The union said that the company had no evidence from the hospital as to why he was out. When the grievant returned to his job, the company had an opportunity to reopen the case because it then had the evidence, but it did not do so. According to the union, the company was prejudiced against the employee and wanted to terminate him because they assumed him to be an alcoholic. In addition, the company had fired him, reinstated him, and then fired him again, which constitutes double jeopardy. Therefore the union argued that the removal was for unjust cause, and he should be reinstated with full back pay. One can see the omission of some facts in the opening statements: by the union in its failure to mention the progressive discipline, and by the company the fact that he was an alcoholic, was fired, reinstated, and then refired. The parties could have added to their opening statement, but they did not.

Often there is a prejudiced selection of facts in the opening statement with the parties referring only to the contract provisions favorable to them. For example, an employer may claim that under the contract it has the right to direct the work force to engage in all kinds of managerial options and clear authority to subcontract. The union may respond that subsection X says that the employer shall subcontract only when employees within the plant are unable to do the work.

The obfuscation sometimes resorted to by parties in opening statements should make an arbitrator wary of these contentions. The arbitrator senses that both sides are not telling the full truth and that it will be difficult to elicit the truth. He tries to find fallacies in the presentations made by the parties. In the case described above, I thought about the extent to which alcoholism is a disease, whether or not it was recognized or treated as a disease, and whether or not the parties had given proper attention to the premise that grievant was an alcoholic. I thought about the newer theories of treatment of alcoholism as a disease, that an employee should be given encouragement to be in Alcoholics Anonymous or a similar type of program, that the employer has an obligation to cooperate in getting an employee into that kind of a program, but that if the employee has refused to respond to treatment, the employer should not be required to continue the uncooperative employee in his employ. Then termination would be for just cause.

I resent it if one of the parties declines to make an opening statement. It makes the arbitrator's and the responding party's jobs more difficult. In this prejudicial theory that I espouse, if the responding party says nothing, either I will believe everything the moving party says, or if I am suspicious, I may go too far the other way looking for skeletons which may not be there. This is very distracting; I will not know the other side's theory of the case. In discipline cases it does not matter much, and the facts do come out, but in contract interpretation cases the responding party—the employer—does itself a disservice by not setting forth its theory of the case. The neutral does not have anything on which to grasp for rebuttal. For instance, if it is a subcontracting case, the union may claim it is entitled to do the subcontracting because it is the essence of its work. There may be a contract clause that gives the employer the right to subcontract. If the employer makes no reference to the contract language in his opening statement, I will not be aware of that fact, and the union's case may be that much more appealing. If the company makes an opening statement giving its theory, I would know the contract clause and there would be some argument in answer to the union's claims. I ask for an opening statement and stop there.

When I refer to opening statement, I mean statements made at the beginning of the case before any witnesses are put on. The parties try to describe what they are going to try to prove. I exclude objections from an advocate during his opponent's opening statement. If they are repeated, I say it is an opening statement and the party will have a chance to respond. If both sides do it, they are going to wash out factual questions.

I am not prejudiced by an advocate who tries to slant an opening statement in the same way that I am prejudiced by an advocate who tries to slant the statement of the issue. The distinction is that the statement of the issue should be a neutral statement of the issue which I am to decide. I do not want to be forced into an issue that does not leave the true question open to resolution.

Exhibits and Stipulations

After the opening statements I ask for the contract, if the contract has not been offered at the onset of the hearing, and any other exhibits that the parties want to stipulate. They may put in the grievance and all the answers. There may be a dispute as to whether they are to be company or union exhibits or joint exhibits. I tell the parties that I prefer to have one set of exhibits. I will call them joint exhibits, and I will note any objections if the parties have them. If they do not accept my suggestion, I will have a set of joint exhibits, a set of union exhibits, and a set of management exhibits. Sometimes the parties will hold back an exhibit for cross-examination in order to trap a witness or challenge his credibility.

Parties may stipulate as many exhibits as they want. If they do so, it is easier for the arbitrator because he can look through these documents and see where the case is going. I prefer to get exhibits at the start of the proceedings because it forecloses many unnecessary questions. If the document is to be admissible anyway, I try to do it faster.

I ask the parties to stipulate the facts. If it appears to be a contract question, I say that there appears to be agreement on the facts. If there is disagreement on the facts, I ask if this or that fact is relevant and try to work out a stipulation. Sometimes the parties do stipulate facts. Usually one lawyer will say wisely that it will take longer to work out a stipulation of the facts than to present them and so urges that all facts be entered. I ask for stipulations of facts after opening statements because after the opening statement the arbitrator has one side's version of the facts. If the other side does not disagree with it, he has stipulation on the facts.

I become annoyed when the parties do not offer the critical facts, but not to the extent that I say I have been faced with an intentional deprivation of evidence that is fatal to a case. However, I reserve the right to say that a party has an obligation in the grievance procedure to get these disputes resolved at the lower steps, that arbitrators are only a fail-safe, and that the party is improperly exploiting the fail-safe. I have wanted to reinstate an employee with full back pay because I was not given the evidence in time, but I have not had the occasion to do it.

I do not resolve requests for documents before the hearing. If it comes as a unilateral request or subpoena is made, I write a letter to the parties saying that I have received a request or subpoena. I cannot judge the validity of such a request at this point because I have not delved into the case. Such a request can be discussed at the opening of the hearing, and I assume that any relevant evidence that is sought will be provided by the other party by that time. If an arbitrator convenes a prehearing conference to rule on such a request, both lawyers would have to go through the whole case to enable the arbitrator to decide what is relevant in what they are asking. An arbitrator should protect an employer against fishing expeditions.

Testimony

At the hearing, the testimony of the parties is presented. In a discipline or discharge case, an arbitrator gets filtered versions of the facts. The arbitrator is given evidence as to the facts of the case, testimony as to the employee's disciplinary record, and evidence as to why he was discharged or given a disciplinary suspension or a written warning.

The arbitrator usually has an opportunity to examine the demeanor of each witness. I had one case involving a teacher who had been given a bad evaluation. When asked what happened when she got the adverse evaluation, the employee testified that she broke down and cried. Under the cross-examination, the grievant was the most hostile, belligerent individual I had ever heard. An arbitrator should be careful to listen to what is said on cross-examination, and counsel should be careful about the questions they ask.

An arbitrator's views influence the parties' presentations. Throughout a proceeding I make marginal notes, recording what I think is important and my reactions to the statements made, and noting facts that I want to hear presented in evidence. If those facts are not forthcoming, I may ask for them.

Sympathy is another factor. The grievant in the previously referenced discharge case was fifty-six years old. I did not know this until the end of the hearing. He looked to be about seventy, maybe because he was an alcoholic. That his three brothers were present offering him great support made an impression on me; I was sympathetic. I felt the presence of the grievant's brothers meant the union was seeking sympathy. Nevertheless, I also thought of grievant as an alcoholic with family support to help him. Perhaps an appeal to sympathy does work against the grievant. I have a negative reaction to the trooping in of wife and family. However, in alcoholism the family is an important element if there is to be rehabilitation.

In the case of the alcoholic, the supervisor testified that the employee said he was not an alcoholic. If he was an alcoholic, failure to acknowledge alcoholism would place him on the disciplinary road more than on the road to rehabilitation. One of the most frequently found syndromes of an alcoholic is his unwillingness to admit that he is an alcoholic, and one of the key stages in treatment is getting him to admit it.

The company contended that the employee had a poor attendance record and was unreliable because he drank. The union, not anticipating the company's position, wanted to establish that someone had called in to cover grievant's absence. The union's theory was that the grievant had gone to the hospital for treatment of a back ailment. Because that explanation had been made for him in advance, they argued that he should have been treated as though he had been legitimately ill. The union queried the foreman if he had refused to let grievant return to work. The foreman answered that he had sent the employee to see the company manager, following the practice for handling employees returning to work from unexcused absences. At this point I made a mental note to ask the supervisor if the employee had been denied permission to come back.

The union asked the foreman if the letter noticing termination for being absent without leave was revoked and received an affirmative reply.

"Did you send out another letter later," the union then asked the foreman.

"Yes."

"Did that letter terminate him again?"

"Yes."

On redirect the company asked the foreman, "Why did you revoke the first letter?"

"This is federal government operations. The union complained that we forgot to insert the paragraph that gives him veteran's rights, and therefore he is entitled to 30-day notice."

"And what did you do?"

The foreman answered, "We paid him for the 30 days and reissued the letter which included the paragraph that his suspension was not effective immediately as it had been in the first letter but it would be effective now."

Then the company asked the foreman on redirect, "Did you see the medical certificate when he came back?"

"No."

"Did you see the medical certificate afterwards?"

"Yes."

"Did the medical certificate say that he had a back problem and say that he was treated for his back?"

"Yes."

"But you still kept the termination?"

"Yes, we did, because the medical certificate also said that he had been referred to an alcoholic ward in the hospital," the foreman answered.

The medical certificate from the hospital read, "Referred to LB aid station, alcoholic ward. Patient has been drinking for the past couple of days, is not eating, complaining of pain and tenderness in the lumbosacral region; had X rays of the lumbosacral spine which were negative."

His brother testified that when he went to the grievant's rooming house and took him to a hospital, he smelled alcohol on the grievant's breath. The personnel manager testified that the employer had a structured program for alcoholic rehabilitation to which grievant was referred in November. Under the company's arrangement, an employee makes a contract that he will go into the program and attend all meetings for whatever period of time agreed upon. Grievant's contract was for one week and was extended weekly. After 9½ weeks, grievant was dropped from the program for being uncooperative.

Grievant testified that he had been employed since January. He stated, "I hurt my back, I had to go to the hospital because my back hurt. I don't know how I ended up in the alcoholic ward, I don't know what was going on there. I just went into a hospital and something happened. I was in such pain I couldn't remember where I was."

On cross-examination the company asked the grievant, "Had you been drinking?"

"I don't remember. I really had terrible back pain."

"Had you left the AA program?"

The grievant answered, "Yes, because the AA counselor said he didn't want to have anything to do with me and he was really being very unfair because I wanted to continue in the program."

"Were you dropped from the program because you were continuing to drink?"

"I guess so."

It was the company's position that grievant was an unreliable employee. The termination order read as follows:

> You are advised that you are being terminated for being absent without leave. This is to put you on notice that the company proposes to remove you from employment no earlier than 30 days from the date you receive this notice. The reason for this proposed action is as follows: Charge number one, you have been absent without official leave on the following dates: January 7–11. You are on a restricted sick leave. You failed to offer any type of acceptable evidence for this absence. The following elements of your past record will be considered in determining any disciplinary action if the imposed charges are sustained. You were suspended for 30 calendar days without appeal; you were suspended for 14 days. . . .

I do not limit past records to a particular period of time. It would be boring to listen to such evidence for a twenty-eight-year employee, but it is admissible. The fact that the company had tolerated that kind of behavior might be to its detriment, so it might not want to introduce the full retrospective record. Usually it is the disciplinary record that the company enters.

In an attendance case the arbitrator must examine the attendance record for any number of years that the company submits. As a matter of fact, if the company enters into evidence a four-year record, the union or the arbitrator may ask what happened five years ago. If the company submits a record and the other side does not challenge it, I do not have to face that issue. If the other side challenges it then I have to deal with that issue.

I am concerned about forcing the witness to testify on cross-examination. At the same time there may be questions that if left unanswered act to the detriment of the employee. I want to get those facts into the record. I can accomplish this by not saying anything, by raising eyebrows the right way, or by asking the right irrelevant question.

It is in the nature of the proceeding that a party will object to something offered into the record. He will ask for a ruling to exclude evidence. The safest way to deal with objections is not to rule too soon. Ask the other party for its response. The party will give a statement as to why the testimony should be allowed. If the parties still want to discuss the objection, they will resolve that issue more often than not, and the arbitrator does not have to face that issue. At some point one of the parties usually will capitulate, withdraw the objection, or rephrase the question. The arbitrator does not have to make very many rulings on evidence. The parties usually take care of those things themselves. That is the way it should be; it is the parties' process. If they can get along with themselves and resolve issues of that type, let them do it themselves.

An arbitrator should not ask questions until both sides have finished their direct and cross-examination and their redirect and recross-examination. At some point a party may ask the question which the arbitrator had in mind. If an arbitrator asks that question prematurely, he may embarrass the party who had intended to ask it. An arbitrator may ask questions of clarification such as, was it the 12th or the 14th, or, are you sure that it was the 13th that they came back because according to the stipulation it occurred on the 11th.

Do not ask a question that is obviously one that someone should have asked and has not done so. I heard a case in which the evidence showed that two employees punched in other people's time cards. The supervisor testified that he watched two employees run a handful of time cards through the machine, put them back on the rack, and disappear. Only one employee appeared at the hearing; he was terminated notwithstanding his protestation of innocence. No reference was made to the other employee. I did not ask about him until I returned to hear another case. The second employee admitted that he had falsified the time cards. Nevertheless, about two weeks later he had been made foreman, a promotion that was already in process at the time. Both sides had agreed to keep out the issue of the second employee. Fortunately, I came out with a penalty for the first employee which was comparable to that given to the second.

Be careful about questions that are obvious. Parties may want to introduce something later in the hearing, particularly in a discipline case, perhaps through a later witness. Sometimes there are obvious questions that are not asked at a particular point in the process. Wait until the end of the hearing, and after all the witnesses have testified, ask the question. At that point the arbitrator will not have undercut one party's intent to introduce crucial evidence through the opposition's witness on cross-examination.

If it is obvious that the grievant wants to testify and the union does not put him on the witness stand, the arbitrator should call counsel into the hall and ask about the duty to provide fair representation. If counsel says he does not intend to have the grievant testify, the arbitrator does not call him as a witness. An arbitrator should call it to the union's attention as prudence may dictate, but it is the union's ultimate decision. If the grievant wants to take the stand despite the admonition of union counsel, and union counsel says that the grievant insists upon taking the witness stand despite the admonition of counsel and that he wants the record to reflect his advice, I let the grievant testify. I probably would not indicate that in my decision even if I were requested to do so.

If there are unanswered questions to which the grievant does not testify, I draw adverse inferences. In my decision I say that the uncontroverted evidence is against him. Sometimes I add that although grievant was in the hearing room, he did not testify.

I have heard several cases in which the employer discharged an employee because he had been arrested. The facts showed that he was arrested for something unrelated to the job or he was acquitted. The company has responsibility in a termination to do so for just cause. Therefore it has the duty to investigate the propriety of the action unless relieved of that authority by the contract. If a collective bargaining agrement says the employer has the right to terminate an employee if he has been arrested for a crime for which there is reasonable cause to believe that he could be imprisoned if convicted, and if the employee is then acquitted, the company has no obligation to give him back pay.

If the company tried to introduce evidence of matters other than those for which an employee was discharged, I would exclude it if the company specified only certain prior reasons for the termination. If grievant was being terminated for getting into a fight and the company introduced evidence of absenteeism or poor workmanship, I would not admit it. The purpose of the termination notice is to inform the employee and the union why such action was taken so that they can utilize the agreed-upon procedure to challenge that action. That procedure, which is very important, cannot be undermined by withholding information, relevant or irrelevant, until the last step. To act otherwise would be to misuse the arbitration process. Arbitrators should be called upon not because the parties want to punish the other side but because the parties in good faith are unable to resolve their own dispute.

In contract interpretation questions, there should be no problem in getting testimony on the facts. If the parties operate in good faith, they are probably going to stipulate the facts that are in the contract interpretation case. An arbitrator reasonably may be suspicious of the party who is reluctant to agree to an obvious fact. I am also suspicious of the party who agrees too readily to the facts. That indicates to me that it is a tough case on the contract, it is a giveaway case, or the spokesmen are incompetent.

The arbitrator needs to understand references to the contract. It is difficult to read a contract, listen to the testimony, and write out notes at the same time. However, an arbitrator must adapt to it, because it is important to read that contract as the parties refer to it. An arbitrator may have questions. There may be standards set forth in the contract which, if not mentioned by the parties, an arbitrator has to ask about, if only to persuade his own conscience that he fully understood the issue. There may be a preliminary clause or a paragraph preceding it that seems to answer the question. The only contract provisions that an arbitrator can rely on in reaching his decision are those that have been mentioned by at least one of the parties. An arbitrator does not have license to roam through the contract to find clauses that come to the conclusion he wants without giving the parties an opportunity to say whether a certain contract clause applies, has been amended by a separate agreement, or simply has been ignored. If in perusing the agreement, an arbitrator sees something that seems relevant, it is incumbent upon him to ask about it at some point, preferably at the end of the hearing.

Closing Arguments and Briefs

Closing arguments are the final phase of an arbitration hearing. In oral argument of the illustrative case, the company contended that the grievant entered a program for alcoholic rehabilitation, that initially he appeared to progress, but was dropped because of his continued drinking. He was repeatedly advised by his supervisor to improve his attendance. He was given two suspensions prior to discharge, to which both the employee and union agreed. Both suspensions were due to unexplained absence and were attributed to grievant's drinking habits. Grievant did not help himself. Because the company requires employees on whom it can rely to run the shop, it had no choice but to terminate him.

The union argued that the removal was not for just cause, since grievant's immediate supervisor said that if he had received the certificate saying the grievant had a back problem while he was still in the hospital, he might not have terminated him. The union argued further that the company did have a timely opportunity to rescind that letter of removal when it received the doctor's medical testimony later, but the company assumed that grievant, having been drunk before, was drunk again. The grievant was removed from the program and should not have been. He should have been given an opportunity to rehabilitate himself. Therefore, because the employer has a commitment to progressive discipline rather than punitive discipline, because a rehabilitation program exists, and because the employee has a record of seven years of service with only two penalties, he should have been reinstated with full back pay because he was absent for reason of a physical disability not alcoholism.

If at the end of the hearing the parties indicate they will file briefs, I insist as strongly as possible that they make an oral argument. It is important to have at least some oral statement from the parties as to what their arguments are to insure that the parties are arbitrating the same issue. An arbitrator wants the issue to be joined and each side to respond to the other. If the issue is not clearly joined at the hearing, the arbitration may not get the joining of the issues in the post-hearing briefs. That places the arbitrator in a very awkward position.

The second reason for closing arguments is to assure that the arbitrator has all the necessary facts. The arbitrator may not have recorded evidence or have recorded it inaccurately if it was introduced at the beginning of the hearing when its relevance was not apparent. Evidence, or an article in the agreement not previously noticed, may become crucial in terms of the parties' arguments.

If the parties refuse to make oral arguments, the arbitrator has no recourse. Usually the parties will comply with an arbitrator's request for closing arguments even though they are going to file briefs.

I make my decision right after I hear a case. That is why it is very important to me to have an understanding of the parties' positions. If a brief is scheduled, I will not write the final decision, but I will outline my expectation of the contentions of the parties and how I am going to decide the case so that when the brief arrives, I can put in my final decision any additional arguments of the parties. I feel much more comfortable by framing the decision quickly because I have a very bad memory for old cases.

I pay attention to the brief, but I am not bound by it. For my personal writing habits, I like to have the oral argument. In fact, after oral argument, one of the parties frequently concludes there is no need to write a brief. Briefs rarely cause me to change my mind. In 60 percent of my cases, I have my decision and an outline of an opinion as to the outcome of the case already implanted in my mind after the hearing. In 90 percent of the cases my conclusion is pretty firm as to who is going to win, the difference being I am not sure exactly how I am going to get there. In 10 percent of the cases, I am uncertain. In 5 percent of the cases, my mind is made up by the briefs, and in the other 5 percent my mind is not made up even after the briefs. I do not mean that I do not carefully consider how I will write the opinion, or what weight to give certain factors. In fact, a brief creates a greater problem because I have already come to a conclusion, and I am trying to buttress it by the evidence and the arguments that are made in the briefs. That may create a problem all the way along the line in 100 percent of the cases.

Writing the Decision

I do not do much research. When I began to arbitrate, I read cases. After about four years I concluded that the cases I was reading were not really relevant to the case that I had to decide. Now I read only about issues that I have not met before and then come to the conclusion very quickly that the printed cases are usually not the case that I have.

If the parties cite cases which they consider important to the issue, I read them but usually I do not pay much attention to the cases cited because my mind is made up. It is very important for a new arbitrator to read the cases. However, he should not go by majority rule, but decide each case on the facts and the agreement presented, using research cases for reasoning modes.

Up to this point, my comments have been about how arbitrators decide cases without doing research. I am very troubled by this lack of research because I am not sure that that is the right way to make decisions. Yet, Benjamin Cardozo writes, "Deep below consciousness are other forces, the likes and the dislikes, the predelictions and the prejudices, the complex of instincts and emotions and habits and convictions, which make the man, whether he be litigant or judge."[1] I think arbitrators are no different from that. I quote also from Jerome Frank:

> The process of judging, so the psychologists tell us, seldom begins with a premise from which a solution is subsequently worked out. Judging begins rather the other way around with a conclusion more or less vaguely formed; a man ordinarily starts with such a conclusion and afterwards tries to find premises which will substantiate it. If he cannot, to his satisfaction, find proper arguments to link up his conclusion with premises which he finds acceptable, he will, unless he is arbitrary or mad, reject the conclusion and seek another. . . . Judicial judgments, like other judgments, doubtless, in most cases, are worked out backward from conclusions tentatively formed.[2]

Consider a hypothetical case in which the company is subcontracting part of the operation, which results in a layoff of 20 percent of the employees. The contract says that there shall be no limitation on the employer's right to subcontract work. There is a line of reasoning, but the contract prevents the arbitrator from reaching the conclusion which equity dictates. The arbitrator must alter his line of reasoning and say that it may appear to be wrong but that the parties negotiated the contract which controls. In most cases intuition will probably be supported by contract language. However, there are times when intuition is wrong and the arbitrator is bound by a contract.

Some arbitrators will adhere strictly to the contract. Others, in order to reach their intuitive judgments, may rationalize their way around contract language and get into negotiating history because they feel that they have a roving commission to do good. Sometimes that may be justified. It depends upon the arbitrator's relationship with the parties and their method of dealing with such matters.

In an alcoholism case, an arbitrator may say simply that the parties have lived with a procedure that calls for termination for alcoholism. They have not done anything to challenge or alter that clear practice; therefore, he will sustain the discharge for alcoholism. In another case an arbitrator may have a relationship with the parties whereby he may say that the parties should set up a system that treats alcoholism as an illness and therefore the employer shall take the employee back. The same may apply to absenteeism. The contract may say absenteeism is grounds for termination, but an arbitrator may conclude that the parties have not followed progressive discipline in a given case, and he may set up standards different from those which the parties have applied traditionally.

---

[1]SELECTED WRITINGS OF BENJAMIN NATHAN CARDOZO, ed. M. Hall 178 (Fallon Publications, 1947).
[2]J. Frank, LAW AND THE MODERN MIND 100 (Brentano, 1930).

It is safer to construe a contract strictly. I think as time goes on an arbitrator feels more comfortable with his relationship with the parties, enabling him to fit into the mode of solving the parties' problems. With experience, one learns how to strike a balance between interpreting the contract and resolving the parties' problems. They are seldom disparate goals, but sometimes they diverge a little. Problem-solving may make an arbitrator unacceptable. Taking the problem-solving approach rather than the contract-adherence approach may seem to be the best device to achieve acceptability, but it is probably the worst.

In writing up a case, first state the facts and contentions of the parties in summary form. Do not spend more than a paragraph or two on the contention for each side. One may take the headnotes of a fifteen-page brief and put them into a summary. An opinion should give an indication to each side that the arbitrator has read the briefs and understands the arguments. Discussion of the case should be in terms of the ruling on it. Sometimes the evidence is overwhelming on one side. An arbitrator may state that the case is without just cause for given reasons. I seldom do that. Usually one should summarize the facts deemed important and reach conclusions that are supported by the contract, the facts, past practice, and the arbitrator's own experience.

At the conclusion of the hearing, an arbitrator may have some inclinations in response to credibility questions. The best single piece of advice that I can give to new arbitrators is to give vent to those leanings and feelings and sit down the first available moment to write out the statement of the facts, the contentions of the parties, and an outline of the opinion discussion. Do it that same day. It is easy to forget the nuances of how somebody reacted to a question. Also, it takes much less time to write a decision immediately than it does to write it a month or two later. Weigh the testimony quickly while it is still fresh and subject to change.

I write my decision the day of the hearing or the next day, and I file it away. I look at it when the briefs are submitted and again when the transcript arrives, if there are some quotations that I want. I may look at it a week later, go through it again, tighten it up, edit it, and send it out. This is good advice for two reasons. It makes an arbitrator's opinions more responsive to the evidence that was presented at the hearing and more responsive to one's own reactions to the hearing at the time it was heard. The best evidence of what transpired is what the arbitrator's thoughts were when very deeply immersed in it, not when reconstructed. Nothing serves better than overcoming the laxity that is ascribed to the majority of arbitrators in the issuance of their awards. One can build a good reputation by issuing awards promptly. An arbitrator is allowed thirty days. Do not let it run for thirty days; get it out in two weeks, if you can.

Transcripts can be inaccurate; take your own notes. If I had not written my award, I would then find it very difficult to do so upon receipt of the transcript. Some briefs are not responsive to the issues and do not raise issues that are as valid as the issues that an arbitrator raises in his own mind right after the hearing. Theories of the case that may not have been raised by either party or that may differ from what is presented by the parties in their briefs may make more sense than either argument made by the parties. Give vent to the urge to postulate the parties' agreements. Put those arguments into writing as rapidly as possible. As illustrated below, I use the case involving alcoholism referenced earlier.

> The parties agreed upon the issue to be decided as follows: Was the termination of Joseph P. for just cause, and if not to what remedy is he entitled?

> Joseph P. has been with the company since January 1971 classified as a custodian. The evidence shows that during that period he has had a problem with alcoholism and his attendance. On November 18, 1976 he entered the alcoholic program and remained therein until January 19, 1977, when according to Counselor Roberts he was, "returned" to the "top boss for not cooperating."

> According to the grievant he left the program because the counselor, "did not want to have anything to do with me." He was absent without official leave from January 18 to April 12, 1977, for which he was given a 14 calendar-day suspension, which was not protested by the union. He was again absent without leave from August 6 to August 23, 1977, and was given a 30 calendar-day suspension effective August 26. This too was unprotested by the union.

> The instant dispute arises from an absence without official leave, which began on January 8, 1978. According to the grievant's brother he was discovered in his bed in the room he rented, having severe pain in his back and "had also taken some drink."

> He was taken by another brother to the Doctors Hospital on his own request but was not admitted to that hospital—which deals with alcoholics—because he lacked his Blue Cross card, and so went to the City General Hospital. There, according to the hospital records supplied later, the grievant was referred to the alcoholic ward where his back was examined and x-rayed.

> The company was informed by telephone that the grievant was in the hospital. Grievant did not report to work. He remained in

the hospital until January 13, 1978, on which date he was issued
a letter of proposed removal based upon "word that he was hospitalized for alcoholism." When the grievant endeavored to return
to work he was referred to the top boss. He apparently brought no
medical certification for his absence. On January 16, 1978, this
was supplied by his brother.

The report from the City Hospital in addition to the reference to
the grievant being in the alcoholic ward reads as follows: "Patient
has been drinking for the past couple of days, not eating, complaining of pain and tenderness in the lumbosacral region and has
had X rays of the lumbosacral region which proved to be negative."
Also on that day the following note was supplied by Dr. Williams,
"The grievant is a patient under my care and is out of work because
of a myotosis hiacitus. Prognosis good."

The grievant protested the termination, appealing the case to
arbitration.

This much I have written. I did not include anything of his medical
record. In a long award there is a tendency to take every objection and
spend a page answering that objection in the opinion; do not do it. In
the instant case, there was a dispute about whether or not grievant had
come into the plant and been allowed to see the top boss or was properly
refused admission to the plant and had his card pulled. I said simply
that he was denied permission. That is a fact; the rest is irrelevant to
the case. Similarly, I ignored the question of the issuance of the two
letters of termination, the charge that one was procedural and it was
double jeopardy. I think the union was satisfied that I believed that it
was only a procedural fault that was corrected at their request, and it
was never pursued by the union.

The discussion part of the decision will be short and probably be
structured as follows. The employee has had a series of disciplinary
penalties. He is an alcoholic. He has been in a rehabilitation program
but has not been successful in his participation in the program. He was
given periods of progressive discipline and ample opportunity to reform
his conduct. It is unfortunate that he is an alcoholic, but the employer
also has responsibilities to operate the enterprise. Because the grievant
has not responded to corrective discipline and the company has proved
that without protest, there is no recourse but to sustain his termination.

I do not say it, but I feel that if I were to put this grievant back to
work and he still believes he is not an alcoholic, he would not reform
because he has been vindicated. The fact that he has been reinstated
without back pay does not matter to him because the money does not

matter. If he is allowed to return to work, he will continue to be a problem for himself and the employer.

I can think of one case of emotional disturbance in which I recommended that the grievant be reinstated as a new employee. The underlying problem had been resolved after the termination and the grievant was an employee who had fifteen years of service. After the discharge the employee had turned around, and I suggested that the parties consider taking him back as a new employee.

Selecting the Remedy

Decide each case as though it is the last. Do not prevaricate on decisions, and do not reinstate all employees without back pay because of the assumption that such action makes an arbitrator acceptable to both parties. It does not.

There are times to compromise on an issue when the language calls for it or to give an employee one last chance. Hypothetically, if an employee with twenty-eight years of seniority has been told that if he is absent one more time he will be fired, and he becomes involved in an automobile accident en route to work and then he is fired, the arbitrator may put him back to work for one last chance.

There are cases where such action is legitimate. However, I heard a case in which a supermarket clerk got into a dispute with a customer. The clerk already had been given one oral warning for not having filled out the shelf. Later, he had been given a second oral warning and told that if he ever failed in that responsibility again, he would be fired. Three weeks later he was given another oral warning for the same thing. A few weeks later, a customer got into an argument with the clerk over the price of lettuce. The customer went to the store manager and said that if the store did not get rid of that employee, he would not come into the store again. The employee was fired and took his case to arbitration.

I found the termination to be for unjust cause. The more acceptable decision would have been to reinstate without back pay because that would have made the employer and the union happy. Grievant would have his job back and the employer would not have to spend money and could fire the employee again the next week. I did not think that was justified because that was progressive discipline. I thought the proper discipline was a disciplinary suspension. The company had used progressive discipline with other employees. I reinstated the grievant with one week's suspension.

Such an award will not be acceptable to the employer. However, I feel much safer, and more comfortable having made a decision that is not acceptable to the employer, than having achieved acceptability to both sides. It is very appealing to reinstate without back pay, but in the long term there are dangers in it. An arbitrator should act as if each case were his last case.

An arbitrator should not keep a scorecard. If the parties think that an arbitrator will decide a case for them because it is their turn and are delighted because he decided the case for them because it was their turn when they had a weak case, they will not hire that arbitrator when they have a hard case because they will be fearful of the same thing on the other side. On the procedural questions as well as on the merits, an arbitrator must decide his cases as though he is the most sought-after arbitrator in the world. If he does, there will be plenty of work for him.

There are three issues to be decided in a discipline case. First, was any discipline justified on the day in question. If no discipline was justified for a particular incident, the employer has no reason to impose any penalty. The second issue is what should have been the penalty for that discipline, in which case the arbitrator looks to grievant's prior record of progressive discipline. Prior progressive discipline in the supermarket case constituted two oral warnings. The first oral warning said the next time the employee does this, he will be terminated. However, he was not terminated but given another oral warning. Indeed, the second oral warning gave him the expectancy that if he violated a rule again he would get an oral warning. That is not progressive discipline.

The third issue is if the penalty imposed was more than the arbitrator thinks was appropriate, how should an arbitrator reimburse the employee for what he lost. In the alcoholism case, if the company had imposed a one-week suspension and I felt discharge was the proper penalty because the grievant was incorrigible, I obviously could not increase the penalty. In the case of the store clerk, I found that he should have been given the next step of progressive discipline, which might have been a written warning. My experience shows that employers do not always give written warnings; they go from oral warnings to suspensions. I found the heaviest suspension which the employer could have reasonably given was ten days. Therefore, that should have been the suspension, and the grievant was entitled to reimbursement for any losses beyond that.

In the course of a hearing I may know very well that I am going to reinstate the employee and that I probably will award him back pay. Should I show my intention by asking what the grievant's interim earnings had been and run the risk of one party feeling that I am dragging out the case for something that I really do not need if the discipline is upheld? An arbitrator does not want to drag the hearing out. At the same time, he does not want to bring the parties back for another day of hearing. Most arbitrators try to formulate language that serves as a guideline to the parties so that they can calculate what the remedy is for a reinstated employee.

The language by which I do this is, for example, to say that the employee's termination is reduced to a ten-day suspension, that he shall be reinstated with full seniority and all rights, and that he shall be reimbursed for all earnings lost beyond the days which would have been the end of the imaginary suspension date. There are a lot of questions that this language does not answer. If the grievant got another job in the interim, presumably that guideline would provide for offsetting those interim earnings. He may have had a nighttime job, and the employer may feel entitled to offset his other job earnings against this earning. The union may counter that the other job was irrelevant to the one at issue. That would create another dispute.

There may be a question of whether or not he applied for unemployment insurance, if the unemployment laws allow him to do so in such circumstances. He has an obligation to offset the damages to the employer by looking for another job. Is that objection met by just signing up for unemployment insurance or does he have to show that he was seriously interviewing for these jobs? Was he making an effort to mitigate the damages? There may be a question of an incarceration during the period of time for which he is to receive back pay. What effect does that have?

These questions should be raised in the hearing. The employer does not want to raise such questions because it does not want to give the suggestion that it is thinking that its cause for discharge might be less than totally meritorious. The arbitrator thinks about them but does not raise them. He is not sure how he will rule on a case, and he does not want one of the parties to say that he prejudged the case. I do not want to extend the case longer by another day of hearings to discover this information, which the parties are usually not prepared to deal with at a hearing. The employer should plead in the alternative more often than it does.

An arbitrator dealing with the remedy question in the decision should formulate what he thinks is the proper remedy. The arbitrator has the option of letting it go at that and removing himself from the case or saying that if there is any dispute as to the appropriate remedy he will retain jurisdiction for a certain period of time. I do not do that. I view it as a separate dispute. I do not feel the parties should be compelled to come back to me, and I will allow them to go to somebody else. Sometimes arbitrators retain jurisdiction. Usually the parties are able to work out their own answers to questions raised by reinstatement.

Mitigation of damages does not usually come up in a hearing unless the union is attempting to impress the arbitrator with the fact that the grievant has obtained other work, or it comes out on cross-examination or by a question from the arbitrator that the grievant did not seek a job. In the standard form of remedy the employee shall be made whole for earnings lost. Let the parties agree on the proper amount, sue in court, or on their own initiative go back to the arbitrator for the determination of mitigation. If an arbitrator limits the award to reimbursement for earnings lost, he is safest. An arbitrator has no authority outside of the employment relationship, and the employment relationship is the obligation of the employer to pay wages.

Promptness

The written decision provides proof of performance by the arbitrator. It shows that one can justify a conclusion by reasonable argument. It provides guidance to the parties for their future use, as in my grocery case, in terms of progressive discipline. It provides an explanation to the grievant about why he is or is not reemployed. It is important for future contract negotiations. When an arbitrator hands down a contract interpretation award, it is a signal to the parties that if they want to change it, they should change it during negotiations or else that decision in fact becomes part of the contract.

Writing provides an opportunity for the arbitrator to think out the decision. I find that in the difficult cases it becomes easier by writing out what I feel. If I do not get to my conclusion, I decide on the other side, and then my writing of the conclusion flows freely. I find it really is much easier to get to a satisfying conclusion by actually writing the decision. I write the decision quickly and make it short. I can think of only two cases in which I have requested an extension beyond the thirty-day period.

I try to get the decision to the parties in approximately two weeks. That is long enough so that the parties will think that I have really thought about the case. I write the decision immediately, let it sit for awhile, and go back over it about a week later. It goes through the typing process, and about two weeks later it is sent to the parties. I find it a great disadvantage to wait any longer than that unless I am forced to by a delay in the receipt of the briefs.

Let me close with three quotations. Lew Gill, a former president of the Academy, said that he frowns on lengthy tomes which, "suggest either an attempt to justify a larger fee or an unbecoming passion for self-expression." Saul Wallen said, "The less you say, the less you have to be taken to account for." Harry Shulman said, "The fear is not that the arbitrator is going to say too little but that he is going to say too much."

Arbitration as a Career

Richard I. Bloch

I want to express very practically about how it feels to be an arbitrator, how I began, and how I intend to proceed in this profession. I will highlight also the good and bad parts of the profession. Obviously I have decided that the good parts substantially outweigh the bad parts; I love my job.

I distinguish between part-time and full-time practice. Mine is a full-time practice; it used to be part-time when I was teaching. In total, I have been in practice for approximately ten years. Although many of my remarks are directed to full-time practice, some apply to the part-time arbitrator. My decision to practice full-time was, I suppose, a slippery one. I had been teaching in Michigan and arbitrating for five or six years. I found myself absolutely exhausted; I risked not doing a good job at either. When my wife secured an appointment as law clerk to Justice Marshall, we moved to Washington. I took a leave of absence from teaching and decided to try being a full-time arbitrator. Thus far I like it.

In the United States today there are about 1,500 to 2,000 people who arbitrate. Of that number, there are about 500 to 700 who do more than hear an occasional case. Of those there are perhaps 100 who call their professional and personal life their own in the context I am doing it. There are a variety of reasons for that. Many are simply unwilling or unable to make that sort of commitment to their own personal lifestyle and workstyle, either because they have grown up in another vein, because arbitration at this point is an older person's profession and at this point they just cannot change logistically, or they choose not to.

Obviously the person who is splitting arbitration with academe cannot have the freedom to come and go. I am not saying that it is easily available, but that it is available and that I recommend that one aspire to it. Arbitration is a great thing to do but it is not great enough, and the downside things are substantial enough, so that if it does not become a meaningful part of one's lifestyle, then I do not think one should do it.

I believe that in my own case one of the things that keeps me active in the profession—and the same holds true for most of the other arbitrators whom I know to be acceptable—is the parties' belief that we do not worry about whether or not we are hired again.

Economics of the Profession

It has been my experience that one makes a very slow start in this profession, and one should steel oneself for that in two ways, either by having another job on which to rely until one's caseload builds up, or by buying a lot of novels to read while waiting for the phone to ring. In my first year I had one case. During the second year my practice exploded: I had six cases. Now my practice is at a very satisfactory level; I hear approximately 150 cases a year. (In some instances, I will hear several cases during a day's session.) However, that is a relatively recent phenomenon. The economics are now satisfactory. I am making a salary probably comparable to law practice, which is 60 percent of what a practicing brain surgeon makes, and 35 to 38 percent of a journeyman plumber. There is another side to that; the money can be very seductive. It is easy to fill up one's entire schedule with hearings and leave no time for the study and preparation that must be given to these decisions if one is a conscientious person. I will return to that later in my discussion of ethics.

Arbitrator as Oracle

I commend a career as an arbitrator. The money is satisfactory; the ego part of it is unbeatable. The arbitrator sits at the end of the table and people turn to him not for a discussion of the important theories of law and life, a mere discussion of theory, but for The Answer. Moreover, the arbitrator *has* the answer. He is being paid to give them an answer, and that is a tremendous ego salver. He walks into the hearing and the parties bow. The grievant, fresh from the plant, notices that management is deferring to this individual. The parties laugh at the arbitrator's jokes and pat him on the back. There is nothing better—during the hearing—however chagrined the parties may be when they read the award and decide not to hire him again.

The arbitrator must give the parties an answer, but he doesn't know The Answer, and to the extent the arbitrator kids himself into believing that he does, he becomes a very bad arbitrator. It is a constant necessity to keep oneself primed and sensitive to the possibility that this case has a different wrinkle and that these parties are talking a little differently than the last parties did. Good arbitrators maintain a sensitivity to the needs of the parties and the particular variances of the cases.

With respect to the really hard case, the answer probably is that there is no answer. I am talking about the two professional parties on either side who come with an absolute mind-blower. At that point I say to myself that I have given this case very conscientious thought. It is the best that I can do, and in fact what the parties have come to me for is an answer. To a certain extent this arbitration process serves a number of functions beyond academic dispute resolution. There is a therapeutic benefit and, finally, there is a necessary resolution goal. To the extent that I have given them a well-reasoned award, there will always be arguments on the other side. Nevertheless, my job has been to give an answer, and I have done so. If I have done this in a conscientious way, recognizing there could have always been other arguments, I have done my job. If one asks whether or not it will ever stop plaguing me, probably it will not. If one cannot live with that, that too is a problem. I can think back to a number of cases where I wonder whether I might not have gone the other way.

There is a lovely Talmudic story about the rabbi who was in his study when two members of his congregation came in. They were having a horrible argument, and the rabbi said, "Let's settle this once and for all." One individual said, "Well, rabbi, here is my side of the story," and he went forward and gave the whole thing. Then the rabbi turned to the other and said, "My son, what is your side," and he went forward in great detail. The rabbi thought about it for a minute and finally he turned and said, "I've listened to your story and I have to say, my son, that you are right." At this point the other man jumped up to speak, and the rabbi said, "Just a minute. I have listened to your story, and you are right." There was a fellow standing in the back of the room while the rabbi spoke, and he said, "Rabbi, Rabbi, I've been listening to this whole business here and you have just said that they are each right, and given the set of facts, Rabbi, they can't both be right." The rabbi turned and said, "and you are right, too." I think that the rabbi's message can be applied to many arbitration cases.

If one does not write an opinion with a healthy respect for one's own flanks, knowing that the language is going to be thrown back at one later, one is seriously abusing one's position. An arbitrator has to write an opinion that will stand the test of time, and to me the pinnacle of success of any arbitrator is to write a well-reasoned, reasonably narrow approach to the specific question that will not cause problems in a different fact situation. If an arbitrator finds himself saying more than once that he cannot live with certain language, he should expect to be removed from that position or remove himself from it.

Workstyle

Another superb part of the job is the workstyle. An arbitrator has reasonable control over how he wants to work. That can be good and bad depending on one's individual motivation and abilities. One works when one wants and for whom one wants, at least when one's practice develops. One need not sit in court waiting for a case to come up or for an appointment with somebody. The parties wait for the arbitrator. That is meaningful to me. In terms of the time spent in one's professional (and indeed personal) life, it is extremely productive time. When the arbitrator gets into the room the hearing begins and when he leaves it is over. He calls his time his own. This may be the most attractive part of the whole process to me.

An arbitrator can choose where to work. I choose to work at home and have my office there. Working at home can be a disadvantage, for there is always the tendency to take a file on a plane or to the beach. Even when jogging one may be thinking about a case. One should not take cases along everywhere. One should learn to turn off, but that is also a risk in anybody's profession.

My own personal commitment is that I should do whatever I can to keep my head open and free to think and to write, which I love to do. To that extent I want at least one full-time secretary to handle typing, make phone calls, and arrange for travel. It is my way of working, but it is not necessary, and other people make other decisions. Many full-time arbitrators who are not otherwise involved in a law firm or academe do not employ anyone. They write up their decision in longhand and bring it to a typist and make their own arrangements. I happen to operate the other way. I generally try to schedule no more than three hearings a week, keeping Mondays and Fridays open in case I want a long weekend. Parties in arbitration do not particularly like to travel to Monday or Friday hearings unless they have to. I try to schedule no more than two nights a week out of town in any given week. That sometimes becomes difficult. It also sometimes becomes a little illusory.

Most cases last a day and no more. By that I mean that they start at approximately 10 A.M. and end around 4 P.M. However, in work that I do for one employer, I schedule hearings in two-day sessions, hearing three or four cases during those two days. I try to arrive the morning of the first day and leave the next day, so I am away only one night. The illusory part of this is that I may get back home at 9 P.M. the next night, and find my children are in bed. I have not seen them, and I cannot truly consider that a night at home. However, I will still maintain my mythical figure of no more than two nights a week away.

I think that on average, I rarely spend less than two days of study and preparation for a day of hearing. I should add that in order to be very effective, every five or six weeks I take a week or ten days out with no hearings whatsoever and spend that time writing and thinking and then go back to the hearing schedule. Remember also that the 150 cases does not necessarily mean 150 days, because parties may present two, three, or four cases, and in some of the very solid umpireship arrangements which I have—where I know the parties and we are very comfortable with each other—they will put in six or seven cases in two-day sessions.

Some cases are settled during the hearing, others after the hearing and before the decision. For certain parties who have a semi- or quasi-expedited procedure, I simply give them a paragraph. They do not want an opinion. One final benefit in a larger spectrum is that it is usually very intriguing work, involving very interesting cases.

The travel is extremely tedious. One can talk about the nicest cities, but they all become the same inside of a chain. One cannot make a leisurely trip when trying to make a living doing this. I do not expect ever to see the cities by daylight, nor do I expect to get out of the hotel at any time except for a meal at night, and then I will see the same cabs and the same airport limousines. I do not enjoy the travel, but obviously I do it because I am willing and desirous of being immersed in these more prestigious or satisfying relationships.

I count a day as six hours in terms of study and preparation. With respect to billing arrangements, per diems in the country range anywhere from $150 on up to $400 or more. Some people charge for travel time; generally, I do not. At the same time, if I come in to a location for a day of hearing and the case is over at 11 A.M. I bill the parties for a full day if I cannot use that afternoon for compensable time. Contrarily, should the case extend into the evening, I do not bill for more than a day. As a general rule, a day of hearing means that I have reserved the day, and I bill for a day. With respect to study and preparation time, if I work from 9 A.M. to 12 noon, putting in three solid hours of work, take a lunch break, and then come back and work, for example, from 1 P.M. to 4 P.M., that is a billable day, and so as a general matter, I define it as six hours. I charge the same amount for hearing days and study days. I think that is a general practice.

There can be pressure. I do not feel the pressure, and I think if one feels the pressure, one should really get out. There are many arbitrators with long experience who are the calmest people in the whole world on the exterior and yet have a heart attack or have ulcers.

Arbitrating on a full-time basis is a very lonely profession. I travel alone, I eat alone, I can assure you I sleep alone, I work alone, and I write my decisions alone. One can be very lonely and very naked when people are reading your innermost thoughts. By definition, the paper the arbitrator gives to the parties should be his best effort. I am keenly aware of that when I sign my name to the award. That is lonely, particularly when one realizes that somebody is a loser in each award and often the loser will feel resentment.

I am still nervous when I begin a hearing. I have nightmares: what if I sit down to hear the parties present their case, and I do not have the faintest idea of what they are talking about, and not only can I not figure out an answer but I do not know what the question is? What if I go through the whole hearing and I cannot understand it all? What if I am the wrong person, and they need somebody smarter? I have such feelings when I go in, but normally at the end of a case I have come to understand, one way or the other, at least what the parties are talking about. I may not have the decision. I think it is the arbitrator's ethical responsibility to be absolutely open with the parties and say he has not understood something that has been said. If an arbitrator is not ready to do this, and does not have confidence in himself to know that if he does not understand an issue that it is probably the fault of the parties, then he really should not be an arbitraator. It is not fair to oneself or to the parties to be misled in any context.

Acceptability

The acceptability question is obviously something with which an arbitrator should be concerned. One gets started by building acceptability. If one worries about it for too long, one is in the wrong job. There are arbitrators who pander to the parties or make frequent phone calls to the appointing agencies, trying to influence FMCS or AAA to send their names out.

Some new arbitrators have generated enormous acceptability. Once acceptability is attained, the problem becomes one of scheduling cases to meet the needs of the parties. Arbitrators doing quality work are needed. One's caseload will grow slowly, but after it gets rolling it will stay there. There is no need for a good arbitrator to campaign. The acceptability and the pressure shows itself in opinions.

In reading opinions in any of these services, one can detect arbitrators who are worried about their acceptability in phrases such as, "the company's case was extremely thorough and very well documented. It was one of the best arguments I have heard in years, but . . . ." That is an apology. That is saying, "You can't imagine how much it hurts me to rule against you, and if I had any other way to go I would. I'm sorry, but I am going to rule against you." Unless one is capable of writing a firm, nonapologetic answer to the question, one should get out of the field.

Ethics

I am involved in the National Academy of Arbitrators, which I think is a marvelous organization; I think that my friends in the Academy are the best people I have ever known. They are good friends, good arbitrators, and good people, and I am flattered to be associated with them. I call them frequently to discuss difficult issues in my cases. I find it by no means unethical to discuss those opinions with other arbitrators; in fact, I feel that an important aspect to doing clients justice is to seek other thinking on the subject, particularly if the case has either been poorly argued or been so magnificiently argued that one is just on the edge of a knife, not knowing what to do.

There is, however, an ethical question in discussing the issues in a case with another arbitrator before a decision is made. There is a trade-off to be made. The quality of the decision is improved by having the input of other individuals who have experience with the same type of case or who have at least given it some thought. Obviously, the other side of it is that the parties are paying for the arbitrator's decision alone, and it must be his decision. I do not rely solely on the codification of this principle, but it is true that in the code of ethics established by the Academy, FMCS, and AAA, this issue was specifically addressed and it was resolved that consultation is permissible.

I do not think it matters particularly with whom the arbitrator discusses a case. At some point the aspects of confidentiality becomes very real, and so obviously if the arbitrator is just bouncing it off a friend, it is an academic question. He is clearly not going to mention the parties. I have no qualms about talking to other arbitrators. I might say I just heard a case with so and so, and the other person asks if John

Doe presented the case for the company and what did I think of his presentation. Obviously, it is my own integrity that matters, and I am not going to let the personalities affect it. If I happen to be with some friends whose mental powers I respect, I will pose a question without revealing the case. I think there is a fine line to be drawn.

On the other hand, I think it is unethical and impermissible that an arbitrator, absent full knowledge of the parties, should have an apprentice draft or prepare the opinion in any context. Aside from Michelangelo doing the Sistine Chapel, there has never been a more personal, service-oriented industry than arbitration. The parties are buying the arbitrator's service and want him to write that award. Ninety-five percent of disputes can be answered by any logical, honest person. However, it is the skilled individual who is able to write a tough opinion, and that is where the craft of this job comes in. I would not draw an analogy to a court decision in which everyone expects clerks to be involved. Such an expectation does not exist in this industry. If the expectation is present, I have no problem with it, but it should be fully disclosed by the arbitrator. Any point when it comes to giving up one's role as arbitrator and delegating the decision-making function to anybody else, is clearly improper.

I am not sure that I rule out the research assistant, but I would draw the line. I might ask a research assistant for a memo on a given topic. I would read his analysis of the cases to make up my mind. That seems to me perfectly proper, and I see no reason to disclose the research done for me. I would not let a researcher set forth the positions of the parties. Setting forth the position of the parties is extremely important and craftsmanlike work. Giving such work to an assistant is like Michelangelo, in painting the Chapel, doing only the faces and permitting his students to do the bodies. I believe the arbitrator has an obligation to reveal that part of the work which has been done by other people. Full disclosure is absolutely required.

Another ethical question is the problem of the parties coming to the arbitrator and wanting a case decided a certain way. I have said no to the parties in such a situation. When the parties come with a political problem and are in agreement as to what the outcome should be, my response is that I will not write an award that contravenes what I find to be the facts. I see no argument against it. Even on a contractual issue, I would tell the parties that they are paying for my decision.

If, after hearing a case, the parties see me outside and both express agreement that the grievant should be discharged, my response would be to tell them to settle the case. Implicit in my remark is the question to them of why have they brought it to arbitration. If they want it in the form of an arbitration award I will write it, but it will be a stipulated award, and they must put their names to it. I will not write it as my decision incorporating their belief. If the parties want just my decision, they take the risk that I am going to decide the other way. They have the option of either settling it or joining me in a stipulated award. I am absolutely adamant on that point, and I am insulted to the extent that they would want me to do otherwise.

I had a case recently which disturbed me a great deal. I heard the evidence, which stated that grievant had rolled over his truck while driving on the highway, spilling the contents. It was alleged that he was driving too fast on the approach. The fellow had fifteen years service with the trucking company and was a good employee. The company wanted to fire him. I stepped outside after hearing the opening statements and asked if the parties could settle, giving them a couple of ways to do so.

The company responded that they had no problems in returning the fellow to work, but that the ICC had been inquiring about its policies with drivers. The company felt the grievant was acceptable as an employee and would be satisfied with imposing a healthy suspension but were afraid simply to return him to work and, therefore, could not settle the case. They had no objection to my returning him to work and allowed it would be much easier. I was not going to do that just because they happened to agree on it, but the real question in my mind was whether I should withdraw from the case at that point because I had heard something so prejudicial that I could not render an honest award in this case. I told the parties that I was considering withdrawing from the case. However, I did not withdraw. Let me give a very clear instance which would have made me withdraw. If the union attorney said in the midst or at the end of a hearing that he really had nothing going for his side at this hearing and expected to get soundly beaten in this case, I would consider that grounds for my immediate withdrawal. Arbitrators may differ, but at that point I would consider that I had been exposed to such a prejudicial remark that my opinion could not help but be questionable when it came down.

I am concerned with some impropriety or improper remark which should not be introduced either in or out of the hearing such as, "It is really a poor case," or "The real reason we are here is because this is a minority employee, and we dare not refuse to take his case to arbitration." Another manifestation of ethical standards with respect to holding oneself out as an arbitrator is that I seldom, if ever, eat with the parties, with one party and not the other, even if I have known them for years. If I do, I clear it with the other representative.

Full disclosure of any possible conflicts in any context is required. After I received appointment on a National Symphony case, it occurred to me that since I played fifteen years ago I have carried a Musician's Federation card. It seemed to me something that clearly had to be revealed to the National Symphony employer, and I did so. When I was appointed as associate umpire for a company some years ago, I sold some stock in their parent corporation that I had bought many years ago. Arbitrators should be aware of possible conflicts of interest. The arbitrator is an adjudicator and is being paid to maintain the system in honesty. It is important to remember that.

If somebody appears before me who happens to be a personal friend, I tell the other side that they should know that Joe is a neighbor of mine, and we see each other occasionally or frequently. I think that is the type of disclosure that should be made. If it is a serious conflict, I make the disclosure before the hearing. I was with a law firm in Chicago for a very brief period of time before leaving the firm to teach. That firm sometimes appears before me, and I think I must make disclosure of my prior association even before I accept appointment in a case. It seems to me not as important if the person just happens to know me well and I do not have an obvious conflict, in which case I can make the disclosure at the hearing, but I always make it.

Arbitrator as Mediator

The question of whether or not an arbitrator should mediate is an on-going one. A party says, "You want to know what this case is really about? Here is why." The arbitrator says to one party "Can't you do this?" And they say, "Look, we can't do that because of this and that," which are all irrelevant to the case at hand but perfectly relevant to why we cannot settle. Should an arbitrator hear that kind of discussion? Can he disregard it and make a sterile decision on the record? If he cannot or if he cannot convince the parties that he can, then he should not mediate. The safe thing is not to mediate.

In eight years of working with one company and its union, I have never tried to mediate a case. On one occasion, I warned the parties of an impending decision which they were both going to hate and which I said was the worst decision I had ever written because they had given me a poor case. I asked if they wanted to try to settle it. That is as close as I have ever gotten to mediating. In other situations with certain parties I never go through a full case without stepping outside and twisting their arms a little bit. That is dangerous. One must be extremely sensitive to the parties to do that, and one has to realize the ethical problems that it could raise. The difficulty is that one may hear something irrelevant to the case, a position, or possibly information that might require the arbitrator's stepping down.

The Acorn

There is the late night thought that comes to me every now and again: that in reality, if viewed from the top of the world, one is deciding little questions. We arbitrators often decide whether Joe hit Sam with a steel bar or not and whether a certain contract provision was properly construed. There can be very meaningful issues, of course, but they are rare and most of an arbitrator's professional life is spent deciding rather small issues. I often wonder whether that is really what one should spend one's life doing. I am not sure that I will not decide against that in the future. I also realize as I talk to law practitioners that they too, for the most part, spend their lives on little issues—in fact, even the big issues are little in the context of day-to-day business.

On the other side are the academics who say how lovely it must be not to attend committee meetings and confront academic nonsense and how great it would be not to worry about badgering students. There is some compelling substance to that too. In deciding these little issues on a case-by-case basis one is making a contribution as significant in its own way to labor relations as those more substantial theoretical contributions made from the academic side. I do have the constant pull from both sides, and maybe that is the way it will always be.

Judges and Arbitrators: Observations on the Scope of Judicial Review

*Lewis B. Kaden**

Twenty years have passed since the Supreme Court determined that an employer's promise to arbitrate would be specifically enforced by the federal courts, under rules of decision drawn from a federal common law of collective bargaining agreements.[1] The Court agreed with Archibald Cox, who had maintained that "the new institutions of industrial self-government and the surrounding legal system can gain strength from mutual support."[2] Cox counseled that the courts proceed empirically in this new undertaking; that "[t]he principles determining legal rights and duties under a collective bargaining agreement should not be imposed from above . . . [but] drawn out of the institutions of labor relations and shaped to their needs."[3]

Injecting the law into the private process of industrial governance has probably contributed significantly to the relative stability of American labor relations. Grievance arbitration, the process of private adjudication of disputes arising during the term of a collective bargaining agreement, has become a major facet of the American system of labor law. The vast majority of collective bargaining agreements contain arbitration provisions, and management as well as labor has come to view arbitration as the preferred means for settling disputes, better than submitting questions of contract application to the courts and better than

*Professor of Law, Columbia University. B.A. 1963, LL.B. 1967, Harvard University.

This Article was adapted from a paper delivered at the annual meeting of the Committee on Arbitration, Labor Law Section, American Bar Association, in Palm Springs, California, February 16, 1979.

I wish to thank Elisa M. Rivlin, J.D. 1979, Columbia University, for her invaluable research assistance.
[1]*Textile Workers Union v. Lincoln Mills*, 353 U.S. 448 (1957).
[2]Cox, *Rights Under a Labor Agreement*, 69 HARV. L. REV. 601, 604–05 (1956). *See also* Shulman, *Reason, Contract, and Law in Labor Relations*, 68 HARV. L. REV. 999, 1024 (1955).
[3]Cox, *supra* note 2, at 605.

resort to bargaining, strikes, or other forms of direct action.[4] But while judges and arbitrators have no doubt heeded Cox's prescription of mutual support, the intersection of the judicial process and grievance arbitration, which bear superficial similarities but are fundamentally different, still shows signs of strain.

Some of the continuing tension between judges and arbitrators is traceable to the Court's own treatment of the relationship. After an initial definition of the roles of judges and arbitrators in settling collective bargaining disputes—in the trilogy of Steelworkers cases[5]—the Court has virtually neglected the area for almost twenty years. In the absence of adequate guidance, the lower courts have had difficulty in formulating and applying standards to determine whether an arbitrator has respected the limits of the authority granted him by the collective bargaining agreement. Similarly, courts have used inconsistent standards in defining those instances when an arbitrator's decision, even though made under proper authority, should not be considered for all purposes final. The Supreme Court's reluctance to return to the subject in the face of demonstrated need has contributed to the wavering and uncertain path of judicial review of arbitration awards.[6]

Recently, the uncertainty regarding the scope of judicial review of arbitral awards has been exacerbated by three critical developments: the increased sensitivity to individual rights affected by the collective relationship,[7] the proliferation of public law impinging on the arbitrator's role in the bargaining process,[8] and the use of grievance arbitration in contracts between government agencies and labor organizations representing public workers.[9] Each development portends more frequent judicial intervention in the arbitration process, and each may generate sound exceptions to the basic principle of finality of arbitration. However, in each case, exceptions to finality should depend upon the formulation of sound reasons for them.

This Article explores the relative roles of judges and arbitrators in resolving disputes arising under a collective bargaining agreement, focusing on the problem of judicial review of an arbitrator's decision. Sections II through IV examine the impact on the relationship between judges and arbitrators of the three developments outlined above. First,

---

[4]A. Cox, D. Bok & R. Gorman, CASES AND MATERIALS ON LABOR LAW 572–73 (1977).

[5]*United Steelworkers v. Enterprise Wheel & Car Corp.*, 363 U.S. 953 (1960); *United Steelworkers v. Warrior & Gulf Navigation Co.*, 363 U.S. 574 (1960); *United Steelworkers v. American Mfg. Co.*, 363 U.S. 564 (1960).

[6]*See* notes 21–26 and accompanying text *infra*.

[7]*See* notes 58–89 and accompanying text *infra*.

[8]*See* notes 90–118 and accompanying text *infra*.

[9]*See* notes 119–52 and accompanying text *infra*.

however, Section I deals with the more traditional doctrine supporting the presumptive finality of the arbitral award.

I. Finality of Arbitration

In *Textile Workers Union v. Lincoln Mills*[10] the Supreme Court decreed that a federal common law of collective bargaining agreements be developed by the courts, and declared as the first rule of decision that promises to arbitrate be specifically enforced. The Court went on in the trilogy of Steelworkers cases to recognize the central place of arbitration in the collective bargaining process. The Court made clear that so long as the parties indicated a desire to submit a dispute to arbitration, a judge must order that it proceed, no matter how manifest the contract violation or how frivolous the claimed infraction.[11] Further, there existed a presumption that the parties intended to submit the dispute to the contract machinery; if there was any rational basis for finding that intention in the agreement, the court must order arbitration— "[a]n order to arbitrate the particular grievance should not be denied unless it may be said with positive assurance that the arbitration clause is not susceptible of an interpretation that covers the asserted dispute. Doubts should be resolved in favor of coverage."[12] Finally, in *United Steelworkers v. Enterprise Wheel & Car Corp.*,[13] the courts were enjoined from reviewing the merits of an arbitrator's performance. Within quite broad limits, the arbitrator's construction of the agreement was what the parties contracted for, and they could not expect the courts to review it.[14]

In *Enterprise Wheel*, a group of employees were discharged for walking off the job to protest the discharge of another employee. The contract provided for arbitration "as to the meaning and application" of the agreement, with the arbitrator's decision "final and binding on the parties."[15] In cases of discipline, if the arbitrator determined that an employee had been "suspended unjustly or discharged in violation of the provisions" of the agreement, the company was obliged to "reinstate

---

[10]353 U.S. 448 (1957).
[11]*United Steelworkers v. American Mfg. Co.*, 363 U.S. 564 (1960). *See* Cox, *Reflections Upon Labor Arbitration*, 72 HARV. L. REV. 1482, 1513–18 (1959).
[12]*United Steelworkers v. Warrior & Gulf Navigation Co.*, 363 U.S. 574, 582–83 (1960).
[13]363 U.S. 593 (1960).
[14]*See* Aaron, *Judicial Intervention in Labor Arbitration*, 20 STAN. L. REV. 41 (1967); Dunau, *Three Problems in Labor Arbitration*, 55 VA. L. REV. 427, 427–62. (1969); St. Antoine, *Judicial Review of Labor Arbitration Awards: A Second Look at* Enterprise Wheel *and its Progeny*, 75 MICH. L. REV. 1137 (1977).
[15]363 U.S. at 594.

the employee and pay full compensation at the employee's regular rate of pay for the time lost."[16]

After concluding that the discharges were unwarranted and that the improper conduct justified only a suspension of ten days, the arbitrator ordered reinstatement of the employees with backpay for the time lost less the period of suspension. Between the discharges and the arbitrator's decision, however, the agreement had expired. The arbitrator rejected the argument that expiration of the contract discharged the employer's responsibilities for reinstatement and additional backpay, but his opinion failed to disclose whether this conclusion was drawn from the contract or was based on some extrinsic principle of law. It was on this issue that the court of appeals upset the arbitrator's award.[17]

Finding that the lower court had simply disagreed with the arbitrator's construction of the contract, the Supreme Court reversed. "A mere ambiguity in the opinion accompanying an award," wrote Justice Douglas, "which permits an inference that the arbitrator may have exceeded his authority [by looking only to enacted legislation] is not a reason for refusing to enforce an award."[18] It was the "arbitrator's construction which was bargained for,"[19] and not that of a judge. Nonetheless, there were limits to the finality of an arbitrator's contract interpretation:

[A]n arbitrator is confined to interpretation and application of the collective bargaining agreement; he does not sit to dispense his own brand of industrial justice. He may of course look for guidance from many sources,

---

[16]*Id.*

[17]*Enterprise Wheel & Car Corp. v. United Steelworkers*, 269 F.2d 327, 331–32 (4th Cir. 1959).

[18]363 U.S. at 598. There is of course a difference between an arbitrator's general authority to hear a particular claim and his specific authority to make an award. Both questions of arbitrability are ultimately for the courts to resolve. The more troublesome questions of the scope of review involve challenges to specific authority. In *Enterprise Wheel*, for example, there was no issue of general arbitrability remaining before the Supreme Court: the company was obliged to submit those discharges to the arbitrator notwithstanding the subsequent expiration of the agreement. Rather, the point of contention was the employer's assertion, accepted by the court of appeals, that the specific remedy selected by the arbitrator—reinstatement with backpay—exceeded his authority under the contract. The Court admitted the possibility that the arbitrator based this ruling on his view of extrinsic statutory guarantees rather than on an interpretation of the contract. It was possible, too, that he had simply looked to extrinsic sources of law to clarify the meaning of the contract, or that he had based his decision solely on his reading of the agreement. Though apparently acknowledging that a court could properly refuse to enforce an award based solely on statutory sources external to the agreement, Justice Douglas was clear that as long as the possibility existed that the remedy was founded in the contract, the arbitrator's construction had to be accepted. *Id.* at 597–98.

If, however, this amounts to a presumption that an arbitrator empowered to make a particular award by the terms of a contract has in fact used that power as the basis for his decision, it is surely not explained in the Court's opinion; nor is it readily squared with the apparent obligation of a judge to find the "essence" of an award in the agreement construed. Perhaps the ultimate meaning of *Enterprise Wheel* is that an arbitrator may be reversed by a court only when his own words betray an unauthorized excursion beyond the bounds of the contract. (This seems to follow from the Court's references to "words that manifest an infidelity to the obligation" to find the essence in the contract, and from the discussion that ambiguity does not allow a court to infer a lack of arbitral authority to make the award. *Id.* at 597, 598).

[19]*Id.* at 599.

yet his award is legitimate only so long as it draws its essence from the collective bargaining agreement. When the arbitrator's words manifest an infidelity to this obligation, courts have no choice but to refuse enforcement of the award.[20]

The problem with this articulation of the limits of finality is that it provides little guidance as to the appropriate standard for judicial review of arbitral awards. Subsequent to the cryptic caveat in *Enterprise Wheel* that finality turns upon whether the arbitrator has drawn the "essence" of his award from the agreement, the lower courts have endeavored to formulate such a standard, with at best indifferent success. An award will be set aside, it has been said, only if it is "palpably faulty";[21] lacks "foundation in reason or fact";[22] shows a "manifest disregard of the agreement";[23] is not "plausible";[24] is "arbitrary, capricious, or not adequately grounded in the basic collective bargaining contract";[25] or discloses an interpretation not "possible for an honest intellect to . . . reach."[26]

Moreover, notwithstanding ritual invocation of the various verbal formulations of the finality principle, reviewing courts frequently do explore the merits of arbitral interpretation, either as an independent ground to sustain a determination to enforce an award, or as an indication of default justifying denial of enforcement.[27] One manifestation of judicial ambivalence toward the finality of arbitral interpretation is the continuing inconsistency in the response to arbitration awards that find just cause for discipline of an employee but not for discharge. Some cases provide examples of judicial intervention in this setting. For example, in *Textile Workers Union v. American Thread Co.*[28] the Fourth Circuit refused to enforce an award based on an arbitrator's finding that misconduct involving improper operation of a machine warranted discipline but not discharge. The contract gave the employer the right to

---

[20]*Id.* at 597.

[21]*E.g., Electrical Workers v. Peerless Pressed Metal Corp.*, 489 F.2d 768, 769 (1st Cir. 1973); *Safeway Stores v. Bakery Workers Local 111*, 390 F.2d 79, 82 (5th Cir. 1968).

[22]*E.g., Machinists Dist. No. 145 v. Modern Air Transp. Inc.*, 495 F.2d 1241, 1244 (5th Cir.), *cert. denied*, 419 U.S. 1050 (1974).

[23]*E.g., Ludwig Honold Mfg. Co. v. Fletcher*, 405 F.2d 1123, 1128 (3d Cir. 1969).

[24]*E.g., Holly Sugar Corp. v. Distillery Workers*, 412 F.2d 899, 903 (9th Cir. 1969).

[25]*E.g., Machinists v. Hayes Corp.*, 296 F.2d 238, 243 (5th Cir. 1961).

[26]*E.g., Newspaper Guild v. Tribune Pub. Co.*, 407 F.2d 1327, 1328 (9th Cir. 1969).

[27]*E.g., Mogge v. District 8, Int'l Ass'n of Machinists*, 454 F.2d 510, 515 (7th Cir. 1971) (enforcing award because it "was not arbitrary and capricious but was wholly justified"); *Baldwin-Montrose Chem. Co. v. United Rubber Workers*, 383 F.2d 796, 798 (6th Cir. 1967) (enforcing award and expressing accord with district court judge's conclusion that "[i]f I were going to rule on [the arbitrator's interpretation of the contract], which I am not, I would say he has done it reasonably"); *H.K. Porter Co. v. Saw Workers*, 333 F.2d 596 (3d Cir. 1964) (enforcing part of arbitral award based on past practice as "fully justified" since court found practice existed, but denying enforcement to part based on past practice court found did not exist).

[28]291 F.2d 894 (4th Cir. 1961).

discipline or discharge employees "for just cause," and the court found that the arbitrator exceeded his authority by invoking a distinction between the just cause required for the lesser penalty and that needed for the greater.[29] Similarly, in *Truck Drivers Local 784 v. Ulry-Talbert Co.*[30] the Eighth Circuit concluded that an arbitrator lacked authority to measure the degree of discipline warranted by an infraction. The agreement provided that the employer's disciplinary action could be reversed only if it were found that the complaint was "not supported by the facts, and that the management ha[d] acted arbitrarily and in bad faith or in violation of the express terms of this [a]greement."[31] Curiously, although the arbitrator had accepted the factual basis advanced by the company for its action, the court itself examined the reasons given for discharge. If the arbitrator was not authorized to determine whether the discharge was arbitrary when the facts showed an infraction, it is difficult to see why the court found a need to explore the company's reason. On the other hand, if the court was testing the arbitrator's determination of "arbitrariness" in the manner of discipline, its inquiry seems to have gone more to the merits of his award than to his power to reach it. In another case, the Tenth Circuit refused enforcement of an award finding just cause for discipline but not discharge when the contract listed the proven infraction—failure promptly to settle collected bills—among the grounds supporting discharge.[32] The arbitrator based his award on the employer's uneven enforcement and failure to use progressive discipline, but the court found the contract unambiguous and the award outside the arbitrator's authority.

Another group of cases involving questions of specific arbitral authority centers around the effect of collective bargaining agreements on management's right to make changes in the terms and conditions of employment during the contract period. The landmark decision in this area is still the Second Circuit's opinion *Torrington Co. v. Metal Products Workers Local 1645*.[33] As all students of labor law recall, the arbitrator in that case upheld the union's complaint against the company's uni-

---

[29]Judge Sobeloff wrote a vigorous dissent, and later wrote for the court's majority in a case raising similar issues. *Lynchburgh Foundry Co. v. United Steelworkers Local 2556*, 404 F.2d 259 (4th Cir. 1968).

[30]330 F.2d 562 (8th Cir. 1964).

[31]*Id.* at 564.

[32]*Mistletoe Express Serv. v. Motor Expressmen's Union*, 566 F.2d 692 (10th Cir. 1977).

[33]362 F.2d 677 (2d Cir. 1966). Commentators have been almost unanimous in their criticism of the *Torrington* opinion. *See, e.g.*, Aaron, *supra* note 14, at 48–51; Dunau, *supra* note 14, at 454–62; Jones, *The Name of the Game is Decision—Some Reflections on "Arbitrability and "Authority" in Labor Arbitration*, 46 TEX. L. REV. 865, 869–77 (1968); Meltzer, *Ruminations About Ideology, Law, and Labor Arbitration*, in NATIONAL ACADEMY OF ARBITRATORS, THE ARBITRATOR, THE NLRB AND THE COURTS (PROCEEDINGS OF THE 20TH ANNUAL MEETING) 1, 9–11 (1967); St. Antoine, *supra* note 14, at 1152–53.

lateral decision to discontinue its practice of granting employees an hour off with pay to vote on election day. The contract offered little guidance, save the commonplace admonition that the arbitration not "add to, modify or alter" its terms. The issue posed was whether the contract included an implied condition that past practices affecting working conditions could not be changed without agreement, or at least that the company could not take such action without prior negotiation. The arbitrator accepted the invitation in the Steelworkers cases to look for guidance beyond the express terms of the contract to "the industrial common law—the practices of the industry and the shop."[34] He found, on one side, the employer's past practice of granting time off, and on the other, a history of prior negotiations during which the company first announced its determination to discontinue the practice, the union demanded its retention, and the new agreement executed after a strike remained silent on the matter. The Second Circuit saw no breach of fidelity to the finality principle in reviewing "whether the agreement authorize[d] the arbitrator to expand its express terms on the basis of the parties' prior practice," and concluded that it did not.[35]

A recent case in the Fifth Circuit affords an illuminating contrast to *Torrington*. In *Boise Cascade Corp. v. United Steelworkers Local 7001*,[36] the union complained when the company paid reduced wages to employees who avoided a layoff by accepting temporary assignment to lower rated jobs. The contract prohibited reduced wages except "when the employee elects to take such lower rated job through seniority rights,"[37] and further provided that an employee who declined a lower rated job could go on layoff until "work is again available for him on his regular job."[38] The arbitrator thought the contract ambiguous, but found in past practice evidence of a distinction between an employee who took a lower rated job in order to avoid layoff and one who voluntarily took a lower rated job "through seniority rights." The district court, however, refused enforcement of the award, finding that the contract clearly supported the employer's position, and thus that an award to the contrary was not drawn from the essence of the agreement.[39] The court of appeals disagreed.[40] Citing Professor St. Antoine's observation that when a court

---

[34]*United Steelworkers v. Warrior & Gulf Navigation Co.*, 363 U.S. 574, 581–82 (1960).

[35]362 F.2d at 680. Judge Feinberg, in dissent, thought it plainly within the arbitrator's prerogative to look outside the agreement to see if under all the circumstances the practice of paid time off for voting was an implied condition of the contract. He criticized the majority for reviewing the merits of arbitral performance under the guise of judicially ensuring that the arbitrator stick to the agreement. *Id*. at 682–84.

[36]588 F.2d 127 (5th Cir.), *cert. denied*, 100 S. Ct. 57 (1979).

[37]*Id*. at 128.

[38]*Id*.

[39]*Id*. at 128. The district court decision is unpublished.

[40]*Id*.

disagrees strongly enough with an arbitrator's reading of contract provisions, "it is simplicity itself to conclude that the arbitrator must have
'added to or altered' the collective bargaining agreement,"[41] Judge Wisdom nevertheless concluded that the contractual proscriptions against
arbitral additions to the agreement did not preclude arbitrators from
looking to extrinsic sources to clarify provisions that may "rationally be
considered ambiguous."[42] Further, the arbitrators' judgments here that
the collective bargaining agreement was ambiguous, and that extrinsic
evidence favored the union's position, could not be said to have no
"foundation in reason or fact."[43]

It may be that the arbitrators were wrong in both *Torrington* and
Boise Cascade—that in *Boise Cascade* the contract provision covered
the particular case, and that in *Torrington* the bargaining pattern effectively created a new status quo eliminating paid time off for voting until
the union managed to secure the benefit in the contract. But to say that
each arbitrator was in error is not to say that the courtroom is the place
to correct his errant ways. No doubt the reviewing judges who felt
compelled to do so acted in the face of what seemed to them the arbitrator's plain mistake. In *Torrington*, the majority in the Second Circuit
also may have been influenced by a view of the bargaining process and
the contract as expressing the full range of limitations on managerial
discretion, rather than as constituting only part of a broader, continuing
process of joint determination of conditions of employment. Certainly
the National Labor Relations Board's wavering course on the duty to
bargain during the term of agreement[44] makes clear that while Judge
Lumbard's view of the collective bargaining agreement may be incorrect,
it is not beyond reason. However, what is reflected in these examples
of judicial intervention is not just the judges' tendency to jump in when
they behold what they believe to be unreasoned interpretations or outrageous results. More fundamentally, they betray some courts' hesitation
to accept the concept of finality as rooted not in arbitral skill, but in

---

[41]*Id*. at 130 n.3. To be faithful to the finality principle expressed in *Enterprise Wheel*, St.
Antoine argued, courts must "recognize that most arbitral aberrations are merely the product of
fallible minds, not of overreaching power." St. Antoine, *supra* note 14, at 1153.

[42]588 F.2d at 130.

[43]This is the standard for review in the Fifth Circuit. *See e.g., Machinists Dist. No. 145 v.
Modern Air Transp., Inc.*, 495 F.2d 1241, 1244 (5th Cir.), *cert. denied*, 419 U.S. 1050 (1974).

[44]*See Allied Mills, Inc.*, 82 NLRB 854 (1949) (midterm bargaining required only as to terms
and conditions not expressly contained in contract); *Jacobs Mfg. Co.*, 94 NLRB 1214 (1951) (terms
and conditions fully discussed or consciously explored although not expressly contained in contract
may also be exempt from midterm bargaining), *aff'd*, 196 F.2d 680 (2d Cir. 1952); *Press Co.*, 121
NLRB 976 (1958) (to be exempt from midterm bargaining union must have made specific and
unmistakable waiver of its right to bargain); *Radioear Corp.*, 199 NLRB 1161 (1972) (waiver need
not be "clear and unequivocal" but depends on circumstances of negotiations). *See also* Nelson &
Howard, *The Duty to Bargain During the Term of an Existing Agreement*, 27 LAB. L.J. 573 (1976).

the collective bargaining agreement itself. Through that agreement the parties have consented to abide by the arbitrator's reading of their contractual obligations, right or wrong, and to correct his decision if need be by the same consensual process of negotiation that gave birth to his authority in the first place.

Perhaps it is foolhardy to expect judges who daily interpret and apply standards codified in contracts, regulations, and statutes to stand aside and enforce interpretations of collective bargaining agreements that seem to them excessively far off the mark. In any event, it is apparent that this judicial instinct will not be stifled by incantations of finality, or by still more verbal formulations of the proper scope of review. Nor will it prove especially productive to parse the distinctions between standards limiting judicial reversal to arbitral interpretations that are "palpably faulty," as opposed to those that are "arbitrary and capricious," or "without foundation in reason or fact." In the end, the courts will be moved, if at all, by an enhanced appreciation of the special qualities of collective bargaining and the enforcement machinery of grievance arbitration. And for this, we must return to the basics—the question of the arbitrator's function, and his place in the bargaining process.

The institution of grievance arbitration is a distinctive and valued American contribution to industrial stability. A process of internal dispute settlement during the term of an agreement permits a species of continuous bargaining to proceed both without interruption of services and without resort to the nonconsensual process of dispute resolution in the courts. And as Professor Cox and others recognized early in the American experience,[45] continuous bargaining is critical when the contracting parties share an ongoing relationship characterized by a high degree of interdependence. As employer and employees live and work together, their agreement adjusts to the experiences they share, and their contract becomes more elaborate. But simply because they coexist by necessity, the agreement will always leave problems unresolved; it will always include deliberate as well as accidental ambiguities; it will always fail to anticipate new events and circumstances generating new problems for joint resolution. As Professor Feller described so clearly,[46] the collective agreement does not introduce rules to the workplace, but rather a new form of participation in the making, application, refinement, and remaking of rules as experience and the needs of those who cohabit the workplace require.

---

[45]See Cox, *supra* note 11, at 1490–93; Shulman, *supra* note 2.
[46]Feller, *A General Theory of the Collective Bargaining Agreement*, 61 CALIF. L. REV. 663, 724 (1973).

Arbitration—the resolution of disputes during the contract period by an impartial person designated by the parties for just that purpose— is a useful but not a necessary invention. At least since Congress made unions subject to suit and collective agreements enforceable in the federal courts, it would be possible to look to the legal process to interpret and apply the contract during its term.[47] But precisely because dispute resolution in this setting involves as much rule-finding and rulemaking as rule-applying, recourse to the courts invites too narrow a view of the problem. In light of their experience with contracts involving single transactions, the courts may take too myopic a view of this function. And the parties have too much at stake to entrust the contours of their relationship to whatever judge happens to come along next on the assignment list in the computer.

Alternatively, whether or not an issue is anticipated in the agreement, the parties could treat the problem of dispute resolution during the contract term as they do the negotiation of a new agreement, leaving each side to its own devices to press its claim. One need only look to the unhappy experience in Great Britain and other jurisdictions[48] that tolerate economic self-help to resolve contract grievances to see the risks that arise if the repose assured by a contract lasts only as long as neither party feels strongly enough about a problem to resort to direct action. Thus, the employer's promise to arbitrate disputes arising during the term is conjoined with the union's promise to avoid midterm concerted activity. The two promises are not always of equivalent scope, and arbitrators' inclinations to find implied assurances against unilateral changes in practice, such as that which gave rise to the *Torrington* decision, may well be influenced by the broad sweep of the no-strike promises in many collective agreements.

The parties' stake in arbitral finality, then, exists not so much because the arbitrator has special competence, experience, or understanding, or even because sometimes he may be filling in gaps in the agreement, making rather than applying rules.[49] Instead, the parties have an institutional stake in finality because the arbitrator is their creation; he functions by their consent and at their sufferance, and his

---

[47]Cox, *The Legal Nature of Collective Bargaining Agreements*, 57 MICH. L. REV. 1 (1958).

[48]Gould, *Taft-Hartley Comes to Great Britain: Observations on the Industrial Relations Act of 1971*, 81 YALE L.J. 1421, 1432 (1972). *See also* ROYAL COMMISION ON TRADE UNIONS AND EMPLOYERS ASSOCIATIONS, 1965–1968 (1968); Fairweather, *A Comparison of British and American Grievance Handling*, in NATIONAL ACADEMY OF ARBITRATORS, DEVELOPMENTS IN AMERICAN AND FOREIGN ARBITRATION (PROCEEDINGS OF THE 21ST ANNUAL MEETING) 1 (1968).

[49]*See* Feller, *The Coming End of Arbitration's Golden Age*, in NATIONAL ACADEMY OF ARBITRATORS, ARBITRATION—1976 (PROCEEDINGS OF THE 29TH ANNUAL MEETING) 97, 107 (1976). *Cf.* St. Antoine, *supra* note 14, at 1161 (arbitrator's special function not limited to application of rules but also includes rulemaking).

powers and roles can and should be molded by them to suit their own purposes. That they freely do so is evident in the wide variety of arbitration procedures, selection mechanisms, and individual umpires selected in major collective bargaining agreements. It might be said in response that resort to judicial review indicates, by definition, the breakdown of continuing consent, and so it does. But more narrowly it usually indicates dissatisfaction with a particular result. Wholesale review of the merits of arbitral awards would import quite different forms and standards into the bargaining process.

Concededly, these observations, standing alone, do little to guide the determination of hard cases. Moreover, some of the decisions mentioned above reflect differences reaching beyond the single question of arbitral finality—most notably, differing perceptions of the collaborative process that national labor policy substitutes for the preexisting unilateral determination of rules for the workplace.[50] Thus, as suggested earlier, Judge Lumbard's conclusion in *Torrington*[51] that the arbitrator exceeded his authority presupposed a "reserved rights" theory of bargaining under which the agreement defined the limited extent to which management had consented to share its authority. Judge Feinberg's dissent,[52] on the other hand, embodied a view more consonant with recent NLRB treatment of the problem, *i.e.*, that there exists a continuing obligation during the term of an agreement to submit to joint determination at least those disputes that concern matters within the statutory scope of bargaining. However, the unenlightened state of the case law and the equally unilluminating array of formulae offered by the lower courts to describe the scope of judicial review do suggest that Justice Douglas's encomium to arbitration in the Steelworkers decisions should have been the beginning, not the end, of the development of a theory of the relationship between judges and arbitrators.

Neither the enthusiastic pronouncement of the finality principle in *Enterprise Wheel*, nor the obscure exception for cases where the arbitrator departs from the "essence" of the agreement, furnished a principled guide for later decisionmaking. What has become known as the "essence" test of *Enterprise Wheel* plainly does not elaborate reasons for finality sufficient to describe either the circumstances in which the principle properly applies, or those in which enforcement of an arbitrator's award

---

[50]*See* Feller, *supra* note 46, at 724–36.
[51]362 F.2d at 682.
[52]*Id.* at 682–84.

may be denied.[53] That Justice Douglas did not supply all the guidance one might have wished is not astonishing. Only three years earlier, he had written the extraordinary opinion for the Court in *Lincoln Mills*,[54] finding in the jurisdictional language and limited legislative history of section 301 of the Taft-Hartley Act a congressional mandate to fashion a federal common law of collective agreements. For sources of this new common law, the Court suggested that judges look to the provisions of the Labor Management Relations Act, "the penumbra of express statutory mandates," the policies behind the statutes, and state rules "compatible with the purpose of § 301."[55] It was a bold stroke and an enticing challenge. However, the tasks of combing these materials for apt rules to apply, and of testing those rules against the exacting standards of industrial relations, have proved to require more direction than may be discerned in a few grand pronouncements by the Supreme Court. The Steelworkers opinions made an important, even historic, start, but they should have been followed after a time by further efforts to elaborate a theory of national labor policy applicable to collective bargaining agreements. Inevitably, a Court thus engaged would have found both need and opportunity to clarify the reasoned justification for the finality principle, and thus to identify a meaningful standard for judicial review of arbitration awards. Yet, in the past two decades, the Court has not returned to the subject.[56] If the mission launched by *Lincoln Mills* and Steelworkers has foundered in the circuits, the Court must share some of the blame.

Occasional confusion and aberrational decisions by the lower federal courts concerning review of arbitration awards are not in themselves intolerable. Recently, however, changes elsewhere in the law affecting the labor contract, the bargaining relationship, and the arbitrator's role have combined to heighten the frequency of conflict between courts and

---

[53]Professor Wechsler set forth the classic test of principled adjudication: "A principled decision . . . is one that rests on reasons with respect to all the issues in the case, reasons that in their generality and their neutrality transcend any immediate result that is involved." Wechsler, *Toward Neutral Principles of Constitutional Law*, 73 HARV. L. REV. 1, 19 (1959), *reprinted in* H. Wechsler, PRINCIPLES, POLITICS AND FUNDAMENTAL LAW 3, 27 (1961). *See also* Greenawalt, *The Enduring Significance of Neutral Principles*, 78 COLUM. L. REV. 982 (1978).

[54]*Textile Workers Union v. Lincoln Mills*, 353 U.S. 448 (1957).

[55]*Id.* at 457.

[56]*See e.g., Holodnak v. Avco Corp.*, 423 U.S. 892 (1975), *denying cert. to* 514 F.2d 285 (2d Cir.), *rev'g in part* 381 F. Supp. 191 (D. Conn.); *Satterwhite v. United Parcel Serv.*, 419 U.S. 1079 (1974) (Douglas J., dissenting), *denying cert. to* 496 F.2d 448 (10th Cir.); *Modern Air Transp., Inc. v. Machinists Dist. No. 145*, 419 U.S. 1050 (1974), *denying cert. to* 495 F.2d 1241 (5th Cir.); *United States Gypsum Co. v. United Steelworkers*, 419 U.S. 998 (1974), *denying cert. to* 492 F.2d 713 (5th Cir.); *Otis Elevator Co. v. Local 453, Int'l Union of Electrical Workers*, 373 U.S. 949 (1963), *denying cert. to* 314 F.2d 25 (2d Cir.); *Local 520, ILGWU v. Glendale Mfg. Co.*, 366 U.S. 950 (1961) (Douglas, J., dissenting), *denying cert. to* 283 F.2d 936 (4th Cir. 1960).

arbitrators. This mounting judicial intervention proceeds in contexts where judges still lack the moorings of "reasons that in their generality and their neutrality transcend any immediate result."[57]

The sections that follow examine the expanded judicial role in three such areas. Section II looks at cases in which an individual employee seeks to reverse an arbitrator's award because of inadequate representation on the part of the union or bias on the part of the arbitrator. Section III deals with cases requiring the application of external "public law" to disputes that are, at least on the primary level, governed by the "law" of the agreement. Finally, section IV focuses on the special problems that arise in the context of public sector grievance arbitration.

II. Challenges to Arbitration Awards by Individual Employees

The place of the individual employee's rights in the collective relationship fostered by national labor policy has been a point of continuing uncertainty. For many years debate flourished on the question whether an aggrieved individual had a right to have his complaint processed through the contract grievance machinery up to and including arbitration: either a right to proceed to arbitration through the union as his exclusive representative, or a right to use the arbitration machinery himself if the union chose not to pursue his claim.[58] Some courts and commentators found such a guarantee in the provision of section 9(a) of the National Labor Relations Act that an individual employee "shall have the right at any time to present grievances to [his] employer and to have such grievances adjusted."[59] Others argued that this provision secured not the individual's entitlement to have his claim heard, but rather the employer's right to entertain it if he wished without committing an unfair labor practice based on circumvention of the majority representative in violation of section 8(a) (5).[60] The Supreme Court added to the confusion by finding that an individual suit for breach of the collective agreement could be brought under section 301 of the Taft-Hartley Act[61] but holding three years later that the action did not lie unless the individual first exhausted his opportunities for satisfaction through the contract machinery.[62]

---

[57]Wechsler, *supra* note 53, at 19.
[58]*See generally* Cox, *supra* note 2, at 616–52; Feller, *supra* note 46.
[59]29 U.S.C. § 159(a) (1976). *See, e.g., Donnelly v. United Fruit Co.*, 40 N.J. 61, 190 A.2d 825 (1963).
[60]29 U.S.C. § 158(a)(5) (1976).
[61]*Smith v. Evening News Ass'n*, 371 U.S. 195 (1962).
[62]*Republic Steel Corp. v. Maddox*, 379 U.S. 650 (1965).

Some of the problems were resolved in *Vaca v. Sipes*.[63] Benjamin Owens is only one of several unfortunate employees whose misadventures fill the case reports in this area of labor law. Owens attempted to resume work after a leave of absence caused by high blood pressure. His own doctor and another pronounced him fit. The company doctor disagreed, and he was discharged. After pursuing the case to the brink of arbitration, the union had him examined by yet another doctor, and on the basis of the latter's negative report refused to take the case to arbitration. Owens sued the union, and a state court jury verdict in his favor was affirmed by the Missouri Supreme Court.

The Supreme Court reversed, determining that Owens had no statutory right to have the union take his claim to arbitration.[64] The union could be held liable to him only if it breached its duty of fair representation—that is, if its conduct was "arbitrary, discriminatory, or in bad faith,"[65] a standard Owens failed to prove in the case. Further, Owens could have sued the employer for breach of contract only after exhausting the contract procedures; and at least when the agreement left the union in control of these procedures, an employee in his circumstances could overcome the exhaustion bar only by showing that the union had breached its duty of fair representation by "ignor[ing] a meritorious grievance or process[ing] it in perfunctory fashion."[66] Left open for later resolution was the question whether an individual could press his grievance to arbitration alone if the union determined not to pursue it and the contract was silent on individual access. This issue was later resolved in favor of the view that section 9(a) permits but does not require an employer to entertain the individual grievance.[67] In sum, the combination of *Vaca* and later decisions yields the conclusion that the collective bargaining agreement confers rights only upon the collective interests who execute it: the union and the employer. The union's basic right is its control of and access to the grievance machinery, which the employer is obliged to respect; the employer's basic right is that of enforcement of the union's promise not to strike during the contract term. The individual employee's right against either his employer or his union turns essentially on the duty of fair representation owed to him by the union.

---

[63]386 U.S. 171 (1967).

[64]By the time the United States Supreme Court sorted out the matter, Owens had died, a misfortune that might have been thought to bear on the issue. His executor received the unhappy news that recovery would not be forthcoming.

[65]386 U.S. at 190.

[66]*Id.* at 191.

[67]*Emporium Capwell v. Western Addition Community Org.*, 420 U.S. 50, 61 n.12 (1975) (citing with approval *Black-Clawson Co. v. Machinists, Dist. No. 137*, 313 F.2d 179 (2d Cir. 1962)).

All of this makes critical the content of this duty. Here, the Court has steered a middle course. After *Vaca*, the duty of fair representation requires something more than subjective good faith and a pure heart, and something less than due care defined objectively as in the law of torts.[68] It requires, the Court tells us, that the union act neither "arbitrarily," presumably an objective standard; nor in "bad faith," seemingly a subjective test; nor "discriminatorily," which could be called objective or subjective, as we know from the tortuous path of antidiscrimination law under NLRA, title VII of the 1964 Civil Rights Act, and the Constitution.[69]

Additionally, the union is obliged to satisfy this duty not just in determining whether to take a case to arbitration, but also in the arbitration proceeding itself.[70] And where the representation has indeed been inadequate, the traditional presumption of the finality of the arbitrator's award does not apply. The leading cases in this area are *Holodnak v. Avco Corp., Avco-Lycoming Division*[71] and *Hines v. Anchor Motor Freight, Inc.*[72] Each exemplifies the proposition that unusual cases make law—some would say, unusual law.

Michael Holodnak published an article critical of both his union and his employer in a political newsletter of the American Independent Movement. He was discharged for violating a company plant conduct rule barring "false, vicious or malicious statements . . . which affect the employee's relationship to his job."[73] The union took his grievance to arbitration, where both the arbitrator and the union attorney seemed bent on extracting repentance from the grievant. The attorney read the article for the first time immediately prior to the hearing; he failed to object to the arbitrator's line of questioning; he failed to raise any first amendment claims of protection for the article; and, perhaps most critically, he repudiated Holodnak's testimony in his post-hearing brief as "oft times wrong and even childlike," and basically argued for mercy. The arbitrator upheld the discharge, and Holodnak sued to vacate the award and for breach of contract, seeking reinstatement and damages.

---

[68]The "reasonable man of ordinary prudence" was first mentioned in *Vaughan v. Menlove*, 3 Bing. (N.C.) 468, 132 Eng. Rep. 490 (C.P. 1837). *See also Delair v. McAdoo*, 324 Pa. 392, 188 A. 181 (1936); W. Prosser, HANDBOOK OF THE LAW OF TORTS, 149–80 (4th ed. 1971).

[69]*Compare Washington v. Davis*, 426 U.S. 229 (1976), *with NLRB v. Erie Resistor Corp.*, 373 U.S. 221 (1963), *and NLRB v. Great Dane Trailers, Inc.*, 388 U.S. 26 (1967).

[70]In fact, a recent survey concluded that one in five fair representation cases challenged the quality of representation in the arbitration hearing. Koretz & Rabin, *Arbitration and Individual Rights*, in THE FUTURE OF LABOR ARBITRATION IN AMERICA 113, 135 n.90 (1976).

[71]381 F. Supp. 191 (D. Conn. 1974), *aff'd in part and rev'd in part*, 514 F.2d 285 (2d Cir.), *cert. denied*, 423 U.S. 892 (1975).

[72]424 U.S. 554 (1976).

[73]381 F. Supp. at 194–95.

Judge Lumbard, sitting in the district court, found first that the arbitrator's bias required vacation of the award.[74] Since Holodnak was seeking reinstatement as well, the court proceeded to deal with the contract claim, finding that the grievant had satisfied the exhaustion requirements of *Republic Steel Corp. v. Maddox*[75] on the ground that the attorney's perfunctory handling of the grievance in arbitration violated the union's duty of fair representation. Having found a breach of the duty of fair representation, the court could proceed to decide the breach of contract claim itself, and it concluded that Holodnak had a constitutional right to publish the article because Avco's activities were sufficiently intertwined with those of the federal government to satisfy the state action requirement. Holodnak was awarded compensatory and punitive damages plus attorneys' fees, and the Second Circuit affirmed all but the punitive damage award.[76]

The *Holodnak* decision clearly applied—perhaps even stretched—the "arbitrary and perfunctory" standard of fair representation to the union's conduct in the arbitration hearing. However, because the arbitrator's bias independently supported the determination to vacate the award, the case left for *Hines v. Anchor Motor Freight, Inc.*[77] the question whether a breach of the duty of fair representation would itself furnish grounds for disturbing the finality of an arbitration. In *Hines*, an arbitrator upheld the discharges for theft of several employees, based on motel records indicating that they had obtained reimbursement for sums in excess of the actual expense of lodging. After the arbitration, new evidence showed that the responsibility lay with a motel clerk who had falsified the records and pocketed the difference. The employees sued for breach of the duty of fair representation and breach of contract. The Sixth Circuit[78] found a breach of the union's duty in its perfunctory investigation and conduct of the case in arbitration, but emphasized the conjunction of this negligent representation with evident political antagonism toward the particular employees.[79] However, the court refused to upset the arbitrator's decision in circumstances where neither the arbitrator nor the employer was guilty of misconduct. On this issue of finality, the Supreme Court reversed, holding that a breach of the duty of fair representation removes the finality bar to an individual's action for breach of contract "if it seriously undermines the integrity of the

---

[74]*Id.* at 199.
[75]379 U.S. 650 (1965).
[76]*Holodnak v. Avco Corp., Avco-Lycoming Div.*, 514 F.2d 285 (2d Cir.), *cert. denied*, 423 U.S. 892 (1975).
[77]424 U.S. 554 (1976).
[78]*Hines v. Local 377, Chauffeurs*, 506 F.2d 1153 (6th Cir. 1974).
[79]*Id.* at 1157.

arbitral process."[80] Justice White, the author of *Vaca*, reasoned as follows:

> The grievance processes cannot be expected to be error-free. The finality provision has sufficient force to surmount occasional instances of mistake. But it is quite another matter to suggest that erroneous arbitration decisions must stand even though the employee's representation by the union has been dishonest, in bad faith, or discriminatory; for in that event error and injustice of the grossest sort would multiply . . . . In our view, enforcement of the finality provision where the arbitrator has erred is conditioned upon the union's having satisfied its statutory duty fairly to represent the employee in connection with the arbitration proceedings.[81]

The Court's treatment of the duty of fair representation in *Vaca* and *Hines* has drawn criticism from all sides. Management representatives find it at least anomalous that their liability turns on the union's virtue, which they must defend even when the union is not a party to the suit,[82] and protest their inability to rely upon the finality of arbitrations won without misconduct on their part. Unions, apprehensive of judicial intervention in their representative functions, plead the drain on staff and treasury that follows when an objective standard of. due care leads to defensive processing of nonmeritorious grievances through arbitration.[83] Some commentators[84] find the scope of the duty defined by the Court unsatisfactory to protect individual employee rights, and argue for recognition of a right in the individual to have his grievance entertained, a standard of breach based on negligence, and even a change in employment law to guarantee all employees, organized and unorganized, access to impartial review of discipline based on a statutory requirement of just cause. Arbitrators wary of these developments in the law have been critical of the Court's acknowledgment of yet another basis for upsetting an award, even when the arbitrator himself has performed unexceptionably.[85] Even the Labor Board, in recent unfair practice cases based on a breach of the duty of fair representation, seems to reject the objective standard, requiring some evidence of bad faith to prove a charge.[86]

---

[80]424 U.S. at 567.

[81]*Id*. at 571.

[82]Bakely, *Duty of Fair Representation Under the NLRA*, in [1974] ABA LABOR RELATIONS LAW SECTION 103, cited in Koretz & Rabin, *supra* note 70, at 123.

[83]*See* Asher, *Comment*, in NATIONAL ACADEMY OF ARBITRATORS, ARBITRATION—1974 (PROCEEDINGS OF THE 27TH ANNUAL MEETING) 31 (1975).

[84]*E.g.*, Summers, *The Individual Employee's Rights Under the Collective Agreement: What Constitutes Fair Representation*, in NATIONAL ACADEMY OF ARBITRATORS, ARBITRATION—1974 (PROCEEDINGS OF THE 27TH ANNUAL MEETING) 14 (1975).

[85]Aaron, *The Duty of Fair Representation: An Overview*, in THE DUTY OF FAIR REPRESENTATION 8 (J. McKelvey ed. 1977); Edwards, *Arbitration of Employment Discrimination Cases: An Empirical Study*, in NATIONAL ACADEMY OF ARBITRATORS, ARBITRATION—1975 (PROCEEDINGS OF THE 28TH ANNUAL MEETING) 59 (1976).

[86]*E.g.*, *Teamsters Local 860 (The Emporium)*, 236 NLRB No. 101 (June 12, 1978).

Striking an appropriate balance between these collective and individual interests is inevitably delicate. More factual data would be useful to evaluate the effect on union representation of expanded availability of judicial protection for individual employees. At present, there is some indication of a cautious march through to arbitration in cases that might have been settled prior to the decisions defining the duty of fair representation; there is certainly more litigation in which breach of the duty is alleged.

Notwithstanding the widespread disapproval in theory and as yet uncertain results in practice, and with an important reservation discussed below, the Court has not done so badly in this corner of labor relations law. If the contract procedures are controlled by the collective interests—a starting point solidly grounded in national labor policy—and the courts are limited in their oversight of the substance of those processes, the duty of fair representation is the principal safety-valve remaining to the individual. In these circumstances, it does not seem too much to ask that the union display something more than lack of bad faith or subjective personal hostility toward the claims of the grievant, or that it afford him minimally competent representation through both the negotiation and administration stages of the bargaining process. One may quarrel with the application of the arbitrary and perfunctory standard in particular cases—indeed, the finding in *Hines* of a breach of the duty, if not tied to the proof of personal hostility, may be troublesome in the standard it sets for union performance in an adjudicative proceeding. In other contexts, however, one may urge a more generous definition of the duty without fearing the consequences of litigation flood tides, for the burden on the individual is still substantial. The reported cases suggest that the unions' proclaimed apprehensions in this regard may exceed the reality of adjudicated matters. Still, there is need for caution in extending the protection too far.[87]

It is not at all shocking to discover that an award may be upset when an individual succeeds in showing a breach of the duty in the union's representation during the arbitration proceeding itself. True, the employer is an innocent victim in this situation, but so also is he in the *Holodnak* example when arbitral bias supports an order to vacate. Leaving aside the matter of the content of the duty, *Hines* presents no more than another aspect of the principle that finality of arbitration depends on the basic integrity of the process. If the arbitrator is biased or bought, or proceeds on a crucial assumption of an erroneous fact, or if the individual's representation fails the test of minimal adequacy in investigation or argument, the process leading to the award is tainted and the

---

[87]*See, e.g., International Bhd. of Electrical Workers v. Foust*, 572 F.2d 710 (10th Cir. 1978), *rev'd*, 442 U.S. 42 (1979).

award itself lacks the integrity essential for finality. This must be true whether or not the employer or the arbitrator is at fault because, in Justice White's phrase, the contractual mechanism "ceases to qualify."[88] Finality is not a goal to be pursued for its own sake; it is useful only so long as the process is honest.

More troublesome than the result in *Hines* is that part of *Vaca* authorizing a court that has found a breach of the duty of fair representation to go on to interpret and apply the contract. The temptation here is surely understandable. The court has before it a matter in which the arbitration process has already failed, either because it was not invoked by the union, or because it was infected by arbitral failings or inadequate advocacy. Further, the union's incremental damage liability depends on the determination of the contract issue—indeed, if there was no contractual breach, the individual has suffered no injury.[89] But notwithstanding these factors, it is a temptation best resisted.

Underlying this *Vaca* principle seems to be a suspicion that the contract machinery, once tainted, will not work effectively. This reflects too low an estimate of the capacity of bargaining representatives to meet their obligations, the very capacity on which the whole process of private dispute-resolution ultimately depends. There is in fact some reason to expect that a union found to have violated its duty of fair representation will be moved to supply excellent representation to the aggrieved employee in the future. In addition, cases such as *Torrington* and *Boise Cascade* confirm the suspicion that judges are not especially apt at reading labor contracts. They are naturally prone to a literalism in contract interpretation that ignores the peculiar nature of the collective bargaining agreement, and naturally more likely to resort to familiar habits and principles of construction drawn from commercial experience. Besides, the parties have contracted for arbitral, not judicial, interpretation of their commitments; a temporary breakdown ought not serve to cast aside a preference so embedded and encouraged in our industrial jurisprudence. The enduring lesson of the Steelworkers cases is that the law best contributes to industrial stability by enforcing the mutual promises of the employer to arbitrate and of the union not to strike, in addition to overseeing the duty of fair representation owed to employees—a duty that makes the principle of majority rule tenable in industrial relations.

III. Application of Public Law to Contractual Disputes

Few subjects have provoked as much debate among arbitrators, management, and union advocates as the question of the role of public

---

[88]*Hines*, 424 U.S. at 571. *See* text accompanying note 81 *supra*.
[89]*Hines*, 424 U.S. at 571.

law in arbitration.[90] The matter arises in several forms. One is the question as to how the courts should treat an arbitrator's determination of contract disputes based upon facts that also give rise to statutory claims. At least with respect to rights protected by title VII of the Civil Rights Act,[91] the Supreme Court resolved this issue in *Alexander v. Gardner-Denver Co.*:[92] the Act embodies too important a national policy to compel an aggrieved individual to choose between his statutory claim and his contract remedies. Thus, an arbitrator's award does not bar an employee from pursuing a discrimination claim before the Equal Employment Opportunity Commission and the courts.[93]

Gardner-Denver has had several effects in practice, the merits of which are beyond the present concern. It has prompted some arbitrators to act on the invitation to "judicialize" the arbitration proceeding, a development yielding both some deference from judges pleased by the imitation, and some cost to the pace and expense of the private dispute-settlement process.[94] It has produced some duplicative litigation, which may not be so bad when the individual or his contingent counsel feels strongly enough to suffer the outrageous delays and complexities of title VII procedures.[95] It has spawned an as yet ignored effort by the American Arbitration Association to provide quasi-judicial arbitration machinery for individual claims of employment discrimination.[96] And it has generated considerable confusion concerning the reach of the principle to other types of statutory interests, with the Tenth Circuit[97] sticking with finality when an individual pursues arbitration rather than judicial or administrative relief for a claim that his employer violated the overtime

---

[90]*See* Cox, *The Place of Law in Labor Arbitration*, in NATIONAL ACADEMY OF ARBITRATORS, THE PROFESSION OF LABOR ARBITRATION (SELECTED PAPERS FROM THE FIRST ŞEVEN ANNUAL MEETINGS) 76 (1957); Howlett, *The Arbitrator, the NLRB, and the Courts*, in NATIONAL ACADEMY OF ARBITRATORS, THE ARBITRATOR, THE NLRB, AND THE COURTS (PROCEEDINGS OF THE 20TH ANNUAL MEETING) 67 (1967); Feller, *The Impact of External Law upon Labor Arbitration* in THE FUTURE OF LABOR ARBITRATION IN AMERICA 83 (1976); Meltzer, *supra* note 33; Mittenthal, *The Role of Law in Arbitration*, in NATIONAL ACADEMY OF ARBITRATORS, DEVELOPMENTS IN AMERICAN AND FOREIGN ARBITRATION (PROCEEDINGS OF THE 21ST ANNUAL MEETING) 42 (1968); Sovern, *When Should Arbitrators Follow Federal Law?*, NATIONAL ACADEMY OF ARBITRATORS, ARBITRATION AND THE EXPANDING ROLE OF NEUTRALS (PROCEEDINGS OF THE 23D ANNUAL MEETING) 29 (1970).

[91]42 U.S.C. §§ 2000e to 2000e-17 (1976).

[92]415 U.S. 36 (1974).

[93]*Id.* at 60.

[94]Edwards, *supra* note 85; *Move to Formality in Arbitration*, 1978 LAB. REL. Y.B. 80, 81–82; *Problems Facing Arbitration Process*, 1977 LAB. REL. Y.B. 206.

[95]When a dissatisfied grievant brings suit to determine his claim under antidiscrimination statutes, the courts have given weight to the arbitrator's determination. *Burroughs v. Marathon Oil Co.*, 446 F. Supp. 633 (E.D. Mich. 1978); *Fort v. T.W.A., Inc.*, Fair Empl. Prac. Cas. 208 (N.D. Cal. 1976); *Swint v. Pullman-Standard*, 11 Fair Empl. Prac. Cas. 943 (N.D. Ala. 1974). The Sixth and Tenth Circuits have held that successful grievants cannot sue for additional relief in the form of damages. *Pearson v. Western Elec. Co.*, 542 F.2d 1150 (10th Cir. 1976); *EEOC v. McLean Trucking Co.*, 525 F.2d 1007 (6th Cir. 1975).

[96]*See* American Arbitration Association, Employment Arbitration (1979).

[97]*Satterwhite v. United Parcel Serv., Inc.*, 496 F.2d 448 (10th Cir.), *cert. denied*, 419 U.S. 1079 (1974).

provisions of the Fair Labor Standards Act, and the District of Columbia Circuit[98] allowing an individual an opportunity to raise again, before the Occupational Safety and Health Administration, a health and safety claim denied in arbitration. After some jogging back and forth, the National Labor Relations Board now defers to arbitration on refusal-to-bargain claims, but proceeds without deference to hear pre-arbitral charges of discrimination in violation of section 8(a)(3) even though these might also supply the material for a claimed contract violation.[99] After an arbitral award, the Board will defer to a procedurally proper determination by an arbitrator unless it detects some important statutory interest being flouted by the private adjudication.[100]

Most of the debate on the role of public law centers on the other side of the issue: the question of how an arbitrator is to respond to a claim that the law should influence his application of the contract. In part, this obsession reflects the extraordinary infusion of law into the employment relationship. Until recently, positive law affecting employment consisted of fair labor standards limiting the labor of women and children and regulating minimum wages and maximum hours, along with a few other state statutes. Today the pertinent law is legion—there are a host of antidiscrimination regulations and complex requirements concerning affirmative action to redress specific or societal injustices to minorities or women,[101] the Occupational Safety and Health Act,[102] the Employment Retirement and Income Security Act,[103] and the Age Discrimination in Employment Act,[104] among many others. Both the NLRA and collective bargaining practices, including arbitration, inevitably rub up against scores of statutory and constitutional policies.

The broad contours of the debate are by now familiar. Does the arbitrator view the contract as existing in an environment of public law that infuses and informs it? Or does he see himself as a creature of the contract, constrained to stay within its limits and leave to the public process of the courts the task of conforming his decisions to external law and societal constraints? The former approach invites visions of arbitrators running amok among legal doctrines neither they nor the parties adequately comprehend. The latter risks futile awards betraying the severe limits of arbitral finality, as courts are obliged to bridge the

---

[98]*Leone v. Mobil Oil Corp.*, 523 F.2d 1153 (D.C. Cir. 1975).
[99]*General Am. Transp. Corp.*, 94 LRRM 1483 (1977), *overruling National Radio Co.*, 198 NLRB 527 (1972); *Collyer Insulated Wire*, 192 NLRB 837 (1971).
[100]*Spielberg Mfg. Co.*, 112 NLRB 1080 (1955).
[101]Title VII of the Civil Rights Act of 1964, 42 U.S.C. §§ 2000e to 2000e-17 (1976); Equal Pay Act of 1963, 29 U.S.C. § 206 (1976).
[102]29 U.S.C. §§ 651–678 (1976).
[103]*Id.* §§ 1001–1381.
[104]*Id.* §§ 621–634.

gap between law and contract. It is the nature of controversies dominated by lawyers that some will find a middle path; thus, it has been urged that only the properly equipped arbitrator may look to the law,[105] or alternatively, that the arbitrator should be empowered to support but not compel the employer's effort to bend the contract to his obligations under the law.[106]

Recent cases reveal that the problem may arise in many guises. The parties may invite the arbitrator to consider law external to the contract either by express statement in the agreement, or by tracking the language of statutes or regulations.[107] In such circumstances, the arbitrator may and indeed must do so to fulfill his function under the agreement, and a court should not review the merits of his performance in any more depth than it reviews the merits of his interpretation of other contractual provisions. In *International Brotherhood of Teamsters Local 117 v. Washington Employers, Inc.*,[108] for example, the parties had asked the arbitrator to determine whether the employer's withholding of contractual wage increases violated a state law that provided for punitive damages in the event of a violation. The employer later sought to vacate the adverse award on grounds that it exceeded the arbitrator's authority and violated the federal policy against punitive damages. Properly concluding that the parties contracted for that liquidated penalty and for the arbitrator's interpretation of the state statute, the Court of Appeals for the Ninth Circuit enforced the award.

At other times the parties' adoption of standards provided by external law may be less explicit. If an employer discharges an employee for using illegal drugs on the job, the arbitrator may have to look to the legal definition of proscribed substances in the pertinent jurisdiction to aid his application of the "just cause" standard for discipline or discharge.[109] Few would quarrel with the proposition that when the parties expressly or implicitly request the arbitrator to consider the law, he must do so.

The matter becomes more controversial when an employer defends a claim of contract violation by pointing to his obligations under the

[105]Sovern, *supra* note 90, at 38–40.

[106]Mittenthal, *supra* note 90, at 50 ("Thus, although the arbitrator's award may *permit* conduct forbidden by law but sanctioned by the contract it should not *require* conduct forbidden by law even though sanctioned by contract.").

[107]*See City of Meriden*, 71 Lab. Arb. & Disp. Settl. 699 (1978) (Conn. Bd. of Med. & Arb.) (contract pension provision incorporated relevant city charter and code provisions); *United States Steel Corp.*, 51 Lab. Arb. & Disp. Settl. 1253 (1968) (Garrett, Arb.) (contract provided that employees returning from military service were to be accorded the rights they were entitled to under the applicable statute).

[108]557 F.2d 1345 (9th Cir. 1977).

[109]*Todd Pac. Shipyards Corp., Los Angeles Div.*, 72 Lab. Arb. & Disp. Settl. 1022 (1979) (Brisco, Arb.); *Keystone Steel & Wire Co.*, 72 Lab. Arb. & Disp. Settl. 780 (1979) (Elson, Arb.).

extrinsic law, or conversely, when he follows the contract and the grievant argues that he should have followed the law. Such cases often involve two employees with conflicting interests. In the classic illustration, a black employee claims entitlement to a promotion at the expense of a more senior white employee, but the contract clearly provides that seniority governs assignments when ability is equal. If the employer abides by the contract and gives the assignment to the white employee, the black employee may complain. If the employer follows the law—assuming he can discern it—and awards the job to the black employee, he may face a grievance from the white worker. What is the arbitrator to do? Presumably he is capable of determining whether each employer is competent to perform the assignment; this question of contract application, though not always easy, is the routine material of the grievance arbitrator's craft. Next, if expressly invited by the contract to consider the law, the arbitrator must do so. He may, however, encounter considerable difficulty in finding it. If not lost, the law may at least be hidden in a maze of regulations, decisions, affirmative action plans, consent decrees, and other sources.

In the rare case when there is no express invitation to follow the law, the proper course for the arbitrator is more difficult to determine. If the arbitrator looks for the law and adjusts the contract to it, his award may withstand judicial review, provided the court agrees with his construction of the external sources. It is unrealistic to expect a court that reads the law differently to accept what it regards as the arbitrator's erroneous view—from the perspective of the reviewing court, the situation is somewhat akin to that arising when an arbitrator has based his reading of a contract on a critical non-fact. In short, an arbitrator's application of uncertain law to the contractual dispute is an invitation to judicial review more rigorous than that anticipated by the *Enterprise Wheel* standard of finality; and such action risks interpretive adventures far beyond the bounds of contract reading that define the arbitrator's commission.

On the other hand, if the arbitrator ignores the law and applies the contract, he may well be performing a futile act, for a court will find the law and deny enforcement if the contract and the award thereunder are determined to be illegal. *Telephone Workers Local 827 v. New Jersey Bell Telephone Co.*[110] exemplifies this result. The arbitrator there enforced a contract seniority rule and sustained a grievance challenging a promotion consistent with a title VII consent decree. Though praising the arbitrator for adhering to the contract, the district judge vacated the

---

[110]584 F.2d 31 (3d Cir. 1978).

award as contrary to the consent decree,[111] and the Third Circuit affirmed. In this case, each party to the proceedings played his proper role. The arbitrator could hardly have denied the individual's valid contract claim on the basis of a litigation settlement in which the grievant had no part. However, the courts properly construed the law and invalidated the contract on the strength of the higher standard of the antidiscrimination statute as expressed in the decree.

A similar conflict arose in *General Warehousemen & Helpers Local 767 v. Standard Brands, Inc.*,[112] where the arbitrator enforced contractual protections for employees affected by a transfer of operations, and directed the employer to offer opportunities for transfer to the new plant under the conditions secured by the old contract. The employer refused to comply, in part because another union had by then been certified by the Board as the representative of employees at the new plant, and had executed a new contract at rates considerably lower than those provided in the old plant agreement. Ultimately the Fifth Circuit, sitting en banc, denied enforcement of the award on the theory that it was repugnant to the National Labor Relations Act in view of the existence of a newly certified union and a new contract. However, the court divided sharply on the question whether the award was illegal. Five members—including the original panel majority, Judges Wisdom and Tuttle—argued persuasively that some form of compliance with the award would not necessarily oblige the employer to commit an unfair labor practice, and that the prospect of friction likely to flow from this result was not sufficient to justify judicial intervention upsetting the arbitrator's decision. It would appear that these dissenters had the better case, in that a remand to the arbitrator, with a direction to modify his award in light of the Board's action, would have been more consistent with national labor policy.

Recent arbitration decisions on this issue show arbitrators to be divided in practice as well as in commentary and debate. In *United Telephone Co. of Carolinas*,[113] the arbitrator rejected a claim of contract violation where the employer, implementing a maternity leave policy drafted in light of EEOC guidelines, refused seniority credit upon the grievant's return from a leave. In *Kentile Floors, Inc.*,[114] however, a discharge based on the contract was upheld, and the arbitrator refused to consider the contention that title VII protected the grievant's unilateral decision to go on leave for religious purposes after the employer had denied permission.

---

[111] 450 F. Supp. 284 (D.N.J. 1977).
[112] 579 F.2d 1282 (5th Cir. 1978). *See* Comment, Standard Brands: *Plant Relocations and the Preservation of Preexisting Bargaining Agreements*, 79 COLUM. L. REV. 1002 (1979).
[113] 66 Lab. Arb. & Disp. Settl. 1, 7 (1976) (Foster, Arb.).
[114] 66 Lab. Arb. & Disp. Settl. 933, 935 (1976) (Larkin, Arb.).

Sensible evaluation of this problem must begin with a better understanding of its dimensions. As noted above, the arbitrator is entirely a creature of the contract. He operates by consent of the parties, and should do what they ask of him in the agreement. Increasingly, this means that, for better or worse, he will find himself engaged in the difficult process of finding and applying external law, either because the parties have made their contractual promises subject to changes in law, or because they have tracked statutory language in a manner inviting resort to extrinsic standards to clarify contractual ambiguities.

Inevitably, this development will result in some undercutting of the finality principle. It is vain to expect a judge commissioned to enforce the law to lend his support to a proceeding he regards as unconscionable.[115] Similarly, an interpretation of law that is necessary to an arbitrator's decision and regarded by a court as egregiously off the mark is likely to provoke judicial intervention, particularly if it touches a critical individual interest. That this is true does not portend either the demise of the arbitral process or diminish its utility. On the contrary, it should inaugurate an era of arbitration that is more exciting and more challenging for the professional arbitrator, albeit one less comforting and less "final."

On the rare occasions involving a conflict between law and contract, the arbitrator ought generally to stick to the contract. As a part of the special process of private rulemaking established for the workplace, his function is to apply the parties' agreement, fill its gaps, and clarify its ambiguities, by reference to outside sources of law if necessary. This is subject to the caveat that when the law is clear—a circumstance perhaps in danger of extinction in contemporary employment relations law—the arbitrator serves neither the parties nor the process by ignoring the law's mandate and issuing a futile award. For example, an arbitrator ought not ignore the unequivocal determination of the Congress to reverse *General Electric Co. v. Gilbert*[116] by flatly barring discrimination against pregnant women in disability pay.[117] To do so would demean the process and oblige the parties to engage in needless litigation. Absent the rare case of manifest illegality, however, the arbitrator should apply the contract, as was done, for example, in *Standard Brands*,[118] and leave it to the courts to import the requirements of law. For arbitrators, as for

---

[115]*See* Cox, *Grievance Arbitration in the Federal Courts,* 67 HARV. L. REV. 591, 605 (1954); *cf. Universal Camera Corp. v. NLRB,* 340 U.S. 474, 490 (1951) (substantial evidence test not meant to preclude reviewing courts from considering reasonableness and fairness of NLRB decisions).

[116]429 U.S. 125 (1976).

[117]42 U.S.C.A § 2000e(k) (West Supp. 1974–1978).

[118]*See* note 112 and accompanying text *supra.*

most professionals, it is generally the course of wisdom to remain within the bounds of one's own charter.

IV. Special Problems in the Public Sector

The recent and widespread introduction of collective negotiations in the public sector[119] has been followed by a proliferation of grievance arbitration provisions in government labor contracts. But just as public sector bargaining is different from bargaining in the private sector—with the constraints attributable more to political than to market forces, and impasse procedures generally barring resort to strikes (in law, if not always in fact)—so, too, is arbitration different in government employment relations, and judicial treatment of arbitral awards often varies from the principles proclaimed in the Steelworkers cases.

In general, collective negotiations between governments and labor organizations ought not to be viewed in the manner of their private sector counterpart, as a new method of rulemaking by joint determination replacing prior rulemaking by unilateral decision. Rather, public sector labor laws have put the force of legislation behind a special procedure for the participation in government decisions of one interest group—employee organizations—while others are left to the more cumbersome and unpredictable avenues of lobbying, petitioning, and other forms of political action.[120] In essence, the obligation imposed on governments to bargain with majority representatives in particular units is a mandate to treat this interest group separate and apart, at least procedurally, from other claimants to public resources.

Further, the negotiated public sector agreement, including the employer's promise to arbitrate grievances, exists in a unique environment of prior law, policies, and decisionmaking processes affecting its implementation. First among these are the constitutional protections afforded individual rights against state abuse or infringement. While the private employer begins with private property rights limited by national labor policy or particular individual and collective rights of access and communication, the government proceeds from a notion of freedom of communication sometimes limited by labor policy. In contrast to the exchange of a promise to arbitrate for a promise not to strike, characteristic of the private collective bargain, public negotiations yield more

---

[119]In little more than a decade, half the states have enacted comprehensive statutes instituting rights of organization and negotiation for state and local government employees. Summary of State Labor Laws, 1 [Ref. File] Gov't Empl. Rel. Rep. (BNA) 51:501–523 (Aug. 20, 1979).

[120]*See* H. Wellington & R. Winter, The Unions and the Cities (1971).

of an agreement to substitute the arbitral process for the review otherwise available elsewhere, such as that provided for in civil service or education law.

The impact of these and other differences on arbitration in the public sector is considerable. Some state legislatures[121] have faced up to the problem of reconciling preexisting regulatory systems with the new process for determining conditions of public employment, with varying results—some giving priority to the agreement in cases of conflict, others giving preference to civil service regulations or other laws. The treatment of arbitration in the courts is similarly varied. The Steelworkers presumption of arbitrability applies in some states,[122] although not in New York.[123] On the other hand, New York courts permit negotiation and therefore arbitral application of the agreement on a range of permissive subjects,[124] while the New Jersey Supreme Court[125] recently decided that joint determination and agreement beyond the scope of mandatory bargaining is illegal in the public sector. Like the *Borg-Warner*[126] rule governing private relationships, this conclusion makes quite a bit turn on the categorization of mandatory and nonmandatory subjects. The difference is that, unlike the situation in the private sector, once an issue is deemed nonmandatory, a provision dealing with it cannot voluntarily be included in an agreement or submitted to an arbitrator for interpretation and enforcement.

Behind both the proscription of bargaining on permissive topics in New Jersey and the denial of presumptive arbitrability in New York lies a contemporary variation of the delegation doctrine once marshalled against any proposal to authorize negotiations with public employee groups. The opinion of the New York Court of Appeals rejecting a presumption of intention to arbitrate made this view explicit: since "the responsibilities of the elected representatives of the tax-paying public are overarching and fundamentally nondelegable, it must be taken, in the absence of clear, unequivocal agreement to the contrary, that the board of education did *not* intend to refer differences which might arise

---

[121]*See, e.g.*, CONN. GEN. STAT. ANN. § 478 (West 1977).

[122]*Kaleva-Norman-Dickson School Dist. No. 6 v. Teachers Ass'n*, 393 Mich. 583, 227 N.W.2d 500 (1975); *County of Allegheny v. Allegheny County Prison Employees Independent Union*, 476 Pa. 27, 381 A.2d 849 (1977); *Joint School Dist. No. 10 v. Jefferson Educ. Ass'n*, 78 Wis. 2d 94, 253 N.W.2d 536 (1977).

[123]*Acting Superintendent of Schools v. United Liverpool Faculty Ass'n*, 42 N.Y.2d 509, 369, N.E.2d 746, 399 N.Y.S.2d 189 (1977).

[124]*See, e.g., Board of Educ. v. Associated Teachers of Huntington, Inc.*, 30 N.Y.2d 122, 282 N.E.2d 109, 331 N.Y.S.2d 17 (1972).

[125]*Ridgefield Park Educ. Ass'n v. Board of Educ.*, 78 N.J. 144, 393 A.2d 278 (1978).

[126]*NLRB v. Wooster Div. of Borg-Warner Corp.*, 356 U.S. 342 (1958) (employer violating obligation to bargain in good faith by insisting to impasse on a nonmandatory subject of bargaining).

to the arbitration forum."[127] Even when such a clear and unequivocal agreement to arbitrate may be found, the courts will still inquire whether the agreement is permitted by public policy. Similarly, the problem of the proper scope of bargaining requires definition of the fundamental limit of public authority. Whether the question arises in the context of an action to stay or compel arbitration or in a petition to vacate or enforce an award, courts will not defer to an arbitrator's judgment, a result that is hardly surprising in view of the constitutional and public policy issues at stake.

The New York Court of Appeals has traced an uneven path through the questions of "public policy" constraints on negotiated public sector agreements and arbitration awards. In the two Huntington cases,[128] the court expressed a policy favoring arbitration and declared that the obligation to bargain over terms and conditions of employment would be limited solely by "express" statutory provisions in other laws. In *Huntington II*, it refused to review the merits of an arbitrator's interpretation of a state law imposing a moratorium on sabbatical leaves.[129] However, in 1974 the tide seemed to turn. In an aside, the court changed the standard limiting bargaining rights from "express" provisions to "plain and clear" prohibitions in statutes or decisions.[130] The next year, while affirming the right to negotiate on a permissive subject such as class size limitations, the court carried the dictum still further: the policy limit might be inferred from the general "governmental interests and public concerns," even if not explicit in statute or decisions.[131] The questions arose again in *Cohoes City School District v. Cohoes Teachers Association*[132] when an arbitrator applied a contractual guaranty of just cause for denial of reappointment. While the education law at issue did not clearly prohibit collective bargaining "with respect to ultimate tenure decisions," this conclusion was deemed "inescapably implicit" in its

[127]*Acting Superintendent of Schools v. United Liverpool Faculty Ass'n*, 42 N.Y.2d 509, 514, 369 N.E.2d 746, 749, 399 N.Y.S.2d 189, 192 (1977).
[128]*Board of Educ. v. Associated Teachers of Huntington, Inc.*, 30 N.Y.2d 122, 282 N.E.2d 109, 331 N.Y.S.2d 17 (1972); *Associated Teachers of Huntington, Inc. v. Board of Educ. (Huntington II)*, 33 N.Y.2d 229, 306 N.E.2d 791, 351 N.Y.S.2d 670 (1973).
[129]Judge Breitel stated:
[While] a small number of problems have been recognized as so interlaced with strong public policy considerations that they have been placed beyond the reach of the arbitrators' discretion, . . . [t]he issue of sabbatical leaves . . . should not . . . be deemed inarbitrable for fear of contravening public policy. . . . [A]rbitration is considered so preferable a means of settling labor disputes that it can be said that public policy impels its use.
33 N.Y.2d at 235–36, 306 N.E.2d at 795–96, 351 N.Y.S.2d at 675–76 (citations omitted).
[130]*Syracuse Teachers Ass'n v. Board of Educ.*, 35 N.Y.2d 743, 320 N.E.2d 646, 361 N.Y.S.2d 912 (1974).
[131]*Susquehanna Valley Cent. School Dist. v. Susquehanna Valley Teachers' Ass'n*, 37 N.Y.2d 614, 617, 339 N.E.2d 132, 134, 376 N.Y.S.2d 427, 429 (1975).
[132]40 N.Y.2d 774, 358 N.E.2d 878, 390 N.Y.S.2d 53 (1976).

provisions.[133] And in 1977, the court enjoined arbitration of a claimed violation of a contract provision limiting school board access to teacher files, finding such a restriction invalid as contrary to [a public policy involving a board of education right to inspect teacher personnel files].[134]

With respect to the scope of judicial review, most states follow the provisions of the Uniform Arbitration Act or some other source that generally tracks the "essence" test of *Enterprise Wheel*.[135] The difference in practice is, of course, that the exception to finality flowing from the requirement that an award not be contrary to law comes into play much more frequently in public sector cases. A new federal statute enacted as part of the Civil Service Reform Act of 1978 addresses this phenomenon directly, providing for review and revision by the Federal Labor Relations Authority when arbitral awards are found to be "contrary to any law, rule, or regulation" or deficient "on other grounds similar to those applied by Federal courts in private sector labor-management relations."[136]

Two phenomena are thus predictable in public sector arbitration cases. First, arbitrators often cannot avoid looking to the law: both the agreements they administer and the statutes authorizing the agreements are intertwined with constitutional and legislative constraints. Second, when they look to the law by invitation or otherwise, or where public policy objections are raised, courts are more inclined to conduct their own unfettered inquiries on the merits before enforcing the awards. Since in most cases the basic distribution of authority between the normal political processes and the specialized procedures of employee relations is affected, this result is appropriate as well as inevitable.

An instructive example of a case where such issues arose is a recent dispute involving an agreement entered by the County of Los Angeles providing that employees covered by the 1974 amendments to the Fair Labor Standards Act (FLSA) would be entitled to time and a half for overtime under certain circumstances.[137] Arguing that the invalidation of those amendments in *National League of Cities v. Usery*[138] excused compliance with the agreement, the employer refused to follow the contract. The arbitrator sustained the grievance, finding, first, that the parties intended the FLSA amendments to define the affected group but

---

[133]*Id.* at 778, 358 N.E. at 881, 390 N.Y.S.2d at 56.
[134]*Board of Educ. v. Areman*, 41 N.Y.2d 527, 362 N.E.2d 943, 394 N.Y.S.2d 143 (1977).
[135]*See* note 20 and accompanying text *supra*.
[136]Pub. L. No. 95-454, sec. 701, § 7122(a), 92 Stat. 1211. The statute also requires that contract grievance machinery include arbitration of most grievances, but permits the parties to agree to exclude any particular matter from the grievance procedure.
[137]*County of Los Angeles*, 68 Lab. Arb. & Disp. Settl. 1132 (1977) (Richman, Arb.).
[138]426 U.S. 833 (1976).

not to determine the entitlement to overtime payments, and second, that *National League of Cities* eliminated the government's statutory obligation but did not nullify its promise. Whatever one may think of the arbitrator's construction of this contract, it cannot be doubted that his function inexorably drew him to judicial opinions to aid his interpretation. Nonetheless, it was the agreement that he applied; he did not exceed his authority in making the award. However, if his award ran afoul of limitations on his powers imposed by *public policy*, a reviewing court could so determine.

In general, the public sector arbitrator, like his private sector counterpart, is well advised to follow the contract and leave claims of its invalidity to the courts. The conflict seems commonly to occur when the parties agree that just cause must be shown to support refusals to reappoint nontenured teachers. Several state courts, including those of New York,[139] Illinois,[140] and Florida,[141] have set aside such agreements, and all arbitration awards based thereon, as contrary to state law and public policy. However, Michigan,[142] Pennsylvania,[143] and Vermont[144] decisons have upheld the legality of such provisions and awards pursuant to them. It seems clear that an arbitrator in another state who is faced with a case raising similar issues should apply the just cause standard, leaving the court to take its side in the debate over the standard's validity.

An arbitrator should also reject claims that a result not mandated by the contract is necessitated by general considerations of "public welfare." A recent decision by the permanent umpire designated in the New York City fire fighters' contract[145] illustrates the potential range of arbitral consideration in this regard. Under a contract providing for specific staff levels but allowing reductions if they were not a "subterfuge" to curtail contractual rights, the employee organization challenged reductions prompted by the city's fiscal crisis. The umpire sustained the city's action, but went on to find "public safety" limitations on the government "implicit within the collective bargaining agreement,"[146] on the basis of which he deemed himself obliged to consider public safety whenever the level, quality, and extent of fire protection were at issue.

[139]*Cohoes City School Dist. v. Cohoes Teachers Ass'n*, N.Y.2d 774, 358 N.E.2d 878, 390 N.Y.S.2d 53 (1976).

[140]*Wesclin Educ. Ass'n v. Board of Educ.*, 30 Ill. App. 3d 67, 331 N.E.2d 335 (1975).

[141]*Lake County Educ. Ass'n v. School Bd.*, 360 So. 2d 1280 (Fla. Dist. Ct. App. 1978).

[142]*Brown v. Holton Public Schools*, 74 Mich. App. 206, 254 N.W.2d 41, *rev'd on other grounds*, 401 Mich. 398, 258 N.W.2d 51 (1977).

[143]*Board of Educ. v. Philadelphia Fed'n of Teachers, Local No. 3*, 464 Pa. 92, 346 A.2d 35 (1975).

[144]*Danville Bd. of School Directors v. Fifield*, 132 Vt. 271, 315 A.2d 473 (1974).

[145]*City of New York Fire Dep't*, 66 Lab. Arb. & Disp. Settl. 261 (1976) (Schmertz, Arb.).

[146]*Id.* at 261.

More specifically, he concluded that no contract "[could] be interpreted to permit personnel and manning reductions in such an essential service . . . below what is minimally required to meet the needs for which the Department was established";[147] the government's obligation to provide an adequate level of service was "an implicit condition of the collective bargaining agreement . . . [which must be] interpreted within the frame of the needs of the public."[148] Although he upheld the workforce reductions, the umpire ordered the city to avoid future reductions based on his determination that the quality of service could not support additional strain, and to raise the force level as soon as funds became available.

This discussion might be dismissed as an example of giving the union the language while denying its grievance, except that the prospective award of a permanent arbitrator must be taken seriously. If the "implied condition" of adequate service had been based on considerations of fire fighter safety, there might be a plausible case for the determination. But the judgment that the bargaining agreement incorporates a level of service delivery or quality to be defined by the arbitrator in the interest of the broader "public" or "community" entails a considerable leap beyond the employment relationship.[149] The arbitrator's task here, as elsewhere, is to interpret the contract, not to substitute his judgment for the political process in allocating public resources. Thus, the arbitrator should avoid defining levels of service or quality except when the contract's provisions require him to make such determinations in order to apply its terms. In view of the wisdom of avoiding arbitral intervention in public policy, a more literal reading of the agreement and a greater respect for its limits are more appropriate in government than in private sector dispute resolution, where industrial practices and the law of the shop properly inform the arbitrator's interpretation of the contract.

Similarly, when a public sector employer claims excuse from contractual duties by reason of fiscal circumstances, the arbitrator should defer to the courts on the issue.[150] As with any other policy limitation

---

[147]Id. at 263.

[148]Id.

[149]The award was not challenged by the city, and the question of the effect of arbitration on governmental authority over the level of services provided—at least in the absence of express contractual provisions on mandatory subjects—awaits further developments.

[150]In cases arising from the fiscal emergencies in Yonkers, New York, arbitral determinations to enforce express contractual protections of job security have been upheld in the courts. Yonkers Fed'n of Teachers v. Board of Educ., 44 N.Y.2d 752, 376 N.E.2d 1326, 405 N.Y.S.2d 681 (1978) (memorandum opinion) (enforcing arbitrator's award of reinstatement with backpay and interest in light of job security clause); Board of Educ. v. Yonkers Fed'n of Teachers, 40 N.Y.2d 268, 353 N.E.2d 569, 386 N.Y.S.2d 657 (1976) (ordering arbitration of job security issue). This result is clearly supported by the fact that the emergency legislation in that city expressly disclaimed any legislative intent to abrogate collective bargaining provisions. New York State Financial Emergency Act for The City of Yonkers, ch. 871, § 3, subd. 3, [1976] 1 N.Y. Laws 3, 5 (McKinney) (1975).

on the contract, the arbitrator's consideration of a public employer's fiscal capacity, when appropriate, should turn on the agreement itself. Certainly a provision permitting workforce reductions for financial reasons compels the arbitrator to hear and determine the union's complaint that the true reason was otherwise. Fiscal limits may also be pertinent to the design of a remedy for contract violations when the parties do not limit arbitral flexibility over the form of relief.[151] Thus, allowance of a reasonable time for compliance with a monetary award presents a fair accomodation with fiscal reality while avoiding improper modification of the agreement.[152]

However the courts may struggle to define the sources and effects of public policy restraints on arbitration awards, the arbitrator will do well to remember that his principal function is to respect the contracting parties' purpose, apply their agreement, and aid their negotiations by resolving the deliberate or unplanned ambiguities in their contract. If he respects his mandate and the limitations on his authority, it should injure neither his pride nor his position when a judge fulfills his own commission by accommodating or adjusting agreements to the more general standards of constitutional and legislative rules. On the other hand, judges should avoid engaging in close scrutiny of awards simply as a result of their own hesitation about the propriety of bargaining between government and employee groups. The values of grievance arbitration in promoting stability in complex working relationships are by now well established; and it is too late to question whether the arbitral function is an essential part of any bargaining process. If, as seems likely, some form of collective negotiation will become a permanent fixture of the governmental process, so too will the grievance procedures designed to interpret and apply the negotiated agreements.

Conclusion

As legal, social, and economic developments affecting the relations between labor and management breed new exceptions to the principle of arbitral finality and new sources of friction between arbitrators and judges, the need for an authoritative and principled examination of the judicial function in reviewing arbitration awards grows more acute. The Steelworkers opinions recognize that the body of rules incorporated in the collective agreement governing the life of the workplace may extend

---

[151]*See City of Newburgh*, 67 Lab. Arb. & Disp. Settl. 559 (1976) (Miller, Arb.) (providing for payment of only ¾ of monetary award in first fiscal year upon the arbitrator's determination that this amount was available).

[152]*See City of Fort Wayne*, 67 Lab. Arb. & Disp. Settl. 529 (1976) (Boals, Arb.) (allowing reasonable time for compliance with monetary award).

well beyond the express terms of the written document signed by parties: "the industrial common law—the practices of the industry and the shop— is equally a part" of the collective contract,[153] and an arbitrator construing an agreement thus defined may therefore properly look to such factors as "the effect upon productivity of a particular result, its consequence to the morale of the shop, [and] his judgment whether tensions will be heightened or diminished."[154]

If the arbitrator's construction of the contract is based on factors such as these, it is final because it is the interpretation for which the parties have bargained. Although an arbitrator's qualities of expertise and familiarity with the shop may initially have commended his selection, they are not really the source of the deference to his judgment. That deference flows rather from the fact that it is the arbitrator's assignment to read the parties' agreement against the backdrop of ongoing practices and habits in the plant, with the understanding that his reading will become part of the agreement itself. It is in this sense that an arbitrator's award is part of a continuing bargaining process that includes rulemaking and rule-applying, and serves the mutual interests of the parties primarily because it avoids the two historic sources of instability in industrial relations: judicial intervention and unrestrained resort to economic self-help.

Looking beyond the agreement, the foundation of finality may ultimately be traced to the preference in American labor law for minimizing governmental involvement in the substantive determinations of working conditions.[155] The Labor Management Relations Act supplies essentially procedural protections, including assurances of rights to organize, to select representatives to engage in collective bargaining, and to use concerted action to support demands. Needless to say, the application of these guarantees and definition of the rules of access, the scope of bargaining, and the circumstances in which economic weapons are permissible, obviously influence the substantive results.[156] Nonetheless, section 203(d) of the Act[157] declares that "[f]inal adjustment by a method agreed upon by the parties" is "the desirable method for settlement of grievance disputes arising over the application or interpretation of an existing collective bargaining agreement." The statute is thus at its root

---

[153]United Steelworkers v. Warrior & Gulf Navigation Co., 363 U.S. 574, 581–82 (1960).
[154]Id. at 582.
[155]See NLRB v. American Nat'l Ins. Co., 343 U.S. 395 (1952).
[156]E.g., Eastex, Inc. v. NLRB, 437 U.S. 556 (1978); Local 761, Int'l Union of Electrical Workers v. NLRB, 366 U.S. 667 (1961); NLRB v. Insurance Agents' Int'l Union, 361 U.S. 477 (1960); NLRB v. Wooster Div. of Borg-Warner Corp., 356 U.S. 342 (1958); NLRB v. Babcock & Wilcox Co., 351 U.S. 105 (1956).
[157]29 U.S.C. § 173(d) (1976).

a charter for private determination of the terms for the sale of labor, and the preference for private processes unequivocally extends to grievance determination.

But to say that the rationale for the finality of arbitral interpretation resides in the parties' agreement to submit contract claims to arbitration and in the statutory preference for consensual adjustment is not to define the extent of permissible judicial scrutiny. Certain qualifications to the principle of finality are well settled. Thus, if a contract clearly denies the arbitrator jurisdiction over a particular complaint, a court must refuse to enforce an award that he was without authority to issue. Similarly, a court will not bend its coercive powers to a decision that is contrary to law; it will, for example, vacate an award sustaining the grievance of a white employee denied an assignment to which he was entitled under the contract when the assignment of a black coworker with less seniority is shown to have been required by title VII. And it is well recognized that a judge must deny enforcement of an award issued by an arbitrator stained with fraud or bias, as in *Holodnak*.[158] The self-evident logic is that the parties have consented to a process of dispute settlement characterized by a basic level of integrity; it can do no injury to their agreement to withhold deference when the process was infected by arbitral misconduct depriving one or both of an honest construction.

The judicial role is more ambiguous and difficult to define when it is claimed that an arbitrator who decided a grievance clearly within his jurisdiction exceeded his authority either in the type of remedy he ordered or in the way he construed the agreement. This is the circumstance that goes to the heart of the "essence" test of *Enterprise Wheel*. However, to say as the Court did in that case that the merits of an arbitrator's reading of a contract must be respected so long as his words show no infidelity to that contract does not really help. In *Torrington*,[159] for example, the question whether the words betrayed infidelity to the agreement could have been answered differently depending on one's views of midterm bargaining and of the extent to which a contract implicitly reflects that part of national labor policy bearing on the duty to bargain. In circumstances where both labor policy and the common law of collective agreements are in flux, gradually unfolding in the same lower federal courts urged to enforce the arbitrator's determination, it may not be appropriate to subject the arbitrator's determination to the court's own review of the policies that affect it.

---

[158]*Holodnak v. Avco Corp., Avco-Lycoming Div.*, 514 F.2d 285 (2d Cir.), *cert. denied*, 423 U.S. 892 (1975).

[159]*Torrington Co. v. Metal Prods. Workers Union Local 1645*, 362 F.2d 677 (2d Cir. 1966).

As suggested at the outset, it may be unrealistic to expect a court to place its authority behind an award without any scrutiny of its merits. However potent the forces constraining judicial review, the courts' temptation to reverse outrageous arbitral excess is likely to be irresistible. No judge would let stand an award by an arbitrator thought to have been incompetent at the time of decision. In a sense, denial of enforcement here resembles the exercise of the mandate acknowledged in *Enterprise Wheel* to protect the procedural integrity of the process by refusing enforcement of awards tainted by partiality or corruption. It is, in effect, not the award of an "honest" intellect. Similarly when an award discloses clear error—*e.g.*, that a crucial fact was wrongly assumed—judges may be predicted to balk at the prospect of using the power of the state to support it. Such awards are also "dishonest"—not in the subjective sense, but in the sense that a crucial piece is missing from the logical chain.

But the cases denying enforcement reach far beyond these deficiencies, because courts often exercise the reviewing authority to substitute their views of the collective bargaining process and collective bargaining agreements for those of arbitrators. It simply cannot be said that no honest arbitrator could reach the result arrived at in *Torrington*[160] or in *Boise Cascade*.[161] A reversal in these circumstances is unwarranted. It is to be hoped that judges will learn to temper their activist instincts with an appreciation that the agreement before them is a unique type of contract, and that an apparently erroneous award may in fact just reflect the creative search for special rules that the parties need from their private judge, and for which they have negotiated.

The Supreme Court may best supply guidance by filling out its elaboration of the substantive common law of collective agreements. If a contract can be said to incorporate past practices affecting terms and conditions of employment, an employer is bound to maintain them unless he either bargains to impasse or negotiates an express waiver of the duty to bargain. Similarly, if the agreement is properly understood to incorporate principles of progressive discipline and, absent explicit limitation, arbitral authority to reduce the measure of discipline, judges would be less inclined to reverse arbitral awards taking this approach. When the law or policy is uncertain, the rationale for finality compels that the arbitrator's view be respected so long as his decision is an "honest" one.

---

[160]*Id.*

[161]*Boise Cascade Corp. v. United Steelworkers Local 7001*, 588 F.2d 127 (5th Cir.), *cert. denied*, 100 S. Ct. 57 (1979).

But this will happen when judges understand not only the line between irrationality and honest error, but also the policies and practices of industrial relations that constitute the common law of labor agreements.

Part II

Selected Training Discussions

The life which is unexamined is not worth living.

Plato

Views of the Parties

The following discussion* on the views of labor and management representatives concerning arbitration includes questions concerning why the parties arbitrate, industry custom and practices, impartiality, intervention, hearing control, subpoena power, scope of authority, admission of evidence, transcripts, duty of fair representation, external law, integrity, expression, timeliness, hard cases, burden of proof, ambiguities, split awards, bias, arbitrator selection, decision publication, predictability, and keeping score.

A Union Viewpoint

Unions are as diverse as companies. I express a union viewpoint, more accurately my own viewpoint or a reflection of my own experience, and hope it reflects the predominant union view. Unions view arbitration in much the same way as it was expressed by the Supreme Court majority in the Trilogy cases. Arbitration is not a substitute for litigation. Rather, it is a substitute for industrial disputes, industrial instability, and strikes.

Arbitration is merely the final step in the resolution of a dispute which, having proceeded through preliminary steps, has remained unresolved. Unions expect that the ad hoc arbitrator—since the problem which I am about to address is much less a problem for the named arbitrator in a contract—will be sufficiently knowledgeable concerning the labor relations settling of the dispute so that his opinion and award will be consonant with the realities of the situation.

This means that the arbitrator should have an understanding of the parties and their working environment. In the industrial context, with which I am best acquainted, this means that an arbitrator dealing with a garment shop should bring to the dispute at least a generally informed knowledge of the dynamics of the industry and the interrelations between the parties.

---

*Led by Max Zimny and Christopher Barreca.

In the typical garment shop, the working pace is hectic. Compensation is by incentive or piece rate. Profitability is small and the pressures are large. The employer is typically small and driven to produce profits. As a consequence, the workers are driven to an even greater extent than is usual in other industries. The arbitrator should have at least a general knowledge of the history of the collective relationship in the garment industry and the particular geographic area within it, since it may vary considerably from area to area.

The union seeks an arbitrator who will be impartial. Partiality rather than impartiality is, in the union's view, the antithesis of what the process is all about. Partiality will result in destroying the process and the therapeutic effect of arbitration, cause dissatisfaction and distrust, and defeats the whole idea of arbitration. It will lead to court challenges and non-finality of the arbitration process, with increased expense and uncertainty in the relations of the parties.

An arbitrator should be cognizant not only of the express contract provisions, but of the interstices, including custom and practice, and this brings us back to knowledge of the industry. What is the custom and practice is a factual and legal determination. But the role of custom and practice in a given situation is an important factor and one which should be addressed.

The history of negotiations can be critical in determining what a particular provision means, and so we expect the arbitrator to be competent enough to understand the impact of contract negotiations upon the resulting agreement. There is in contract negotiations a give-and-take and in some cases an intentional avoidance of a particular solution. The negotiating history can have considerable consequence in determining what the contract means. We expect that an arbitrator will be mature and competent enough to understand this aspect of the case.

We do not ordinarily expect an arbitrator to be interventionist with counsel on both sides of the case. The arbitrator should expect that counsel will address the issues which the parties feel are important. This does not, of course, mean that an arbitrator should not attempt to satisfy a need to flesh out a position or argument addressed by the attorneys. We do not expect that an arbitrator will merely be a receptacle. On the other hand, we do not expect the arbitrator to take over the hearing, as one arbitrator did in a case[1] that ultimately went to court, I think to his regret. We expect arbitrators to be mature and to have the comprehension and emotional and intellectual balance which permit a full examination and consideration of the relevant issues.

---

[1]*Holodnak v. Avco. Corp.* 387 F. Supp. 191, 87 LRRM 2337 (D. Conn. 1974), *aff'd in part*, 514 F.2d 285, 88 LRRM 2950 (2d Cir. 1975).

We expect the arbitrator to control the hearing. We expect the arbitrator to be aware of the intrusion of external law, which comes more and more to the fore as a result of decisions such as *Spielberg*,[2] and *Gardner-Denver*.[3] An arbitrator who cannot control or properly order a hearing cannot begin to develop a record that is necessary to satisfy doctrine in these areas. Certainly, a well-ordered hearing is necessary to a well-ordered record, and a well-ordered record is necessary to a determination which will result in deferral under *Spielberg* and due consideration by a reviewing court in an equal employment context under *Gardner-Denver*. A well-ordered hearing includes the opportunity for opening statements, as appropriate, and a full presentation of evidence, both oral and documentary.

Hearing control includes the proper use of subpoenas where the accurate development of the record in a complicated case requires it. Proper use of the arbitrator's subpoena powers will depend on the U.S. Arbitration Act, other applicable federal law, as well as applicable state law. At the very least the arbitrator has a right to issue subpoenas, and under the laws of many states, attorneys for the parties also have the right to subpoena material and witnesses for the hearing.

If a subpoena is not complied with and if the noncomplying party chooses not to go into court to challenge the subpoena, the arbitrator may be confronted with a difficulty. I had a very important case in which an employer tried unsuccessfully to stay an arbitration. When he failed, he refused to comply with subpoenas for the production of his books and records which went to the heart of the issues in the case. The union had the right to go into court to enforce the subpoena, but court proceedings would have unduly lengthened the proceeding and, under the circumstances, all or a good deal of the benefit which would flow from a favorable award would have been lost. The union decided to follow a different path. It requested that the arbitrator permit the union to introduce secondary evidence and prohibit the employer from rebutting the secondary evidence except by use of the primary evidence in his possession, which he had refused to produce. It was a difficult issue for an arbitrator to confront. An arbitrator is accustomed to receiving evidence, but he is not accustomed to refusing to receive evidence.

There is substantial legal authority supporting such a request before the NLRB and in court proceedings; it is uncommon in arbitration. We expect in such a case that an arbitrator will use every proper device at his command to see that the best evidence is introduced and that the party who refused to produce such evidence does not profit thereby.

---

[2]*Spielberg Mfg. Co.*, 117 NLRB 1080, 36 LRRM 1152 (1955).
[3]*Alexander v. Gardner-Denver Co.*, 415 U.S. 36, 7 FEP Cases 81 (1974).

One of the good mechanical techniques in arbitration is for an arbitrator to record what is taking place not only mentally but on paper. This should be done within the view of the parties. The parties tend to look with considerable favor on an arbitrator who is attentive and takes notes.

We expect the arbitrator to base his decision on the contract when the contract defines the right and obligations in issue, but when the arbitration provision provides broad authority—even going beyond the specific terms of the contract, as it does in the apparel industry—we expect the arbitrator to discharge his obligation, without reticence, and to carry out the mandate of the contract. The Trilogy cases support such a determination. I believe that such a determination is faithful to the contract and that it will be enforced by a court.

Broad arbitration provisions are quite common in many industries. *Wiley*,[4] the preeminent successor case, is an example of an arbitration case which dealt with rights which vested during the life of a contract and survived the expiration of the contract. This was also at issue in the Supreme Court's decision in the *Nolde* case,[5] in which you will find an example of a broad arbitration provision such as exists in the garment industry.

Garment industry arbitration provisions go back to the early 1900s. Their growth over the years has produced very broad arbitration provisions. Under such arbitration provisions, the arbitrator has the authority, in the disjunctive, to consider not only disputes arising under the contract but also any other differences between the parties. There is no provision in such contracts that the arbitrator must confine himself to the contract or that his authority expires with the expiration of the contract. We expect arbitrators to pay as strict attention to a broad provision as to a narrow provision which strictly confines the arbitrator's jurisdiction.

An arbitrator should have the skill to develop a submission agreement which will frame the issues and result in an orderly hearing and a good opinion and award. We expect that where the contract is sufficient without a submission agreement and where the parties cannot agree upon the issues—and that is not unusual—that the arbitrator will be able to derive the issues from the contract and the arguments and positions of the parties and render a proper opinion and award.

The arbitrator should be liberal in the admission of evidence. Although legal rules of evidence have a place in arbitration, we oppose the idea that rules of evidence should be strictly applied in an arbitration

---

[4]*John Wiley & Sons, Inc. v. Livingston*, 376 U.S. 543, 55 LRRM 2769 (1964).
[5]*Nolde Bros., Inc. v. Local 358, Bakery & Confectionery Workers*, 430 U.S. 243, 94 LRRM 2753 (1977).

hearing. We think that it is inappropriate to do so, and the law does not require it.

There is a place in an arbitration hearing for secondary evidence, hearsay, and all kinds of reliable information. Arbitrators should err on the side of admissibility, and they should apply their expertise in according proper weight to evidence. This does not mean that everything that anyone at the hearing wants to say or do or introduce should be allowed. A rule of reason and order should be used, but reasonable doubts should be resolved in favor of admissibility.

We think that a hearing should close after a fair and reasonable opportunity for a presentation of evidence and argument. This should ordinarily include an opportunity for closing argument and the filing of briefs, except in the simplest cases where the filing of briefs serves to delay an award and is antithetical. Filing and consideration of briefs where they are not necessary adds to the cost of an arbitration, and the cost of arbitration has become increasingly burdensome to unions, especially small unions which cannot afford the expense of arbitration.

An AFL-CIO study done not too long ago found that the typical costs of arbitration was about $2,000. That is a lot of money for a small local union, and especially so in right-to-work law states which impede unions in the collection of dues which, in turn, interferes with the ability to process grievance arbitration. In such states, it is not unusual for a small percentage of people within the bargaining unit to be union members, and such a union has only a limited amount of money to apply to the cost of administering the contract, including arbitration.

We expect too that the arbitrator or the parties may want a transcript in certain cases, although the transcript is unnecessary in the ordinary case. The ordinary rule is varied where the circumstances indicate that a transcript is desirable. An arbitrator should not impose a transcript on parties if neither of them wants it.

Vaca[6] and *Hines*[7] are two of the many cases dealing with the duty of fair representation, an area in which litigation is proliferating. The duty of fair representation imposes additional burdens on the parties, the arbitration process, and the arbitrator. The arbitrator must consider whether or not to allow personal attorneys for grievants to participate in the case. Special consideration must also be given to the use of a transcript in such circumstances.

We expect the arbitrator to look to external law infrequently. We do not feel that external law should displace the contract, even under

---

[6]*Vaca v. Sipes* 386 U.S. 171, 64 LRRM 2369 (1967).
[7]*Hines v. Anchor Motor Freight, Inc.* 424 U.S. 554, 91 LRRM 2481 (1976).

a theory of incorporation of such law into the body of the contract. My union had a case in which an arbitrator failed to reinstate an employee clearly discharged without just cause, simply because the employee was an illegal alien. The arbitrator felt that reinstatement would impose too much of a burden on the employer because of the possibility of raids by the Immigration and Naturalization Service.

An arbitrator should have firm control of the parties. Maintaining order tests an arbitrator's ability to act with the degree of control necessary to assure the integrity of the proceedings and the confidence of the parties. It is not an easy job.

It almost goes without saying that an arbitrator must have integrity. The appearance as well as the fact of integrity is critical. When the arbitration case ends, both parties should be left with the feeling that they have participated in a fair and constructive process.

An arbitrator must have the ability to express himself clearly and persuasively. Awards should be rendered promptly. Undue delay in issuing an award often reduces satisfaction with the award, the arbitrator, and the arbitration process.

We expect the arbitrator to be able to handle the hard case as well as the easy case. The hard case may involve a request for interim injunctive relief or a request for liquidated damages. This is generally defined as actual damages which are difficult to determine with mathematical precision. Such damages may be critical to proper remediation of a serious violation of the contract. We also expect an arbitrator, confronted with a request to award relief for rights which vested before the contract expired, to do so even after the contract expired, that is, we expect the arbitrator will follow *Wiley* and *Nolde*.

We expect the burden of proof in the ordinary discharge cases to be placed on the employer rather than on the grievant. We believe that procedural questions will be decided by the arbitrator. Finally, we expect a good deal from arbitrators because we believe that the success of the collective bargaining process is substantially influenced by the performance of arbitrators.

A Management Viewpoint

Mr. Justice Douglas, speaking for the Court in the *Warrior and Gulf*[8] case, gave what has generally been viewed as the romantic view of arbitrators. Professor Hayes, in commenting on the Supreme Court's decisions of the 1959 term at a 1960 American Bar Association Labor

---

[8]*United States v. Warrior & Gulf Navigation Co.* 363 U.S. 574, 46 LRRM 2416 (1960).

and Employment Law Section meeting, suggested that the parties choose arbitrators because they "have looked up their record and think that they have shown themselves to be impartial for their side, or because they decided the last case for the other side and now may be expected to give *them* a break, or because they have had absolutely no experience in industrial relations, and no knowledge of the subject, and therefore each side will at least have a 50-50 chance, or because they don't expect to win anyway, and so any arbitrator will do."[9]

As a management attorney I do not think either the Douglas or the Hayes description of arbitrators reflects how management or union lawyers view arbitration or arbitrators. To illustrate how some management lawyers view arbitrators, I am going to discuss a few questions which management representatives ask each other when selecting an arbitrator.

One question relates to the control of the arbitration hearing. Does the arbitrator conduct an orderly hearing? The arbitrator must be in control to be effective, and that is not an easy role. It requires a great deal of maturity and judgment in terms of how far the arbitrator lets the parties go. Control does not mean arrogance. Arrogance can lead to the loss of control in this process. The arbitrator must be firmly in charge so that the parties understand that they cannot run away with the hearing. Some parties try to do that, particularly with a new arbitrator whom they may be testing.

Does the arbitrator understand industrial relations problems, and does he appear to grasp the issue in the case? The latter can be particularly difficult for a new arbitrator who may be tempted to pose as an expert to impress the parties. I do not recommend that. It may be better to remain silent than to display ignorance.

In this same vein, while management representatives want to have confidence that the arbitrator is knowledgeable about the issues, they do not want an arbitrator to assume their advocacy role. However, I am not suggesting that the arbitrator should not ask questions after the parties have completed their questioning of a witness, when the arbitrator feels a need to pursue a particular subject further. To intervene earlier can seriously undermine the presentation of a case.

Many contracts say that the arbitrator cannot add to or detract from the contract. What does that mean? To some it means that the arbitrator simply should respect the integrity of the agreement between the parties. While the parties may be reluctant to seek judicial review of an award even when they believe that an arbitrator has exceeded his authority, they do not want to undermine the finality of the process or ongoing

---

[9]60 Col. L. Rev. 901, 931 (1960).

relationships under a collective bargaining agreement, and they will not hesitate to subsequently reject those arbitrators whom they find do not respect the plain meaning of the contract. Where there are ambiguities in contract language, the question is whether or not the arbitrator makes the decision in the context of negotiation history and past practice. The measure is whether the arbitrator is trying to understand what the parties intended the contract language to mean.

Management representatives also ask each other if an arbitrator makes compromise decisions or splits awards. Most representatives I know do not like split awards. That does not mean that there are not circumstances under which a split award is appropriate. That is different from the concept which some arbitrators may have that the only way they can please both sides and maintain acceptability is to give something to everybody. The representatives whom I know do not respect that kind of judgment.

Initially it does take courage to call a case plainly one way or the other. If the facts support it, that is the way of gaining the respect and acceptability of the parties. If an arbitrator treats each case as though it was his last one, he is more likely to be asked to arbitrate additional cases.

It is sometimes difficult for an arbitrator to maintain the appearance of neutrality when parties may seem offensive in the way they present themselves or their case, yet the appearance of fair play is itself a very important element in the arbitration process. Nor only are the advocates for the parties there, but also grievants, union stewards, and first line supervisors, all of whom may be in the only arbitration case that they will attend in their careers. How they perceive arbitration is very important to the effectiveness of this process. If they perceive arbitration as an unfair game, it can undermine the ongoing relationship in the shop in a very important way.

If I were an arbitrator, no matter how well I knew the advocates, I would refer to them by their last names even though we say we want the arbitration process to be informal. It is important to know that the appearance of fair play can manifest itself in seemingly unimportant little details such as how the arbitrator addresses people and with whom he goes to lunch. I do not think that an arbitrator should go to lunch with either of the parties during a hearing. It is important that an arbitrator not talk to one of the parties individually about a case without the presence or concurrence of the other party. These are small things. However, one of the aspects about voluntary arbitration of rights in our society is that the arbitrator serves only as long as the parties continue to want the arbitrator to serve. This concept of fair play must be understood by those who wish to serve as arbitrators.

QUESTION: Are new arbitrators chosen to arbitrate certain types of issues as opposed to other types of issues? Do counsel for the parties tailor their presentations to new arbitrators in certain ways?

MR. ZIMNY: We try to select arbitrators to fit cases, and new arbitrators are ordinarily selected for simpler cases. Both parties are usually well aware that an arbitrator is new, and they tailor their presentations to the individual arbitrator. Presentation of a case to a new arbitrator may also differ.

MR. BARRECA: We have talked about arbitrators understanding the background of the shop. Unfortunately, I do not think we find many arbitrators who do understand the industry or the background. Many advocates nevertheless tend to assume that arbitrators do understand their case and jump into the middle of it. This is less likely with a new arbitrator.

QUESTION: How does one get to know an industry?

MR. ZIMNY: The arbitrator knows an industry through personal experience with it or through testimony at the hearing. If we think we will benefit from having the arbitrator know more about the industry, we present appropriate proof, including expert testimony, which helps with an understanding of the work environment and the immediate issues at hand. It is very unusual for a given arbitrator to know the precise details involved in the problems at hand, but his personal experience enables him to better understand the issues and the contentions. The acceptability of an arbitrator depends on his success in absorbing the presentations and fulfilling the needs of the parties. Arbitrators do not ordinarily know more about the smell of the shop than anybody else. However, an arbitrator should thoroughly understand the case before leaving the hearing.

QUESTION: To what extent can the arbitrator ask questions and not usurp the role of the parties?

MR. BARRECA: He can ask questions to the extent that it is necessary for him to have a clear view of the facts and issues before him. Depending upon the case and the presentations of the parties, questions by an arbitrator may be fairly extensive or very limited. I would suggest that an arbitrator hold any questions until the parties have completed their own questioning. There are very different views among arbitrators as to the degree of involvement which an arbitrator should have. Some arbitrators believe that the arbitrator should sit like a sponge; others hold the opposite view.

MR. ZIMNY: It seems to me that there are two approaches: the arbitrator may ask the question, or the arbitrator may ask the parties to address themselves to the question. The latter approach might be more useful in certain cases. The arbitrator could indicate to the parties that he has further interest in a given area and wants the parties to address themselves to it. Such an approach may not be considered unduly interventionist. Giving the parties the first opportunity to cover an area might be the better way of approaching the problem.

Under circumstances in which the parties are not going to delve into an area no matter what lead given them, the arbitrator should ask questions for clarification.

QUESTION: On what criteria do you as advocates ultimately rely in choosing an arbitrator?

MR. ZIMNY: Advocates look for a person who is going to call it as it is. A careful advocate does research. Advocates will look at other opinions and awards made by the arbitrator on the same or similar questions, and if that arbitrator shows evident predilections towards conclusions we do not want, we will try to avoid that arbitrator. Advocates also look for an arbitrator who can express an opinion clearly, pointedly, persuasively, and fairly. The arbitrator who fails to do that is the arbitrator the parties will avoid.

MR. BARRECA: We look at the decisions with respect to the issues involved. However, the point is that the box-score person is not the arbitrator the parties look for, because the box-score kind of person is most unpredictable. In terms of selection, recognize that most selections are not really made in the abstract. There is a universe of arbitrators to select from. The selection is being made from a limited list provided by an agency.

Candidly, the first thing that I do is cross off everyone I do not know. I think one must recognize that parties who are arbitrating on a regular basis cannot afford to take a chance on an unknown.

MR. ZIMNY: If there is someone on the list before whom I have tried a dozen cases, I know how they rule and how they think. I know I am going to get a fair and well-reasoned decision. Win or lose it is going to be based on the contract and the facts. That is the person I will choose.

Assuming there is no one who fits those criteria, when I say someone I know, I mean someone whose decisions I can read. If I read three or four decisions of the arbitrator and recognize that the arbitrator understands basic principles of industrial relations and has reached a reasoned conclusion based upon what has appeared to be a logical chain, I will select that person.

Advocates have responsibility for winning cases for their clients. That is a central point, and it should be understood. In selecting arbitrators, if one can select someone who makes a victory for that side more likely, that is obviously the one he will select. The advocate is there to win a case. Most often the list of potential arbitrators is less than predictable.

I do not strike all the names of people I do not know, they may be the best people. I find out about those people first. I may call some people whose judgment I trust and who may have had some experience with these arbitrators. Only then do I make a decision.

QUESTION: Do you refer first to published awards?

MR. ZIMNY: Yes.

QUESTION: If only 10 percent of the awards are published, and one is looking for someone who has had a decision published, and the agencies publish decisions which are new and innovative, should new arbitrators write innovative and creative decisions?

MR. ZIMNY: I caution against being creative. As an advocate I am not looking for creative arbitrators in most cases.

QUESTION: How much propagandizing or advertising is the arbitrator doing in terms of future cases so that people who read these decisions might know a little bit more about him and what he is doing in this particular case?

MR. BARRECA: I feel that the arbitrator who advertises will over-advertise and defeat his purpose. An arbitrator who renders a clear, conscientious, and concise award, supported by an opinion written in like manner, will do himself and the parties service in most cases. I believe that such opinions, if they properly fulfill those criteria, are also published. Innovation for the sake of publication simply will not work; it should be avoided.

MR. ZIMNY: I think one should not predicate his career on rating services or internal union communications.

MR. BARRECA: If an arbitrator worries too much about his acceptability, he will never become acceptable. I doubt that there is an Academy arbitrator whom somebody does not find unacceptable. I would say that any arbitrator worth being selected is going to be unacceptable to somebody.

QUESTION: Have you ever used the opinion in an award to convince your client that your case was properly explored, properly explained, and the decision was sound because the reasonableness of the arbitrator's thought processes was set out?

MR. ZIMNY: Decidedly yes. It is used at the most sophisticated as well as the local level. A well-reasoned, well-ordered arbitration decision can often be a great boon in a difficult situation. For example, I had a situation which involved a plant which was subject to one wildcat strike after another. Both union and management were at wits end. It was finally decided that a fairly-conducted arbitration by a highly competent person in the proper setting might provide the therapy which would bring peace. We undertook this, and the arbitration succeeded. The way in which the arbitrator handled the hearing and wrote his opinion and award was essential to success.

MR. BARRECA: I would like to add another negative dimension about keeping score. Lawyers want to be able to predict results for their clients, sometimes to persuade their clients not to go further with a case. Even a winning advocate is reluctant to select an arbitrator who is perceived as dividing his decisions because such an arbitrator cannot be trusted to make a fair decision in a critical case.

Determining Facts and Decision-Making

The following discussion* on determining facts and decision-making includes an analysis of the Acme Manufacturing Company case** and questions concerning admission of disputed evidence, reserved rulings, credibility of witnesses, objections, arbitrator's role as an evaluator of facts, relationship of the contract grievance procedure, exclusion of testimony, conflicting evidence, ambiguity, inconsistencies, incompleteness, alternative remedies and appropriateness of penalties.

Case for Discussion

In the Matter of Arbitration	OPINION & AWARD
between	
Acme Manufacturing	Grievance dated February 30, 1981
and	Mary Smith and Marvin Brown Discharge
XYZ Union	

Arbitrator: Jane Doe, Amityville, Florida

Appearance:
   For the Company: Arlo J. Johnston, Attorney, Cascade, Cooper and Codefish, Philadelphia; Felix E. Smith, Manager, Industrial Relations; Robert J. Chickering, Senior Manufacturing Engineer; Daphne Z. Kramer, Unit Manager, Finishing Unit.
   For the Union: Diana L. Rae, Manager, XYZ Union; Nicholas G. Meiers, President, Alfred Lawson, Vice President, Local 531; Mary

---

*Led by Richard I. Bloch.
**The arbitrator's statement of the facts in Acme is set forth before the group discussion. The arbitrator's decision in Acme follows the discussion.

Smith and Marvin Brown, Grievants; Howard Whimpling and George Smith, Witnesses.

* * *

Pursuant to the terms of the collective bargaining agreement between the above named parties dated May 9, 1979, the undersigned was named by the parties as Arbitrator to hear and decide the above grievance. A hearing was held June 1, 1981, at Sunnyview Inn, Amityville, Fla. Both parties were given full opportunity to be heard through the presentation of the testimony of witnesses, other evidence, and arguments.

Introduction

Grievants were discharged for falsification of expense reports submitted by them following an eight-day customer service trip made December 27, 1980 through January 3, 1981. Grievants deny having changed any of the supporting tickets which were turned in to the company or having falsified any records.

The company manufactures reinforced heavy-duty fabric expansion joints used in heavy manufacturing in exhaust systems for heat, chemical, and other waste products. The joints are made for each order and are sometimes 100 feet long. It also installs and services the joints at the customer's site. It sends field crews to perform the work as needed; often they work in several different locations over a period of several days before returning to the plant. The service is nationwide. The trip taken by the grievants included locations in Montana, California, and Nebraska.

Field crews, consisting of two employees, are paid one and one-half times their normal hourly rates, including all overtime premium rate while on a trip. If they are out over a weekend, they are also paid at the premium, even if not working. One employee is named as the crew leader and has responsibility for reporting all expenses for both employees. The crew leader is given instructions that he or she must maintain the expense report sheets and provide receipts where necessary and turn them in with the report upon return.

The leader in this crew was grievant Smith, who was given a sum of cash with which to cover the estimated expenses that would not be covered by direct billing through credit cards. In this instance the amount of cash was $850 and the submitted expense report total was $869.70. Thus, the grievant was entitled to reimbursement for $19.70.

When the report and receipts were turned in a day or two after the return from the trip, Mr. Chickering, who oversees the field trips, sorted out the receipts, checked them against the figures on the report, consolidated the information onto new expense sheets, and then asked Ms. Smith to check them for accuracy and sign the sheets, as did Mr. Chickering, approving them as department head. They were then sent to Ms. Kramer, head of Finishing, who also had to approve them.

It should be noted that in some instances all expenses of the field crew are billed to a customer and in others it may be divided or paid entirely by the company. In her review of the report, Ms. Kramer noticed that costs of some meals seemed to be very high and that upon examination, some of the receipts appeared to have been altered. The numeral 1 had been added preceding the amount of some receipts to increase them by $10. When these were called to Mr. Chickering's attention by Ms. Kramer, they agreed to contact the inn which had provided the meals and restaurant receipts.

Mr. Chickering called the night manager of the inn and learned that the original restaurant checks in the inn's file reflected an amount $10 less than what had been reported on the receipt. With this information, Mr. Chickering and Ms. Kramer asked the grievants separately, in a meeting on January 29, 1981, if the amount of $14.84 listed as the cost of lunch for Friday, January 2, 1981 on the expense report and the attached receipt was the correct amount spent for the meal. Each answered that it was the amount paid. They were then told that the night manager had said it represented the amount for the meals, but without the "1" someone had added in front of it, and the company would be in touch with them further about the matter.

Meanwhile, the company contacted the inn again to request the original tickets (all of which are serially numbered) for the individual meals listed on the expense report to match the receipts. This information revealed additional alterations made to the meal receipts which had been turned in by the grievants. The grievants were then questioned separately by Mr. Chickering and Ms. Kramer again on February 20, 1981. Grievant Brown was questioned first and asked if the information on the reports was correct and he said that to his knowledge it was. Grievant Smith was then brought in and questioned, and she said the information was correct. Mr. Chickering then told her the company believed it to be incorrect, showed her the receipts from the inn, and informed her she was discharged. The receipts from the inn were then shown to grievant Brown, and he was asked if he had any comment. He answered, "No, that is what we paid." He too was then discharged.

Contentions of the Parties

The company emphasizes that the grievants were not discharged for overspending items listed on the expense report. It was the apparent excessiveness of the amounts listed for certain items that caused the company to investigate further and ask the grievants for an explanation. Had they given an explanation which could be supported, there would have been no discipline, but upon investigation and being confronted with the company's information, the grievants' attempted explanation clearly established their falsification of the records for which they were discharged.

The union points out that the grievants were under no obligation to furnish any meal receipts except for ones in excess of $25. It acknowledges that grievant Smith made mistakes but points out this was the first time she had been on a trip as a leader. It argues that Smith's testimony that she did not alter or modify any receipts was unrefuted and the fact that she brought back meal receipts in itself indicates honesty on her part. The union urges that this trouble arose out of the fact that the company did not properly instruct the employees prior to their leaving on the trip, which took more than a week and included three different cities in three different states. In conclusion, the union argues that grievant Brown had no responsibility for handling any money or keeping any records, that he did not furnish or handle any receipts or prepare or sign any report, and his discharge is unjustified.

Issue

The Arbitrator states the issue:

Were the Grievants, Mary Smith and Marvin Brown, discharged for just cause? If not, what shall be the remedy?

* * *

LEADER: It will be helpful in discussing the decision-making process to employ a classic Socratic case approach. The critical part of these cases is the facts. Will someone state the facts in this case?

VOICE: Two employees were discharged for submitting allegedly altered receipts from a field trip. The company produced evidence from the inns and restaurants that allowed comparisons to be made of these records against grievants' receipts, which showed a discrepancy. The employees denied altering the receipts.

LEADER: To be sure we understand precisely the nature of the discrepancy, start with the actual charges incurred.

VOICE: From my reading of the case, not all but some of the receipts were altered. Apparently, there was a $10 difference in some of the receipts. A "1" had been added preceding the initial amount, changing the bill from $4.50 to $14.50.

LEADER: How did these grievants pay for their expenses?

VOICE: They paid for those expenses which were not covered by direct billing from credit cards with cash. The senior employee had approximately $800.

LEADER: It was not approximately $800, it was $850.

VOICE: At the end of the trip she submitted the receipts and vouchers and claimed she was entitled to $19 and something.

LEADER: The expenses totaled $869.70. Why did this case come to light?

VOICE: Apparently it was Smith's responsibility to collect all the receipts and turn them in to her department head, and the responsibility of the department head to check and enter on another sheet. He had called Smith back in to ask if it was right. Smith and the department head signed the sheet and forwarded it to a third person.

LEADER: What caused the department head to question the receipts initially?

VOICE: The department head did not question it. It was the department head's boss who questioned it. I am not sure what happened. I think she noticed that something appeared to be altered.

LEADER: Was not the first thing she thought that some of the meals were unusually expensive?

VOICE: Yes.

LEADER: Did she then check the receipts?

VOICE: After she checked with the person who had submitted them, they decided to conduct a company investigation.

LEADER: At what point did the company indicate to the grievants that something was wrong?

VOICE: The company made its allegations after calling the inn.

LEADER: The decision states that the company was told by the night manager of the inn that the unaltered receipt set forth the amount paid. The department head called Smith in and found that there was an apparent $10 discrepancy with what had been reported. What happened next?

VOICE: Both employees involved stated that was the amount which had been paid.

LEADER: What were the employees told at that point?

VOICE: The company told them it would be in touch with them at a later time.

LEADER: The company put the employees on notice at that point. Were they interviewed jointly or separately?

VOICE: Separately.

LEADER: Then the company contacted the inn again.

VOICE: It is ambiguous as to whether they were together at that meeting or whether they were interviewed at separate meetings that first time.

LEADER: Let us assume there is an ambiguity there. The company contacted the inn again and they sent the original bills. Apparently there were additional alterations. The company questioned the employees again separately but not at the same meeting; there is a distinction. The first time the company questioned them at the same meeting but separately and in the second instance separately. I do not understand why you assume it was at different meetings the second time.

VOICE: I just picked that up; I do not know if it is material. The case states, "with this information they asked the grievants separately in a meeting. . . ."

LEADER: In a meeting.

VOICE: I do not know what that means.

LEADER: Separately. It says that the grievants were then questioned separately . . . again on February 30. It is not entirely clear.

VOICE: No, it goes on to say that grievant Smith was then brought in.

LEADER: The second meeting was not ambiguous, it was "separate."

VOICE: It does not say "separately again," it says "separately by Mr. Chickering and Ms. Kramer again."

VOICE: It was in the first meeting that it was ambiguous whether or not they were at the same meeting. The second meeting was not that ambiguous, at least as to the first person.

LEADER: It seems clear that they were interviewed separately. Receipts from the inn were then shown to grievant Brown and he was asked for his comment. He said, "That is what we paid." He was discharged. Grievant Smith claimed the information was correct.

It is apparent what the parties' positions are. The company said it was concerned about the discrepancies. The union's first claim was that the grievants did not have to furnish any meal receipts except for more than $25. What does the next sentence mean? It acknowledged that grievant Smith made mistakes. Specifically, what mistakes are the union acknowledging, or is that a general affirmation? Does anybody know? What is the union admitting?

VOICE: I do not know if the union is acknowledging an error in judgment or a mathematical error in adding up the expense items.

LEADER: Do we know of any mathematical error?

VOICE: No, the case does not say.

LEADER: What is the error?

VOICE: I would say the grievants made the mistake of turning in the receipt in the first place because they did not have to do it.

LEADER: Is that the mistake they made?

VOICE: There was some testimony that grievant Smith went to the inn clerk and claimed that there had been mistakes made on the receipts.

LEADER: At what time?

VOICE: At the time Smith and Brown checked out, employee Smith went to the clerk, who said the number on the receipt would be changed. When the company went back to the inn to ask whether or not the receipts had been changed, the inn denied having made any changes on the receipts.

LEADER: That does not mean anything in the case.

VOICE: Did the arbitrator choose to leave that fact out?

LEADER: Do you have any idea why that explanation was left out of the statement of facts?

VOICE: The arbitrator included that in her decision, but as an explanation of Smith, that she went to the hotel clerk and asked him to make corrections.

LEADER: What did Smith claim she said to the hotel clerk?

VOICE: She said the receipt does not reflect the money paid, it is too low. She alleges the inn clerk agreed to make a correction on the receipts. There are some initials that appeared on the receipt, which the union contends are the inn clerk's initials.

LEADER: Do the initials appear only on the copy, not on the original?

VOICE: Yes.

LEADER: That is something of interest.

VOICE: The inn was called.

LEADER: More than once.

VOICE: Yes, for several receipts.

LEADER: Were several receipts changed and initialed and with the same initials?

VOICE: Yes. I do not know the exact number of receipts.

LEADER: The description you gave us does not indicate a mistake on the grievant's part, but it does say that the union acknowledges that a mistake was made.

VOICE: Should not all this information be in the statement of facts?

LEADER: I suggest it is cleaner if it is in the statement of facts, not in the position of the parties. An arbitrator should not bring it up for the first time in the discussion of the case. I think we all find that all the evidence is pivotal and critical to a proper decision. This illustrates the value of putting the facts in one statement, not interspliced throughout the award.

VOICE: Is grievant Smith's explanation of the altered receipt a fact or a contention of the grievant?

LEADER: It is a disputed fact. I identify a disputed fact in the statement of facts, and if there is a dispute about a fact, say that grievant says such and such, and company denies it. I try to keep the positions of the parties relatively brief.

VOICE: In the meetings which occurred with the company, did grievant Smith say that the bill was all right, but that he wanted the original bill? Was it the impression of the grievant that it was the altered bill or the original one which the company had?

VOICE: The company had the altered receipts on which it questioned the grievants.

VOICE: Yes, but the company also showed grievant Brown the original from the inn, who identified it as what was paid. It was not clear whether he was saying they paid four or fourteen dollars.

LEADER: That makes the case more complicated. Was there testimony from the inn which showed the receipts that the company had were accurate or inaccurate, whether they reflected the menu prices?

VOICE: The inn responded that it knew of no changes in receipts made while the grievants were there.

LEADER: How did the inn respond? Did someone from the inn testify? Did that witness undergo cross-examination?

VOICE: A letter was introduced from the inn to the company.

LEADER: Did the letter mention the initials on those receipts?

VOICE: No.

LEADER: Consider the actual presentation of the case. The company introduced receipts, and it was admitted that they had been altered. The company introduced a letter from the inn. Did that letter say that the receipts reflected the prices on the menu?

VOICE: The inn provided a letter and copies of the inn's receipts which were unaltered.

LEADER: The company came forward and said that is our case. It also called the supervisors who testified as to what happened in the interviews. If you were the union representative when that evidence was presented, what would be your first objection to the company's evidence? You have the testimony of the supervisor as to what happened at the disciplinary interviews. You also have the letter from the inn along with the receipts, as well as the receipts from the grievants. The company seeks a stipulation from the union that there was in fact an alteration on the receipts. The union acknowledges that it was done at the request of the employees. Should the union object to part or all of the evidence? How?

VOICE: I do not understand when you say the union stipulated. I do not know to what I would object. I would argue that perhaps the inn might seek a discharge of the cashier for pocketing the difference between the actual cost and the receipts the grievant was given.

LEADER: Assume that the union's first objection is to hearsay as to the inn's letter. It was presented by the company without proper qualification.

VOICE: I would make an objection.

LEADER: As arbitrator, would you sustain the objection?

VOICE: It is going to be an essential point. The questions are why the alterations were made and by whom, and whose initials they are. Because these are essential parts of the case, I would sustain the objection. The writer of the letters from the inn is not subject to cross-examination and that would be rather critical here.

LEADER: The letter is really hearsay. Remember the quickie hearsay rule: can you cross-examine it and do you want to. Is it being submitted to prove the truth of the matter asserted?

VOICE: It is. It is being submitted to prove that there was an alteration.

LEADER: It is a key argument in the company's case.

VOICE: But you said the alteration was admitted.

LEADER: The alteration on the receipt was admitted.

VOICE: The reasons for the inn's letter is to prove the absence of alteration by the inn, not the existence of alterations.

VOICE: I think I might admit it, but I find it does not prove anything for the company.

LEADER: What does it prove? It proves that there were not alterations on the originals, but it is being submitted for another purpose as well. What is the other purpose?

VOICE: Credibility. It supported the employer's reasoning for his actions. Whether or not it is true, it is the support that the employer is using for the basis of its discipline. The company is not acting capriciously.

LEADER: An arbitrator could admit the letter to show why the employer took the discharge action, but the arbitrator certainly requires not only that the company acted reasonably, but that it was correct in a discharge case. One could say, from what I see, that to discharge the grievants was a totally reasonable thing, but if it could be shown that while reasonable it was wrong, obviously the grievants go back to work.

VOICE: The company may do something else to show that it was correct.

LEADER: A second and critical factor is that the inn's letter says the unaltered receipt reflects the money it received. That is a critical piece of information. Surely the arbitrator wants to ask somebody about that. What are some of the questions that an arbitrator would want to ask?

VOICE: One should ask if the total on the receipt has been checked against the register which the inn has to record the amount of money that is taken in to pay for a bill of that type.

LEADER: How do you know that the receipt reflects the money the hotel received? If the inn's clerk received the money, did he verify the receipt? In *Hines v. Anchor Motor Freight*,[1] three truck drivers were discharged for falsifying their hotel receipts, and it was subsequently found that it was the hotel clerk who was pocketing the money. Because the questions we are discussing were not answered in *Anchor Motor Freight*, the Supreme Court found a breach of the duty of fair representation. Who received what money is a critical piece of information. Assume that the objection to the letter is sustained on the basis that it is hearsay. All that is left are the altered slips. If, as arbitrator, you reject that evidence, is the case over as far as you are concerned? I suggest that the company would not have to withdraw the case at that point. Assume that the company goes forward. What is the company's next claim?

VOICE: The company has the admissions which were made by the grievants during the investigation. If the arbitrator would admit those admissions over some objections about not having union representation during the investigation, it could be critical.

LEADER: Consider the procedural aspects of the investigation. Suppose the union said that questioning of grievants was wholly without union representation and that the grievants should have been offered the opportunity to have somebody by their side. What would be your response as arbitrator?

VOICE: What does the contract provide for?

LEADER: That is a good response. First question for the arbitrator to pursue is, where does the contract say that grievant has a right to representation during investigation? There is no right to union representation. There is no due process overlay. Unless there is a contractual right to union representation, there is no procedural defect. An arbitrator should, however, inquire into the procedural requirements of fair representation under the contract.

VOICE: What if the contract provides for union representation during investigations and that fact has never been mentioned at all in the grievance procedure up to the point of arbitration, at which time that

---

[1]*Hines v. Anchor Motor Freight, Inc.*, 424 U.S. 554, 91 LRRM 2481 (1976).

fact is brought out by the union, and the employer is totally unaware and is not prepared to discuss that issue?

LEADER: The question for the arbitrator is whether or not a party waives procedural objections by not raising them earlier. I would probably allow a party to raise such arguments at the hearing, but there may be some dissent on that. What do you think?

VOICE: I would permit a party to raise fresh procedural arguments at the hearing. I would decide at the time of writing the award what effect to give it.

VOICE: Does *Weingarten*[2] provide that when an employee senses an investigation might result in disciplinary action, he should raise the question of representation at that time?

LEADER: That is a different question. *Weingarten* does not stand for the proposition that you have the *per se* right to that representation.

VOICE: Assuming the contract is silent and the grievant did ask for union representation here, do you impute NLRB rights into the situation?

LEADER: The grievant does not have a right to union representation even though he asked for it, unless it is a contractually guaranteed right.

VOICE: Would you not consider NLRB case law?

LEADER: I would not.

VOICE: If the contract did provide for union representation and grievant did not ask for it, and at the hearing the union objected to admission of the discussion with the grievant where union representation was not present, how would you deal with the objection?

LEADER: That is difficult. My inclination would be to allow the union to raise such a procedural claim rather than permit a waiver in this context.

VOICE: What is the remedy if the arbitrator finds that the company violated the procedural rule?

LEADER: The arbitrator could exclude whatever evidence arises out of the meeting.

VOICE: Would you exclude the grievant's statement?

LEADER: Procedurally, if the company claims surprise, I would grant a continuance to respond. Assuming I sustain his objection on the ground that he was improperly denied representation, I would apply an exclusionary rule.

VOICE: I do not understand. If the union claimed rightly that the grievant had been deprived of representation in violation of the contract, is the case moot?

---

[2]*NLRB v. Weingarten, Inc.*, 485 F.2d 1135, 84 LRRM 2436 (5th Cir. 1973), 420 U.S. 251, 88 LRRM 2689 (1975), *enforced on remand*, 511 F.2d 1163, 89 LRRM 2192 (5th Cir. 1975).

LEADER: No. There may be evidence beyond that.

VOICE: Do you ever reserve rulings?

LEADER: Sometimes.

VOICE: Might you do so in this case?

LEADER: Yes, because I would want to see what the other evidence is. I might say, "Even assuming the union's objection is well taken, I nevertheless sustain the discharge on the basis of other facts." I think there are some procedural improprieties in certain collective bargaining relationships where the arbitrator would say that the company did not follow the correct procedure, and the case is therefore moot.

VOICE: How would you handle such an issue at the hearing?

LEADER: In most cases, I would reserve the ruling and say that I consider this a very serious procedural objection and I might base my decision on it. I might close the case at that point. I might simply exclude certain testimony from the hearing. I did not mean to suggest that on all cases I would say the case is over.

Returning to the facts in the arbitration, what happened in the interview? What was said?

VOICE: Based on what we know, the company did not refute the grievants' testimony about what occurred in the interview.

LEADER: What did they say?

VOICE: The first interview had to do with one particular receipt. The grievants were asked separately whether $14.84 was the cost of the lunch. They said that was the correct amount which was spent for the meal.

LEADER: Assume that is all that was said.

VOICE: That is all that is in the decision.

LEADER: Reconstruct what happened at the disciplinary interview. The grievant knows he was in trouble. He had a receipt with an obvious alteration on it. There are also initials on it. The company asked if that was what grievant paid, and the grievant responded affirmatively.

What about the initials?

VOICE: The statement of facts shows that was raised subsequently in the interview. If the fact had not been raised, and if I were the grievant, I would have remarked on and began to explain the reason for the initials.

LEADER: On the other hand, recognize there are some other viable responses. Assume that at the hearing the arbitrator asked the grievant if she knew she was in trouble and she answered yes. If asked why she did not explain, she responded that she did not want to say more than she had to say because she knew her job was on the line. That could be quite persuasive under the circumstances.

VOICE: Is it implied that the amount was for three meals?

LEADER: There are many questions which I would have expected to be raised and answered at the hearing. First, refer to the facts and put yourself in the position of the arbitrator to judge credibility. The procedure followed above is what happens time and again. One has to reconstruct the facts.

VOICE: To what does the "grievants' attempted explanation" refer? In the contentions of the parties, the decision reads, "Upon investigation and being confronted with the company's information the grievants attempted an explanation." Is that an attempted explanation at the first interview or the second interview?

LEADER: I do not know. That is ambiguous language. I read that as meaning that the grievants' answers, when they individually said that that is what was paid, was interpreted by the company as an admission that they had falsified the records.

VOICE: The information with respect to the explanation of the clerk at the inn was the grievant Smith's testimony at the hearing.

LEADER: Was it the company's testimony as to the response of these grievants at the investigation that caused the arbitrator to draft the sentence referring to "attempted explanation?"

VOICE: The company contends that the receipts did not match the inn's receipts, and the grievants had not provided an adequate explanation of the alteration.

LEADER: Assume that the second disciplinary interview is essentially abbreviated, as was the first, to the question asked of the grievants whether the information is correct. They answered yes. That answer is consistent with the grievants' position if they did pay that amount.

Assuming again that no information came from the grievants at the second disciplinary interview with respect to the nature of the alterations, when did grievant Smith first offer an explanation of the alteration? Was it at the hearing?

VOICE: It was at the hearing, and the company presented no testimony to refute it.

LEADER: Go back to the hearing. The company has put on its case. Suppose the union makes a hearsay objection on the inn's letter and it is sustained because it is such a critical piece of evidence. The company rests. The union calls the grievant who offers an explanation for the alteration of the receipt for the first time, and the company says, "We object. We have never heard this before." Do you sustain the objection on that ground?

VOICE: No, but one may draw inferences from the fact that the parties have not used the contract grievance procedure properly.

VOICE: No, because the company did not ask the grievant to tell exactly what happened. Instead it showed grievant two documents and asked if the amount shown on the receipt was correct. If I had been the grievant, I would have answered exactly what was asked.

LEADER: The failure of the company to ask for an explanation is a strong reason to overrule the objection and let the testimony in. An arbitrator should be careful before extending admission of evidence to undercutting any inference which may be drawn from specific events.

VOICE: Would the parties have already gone through about three steps of the grievance procedure?

LEADER: Yes, perhaps four.

VOICE: Would not the company at this point say, "We have had three or four steps of the grievance procedure and we have had opportunity for both parties to put forth evidence."

LEADER: The failure of the grievants to offer an explanation before the arbitration hearing would be the company objection. The arbitrator overrules the objection, but is free to draw whatever inferences are appropriate.

VOICE: Grievant Smith, the crew leader, was not asked if she had any comment but was simply informed that she was discharged. The other grievant, who did not make out the vouchers, was asked if he had any comment and he said no.

LEADER: In fact, that is the union's advice to its members, "Say nothing when you are questioned and come to us. We are going to represent you."

VOICE: Is that before the grievance has reached the arbitration stage?

LEADER: Yes, and it may even be before a dispute gets into the grievance procedure. There is good cause to ask why the explanation of the alteration was not offered before the arbitration hearing.

VOICE: I have a lot of difficulty with the notion of putting the burden on the union for an explanation. The company has a basic just cause discipline burden, and you are saying that an arbitrator may be able to sustain the discharge here by the testimony of the grievants, without the company having done anything more than showing altered receipts. The company has given a reason, and the arbitrator has excluded the evidence that supports that reason. Whether the arbitrator closes the hearing at that point or continues it, how can discharge be sustained based on the evidence as presented?

LEADER: Of the two remaining elements in the company's case, one is the altered receipt itself, and the other is the evidence from the supervisor as to what went on in the disciplinary interview.

VOICE: Even accepting your premise that there are two elements remaining, how can the discharge be sustained without proof that the grievants altered the receipts?

LEADER: There is a very real question as to why no other evidence of alteration was submitted. However, before we discuss how an arbitrator should rule, without such direct evidence, consider the union's case. The union witnesses have told their story, which we now understand to be that they paid the amount on the altered receipt which was initialed by the inn.

VOICE: Then the company claims surprise.

LEADER: That is right.

VOICE: Is surprise cause for an arbitrator to adjourn the hearing?

LEADER: I do not think so. Is there more evidence?

VOICE: No.

LEADER: The company argues that even if the inn's letter is excluded, the clearly incredible testimony on the part of the grievants was never told in the grievance procedure. Even assuming that the story the grievants have told is true, the company contends that the grievants should still be discharged because they are dealing with company funds every day and if they had asked somebody to alter their copy of the receipts, the burden should shift to them to prove it. The grievants should have brought in a letter from the inn.

The union argues that the burden is on the company to prove just cause. The union does not have to prove innocence. While there may have been better bookkeeping ways to handle the altered receipts, the grievants are not bookkeepers. It is still the company's burden, and they have failed to show just cause. You are the arbitrator, you decide the issue.

VOICE: I would like to know the seniority of the grievants.

LEADER: They both have twenty-eight years with clean records, but it does not matter because the penalty for stealing, unless you can make a tremendous argument, consistently is discharge. Progessive discipline normally would not apply.

VOICE: I would find for the union. I would say the company has not proved its case and the union's position has been consistent from the beginning because the initials on the receipts were there at the time the grievants submitted the receipts to the company. The union explanation of why those initials were there was consistent with their explanation of why the bill was raised by $10, and that has never been discredited by any testimony.

LEADER: Why did you feel the necessity of going beyond your first point which was that the company had to prove its case?

VOICE: One might say an arbitrator should go beyond burden of proof in terms of responding to the company's argument.

LEADER: Yes, but the arbitrator must first decide whether or not the company has proved its case.

VOICE: I would concur that the company has not sustained its burden.

LEADER: Are you not bothered by the fact that the grievant made no explanation prior to the hearings in the three steps in the grievance procedure as to why she admittedly altered the receipts?

VOICE: No, that is not enough.

LEADER: You believe her story fully.

VOICE: I do not have to.

LEADER: What do you think?

VOICE: Well, I am not sure why the inn's letter was excluded but apart from that, I think the company initially made a case. What credibility to attach to the grievants' explanation is the key question.

LEADER: I agree. The company has made a prima facie case and therefore gets the case beyond dismissal for failure to state the case. It is beyond that threshold.

VOICE: I would put a great deal of weight on the grievants' failure to offer an explanation before the arbitration hearing. I would attach weight to that failure in the sense that the explanation is less credible.

LEADER: Would you sustain discharge of both grievants?

VOICE: I would sustain the discharge of grievant Smith. I do not see enough evidence showing what grievant Brown's relationship was with grievant Smith to sustain Brown's discharge. That conclusion is only from reading this arbitrator's statement in the record.

LEADER: Would you reinstate Brown with full back pay?

VOICE: I would want to read the record. My guess is that he was involved. My guess is that I would probably sustain the discharge on grievant Brown, based upon the record.

VOICE: I would sustain Smith's discharge. I do not know what I would do with Brown.

LEADER: What is the strongest part of the company's case?

VOICE: The strongest factor is the grievants' failure to explain at the meetings why there were alterations of the receipts. More importantly, at the hearing I could see a mistake in billing on one receipt. I just do not believe that there were mistakes made on ten of them at three different inns and three different meals in three different places.

LEADER: So you sustain Smith's discharge. What actions do you take with respect to Brown?

VOICE: I do not know what role he played.

LEADER: Even if you do not know, as an arbitrator you must decide.

VOICE: I would probably not discharge him but give him a disciplinary suspension.

LEADER: For what reason?

VOICE: I do not know what to do with him.

LEADER: My inclination is that I would sustain Smith's discharge and restore Brown with full back pay based upon the company's failure to sustain its burden. The company introduced an altered document which grievant Smith acknowledged she altered. That is meaningful evidence, and through the entire steps of the grievance procedure, she offered no explanation.

VOICE: Do you think that the company has the responsibility to bring in the direct evidence from the inn manager?

LEADER: Yes.

VOICE: Why did you restore Brown with full back pay? I returned Brown without pay because I felt he probably knew what Smith was doing.

LEADER: Probably? How did he know? The company has not shown that he knew anything.

VOICE: That is true. That is a false presumption on my part.

VOICE: The company also should have brought in the inn's clerk to testify. The company could have asked the inn representative to explain how two people could eat lunch for $4.52.

LEADER: I find the rest of the evidence persuasive enough.

VOICE: I see three or four very plausible stories. Could not Smith's story be entirely accurate, based on the evidence that came in?

LEADER: Yes, but I would have expected an explanation to be offered during the grievance steps.

VOICE: I still would not say that the company proved its case.

LEADER: Did the company prove that there was an altered slip?

VOICE: Yes, the grievants admit that.

LEADER: If it were just at the disciplinary interview when grievants failed to explain the alterations, I would readily put both grievants back with full back pay.

VOICE: If the union had not put forth any evidence, would you have found the other way?

LEADER: No.

VOICE: Why not? You would have only the receipt with initials on it. You would not know that it was altered, because you have excluded the inn's letter. You have only the grievant's statements that the receipts are correct.

LEADER: Are you telling me that I do not know that the receipt was altered?

VOICE: The company put on its case. You excluded the letter from the inn which indicated that its records showed $4.54. All you have is a receipt in evidence with some initials and statements by the grievants that they were questioned about the receipt and said that it was accurate.

LEADER: If I cannot be assured that the receipt was altered, the case goes the other way. But, for union counsel, what a dangerous game to play. Most arbitrators would never rule until the case was closed, unlike a motion to dismiss in a court proceeding.

Decision

Although the grievants were discharged at the same time and for the same reason, the facts relative to each are different. Because Ms. Smith was the leader of the crew, her case will be discussed first. The case of Mr. Brown will be discussed thereafter.

When a crew leader is named by Mr. Chickering, he or she is given a packet which includes instructions as to where to go, what to do, where to stay, what route to travel, and what means to use. Also included are expense report forms which cover a period of one week. They include columns for each day, Sunday through Saturday. They include lines for each of the three meals, lodging, transportation, leased auto, parking/toll/storage, taxi and limousine, tips (other than meals), and other similar items. Unless the items are marked in the left margin with a symbol, no receipts are required. Certain other items are to be explained in a space provided.

Although the evidence was not specific on the point, apparently it was not an uncommon practice for Mr. Chickering to rewrite the expense reports by relocating certain items to the proper columns, consolidating sheets where possible, and submitting them to the leader to check and sign before approving them himself. At least this procedure was followed in the instant case. There is no dispute about the accuracy of Mr. Chickering's transfer of the items to another report form.

The question is whether or not the reported amounts for the meals listed were in fact spent for the meals. Grievant says the amounts were reported correctly; the company says they were not and that the physical evidence proved they were not.

The Arbitrator agrees with the union that a signed statement by the inn manager in the presence of a witness is not sufficient proof of misconduct by the grievants without the opportunity to cross-examine the manager. The original restaurant checks (or bills) which were given to the customer, who then handed them to the cashier when paying the bill have serial numbers on them which match the serial numbers on the receipts turned in by the grievant. This is conclusive evidence as to the amounts paid when the cash register imprints also match the amounts on the check and the same numbered receipt. When several receipts which otherwise match exactly with the amount of the check have a noticeably different handwritten "1" added in front of the figures to increase the amount by $10, the Arbitrator has no doubt that they were altered.

Ms. Smith's explanation of the alterations at the hearing was that she had tried to keep some accurate records but got them all mixed up. She stated that she went to the desk at the inn and told the manager about her problem, that the manager asked for the receipts she had, that he then said that there was no problem and just changed the receipts. On cross-examination, she could not recall which ones had been changed. She did not know, but thought the initials on the receipts were those of the manager who changed them. She testified on direct examination that she went to the manager on two different days and had some changed. On cross-examination, she stated without questioning on the point that they were all changed at one time. On cross-examination she testified she had kept a little pad on which she listed expenses, but said she did not think to keep it after she turned in her report. Before turning in her report to Mr. Chickering, she had gone to another employee and experienced leader, John Savoir, to get help in filling out the report. She did not think to explain any of this to him, nor had she mentioned it at any time before the hearing to Mr. Chickering or Ms. Kramer, nor made any effort to contact the inn to get the name of the manager whom she said changed the receipts. Finally, grievant Brown's testimony included no support for any of the explanations offered by grievant Smith.

The Arbitrator listened carefully and took thorough notes as to all the testimony by grievant Smith. She also had in mind the United States Supreme Court decision in *Hines v. Anchor Motor Freight Co.* and the unreliability of hotel receipts. Although hotel receipts may be unreliable, in this case the receipts matched the serial numbers on the restaurant checks from which they were detached when paid. The cash register printing on the checks matched the original amounts paid on the receipts which had been changed. Furthermore, grievant Smith's testimony on cross-examination was evasive and together with her inability to recall any of the simplest facts about her trip, persuaded the Arbitrator that she was not a credible witness. Therefore, the Arbitrator finds that the expense report provided by grievant Smith was a false report of her expenses.

Turning to grievant Brown's case, the Arbitrator finds no evidence to support the conclusion that he falsified any records or supported any falsification of the expense report. The company's contention that his responses to the questions by Mr. Chickering and Ms. Kramer as to the accuracy of the report were false is built on the assumption that he had knowledge to the contrary. There is no evidence that Brown even saw any of the restaurant checks, much less participated or knew of any changes in the receipts.

The fact that the report covered his expenses as well as those of Smith does not in and of itself cast any responsibility on him for its accuracy or give cause to hold him accountable for its inaccuracy. This is especially true when the only question put to him was whether or not the amounts on the report were accurate. If he did not keep the records or have intimate knowledge of the details, he could not be expected to answer differently from the way he did. To prove someone has falsified a record requires much more than his statement that it was accurate to the best of his knowledge, when there is no evidence that he had any information to the contrary. In fact, Mr. Chickering's approval of the report as initially submitted before Ms. Kramer's questioning of it is evidence that a fellow employee who was on the same trip but with no supervisory authority or responsibility for expenditures or accounting for them could not be held responsible as to their accuracy. There is absolutely no evidence that he knew anything about the accuracy of the report. Such guilt by association is not enough to uphold a disciplinary layoff, much less discharge.

Award

Based upon a careful consideration of all the evidence and arguments heard in this matter, it is the Award of the Arbitrator that grievant Mary Smith was discharged for just cause and her grievance is denied.

Grievant Marvin Brown was discharged without just cause. It is therefore ordered that Brown be reinstated to his job with full seniority and that he be made whole for all earnings and other rights lost because of his discharge.

Jane Doe
Arbitrator

Amityville, Florida
July 18, 1981

Administrative Practices and Lifestyle

The following discussion* on administrative practices and arbitrator lifestyle includes questions concerning tape recording of hearings, the use of court reporters, filing of briefs, recording of expenses, billing for services, determining a work day, collection of fees, travel time, scheduling, academic conflicts, length of hearings, preparation time, availability, cancellations, disclosure of relationships, ethics, and gaining acceptability.

LEADER: I am not sure what to say about lifestyle. I know that I want to remain an arbitrator because arbitration is one of the few professions in which one has total control over one's time. The single most satisfying reward is the ability to schedule work and time off at will. When the pace of an arbitrator's work quickens, he should be very selfish in terms of putting aside time for himself and his family.

QUESTION: Do you tape record your hearings?

LEADER: I do not make tape recordings of the proceedings as do some arbitrators. I find it terribly inconvenient to listen to a hearing twice. I believe tape recordings stultify the proceeding and inhibit the parties.

QUESTION: Why do some arbitrators tape record hearings?

MS. GOOTNICK: There are several reasons why tape recordings are used extensively by arbitrators in the absence of a transcript. The testimony may be extremely technical. If there is a credibility question as to whether or not one witness said something, the arbitrator may want to refer back to it. I do tape record if I sense it is a technical case and there is no question of embarrassing people.

QUESTION: What about court reporters?

LEADER: They are used far more than they should be. In my practice, there is a transcript in 25 percent of the cases.

MR. SCHULTZ: That is about right for total FMCS cases.

LEADER: What percentage of FMCS cases have briefs?

---

*Led by Arnold M. Zack.

MR. SCHULTZ: 60 percent.

LEADER: This would vary by industry. The airline industry representatives always file briefs and the postal service cases usually have briefs. On the other hand, I have some clients who never file briefs.

QUESTION: I assume you charge for normal expenses such as transportation, hotels, and meals. Do you charge for photocopying costs and other incidental expenses?

LEADER: I do not charge for incidental expenses, overhead, or typing. I think it is deplorable when arbitrators, who are charging the rates they do, gild the lily by charging additional amounts for normal operating expenses. I know there are some arbitrators who do, but the only time I have charged for telephone costs is if I arranged a conference call or something extremely unusual. My impression is that there is nothing that annoys the parties more than being billed by an arbitrator for normal overhead. If you are billing for $200 or $300 a day, to charge 75 cents for a phone call or $2 for lunch just shows up like a red light.

MR. COOK: If the bill is otherwise reasonable, I do not care if incidental items are included. If the total bill is high, there may be an adverse reaction.

LEADER: A new arbitrator is going to be marginal in terms of selection by the parties. Why run the risk of antagonizing the parties by an excessive bill when, by keeping your costs down, you may increase your appeal to the parties for a subsequent case.

QUESTION: How do you handle billing when you are away from home for two days?

LEADER: If the cases are in the same town, there is no problem. I just split the expenses. If I am going to be in New York overnight for two separate clients, I charge one way fare to each and split the hotel bill and meals. I split everything. If I am going from New York to Minneapolis and back I will try to work out a prorated amount. I will charge the first client the one-way fare to New York and the second client the one-way fare from Minneapolis back to Boston. I will somehow prorate the fare so that it is a little less than normal for each side.

QUESTION: I do not understand why you would charge the New York client the fare to Minneapolis.

LEADER: It is less than the New York to Boston return than they otherwise would pay. If I rent a car for three days, and go to Manchester one day, Rutland the next day, and Providence the third day, I prorate charges on the basis of mileage. I try to give a rough estimate to the parties and the approach has never been challenged.

QUESTION: How do you define a day to set a per diem charge?

LEADER: A day is a regular workday, ten to suppertime.

QUESTION: If you start at ten o'clock and go beyond supper in an arbitration hearing, do you charge an extra half day?

LEADER: I have never done it. If the hearing only goes from ten to twelve in the morning, I charge a minimum of a day.

QUESTION: How many study days do you average for a one-day case?

LEADER: I do not know. There are as many that are two as there are one, and there are very few that are three, so it may be a little more than one.

QUESTION: Has a party ever not paid?

LEADER: It happens once a year, and I hear 125 or 150 days.

QUESTION: Do you charge the same rate for AAA as a direct contact?

LEADER: Yes.

QUESTION: Do you charge travel time if you go to the west coast?

LEADER: I do not charge travel time when I go west. I do charge travel time if I have to take the red eye for the next day coming home.

MR. SCHULTZ: Some arbitrators charge travel time.

LEADER: If I have to drive to southern Vermont, I do charge four hours of travel up and four hours of travel back. I tell the parties if they are going to have the case up there, it is going to cost them a day of travel time. If they hold it near an airport in a city, I do not charge travel time. Except for New England, where I feel an obligation to take most of the cases, I do not travel to places other than airport cities.

QUESTION: How many days do you work?

LEADER: I hear cases about four days a week.

QUESTION: How many weeks do you work?

LEADER: I do not work in July and August. I take off ten days in October, ten days in December, five days at Christmas, and ten days in February.

QUESTION: When you say that you do not work in July and August, what do you do? Do you have the appointing agencies take you off the panels?

LEADER: I do not schedule cases. At the beginning of the year I sit down with my wife and say, "When are we taking our vacation?" Then, I block those days out and they stay blocked out. I work about nine months, four days a week.

MS. GOOTNICK: Arnold Zack is not a typical arbitrator. He is in demand, and he can say he will only go to airport cities. I do not suggest new arbitrators say that. I would like to, but I do not.

LEADER: I am convinced that I stay busy because there are enough people out there with little cases who want short awards issued rapidly.

QUESTION: What about arbitrators in academe?

MR. SCHULTZ: For arbitrators in academe three cases a month is a lot.

LEADER: I know a very good teacher and excellent arbitrator who had a sabbatical last year and spent all his time arbitrating. Then, he threw up his hands and said, "I cannot take it. It is just too much. I want to teach and I want to arbitrate. I want to do both." I would not want to do any teaching because I am having too much fun arbitrating.

QUESTION: When you schedule four days of different cases in different places, what do you do when you have a hearing that goes over?

LEADER: That does not happen. Hearings seldom run past one o'clock. In New England, an arbitration case is conducted very expeditiously. The parties stipulate a lot of facts. If I am traveling among cities, I tell the parties when I schedule the hearing that I have to leave by a certain time. Usually the parties will talk for as long as you give them. If you give them less time, they will present their case in a shorter period of time.

QUESTION: How should expenses be itemized?

LEADER: Some arbitrators list everything. I break expenses down into categories. Transportation, taxis, hotel, and meals are the four categories. Do not pad your expense account and you will not be challenged. If you are going to two places, divide your expenses right down the line. It is extremely important to keep your expenses and per diem billing down, particularly when you are a new arbitrator. If you think billing is marginal between one day and two days, charge a day and a half. If you cannot limit your billing to one day, charge a day and a half. Keep expenses down because the parties do look at it, particularly with the increase in arbitration costs. It will have an impact on your future business.

QUESTION: Does preparation time have an impact on future business?

LEADER: I think so. Get out your awards quickly; do not wait for thirty days. Get your decisions out within two weeks. When my apprentice walks out of a hearing, he is to tell the parties they will have their decision in two weeks. Make a commitment to the parties, and impose the earlier deadline on yourself to get the case out to meet that deadline.

QUESTION: What if the parties do not file briefs until thirty days after the hearing?

LEADER: Make your decision deadline two weeks from the time when you have the complete record.

MR. COOK: In the Midwest, we expect to get charged travel expense and travel time if the arbitrator is from another area.

LEADER: I have very seldom charged travel time because the only time I would charge travel time is when it has an impact on another workday, and it very seldom does that. If it means arduous driving, I charge it as a really punitive measure because I do not want to go there again. In most cases, you can fly anyplace and get there in two hours of elapsed flight time and still have a full day of work. You can go to the West Coast the same day.

MR. KADEN: When you fly, do you fly first class so you can work?

LEADER: Yes.

MR. KADEN: Have you ever been questioned on that practice?

LEADER: No, but I did not always fly first class. When I started to get busy, I started to fly first class.

MR. COOK: A new arbitrator is going to spend a week or two on some of the early decisions but should not charge the parties for all that time. Some new arbitrators have done that and it has made it difficult for them to achieve acceptability.

LEADER: If I get into a subject area with which I am unfamiliar and I want to read about it, I will spend time that is out of proportion to the length of the decision and to the amount of time I would have spent on that case if I had known the subject. I do not bill for the extra time.

QUESTION: What if an arbitrator has an unusual case?

LEADER: I feel very bad about charging more than a day or two for a hearing day. If there are many cases cited which I must read, long briefs, a long transcript, or something special, I will charge but I do not like to do it.

MR. COOK: Our law office keeps records of what arbitrators charge. We list the issue, the arbitrator, how the case was decided, what the charges were, how long the hearing was, and what the remedy was. That does not automatically determine what we are going to do with that arbitrator in the future. If one begins to get what is considered to be high charges repeatedly from the same arbitrator, one may still use him. The charge is secondary to getting what one thinks is an arbitrator who is important in that case, but if there is a choice between arbitrators then the charges come into play. Some companies and unions have to watch their pennies; it then becomes a more definite factor.

LEADER: That is why I say that if an arbitrator's decision is for circulation to those who decide which arbitrators are acceptable, the bill has the same effect.

MR. SCHULTZ: I have seen the evaluation sheets by arbitration rating services, and I do not think there are any questions on charges. The questions relate to how they conducted the hearing and how they wrote the decision.

LEADER: Someone is going to call up a lawyer acquaintance and say, "Have you ever used so-and-so?" He is going to look up the charges and say, "Yes, good decision, but his rates are high." Word of mouth is far more effective than a rating service. In choosing an arbitrator, the parties are not looking for a person who has decided all his cases pro-management or pro-union. They are looking for an arbitrator who has had good judgment and not at how the bottom line came out on past cases. In that kind of quest, they can obtain reliable information by calling parties who have had experience with an arbitrator.

QUESTION: Is there a simple way for an arbitrator to keep a record of expenses?

LEADER: I suggest a device for keeping your expense records. I keep a week-long form, from Sunday through Saturday. It lists, on the top, the date I wrote it, where I traveled, from what city to what city. The top three-quarters of the page contains spaces for all the different categories of cash expenditures including tolls, telephone calls, laundry, and tips. On the bottom quarter of the page, the same column lists the client for each day and the charges devoted to transportation, taxi, hotel, automobile, meals, and other. I keep the top portion as a daily entry for my tax record. The bottom, which I fill out at the same time, indicates what is to be attributed to each client for that particular case. On my prorated trip for two different clients in New York, it will show just what is to be billed, such as, half the hotel, half the meals, half the automobile rental. I don't have to look at that expense sheet again and it is all ready to be pulled out at tax time.

From the first paragraph of the decision, my secretary learns that a hearing was held on a certain date. She looks up that date, and there it is for her to bill. At the top of my draft decision, I indicate "one plus one," or "one plus one and a half," or "one plus three." That is the only instruction I have to give to my secretary on expenses. My secretary also keeps all my accounts and does all my scheduling. She tries to put me in the right cities at the right times.

I have another rule on travel. I do not stay away overnight more than one night a week. That is a goal. There are some times that I will stay away two nights. We live right in Boston, which has very good air transportation, so it is easy to do that.

QUESTION: Earlier you mentioned that unless the parties cite cases of other arbitrators, you really do not spend time looking up arbitration decisions. Is that the general rule of arbitrators?

LEADER: I read every case cited and I researched every case when I started as an arbitrator. I still look up law or arbitral decisions on occasion. After several years, one begins to realize that there are often no reported cases on an issue one must decide. That may be very distressing, but one ultimately comes to that conclusion. If cases involving both the parties are submitted, I will read them. If cases are cited in the brief, I will read them. It is very unlikely that I will do independent research.

QUESTION: If your name is submitted on a panel and the parties choose you and for some reason you do not want to be an arbitrator for those parties, do you simply decline?

LEADER: I try to get them to take my apprentice.

QUESTION: If they refuse to accept your apprentice, would you take the case?

LEADER: I would give them a date in the future. There are places I do not want to go because of the inconvenience of travel, but there are no clients with whom I do not want to deal.

MR. SCHULTZ: If someone on the FMCS panel does not want a case, he can notify us. We have a form letter which says that he is not available.

QUESTION: How do cancellations affect an arbitrator's schedule?

LEADER: I did not work last Friday and Thursday and I am not working this Thursday and Friday because I had cancellations. We are as much victimized by the lawyer's day in scheduling as we are by our own. It is very hard when you are scheduling days and the parties have not firmed up their schedules.

QUESTION: How does a new arbitrator fill the schedule?

MS. GOOTNICK: In the beginning, I contacted some of the administrative agencies in New York, which hire arbitrators on an ad hoc basis to hear administrative cases in the Human Rights Division and other areas. It is not unprofessional to apply to the various agencies who may indeed need arbitrators, and these cases will provide good experience because the hearing itself is reasonably similar. At the beginning it was a very good way for the advocates to get to know me. Some of the same advocates who are doing state hearings may pick you as an arbitrator subsequently. I think that approach is something for a new arbitrator to investigate.

QUESTION: Who should be contacted? What agencies should be approached?

MS. GOOTNICK: In New York, the state health, education, human rights, and environmental conservation departments are all possibilities. I am sure this will vary from state to state.

LEADER: It is important to attend arbitration conferences. Any meeting in the labor-management field where you can meet the parties is important. In New England we have a very active AAA office which runs "Meet the Arbitrator" sessions, and union and management people are introduced to the newer arbitrators. That is a very good opportunity.

QUESTION: What advice would you give about cancellations?

LEADER: I do not think new arbitrators should charge for cancellations. I charge as a deterrent to uphold my schedule.

QUESTION: What sort of materials do you recommend new arbitrators read regularly?

LEADER: Read right through the Academy proceedings. The older volumes are just as pertinent now as they were then, and they are better written. The Academy proceedings contain a number of essays on a lot of different subjects that are very important. There is the whole debate that occurred in the early '60s on NLRB arbitration arrangements and the brewing external law which is just as pertinent now, when you are dealing with the EEOC questions, as it was then in dealing with NLRB questions. The paper on subcontracting is excellent and is still pertinent. That is probably the best reading you can do.

MR. SCHULTZ: The LRR series of BNA is valuable. I have a subscription to the *Labor Law Journal*. I think one ought to look at the *Industrial Relations Law Review*, and the AAA's *Arbitration Journal*.

QUESTION: Is the annual meeting of the National Academy restricted to Academy members?

LEADER: Part of it is restricted to Academy members. The last two days of the sessions are open to invited guests.

QUESTION: What if someone was interested in presenting a paper they thought would be acceptable to the Academy?

LEADER: The Academy does not accept unsolicited papers.

QUESTION: Is the Society for Professionals in Dispute Resolution (SPIDR) a good organization to join?

LEADER: You ought to join SPIDR. Their office is at 1730 Rhode Island Avenue, Washington, D.C., in care of the AAA office there. By becoming active in these things, one can get the chapters to do more, such as running training programs or getting together meetings of arbitrators.

QUESTION: What relationship should an arbitrator have with the parties?

LEADER: One has to be very careful not to give the appearance of being closer to one side than to the other side. We have friends in Boston with whom I will not socialize when I have a pending case with that party.

When parties are comfortable with each other, an arbitrator can take certain liberties where the parties recognize that there is not going to be any effort to exert influence. A new arbitrator should go to the hearing by himself, eat by himself, and not talk to anybody outside the hearing room unless both parties are present.

QUESTION: Do you disclose social relationships with one of the parties?

LEADER: Yes. I do not want to be at a hearing wondering whether I should or should not have disclosed something. The first time I heard a Telephone Company case, I said, "I have to tell you I own Telephone stock." The union representative asked, "How many shares?" I said, "132." The union representative said, "Is that all you have? We have more than that."

An arbitrator must decide what to disclose. The possible consequences of not doing so is just not worth the anguish.

QUESTION: If an arbitrator is asked to withdraw from a case because of a disclosure, should he charge for transportation expenses?

LEADER: I might charge just for transportation expenses. However, when an arbitrator discloses, the parties usually are not going to ask him to withdraw. I do not know of any situation where an arbitrator has made an offer of disclosure where he has been asked to withdraw from the case.

I have always operated on the theory that the best thing that can happen in this profession in terms of ego satisfaction is to be selected for a case. If an arbitrator is unable to handle that case, either because he is too busy or because of a disclosure, he retains two loyal supporters. If an arbitrator holds the case and writes a decision, he has lost one.

QUESTION: How much disclosure do arbitrators make about what their relatives do? I have relatives who do not have the same last name.

LEADER: How related?

QUESTION: It is my father and he is a partner in a very prominent law firm. It is very likely that I could show up at a hearing with counsel from his firm.

LEADER: I would disclose my relationship to the firm representing one of the parties.

QUESTION: Should an arbitrator disclose prior representations?

LEADER: My apprentice lives in Manchester, New Hampshire and had a case involving the Manchester School Department. He told me that he worked on a case for the City Solicitor in Manchester in which he determined eligibility for disability insurance for females and asked me if the arbitration case had to do with that issue. I did not know whether it did or not and told him to disclose his prior activity to the parties. He told them and they said that they already knew about that.

MS. GOOTNICK: In a hearing I had recently, I was very impressed with the company and thoroughly enjoyed the case. At home I remarked on the company by name to my husband, who said he had stock in the company. I found myself in a quandary, having already heard the case. I wrote to the parties telling them that I had discovered the fact of ownership. The parties replied with a thank you and directed me to go ahead and write the decision.

LEADER: It is not a question of what the arbitrator thinks is important; it is what the parties' perception of the disclosure is.

QUESTION: What does an arbitrator do at night in a strange city?

LEADER: I stay in that hotel room. That is the best time for sitting down and writing, but it saves time because I have the weekends free.

QUESTION: What happens when you have an arbitration panel, you finish the hearing, and there are three of you. Who writes a decision in a three-member panel?

LEADER: In a three-member panel, my practice is to write the decision and bring it to the board meeting. I think that three-member panels are a waste of time and money. If the parties are insistent on having a panel, I have been equally insistent on having a board meeting. If I am going to make the decision solo, it is going to be my decision. I am not going to send a decision out and have both parties say we disagree.

For instance, in a case of reinstatement without back pay, neither party would agree with my award. I do not want to be placed in a position where I have to negotiate against my own decision to get another vote.

At the board meeting I have with me the completed and typed statement of the issues, facts, and contentions of the parties. I also have my typed discussion but do not supply it to my fellow board members. We talk about the case for as long as is necessary to determine its outcome. In most cases the discussion will not change my previous decision. In some cases it may change my approach. In a few cases it will change my mind about the outcome. If the discussion does not change anything, I give them the decision and they can take it with them.

QUESTION: Are tripartite panels common in certain industries?

LEADER: Yes. The airline industry uses three- or five-person panels. Utilities also frequently have panels. There is an impression that the second bite of the apple is very helpful. It is not helpful to the neutral because the neutral cannot really gain very much insight. If the parties try to put in additional facts or practices, I will not listen to them.

QUESTION: Should a new arbitrator be discouraged if cases are not available?

LEADER: Rick Riley says that a new arbitrator should get two cases the first year, four the second, eight the third, sixteen the fourth, and if you have not really achieved acceptability by then, look for something else. It is slow, and it is arduous. Establish friendships with the people in the AAA office, and get your name out. Get on the list of the AAA and you will get on the FMCS list.

Use the fact that you are on the FMCS and AAA lists to go to state agencies to be put on their list as well. There is nothing wrong with calling up the neutral agencies and saying that you are available and would like to get on the list of arbitrators. Do not pressure agencies by calling to ask if your name has gone out.

The worst thing a new arbitrator can do is to solicit cases. It is good to go to those meetings of organizations where people see you and get to know that you are an arbitrator but do not try to get them to use you. It is very dangerous. It is a reflection that you need the work and that you are not getting work on your own qualifications. It also raises the question of whether you are pursuing the other side more than you are pursuing the side you are talking to. Do not do it.

Read the Code of Professional Responsibility. There are and will continue to be questions raised as to whether certain types of conduct are ethical or unethical. Always err on the side of caution and ethics. I know of no profession that has such a "jungle telephone" as does the arbitration profession or the labor-management profession. That is true on the union side and that is true on the management side. You can destroy yourself professionally in short order if you are perceived to be unethical.

Trainee Role and Expectations

The following discussion* on the trainee's role and expectations in labor arbitrator development includes questions concerning trainee conduct at hearing observations, hearing procedures, development timetables, ethical considerations, part-time commitments, clerical requirements, length of opinions, training value, publication of decisions, appointing agency rules, fees, and acceptability.

LEADER: When I went into the GE-IUE program, I had had no experience in arbitration, although I was an experienced labor lawyer and had specialized in the field for a number of years at the NLRB, the City of New York, and a private law firm. At the time, I was teaching labor law. The GE-IUE training program was enormously useful to me in many ways. I am very happy with both my arbitration career today and my expectations, even though the phone may stop ringing next week.

Fundamentally, the training program gave me a great deal of very useful substantive and procedural information. When I started arbitrating, after the first academic session, I read my notes on procedural matters before every arbitration. That gave me confidence to handle the arbitration proceeding. The training program put a pattern to a lot of the problems we have in arbitration. Since I have been arbitrating, I see that some of the issues which were raised in the training sessions have occurred including, surprisingly enough, ethical problems. I would have been more confused about how to handle such problems had I not been in the program.

During the observation period, program participants attended GE-IUE arbitration cases, singly or in groups of two or three. We sat, took notes, but did not participate in the proceedings. We wrote a mock opinion and award based on the transcript or our notes.

QUESTION: What was your relationship with the arbitrator either before or during the hearing?

---

*Led by Janet Maleson Spencer.

LEADER: Limited, but most hospitable. Participants were careful not to discuss the particular case that was before us. Subsequent to the arbitrator's submission of his opinion and award, the arbitrators did comment upon our opinions and it was interesting for us to compare not only the decision but also the way the decision was reasoned. Our opinions were reviewed by Jean McKelvey and Ted St. Antoine, who was the dean of the law school at Michigan and the academic director of the GE-IUE program.

QUESTION: What did your training program consist of? Was it very similar to the ABA pilot program?

LEADER: From what I have seen, it is virtually identical in the sense that there are sessions on procedure and also on substance.

COMMENT: I think there was a good deal more on substantive issues in that program. Professor Kaden emphasized procedure because one of the major criticisms from the participants in the GE-IUE program was that they wanted more on the procedural aspects of arbitration.

LEADER: Yes. We had sessions on seniority and other substantive areas, but they were not nearly as useful as the discussions of procedure.

COMMENT: Substantive issues can be read about afterwards.

LEADER: Yes. It was very nice to have the inside of the procedural matters such as evidence, rulings, and sequestering of witnesses; all those questions come up in a real hearing. Those who have had some arbitration experience can benefit even more from the training program. I wish I could go through another program now to talk about some of the problems that one meets. During the training program, those problems did not mean as much as they do now.

QUESTION: What can you tell us about the evolution of your career, both in terms of what you wanted to do when you got started and where you are now?

LEADER: This is one of the mysteries of this whole arbitration business. One of the things about going through a training program is that not only does it benefit me in terms of my ability to be an arbitrator, but it also gives the parties confidence that those who have gone through a training program are not complete novices and will not embarrass anyone.

I feel that there were a lot of people encouraging me and helping me to get started in my arbitration career. I do not know how it evolved. I only know that I got designations as arbitrator through the AAA, FMCS, and some private designations from people who knew that I was a new arbitrator. Many people assumed that, because I was new, my schedule would not be as tight. If they had an arbitration that had to be handled expeditiously, they would call me.

QUESTION: When did the GE-IUE program start? When did you get your first case?

LEADER: I got my first case immediately after the first academic session. I thought it was a mistake, and I called AAA and said I was not ready.

QUESTION: Was the publicity about the GE-IUE program and the knowledge that you were participating in the program a factor?

LEADER: Yes.

QUESTION: Did you turn that case down?

LEADER: No. I went ahead with it.

QUESTION: What about time frame?

LEADER: We finished the first academic session in October of 1975.

QUESTION: Are you talking roughly about two and a half years?

LEADER: Yes. At the beginning I received a few private designations through the AAA, and I went on a Post Office disciplinary expedited arbitration panel, which was ideal, and I did a lot of expedited cases. The more cases one has the more confident I believe one becomes in running a hearing. The expedited cases did not require writing a long opinion and they were all disciplinary. That was very good experience and I did some expedited postal cases the first year.

QUESTION: Did you travel?

LEADER: I traveled a little but I limited myself geographically to some extent to the eastern seaboard for personal and professional reasons, because I have a teaching schedule which I have to accommodate. That first year was relatively quiet, truthfully, and I geared up for those GE-IUE cases in a big way. I read over my books and notes and I went in prepared to do it procedurally right. In the second year my arbitration career really started to develop. I have a limited number of days that I can give to arbitration, and I do not know how much faster it would roll along if I had more time. I have received some private cases directly, and I do not know how my name went to the parties in those situations unless it went through the grapevine. Some lawyers with whom I do committee work have also selected me as arbitrator.

One of the first private designations was one which immediately raised a problem that we had discussed in Ann Arbor. The phone rang and a man said, "I have an arbitration for you." "Great," I responded. "Let me get out my pad." Then, he told me that the union and the employer had agreed on the decision. Imagine my surprise when that really happened. I turned the case down and after I hung up the phone, I thought, "Oh, my, the first one that comes and I turn it down."

I have since been called upon to serve as an arbitrator twice by that same lawyer. This was interesting, because I thought that lawyer might think that I was too rigid because that is the way it was put to me. When he inquired if I would do it, I said no. Then he said, "You are the new breed. You have been talking to those guys out in Ann Arbor," but I do not think he was surprised.

COMMENT: At least, that lawyer established to his own satisfaction that if the other side in the second case had come up to you and said, "We want to win this case," you would pay no attention to them.

LEADER: I think that is right, but it was interesting that my refusal did not change my acceptability.

QUESTION: How did Janet receive the GE-IUE cases when she completed the program? Is that what the parties usually try to do?

MR. BARRECA: The union and the company agreed that each of the individuals who successfully completed the first three phases of the program would be the arbitrator of record in three cases involving IUE and GE, and BNA said that they would publish those awards. However, it was not easy to schedule those cases. Even in the part of a program where participants were only observing, they would be scheduled to go somewhere for a case and they would then learn that the case had been settled or postponed. In fact, a training program has a broader impact, which is worth describing on the basis of Janet's experience, because in the course of the GE-IUE program, other opportunities opened up as Janet has described.

QUESTION: Janet, one of the things we have been talking about is different ways of packaging a working life. Rich Bloch told us that he works full-time out of his home and hears 160 cases a year. As a younger law professor for whom arbitration is an important activity, whether you put it first, second, or third, how do you see it fitting into the rest of your professional life? How much do you hope to do eventually?

LEADER: That is something I am not fixed about at the moment. Fortunately, my arbitration career came sufficiently late in my teaching career so that I can now handle more arbitrations. When I first began the GE-IUE training program, it was fortunate that I did not have more cases because I was very busy trying to teach my classes. As I have become more adept and more experienced in teaching, I have been freed-up to take on more arbitrations. Still, I have a limited number of days, and I am not even sure in my own mind how many arbitration cases I can comfortably handle and still do what I think is required of me as a law professor. Law professors usually have one or two free days in a week and I can schedule arbitration hearings on those days. However, one has to devote the time to writing opinions. One arbitrator told me he was scheduling two cases a week and teaching full time. He said that was too much, and he had to cut back.

I am not sure where arbitration fits into the rest of my professional life. There are times when I think arbitration is going to supplant my teaching eventually. At the moment it is a balance. I have four or five days scheduled each month and that is now an absolute maximum for me. I do not think I can absorb any more and still do everything else that I want to do, including care for my young family.

QUESTION: How do you handle the mechanics?

LEADER: I have just gotten sophisticated dictating and typing equipment in my home, and I have a typist come in on a free-lance basis. I do not have a secretary of my own at school, and I do not have enough confidence that I am going to have a steady flow of cases to justify committing myself to a part-time secretary.

QUESTION: Do you dictate your awards or write them out in longhand?

LEADER: I was writing them in longhand, but I got dictating equipment which I hope will revolutionize my life.

MR. ZACK: Having tried equipment, I still handwrite my awards. However, that is really a function of the way in which I handle a decision. Sixty or 70 percent of my cases involve plane trips, and I start writing the decision when I get on the plane, I find it easier for me to edit from a written document. I write it out, correct it, and edit it by hand. I feel very sorry for my secretary, but that is what she has to work with. I do not see the opinion again until it is time for proofreading. I might change 5 percent of the decisions after I see the opinion, so I find that this method saves me a lot of time.

QUESTION: Janet, when you look back at the program you went through at the University of Michigan, what would you delete and what would you add?

LEADER: One of the things that we did not have was a discussion about remedies. I would add that, because I think the procedural and ethical information—the opinions and how you approach the problems—are of most value.

QUESTION: How do you evaluate the followup to the GE-IUE training program, and what has happened so far?

LEADER: It is wonderful. This is a great opportunity to be able to arbitrate GE-IUE cases, which I would not have had otherwise. I understand that this aspect of the program is to help make us known to other parties and to get our decisions published. I have not had many of my decisions published, which is a whole aspect of being an arbitrator which befuddles me. I have had people say to me that I really should get my arbitration decisions published because that is what the parties look at. I do not know what to do about it. I wish somebody would tell me. I have not been submitting decisions for publication myself because I understand it is up to the parties.

MR. BARRECA: Publication is an important part of the acceptability process.

LEADER: How do I find out whether or not the parties agree to have my decision published?

MS. MILLER: An arbitrator should ask the parties for their written permission.

QUESTION: What about the AAA?

MR. BARRECA: AAA receives the award before the parties do. When AAA sends the award to the parties, there is a card with it which says, "May we have your permission to publish this award?" If they do not receive permission from both parties, they do not publish.

MR. SCHULTZ: There is a new service called Labor Relations Press and their intention is to index every arbitration decision. Each decision, whether published or not, will be indexed and accessible to the parties.

QUESTION: Does FMCS distribute the decision to the parties?

MR. SCHULTZ: When you have an FMCS case, the minute you get that letter of assignment, it is your case. You take care of anything directly with the parties including arrangements for the hearing. You even collect your own fees. You send in a final report to FMCS.

QUESTION: Janet, considering the fact that you are carrying on another career at the same time, what is your median time for writing an opinion and getting it to the parties?

LEADER: I do it within thirty days. I have had to ask for an extension only once.

QUESTION: Does it take thirty days?

LEADER: No, it does not take me thirty days to write the decision, but I usually do not get it out in much less than thirty days because of other responsibilities. At this point it does take me longer to write an opinion than I can bill. For example, I do not have the ability to write easily, which I am sure that a more experienced arbitrator has. I dictate a draft, study, edit it, and study it again. I feel that is part of the learning process.

QUESTION: What are your average study and preparation times compared to hearing days?

LEADER: One to one, but I may not charge a second whole day for study and preparation if I have had two full days of hearing.

QUESTION: Do you ever have any trouble getting your bills paid?

LEADER: The first case I had the company went bankrupt, and I never got paid. I have had times where pay was very slow, and I have some that are now three months in arrears.

QUESTION: Have you ever pursued them?

LEADER: Sometimes. The furthest I have gone is to send a letter to the party, following which I received payment.

MR. ZACK: I once caused a company to go bankrupt by deciding, when they had an enormous layoff, that they were liable for separation pay, which pushed them into bankruptcy, and which resulted in my not getting paid. I did not pursue that one. Out of 125 cases a year, I may have one or two parties which I will pursue after two or three months. I send letters, but I never threaten to do anything.

QUESTION: When you send out a letter after three months, do you send copies to the other side?

MR. ZACK: No, I do not, although some arbitrators I know say that works.

MR. BARRECA: If you do not get paid in a reasonable amount of time, I would urge you to send a letter because the problem usually is that the bill was lost in the bookkeeping process and not that a party refuses to pay.

MR. ZACK: More often it will happen on the union side, where the bill will get lost between the local and the international.

QUESTION: Do you charge a cancellation fee?

LEADER: This is something I have recently been considering. I have not up to now.

MR. ZACK: If time is of limited availability, an arbitrator should be compensated for the loss of that time. When first starting out, I would not use a cancellation fee. My practice originally was to charge a fee where the cancellation was less than one week before the hearing. Now my letter to the parties says, "You may be subject to a cancellation charge." I charge a cancellation fee on two weeks' notice. I do not get very many cancellations. The parties usually do cancel far in advance if they are going to cancel.

QUESTION: Are the parties sensitive about fees?

MR. BARRECA: Both management and union people generally do express concern about arbitrator fees as well as the other costs of arbitration.

QUESTION: In relationship to the one-day hearing, how many days for research and writing the opinion is normally charged?

LEADER: The average would be one to one.

MR. ZACK: I have more one and ones than I have anything else. Once in a while I will have a case that will go one to four, but that is very rare.

QUESTION: How long is a decision in your run-of-the-mill case?

MR. ZACK: Do not go by the length of the decision in determining study time because one can jack up a bill by just sitting there and writing out a repetition of all the testimony or long quotations from the contract. The parties are going to look at that and think that is the basis of the bill.

QUESTION: What is the average length of your award?

MR. ZACK: On average, my award is five to six pages. I believe very strongly in short awards for several reasons. I am concerned about the cost to the parties and more important, the less I say the fewer mistakes I will make and the less I will be challenged.

LEADER: On average, my awards are about ten or twelve pages. I feel an obligation to explain how I reached my decision. I feel I have to say why I found there is no merit. I wonder if one can write a shorter opinion if one is better known to the parties and they have more confidence in the arbitrator.

MR. FELLER: One has to sense a given situation. If a union has made a lot of arguments and has a lot of explaining to do to its members, an arbitrator has to spell out what they have argued, so that it is clear that the union has done its job. The same situation can occur on the employer's side. This is not always so; there is no pattern. An arbitrator should have a sense of the situation in the hearing as to whether or not he has to go through every argument and contention, making clear what was argued and why he rejects those arguments.

MR. BARRECA: Whether they won or lost, the parties are very much interested, for possible future use, in how a new arbitrator arrived at the decision. Even when they have lost, if they are satisfied with the logic of the decision, a new arbitrator stands a good chance of getting greater acceptability. On the other hand, if your opinion is not well-reasoned, a new arbitrator may not be selected again even by the party he ruled for.

MR. ZACK: Particularly if it is published.

QUESTION: Would you give the same response on study time if the parties each submitted a fifteen-page brief?

MR. ZACK: No, I might have an extra paragraph in my "Contentions of the Parties."

QUESTION: If a case has a stenographic record and extensive briefs, would the ratio normally remain one to one?

MR. ZACK: No, it would be more likely two to one. However, I do not charge a day for a transcript which I do not read. I usually have my decision written by the time the transcript comes, but I do have to pay attention to the briefs. If I receive a thirty-page brief and have a unique situation with many citations and both parties arguing the relevancy of particular cases which they claim are stare decisis involving those parties, I have to read those decisions. However, if I receive a brief in which someone has pulled out all the pertinent cases from *Labor Arbitration Reports*, volumes one through ten, I am not going to pay any attention to that.

QUESTION: When briefs have not been submitted, how much additional research do you do in terms of other arbitrators' opinions?

LEADER: It depends on the particular issue. I do some research usually, but not much.

QUESTION: Do collective bargaining agreements usually stipulate the choice of an arbitrator from a particular appointing agency list exclusive of the others?

MR. BARRECA: Very few contracts would be silent on the selection procedure. Contracts that are negotiated between a company and a union will usually specify the procedure for the selection of the arbitrator. Contracts with major companies involved in interstate commerce will normally specify either FMCS or AAA as the appointing agency. They select those two for different reasons. AAA provides certain kinds of administrative services which certain parties want and others do not want. The parties can also name their arbitrator in the contract.

Part III

A Review of Arbitrator Development and Training

It is indeed desirable to be well descended, but the glory belongs to our ancestors.

Plutarch

Creature of the Parties

In one of the now landmark 1960 trilogy of Steelworkers cases, Justice William O. Douglas lauded the function served by the labor arbitrator.

> The labor arbitrator is usually chosen because of the parties' confidence in his knowledge of the common law of the shop and their trust in his personal judgment to bring to bear considerations which are not expressed in the contract as criteria for judgment. The parties expect that his judgment of a particular grievance will reflect not only what the contract says but, insofar as the collective bargaining agreement permits, such factors as the effect upon productivity of a particular result, its consequence to the morale of the shop, his judgment whether tensions will be heightened or diminished. For the parties' objective in using the arbitration process is primarily to further their common goal of uninterrupted production under the agreement, to make the agreement serve their specialized needs. The ablest judge cannot be expected to bring the same experience and competence to bear upon the determination of a grievance, because he cannot be similarly informed.[1]

Although Fleming observed that labor arbitrators must have taken a second look at themselves in the mirror after reading this glowing description of their role,[2] it is not an overstatement to acknowledge the important role and responsibilities of the labor arbitrator in America. Jobs, tenure, promotion, compensation and, at times, even the survival of the enterprise are at stake in an award rendered by a labor arbitrator. The adjudication of a single grievance normally affects many other individuals. Contractual precedents may be established which will affect future collective relationships.

Nevertheless, unlike the well-established intellectual professions, labor arbitration lacks a formal course of clearly defined study. Any individual aspiring to be one can simply choose to be called a labor arbitrator. The reality of being a labor arbitrator is more complicated.

---

[1]*United Steelworkers of America v. Warrior and Gulf Navigation Co.*, 363 U.S. 574, 582, 46 LRRM 2416 (1960).

[2]R. Fleming, THE LABOR ARBITRATION PROCESS 24 (University of Illinois, 1965).

An individual must attain a status which results in his acceptability by the parties to make a final and binding determination of their dispute. Acceptability is the elusive aura, status, or quality that aspiring labor arbitrators seek, but few seem to attain. Acceptability can be described as that combination of practical experience and substantive knowledge coupled with a generous sprinkling of judgment, insight, and good luck which persuades both parties to a labor dispute to request a particular person to settle their dispute.

The following review of labor arbitrator training and development in the United States, with particular emphasis on formal programs, examines the history of labor arbitration and arbitrator training, and the structures, goals, and experience in increasing the acceptability of arbitrator trainees.

Although the origins of the American experience in labor arbitration can be traced to the latter part of the nineteenth century, little was written contemporaneously about labor arbitration or the qualifications of arbitrators. Binding third-party resolution of disputes between labor and management was uncommon and the procedural mechanisms and dynamics of the process were rudimentary.

Little information concerning arbitrator selection criteria can be gleaned from the early sources other than that the parties made a general search for educated and impartial individuals possessing the general qualities of fairness, experience in dispute resolution, and insight into human nature. During this early period there was a difference of opinion over whether the labor arbitrator should be someone far removed from the contending parties, their particular line of business and interests, or someone closely associated with the disputants and intimately familiar with their industry. Similarly, there were differences as to whether the arbitrator should be skilled in making sound economic judgments based upon a proper analysis of underlying facts or a facile bargainer versed in labor relations.[3]

The first employment of an outside neutral to make a binding determination in a labor dispute occurred in 1871 when the coal industry's Anthracite Board of Trade and the miners' Workingmen's Benevolent Association chose Pennsylvania Judge William Elwell as outside umpire to settle their dispute over concerted activity and employee discipline. Other reported instances of genuine third-party dispute resolution during this period are rare.

---

[3]*Compare* Taylor, *The Factual Approach to Industrial Arbitration*, ARB. J., O.S.2 (1938) *with* F. Kellor, ARBITRATION IN THE NEW INDUSTRIAL AGE 133–60 (McGraw-Hill, 1934).

While management and labor, on occasion, made provision for boards of arbitration, these were usually bipartite boards composed of representatives of the parties themselves. Few agreements provided initially for the employment of a neutral, but by the turn of the century many states and localities had established neutral arbitration boards, which functioned, for the most part, solely as mediation agencies. In retrospect, the infrequent resort by industry and labor to binding third-party determination of disputes was not surprising because during this period, companies were reluctant to recognize unions, much less agree to binding arbitration over the interpretation and application of contract terms.

Neutral arbitration remained infrequent in the early 1900s, except to promote industrial peace in such critical national industries as coal and the railroads. A notable exception was the establishment of a private arbitration mechanism in an agreement reached between newspaper publishers and the typographical union in 1901. A two-tiered appellate system of arbitration boards was established with provision for the inclusion of an impartial member chosen by the parties if they failed to agree. This approach was subsequently widely adopted throughout the printing industry.

Protocol of Peace

A significant development in the establishment of labor arbitration followed a long and bitter strike in the New York cloak and suit industry in 1910 with the establishment of permanent machinery for conciliation and arbitration as part of a protocol of peace designed by Louis D. Brandeis, who subsequently served as the impartial chairman of the arbitration board. Although the settlement collapsed in 1916 as a result of an industry-wide strike-lockout, the protocol's impact became the foundation for a comprehensive system of binding arbitration, which continues to function successfully in the ladies garment industry. The 1911 agreement between the Amalgamated Clothing Workers of America and Hart, Schaffer and Marx, then the largest producer of men's clothing in the country, was modeled after the protocol and established negotiation and arbitration machinery which endures to this day. Sidney Hillman, later president of the Amalgamated Clothing Workers of America, sponsored arbitration machinery similar to the protocol in other cities in the United States and Canada which included an impartial chairman on the arbitration board who was familiar with the industry.

Early Government Intervention

Concurrent with private efforts to develop labor arbitration machinery, public efforts resulted in the creation of the United States Conciliation Service within the Department of Labor in 1913. Although it was primarily a mediation agency, the Conciliation Service could suggest arbitration and name or assist the parties in selecting arbitrators. More than a dozen new labor dispute agencies were established during World War I, the most important being the War Labor Board, which was empowered to intervene in most domestic labor disputes affecting war production.

Rights and Interests

During the 1920s and early 1930s, labor arbitration machinery remained primarily centered in a few industries such as the garment, hosiery, and bookbinding industries. In this period, the line between arbitration of rights under an existing contract and interest arbitration was blurred. Landis observed:

> Most arbitrators still did not clearly differentiate between grievance and interest arbitration. . . . In most situations when arbitration was called for, the parties generally appointed a permanent arbitrator to settle all disputes arising during the life of their agreement. The popular present-day practice of selecting a different ad hoc arbitrator for each case that arises was uncommon. Since most of the arbitrators of this period had a close, continuing relationship with the parties, it consequently was easy for them to become involved with interest disputes as well as with questions of contract interpretation.[4]

American Arbitration Association

As commercial arbitration became more popular, labor arbitration gained in acceptability. Following passage of the Wagner Act in 1935 and the Supreme Court's *Jones & Laughlin* decision[5] upholding its constitutionality, there was a dramatic increase in the demand for labor arbitration and arbitrators. In response, The American Arbitration Association established in 1937 a voluntary industrial tribunal, maintained a panel of labor arbitrators available to the parties, and recommended model arbitration clauses for inclusion in agreements.

---

[4]B. Landis, VALUE JUDGMENTS IN ARBITRATION: A CASE STUDY OF SAUL WALLEN 3–4 (New York State School of Industrial Relations, Cornell University, 1977).
[5]*NLRB v. Jones & Laughlin Steel Co.*, 301 U.S. 1, 1 LRRM 703 (1937).

National War Labor Board

World War II established labor arbitration as a fixture in the American industrial workplace. To avoid industrial strife disruptive of the war effort, President Roosevelt created the National War Labor Board by Executive Order and gave it ultimate authority to settle any disputes within its jurisdiction by mediation, voluntary arbitration, or arbitration under its rules. The War Labor Board encouraged the parties to include grievance arbitration clauses in their collective bargaining agreements by strict interpretation of agreements to arbitrate and limitations on the scope of authority of arbitrators.

> Where it was reasonably clear that the arbitration clauses meant to exclude a subject from arbitral review, the NWLB denied arbitration. The only exception was the issue of discharge for cause, which the board held arbitrable regardless of the contract language. Where the arbitration clause failed to define adequately the arbitrator's jurisdiction and a dispute later arose, the board's policy was to confine jurisdiction to disputes over working conditions or the interpretation of specific contract language. The NWLB made it clear that the arbitrator could not modify, alter, or amend contract language. It further specifically defined grievance arbitration as a judicial process, limited in jurisdiction and limited to an award based solely on the evidence presented at a hearing.[6]

The Final Report of the Conciliation Service in 1947 illustrated the growth in the number of voluntary arbitrations during the years. From less than 200 arbitrators appointed by the Service in 1940, the report showed the wartime annual average exceeding 1000.[7]

In evaluating this increase in arbitrator appointments, Fleming wrote:

> In retrospect it is clear that World War II did three things insofar as voluntary arbitration is concerned. First of all, it encouraged widespread adoption of arbitration techniques. Second, it sharpened the distinction between arbitration over 'rights' and 'interests' . . . . Finally the War Labor Board served as a training ground for the men who subsequently served as arbitrators. This cadre has ever since constituted the hard core of the arbitration profession. Without the understanding which they brought to the job it is possible that grievance arbitration would have been less readily accepted.[8]

---

[6]*Supra* note 4, at 5–6.
[7]FINAL REPORT OF DIRECTOR OF CONCILIATION [E.L. Warren] TO SECRETARY OF LABOR [L.B. Schwellenbach], 11–12 (August 21, 1947) (available from Federal Mediation and Conciliation Service).
[8]*Supra* note 2, at 19.

When the National Academy of Arbitrators was established in 1947, its founding members were primarily the graduates of the War Labor Board. Given the opportunity to serve in a neutral capacity, their wartime experiences were crucial to their later acceptability as arbitrators.

Chronicle of Training and Development

The American Arbitration Association convened a conference on the state of the art of dispute resolution training at the Johnson Foundation's Wingspread Center in June 1977 at which Edwin R. Teple reviewed the American experience in the development of labor arbitrators after World War II, and some of the principal architects of labor arbitrator development efforts described their particular programs. Part of Teple's review and the separate program descriptions are reprinted here* because these papers personalize the training efforts and capture the continuity as well as the chronology of events from 1946 through mid-1977.

American Experience in the Development of Labor Arbitrators

Edwin R. Teple

Since the demise of the War Labor Board after World War II, there has been nothing similar in scope or significance in the United States to the accomplishments of the Board program in the development of labor arbitrators. From time to time there have been sections of the country in which a shortage of labor arbitrators appeared imminent. In 1961, the Arbitration Committee of the Labor Relations Law Section of the American Bar Association issued a report on the development of arbitrators and recommended a pilot program for training new arbitrators, supplemented by a panel of labor and management representatives who would try to induce the parties to accept the people trained in such a program. Little was done at that time, however.[1] Since then, more than

---

*DISPUTE RESOLUTION TRAINING: THE STATE OF THE ART (Selected Proceedings of the Second Wingspread Conference, June 9–10, 1977) (AAA, 1978).
[1]*Report of the Committee on the Development of New Arbitrators*, in ARBITRATION AND THE PUBLIC

a dozen formal training programs have been instituted in the United States, with varying degrees of success.

The first of these was attempted in Chicago in 1962, under the auspices of a training committee established by the National Academy of Arbitrators (NAA), and in conjunction with the American Arbitration Association (AAA) and the Federal Mediation and Conciliation Service (FMCS). The program began with 14 candidates and ended with 10. Candidates attended a one-day training institute and then observed hearings conducted by members of the Academy. Only a few prepared their own awards for review by the arbitrator.[2] The next training program, conducted in Pittsburgh in 1963, followed a somewhat similar pattern. Seven candidates were selected.[3] There have been no reports that either of these early programs resulted in the achievement of significant acceptability as labor arbitrators by those who took part.

A training program was undertaken in Cleveland in 1965, sponsored by the AAA and the FMCS, with the full cooperation of the National Academy. There were nine candidates in this group initially, but three did not finish the program. The primary method of training was basically similar to the Chicago program, with indoctrination sessions at the Cleveland Regional Office of the AAA and attendance at hearings conducted by experienced arbitrators. More of an effort was made in this instance to have the candidates submit practice opinions and awards, based on their own notes of the hearings they attended, after awards were issued by the arbitrators. Six candidates were recognized as having completed the program at a jointly sponsored dinner held in Cleveland and attended by representatives of labor and management. The results in this instance were outstanding, due in large part to the exposure the candidates received on AAA and FMCS lists. Five of them are now members of the Academy, and a sixth member of the group had heard several labor cases at the time he became the full-time executive secretary of the Cleveland Bar Association and could no longer handle arbitration work.

A second training program was instituted in Cleveland in 1971 with the regional office of the AAA and the National Academy cooperating. One of the chief purposes of this new Cleveland program was to obtain female and minority candidates, but only one woman and one black

---

INTEREST, (Proceedings of the 24th Annual Meeting, National Academy of Arbitrators) 309–10 (BNA Books, 1971).

[2] *Report of the Committee on the Training of New Arbitrators*, in LABOR ARBITRATION: PERSPECTIVES AND PROBLEMS, (Proceedings of the 17th Annual Meeting, National Academy of Arbitrators) 322–24 (BNA Books, 1964).

[3] *Ibid.*, pp. 326–27.

(male) enrolled. Heavy reliance was again placed on attendance at hearings conducted by experienced arbitrators, mostly members of the Academy, arranged through the Cleveland Office of the AAA. This was supplemented by a full semester course at the law school of Case Western Reserve University. Eighteen people were enrolled in the course, all but one of whom were lawyers; two had been in the first Cleveland program. Seven members of the Academy participated in the course lectures. Twelve of the candidates attended one or more hearings, one of them observing six different cases. The 12 who completed this program were recognized at a luncheon during a two-day arbitration seminar jointly sponsored by the Cleveland Bar Association, AAA, and the Academy.

Acceptance of the candidates in this second Cleveland group has not been as spectacular as with the first group, despite the fact that several of them had limited experience as labor arbitrators before the program was initiated. The black candidate, however, is now a member of the Academy, several others are serving regularly on expedited labor panels, and the general acceptance of at least five is gaining rapidly.

The St. Louis Bar Association, in conjunction with FMCS and AAA, conducted a training program in 1970 based mainly on attendance at hearings with experienced arbitrators. There has been no report concerning the formal completion of this program. A training program was conducted in Philadelphia in 1971 with 15 candidates who received a one-day training session at Temple University, followed by attendance at hearings conducted by experienced arbitrators and a final reception to meet management and labor people; there has been no evidence of firm results from this effort, either. [4] Two training programs were conducted in the state of New York during 1971. One of these was jointly sponsored by the AAA and the International Association of Machinists, which cooperated in the selection of 18 candidates who were given a three-day seminar for orientation, after which arrangements were made for attendance at hearings with experienced arbitrators. This group had limited experience as arbitrators before the program, mostly in the public sector. Twelve of the candidates attended hearings and wrote one or more practice awards for review by the arbitrators of record. One of the candidates in this program achieved wide acceptance and is now a

---

[4] McDermott, *Evaluation of Programs Seeking to Develop Arbitrator Acceptability*, in ARBITRATION—1974 (Proceedings of the 27th Annual Meeting, National Academy of Arbitrators) 342 (BNA Books, 1975); Proceedings of the 24th Annual Meeting, *op. cit.*, 311; and McDermott, *Activities Directed at Advancing the Acceptability of New Arbitrators*, in LABOR ARBITRATION AT THE QUARTER-CENTURY MARK (Proceedings of the 25th Annual Meeting, National Academy of Arbitrators) 337 (BNA Books, 1973).

member of the Academy, while six others have been receiving increased acceptance in the public sector.[5]

The Western New York State Arbitration Program
1971–1972

Jean T. McKelvey
Alice B. Grant

The Western New York Arbitrator Development Program evolved through the cooperation of the New York State School of Industrial and Labor Relations at Cornell University, the American Arbitration Association, the Federal Mediation and Conciliation Service, the National Academy of Arbitrators, and the Western New York Chapter of the Industrial Relations Research Association.

The need for such a program was discussed initially during the May 1971 Annual Meeting of the National Academy of Arbitrators in Boston. Representatives of the AAA and the FMCS reported to the Academy's Committee on the Training of New Arbitrators on the shortage of available and acceptable arbitrators in the Western New York area. On June 8, 1971, a meeting held at the General Counsel's Office in Washington was attended by Thomas J. McDermott, Seymour Strongin, and Jean T. McKelvey, along with Joseph S. Murphy of the AAA, and William Kilberg, L. Lawrence Schultz, and James Power of the FMCS. At this meeting the basic structure for the initiation of the Western New York program was discussed and tentatively adopted.

It was determined that the training program would be confined to the Western New York area, including Buffalo, Syracuse, and Rochester. One part of the program was to consist of academic training under the direction of Jean McKelvey and Alice Grant from Cornell's School of Industrial and Labor Relations. A second part of the program would involve the assignment of the candidates to hearings with experienced arbitrators who have cases in the general area. These arbitrators would be asked to work as closely as possible with the candidates through discussions and through critical evaluations of the decisions that the candidates would prepare from their own notes and submit to the arbitrator after the actual decision had been released to the parties.

---

[5]Proceedings of the 24th Annual Meeting, *op. cit.*, 312–13; Proceedings of the 25th Annual Meeting, *op. cit.*, 336.

In August 1971 the Chairman of the Committee for the Development of New Arbitrators circularized 99 Academy members in New York State and in the contiguous regions of Philadelphia, Pittsburgh, and Cleveland to secure the names of individual arbitrators who would assist in the training program. Specifically, the members were asked if they would agree to have the selected candidates sit in on their hearings, and whether following the hearings they would spend some time with the candidates answering questions and discussing some of the procedural matters that might have arisen. They were also asked if they would at a later date review decisions written by the candidates. The willingness of members to cooperate in this program was excellent. Of the 99 surveyed, 57 offered their services. Of those who declined, several wrote their regrets, for reasons of health, or not being available at that time for arbitration, or because their activities were limited and they would not, therefore, be in the Western New York area.

Meanwhile, the Western New York Chapter of the IRRA had established a joint Labor-Management Committee to process applications for admission to the program and to formulate criteria for selecting the twenty most promising candidates. The Committee consisted of seven attorneys active in representing company and union clients, plus 20 others, who were union or company representatives; it was under the direction of Robert R. Logan, President of the IRRA Chapter and Secretary of the Western New York Master Builders Association.

Applications were received from over 100 persons. Copies of all résumés were circulated among all members of the Labor-Management Committee, who were requested to list 25 choices in preferential order on the basis of criteria established by a Criteria Committee. These lists were then turned over to a special subcommittee of four members, who had the task of narrowing the group to 20 candidates.

The criteria used for the selection of candidates were as follows:

AGE: Every consideration and encouragement should be given to younger individuals who have some experience or to those in older age brackets who have an immediate chance of acceptability because of their standing in the labor relations community.

EXPERIENCE: At least five years experience in labor-management relations with labor, management or both, including exposure to a wide range of labor relations problems and activities; appropriate government service in the labor field; college-level teaching experience in pertinent subjects including labor relations, collective bargaining, labor law, and related subjects. Consideration should also be given to experience in research in labor relations fields or in educational or nonprofit organizations having contact with the labor relations community. Education degrees in industrial relations, law, personnel, management, industrial engineering, or related fields, or the equivalent in training or experience. Actual degrees are unnecessary in instances where there is appropriate and extensive experience in diversified phases of labor relations work; e.g., 10 years as a union representative, labor relations representative, or a combination of both.

OCCUPATION: Candidates should normally be selected from those currently engaged in (1) labor relations and/or related industrial relations work, (2) attorneys with an interest and experience in labor relations, or (3) educators with qualifications and experience in teaching labor relations and collective bargaining and related industrial relations courses. Before final selection of any candidate, determination should be made that the individual will be available as required for training and subsequent use as an arbitrator with no remuneration during training.

GEOGRAPHICAL AREA: Candidates for the recruitment program should be located in the Western New York State area, preferably in the Rochester, Jamestown, Buffalo, Syracuse, Ithaca, and Niagara Falls area.

NON-DISCRIMINATION: In consideration and selection of applicants there shall be no discrimination based upon race, creed, color, national origin, age, or sex.

WAIVER: In those instances where a candidate's total qualifications are clearly exceptional, yet in fact do not meet each of the listed criteria, the Selection Committee may, by unanimous vote, find such candidates to be qualified for the training program.

This set of criteria was based upon specific proposals made by the AAA and the FMCS to the Subcommittee on Criteria.

A profile of the 20 arbitrator designates finally selected for this program is as follows: The accent was on youth, as arbitrators go, with one person under 30, eleven between 30 and 35, two between 35 and 40, and six between 40 and 50. One female and two blacks were among those selected. A large majority, 14, were nonattorneys. Of the six with legal backgrounds, three were practicing attorneys, while the other three were full-time law school faculty. Nine candidates were from university faculties. In general, the group presented very impressive credentials for a program of this nature.

Although nine of the designates were listed on an appointing agency panel of arbitrators, most of them with the Public Employment Relations Board of New York, only six had had any prior arbitration, fact-finding, or mediation experience. Two of these had had a few arbitration cases in the public sector, and two had had a few in the private sector.

Before their selection was announced, and in order to stimulate interest in the program and commitment to its success on the part of the industrial relations community in Western New York, the IRRA Chapter sponsored an all-day conference on labor arbitration in Buffalo on October 15, 1971. Participating in the program were George Hildebrand and Jean McKelvey of the ILR School, Professor Bernard Meltzer, and arbitrators Lewis Gill and Jacob Seidenberg. Joseph Murphy spoke for the AAA and Lawrence Schultz for the FMCS. The conference was attended by over 500 persons and generated extensive and favorable publicity in the press.

The academic program, which consisted of eight monthly full-day seminars conducted on Saturdays either in Rochester or Buffalo, began in February 1972 and ended in December 1972. Each session covered a different aspect of the arbitration process and featured visiting speakers, panel discussions, role-playing, and the use of audio-visual material. Two text books and mimeographed cases comprised the reading assigned as preparation for each session. Among the topics covered were labor-management responsibility in arbitration, legal aspects of contemporary arbitration, the use of evidence, the arbitrator's award, past practice, contract construction, mediation-arbitration, what labor and management look for in an arbitration case, seniority versus ability, arbitrator misconduct, how to write an award, fees and charges, due process, remedy power, and public sector arbitration.

To supplement the academic program, each candidate was required to attend a minimum of six arbitration sessions and to complete six mock awards. The administration of this part of the program, which included the notifying of the designates, the obtaining of clearances from the parties, and practically all other details, was carried out by Samuel Sackman, Commissioner of Conciliation, Buffalo Office of FMCS, and Robert E. Meade, then Regional Director, AAA, Syracuse (now AAA Regional Director, New York City area). The latter was responsible for administration of cases in the Rochester-Syracuse area, while the former handled assignments in the Buffalo area. For FMCS appointments, three postcards were sent to the cooperating arbitrator along with a notice of appointment. One was to be used by the arbitrator to notify the appropriate office of the date for the hearing. A second was to be used should that hearing subsequently be cancelled, and a third was for notification by the arbitrator of the date of release of the decision.

The designate's decision was routed through the administrative offices and sent to the arbitrator. A relatively simple evaluation form, which the arbitrator was asked to complete, accompanied the decision.

In addition to the arbitrator's own evaluation, the awards were appraised by Jean McKelvey, Alice Grant, Joseph Murphy, and Lawrence Schultz before they were returned to the trainees.

What were the program's results and how was it regarded by the participants? Seven of the original 20 dropped out of the program during 1972 either because of job transfers, relocation outside the area, or lack of time to fulfill the program requirements. Two of the latter are still hoping to complete the field assignments.

By May 1973 thirteen had successfully completed all phases of the training program, ensuring that their names would be placed on the AAA, FMCS, and PERB rosters of arbitrators. About half of this group were also selected for the special expedited panels set up by the steelworkers and textile workers. Several hundred representatives of the industrial relations community attended the graduation ceremonies held in Buffalo on May 21, 1973. Before the evening was over, one of the graduates had been offered and accepted a permanent umpireship in a large industrial plant in the area. (He had, fortuitously, sat at a table with the union and management representatives from the plant in question.)

Three and a half years later, by the end of 1976, ten of the graduates had gained acceptance as arbitrators and reported a steadily increasing case load. (One of these has just died.) One achieved meteoric success and is now a member of the National Academy of Arbitrators.

Of the three who have not yet gained acceptability, two were out of the area for a year on sabbatical leave and one is well known as a management advocate.*

The thirteen graduates of the program were asked to evaluate it in a questionnaire sent to them in 1974 by C. Richard Miserendino, then a graduate student at the New York State School of Industrial and Labor Relations. Mr. Miserendino concluded that:

> "The participants' opinion of the program was very favorable and its continuation was stongly recommended. The stated objectives of the course corresponded with the outcome. The mock awards and field experience were thought to be an extremely valuable part of the program.

---

*Further details on the progress of each graduate can be found in the annual reports of the Committee on the Training of Arbitrators published in National Academy of Arbitrators Proceedings from 1974 to 1977.

"The major criticisms were as follows:

(1) The program did not adequately deal with the legal aspects of the arbitration process. It was felt that more emphasis should have been placed on the basic legal concepts of contract interpretation, due process, admission of evidence, and labor law.

(2) The arbitrators' criticisms of the mock awards were superficial. Adequate constructive criticism of each participant's awards was lacking.

"Minor criticism: The program could have been more structured in terms of session to session assignments."

As a result of these evaluations the program planners had a follow-up seminar for the alumni(ae) in 1975 to discuss legal problems confronting arbitrators—a subject which many thought had been slighted in the seminar presentations. More such "reunions" are planned for the future.

On the whole, the sponsors of the program are pleased with the results. Whatever success the graduates have achieved is attributable in our opinion to the careful planning which preceded the program, the cooperation of the appointing agencies, and the sponsorship of the labor-management community.

The University of California at Los Angeles U.S. Department of Labor Program for Mediators, Fact-finders, and Arbitrators 1972–1973

Paul Prasow

From July 1972 through June 1973, the UCLA Institute of Industrial Relations cooperated with the U.S. Department of Labor in conducting an extensive training program for third-party neutrals: persons who serve as mediators, fact-finders, and arbitrators in impasse resolution in both the public and private sectors. Also working on the project were the American Arbitration Association, the Federal Mediation and Conciliation Service, and the California State Conciliation Service. The agencies were on an advisory committee for the program.

Twenty-two participants were selected from among some 80 applicants by a tripartite steering committee, composed of labor and management representatives from the public and private sectors, and neutral experts in mediation, fact-finding, and arbitration. Evaluation and selection were based on criteria which emphasized broad experience in labor-management relations. In terms of their subsequent acceptability to serve as neutrals, the committee would have preferred persons not currently engaged in either labor or management representation; a sufficient number of such nonpartisan candidates, however, was not available. In some cases, therefore, the committee's choice was between nonpartisans with little or no labor relations background and advocates (namely, labor or management representatives) with extensive relevant experience. After deciding that experience in the collective bargaining process was the most important criterion for selection, the committee chose 22 participants for the training program, including those who were serving as representatives of management or labor. The candidates selected may be classified as follows:

Age		*Sex*		*Race*		*Professional Background*	
28–35	: 7	Female	: 5	Caucasian	: 14	Management	: 7
36–46	: 8	Male	: 17	Black	: 8	Labor	: 4
47+	: 7					Attorneys	: 5
						Other	: 6

The content of this comprehensive one-year program was developed with the assistance of the steering committee and included classroom seminars as well as experiential involvement. Approximately 30 evening seminars were held weekly on various aspects of labor-management relations. These sessions, conducted by leading experts in labor-management relations, were concerned with providing a thorough understanding of the mediation, fact-finding, and arbitration processes. The second phase emphasized experiential training. The participants attended actual mediation, fact-finding, and arbitration sessions conducted by professionals, and then prepared written opinions that were evaluated by the faculty in private consultation with each student. In addition, the entire group took part in several simulated fact-finding and arbitration sessions.

Since July 1973, a number of the participants have been placed on lists of neutrals maintained by various administrative agencies, including the American Arbitration Association (Labor Panel and Public Employment Disputes Settlement Panel), the Federal Mediation and Conciliation Service, the California State Conciliation Service, the Los Angeles County Employee Relations Commission, and the Los Angeles City Employee Relations Board. It is hoped that eventually all graduates of the program will be included on the panels of the FMCS, CSCS, and AAA. Although the formal training program was completed on June 30,

1973, the Institute staff continues to work with the graduates. Thus, selected faculty members meet with them on both a group and an individual basis to give counseling and to render assistance as needed. The Institute also maintains a close working relationship with the appointing agencies, as well as with union, association, and employer representatives to encourage selection of the graduates as third party neutrals. In addition, "practitioner luncheons" are scheduled periodically, at which labor and management representatives gather to meet informally with the graduates. Some of the graduates have participated as instructors in Institute training programs, and many are now members of the Society of Professionals in Dispute Resolution (SPIDR) and take part in regional activities of that organization.

The University of California at Berkeley Minority Neutral Training Project 1972–1973

John L. Bonner

In April 1972, the Institute of Industrial Relations at the University of California, Berkeley, submitted a proposal for "Training Neutrals for the Public Sector." The project was in cooperation with the American Arbitration Association, the Federal Mediation and Conciliation Service, the National Center for Dispute Settlement (now AAA's Community Dispute Services), and the California State Conciliation Service.

The project had three major objectives: to train effective, acceptable neutrals to meet the increasing demand in public sector labor relations, to open the occupation to minorities and women, and to determine the feasibility and effectiveness of one particular kind of training format.

These objectives rested on the assumption that trainees will be perceived by adversaries in a public sector labor dispute to be "acceptable" primarily as a result of demonstrated performance in the Institute program and in counterpart practice.

The Institute's central objective was to create and evaluate a pilot training project designed not only to produce a continuing supply of public sector neutrals, but also to show that minorities and women represent an untapped source of competent, acceptable neutrals.

The project had three phases: formal classroom training (four months); counterpart (apprenticeship) training (five months); and a referral system (three months).

Because the selection procedure was expected to result in trainees with different levels of education and experience, they anticipated the need to be flexible in their time allocations. The classroom training was scheduled for 102 hours; as much as 216 additional classroom hours could be added to the curriculum as necessary or desired.

Counterpart training was to be about 160 hours, with the trainees serving as observers or assistants in dispute settlement forums or in meetings or work sessions in a wide variety of dispute situations. It was planned to use both collective bargaining disputes and community disputes as training vehicles. Trainees would work with advocates, as well as with neutrals.

Trainees were to be selected from the 25 to 40 age group; females were favored over males; minority groups were favored; and participants had to be high school graduates or have the equivalent education, with some training in labor relations or experience in adversary proceedings. Fifteen trainees and five alternates were to be selected.

Some early problems developed when it became apparent that the FMCS and NCDS were not really wired into the project. FMCS indicated that neutrals with questionable credentials would not be added to their panel. NCDS expressed some doubts about Berkeley's ability to do the job, since Berkeley's prior experience had been with advocates. NCDS also questioned the heavy emphasis on arbitration.

Following considerable publicity in minority communities, 562 applications were received. These were screened and reduced to 120 individuals, who were then interviewed. Seventeen candidates were ultimately chosen. Nine were male; eight, female. The racial breakdown was seven black, three Oriental, three Hispanic, one Indian, and three white. Five were attorneys, four had master's degrees, six had bachelor's, and only two were nongraduates. Only two of the candidates (both female) had previous labor relations experience.

It became apparent early in the project that a more extensive follow-up effort would be required than was anticipated or could be performed by the Institute. Accordingly, we encouraged AAA to assume this responsibility.

A second year contract with AAA provided (1) a referral system, (2) a promotional system, (3) a review system to identify and correct weaknesses of the graduates, and (4) a prestige agency to enhance acceptability.

The anticipated outcome of the follow-up contract was that all of the graduates would be fully qualified and at least 10 of the 17 would become fully accepted and substantially utilized as neutrals.

As a matter of fact, the contract anticipated the need for a considerable amount of "propping up" of the graduates. It proposed to (1) fully assess each graduate's weaknesses, (2) develop a plan of action to remedy the weaknesses, (3) arrange with arbitrators and parties to use the graduates, (4) arrange for an arbitrator to attend the hearings of the first two cases of each graduate, (5) review the decision in these first two cases, (6) use these reviews and interviews with the graduates for devising continuing training assistance, and (7) provide other efforts as necessary.

AAA further agreed to place each graduate on its panel and to make "special efforts" to obtain the first two or three cases for them. Thereafter, they would have the same status on the panel as any other "fully qualified professional neutral."

There were numerous early indications that the program was floundering. The graduates were grumbling about lack of assistance in obtaining work. There was a feeling that not all of the graduates were qualified. There was grousing about lack of involvement from the "cooperating agencies." Support from using agencies all but disappeared. AAA was processing applications for its panel and was hedging about putting them all on. FMCS refused entry to their panel. Four of the graduates dropped out.

The final report from AAA claimed little success. Only five of the graduates had been placed on its panel; two others had received some work as neutrals. Many of the remaining graduates were labeled as lacking in aggressiveness (did not apply for the panel or did not attend seminars and conferences for contacts and exposure). Others were identified as being too advocate oriented to gain acceptability as neutrals. There was no information on, and no apparent attempt to determine, the impact that the selection of minorities and females may have had on the outcome of the program.

The report identified a number of problems encountered by the project. Most of them were already known to us; none should have been insurmountable. The most significant new piece of information in the final report was that "the San Francisco Bay Area was a poor choice of locale to fund such a pilot program, because there is definitely no shortage of qualified labor arbitrators [in that area]. If anything, I would say there is an overabundance of highly qualified neutrals. There is perhaps no place in the United States that has such a high concentration of neutrals. The funding of this program should not have been predicated upon an immediate need for neutrals in this area. . . ."

There were several differences between the Berkeley and the UCLA (Prasow, pp. 253–55) projects. At UCLA, the cooperating agencies (AAA, FMCS, and the California State Conciliation Service) were also on the advisory committee, thus involving them in the planning and execution of the project and also committing them to help make it succeed. The project's primary focus was on the training rather than on the trainee. This would provide different criteria for measuring success even though the two programs looked a lot alike.

There was no referral component in the UCLA project. It was expected that "each prospective neutral satisfactorily completing the prescribed program of academic and field training would be placed on the lists of various appointing and selection agencies. . . ." UCLA's selection process also differed significantly from Berkeley's. UCLA used the standards set forth by the National Academy of Arbitrators. It enhanced its chances of success by seeking out the best qualified candidates. Another difference in approach was that UCLA covered mediation and fact-finding as well as arbitration. Also, the program was concentrated exclusively on the public sector as opposed to Berkeley's emphasis on community disputes.

In the final report, it was indicated that all 22 graduates would be placed on the AAA and the California State panels. FMCS had also indicated a willingness to cooperate. A number of the graduates were already on the Los Angeles City and County boards' panels.

Much of the success of the program was attributed to the continuing involvement of the tripartite Advisory Panel. In the area of problems, they felt underbudgeted and short of time. As in the Berkeley program, there was also the need for a follow-up contract. It was primarily for evaluation, group and individual conferences, general "hand-holding," and a continuing placement effort.

It is tempting to evaluate programs such as these solely on the numbers of graduates who are now successful, practicing neutrals. It is also tempting to take full credit for those who made it. Neither approach is completely fair. But they are nevertheless important indicators.

Each project generated six to eight people who are still "active" in the field to some degree, some on a full-time basis. Both projects had trouble with the people who were too heavily advocate-oriented. These people were simply unable to cut their financial ties to enhance their prospects of being hired as neutrals. There were, however, some spin-off benefits attributable to the programs. At Berkeley, three of the graduates have become judges, three of the women are in law school and may reenter the field, and one person is in General Electric's apprenticeship program for neutrals.

At UCLA, one person is now a judge, one was hired by the Institute, one is a member of the California PERB, and one is a member of the San Diego PERB. And most interesting—the assistant project director, as a direct result of his participation in the program, is now a full-time practicing neutral.

The General Electric Company
International Union of Electrical, Radio and Machine Workers (AFL-CIO) Labor Arbitrator Development Program 1975–1976

Theodore J. St. Antoine
Michael F. Hoellering
L. Lawrence Schultz

The academic portion of this program was administered by the Institute of Continuing Legal Education at the University of Michigan. The Institute is the continuing education arm of the University of Michigan Law School, Wayne State University Law School, and the State Bar of Michigan.

Administrative support was provided by the American Arbitration Association and the Federal Mediation and Conciliation Service, the International Union of Electrical, Radio and Machine Workers (AFL-CIO), the General Electric Company, and the G.E.-IUE panel of contract arbitrators.

The Institute was responsible for the employment of the academic director and faculty. It was also responsible for making arrangements for physical facilities, publications, and the housing of trainees while in Ann Arbor. Theodore J. St. Antoine, Dean and Professor of Law, Law School, University of Michigan, served as academic director of the program. Austin G. Anderson, Director of the Institute of Continuing Legal Education, University of Michigan, served as the administrative director.

The program was divided into three phases. Phase one involved the selection of trainees. Fifteen trainees participated. Candidates were nominated on the basis of experience, education, and potential for development as an arbitrator. Experience as an arbitrator was not required, nor was legal training. The program was not announced nationally; recruitment, however, was conducted nationwide. One-third of the group of 15 trainees were women and minorities. The procedure followed found the FMCS and the AAA each submitting a preliminary list of 50 candidates. From the initial list of 100, the IUE and General Electric jointly recommended 30 "qualified" candidates to the academic director, who selected the 15 trainees to be enrolled in the program. Although he selected from the list submitted, the academic director retained the right to select persons not included on the list of 30.

Phase two included two weeks of academic training in Ann Arbor. The first one-week training session was offered from September 29 through October 3, 1975. (See Appendix A at the end of this paper for the curriculum.) The second in-residence session of two and one-half days duration was held September 27–29, 1976. (See Appendix B, also at the end. Appendix C contains a model curriculum.) The intervening period was used to provide the trainees with field experience. These arrangements were handled by the office of the Vice President for Case Administration at AAA. The trainees observed at least two, and up to five, arbitration proceedings to give them exposure to various approaches used by arbitrators. Each trainee prepared mock awards for at least two of the hearings. These awards were critiqued first by the arbitrators who conducted the hearings and later by Jean T. McKelvey and Theodore J. St. Antoine, following which they were discussed in the second week in-residence session. The first week's curriculum introduced the trainees to labor arbitration, philosophy, and procedures. The second week's curriculum built upon both the first week's academic training and the trainee's field experience. The faculty included leading labor arbitrators and law school faculty with expertise in labor arbitration.

Phase three provided for each trainee who completed the program to be assigned by the AAA as the arbitrator of record to three actual nonprecedential cases (designated by the parties). Awards were submitted to the various services for publication.

The budget for the full-year's course was $70,029.10. The enthusiastic response of both the participants and the sponsoring organizations and the selection of some of the candidates as arbitrators by parties in other cases testify to the fact that the program was a success. Each of the elements of the program (involved cosponsors, limited number of committed students, the effective use of both academic and on-the-job training) contributed to this achievement. Each is a necessary ingredient in such a program. Finally, academic direction must be provided by an authority in the labor field (who, in this instance, was Dean St. Antoine). This insures a carefully designed program, personal knowledge of prospective faculty members, and recognition by the sponsors. When combined, these elements will insure a meaningful educational exercise.

Appendix A: Curriculum for First Training Session

Historical Background and Legal Framework

(1) Growth of arbitration in the U.S. and elsewhere
(2) Grievance or rights arbitration; interest or new contract arbitration
(3) Private sector and public sector
(4) Common law and state statutes
(5) The Railway Labor Act
(6) §301 of the Taft-Hartley Act
    (a) Federal substantive law: *Lincoln Mills*
    (b) Arbitrability and judicial review: *Warrior* and the Trilogy
    (c) Arbitration as a prerequisite to suit: *Atkinson; Drake Bakeries; Boys Markets*
    (d) Relationship to courts and NLRB: *C & C Plywood, Collyer, Gardner-Denver, Electronic Service Reproduction Corporation*

Selection and Appointment of Arbitrators

(1) Appointing Agencies
    (a) Procedures
    (b) Rules and regulations
    (c) Relationship with arbitrators
    (d) Objectives
(2) The Arbitrator
    (a) Qualifications for selection
    (b) Qualifications for retention
    (c) Ethics, independence, the Code of Professional Responsibility for Arbitrators of Labor-Management Disputes
(3) Fees and charges

Arbitration Function and Arbitrator's Role as Viewed by Arbitrators and Parties

(1) Function of arbitration in collective bargaining
    (a) Source and extent of arbitrator's authority
    (b) Importance to industrial peace
    (c) Suggestions for improvement
(2) The arbitrator
    (a) The "ideal" arbitrator
    (b) Active or passive at hearing?
    (c) Judge v. mediator
(3) Arbitration clauses

      (a) Grievance procedure, final step
      (b) Contract language: narrow or broad
(4) Preliminary steps upon appointment
      (a) Initial contact with the parties
      (b) Submission agreement and stipulations
      (c) Prehearing briefs (if any)
      (d) Prehearing conference (if any)
      (e) Notice of hearing
(5) Characteristics of serving as
      (a) An ad hoc arbitrator
      (b) Permanent arbitrator
      (c) Member of tripartite panel
      (d) Member of a neutral panel
      (e) Expedited procedure arbitrator

Procedure and Rules of Evidence

(1) Applicability of legal rules of evidence
(2) Admissibility, relevancy
(3) Confrontation and cross-examination
(4) Hearsay, affidavits
(5) Employee's past record
(6) Right to call opposing witness
(7) Right to information
(8) Burden of proof
(9) Authority of arbitrator to issue subpoenas
(10) Plant or site visitation

An Arbitration Hearing—Movie

The Arbitration Hearing

(1) Location, responsibility for arrangements
(2) Attendance by observers, including friends of grievant
(3) Transcripts, tape recordings
(4) Order of presentation
(5) Opening statements
(6) Witnesses
      (a) Oaths, affirmations
      (b) Examinations
      (c) Cross-examination
      (d) Limits on further examination?
(7) Documents and exhibits

(8) Closing arguments
(9) Post-hearing briefs

The Arbitrator's Bench Rulings

(1) Issues to be resolved during hearing and issues to be postponed for post-hearing resolution
(2) Arbitrability: substantive and procedural
(3) Objections to evidence
(4) Requests for information
(5) Interlocutory orders, stays
(6) Trilateral dispute (two affected unions)
(7) Right of aggrieved employee to own counsel
(8) Ex parte hearings
(9) Recesses and adjournments

The Arbitrator's Opinion and Award

(1) Format and length of decisions
(2) Soliciting parties' views as to length and format
(3) Dicta—helpful or hurtful?
(4) Pitfalls to avoid, how not to heal wounds
(5) The bottom line: the art of writing concise, precise, and viable awards
(6) Retention of post-award jurisdiction

Wages, Hours, and Job Classification

(1) Job classification and job rates
    (a) Job evaluation
    (b) Reclassifications
    (c) New or changed jobs
(2) Wage systems
    (a) Fixed rates
    (b) Incentive rates
    (c) Automatic or renegotiated adjustments
(3) Hours of work
    (a) Premium pay provisions
    (b) Distribution of overtime

General Standards for Decisions

(1) Contract language: plain meaning
(2) Prior arbitration awards as precedent
    (a) Same parties

(b) Different parties
(3) Legal or public policy considerations: what weight should be accorded them?
    (a) Court decisions
    (b) Administrative rulings and regulations
    (c) Pending actions

Management Rights and Union Concerted Action

(1) Residual rights v. implied obligations
(2) Management rights clauses
    (a) Broad statements
    (b) Detailed statements
    (c) Special G.E.-IUE provisions
(3) No-strike and no-lockout clauses
    (a) Broad v. narrow provisions
    (b) Relationship to arbitration coverage
    (c) Special G.E.-IUE provisions
    (d) Wildcat strikes
    (e) Picket line clauses
    (f) Remedies for breach, damages

Individual and Minority Rights

(1) Union duty of fair representation: *Vaca v. Sipes*
(2) Employer responsibility
(3) Racial or other minorities and possible third-party representation
(4) Remedies by arbitrator or courts for unfair representation
(5) Possible conflict between contract and statutes

Discipline and Discharge

(1) Just Cause
    (a) Incompetence on job
    (b) Insubordination
    (c) Misconduct: theft, drunkenness, absenteeism, fighting, drugs, off-the-job conduct, etc.
(2) Special procedural problems
    (a) Burden of proof and quantum of proof
    (b) Prior warnings and previous record of employee
    (c) Arbitrator's power to modify penalty

Due Process and Fair Procedure

(1) Effect of procedural irregularity in applying contract

(2) The "agreed" case

(3) The "surprise" case

(4) Privilege against self-incrimination, improper search and seizure

(5) Employee's right of privacy, including wiretaps and hidden cameras, lie detector tests, blood tests, etc.

Appendix B: Curriculum for Second Training Session

Appointment through Hearing

(1) Contacting the parties, arrangements

(2) Attendance by observers

(3) Submission agreements

(4) Transcripts, recordings, notes

(5) Witnesses

(6) Evidentiary rulings

    (a) Pros and cons of flexibility

    (b) Hearsay, affidavits

    (c) Documents, exhibits, photographs, site inspections, etc.

(7) Discovery, subpoenas

Opinion and Award

(1) Critique of common problems

(2) Format

(3) Use of briefs and record

(4) Use of precedent (arbitral and legal)

(5) Fashioning remedies

(6) Back pay: deductions? interest?

(7) Finality of awards, judicial review

Appointing Agencies and the Appointment Process

(1) Differences in appointment and administrative procedures

(2) Differences between G.E.-IUE and other union-employer arbitration procedures

Roundtable Discussion

Seniority

(1) Uses of seniority

    (a) Layoffs and recalls

    (b) Promotions and transfers

(c) Vacations and overtime
(2) Determination of seniority
(3) Seniority v. affirmative action in a slumping economy

The Use of Past Practice

(1) Nature of a custom or practice
(2) Clarification of ambiguities
(3) Past practice v. apparently unambiguous language
(4) Past practice as separate, enforceable condition of employment

New Contract Arbitration in the Public Sector

(1) Survey of developments
(2) The collective bargaining environment in the public sector
(3) Guidelines or standards in deciding interest arbitration cases
(4) Open-ended v. last-best-offer arbitration
      (a) Michigan and Wisconsin experience
      (b) Union and employer reactions
(5) Appraisal of the past and speculation on the future

Summary of week and review of activities to come

Appendix C: Model Curriculum

(I) General Introduction to Arbitration
      Registration
      Welcome
      Historical background and legal framework
      Selection and appointment of arbitrators
      Arbitration function and arbitrator's role
(II) The Arbitration Hearing
      Procedure and rules of evidence
      Movie: an arbitration hearing
      The arbitration hearing
      The arbitrator's bench rulings
(III) Fundamental Rights: Standards for Decision
      Due process and fair procedure
      Individual and minority rights
      General standards for decision
      The use of past practice
(IV) Major Problem Areas
      Management rights and union concerted action

Discipline and discharge
Wages, hours, and job classification
Seniority
(V) Summary and Conclusion
The arbitrator's opinion and award
New contract arbitration in the public sector

Arbitrator Development in New Jersey
1975–1976

Jeffrey B. Tener

There have now been a number of programs throughout the country which have been designed to develop new arbitrators. These programs have shared two basic assumptions: first, that there is a need for more arbitrators and second, that new arbitrators can be produced or developed through training programs.

An Arbitrator Development Program was conducted in New Jersey with its formal phase occurring between September 1975 and June 1976. Although the concept of an arbitrator training program had been discussed for several years by officials of the American Arbitration Association and representatives of the Institute of Management and Labor Relations, Rutgers University (IMLR), this program began to take shape in the fall of 1974 when, at the invitation of AAA's New Jersey Regional Office, representatives of the Federal Mediation and Conciliation Service, the New Jersey Board of Mediation (BOM), the New Jersey Public Employment Relations Commission (PERC), the Labor Law Section of the New Jersey State Bar Association, and the IMLR were invited to meet in order to discuss the development of such a program. A committee was established and the project launched.

Taking advantage of the experience of earlier programs, it was readily agreed that two elements were essential to success: first, the participants would have to obtain sufficient training, skills, and expertise to be able to serve as arbitrators and, second, the participants would have to have not only the potential for acceptability, but would in fact have to attain acceptability. The first element is far easier to accomplish than the second.

As the program developed, the AAA, BOM, PERC, Labor Law Section, and the IMLR served as official sponsors. The participation of the IMLR as a division of Rutgers, the State University, provided academic acceptability as well as expertise to the program.

Applications for the program were solicited through public announcements, an announcement in the *New Jersey Law Journal*, posting at colleges and universities, and word of mouth. Additionally, AAA, BOM, and PERC went through their files of applicants in an effort to identify potential candidates among those who had indicated an interest in this field by applying for panel membership but who had minimal experience, acceptability, and background in arbitration. These individuals were contacted directly and invited to apply. Also, the Women's Section of the State Bar Association was contacted and asked to notify its members of this program.

A selection committee was established that consisted of ten representatives each from labor and management. Some had public sector connections, but the majority were from the private sector. This committee reviewed the 73 applications submitted and, after a screening process, arranged interviews with the 34 remaining candidates. These candidates were personally interviewed by members of the selection committee, usually with two labor and two management representatives participating in each interview. Ultimately, 20 candidates were invited to participate in the program and 18 accepted.

To assure a real commitment by the participants, as well as to defray the costs of the program, participants were charged $350 for each of two semesters. All participants paid the fee, although several were extended credit and two Rutgers faculty members enjoyed the usual fee reduction.

Of the 18 participants only two were female and one was a black male. The participants ranged in age from 27 years to the mid-fifties. Seven were trained as attorneys; five were predominantly engaged in the field of education in academic or administrative capacities; four were management representatives; and two with academic backgrounds in industrial relations were committed to the development of careers as professional neutrals. Some of these people had a wide range of experience in labor relations, some had academic backgrounds in the field, and some had had almost no prior interest or commitment. Several of the attorneys practiced labor law, representing unions or management, and several of the participants were already members of one or more arbitration panels when the program began.

The course ran a full academic year and it generally met once a week for two and one-half hours per session. There were midterm and final examinations, as well as numerous written assignments. In the first semester, taught by Jonas Aarons, the legal framework of arbitration was emphasized: the legal status of arbitration, the jurisdiction and authority of the arbitrator, framing the issue, rules of evidence, standards of interpreting contract language, the role of the arbitrator, stays of arbitration, enforcement of awards, and the conduct of hearings.

The second semester concentrated on the arbitration process and was intended to be pragmatic and practical. Daniel House served as the chief instructor, although a number of guests also participated in this aspect of the program. Arrangements were made for the participants to attend several arbitration hearings and to prepare mock opinions and awards. These awards were then discussed in class and critiqued by the instructor.

In addition, each participant was assigned to an active member of the National Academy of Arbitrators who had volunteered to take on a student, thereby affording each a mini-apprenticeship. The participants attended at least two arbitrations with their master arbitrators and wrote mock determinations which were analyzed by the master arbitrators.

The second major component of the program, and the one that is generally recognized as the chief barrier for aspiring arbitrators, related to the effort to assist the participants in developing that elusive, but indispensable, commodity called acceptability. This program placed very great emphasis on that aspect.

The program sponsors included the major appointing agencies in New Jersey: the AAA, the Board of Mediation, and PERC.[1] Another sponsor, the Labor Law Section of the State Bar Association, is composed of many of those who represent both labor and management and who do the actual striking and selection of names once a panel is sent out.

In addition to serving as sponsors and assisting in developing the program, the appointing agencies made commitments to look favorably upon the applications of those who successfully completed the program. It was generally understood that the successful participants would be placed on panels unless there was a good reason to exclude them. Also, it was understood that the agencies would list these applicants so that they would have a real chance of being selected by the parties.

The selection process was designed with several aims. It was, of course, intended to identify those applicants who, in the eyes of labor and management officials, had the potential to become acceptable arbitrators. At the same time, however, it exposed each applicant to (usually) four representatives of labor and management. Thus, the applicants had a chance to meet and spend about 45 minutes with two union and

---

[1]FMCS was originally slated to be part of this program, but scheduling conflicts interfered.

two management representatives, contacts which could prove helpful to graduates of the program.

Also, several labor and management attorneys and members of the Labor Law Section appeared as guest lecturers during the course of the formal training. Again, this gave the participants an opportunity to meet individuals responsible for the selection of arbitrators.

The training included three plant tours. The dual purpose is obvious. Not only did the participants get to see several manufacturing processes and plants, which would contribute to their ability as potential arbitrators to understand the context of industrial disputes, but they also met the personnel directors or labor relations officers of these firms.

In addition, the program hosted a formal dinner at the beginning of the program with 60 individuals in attendance, and a cocktail party and graduation ceremony at its completion. The graduation-cocktail party was attended by representatives of the appointing agencies, members of the Labor Law Section, members of the initial selection committee, and others. The program was briefly reviewed and each successful graduate was identified and given a certificate.

An attractive brochure was prepared, which not only described the program, but also included brief biographical sketches of each of the graduates. This brochure was printed in large quantities and was widely, if somewhat redundantly, distributed throughout the labor-management community in New Jersey.

Also, at the end of the program, all members of the Labor Law Section were sent a communication from the Chairman of the Section that reminded members that the Section had participated in the program just completed. The letter concluded with the following statement about the graduates: "We commend them to your consideration and are confident that their performance will be equal to the high standards established in the field by their fellow arbitrators."

The program has been discussed at a number of meetings in the area, including a session at the October 1976 Annual Meeting of the Industrial Relations Research Association in Atlantic City, New Jersey. Sometimes graduates of the program have been invited to discuss it and at other times AAA representatives have spoken about the program.

Last, and probably most important, the AAA to date has sponsored three "meet-the-parties" programs, which the graduates have been invited to attend. One of the programs was a session with the approximately 30 New Jersey Education Association UniServ representatives, another was with the field representatives and other officials of the New Jersey School Boards Association, and the last one involved the Employers'

Association of New Jersey. Each of these programs included an informal session during which, it was hoped, the graduates of the program, as well as other arbitrators, mingled with and met representatives of parties who select arbitrators.

The program was designed to make its graduates available to the parties as arbitrators, thereby increasing the supply of qualified and acceptable arbitrators. In the end, success of the program must be measured by the number of acceptable, qualified arbitrators produced.

It has now been one year since the formal program ended. That period of time is too short to allow final conclusions about the program's success. The following is a review of the results to date: how the participants have fared in terms of being placed on panels, being listed by the appointing agencies, and being selected by the parties.

Several of the participants were already panel members when the program began. It is safe to say, however, that they had not, at that time, received many appointments. It is difficult, if not impossible, to know how many extra listings and appointments they received because they completed the program.

Most of the participants have submitted applications to the appointing agencies. Particularly in the case of the AAA application, which requires the submission of 16 letters of recommendation—itself an imposing requirement—this would seem to indicate that the participants are interested in serving as arbitrators. Undoubtedly, the application process was easier for them in that they had met people during the program who could serve as references.

Not all of the applications for panel membership have been approved. Three of the ten post-program applications at the BOM are still pending. Only one has been rejected. There was a considerable delay in acting upon applications and in listing the new panelists at the BOM because the BOM has just recently completed a comprehensive review and revision of its entire arbitration administration procedure. That review is now complete and the BOM is implementing its new procedures, including its new selecting processes. While that review process has resulted in a substantial delay in terms of processing and listing of new panelists, the result of that review and the revised procedures will be extremely beneficial to the program participants, as well as to other new arbitrators who are included on the panel. The BOM intends to list each of these people and others 50 times on a regular, rotational basis and, after that number of listings, to review the results in terms of the number of selections. People who were never selected will be dropped. Also, there will be a review every two years of all panelists and, as a result, some may be dropped and others may be listed more often.[2]

At the time of this paper, the AAA has added five new panelists of the ten who applied, has rejected two, and has three applications pending.

PERC has rejected more applications than the other agencies. This can be attributed mainly to the fact that a number of the graduates are management representatives in either the public or private sectors. PERC has been unwilling to list individuals presently identified or affiliated with either labor or management, without a strong showing of established acceptability as a neutral. This applies to those graduates of the program who have present partisan ties.

The number of graduates of the program whose applications for the various panels were rejected by the appointing agencies could have been reduced if the appointing agencies had been asked to review the résumés of the program's applicants prior to their acceptance in the program. This might have created more "political" problems for the labor-management selection committees, however, than it was worth.

The data regarding the numbers of listings and actual appointments are very limited. The BOM's new procedure assures applicants of 50 listings. Time will tell whether the parties are willing to choose these new, inexperienced panelists.

The AAA did not have this information available in easily retrievable form. It is known, however, that eight of the ten graduates who have been included on the panel have actually heard one or more cases. This includes three of the five people who have been admitted subsequent to and presumably as a result of the program.[3]

More information is available regarding PERC. The eight people who are on PERC's arbitration panel have been listed 59 times and have been appointed as arbitrators in eight cases. An analysis of the raw data reveals that 37 of those listings were confined to the three individuals who were already on the panel prior to the program and six of the eight actual appointments went to one individual who was already on the panel. It is not possible to say how many listings those people would have received had they not completed the program. If the listings of the three people who were on the PERC panel before the program began are added together, they constitute almost two-thirds of the listings and three-fourths of the appointments.

PERC also maintains panels of mediators and fact-finders. The same graduates who have been admitted to the arbitration panel have

[2]Discussion between John Tesauro, Executive Director, and the author, May 23, 1977.
[3]Discussion between Patrick Westerkamp and the author, May 25, 1977.

also been admitted to the mediation and fact-finding panels. PERC has tended to utilize new people as mediators, where direct appointments are made, more readily than as arbitrators or fact-finders. Thus, all of the graduates who have been placed on the PERC panels have received one or more appointments as a mediator. Additionally, several have been listed on a total of ten fact-finding panels that have been sent to the parties for their selection and this has led to four actual appointments as fact-finders. All four of these appointments went to individuals who were already on the fact-finding panel prior to the program.

Arbitration is undoubtedly one of the professions in which it is most difficult to become established and in which it is least possible to predict success. There are only several hundred full-time arbitrators nationally and the work is highly concentrated in the hands of a few. The BOM reports that 65 percent of its approximately 1,300 cases per year are heard by 11 percent of the 200 panelists. That situation is repeated throughout the country.

Additionally, it is well known that it usually takes some years for individuals to develop acceptability as arbitrators. Many who today are overwhelmed with cases report that it was literally years before they had heard five or ten cases. The author is aware of no statistics regarding the number who have tried but failed.

The development of new arbitrators thus appears to be a formidable if not almost a presumptuous task. The results of any efforts to develop new arbitrators must be realistically examined. One could not expect all 18 graduates of a program to become successful, full-time arbitrators, even after five or ten years. If they did, this one program would augment the ranks of the arbitrators appreciably.

No final conclusions about the success of the New Jersey Arbitrator Development Program can be drawn at this time. The results are not in and it will require follow-up studies for a period of years to discover how many of the program's graduates make it as arbitrators.

Conceptually, this program seems to have been excellent, both as to its technical or skills component and as to its efforts to assist the participants in obtaining acceptability. The participation of the appointing agencies and the Labor Law Section assured the cooperation, to the extent possible, of those most able to control the arbitration panels.

The selection process also was designed to lead to the selection of participants who had the imprimatur of a labor-management committee. The course was taught by two highly respected members of the National Academy of Arbitrators. Its content was comprehensive and well planned.

One thing that might have been done was to involve the appointing agencies in the selection process along with the labor and management representatives. At least as far as PERC is concerned, perhaps one-third of the participants were unacceptable because of partisan connections with management. Some even represented public employers or public employee organizations as administrators or as attorneys. The other appointing agencies may not share this reaction. Nevertheless, in these times of rapidly expanding public sector negotiations, it is the public sector, where experience is most limited, that is easier for new arbitrators to break into. Thus, a significant portion of the graduates is in effect cut off from a major potential user of their new skills.

The program did not attract large numbers of women and blacks. Contacts with the Women's Section of the State Bar Association yielded no applications. While attracting women and blacks was not an initial goal, perhaps a greater effort should have been made to appeal to these groups. The program, however, was designed to increase the supply of New Jersey arbitrators. [4] New Jersey, with its location between New York and Philadelphia, has a shortage of New Jersey-based arbitrators and the parties in the state, especially in the public sector, seem to prefer residents of the state as arbitrators.

One other point that might be made, although this is not the place to develop it fully, is that the interest of appointing agencies are not necessarily the same as those of the individual arbitrators, even though they do need each other.

The appointing agencies are performing a service for the parties: the provision of panels of arbitrators. Agencies tend to be oriented to the needs and desires of the parties. There may even be a degree of competition among the appointing agencies for this business. Although the parties may complain about the increasing costs and delays associated with the arbitration process, the evidence is not strong that they are willing to give up the services of the well-known and established arbitrators who are booked several months ahead for a well-trained but new, inexperienced, and unknown arbitrator who is available the day after tomorrow. The agencies seek to provide panels that include the names the parties prefer.

Some of the newer arbitrators, on the other hand, seem to think that they should have a right to be listed and, furthermore, that they should not be matched against the well-established arbitrators. These positions cannot easily be reconciled.

In summary, the New Jersey Arbitrator Development Program was well conceived and well executed. One year after the program ended, there is little evidence, based on appointments so far, that the graduates

---

[4] Two of the participants were from New York State and one of these was a woman.

have become arbitrators. But one year is too short a period to assess such a program. Several factors, including the procedural revisions at the BOM, slowed the flow of the graduates into the process but promise to give them a real opportunity in the future. Furthermore, the graduates have not given up. In fact, a group of the graduates has been meeting monthly with one of the instructors. During these meetings they discuss such matters as their progress, development, problems, and case assignments.

If this program does not produce at least several successful arbitrators, and in my judgment that alone would make the program a success, then the entire concept of training programs for the development of new arbitrators would be seriously undermined. But I expect several successful arbitrators to emerge from this program.

The Michigan Arbitrator Project
1977

Robert G. Howlett

Late in 1975, a number of labor relations professionals discussed the possibility and advisability of developing a training program in Michigan for persons interested in labor dispute resolution. The discussants included representatives of Wayne State University, headed by Edward Simpkins, Dean of the College of Education; Harry R. Payne II, Director of the American Arbitration Association's Regional Office in Detroit; David Tanzman, Assistant Regional Director of the Federal Mediation and Conciliation Service; and Robert Pisarski, Director of the Michigan Employment Relations Commission. The group decided to discuss the proposed project with a larger group of arbitrators and employer and union representatives. A meeting, held on February 23, 1977, at Wayne State University, was attended by several arbitrators and representatives of employers and unions. It was decided to proceed with the project. Dean Simpkins undertook to provide the administration service necessary for the project and to serve as chairman of the committee.

Three committees—Program Planning, Heavy Users (frequent users of arbitration), and Candidate Selection and Education—were established.

No formal announcement of the program was made. The "word got out" primarily through the participating organizations and individuals.

AAA's Harry Payne was a prime mover in securing candidates. No application form was sent to persons expressing interest. Each was asked to submit a résumé or vita detailing educational background, occupation, professional or other work performed, outside activities, and publications. There were over 60 applicants. Twenty-two were chosen. Two subsequently dropped from the program.

Each participant was assigned to a well-known and experienced arbitrator as advisor, and attended at least three arbitration hearings with the advisor or another arbitrator.

A participant wrote an opinion following each of the hearings attended, which was critiqued by the advisor and rewritten, if necessary. The opinions were discussed further at the lecture and study course.

Following the completion of the active arbitration program, a lecture and study course covering five days (not consecutive) will be held. Subjects (subdivisions omitted) are: historical background and legal framework of arbitration; selection and appointment of arbitrators; arbitration function and arbitrator's role as viewed by arbitrators and parties; the arbitration hearing (procedure and rules of evidence); a movie of an arbitration hearing; the hearing per se; arbitrators' bench rulings; fundamental rights and standards for decision; the arbitrator's opinion and award; wages, hours, and job classifications; general standards for decision-making; management rights and union concerted activities; individual and minority rights; discipline and discharge; due process and fair procedure; seniority; use of past practice; and new contract arbitration in the public sector.

When the course has been completed, the AAA, the FMCS (through contact by the Detroit mediators with the arbitration service in Washington), and the Michigan Employment Relations Commission will seek to secure assignments for the successful participants in the program.

1978 ABA Pilot Labor Arbitrator Development Program

A detailed description of the ABA pilot labor arbitrator development program in the form in which it was submitted to the Ford Foundation is included in Part VI.

1978 Cornell Program

A special program to train women to become labor arbitrators was initiated in the spring of 1978 under the direction of Jean T. McKelvey in cooperation with the AAA and FMCS. The program had twenty-three participants, who were recruited and screened on a national basis. There were three two-day workshops scheduled over an approximate one-year period. Because the majority of the participants had already completed academic courses in arbitration, collective bargaining, and labor law, the instruction concentrated more on procedural and evidentiary problems and relied on each participant to do her own research. In the interim between workshops, participants were assigned to attend hearings under arrangements handled largely by AAA regional officers. Mock awards were evaluated and returned to the participants. The writing of a minimum of six awards was required for the successful completion of the program. Participants who successfully completed the program were accepted on the labor panels of both the AAA and FMCS.

1978 Wisconsin Program

The Wisconsin training project was carried out under the direction of Professor James L. Stern of the Industrial Relations Research Institute (IRRI), University of Wisconsin at Madison. The content of the program as well as the selection of the trainees was developed by Stern in conjunction with an IRRI advisory committee.

Fourteen prospective interest-arbitrator trainees were selected by the committee. Eight trainees were residents of Wisconsin, the rest from the contiguous states. Seven trainees had been previously listed on the Wisconsin Employment Relations Commission (WERC) roster for grievance panels.

Following the initial one-week session in September 1978 of classroom instruction including simulation exercises, all trainees were encouraged to participate in a ride-along program to observe an experienced mediator-arbitrator during actual cases and to discuss these cases and draft mock arbitration awards to be critiqued. Nine of the fourteen trainees participated in this aspect of the program. A further training session was held the following spring.

A follow-up survey of about nine of the fourteen trainees indicated that the most important factor contributing to the poor selection ratio of the trainees as arbitrators was their lack of experience. Of the twenty-four respondents who rejected trainees, ten claimed that they had no information about the trainee in question. Analysis of the selection statistics indicated that those trainees who were experienced grievance arbitrators were more readily acceptable as mediator-arbitrators than those trainees who were recently added to the WERC roster. Overall, the respondents indicated that information contained in previous awards was an important factor in selection decisions.

Respondents generally did not consider the rejected trainee's personality as a factor in their decision-making. However, most admitted that they did not know the trainees and, therefore, had no basis on which to evaluate their personalities. Respondents who did select trainees stated that they had some knowledge about them. Most respondents indicated that they were willing to select a trainee because all other names on the panel were unacceptable or were less well known than the trainee. Respondents generally claimed that the track records of the more experienced arbitrators on the panels contributed to their rejection and, therefore, to the trainees' selection. Here the trainees' lack of knowledge on the issues worked in their favor. In all but one instance, cost and availability of the trainees were said not to be factors in selection decisions. The single respondent who did state so suggested that cost was considered in all selection decisions and was not a factor unique to the case in question.

All respondents reported that they were pleased with the selected trainee's personality and that personality was not considered in their selection. Responses to questions pertaining to the trainee's ability and performance exhibited during mediation, arbitration hearings, and in the subsequent award were quite favorable. Further evidence of the trainees' capability was reflected in the responses pertaining to future acceptability. Nearly all respondents stated that, depending upon the issues involved, they would definitely select the trainee in the future.

Comparisons of selection ratios indicated that when graduates of the training program were included on a panel, they were more likely to be selected than all other arbitrators in mediation-arbitration grievance and in all types of cases combined. This was attributed to WERC, and management and association representatives' support of the training program. The panel/arbitrator comparisons reflected the involvement of WERC and that agency's confidence in the new arbitrators.

Trainees who had completed the training program were invited to discuss their experiences as mediator-arbitrators, give their impressions of the training received, and offer recommendations and suggestions on possible future programs. Nine trainees expressed overall satisfaction with both the methods and results of their training. In the evaluation process, trainees discussed each component of the formal one-week training program and were encouraged to identify both positive and negative aspects. The trainees indicated that the sessions devoted to mediation and the application of statutory criteria were most helpful and future programs should include more intensive role playing and feedback on performance in mock mediation, arbitration, and award-writing sessions.

The trainees' reactions of the ride-along component of the program were positive. In fact, many felt that it was the most valuable aspect of their training. Information obtained from trainees suggested a positive correlation between the number of ride-along experiences and the number of selections as mediator-arbitrators. Trainee recommendations for future programs included a restructuring to permit ride-alongs with both WERC investigators and experienced mediator-arbitrators prior to the formal training session, more role playing particularly in the area of mediation, less emphasis on school and municipal statutes, more emphasis on school financing and comparability issues, and a more realistic time period in which to write the mock arbitration awards. Several trainees indicated that review of drafts of their first few arbitration awards by an experienced arbitrator would have been helpful. All expressed a desire to receive substantive material from WERC explaining related court decisions and WERC policies.

Analysis of the selection statistics and the survey data suggested that although management and association representatives were reluctant initially to select trainees because of their lack of experience, those selected were considered capable and were selected again. Respondents indicated unanimously that knowledge about the trainees, including information on past performance and positions on particular issues, was the most important factor in their selection of an arbitrator. The trainees considered the training program to be a success.

1979 Michigan Bar Program

The Young Lawyers' Section of the Michigan State Bar Association conducted a training program in early 1979 following the format of the American Bar Association pilot program. Candidates for the program were solicited through the Michigan State Bar Journal, the Young Lawyers' Section publication, and internal communications of the AFL-CIO, UAW, and Employers' Association of Detroit. A total of 190 candidates were screened by a nine-member committee with equal management, labor, and neutral representation, each applicant paying a fee of $10 to defray administration costs. The fifteen trainees were selected and each paid a course fee of $150. Additionally, fifteen alternates were chosen.

Classes were held on Saturdays and weekday evenings by the Institute of Continuing Legal Education, University of Michigan, Ann Arbor. Mock arbitrations were conducted during two of the class sessions. Lecturers for the program included Academy members. Arbitration participation followed the academic part of the program. The Young Lawyers'

Section has followed up the program by publicizing the course and its graduates.

1979 Southern California Program

Based upon their premise that users of arbitrators would use aspiring neutrals if they had the power to select canidates for training as arbitrators and had a hand in the design and implementation of training, the Southern California Chapter of the Industrial Relations Research Association (IRRA) designated an executive committee of twenty-four persons from a wide spectrum of labor, management, and attorney representatives in Southern California to coordinate this program. The Institute of Industrial Relations (IIR) at the University of California, Los Angeles (IIE, UCLA), FMCS, AAA, and the labor law sections of the Los Angeles County and Beverly Hills Bar Associations supported the project. Underwritten by a $12,500 commitment from the IRRA's Executive Board, the committee developed the program's objectives, contracted with UCLA for academic training, defined eligibility rules, encouraged labor-management support, and publicized the opportunities available to Southern Californians outside the San Diego and Orange County areas where sister IRRA chapters functioned.

Over 1700 people from all walks of life responded to the program announcement in a Los Angeles Times feature article in the fall of 1978 by requesting applications. Eight hundred ninety-three individuals paid a $10 filing fee and applied for consideration. After a preliminary screening, about 250 candidates remained. Five subcommittees each comprising a union, employer, and attorney member of the executive committee, culled the 250 applications and listed the fifty candidates each deemed best qualified for further consideration. This pooling of judgments produced a group for further evaluation of forty-three candidates mentioned by three or more of the subcommittees.

A selection committee consisting of seventy-four people equally divided between labor and management in the Los Angeles metropolitan area ranked the top thirty candidates who were then interviewed individually by either of the two tripartite subcommittees of the Executive Committee. For purpose of evaluation, each candidate was asked also to analyze and write an opinion in a limited time period based upon a hypothetical grievance. The Executive Committee chose the final twenty candidates of which five were women attorneys, three of them black. There were also two black and two Hispanic men. Two men in the training group actively represented union members, one as a staff attorney. The occupational affiliations of the others included education, government, law, and private industry.

The academic portion of the program began in January 1979 with an orientation and discussion of the historical background and legal basis of grievance arbitration. Sessions continued through 1979 and involved ten days at UCLA's Institute of Industrial Relations: one Saturday each month except for July and August. The academic curriculum covered the grievance arbitration process and its legal basis, elements and structure of arbitration hearings, evidence and proof, decision-making criteria, essentials of arbitration opinions and awards, remedies available to arbitrators, and specific kinds of grievances involving discipline, discharge, seniority and work assignments. The influence of external law on discrimination cases and other types of cases was also reviewed. The final session was devoted to a survey of administrative practices and the ethical conduct of arbitrators. The academic portion of the program was the responsibility of UCLA's IIR and was conducted under the guidance of UCLA Law Professor Reginald Alleyne.

On-the-job training, which extended from March 1979 through June 1980, was the responsibility of FMCS and AAA. They arranged for pairing trainees and arbitrators, processing forms and reports, and handling cancellations and reschedulings with the assistance of an advisory committee.

The trainees were evaluated on their handling of the contact with the arbitrator and attendance at the hearing, their understanding of the issues and positions of the parties, and their logical thought processes. The mock awards, prefaced by a brief summary of the dispute and a statement identifying and explaining underlying theories or relevant principles, were evaluated by the arbitrators of record. The trainees were required also to submit addenda responding specifically to questions about their own actions at hearings and their impressions of techniques used by the arbitrator in charge of the case.

Phase One of this part of the program involved attendance at three arbitration hearings. In lieu of a mock award, completion of an evaluation form was required. Two mock awards were required for cases observed in the second phase, in addition to completion of the standard evaluation form. In a final phase, candidates attended three additional hearings for which they prepared mock awards and evaluation forms. Early in this phase, trainees met with labor and management representatives of the executive committee and representatives of AAA and FMCS to discuss their experiences in the program and to learn from committee members what the users expected from professionals in labor arbitration practice. The people who participated in the final selection process also took part in these sessions to provide continuity for evaluating the effect of the program on trainees one year after their entrance into it.

At each of the three phases, counseling was provided based upon the record made by each trainee. Both the academic and training phases of the program were subject to pass-fail evaluations by those who provided instructions.

1979 Ohio Internship Program

In February 1979, an indoctrination meeting was held in Columbus where potential interns heard talks by Academy members led by Edwin R. Teple. When the Committee on the Development of Arbitrators reported at the Academy's annual meeting in May 1979, most of the eleven interns had already attended hearings with members of the Academy. It was announced that the program was to include attendance of at least six additional hearings to be arranged over the next one or two years, with the candidates drafting practice opinions for review with the arbitrator of record in each case.

Contemporaneously, all participants were to be advised of seminars, meetings, and other programs with labor arbitration content scheduled in their geographic area. Where appropriate, university courses were also to be taken by the interns. It is intended that the program will continue indefinitely, with individual interns finishing at their own pace and new interns joining from time to time. Five new interns have joined the program since its inception, and one has finished. Other areas, including Philadelphia and New York, are considering similar internship programs.

1980 St. Louis Bar Program

Sponsored by a broad cross section of the labor and management community, the Labor Law Section of the Metropolitan St. Louis Bar Association undertook an arbitrator development program in 1980 which was described as an extension and intensification of the 1970 St. Louis effort. A committee balanced with labor, management, and neutral members developed standards of eligibility, reviewed sixteen solicited applications, and selected six trainees. In developing the program, the committee reviewed the ABA national pilot labor arbitrator development program along with other training information available and adapted its own format with a $5,000 budget to meet professional and administrative expenses.

Professor John Dunsford of the St. Louis University School of Law was the academic instructor for three separate days of training which began in March 1980. The first session included the theory of labor arbitration, the relationship of arbitration to the courts and administrative agencies, the source of grievances, and procedural and substantive problems. The second session in May 1980 centered on evidentiary issues, subpoena power, burden of proof, substantive arbitration law, and remedial power. The third session in October 1980 concerned the writing of opinions and awards, ethical considerations, and scheduling and billing matters.

Attendance at arbitration hearings began concurrent with the academic program in March 1980. Trainees were referred to hearings of participating parties including thirty-five companies, ten unions and fifteen arbitrators. Given instructions with respect to their conduct at the hearing, each participant attended at least five hearings and prepared a mock award and opinion for each case. Professor Dunsford, the arbitrator of record, and the committee separately reviewed the mock awards. Professor Dunsford subsequently critiqued each trainee in a personal discussion.

As a consequence of their experience with the 1970 program, the committee concluded that more emphasis should be placed on academic training, which was done in this program. A comprehensive report was also sent to members of the Labor Law Section of the St. Louis Bar Association in the spring of 1981 to encourage the parties to utilize as arbitrators of record the five participants who completed the program. The committee is confident that they will become acceptable arbitrators.

1982 Cornell Survey of Program Participants in Selected Programs

In the spring of 1982, the Graduate Student Association of the Industrial and Labor Relations School at Cornell University (GSA) completed a survey, in connection with an American Arbitration Association and GSA conference on the training and development of third-party neutrals, of participants in several arbitrator training programs. Over 60 percent of the survey forms received by the participants, who included graduates of eight programs, were returned.

The survey shows that about half of the respondents were lawyers and almost half were women. This ratio of female participation in training programs may be overstated due to the high response rate of participants in the Women's Arbitrator Development Program. Before the respondents' training program, less than 10 percent had heard more than five cases, and approximately 60 percent had never heard a case. After the training program, only 10 percent of the respondents had heard no cases, and approximately 40 percent had heard more than fifteen cases. Although 30 percent were already members of a neutral panel before participating in a training program, 75 percent were appointed to neutral panels following the completion of training.

The respondents rated the most beneficial elements of the training program as follows: program readings 74 percent, interaction with advocates 69 percent, and lectures 50 percent. Thirty-three percent of the respondents felt that there were unspecified features which detracted from effective training; 20 percent of the respondents found some administrative problems.

Almost 80 percent of the respondents thought that there was no commitment by the parties to use program graduates to hear cases after their training. Nevertheless, over 75 percent felt that their program was successful and about half believed that the training program helped them gain acceptability as arbitrators from the parties. Almost 80 percent of the respondents rated their training program as good or excellent.

Although the survey indicates that there is substantial room for improvement in labor arbitrator training and development, the results confirm that programmed training contributes significantly to attaining acceptability. Even though the opinions of the respondents do not provide all the answers to possible training improvements, architects of future development programs should carefully review the survey results.

The numerical results of the survey are shown below, with the permission of the AAA and GSA. No attempt has been made here to categorize other occupations of those participants who arbitrate on a part-time basis or to summarize comments of participants' commitment to the program or their expectations of gain from it.

SURVEY RESULTS

Questions	Responses by Programs*									
	1	2	3	4	5	6	7	8	9	Total
Background										
Number of Respondents	3	14	2	10	4	8	2	8	3	54
What is your age? (average)	56	35	61	40	49	36	65	44	56	
What is your sex? (male)	3	0	2	8	3	4	2	7	1	30
(female)	0	14	0	2	1	4	0	1	1	23
What is your race? (caucasian)	2	13	1	9	0	6	2	8	2	43
(black)	1	0	1	0	2	1	0	0	1	7
(Hispanic)	0	1	0	0	1	0	0	0	0	2
(other)	0	0	0	0	1	1	0	0	0	2
What is your educational attainment? (bachelors)	0	3	0	2	1	0	0	1	0	7
(masters)	0	2	1	3	1	0	0	1	0	8
(J.D.)	3	6	1	2	2	5	2	2	3	26
(Ph.D.)	0	3	0	2	0	3	0	4	0	12
(other)	0	0	0	1	0	0	0	0	0	1

	1	2	3	4	5	6	7	8	9	Total
What is your professional training?										
(lawyer)	3	6	1	2	2	5	2	2	3	26
(economist)	0	0	0	1	0	1	0	0	0	2
(business)	0	1	0	1	0	0	0	0	0	2
(government)	0	1	0	1	0	0	0	0	0	2
(industrial rel.)	0	6	1	4	1	2	4	4	0	18
(other)	0	0	0	1	2	0	2	2	0	5
Do you arbitrate full or part-time?										
(full-time)	0	3	1	2	1	1	0	1	2	11
(part-time)	3	7	1	8	1	6	2	7	0	35
(neither)	0	3	0	0	2	1	0	0	0	6

Training Program

	1	2	3	4	5	6	7	8	9	Total
What training program did you attend?	3	14	2	10	4	8	2	8	0	51
How many cases had you heard before entering the training program?										
(-0-)	2	13	0	5	3	4	0	3	0	30
(1–5)	1	1	2	4	1	2	2	4	0	17
(6–10)	0	0	0	1	0	0	0	1	1	3
(11–15)	0	0	0	0	0	1	0	0	0	1
(over 15)	0	0	0	0	0	1	0	0	0	1
Were you a member of any neutral panels prior to the program?										
(yes)	1	5	0	3	2	3	0	2	1	17
(no)	2	8	2	7	2	5	2	6	1	35

*1. Cleveland (1971)
2. Women's Program (1978)
3. UCLA (1972)
4. New Jersey (1975)
5. Berkeley (1972)
6. ABA (1978)
7. St. Louis (1970)
8. Western New York (1971)
9. No program identified by respondent

Responses by Programs*

Questions		1	2	3	4	5	6	7	8	9	Total
How many cases have you heard since completion of the training program?	(-0-)	0	4	0	0	1	1	0	0	0	6
	(1–5)	0	4	0	3	0	3	1	0	0	11
	(6–10)	0	1	0	2	1	1	0	0	0	5
	(11–15)	0	1	0	1	1	0	1	1	0	5
	(over 15)	3	4	2	4	1	2	0	7	1	24
Have you been appointed to any neutral panels since completion of the training program?	(yes)	3	12	2	7	2	4	1	8	1	40
	(no)	0	2	0	3	2	3	1	0	0	11
Were you required to write practice/mock awards?	(yes)	2	14	1	9	4	8	2	8	0	48
	(no)	1	0	1	1	0	0	0	0	0	3
Did you have a mentor as part of the program?	(yes)	1	6	1	6	2	3	2	2	0	23
	(no)	2	8	1	4	2	5	0	6	0	28
Were you introduced to any advocates during the training program (other than at arbitration hearings)?	(yes)	2	8	1	9	3	6	2	4	0	35
	(no)	1	6	1	1	1	2	0	4	0	16

Question		1	2	3	4	5	6	7	8	9	
Was there any commitment by any labor/management parties to give you cases to hear upon completion of the program?	(yes)	0	0	0	1	1	7	1	1	0	11
	(no)	3	14	2	9	3	1	1	6	0	39
Was there commitment by sponsoring parties/neutral agencies to "promote" you after the program?	(yes)	1	8	1	9	2	6	2	4	0	33
	(no)	2	6	1	1	2	2	0	4	0	18
Do you feel the program was successful?	(yes)	2	9	2	7	4	3	2	8	1	38
	(no)	1	2	0	3	0	4	0	0	0	10
Do you feel the effectiveness of the program was affected by class size?	(yes)	2	6	0	4	1	3	2	5	0	23
	(no)	1	8	2	6	3	5	0	3	0	28
Do you feel the effectiveness of the program was affected by the homogeneity of the group (i.e., experience, knowledge, motivation)?	(yes)	2	6	0	1	3	5	1	5	1	24
	(no)	1	5	2	7	1	3	1	5	1	26

*1. Cleveland (1971)
2. Women's Program (1978)
3. UCLA (1972)
4. New Jersey (1975)
5. Berkeley (1972)
6. ABA (1978)
7. St. Louis (1970)
8. Western New York (1971)
9. No program identified by respondent

Responses by Programs*

Questions		1	2	3	4	5	6	7	8	9	Total
Do you believe the training program facilitated your acceptability with labor/management parties?	(yes)	3	8	1	3	1	3	2	6	0	27
	(no)	0	5	1	7	3	4	0	2	0	22
What aspects of the program did you find most beneficial?	(lectures)	0	11	1	2	1	3	0	6	0	24
	(readings)	1	12	2	7	3	7	1	7	0	40
	(attendance at hearings)	1	3	2	4	2	5	0	1	0	18
	(mock awards)	1	2	2	4	1	4	1	2	0	17
	(interaction with arbitrators)	1	1	1	4	0	3	1	0	0	11
	(interaction with advocates)	3	10	1	9	2	6	0	6	0	37
Were there any features of the program which you felt detracted from the training?	(yes)	0	7	0	3	1	4	0	2	0	17
	(no)	3	7	2	7	3	4	2	6	0	34
Were there any administrative problems which detracted from the training?	(yes)	0	3	0	1	0	6	0	0	0	10
	(no)	3	10	2	9	4	2	2	8	0	40

Rate the program

Program	(poor)	(fair)	(good)	(excellent)
*1. Cleveland (1971)	0	1	1	1
2. Women's Program (1978)	0	2	6	6
3. UCLA (1972)	0	0	2	0
4. New Jersey (1975)	1	1	5	3
5. Berkeley (1972)	0	0	1	3
6. ABA (1978)	1	3	2	2
7. St. Louis (1970)	0	0	0	2
8. Western New York (1971)	0	1	4	3
9. No program identified by respondent	2	8	21	20

Part IV

A Manual for Training

*For the things we have to learn before
we can do them, we learn by doing them.*

Aristotle

A Manual for Training

Organization for Training

There is no established single organizational structure for the training of acceptable labor arbitrators. Various development programs illustrate widely divergent organizational models suitable to particular situations. Whatever the structure for a development program, a critical element of effective organization for arbitrator training is the assignment of responsibility. While leadership is critical to the success of any undertaking, the difficulty of scheduling training program activities requires special emphasis. For most participants, arbitrator training will be an avocation. Program activities must usually be superimposed upon widely divergent individual schedules. Failure to address simple logistical problems can easily undermine the success of training efforts. Extensions in the schedule of the American Bar Association pilot program are a good illustration of such problems. Attention to detail is a clear hallmark of successful programs.

Program Elements

Apart from the one-to-one internships, a pattern of arbitrator training has evolved over the years. The programs described in Part III show this pattern to include some or all of six elements: selection of trainees, academic content, attendance at hearings, mock awards, serving as arbitrator, and publication of awards. These elements emerged without the benefit of planned coordination or established requirements. The history of arbitrator training suggests that the common elements of the various programs are more the result of independent decisions of those concerned with the needs of the arbitration process than of recognition of the validity of other programs. There is little evidence of extensive communication between the various sponsoring groups. The relative consistency of program elements is therefore noteworthy and should be considered by those planning future programs.

Costs

There is no fixed cost for arbitrator training and development. Costs vary substantially depending upon the structuring of training elements alone. The ABA pilot program, for example, included in-residence academic sessions. This arrangement was necessary because of the national scope of the program, and it provided a greater interaction among the program participants and between participants and faculty. Some of the most penetrating discussions took place in informal sessions. Other programs limited academic training to a series of evening or weekend sessions at a location accessible to all participants on a commuting basis. Costs vary significantly because of facility and transportation differentials.

Attendance at arbitration hearings is another cost consideration, which can be controlled by geography and time limitations. The number of hearings to be audited is also part of the cost equation for either the program or participants. Whether or not the faculty is paid or contributes its service *pro bono* is also a policy decision which has impact upon the costs of training. The same decision applies to administrative expenses.

The budget for the ABA pilot program (see Part VI) can help establish a reference point, but even apart from inflationary costs, these figures should not be viewed as typical because of the national scope of the program and the fact that it was a pilot project. Reviewing this data will indicate the cost implications of various options. Careful budgeting is an important part of organizing for arbitrator development. Costs, funding, and program structuring are necessarily interrelated.

Funding

Foundations are one source of funding. Arbitrator development serves a useful purpose which can be attractive to foundation administrators if persuasively articulated. The support of the ABA pilot program by the Ford Foundation and others is a case in point.

Union and management, who use the services of arbitrators, should be a prime source of funding. The listing of the sponsors for the ABA pilot program illustrates the breadth of this interest. Those interested in becoming arbitrators are likely to be willing to invest in a program perceived as helping them to enter into the circle of acceptability. Fees paid by participants can also be used to defray costs. This alternative should be carefully handled, if commercial implications are to be avoided.

Selection of Trainees

Goals

In order to promote the successful selection of trainees, a sponsoring group should first determine the goals of its program. The goal of the ABA pilot labor arbitrator development program was to develop a training program useful as a basis for locally sponsored programs and, only incidentally, to train a group of acceptable arbitrators drawn from a national pool. The primary thrust of local programs should be the training of arbitrators to fulfill local needs and only incidentally to improve the framework for future training.

The sponsors must determine the format of the program, assign administrative tasks, and perform other planning operations. In the exceptional case, a local group may develop a program after having identified an appropriate group of people who wish to become arbitrators. In most cases, however, the sponsors will need to seek and identify qualified participants.

Questionnaire

A uniform questionnaire should be prepared for completion by each aspirant as a basis for evaluating applicants. It will also provide a first step in the necessary weeding-out process. As the sponsors discovered in the 1979 Los Angeles program, payment of a processing fee demonstrates an applicant's interest in the program beyond mere curiosity and also helps to defray some of the costs of the program. In some local programs, applicants are likely to be known to the sponsors, and the preliminary screening of applications may not be necessary. In almost any program, however, objective requirements should be helpful in averting charges of favoritism or discrimination.

Criteria

Those involved in the arbitral process recognize that prior experience and education, be it ever so impressive, do not guarantee a successful arbitration career but may be helpful in selecting the participant and in predicting the arbitrator's success. Although local programs will normally differ in structure and size, certain considerations in choosing participants are common to most programs. Criteria should be decided upon before selection of trainees begins, but it need not inhibit flexibility. The focus should be on future acceptability to the parties. Four general areas for consideration for choosing participants are educational background, employment history, labor-management experience, and experience as a neutral.

Writing Samples

A request for writing samples from participants under serious consideration is useful because the ability of particpants to write clear and concise arbitration decisions will contribute significantly to their success. Few programs provide instruction in expository writing although writing skills can be developed. The extent to which program sponsors are willing to provide for such training should be determined in the planning stage.

Screening Committee

A screening committee should be appointed to interview an applicant and check references. The rule of the committee requires a substantial commitment of time and energy. During the interview, an applicant should be given a description of the profession of arbitration as well as an explanation of the schedule procedures of the program. An applicant intrigued by the mystique of arbitration may not be ready for the realities of the arbitration practice, and such description may persuade unqualified applicants to withdraw.

Commitment

Program sponsors should require a commitment from participants to fulfill the goals of the program. The commitment may involve withdrawal from all advocacy in labor matters and a pledge not to identify oneself as a participant in the program until successful completion of it. Whatever the nature of commitment, it should be formally accepted by the applicants prior to their final selection as participants. When one considers the range of talent and intelligence of practicing arbitrators found acceptable by the parties, the conclusion is inevitable that there is no single formula for predicting success. Commitment can make the difference.

Academic Content

Some training programs have been limited to an academic dimension as opposed to inclusion of clinical training. Many law and industrial relations schools offer seminars in labor arbitration at varying levels of sophistication and practical value. Labor arbitration programs have consistently included academic training as an important part of a comprehensive program. Formal academic training provides a sound foundation of basic information and stimulates continuing growth in mastering knowledge of the arbitration process.

Part of this academic emphasis is due to the judicial nature of labor arbitration, which by itself may require a didactic exposure to the adversary aspects of this process. For instance, while an understanding of the application of the rules of evidence might be achieved through experience, a focused academic exposure heightens sensitivity to subtle dimensions and issues which abound in the arbitration forum.

A review of the academic training element in arbitrator development programs suggests serious consideration of the following scope of subjects:

History

> Arbitration under common law
> Distinction between labor and commercial arbitration
> Development under various statutes
> *Lincoln Mills*
> Effect of Steelworkers Trilogy

The collective bargaining agreement

> Nature and content
> Grievance procedures
> Rights arbitration
> Interest arbitration
> External law
> Judicial review

The Arbitrator

> Selection
> Authority
> Procedures
> Ethics

Hearing

> Record
> Submissions
> Stipulations
> Opening statement

Order of presentation
Closing arguments
Brief

Evidence
Application of rules
Burden and quantum of proof
Admissibilty
Direct examination
Cross-examination
Hearsay
Subpoenas

Discipline
Just cause
Disparate treatment
Condonation
Provocation
Due process
Progressive discipline
Work rules

Contract Interpretation
Plain meaning
Bargaining history
Past practice
Precedent

Opinion and Award
Form
Remedy

Attendance At Hearings

Responsibility of the Planners

An opportunity to attend arbitration hearings is an essential part of the training of arbitrators. Because the arbitration process is a private one, the program sponsors must obtain agreement of both management and union. It is also desirable to have the cooperation of the arbitrator of record. Obtaining such agreement and cooperation is not difficult because there is broad support for arbitrator development. Arbitrator appointing agencies such as AAA and FMCS can be helpful in obtaining access to hearings.

Greater difficulty lies in administration of the auditing program. The degree of difficulty varies with the number and availability of participants, the cooperation of arbitrators and/or an arbitrator appointing agency in scheduling cases, the number of cancellations among the scheduled hearings, and the number of cases each participant is required to audit. The time necessary to administer and complete this basic part of the program must be budgeted. The number of hearings which a participant should attend varies with the experience and background of the individual. If a point of diminishing returns in auditing cases exists, it is unlikely that point will be exceeded in most training programs. Past programs have scheduled two to five hearings. Most participants will benefit from the greater number of hearings.

When the mechanical process for assigning cases for audit has been established, the sponsors should attempt to vary the distribution of cases among the participants by arbitrator, subject matter, and manner of presentation. When a case is scheduled for auditing, the parties and the arbitrator should be informed of the identity and sole purpose of the program participant.

The arbitrator of record should be available to answer questions by the participants at the close of the hearing and substantive questions after the decision has been made. Such cooperation from the arbitrator should be sought prior to the hearing. If the sponsors encounter a community of arbitrators reluctant to become more involved than simply allowing trainee attendance at the hearing, the sponsors should provide a vehicle for discussion of the events at the hearing and a conditional response to the questions raised by the trainee concerning those events.

The sponsor should request the parties to provide program participants with copies of all documents introduced at the hearing with which the trainee can not only more readily follow the substance of the hearing but also acquire the material necessary for the preparation of a mock decision. Should arbitrating parties decline to provide documents, the trainee will rely on notes taken at the hearing and must know this fact before the hearing begins.

Finally, the sponsors should inform each participant before he attends a scheduled hearing of his role at that hearing. Failure to do so can lead to serious embarrassment for everyone involved.

Role of the Participant

It is the trainee's responsibility to attend the hearing on time, refrain from inserting himself into the proceedings, and remain until the hearing ends. A trainee must understand that his opinion about the case, however perceptive, will not be welcomed by the parties. The auditing participant will experience varied receptions from the parties and the arbitrator. The ability to adjust to the expectations of the parties in each situation should have a positive effect on those parties and will contribute to the recognition factor when those parties subsequently find the trainee's name upon a panel of prospective arbitrators. The intrusion of a trainee into the proceedings at the hearing is likely to have a negative effect. When in doubt, the participating trainee should occupy hearing time with note taking and assume the role of listener during breaks in the hearing.

A letter thanking each of the parties for making the hearing available for auditing will assist in reinforcing the recognition factor which is necessary to all fledgling arbitrators. Such a letter, however, should be limited to gratitude and avoid any comment on the hearing.

Mock Awards

The preparation of two or more mock awards of acceptable quality is an invaluable exercise. Consequently, one decision to be made by the sponsors at an early stage of the program and conveyed to each trainee is what does and what does not constitute a mock award of acceptable quality. Achieving the standard could require auditing additional cases or rewriting submitted awards.

One of the most effective contributions to the development of an acceptable arbitrator is the conscientious criticism of the mock awards submitted by program participants. While arbitrator acceptability is not dependent upon the literary excellence of written awards, one way a new arbitrator is able to expand acceptability is by demonstrated ability to support conclusions through incisively written awards. This alone may persuade parties to choose a new arbitrator for future cases.

Documentary Evidence

In preparation for writing a mock award, the trainee should have copies of all documentary evidence and the transcript if a record is taken. In some cases, either because of logistical difficulties or the parties' insistence on privacy, it may be impossible to obtain all the relevant materials. These circumstances should be anticipated. For instance, as fewer court reporters are used in arbitration, the absence of a transcript of record can provide an opportunity to develop the skill of record taking. The lack of copies of documentary evidence, however, can inhibit the writing of a coherent decision, particularly in a complex case. This is a problem for the program's administrators as well as for the program participants if mock awards of proper quality and depth are to be available for criticism. It would be well to require a mock decision for each of the audited hearings. Two or three decisions in which the trainee has had the most opportunity to share the evidence could be chosen for criticism.

Time Limits

A time limit should be established by the sponsors for the completion of mock awards. The typical practice of thirty days from the close of the hearing would be desirable training discipline. The administrator could, if necessary, grant extensions of time for good reasons, but satisfaction of the deadline should count toward satisfactory completion of the program.

Criticism

Useful as the discipline of writing an award is, equally or more useful is a responsive criticism of that award. Again, this is a time consuming project for the sponsors. Two criticisms are usually better because they supply two points of view and reduce the possibility of criticism based upon stylistic differences. In some cases it is valuable to have the arbitrator of record criticize the decision after his has been dispatched to the parties. The local sponsors will have the advantage of familiarity in identifying those arbitrators whose criticisms would be most helpful to the trainee.

Writing Decisions

In writing decisions a new arbitrator prepares his best advertising copy. A well-reasoned decision encourages its readers to take a chance on the author to arbitrate a case. Each arbitrator develops his own style in decision writing, which may vary with the complexity of the issue in the case. Reading decisions written by acceptable arbitrators, such as those included in Part V, can help in writing one's own. The following suggestions should be helpful up to and beyond the first few decision-writing experiences.

The introductory paragraph. State the basis for the arbitrator's authority, the date of the hearing, the date briefs were received, and the date of the decision.

The issue. Unless the parties authorize the arbitrator to formulate the issue, strive for their agreement on as objective a statement of the question to be resolved as possible. Suggest the inclusion of the remedy as a second question. Repeat the statement of the issue as submitted by the parties at the beginning of the opinion.

Arbitrability. If one party challenges the arbitrability of the issue before the arbitrator, that becomes a threshold issue to be stated and answered in the opinion. An award stating that a grievance is not arbitrable disposes of the case. The parties should be encouraged to frame the substantive issue and present the case. If that is done, the arbitrator, after finding and stating that the grievance is arbitrable, can reach the substantive issue and provide a remedy if appropriate.

The statement of facts. Include in the statement of facts all the record evidence upon which the decision is based. A chronological recitation of the events giving rise to the grievance is, perhaps, the easiest method for the writer, and for the reader. Resolve credibility issues in the statement of facts. If the decision rests on an issue of credibility, juxtapose the evidence presented by each side, and resolve the issue in the discussion portion of the decision.

Contract provisions. Quote only those portions of the contract which are relevant to the decision.

Contentions of the parties. Spell out the contentions of each of the parties. Summarize those contentions. If the statement of facts is complete, the positions of the parties with respect to those facts does not require a lengthy repetition of the evidence.

Discussion—Reasoning. Answer relevant arguments and set forth the reasons for the decision.

Decision—Award. At the end of the discussion, answer the question stated in the issue, and order any remedy.

Serving As an Arbitrator

Acceptable arbitrators are those whose qualities are appealing to those who select arbitrators. These qualities include judicial temperament, an authoritative presence sufficient to keep an adversary proceeding under control, sound judgment, impartiality, fairness, and an ability to write a succinct, persuasive decision.

A few of these qualities can be demonstrated through the preparation of mock awards, others by serving as arbitrator of record. Without the opportunity to serve as an arbitrator of record, the efforts expended in training may do little to add to the still small cadre of acceptable arbitrators. Those planning arbitrator development programs should require participants to serve as arbitrators of record as part of their training.

Securing case commitments, however, is difficult. The ABA survey of Labor and Employment Law Section members shows wide support for training more acceptable labor arbitrators. Most labor and management representatives who use the process apparently favor development programs as an important source for new arbitrators. Although almost everyone is in favor of developing new acceptable arbitrators, few are eager to risk providing the initial hearing experience. Adversary parties are reluctant to give the responsibility for binding decisions involving disputes between them to individuals without established acceptability. Too much is thought to be at stake.

If this dilemma is recognized, participation of the parties to collective bargaining agreements in sponsoring groups can help to obtain arbitration hearing assignments. It does not assure case assignments. Although commitments for cases may be obtained at the outset in the planning process, such commitments do not assure case assignments. The experience of the ABA pilot program indicates that availability of cases is affected by hearing cancellations, erosion of commitments to provide cases, and unavailability of appropriate cases when needed. A significant disappointment for participants in the ABA pilot program has been the failure to provide the fledgling arbitrator with timely case assignments. Persistent prodding of the parties by program sponsors is necessary, if serving as arbitrator of record is to be part of a training program.

Publication of Awards

Publishers are faced with an increasing number of awards each year and are compelled to apply standards in selecting awards for publication. The Bureau of National Affairs, Inc., for example, utilizes essentially a two-step selection process. In the first instance, cases that turn on the credibility of witnesses, those that involve factual situations which have no general application, or those that involve routine principles or situations are eliminated. That the last category is a small one is a testament to the growing competence of management and unions in settling routine grievances short of arbitration.

BNA's criteria for inclusion is met by decisions which present issues of general interest and in which the arbitrator's opinion and reasoning can be clearly understood by persons other than the parties. However, no consideration is given to which party won the case or the name of the arbitrator who decided it, except in the case of a new arbitrator.

It is important to new arbitrators to have awards published so that users of the reporting services may have access to the arbitrator's work in making future selections. The American Arbitration Association also makes awards available for publication if the parties give their approval. Publishers will give some preference to new arbitrators in selecting awards to be published in order to aid in the development and acceptance of more neutrals. New arbitrators should send copies of their awards to publishers with an appropriate notation. Names and addresses of the principal publishers of awards in full text are:

> Labor Arbitration Reports
> The Bureau of National Affairs, Inc.
> 1231 25th St., N.W.
> Washington, D.C. 20037

> Labor Relations Press
> Highland Office Center
> P.O. Box 579
> Fort Washington, Pa. 19034

> Labor Arbitration Awards
> Commerce Clearing House
> 4025 W. Peterson Ave.
> Chicago, Ill. 60646

Self-Development

There have been a limited number of formal training programs or internships available to those seeking to become labor arbitrators. Although formal training opportunities are likely to increase, it is unlikely in the foreseeable future that the majority of new arbitrators will have had the benefits of such training.

Given this assumption of need outpacing formal training opportunities, those seeking recognition as labor arbitrators can substantially improve the chances of attaining it through self-development. However, before investing the time and effort necessary, one should first determine as objectively as possible whether one is likely to be selected by both labor and management representatives—initially, and then again and again.

Do you have academic credentials indicative of superior reasoning ability? Do you have a practical knowledge of labor relations? Does your current employment record show a neutral position on labor relations issues? Will your personal convictions permit you to make hard decisions without partiality? Can you write cogently and incisively? Do you have the leadership ability necessary to control an adversary proceeding? Do you understand the nature of a quasi-judicial process? Do circumstances permit you to schedule hearing dates intermittently during normal working hours? As part of this self-evaluation process, it will also be useful to review the results of the ABA survey of the qualification and training of arbitrators as reported in Part VI. The statistics of that survey indicate a hard objective standard by selecting parties.

Attendance at Hearings

Several films dramatizing labor arbitration hearings provide a good picture of the nature of a hearing. Mock arbitrations conducted at a university or other seminar can contribute also to an understanding of what is involved. There is, however, no substitute for being present at several actual hearings. The reality of involvement and interaction has special dimensions in arbitration of rights in labor cases because of labor arbitration's unique function at the end of a multi-step grievance procedure.

There are several approaches to gaining access to arbitration hearings as an observer outside the framework of a formal training program. One direct way is to contact a known acceptable arbitrator and ask for an invitation. Although arbitrators generally serve at the will of the parties and are not likely to invite an audience to a hearing, successful arbitrators and contesting parties are generally willing to provide such opportunities for individuals interested in becoming arbitrators. Members of the National Academy are likely to be responsive to such requests.

A positive approach in this regard might include an introductory letter setting forth interest and background as well as availability to attend hearings. A follow-up telephone call is useful after an interval of a few weeks. Do not be discouraged if a first request to be invited is not received with enthusiasm. Some arbitrators receive many such requests, and the opportunites to permit outsiders to be present may be limited.

One may also contact the arbitrator appointing agencies explaining one's interest and goals. The agencies will use their good offices to help you obtain invitations to attend arbitration heaarings under their auspices. The arbitrator appointing agencies regard assisting in the development of new arbitrators as being consistent with their function; they will welcome your request.

Mock Awards

The ability to express effectively a decision in a dispute before an arbitrator requires uncommon writing skills. While the disputants usually want brevity, they also want clarity. While they do not want equivocation, they do want an exposition of conflicting positions. To the extent that incisive writing skill in the framework of an arbitration decision can be acquired, the preparation of mock awards is a necessary exercise. Although the form of opinions and awards can be gleaned from studying the decisions of leading arbitrators, the effective articulation of a decision must ultimately be of your own expression. For a self-made golfer, the practice tee is the answer. For a self-made arbitrator, mock awards serve the same purpose.

It would be desirable to obtain criticism of your mock awards from seasoned arbitrators. It would be helpful if the arbitrator of record in a case where you attended the hearing as an observer would review your mock award for that case. From a self-help perspective, one should continually compare one's own efforts with those of acceptable arbitrators. This will work, however, only if the student writer is a tough self-evaluator.

Serving as Arbitrator of Record

The test of one's efforts will be selection as an arbitrator. Acceptability is the established standard, but acceptability can appear to be an impenetrable ring of the chosen. It is difficult for a potential arbitrator to become acceptable where the criterion for determining acceptability is past performance. How does one enter the inner circle? One solution to this puzzle is found in the local public sector, where there has been a growing demand for new arbitrators because established arbitrators have generally not been interested in hearing these cases. Such arbitrator assignments are a natural opportunity to make a record.

Expedited arbitration is another avenue to enter the circle of acceptability. An increasing number of opportunities to serve as arbitrator exists under expedited procedures. Although these procedures usually limit time of and for hearings as well as the nature, scope, and length of the arbitrator's opinion, they do provide the opportunity to conduct a hearing and render an award. These cases also provide the opportunity to be observed by those parties who make the arbitrator selection for more critical issues. Application to serve as arbitrator in expedited cases may be made to the parties themselves or through the appointing agencies. Both approaches are recommended.

Publication of Awards

Once an arbitrator has served in a few cases, his reputation can be enhanced if one or more of his decisions is published. Fortunately, publishers are sympathetic to new arbitrators. Do not, however, assume an automatic right to seek publication of a decision. The award belongs to the parties. Either one of the parties may not want the decision published. Consent must be obtained from both the union and company before publication is sought, unless release for publication is arranged by an appointing agency such as FMCS or AAA.

A primary consideration is the quality of the opinion. Will the parties who read a published opinion want that arbitrator to serve as their arbitrator? It may sometimes be better to be unknown than known too well before one has developed the writing style and judgment upon which one is willing to be assayed.

Part V

Selected Decisions

> *The Court bows to the lessons of experience and the force of better reasoning, recognizing that the process of trial and error, so fruitful in the physical sciences, is appropriate also in the judicial function.*
>
> Louis D. Brandeis

Selected Decisions

The decisions reproduced in this Part, a sampling of opinions and awards written by a few of the many acceptable arbitrators who have shaped the law of arbitration, are presented as models or instructional aids. Clarity of expression, a sense of balanced judgment, and persuasive and fair-minded conclusions are characteristics common to all of them. However, they vary in writing style and length as well as in the structure of the opinion. It is apparent from reading these decisions that there is no rigid format or single formula for successful decision writing.

The full text of each decision is given and identified by BNA reference number, as relevant. Suggested questions designed to elicit discussion follow each decision.

Ford Motor Company

Arbitrator Harry Shulman
September 4, 1952
19 LA 237

ASSIGNMENT OF WORK

These two cases were specially submitted at different times; but they involve similar questions and may be disposed of together.

Background

A project relating to the spray booths in the Dearborn Assembly Plant required the construction of a long system of pipe. The work was assigned to the Company's Pipefitters. Some of the pipe was to be overhead, about twenty feet above the ground. The pipe was of approximately twenty-foot lengths with various diameters, much of it eight inches or more. In order to lift the lengths of pipe to the overhead positions, it was necessary to use chain or rope falls rigged on a steel beam under the roof. After the work had proceeded for some two weeks, the Pipefitters refused to rig and lift the pipe; their contention was that this was work for a Rigger, not a Pipefitter. Discussions and threats of discipline were unavailing; the Pipefitters were adamant in their refusal. The Company thereupon submitted the matter to the Umpire under Article VII, Section 25. It considered the alternative of letting the completion of the work to an outside contractor; but, on my suggestion and in order to provide adequate opportunity for decision, it proceeded to complete the work with its own Pipefitters, supplying a Rigger as demanded, without prejudice. That is Case No. 12049.

Case No. 12274 comes from the Fab Shop. A Welder was assigned to welding anchors in curb angles which were subsequently to be set in concrete on the ground. He was directed to hold the anchor (a straight piece of iron under a foot in length) in the angle while welding it. He refused to do so on the ground that the holding of the anchor in the angle was a Fitter's work and had always been done by a Fitter. Upon his continued refusal to do the job as directed, he was discharged. Meetings between the parties followed promptly and the Welder was reinstated upon the understanding that the case would be specially submitted to the Umpire. The Welder's penalty was thus reduced to a Reprimand with time lost prior to his reinstatement. The specific penalty is, however, only an incident of the primary issue involved in the case, namely, the situation out of which the penalty arose.

Discussion

The two cases are but illustrations of an old controversy which recurs with particular virulence in the Maintenance Unit at Rouge, the controversy relating to "working out of classification" or "crossing lines of demarcation." With respect to production classifications the issue has long been settled. It is recognized that production classifications denote the rates of pay for types of work and are not areas of jurisdiction. An employee on a production classification may not refuse an assignment on the ground that it is, even admittedly, work of a different classification (Opinions A-116 [3 LA 779] and A-215). The parties' Agreement provides specifically for the loan of employees "from one classification to another" (Article VIII, Section 14) and for the grouping of occupations for the purposes of layoff. A production employee who refuses to do a work assignment solely because the work is outside his classification is properly subject to discipline; and this well established principle is no longer challenged in the grievance procedure.

A differentiation with respect to the skilled trades is also established. Opinion A-223 [3 LA 782] reversed a disciplinary penalty imposed on a skilled tradesman for refusing an assignment of work in an admittedly different trade. It held that "the duty of obedience to orders" did not extend "to assignments of work in admittedly skilled trades constituting different seniority groups." Because of the reliance placed on that Opinion, its precise limits need to be re-emphasized. The Opinion dealt with "a bald case in which a skilled tradesman was assigned to work wholly from and unrelated to his classification because of a shortage of work in his own classification or a desire to get the other work done." It therefore pointed out that, under the parties' seniority agreements, a "skilled tradesman for whom there is no work in his trade," unlike a production worker, "is entitled to refuse a transfer to another trade" and take a layoff instead. The Opinion expressly limited the right of refusal to clear cases like the "bald" one there involved. It was at pains to point out that it did not extend to "situations where there is reasonable dispute as to whether the work assigned does or does not fall within" the tradesman's classification. For "such instances of reasonable dispute," the duty of the obedience as explained in Opinion A-116 was stated as the applicable rule.

Two questions are involved in the situations illustrated by the cases here for decision: (1) the propriety of the work assignment and (2) the method by which the propriety of the assignment is to be challenged and determined. While the answer to the first question must necessarily depend upon the facts of the particular case and cannot be generalized, the answer to the second question can be generalized and should be so clear in advance as to admit of very little, if any, doubt in its application to specific cases.

Right to Refuse Assignment—The regular method for determining the propriety of a protested assignment is not by refusal to do the work, but by invoking the grievance procedure or by special submission to the Umpire. That is the method always safe and always proper. It is the required method in the usual run of cases. Only in the rare cases defined in Opinion A-223 may a refusal to do the work be justified, that is, cases in which the assignment is admittedly or beyond reasonable dispute to work in a different trade constituting a different seniority group. Such cases should be rare, indeed, since Supervision can now well be expected not to make such plainly improper assignments. Refusal to do the work is therefore always risky. For, if it is determined that the assignment was not improper beyond reasonable dispute, the refusal is proper ground for disciplinary measures. And, of course, a stoppage of work by other employees in protest against the assignment or against a disciplinary penalty for refusal to perform it would be a violation of Article V of the Agreement, regardless of whether the refusal was justified or not. For it is specifically the purpose of Article V to confine the parties to the contractual procedures for the redress of grievances and to prohibit them from resorting to strike or lockout as a means of rectifying alleged violations.

The idea that the work is to be done as assigned pending determination of the propriety of the assignment is not an invention for the Ford plants. It is now the generally accepted method of dealing with jurisdictional disputes. The home grounds for jurisdictional disputes are, of course, the building trades. There the disputes are not only with employers; the disputes there are also between Unions. For some years now, agreements between the A.F. of L. building trades and associations of contractors have provided, on national and local levels, procedures for the adjustment of jurisdictional disputes as to work in the construction industry. And a basic feature of the established procedures is that there must be no stoppage of work because of the dispute and that the work must be performed as assigned by the employer pending the determination of its propriety through the procedure. That is the self-regulation adopted in the construction industry not merely for the purpose of avoiding the relevant procedures of the Taft-Hartley Act but also for the purpose of providing a rational, economical, and peaceful method of adjusting controversies which had been a constant source of costly strife and embarrassment.

It may be objected that to require employees to do the work as assigned pending determination of the propriety of the assignment through the contractual provisions is to enable the employer to enforce what may be an improper assignment for the period that the case is pending,— and that may be a long time. The grievance procedure may, of course, provide appropriate redress for loss unjustly suffered in that period. And the time need not always be long; the procedure for special submission provides means of expedition when necessary. But to the extent that some time is necessarily required, the answer is that the result is inevitable and must have been contemplated and accepted by the parties when they entered their collective Agreement. Business enterprise, whether private or public, requires management. And management requires administrative initiative, one important phase of which, as expressly recognized in Article IV, Section 1, is the assignment of work. The whole idea of establishing a grievance procedure is based on the assumption that Management will act and that its action may be in violation of the Agreement. And it is precisely for such alleged violations that the Agreement prescribes its procedures and prohibits resort to work stoppage. Of course, these procedures, and the whole Agreement, can work effectively for the accomplishment of their goals only if both parties act in good faith, with a modicum of good sense, and with respect for each other and for their commitments. Acting in this way, an employer will rarely make blatantly improper assignments; and when he does, Opinion A-223 recognizes exceptional defensive action by the employees.

Great reliance is placed by the Union in these two cases upon prior practice. It seems to be thought that, while what has been said above may be true generally, it is not true where the protested assignment deviates from prior practice in the plant and that in such cases a refusal to do the work as assigned is proper. This is an erroneous notion. In the first place, as will be more fully stated below, past practice is not necessarily controlling in an inquiry as to the propriety of an assignment. And secondly, there is generally considerable dispute in these cases, based on reasonable grounds, as to the nature of the past practice. A general exception to the duty of obedience based on belief as to past practice is neither reasonable nor practicable.

In these cases, the Company rescinded the protested assignment pending determination by the Umpire; and in one of them it invoked the Umpire's jurisdiction under Article VII, Section 25. This is an example of a flexible and conciliatory attitude which is commendable and which, with respect to the use of the Umpire, is found more frequently at Ford than elsewhere. The method thus employed is an available one. The desirability of its use in particular circumstances should always be explored. Maintenance of desirable labor relations and plant operation requires flexibility of mind and wise choice between available procedures in the light of special circumstances. But by that very token, the employment of this method in all cases cannot properly be demanded. It is a deviation from the general rule of administrative initiative in management and the right of challenge by the Union through the contractual procedures. It provides the elasticity desired to ease special tensions in unusual circumstances. It is not the basic method established by the Agreement.

Effect of Past Practice—The next question concerns the propriety of the assignments in the two cases.

As is well known, jobs at Ford are classified by classification titles only. With few exceptions, there are no descriptions of job content, except such as may be inferred from the titles themselves. While the

Agreement freezes the rates of pay for the classifications, it does not freeze jobs or job content. On the contrary, the Agreement expressly recognizes the Company's right to discontinue or change jobs and it makes provision with respect to seniority rights and rates of pay in the event of such changes. Indeed, changes in methods and job content are a common characteristic of the automobile industry. While there are a great variety of classifications, the trend with respect to classifications other than the skilled trades has been to place them into larger seniority groups of interchangeable occupations and to recognize seniority rights in a group of jobs rather than in a single job or classification. Consistent with this trend, the Agreement recognizes that an employee in such classifications may be assigned to work out of his classification, subject to limitations not here relevant.

The situation with respect to the skilled trades is different. It is true that here, too, there are only classification titles, without job descriptions; and the Agreement does not in so many words prohibit the crossing of trade lines and working a tradesman on a job not in his trade. But other guides point in that direction. The classification titles are identification of skills, trades or crafts of long tradition outside as well as within the automobile industry. Many of the trades are apprenticeable and the nature of their work is indicated by their apprenticeship standards. Generally, each trade is a different seniority group; seniority is reckoned from the date of entry into the particular classification, rather than from the date of hire by the Company; the classifications are not interchangeable for seniority purposes; seniority may not be carried over from one group to another; on a reduction of force in his trade, an employee may choose a layoff instead of a transfer to work outside his trade. A tradesman is hired not so much for a job as for his trade; he is a journeyman when he is placed on the classification. When it was necessary to use non-journeymen, the parties provided for upgraders or trainees by special agreement which safeguarded the claims and the status of the journeymen. There have thus been recognized, albeit without precision and with some variations, the complementary principles that the work of a trade should be done by employees in that trade and that a tradesman should not be required to do work in a trade other than his own.

This necessitates, of course, some knowledge of the content of the individual trades or of the so-called lines of demarcation between them. The Maintenance Unit has long sought an agreement specifying in detail the content of the individual trades and the parties have many times discussed the matter. But they have been unable to reach agreement on the preliminary question of whether such specification is desirable or feasible. The Unit has also suggested at times that I specify the lines of demarcation through a decision; but I have had to decline the task as beyond my jurisdiction and competence. The result is that each case must be considered on the basis of its own facts and circumstances, and only unconnected points can be marked by case to case decision as the cases arise. Fortunately, there is no dispute with reference to the great bulk of the work—that is, for example, what trade is to paint a wall, build a wooden cabinet, repair conveyors, lay brick, care for electric wiring and so on. The disputes that do arise, while numerous, concern principally the edges—that is, incidental tasks that must be performed in conjunction with the conceded work of the tradesman, as, in these cases, the lifting of the pipe to be connected by the Pipefitters or the holding of the anchor to be welded by the Welder.

Determination of the propriety of disputed assignments must necessarily rely on accepted notions in the trades generally, that is, outside the plant and not merely in the plant. For, as must be apparent, the trades are not just Ford classifications of work and rates of pay. They are specifications of skills, status and ethics, having an independent existence. Their relationship to standards of the trade generally is comparable to the relationship between Company doctors or lawyers and the standards of their professions. The Union commonly espouses this view and seeks to secure at Ford whatever advantageous standards exist in the trade outside.

But while espousing this view, the Union also invokes restrictions not found in the trade generally but claimed to be based on prior practice at Rouge. The contention is that even though a particular assignment may properly be made in the trade generally, it may not be so made at Ford because the prior practice there was otherwise. As a broad statement of principle this contention is erroneous. That is not merely because the two positions seem inconsistent. (Both parties are frequently found in this puzzling position. Each insists on the compulsion of prior practice in some cases and on the right to have practice changed in others; and each points, with perhaps histrionic indignation, to the inconsistency of the other.) It is erroneous rather because it does not accord with the parties' basic philosophy and contractual arrangements as set out above.

The differentiations between the skilled trades and production classifications, as set out and as sharpened by Opinions A-116 and A-223, were made in recognition of the external and independent existence of the trades and their standards, comparable as I have said, to the professions. To the extent that special arrangement with respect to skilled trades may exist at Ford, they are not features of the trade but, rather, features of Ford employment or Ford classifications. Nothing in reason or in the Contract requires differentiation between the skilled trades and production classifications with respect to features which are peculiar to Ford employment and are not general standards of the trade. No such differentiation is made, for example, with respect to the rules for holiday eligibility, vacation pay, discipline, and so on. And no such differentiation is required with reference to practices as to work assignments which have no standing as general trade practices. To the extent that the practice is peculiar to Ford and is not a feature of the trade, it is as binding or as subject to change as is a practice with respect to production classifications.

A practice, whether or not fully stated in writing, may be the result of an agreement or mutual understanding. And in some industries there are contractual provisions requiring the continuance of unnamed practices in existence at the execution of the collective agreement. (There are no such provisions in the Ford Agreement or in those of the automobile industry generally.) A practice thus based on mutual agreement may be subject to change only by mutual agreement. Its binding quality is due, however, not to the fact that it is past practice but rather to the agreement in which it is based.

But there are other practices which are not the result of joint determination at all. They may be mere happenstance, that is, methods that developed without design or deliberation. Or they may be choices by Management in the exercise of managerial discretion as to the convenient methods at the time. In such cases there is no thought of obligation or commitment for the future. Such practices are merely present ways, not prescribed ways, of doing things. The relevant item of significance is not the nature of the particular method but the managerial freedom with respect to it. Being the product of managerial determination in its permitted discretion such practices are, in the absence of contractual provision to the contrary, subject to change in the same discretion. The law and the policy of collective bargaining may well require that the employer inform the Union and that he be ready to discuss the matter with it on request. But there is no requirement of mutual agreement as a condition precedent to a change of a practice of this character.

A contrary holding would place past practice on a par with written agreement and create the anomaly that, while the parties expend great energy and time in negotiating the details of the Agreement, they unknowingly and unintentionally commit themselves to unstated and perhaps more important matters which in the future may be found to have been past practice. The contrary holding would also raise other questions very difficult to answer. For example, what is properly a subject of a practice? Would the long time use of a wheelbarrow become a practice not to be changed by the substitution of four-wheeled buggies drawn by a tow tractor? Or would the long time use of single drill presses be a practice prohibiting the introduction of multiple drill presses? Such restraints on technological change are alien to the automobile industry. Yet such might be the restraints, if past practice were enshrined without carefully thought out and articulated limitations. Again, when is a practice? How frequently and over how long a period must something be done before it is to be called a practice with the consequences claimed? And how is the existence of the past practice to be determined in the light of the very conflicting testimony that is common in such cases? The Union's witnesses remember only the occasions on which the work was done in the manner they urge. Supervision remembers the occasions on which the work was done otherwise. Each remembers details the other does not; each is surprised at the other's perversity; and both forget or omit important circumstances. Rarely is alleged past practice clear, detailed and undisputed; commonly, inquiry into past practice of the type that is not the result of joint determination or agreement produces immersion in a bog of contradictions, fragments, doubts, and one-sided views. All this is not to say that past practice may not be important and even decisive in applying provisions of the Agreement. The discussion is addressed to the different claim that, apart from any basis in the Agreement, a method of operation or assignment employed in the past may not be changed except by mutual agreement.

Propriety of Assignments—Now to the specific assignments here in question.

The Pipefitters' position was that they could not properly be required to lift and position overhead, by means of rope or chain falls attached to an overhead beam, pipe that is over four inches in diameter. This, they said, was Riggers' work. Whether they were seeking thus to protect the Riggers' jurisdiction or to advance their own trade claims is perhaps immaterial. What is material is that their refusal to do the work was based soley on the jurisdictional ground. At the hearing it was suggested that the four-inch specification is not the decisive point and emphasis was placed on the height and nature of the lift and the attachment of the falls to the beam under the roof; but the four-inch factor continued to be stressed.

The Pipefitters' claim is not based on standards generally accepted in the trade. It cannot be so based because those standards lend no support to the claim. In the Pipefitters' trade generally, the lifting and positioning of pipe, manually or with the aid of chain falls, is accepted as a normal incident of the craft, within the conception of "tools of the trade." A. F. of L. Pipefitters claim this work and the other trades concede it to them. Whatever question there may be about Ford practice, it is entirely clear that it is a normal incident of the Pipefitters' trade to lift and position pipe, with the aid of rope and chain falls, regardless of the pipe diameter or the height of the lift.

The Pipefitters' claim is based on the ground that, for numberless years at Rouge, Riggers rather than Pipefitters did the lifting and positioning of pipe over four inches in diameter. It is not claimed that this was the result of any agreement between the parties, or even of any joint discussions. On the contrary, the practice is said to date from years prior to the beginning of the parties' relations in collective bargaining. The Company denies the existence of the practice. It concedes that Riggers have been used to aid Pipefitters as claimed; but it insists that Pipefitters have also made the lifts themselves; and it disclaims any knowledge of a rule, commitment or stated policy of the kind claimed by the Pipefitters. This conflict of testimony is understandable and, in all likelihood, quite honest. The higher levels of Supervision did not concern themselves with the detailed assignment of tasks on the job. That was taken care of by the immediate foreman and to some extent by the crew leader. With Riggers readily available (as they were more particularly when maintenance and construction were centralized in a single plant-wide department) they were probably used as claimed by the Union, with and without express direction from immediate Supervision. But this is a long way from a commitment as to how the work must be done.

As already stated, if the parties as a result of joint consideration reach an agreement as to the distribution of tasks in the skilled trades, that agreement is binding and the agreed upon distribution must be observed until the agreement expires or is changed by mutual consent, regardless of whether or not the agreement conforms to standards of the trades outside. But in the absence of such limiting agreements, the Company is entitled to use its skilled trades employees in accordance with the generally accepted standards of their trades. The fact that it does not avail itself of the full scope of their crafts for a time does not mean that it may not do so at another time when it deems it desirable.

A different rule, in the absence of a deliberate choice to the contrary by the parties, would be disadvantageous to the interests of both. While there has been considerable controversy between the parties as to the letting of work to outside contractors, it is undisputed that Ford at Rouge does much more of its maintenance and construction with its own employees than does any other unit in the automobile industry. (Indeed, some of the maintenance classifications do not even exist in some of the automobile companies.) To safeguard this condition and to discourage greater resort to outside contractors, the Company should not be placed at a disadvantage with respect to its competitors or the outside contractors by jurisdictional restrictions which are not generally accepted features of the trades and which are not negotiated or deliberately adopted.

To the extent that the Pipefitters' refusal in Case No. 12049 was based on the jurisdictional claim, it was improper. Pipefitters may properly be required to lift and position their pipe without limitation as to its size, and to fasten and use the manual chain or rope falls necessary for that purpose. That kind of rigging is part of their trade as, indeed, it is part of some other trades.

This holding is addressed to the general question of craft jurisdiction only. In special circumstances other considerations may be involved and may call for the auxiliary services of a Rigger. This the Company concedes. For example, the pipe may have turns or joints or be so fashioned as to constitute an unbalanced load. Or it may have to be guided in the air around obstructions or corners. In cases of this nature, the hazards may be such as to require the more specialized skill of a Rigger. But the reason then would be, not a general rule or craft jurisdiction, but rather the dictates of safety in the light of the special hazard. Again, even in a normal case, a particular Pipefitter may, because of his age or some other physical disability, be unsuited for climbing to a beam in order to attach the falls. Here, too, his assignment to the task may be improper for reasons peculiar to him, but not because of lines of jurisdiction.

In the Welder's case, too, the claim is based solely on prior practice. Here the area of the practice is even narrower than the Rouge. The claim is, and it is substantiated, that in the Fab Shop a Fitter would hold the anchor in the curb angle while the Welder welded it. But it is equally clear that "in the field," that is, elsewhere at Rouge, if a similar weld were necessary, the Welder would hold the piece himself. Here, too, there is no suggestion that the Fab Shop practice was ever adopted as a result of discussion or negotiation. It seems just to have grown up— perhaps, in part at least, because in the Fab Shop Fitters and Welders worked in close proximity and were not always fully occupied.

The disputed task is the mere holding of the piece while it is being welded. No fitting, in any realistic sense, is involved. The anchor does not have to be welded to any particular specification or at any particular angle so long as it is welded at an angle. It might perhaps be more convenient and even speed the work to have some one other than the Welder handle and hold the anchor. But there is no rule in the trade or adopted by the parties that a Welder may not hold the piece he is welding or that the placing of a piece in position for welding, when the position is so unrestricted as in this case, is the exclusive province of a Fitter. Insofar as the Welder's refusal in Case No. 12274 was based solely on the claim that the placing and holding of the anchor was Fitter's work not to be done by a Welder, the refusal was improper. This determination, like the preceding one, is addressed to the general question of jurisdiction only. In particular cases, other considerations may be involved, as for example, fitting the pieces to precise limits, or special difficulty in holding and welding at the same time.

This opinion is oriented primarily by the situation at Rouge. So far as the procedures discussed are concerned, the discussion is of general relevance, applicable to the other Ford plants as well as Rouge. But so far as the so-called "lines of demarcation" are concerned, the situation at Rouge is unique and quite different from that at other plants, particularly the Assembly Branches and Parts Depots,—because of the amount and variety of maintenance and construction at Rouge, the size of the maintenance and construction force, the variety of trades found in that force, and other reasons. Accordingly, some different arrangements, more suited to the different needs of flexibility and employment at the Branches, are necessary and have been worked out.

Questions for Discussion

What elements does Arbitrator Shulman suggest are required to establish a binding past practice?

How does Arbitrator Shulman's view of past practice compare to current thinking?

What is the essence of the work and grieve method of protesting a work assignment?

Under what circumstances would Arbitrator Shulman have permitted an employee to refuse a work assignment?

Compare the style, form, and substance of this opinion and award with the other decisions included in this Part.

Maremont Automotive Products, Inc.

Arbitrator Bert L. Luskin
September 2, 1955
25 LA 171

ARBITRATION: PROCEDURE

An Arbitration Hearing was held at the office of the Arbitrator on August 22, 1955. A Post Hearing Statement of position was filed by both the Company and the Union.

Background

Grievances Nos. 16, 68, and 80 had been filed and were processed through the various steps of the grievance procedure. At grievance meetings held on April 21, May 5 and May 19, 1955, the Union certified one of the three grievances to Arbitration on each of those dates. Following notice of intention to arbitrate by the Union, the Company by letter confirmed the receipt of such notice and commenced the processing of the respective grievances to Arbitration. The Union subsequently requested that all three cases be processed in a single Arbitration proceeding, to be heard by a single Arbitrator. The Company refused to agree to such a procedure on the grounds that the grievances involved had been certified to Arbitration at different grievance meetings and should properly be construed as separate cases to be arbitrated one at a time. That issue became the subject matter of a grievance which the parties were unable to resolve and the issue is presently before this Arbitrator for disposition.

Union Contentions

The Union contended that historically Arbitration was urged by management as a means of peaceful disposition of problems arising under agreements between the parties. That Unions were suspicious of the process because of their fear that Arbitration would prove too expensive, and there was an insufficient history to convince the Unions that Arbitrators were equipped by experience and temperament to issue Awards on the type of problems arising out of Collective Bargaining Agreements. That Unions have accepted the process which is now being distorted by a management insistence on a case by case approach. That such a procedure destroys efficiency, adds time and cost to the Arbitration process and affects good labor relations. That the judicial system has developed to a point where multiple issues between two parties can now be tried and disposed of in a single case. That Arbitration was intended to serve the purpose of disposing of all pending grievances certified to Arbitration with a minimum of cost and delay, avoiding the problem of establishing multiple hearings by grouping as many issues as possible into one case to be presented before a single Arbitrator. That experienced Arbitrators do not attempt to compromise or trade awards between the parties and decide cases on their individual merits regardless of the number of issues heard at one time. That in the past, in every instance where a number of issues were present, all pending grievances were certified to Arbitration in one case before a single Arbitrator. That this is the first instance where the Company has made an effort to require individual processing of individual grievances.

Company Contentions

The Company contended that under the provisions of Article 4, Section 1, Sub-section (4) the word "grievances" while in the plural, subsequently refers to a grievance in the singular. That the parties specifically negotiated the provision in question which required an Arbitration to be heard within 30 days from the date that the grievance had been submitted to the 3rd step of the grievance procedure. That the Company is in agreement that grievances awaiting Arbitration should be expeditiously heard and disposed of. That its position in the instant case is based upon such premise since the Union appears to desire that Arbitration on any single case be withheld until several cases had been processed in order to group them as one case, whereas the Company is desirous of having grievances arbitrated quickly and expeditiously as they arise. That the Company has no objection to certifying a group of cases to one Arbitrator provided that all cases so grouped should be certified at one time. That if all three grievances involved had been certified to Arbitration at one grievance meeting, the Company would have been willing to submit the three issues to a single Arbitrator. That allowing grievances to accumulate defeats the intention of the parties for speedy and expeditious handling of grievances and would encourage delays which the parties intended to avoid under the language of the provision in question.

Discussion

The provision of the agreement which establishes the Arbitration process and the formula thereunder is Article 4, Section 1, Sub-section (4) thereof which reads as follows:

"(4) Grievances that have not been satisfactorily settled under the foregoing procedure shall be referred to an arbitrator agreed upon by the Company and the Union. The decision of the arbitrator shall be final and binding on the Company and the Union, and any employee or employees involved. The expense of arbitration, including the arbitrator's charges, shall be divided equally between the Company and the Union. All arbitrations shall be heard within thirty (30) days from the date a grievance has been submitted to the third step of the grievance procedure. This thirty (30) day period can be extended by mutual agreement between the Union and the Company. The schedule regarding the arbitration of the grievance is to be set up with the arbitrator within thirty (30) days of the incident. The matter shall be considered closed if above has not been affected."

This is the first time in the relationship between the parties that the issue has arisen. In the past whenever multiple cases were pending Arbitration, they were grouped together and heard as a single case by a single Arbitrator. It should be noted at the outset of this discussion that the Company does not object to grouping grievances referred to Arbitration in one case. It contends, however, that each grievance or grievances certified at one meeting creates a separate case, and all grievances which may be certified to Arbitration at any specific grievance meeting of that nature should be treated separately. In other words, if the grievances which gave rise to the instant issue had all been certified at the same meeting, the Company would have been willing to have them heard at one time by a single Arbitrator. The Union does not agree with that view, and that limitation, and contends that all grievances pending at the time the Arbitration procedure is invoked and an Arbitrator selected may be submitted to that Arbitrator and heard in that proceeding.

An analysis of the provision hereinabove set forth indicates that although the Arbitration procedure has been established by the parties, and the Arbitrator is to be selected and agreed upon by the parties, the provision is silent with respect to any procedure to be followed in the selection of the Arbitrator. It is also required that Arbitrations must be heard within thirty (30) days from a date that the grievance has been submitted to the 3rd step of the grievance procedure. Grievances are referred to both in the singular and in the plural. Based upon the position of the parties, it is apparent that multiple grievances can be heard in one Arbitration Hearing before a single Arbitrator, and that procedure has been followed in the past. The issue resolves itself around the problem of the grouping of grievances into one case where those grievances have been certified to Arbitration at different times. There can be no question that once the Arbitration process has been established, an Arbitrator selected, and pending grievances submitted to the Arbitrator, that additional grievances arising subsequent thereto and prior to the date of the hearing, can thereafter not be submitted in that proceeding without the joint agreement of the parties. Once an Arbitrator has been selected and grievances have been submitted by whatever process the parties may follow, a submission has been created and new cases cannot thereafter be added without agreement. However, prior to the time that an Arbitrator has been selected, the submission is not complete. It would appear that the language of the provision in question allows and permits the submission of multiple issues to a single Arbitrator. It must follow therefore, within certain limits, that grievances which have been certified to Arbitration prior to the formal selection of an Arbitrator can be joined into one case for submission before the Arbitrator to be selected. The limits, however, appear to be a 30-day period which the parties have established under the contract within which Arbitrations are to be heard after a grievance has been submitted to the 3rd step of the grievance procedure. That thirty (30) day period may be extended by mutual agreement. However, if the 30-day period is not extended, then and in that event, grievances which are thereafter certified to Arbitration fall within a different grouping and cannot be combined excepting by mutual agreement. In effect therefore, the specific grievances which were pending Arbitration at the time the instant issue arose were certified to Arbitration on April 21, May 5, and May 19, 1955. They were therefore certified within a 30-day period and could have been grouped within one case for submission to a single Arbitrator. To allow a grievance to be certified to Arbitration without completing the process within the time established by the parties acts to defeat the very purpose that it was intended to effectuate. Extensive delays in the selection of an Arbitrator and the submission of the grievance or grievances to Arbitration creates a condition which could conceivably result in the very delay and inefficiencies which the Union contends should be avoided.

The provision also refers to the scheduling of cases with the Arbitrator within thirty (30) days of the incident. That language was changed from the prior contract where it followed the provision referring to discharge or discriminatory layoff or recall grievances. This language clearly supports the interpretation placed upon the provision by the Arbitrator to the extent that the parties intended under this section to permit cases to be scheduled for hearing within thirty (30) days after they are certified to Arbitration without limitation as to number but with the specific limitation with respect to the time at which they were certified within the 30-day period.

It must follow therefore that the 30-day period set forth in the provision in question appears to be the limitation set upon the procedures by the parties. In other words, grievances may be grouped within a single Arbitration hearing, provided they were certified to Arbitration within a 30-day period. Since Grievances Nos. 16, 68 and 80 were certified to Arbitration within the 30-day period referred to, they should properly be grouped in one Arbitration proceeding and heard by a single Arbitrator to be jointly selected by the parties.

Award

1. It is the award of the Arbitrator that grievances certified to Arbitration within a thirty (30) day period may be grouped into one submission and heard by a single Arbitrator.

2. Grievances Nos. 16, 68 and 80 having been certified to Arbitration by the Union within a thirty (30) day period should be submitted to a single Arbitrator to be heard in one proceeding instead of establishing separate arbitration hearings for each individual grievance.

Questions for Discussion

On what basis did Arbitrator Luskin conclude that several separate grievances may be grouped within a single arbitration hearing as a matter of right?

What effect did evidence of bargaining history and past practice have on Arbitrator Luskin's interpretation of the contract language?

How could the contract language have been framed to avoid ambiguity and to support clearly the position of either the union or the company?

Why would a procedural arbitrability question (as distinguished from substantive arbitrability) be within the scope of an arbitrator's authority today?

Compare the style, form, and substance of this opinion and award with the other decisions included in this Part.

Fafnir Bearing Company

Arbitrator Saul Wallen
November 28, 1955
25 LA 657

WAIVER OF BENEFITS

Introduction

Pursuant to Article IV of the currently effective collective bargaining agreement between the above parties, the undersigned was selected as impartial arbitrator in the determination of this dispute. At a hearing held at New Britain, Connecticut, on October 12, 1955, the parties agreed that the issue was as follows:

> "Was there a violation of the contract dated 1/26/55, when the Company compelled X, an employee, as a condition of returning to work, to sign a waiver, referred to in Section 7465 of the Connecticut Workmen's Compensation Act, for a condition resulting from non-occupational illness or injury?
>
> "If so, shall the Company be ordered to void the waiver signed April 14, 1955, by X.?
>
> "If so, is X entitled to retroactive pay for the period she was not allowed to resume employment for not signing the waiver?"

At the hearing the Company was represented by Keith Middleton, Vice-President, and Fred Senf, Personnel Director; the Union was represented by William Zeman, Attorney. Briefs were subsequently filed by both parties.

The Facts

X has been employed by the Company since 1942. On March 18, 1955, she complained of some trouble with her leg, and [was] told that she would have to be examined by the Company physician. On March 24, she was examined by Dr. Livingston who found that she had the following defects:
1. Obesity
2. Bilateral Varicose Veins
3. Hypertensive C.V.D.—blood pressure 216/100

Dr. Livingston told Mrs. X that with conditions such as these, she would have to sign a waiver as permitted by Connecticut law, designed to release the employer from all Workmen's Compensation claims which she might otherwise have in the future as a result of work-induced aggravation of these non-work-induced defects. Mrs. X said she would like to think the matter over, and meanwhile returned to her job.

On April 7, she was examined again, and was told by the Personnel Department that she could not work any longer unless she executed the waiver. On April 14, she signed the waiver under protest, returning to work on April 18, and the present grievance protesting the waiver requirement was subsequently filed.

Position of the Parties

The Union contends that the waiver requirement, while concededly valid as to newly hired employees, is the unilateral introduction by the employer of a new condition of employment as to present employees. Consequently, according to the Union, a discharge for failure to sign such a waiver, is not a discharge for cause but a violation of seniority rights under the Agreement. Moreover, says the Union, the Connecticut law expressly only *permits* such waivers, thus, impliedly prohibiting their compulsion. Finally, the Union relies on the *Royal McBee Corp.* case, 24 LA 243, which it says is completely in point here, in that it held the involuntary layoff of an employee for refusing to sign such a waiver to be an act not justified by the collective bargaining contract.

The Company, on the other hand, strenuously contends that the discharge of an employee for refusing to sign a waiver exempting the employer from liability arising out of non-work-connected disabilities is a discharge "for proper cause." After all, says the Company, an employee who has a serious disability can be discharged altogether. So why should the employer, if he is willing to retain the employee, not be entitled at least to limit his extraordinary Workmen's Compensation liability on account of the employee? The employee here in question has varicose veins, which according to the medical evidence can bring a varicose ulcer in case the employee suffers a mild "scrape" or abrasion; similarly, the employee's high blood pressure subjects her to danger of dizzy spells and shock. Surely an employer is entitled to protect himself against such undue risks. Finally, the Company, in turn, points to the *Allen Mfg. Co.* case, 25 LA 216, which it says sustains its position in this controversy; and while the Company does not accept the Union's contention that that case distinguished the *Royal McBee* case solely on the grounds of a clearly established past practice requiring such waivers, even if this were so, the Company says, in the instant case there was an equally well-established practice of requiring such waivers.

Discussion

It seems appropriate to point out at the outset that I do not think the Connecticut statute dealing with Workmen's Compensation law waivers is of any aid in solving the problem before us. Concededly, that provision *permits* waivers such as are here involved. On the other hand, the law itself clearly does not compel them. Therefore, so far as the Connecticut statute is concerned, an employee may, but need not, sign a waiver. But the issue here goes beyond that and addresses itself to the question whether, if an employee resorts to his statutory right not to sign a waiver, this is "proper cause" under the collective bargaining contract for the employee's discharge.[1]

The parties have referred me to two recent arbitration decisions with the general question of Workmen's Compensation law waivers, *Royal McBee Corp.*, 24 LA 243; *Allen Mfg. Co.*, 25 LA 216. But I think that the instant case falls somewhere between the two decisions; and that neither of those decisions is dispositive of the problem here presented.

In the *Royal McBee* case, an employee who had had leg trouble three times before, suddenly was required, upon return from his fourth absence, to execute a Workmen's Compensation law waiver of future claims arising out of the leg trouble. The arbitrator, while also relying on the Connecticut provision permitting waivers, stated that since there was nothing in the Agreement authorizing such waivers and since no such waivers had ever been required of this employee after his three prior absences, the refusal of the Company to reinstate the employee unless he signed such a waiver was improper.

In the subsequent *Allen* case, however, there was a fairly clear past practice of requiring such waivers. Indeed the very employee there involved had signed two waivers before. Moreover, for more than a year before the grievance was filed, there had been a notice on the bulletin board making explicit this waiver requirement. Conceding that in the absence of such a clear notice the decision "might be more difficult," (25 LA at p. 225) the Board of Arbitration there concluded that by notice and practice in this plant it had become a condition of continued employment for returning employees with non-work-connected disabilities to sign such waivers, and that therefore the refusal to do so constituted a proper ground for discharge.

---

[1]Moreover, even though the state law must be "read into" the collective bargaining contract, as the Union contends, that does not dispose of the issue because it is clear that the Connecticut law here involved is merely a declaration of state policy that Workmen's Compensation law waivers are not against public policy in Connecticut (as they are in some states); but the Connecticut law leaves to the area of private industrial relations the questions of what consequences, if any, an employer may attach to an employee's refusal to sign such a waiver.

In the instant case, however, I do not think there has been any such invariable practice, and certainly no notice setting forth such a requirement was ever posted. Indeed, the Union points out that the posted Shop Rules and Regulations expressly omit reference to this matter. The Company has introduced convincing evidence to show that many employees (including some union officers) have signed such waivers in the past. However, according to its own testimony, very few employees refused to sign, and in those few cases some individual adjustment was arrived at. Thus without going into further detail on this question of past practice, it would appear that the issue presently before me simply has never been squarely posed before, and I therefore conclude that I must decide it on the basis of other considerations.[2]

The issue, as I have said before, therefore is whether the refusal to sign a waiver constitutes "proper cause" for discharge under the agreement. The Company's argument seems to be that since the waiver requirement is the only legal means by which Management may limit its contingent liability under the Workmen's Compensation Act without depriving employees of protection in cases of occupational illness or injury, it is essentially a reasonable requirement and a discharge based on the refusal to sign such a waiver would be for "proper cause."

It seems to me that this argument is much too broad. While it is reasonable for the Company to seek to limit its contingent liability by securing the voluntary assent of its employees to waivers, it does not follow that their unwillingness to give such assent is an act which constitutes "proper cause" for discharge. "Proper cause" for discharge exists when an employee either departs from accepted norms of behavior in his work environment or constitutes so potent a hazard to his fellow-employees or himself as to make his continued employment clearly unwarranted. Mrs. X fits into neither of these categories.

Her refusal to sign a waiver was not an act of misconduct of the same character as fighting in the plant, chronic absenteeism or other behavior for which it is commonly recognized Management has the right to discipline. At the same time, Mrs. X's physical condition—obesity, varicose veins and high blood pressure—was not alleged *of itself* to justify her discharge. The Company seeks, in effect, the right to discharge an employee whose physical condition is not of itself such as to justify it, solely because she is unwilling to opt in its favor in a matter in which the law gives her an option. This can hardly be classed as an impropriety of behavior or an act of misconduct which can fairly be

---

[2]As I understand the contentions of the parties, they both are in accord with this conclusion. Company brief, P. 11; Union Brief, pp. 5–8.

deemed "proper cause" for discharge. Employees enjoy numerous rights which, if surrendered, would advantage or protect their employers. For the employer to seek their surrender is understandable. But it does not follow that he may insist upon their surrender to the point of discharge on the basis that refusal of surrender would be "proper cause" for discharge.

The point is, while I fully appreciate the Company's understandable desire to limit its undue Workmen's Compensation liability, the employee's right to claim workmen's compensation is a substantive right conferred upon him by state law which he may bargain away when, as here, permitted by state law but which cannot be taken away from him through a general discharge clause. I might add that there is a very logical place in this Agreement where such waivers might have been specifically required, if that had been the intention of the parties drawing up this Agreement[3] to wit, it is in the general provision dealing with conditions under which employees out on personal illnesses may return to work.[4] But there is nothing whatever mentioned here or anywhere else in the Agreement about the Company's right to require such waivers.

One other matter requires some discussion. The Company argues that since an employee with a serious disability can be discharged altogether, surely the lesser course of retaining him on condition he signs a waiver is justifiable. Perhaps as applied to a clearly dischargeable employee, such an argument has merit. Presumably, since such an employee, by hypothesis, has no right to his job quite apart from the waiver requirement, he would most likely be quite agreeable to signing the waiver as a means of regaining his job. As noted earlier, however, that situation is not the one presented by this case. Rather, the sole issue here is whether her refusal to sign a waiver is, *in itself*, sufficient to deprive her of her otherwise secured seniority status. For the reasons above, I conclude that the answer to this question must be in the negative.

Decision

There was a violation of the contract dated January 26, 1955, when

[3]The evidence indicates that when the present Agreement was being negotiated, the *Royal McBee* case holding that, in the absence of a specific provision in the Agreement, the Company there had no power to compel such waivers, had just been decided and was well known to the present Company; yet the latter made no effort to have such a clause included in the present Agreement.

[4]Section 6.8 "When an employee is granted a leave of absence by the Company for reasons of personal illness such leave of absence shall not exceed the employee's length of service or two years whichever is shorter. When such employee is able to return to work with the approval of his physician and/or the Company Employee Relations Director and provided he returns not later than the end of his leave of absence, the Company will place such employee on work for which he has the necessary skill and ability and is physically able to perform . . .."

1. The Company compelled Mrs. X to sign the waiver as a condition of returning to work and the waiver signed by her under protest must therefore be voided.

2. Mrs. X is entitled to back pay for the days that she was able to work but was denied the right to work solely on account of her refusal to execute the waiver.

Questions for Discussion

On what basis does Arbitrator Wallen conclude that requiring the grievant to sign a waiver of workers' compensation claims for work-induced aggravation of non-work-induced defects was not a proper condition of employment?

Why does Arbitrator Wallen decide that the authority for waivers of workers' compensation claims under the Connecticut statute was not controlling?

How does Arbitrator Wallen distinguish this situation from other cases cited by the parties?

What is the significance of Arbitrator Wallen's observation regarding the negotiation of section 6.8 of the collective bargaining agreement between the parties?

Compare the style, form, and substance of this opinion and award with the other decisions included in this Part.

National Supply Company

Arbitrator Benjamin Aaron (chairman)
May 7, 1956
26 LA 666

CHANGE IN JOB CONTENT

This decision is rendered pursuant to the terms of an arbitration agreement executed by the above-named parties on February 23, 1956, which designated the undersigned as Chairman of an Arbitration Board and submitted the following issue for final and binding determination:

Was the assignment of the lubrication and cleaning duties to the Ladle Craneman a violation of our current Articles of Agreement?

A hearing was held on April 12, 1956 at the Company's plant in Torrance, California, before an Arbitration Board whose members were Scott F. Albright, representing the Company; O. O. Clayton, representing the Union; and the undersigned, acting as neutral member and Chairman. Both parties appeared and were offered a full opportunity to present evidence and argument bearing upon the issue. Each side was permitted to file a post-hearing brief, but only the Company elected to do so.

On the basis of the entire record in this case, the Arbitration Board makes the following

Award

The assignment of the lubrication and cleaning duties to the Ladle Craneman was not a violation of the current Articles of Agreement.

Facts

This case arose under the terms of the Articles of Agreement between the parties (Joint Exhibit 1), dated November 10, 1954, as subsequently supplemented and revised.

The following facts were established at the hearing:

Prior to June, 1955, foundry crane #615 was replaced by a new crane, #2211, at a cost of about $80,000. Much of the trouble with crane #615 had been caused by excessive oiling and the consequent accumulation of dust, dirt, and muck caking on the equipment.

After investigating, management concluded that the crane operator should do the cleaning in his work area and should also perform the manual operation of the pump handle on the one-shot lubrication system on the new crane and on crane #617. Previously, the lubrication of all overhead cranes had been the responsibility of the oiler.

The reasons for management's decision, and the steps taken to carry it out, were explained in detail by J. T. Evans, Jr., Superintendent of the Melting Department, Evans' undisputed testimony was that the accumulation of the residue of over-oiling and dirt resulted in a muck that was both damaging to the equipment and hazardous to the employees. Prior to the change in procedure, numerous complaints had been received and warnings against over-oiling had not been heeded. As an illustration, Evans cited the fact that, in making the change-over on crane #617, 135 hours of work were required to clean up the accumulation of oil and dirt in order to get the crane in proper condition.

According to Evans, the new lubrication operation assigned to the craneman takes about five to ten minutes, once a week. Since he is otherwise occupied only about 50 per cent of the time, he can readily accommodate the added duty.

Evans also testified that, prior to making any change in the crane operator's job duties, he described the proposed plan to each craneman and asked if he had any objection. Only one man raised a question, and this concerned not his own performance of the new function, but rather the possibility that the proposed new arrangement might put one or more of the oilers out of work. When advised that the oiler would still be required to perform other lubrication not covered by the one-shot system, the craneman withdrew his objection.

Following these discussions with the individual cranemen, Evans initiated the new procedure, effective July 1, 1955, in a "Memo to Supervisors" (Company Exhibit 1). The memorandum drew a distinction between "service" and "maintenance," defining the former as "cleaning, minor adjustments, lubrication and replacement of non-critical parts," and the latter as "repair, installation, major adjustment or replacement of critical parts." The memorandum then continued:

> In keeping with this program we are having our cranemen take over two services on their cranes. These are:
> (1) Daily cleaning of the cranes on all shifts. This includes blowing off as much of the crane as can be reached safely with the air hose and wiping up grease and other dirt that the air will not handle.
> (2) The operation of the centralized lubrication systems on #617 and #2211. This service is to be performed on the day shift each Monday. Each craneman will be instructed in the proper method of operating the lubrication systems prior to the effective date.
> Please make it clear to the cranemen that they are not being held responsible for the efficiency of the lubrication systems. They are responsible for operating the lubrication pumps according to maintenance instructions at the proper time. The maintenance department is still responsible for keeping the system operating so that if the schedule is followed the crane will receive proper lubrication. The regular preventive maintenance inspections will be performed as in the past by qualified personnel. . . .

Position of Parties

On July 29, 1955, the Union filed a grievance (Un. Exhibit 1), asserting that "Craneman in Foundry are (sic) being required to do Maintenance classification of work which is in violation of Article 3— Paragraph 1 of our current Articles of Agreement." The provision of the Agreement referred to in the grievance reads as follows:

> The Company and the Union have agreed upon the wage rates which will prevail under this agreement with proper consideration to the differential which will prevail in view of different responsibilities and skills required

by the various jobs and operations in the plan and such rates of pay are appended hereto as Supplement "A" and are made a part of this agreement.

In its argument before the Arbitration Board, however, the Union also invoked Paragraphs 2 and 3 of Article 3, which read as follows:

> The Company agrees to provide the Unit Chairman with a complete list of all changes in wage and job reclassifications, termination, recalls and new hires weekly.
>
> It is understood and agreed that no right of appeal to an umpire as provided in Article 8 shall exist in respect to wage rate matters of any kind, except in the establishment of rates for new operations creating jobs of such nature that previously established rates are not applicable thereto, or a grievance alleging improper individual classification in accordance with established job classification.

The Union's theory in this case can be summarized as follows. The job description of Craneman, Ladle (Un. Exhibit 2–A) makes no reference of any kind to service or maintenance functions. On the other hand, the job description of Oiler, Maintenance Cranes (Un. Exhibit 2–B) specifically states that he shall "Lubricate all overhead cranes in plant . . . at regularly designated times with proper lubricant." The Union contends, therefore, that the Company has unilaterally altered the content of the two jobs by removing a vital function from one and including it in the other. Since the job evaluations are mutually agreed upon by the parties, the Union asserts that the unilateral change by the Company violates both the Articles of Agreement and past practice at the plant.

The Company's position is that, while the Union has the right to request a re-evaluation of the Craneman, Ladle classification in order to determine what, if any, change in the rate should be made as a result of the added duties, it has no standing to challenge management's right unilaterally to change the nature of the job. The Company bases its contention on Article 9 (Management), which reads as follows:

> The Management of the works and the direction of the working forces, including the right to hire, suspend or discharge for proper cause or, transfer and the right to relieve employees from duty because of lack of work or for other legitimate reasons is vested exclusively in the Company provided that this will not be used for purposes of discrimination against any member of the Union.

Discussion

In discussing issues of this type I think it is more helpful to concentrate on specific details than to speculate upon the theoretical extent or limitation of abstract rights. From the testimony given at the hearing and my personal observation I conclude that the Company's action in reassigning certain duties from the oiler to the craneman was neither arbitrary nor discriminatory, but was in fact based upon the considered and reasonable judgment of responsible management. The transfer of job functions did not diminish the sum total of work previously performed by employees within the bargaining unit, nor did it result in any layoffs or wage rate reductions. I also conclude that the references to past practice made by the Union are inapposite to the instant case.

The one relevant possibility that has not yet been jointly explored by the parties is whether the transfer of the lubrication service function from oiler to craneman justifies a higher evaluation of the latter's job. That the Union has the right to raise this question is freely conceded by the Company, but the question which the Union has raised in this case goes to the Company's right to change the job functions, rather than to the consequences of such a change.

In my judgment the Company had the right in this instance to make the disputed change in job functions without the Union's consent. I do not think that right was affected one way or the other by the Company's prior consultations with the individual employees involved, which were neither required of the Company nor binding upon it or the Union. The current Agreement places no restriction upon the Company's right to reorganize work for more efficient performance; it protects the Union's interests in this regard simply by affording it the right to bargain over the terms under which new or changed jobs shall be performed.

It is significant that Article 3, upon which the Union relies in this case, deals with only one subject: Wages. I do not read the article as preventing management from changing the nature of work operations. This is the normal and accepted function of management, comprehended by the phrase, "Management of the works and the direction of the working forces," in Article 9, and it must be so recognized unless expressly limited or foreclosed by the terms of the Agreement.

My conclusion, therefore, is that the Union has mistaken the remedy afforded by the Agreement in the instant case. If the Union contends that the craneman should be paid more money for the job he is now required to perform, there is a procedure under the Agreement to explore and to resolve that issue. On the other hand, the initial decision to revise the job duties of the craneman and the oiler was within the authority and discretion of management to make, and it was made carefully, reasonably, and without violating any rights of the Union provided in the Agreement.

Questions for Discussion

Is the reserved rights doctrine a factor in Arbitrator Aaron's decision?

Why does Arbitrator Aaron conclude that the past practice arguments "are inapposite"?

Could Arbitrator Aaron have retained jurisdiction to decide the proper evaluation for the changed Ladle Craneman classification under the submission to arbitration?

How can one member of the Board of Arbitration also represent one of the parties?

Compare the style, form, and substance of this opinion and award with the other decisions included in this Part.

United States Steel Corporation

Arbitrator Sylvester Garrett
June 15, 1956
26 LA 812

REVISION OF INCENTIVE RATES

Statement of Grievance

Case No. G-60: "We the undersigned Charging Machine Operators, feel the Company is in violation of Section 9 of the August 15, 1952 Agreement; in changing the existing incentive plan, thereby reducing our earnings. We request the present plan providing the same amount of earnings remain in effect."

This grievance was filed in the Second Step of the grievance procedure on December 18, 1953.

Case No. G-61: "We, the employees of the Open Hearth Department feel the Company has reduced our incentive earnings without proper justification by the installation of the revised incentive on #6 Furnace. This revision requires increased production from 6 to 10 percent in order to maintain our existing incentive earnings as comparable on eight other furnaces.

"Therefore, we request that the fair day's work application as originally installed in furnace production be retained without change and that we be reimbursed for all monies lost."

This grievance was filed in the First Step of the grievance procedure on April 1, 1954.

Contract Provisions Involved

These grievances claim violation of Section 9-C-2, -3, and -4, and Section 9-F-2 of the August 15, 1952 Agreement because of changes made by the Company in existing Open Hearth incentives for (1) the Furnace Charging Crew, and (2) the No. 6 Furnace Crew, at Geneva Works.

Among the more important provisions of the 1952 Agreement directly involved in decision of these cases are the following:

"Section 9-C. New Incentives.

. . .

"2. The Company shall establish new incentives to replace existing incentive plans when they require revision because of new or changed conditions resulting from mechanical improvements made by the Company in the interest of improved methods or products, or from changes in equipment, manufacturing processes or methods, materials processed, or quality or manufacturing standards.

. . .

"3. Such new incentives shall be established in accordance with the following procedure:

"a. Management will develop the proposed new incentive;

"b. The proposal will be submitted to the grievance or assistant grievance committeeman representing the employees affected for the purpose of explaining the new incentive and arriving at agreement as to its installation. Management shall, at such time, furnish such explanation with regard to the development and determination of the new incentive as shall reasonably be required in order to enable the Union representative to understand how such new incentive was developed and determined and shall afford to such Union representative a reasonable opportunity to be heard with regard to the proposed new incentive;

"c. If agreement is not reached, the matter shall be reviewed in detail by designated representatives of the grievance committee and Management for the purpose of arriving at mutual agreement as to installation of the new incentive;

"d. Should agreement not be reached, the proposed new incentive may be installed by Management and the employees affected may at any time after thirty days, but within sixty days following installation, file a grievance alleging that the new incentive does not provide equitable incentive compensation. Such grievance shall be processed under the grievance and arbitration procedure of this Agreement. If the grievance is submitted to the arbitration procedure, the Board shall decide the question of equitable incentive compensation and the decision of the Board shall be effective as of the date when the new incentive was put into effect;

"e. In the event Management does not develop a new incentive, as provided in Paragraph 2 above, the employee or employees affected may, if filed promptly, process a grievance under the grievance and arbitration procedures of this Agreement requesting that a new incentive be installed in accordance with the provisions of this Subsection. If the grievance is submitted to arbitration the decision of the Board shall be effective as of the date when the grievance was filed.

"4. When an incentive plan is replaced, the average hourly earnings on any job which was covered by the replaced incentive shall not be less than the average hourly earnings received by regularly assigned incumbents of the job under the replaced incentive plan during the three months immediately preceding cancellation of the replaced incentive plan, provided that the average performance during such three-month period is maintained.

. . .

"Section 9-F. Existing Incentive Plans.

. . .

"2. All existing incentive plans in effect on April 22, 1947, including all existing rates incidental to each plan (such as hourly, the addition in Paragraph 1 above, base, piecework, tonnage, premium, bonus, standby, etc.), and all incentives installed after April 22, 1947 shall remain in effect until replaced by mutual agreement of the grievance committee and the plant Management or until replaced or adjusted by the Company in accordance with Subsection C of this Section."

Background

When these grievances arose, there were 10 furnaces in the Open Hearth at Geneva Works. Incentives had been installed for the various operations by mutual agreement May 28, 1950, and included:

Application 32.1-1 Stockyard Crew (Stockyard Craneman; Stockers)

Application 32.2-1 Furnace Crew (First and Second Helpers)

Application 32.2-2 Charging Crew (Charging Machine Operators; Floor Cranemen)

Application 32.2-3 Third Helper Crew (Third Helpers)

Application 32.2-4 Mixer Crew (Mixer Operators; Mixer Cranemen; Transfer Car Operators)

Application 32.3-1 Pit Crane Crew (Ladle Crane Operators)

Application 32.3-2 Casting and Pit Crew (2nd and 3rd Castingmen; Castingmen Helpers)

Application 32.3-3 First Casting Man Crew (First Castingmen)

All of these were in one brochure, with many elements in common. Each application here (Charging Crew and No. 6 Furnace Crew) is treated as a separate incentive by the parties.

Case G-60 relates to the Charging Crew (Charging Machine Operators and Charging Floor Cranemen) servicing all furnaces. Their incentive sets forth:

1. Statement of principles governing application of performance standards and incentives.

2. List of the jobs covered, and standard crews per turn at various levels of operation. Before the addition of the third floor crane the standard crew was as follows: [table omitted]

3. Statement of performance standards. The incentive uses a "calculated process allowance" method with two sets of performance standards: (a) "true work" performance standards (reflecting required man-hours of actual work at normal pace with allowance for rest and personal needs) stated in terms of Standard Man-Hours per 100 tons of prime product, broken down by percent hot metal charged; and (b) equipment performance standards, stated in terms of furnace hours per 100 tons of prime product, broken down by variable conditions. The product and conditions to which the performance standards are applicable are carefully defined. As a footnote to each page of the performance standards there appeared:

> "Note: The above performance standards: (1) are established to cover the conditions specified as of May 28, 1950; (2) reflect the performance requirements as related to a fair day's work for a fair day's pay; (3) will remain unchanged as long as all of the conditions under which the performance standards were established prevail; (4) shall become null and void when and if conditions under which they were established are changed; and (5) will be replaced by new standards which as compared to such expired standards shall reflect only the change of conditions."

This same limitation is among the points covered by the statement of principles mentioned under Item I above.

4. Statements defining units of production on which the performance standards are based, outlining the reports by which records of production are secured, and defining conditions under which work is unmeasured.

5. Statement of method by which incentive earnings are calculated.

6. Description of working procedures of the Charging Crew.

7. Tabulation showing pay performance at normal capacity under different operating conditions.

8. Statement showing a "special allowance job differential" for men on the job of Stocker. There is no such differential for Charging Crew jobs.

On December 6, 1953, a third floor crane was installed for use at eight, nine or ten furnace level of operations. To reflect this change the Company changed Incentive Application No. 32.2-1 as follows:

1. Statement of standard crew: [Table omitted. Shows reduction in standard floor cranemen on Furnace 4 and increase in standard crew for furnaces 8, 9, and 10.]

2. Description of equipment was changed to show three floor cranes instead of two.

The Company found no reason to change any other element of the incentive. No change was made in either "true work" or "equipment performance" standards because Management believed:

1. The true work performance standards already reflected the time per 100 tons of steel required by members of the Charging Crew to perform all necessary work at normal pace, with allowance for rest and personal needs.

2. The equipment standards reflected the furnace time requirements per 100 tons of steel when operating at normal capacity. The third floor crane at the 8- to 10-furnace level of operation was expected to reduce delay time and increase capacity, with shorter furnace cycle time.

In changing the Furnace Charging Crew incentive on December 6, 1953, the Company felt that it was acting under 9-F-2 as well as the brochure footnote quoted above.

Apparently this footnote, or statement of principle, was included on each page of all performance standards in all incentives installed between April 22, 1947 and some time in 1951, after the May 5, 1951 Award in Case A-372.[1] The Company believes it therefore is not required to observe either Section 9-C-2 or -4 of the August 15, 1952 Agreement when changed conditions require changes in existing incentives installed after April 22, 1947.

Second Grievance—The grievance in Case G-61 asserts that the No. 6 Furnace Crew incentive was improperly revised on March 25, 1954, in violation of Section 9-F-2 of the August 15, 1952 Agreement. In the alternative it claims that (1) the new incentive fails to provide equitable incentive compensation and (2) Section 9-C-4 was not applied properly.

In June 1953 the Company enlarged No. 6 Open Hearth from 936 square feet to 1062 square feet, with increase in standard heat size from 240 to 257 tons.

In May 1953 Incentive 32.2-1 was cancelled to the extent that it covered No. 6 Furnace, and the No. 6 Furnace Crew members were paid interim differentials until entirely new standards for all No.6 Furnace production were installed March 25, 1954.

---

[1] At some date after the decision in Case A-372, Item 2 of the form footnote was dropped.

As in Case G-60, the Company believes this overall revision of the No. 6 Furnace incentive to be authorized under Section 9-F-2 and the brochure footnote, without necessity for compliance with requirements of Section 9-C-2 or 9-C-4.

The incentive pay of the No. 6 Furnace Crew would have increased from 123 percent to 132 percent had the old standards been applied, without change, to production from the enlarged furnace. In revising the No. 6 Furnace incentive, the Company acted on the basis that around 8 percent greater tonnage would result from the increased furnace capacity, and that the new standards would yield earnings comparable to those under the old standards before the furnace was enlarged.

Earnings of the Furnace Crew for six pay periods prior to cancellation in May 1953, compared with earnings on other furnaces are set forth in Table A. Comparative earnings for six pay periods following installation of the new standards are set forth in Table B. [Tables omitted. Indicate an average two percent drop in earnings.]

Earnings on No. 6 Furnace traditionally have been lower than those on the other furnaces, and it has been regarded as the stand-by furnace. It normally is manned by crews from other furnaces when the latter are down for repairs.

Union Contentions

The Union believes that neither the August 15, 1952 nor the July 1, 1954 Agreement permits the Company to make any change in an incentive plan installed after April 22, 1947, unless either (1) Section 9-C is applicable, or (2) there is mutual agreement as contemplated in 9-F-2.

Section 9-F-2, in both the 1952 and the 1954 Agreements, provides that:

> ". . . all incentives installed after April 22, 1947 shall remain in effect until replaced by mutual agreement of the grievance committee and the plant Management or *until replaced or adjusted by the Company in accordance with Subsection C of this Section*." (Emphasis supplied)

Section 9-C, in both the 1952 and the 1954 Agreements, makes no provision for "adjusting" incentives.

Section 9-C-1 deals with *establishment of new incentives* to cover (a) new jobs; (b) jobs not presently covered by incentive applications; or (c) jobs covered by an existing submerged incentive plan.

Section 9-C-2 deals with *replacement* of existing incentive plans *whenever they require revision* and provides an interim period where necessary pending installation of the new incentive application.

Section 9-C-3 sets forth further procedures for *establishment of new incentives* and requires that a *new* incentive provide equitable incentive compensation.

9-C-4 provides for a minimum earnings guarantee on any job covered by a new incentive and which was covered by the *replaced incentive plan*.

Thus, the Union believes it clear that Section 9-C applies only (1) to initial establishment of new incentives, and (2) to subsequent *replacement* of existing incentives by new incentives when they require revision, or when earnings have been submerged. The "adjustment" of incentives is not contemplated at all in Section 9-C of the 1952 and 1954 Agreements, hence it believes use of the word "adjusted" by the parties in revising 9-F-2 in 1947 did not give any sanction to any form of incentive change save as already contemplated by 9-C, or as the parties might mutually agree under 9-F-2.

These conclusions, in the Union view, were required even more clearly under the 1947 Agreement where the parties used care to assure that whenever existing incentives *required revision* under 9-C-2, they would be *replaced* with new incentives rather than merely adjusted to meet the change in conditions.

The Union agrees that addition of the words "or adjusted" to Section 9-F-2 in 1952 suggests that the parties did not intend to rule out "adjustments" of post-1947 incentive plans. But the parties did not make any change in Section 9-C to effectuate the new language of Section 9-F-2. Moreover, the only language in the 1952 Agreement which provides clearly for *adjustment of post-1947 incentive was Section 9-G* dealing specifically with the adjusting of "out-of-line differentials."

Both parties recognized a need for some changes in the language of 9-C during negotiations in 1952 and particularly 1954. Both sides made proposals, but no agreement was reached.

Since the parties thus failed to resolve the problem, the Board can do no more than interpret and apply Section 9-C of the 1952 and 1954 Agreements in substantially the same manner as Section 9-C of the 1947 Agreement.

In Case G-60 the Union stresses that the theoretical earnings impact of the addition of a Floor Crane at certain levels of operation, under the incentive, was not more than about a 3 percent decrease. Since this decrease (even if realized) would be only relatively minor, the Union urges that conditions were not changed sufficiently to invoke Section 9-C-2. Hence it sees no basis for the Company to modify the old incentive by inclusion under it of the added Floor Craneman.

Further, the Union stresses that earlier a new (No. 10) furnace was added and No. 6 Furnace was enlarged, without any adjustment of the Charging Crew incentive. According to the Union these changes increased workload of the Charging Crew. Thus it holds that addition of a Floor Crane and Floor Craneman at the 8- to 10-furnace level of operations only had the effect of offsetting somewhat the increase in workload growing out of increased capacity of No. 6 Furnace and addition of No. 10 Furnace.

The Union stresses that—in agreeing to the incentive plan—the Local Union did not thereby intend to agree to a set of principles covering incentive adjustments (such as in the footnote relied upon by the Company) which were inconsistent with the criteria of the Basic Agreement.

With specific reference to Case G-61, the Union also invokes the argument that there was no authority under the Agreement for any change or revision of the incentive. In the alternative, however, it urges that the new incentive does not provide equitable incentive compensation and that in any event the Company has failed to apply the minimum earnings guarantee of Section 9-C-4. The Union sees no escape from the conclusion that if the Company was authorized to install completely new standards for the No. 6 Furnace Crew, it could only be by virtue of 9-C-2 with consequent applicability of 9-C-4.

Company Contentions

(a) *Under the 1947 Agreement*—The 1947 Agreement contemplated that the immense variety of incentives then found throughout the basic steel plants of the Corporation were to be converted to an entirely new incentive approach under certain circumstances. The circumstances requiring such a conversion were set forth in 9-C-2.

In Section 9-F the Company was required to maintain existing incentive plans in effect "until replaced in accordance with Subsection C . . ." or by mutual agreement. And the basis upon which the new incentives must be built appeared from Section 9-B-2-b and 9-C-3-e.

Thus, the normal process of simply modifying an existing incentive plan to the extent necessary to meet a new or changed condition was blocked because of the agreement that existing incentive plans (those in effect prior to April 22, 1947) were to be *replaced* by an entirely new incentive application. This was well recognized by the Board in Case A-372.

The 1947 Agreement had no specific provision requiring that a "post-1947 incentive" application must be maintained in effect. Nor was there provision covering the role of the Board with respect to actions taken by the Company in preserving or adjusting post-1947 incentives.

While this might appear anomalous to the uninitiated, it should be viewed as practical confirmation that what was done was all in accordance with the original intentions of the parties and nowise a contractual violation. From the beginning, each of the post-1947 incentive brochures contained provisions which, in the Company's view, were as much part of the incentive as the standards themselves. Thus, the form footnote (as set forth above) appeared on each page of the standards and the same concept was set forth on the first page of each incentive brochure.

Hundreds of incentives including these provisions were agreed upon. Other hundreds went into effect without grievance. Thousands of changes— or "adjustments"—were made in maintaining post-1947 incentives with the same type explanation being given the employees as set forth in 9-C-3.

This situation suggests to the Company two overlapping questions: (1) can the Board enforce the above principle set forth in post-1947 incentive applications? and (2) is such a result in harmony with the Labor Agreement if applied by the Company?

Under the 1947 Agreement no one expected life to come to a standstill with no further changes in equipment or processes and no need to modify or adjust the new incentives installed under 9-C-2 and 9-C-3. There were no limitations upon Management's right to make changes in methods, equipment, processes, etc., which would require conforming the new incentive applications to the changed conditions. No one could have expected the new incentive applications to remain static in the face of changes in the conditions on which they had been predicated. Unless there were adjustments in post-1947 incentive applications to meet changes in conditions, the Company believes they could not continue to provide "equitable incentive compensation."

As the Company views it, neither 9-C-2 nor 9-F said anything about post-1947 incentives until the 1952 changes were negotiated. In this view, the only provisions about new incentives were those saying how they should be installed; those stating that they should have a new basis (9-B-2-b) and those stating that they must provide equitable incentive compensation (9-C-3-c).

If an incentive provided equitable incentive compensation at the outset, then any change in it because of changed conditions which did not merely adjust to, or reflect, the change of conditions would impair the integrity of the incentive as originally installed. Hence such a change would not represent a continuation of equitable incentive compensation.

Thus the Company holds it to have been implicit under the 1947 Agreement that the Board could require it to make new incentives continue to provide equitable incentive compensation despite changes of conditions. Likewise employees who felt themselves aggrieved (either by the action or inaction of the Company) in this regard would have had recourse to the grievance procedure.

In view of this, it was natural for each incentive brochure to provide that:

> "The standards will become . . . void when the conditions under which they were established are changed . . . and . . . new standards . . . which reflect only the change of conditions."

This language resulted in a binding agreement in each incentive application. There is a practical inseparability of the standards originally installed and the qualifications and conditions which gave them meaning.

(b) *Under the 1952 and 1954 Agreements*—By 1952, problems between the Company and the Union concerning incentives were manifest. The Union felt there should be no difference in treatment of pre-1947 and post-1947 incentives and that the only conditions on which post-1947 incentives would be changed were those set forth in 9-C-2, in the absence of mutual agreement. The Company, however, saw need for indication in the Agreement that it could continue to take action to preserve the integrity of post-1947 incentives in light of changing conditions. It felt that the distinction which it believed to exist between (1) "replacement" of pre-1947 incentive plans and (2) conforming of a post-1947 incentive to changed conditions, must be preserved.

The Company proposed a separate procedure applicable to post-1947 incentives, but as the negotiations concluded the principal changes were in 9-F and 9-C-4. The Company believes these changes to be of vital significance.

Whereas the title of 9-F previously read: "Existing Incentive Plans That Were in Effect on April 22, 1947," it was changed to "Existing Incentive Plans."

Prior to 1952, 9-F applied only to incentive plans in effect on April 22, 1947, and provided that they would remain in effect, (in the absence of mutual agreement to the contrary) "until replaced . . . in accordance with Subsection C." Since 9-F was broadened in 1952 to apply to both pre- and post-1947 incentives, the words "or adjusted" were added—so that pre- and post-1947 incentives were to remain in effect "until replaced *or adjusted* . . . in accordance with subsection C."

The question now is whether the words "or adjusted" mean anything different from "replaced" and if so, are they applicable *only* to post-

1947 incentives. The Company believes both of these questions must be answered affirmatively. It stresses:

1. "Adjusted" cannot be read to mean the same thing as "replaced" because this would assume the parties did a meaningless act in adding the new words.

2. In August, 1952, the parties knew what was meant by the word "replace." It clearly meant to start from scratch on a new basis, as reflected in Case A-372.

The word "adjust" seems adequate to the Company to describe what it had been doing with post-1947 incentives under the 1947 Agreement and to distinguish that from what was required with respect to change-over of a pre-1947 incentive to a post-1947 incentive. It cites definitions of "adjust" both from *Winston's Simplified Dictionary* (Advanced Ed. 1934) and *Webster's Collegiate Dictionary*, (Fifth Ed. 1948) to support its interpretation of the word here.

The Company holds that the "adjustment" concept is applicable only to changes in post-1947 incentives, because of the manner in which the words "or adjusted" were added. This is based on the view that 9-F previously applied only to pre-1947 incentives, and when its coverage was broadened in 1952 to include post-1947 incentives, the word adjusted was added.

Unless this approach is adopted, there is only one other possibility, i.e., that both methods of treatment were made applicable to both the pre- and the post-1947 incentive areas. But a conclusion to adopt this approach would have obstacles, since the Board has made clear in three decisions that "replacement," and nothing else, is what is applicable to pre-1947 incentives. These decisions (N-126, T-307 and A-372) were rendered after as well as before the 1952 Agreement. If only *one* of the two words, i.e., "replaced," is applicable to pre-1947 incentives, what basis can there be for applying *both* words to post-1947 incentives. To do so would constitute marked inconsistency with prior Board rulings and make very little sense.

It was only because 9-C-2 contemplated a complete change from one type incentive to another, that the 1947 Agreement included the protection provided by 9-C-4. Hence when 9-C-4 was amended in 1952, it did more than merely change the "personal" protection to a "job" protection. It added specific language stating "*when an incentive plan is replaced . . . .*" The Company urges that this specific reference to "replaced" at the very time when 9-F-2 was expanded to refer both to "replaced" and to "adjusted" makes clear that 9-C-4 is not applicable in cases of "adjustment" pursuant to 9-F-2.

As applied to Case G-60, the Company believes that the foregoing supports its major conclusion that the adjustments of the Charging Crew incentive is of the type contemplated by Section 9-F-2 and that Sections 9-C-2 and 9-C-4 are inapplicable. The necessity for adjusting the incentives to meet the changed condition not only is apparent as a matter of good sense and common practice, but also contemplated in the incentive brochure itself, to which the parties agreed. The Company believes none of the essential features of the incentive were materially affected by addition of the third Floor Crane. Since the Charging Crew was receiving equitable incentive compensation before the third Crane was added, the Company believes it plain that they continue to receive equitable incentive compensation.

Concerning Case G-61, the Company believes the inapplicability of Sections 9-C-2 and 9-C-4 to be apparent for the same reasons as in G-60. It sees no merit in the Union evidence to support the claim that the earnings under the changed standards do not constitute equitable incentive compensation. Rather, it concludes that the changed standards for No. 6 Furnace reflect only the changed conditions and no more. Hence, since the standards yielded equitable incentive compensation before the changed conditions, the ensuing adjustment in its view must necessarily produce equitable incentive compensation after the change.

Contract Interpretation

The Board approaches the intricate interpretive problems here mindful of the extreme difficulty of the 1952 negotiations between the parties, covering a wide range of critical subjects. While the incentive situation was sorely confused under the 1947 Agreement and urgently needed attention, there were yet other problems of transcendent importance to absorb the best efforts of the negotiators. The parties could not reasonably have hoped in this context to attain perfect expression of agreement concerning long-range administration of the incentive program which the Company had launched under the 1947 Agreement. If the 1952 Agreement thus does not cover all present and potential disputed issues as clearly as some might desire, it is only the parties who may remedy such deficiency, in future negotiations. The Board meanwhile must work with the tools at hand in providing as fair and practical an interpretation of the Agreement as is possible objectively under the language used in 1952.

Considering the myriad difficulties which beset them in the incentive area under the 1947 Agreement, one may suppose that one party or the other—or both—felt real uncertainty as to the manner in which

Section 9-C, as it then stood, might be held to apply to post-1947 incentives. Looking back to the actual language of the 1947 Agreement, however, it seems hardly proper to infer that this section was inapplicable to replacement of post-1947 incentives.

Thus, Section 9-C on its face seemed to apply to all instances where new incentives might be installed to replace existing incentives (save as there might be mutual agreement to a replacement not required or authorized under 9-C). Nothing appeared in 9-C to limit its scope to establishment of new incentives replacing those which were in effect on April 22, 1947. While the Company feels that in 1947 Section 9-F indirectly provided a definition of "existing incentive" for purposes of Section 9-C, adoption of this view would entail an inference that the post-1947 incentives were not thereafter governed by the Basic Agreement at all. Such a surprising conclusion—bearing in mind the original two-year term of the 1947 Agreement—should require clear support in language of the Agreement before embraced by the Board.

When 9-F first was written in 1947, moreover, it served three broad purposes. Section 9-F-1 covered application of the general wage increase simultaneously negotiated, and made this effective *April 1, 1947* for "each employee on an incentive job." Section 9-F-3 provided a sort of earnings guarantee for employees under existing incentives, based on the applicable single or multiple number of eight-hour turns "in effect *as of January 13, 1947*." Thus both 9-F-1 and 9-F-3 were of limited purpose, each with clear reference to a date giving the clause its precise meaning. It is of more than passing interest, too, that in each instance the limiting date was a date other than April 22, 1947.

Section 9-F-2 was not similarly circumscribed. It contained no date to limit its scope, or to suggest the meaning urged by the Company. In the 1948 wage reopening, it is true the caption of 9-F was changed to refer only to "Existing Incentive Plans that were in Effect on April 22, 1947," where 9-F-1 was substantially changed to reflect a different method of applying the general increase which related only to incentives in effect on April 22, 1947. There was no such change in the actual language of 9-F-2. Such a change in caption in the 1948 reopening seems not a reliable guide, in these circumstances, to what the parties meant when they wrote 9-C more than a year earlier. Had the parties so intended they as easily could have put a limiting phrase into 9-C itself.

The evidence leaves no doubt, however, that under the 1947 Agreement the Company made numerous changes in post-1947 incentives, without replacing such incentives under Section 9-C-2. Changes of this sort were not necessarily precluded by the Agreement. Section 9-C-2 required *"replacement"* of an existing incentive only where changed conditions were sufficiently significant to *require revision* of an existing incentive. This was recognized in Case N-146 as follows:

> "This language presumably was drafted with great care by the parties in view of the obvious importance of providing a clear statement as to when Management was both authorized and obliged to install new incentives. It does not purport to convey a broad and unlimited authority. The words chosen by the parties preclude such an interpretation. This is apparent in use of the phrase 'require revision.' This recognizes that not every minor change in equipment or manufacturing methods, standing alone, will provide occasion for installation of a new incentive. To require revision of the old plan, the changed condition must be of such nature as to appreciably affect the operation of the existing plan, or earnings under it."

It is not open to argument that countless changed conditions may arise in the normal course of operations which are not sufficiently important to require revision of a post-1947 incentive under 9-C-2, but which it may be desirable to recognize through appropriate modification of the incentive to preserve its effectiveness. Perhaps the simplest illustration is provided by introduction of a new product or specification affecting a portion of total production under the incentive. The advisability of adding an appropriate rate or standard—preserving the effectiveness of the incentive—is commonly recognized.

Such modifications maintain the basic integrity and effectiveness of an incentive without serious distortion through cumulative changes. The evidence leaves no doubt that the Company since 1947 has followed this type of policy as to post-1947 incentives. Under normal conditions adjustments of this general nature represent such a natural and well recognized process that it would seem an abuse of the Board's discretion not to deem them reasonable steps to administer incentives under 9-F.

The fact that the Company's post-1947 incentive program differed radically from the earlier program may have caused confusion here. As an incident of the Inequities Program, it was the Company's policy broadly to replace pre-1947 incentives with new-type incentives, rather than to preserve the old incentives by interpolation or extension of rates. Also, as a practical matter, pre-1947 incentives differed from post-1947 incentives in the manner in which 9-C-2 might be applied on a case-by-case basis. Some reasons for this were suggested in the February 3, 1952 Decision in Case A-372, particularly the requirement that a replacement incentive under 9-C-2 must conform with Section 9-B-2-b. Since the Company was concerned to maintain the effectiveness of post-1947 incentives, as distinct from the earlier types, the new incentives were formulated to facilitate adjustment without wholesale revision.

The parties in 1952 made no change in Section 9-C to indicate that it did not apply to post-1947 incentives in whole or in part. On the other hand, they changed the language of 9-F to reflect unmistakably their recognition of the desirability of adjusting post-1947 incentives.

The Company believes the new language in 9-F reflects that 9-C-1 and 9-C-3 would apply to changes in post-1947 incentives (save by mutual agreement), but 9-C-2 and 9-C-4 would not apply to any such changes.

The Union relies on the same language to urge that the parties thereby made plain that no post-1947 incentive adjustment of any sort was to be permitted unless by agreement or where changed conditions arose sufficient to require a replacement under 9-C-2.

Of course, the parties had no express understanding that the 1952 additions to 9-F-2 would produce the result urged either by the Company or by the Union. The word "adjusted" was new in Section 9—RATES OF PAY, although it had appeared in Section 4-F of the March 13, 1945 Agreement (contemplating that substantial changes in job duties or requirements would necessitate adjustment of hourly, incentive, piecework, or tonnage rates). Its use in Section 9-G of the 1952 Agreement was for a specialized purpose only, providing no guide to interpret 9-F-2. Nor had the Company itself used the term generally to describe the various modifications or changes it made in post-1947 incentives during the life of the 1947 Agreement.

Here the language of the Board in USC-316, Interim Award No. III, seems apt:

> ". . . As the Board pointed out in Case N-146, neither party in negotiations is entitled to rely upon its own impression, or hope, as to the meaning of the language adopted. Where the parties *reasonably can have differing views as to the effect of language in the agreement,* as is the case here, the Board must interpret the actual language in light of the known facts to which it was addressed."

In August 1952 the term "adjusted" was not used in a vacuum. It is not to be denied that the negotiators knew that the Company had been making changes in existing incentives (where changed conditions arose) and desired to deal with this matter in some way in the new contract.

No doubt each party would have liked to include more language to make clear that its own view as to proper disposition of all substantive and procedural problems clearly had been adopted. Each was unable to attain its objective, however, so that the expedient result was to let the matter rest with the modest additions made to 9-F-2. Viewing the interpretative problem from the distance of some years after the event, the Board is not prone to infer that this type of limited action accomplished—

or fairly was intended to accomplish—a drastic change in the practical situation which the parties faced when the new language was written.

Some of the significant elements of that situation for present purposes were:

1. After protracted effort to develop principles for determining a fair day's work (in completing the Inequities Program as reflected in the May 8, 1946 Agreement), the parties were now in agreement that the effort should be abandoned. In recognition of this, it was possible in the 1952 agreement to eliminate 9-K-2 of the 1947 Agreement. Related significant changes also were made in 9-C-4 and 9-G. After these steps it remained to clarify application of the Agreement to ordinary and long range problems of incentive administration.

2. During the 1947 Agreement the Company had sought to maintain the integrity of post-1947 incentives through modifications to meet changed conditions. This policy fell outside Section 9-C, but might have been regarded as an implementation of Section 9-F-2 in proper cases.

3. Section 9-C-2 made no clear distinction between pre- and post-1947 incentives in requiring that incentives must be placed upon occurrence of changed conditions sufficiently important to require their revision.

4. Post-1947 incentives differed from pre-1947 incentives in that the former had been installed in accordance with the 1947 Agreement (and notably Section 9-B-2-b). Also, the Company had embarked upon a program of maintaining the effectiveness of its post-1947 incentives to the extent practicable by changes to meet changed conditions. This program differed from the Company policy concerning pre-1947 incentives, but to an extent not fully revealed in this record since the pre-1947 incentive adjustment situation was not the subject of any comprehensive review in these cases.

Against this background the Board finds no reasonable basis for either party to infer that the changes in 9-F-2 accomplished the respective objectives now claimed.

The words added to Section 9-F could not have been intended to exclude post-1947 incentives from the scope of Section 9-C-2 and 9-C-4, for all purposes. The use of the specific phrase "until replaced or adjusted by the Company *in accordance with Subsection C of this Section*" precludes such an interpretation.

Nor is there support for the Union view that the new language in 9-F-2 ruled out thereafter any possibility of adjusting post 1947 incentives, save as Section 9-C-2 might apply to require replacement. Had the parties intended this result, the words "or adjusted" would not have been used as distinct from the term "replaced." If it is reasonably possible to do so, therefore, the word "adjusted" as well as the word "replaced" must be given substantial meaning by the Board.

Since Section 9-C-2 refers only to replacement of incentives where changed conditions *require their revision*, the parties in 9-F-2 must have contemplated the making of adjustments to post-1947 incentives which differed from "revisions" of such incentives as contemplated under 9-C-2. It is true that some dictionary definitions, or common usage, of the words "revision" and "adjustment" may overlap to an extent. This serves only to emphasize that the parties and the Board must find the meaning of words used in the Agreement primarily from the Agreement itself and in the context of the specific bargaining relationship.

Hence when new or changed conditions are of such magnitude as to require revision of a post-1947 incentive, then a replacement under 9-C-2 is in order. But where the new or changed condition is not of such far reaching significance, but may be met by a modification or addition specifically adapted to meet the change, this constitutes an adjustment essentially to preserve the effectiveness of the incentive under 9-F-2.

While this type adjustment may be regarded as an implementation of 9-F-2, the express language there used makes plain that relevant procedure of 9-C must be observed. For example, Section 9-C-3 provides the appropriate machinery for handling adjustments in the same manner as a new incentive would be handled. This includes the right to file a grievance where a necessary adjustment is not developed and presented by Management as required. While the Union seems particularly concerned also about 9-C-4, application of this Section should not present any serious difficulty, as noted below in the specific discussion of Case G-60.

The validity of these conclusions is not impaired by the form statement, or footnote, in all post-1947 incentives, and embodied in the brochures here. The Company suggests that each post-1947 incentive brochure constituted a complete and binding local agreement, with the form footnote an integral part. This contention warrants scrutiny and discussion since, if sound, it might control the issues here to an important extent.

The argument assumes that the parties locally were called upon under Section 9-C-3 of the 1947 Agreement to reach agreement upon (or pass to the Board for decision) many aspects of the Company's incentive program not related to determining whether the new incentive provided equitable incentive compensation. But under 9-C-3 the only basis for grievance (and the only issue arbitrable) was a claim that the new incentive failed to provide equitable incentive compensation. Section 9-C-3 provided only a procedure to determine questions of equitable incentive compensation, where the employees involved felt that the earnings they received under the incentive were too low and pressed a grievance.

This limited scope of 9-C-3 was recognized in Case USC-316, where the Board in effect held that issues of claimed arbitrary and unreasonable incentive grouping could be determined only on the basis of whether there was actual failure in any given instance to provide equitable incentive compensation as a result of the protested grouping of jobs under separate incentives.

Material which Management elects to include in a brochure, but which in no way relates to determination of compensation provided, scarcely could be said thereby to become part of a binding local agreement. To hold otherwise would obstruct application of Section 9-C-2 and -3 by permitting the Company to require agreement—or determination in arbitration—concerning matters not reasonably within the scope of 9-C-3.

The necessary consequence of the First Award in Case A-372, is to strike down a key provision of the form footnote. The footnote includes typically the following:

> "Performance standards shall: (1) be established for a specified set of conditions; (2) reflect the performance requirements as related to a fair day's work for a fair day's pay; (3) remain unchanged as long as all of the conditions under which the standards were established prevail; (4) become null and void when the if conditions under which they were established are changed; and (5) be replaced by new standards which as compared to such expired standards shall reflect only the change of conditions."

Item (2) of this language would seem to be inoperative and without the scope of permissive local agreement under Section 9, as interpreted in the May 5, 1951 Award in Case A-372. Item (5) of the footnote, as the whole footnote is written, could not have been read without reference to Item (2). Without Item (2) a significant purpose of the footnote thus was lost. This seems to have been recognized, properly, in the second hearing in Case A-372, where the Company avoided a Union challenge to the footnote. Counsel stated:

> ". . . with respect to the Union's comment that it is not bound by what we have called the brochure, in each one of these cases, and its request for a ruling, as I understood it, that it is not so bound. There has never been any claim, and there is not any claim now by the Company, that the Union is bound by such brochures." (Tr. Oct. 31 p. 5)

This statement in any event was consistent with the parties' understanding under the 1947 Agreement that the Company should proceed with installation of incentives under its new program—even though the parties had failed mutually to define a fair day's work—leaving to the employees in each instance the choice of filing a grievance under 9-C-3.

In sum, therefore: (a) the observance of the procedure of 9-C-3 in any given case did not of itself reflect mutual intent to be bound by the brochure footnote, and (b) even if express agreement were reached to the terms of the footnote in some isolated case—which is not suggested here—such agreement would have been invalid under Section 9 as interpreted in the May 5, 1951 Award in Case A-372.

Finally it remains to note that the brochure footnote nowhere speaks of "adjusting" incentives, but only of "*replacing*" standards, which become "null and void" because of *any change* in the conditions under which established.

Specific Cases

Under the foregoing analyses, Case G-60 involves an incentive adjustment authorized by 9-F-2 rather than an incentive revision requiring replacement under 9-C-2. The changed condition—use of the new third crane—was applicable only at 8, 9 and 10 furnace level of operations, and it remained possible to operate, even at these levels without use of the third Floor Crane. The incentive at lower levels of operation was in nowise affected by the change. The impact of the changed condition hence was not of such magnitude as to require replacement under 9-C-2.

This leaves the questions of (1) whether the adjustment here made sufficed to maintain the integrity of the incentive under 9-F-2, and (2) whether there was full observance of applicable provisions of 9-C.

The evidence shows that overall effect of the protested adjustment, in light of the changed conditions, was to reduce earnings of the Charging Crew by 2 percent. If properly an implementation of Section 9-F-2, an adjustment should not materially affect the provision of equitable incentive compensation, or measurably alter earnings opportunity, under the specific incentive. Since under Section 9-C-3 this incentive yielded equitable incentive compensation, when the changed condition arose, any resulting adjustment under 9-F-2 must be on this basis. Hence the earnings yielded here must be adjusted retroactive to December 16, 1953, so as to make whole the employees whose earnings have been adversely affected. The adjustment required is such that actual earnings of the Charging Crew at 8, 9, or 10 furnace level of operations, when the third Floor Crane is in use, will be 2 percent higher than were realized in such circumstances after December 16, 1953.

Since the Charging Crew incentive was installed under 9-C-2 to replace a pre-1947 incentive, there is no doubt of the application of 9-C-4 to this incentive. The present adjustment, of course, is not a replacement, but serves only to maintain integrity of the incentive. Thus it does not affect the continued application of 9-C-4, or call for determination of any new earnings guarantee thereunder.

Case G-61 unmistakably falls under 9-C-2, since overall revision of the incentive was required. While the Company has asserted that there was no necessity for replacement of the old incentive, what actually was done here sufficed to satisfy the requirements of Section 9-C-2. The requirement of equitable incentive compensation under 9-C-3 has been met, moreover, under the case-by-case test enunciated in Cases A-372 and USC-316.

This conclusion is required despite the fact that the Company offered to loosen the incentive slightly in the grievance procedure in an effort to settle this case. The Union urges that—at the least—such an offer must be regarded as an admission that the incentive did not provide equitable incentive compensation, thereby entitling grievants to a retroactive adjustment. The Board cannot accept this rationale. To do so would be to prejudice the fundamental interest of both parties in effective operation of the grievance procedure without excessive resort to arbitration—it would, in short, undercut effectiveness of the parties' representatives striving for compromise in the grievance procedure. These men must enjoy full freedom to advance whatever propositions seem calculated to induce practical settlement without fear that thereby they prejudice their position should the case later reach the Board. In evaluating the present evidence, therefore, the Board has given no weight to offers of settlement in the grievance procedure.

There remains only the question of whether there was adequate observance of Section 9-C-4, since this is a replacement situation within its meaning. This matter was not considered in detail by the parties, or presented to the Board in such manner as to permit decision, save on the bare question of whether 9-C-4 is applicable at all. With this issue clarified, the parties now are free to consider in the grievance procedure whether any specific problems of application of 9-C-4 are presented, and if so, what disposition should be made of them.

Awards

Case G-60: (1) An adjustment of the existing incentive was required under Section 9-F-2, and in accordance with the applicable provisions of Section 9-C; (2) The Adjustment of December 16, 1953 fell short of meeting the requirements of Section 9-F-2; (3) Under 9-F-2 the earnings of the employees during periods when the new conditions were applicable as outlined in the above Opinion, should have been 2 percent greater than the earnings actually realized under the incentive; (4) The employees affected are entitled to an adjustment in their incentive earnings of 2 percent, retroactive to December 16, 1953, for all appropriate periods when the changed conditions are operative.

Case G-61: (1) Cancellation of the old incentive in May 1953, and its replacement, was required in accordance with Section 9-C-2; (2) In practical effect, there has been adequate compliance with the requirements of Section 9-C-2 in this case; (3) The earnings received by affected employees under the new incentive installed March 25, 1954, meet the test of equitable incentive compensation under 9-C-3; (4) Section 9-C-4 is applicable to this incentive replacement, but lack of full exploration of this aspect precludes expression of opinion now as to whether any specific problems may exist under 9-C-4 in this case. This matter may be considered further in the grievance procedure, if necessary.

Questions for Discussion

What are the differences between an arbitrator who serves throughout the term of a contract and an ad hoc arbitrator? How do the differences affect decisions?

What was the nature of the Board of Arbitration in this case? How did its decision reflect its status under the contract?

What was the role in the decision of:
(a) the doctrine of stare decisis; and
(b) the history of contract negotiations?

Compare the style, form, and substance of this opinion and award with the other decisions included in this Part.

Bethlehem Steel Company

Arbitrator Ralph T. Seward
June 5, 1956
26 LA 874

DISCHARGE: FIGHTING

This grievance presents the question of whether or not Management was justified in discharging James W. Daniels, the grievant, for participating in a fight with Carl Snow, another employee. The fight took place on February 14, 1955. Both men admitted participation in it, and each alleged that he was the victim of an unprovoked assault by the other. No supervisory employee witnessed the fight, and while other employees saw both men fighting, no one other than Daniels and Snow, themselves, admitted to a knowledge of how the altercation began.

Company Policy

It is the Company's general policy, when two employees have a fight in the plant, to discharge both participants. In accordance with this policy, after completion of the various proceedings required by Article XII of the Agreement, both Daniels and Snow were discharged. Though the Union represented both employees at their discharge hearings, it now claims that Snow was the aggressor and the sole individual at fault and that Daniels did nothing more than defend himself against two unprovoked attacks.

Snow did not testify at the Umpire hearing. As no representatives of Management or Supervision saw the fight, all the testimony concerning it comes from Daniels and from two employees who testified on his behalf. On the basis of their testimony, the facts appear to be as follows.

Testimony of Witnesses

On February 14, 1955, Daniels who was a Chipper and Shop Steward in the Billet Yard Department, reported for work on the afternoon shift. Shortly after he entered the General Welfare Building to punch his time card, some of the employees complained to him that Carl Snow had unfairly persuaded the Foreman to assign him for three consecutive days to the chipping of 7³/₈ inch bars—an assignment which offered exceptionally high incentive earning opportunities. As there had been an understanding that the assignments to this work would be rotated daily, Daniels—as a Steward in the Department—decided to speak to Snow about this complaint.

Daniels then went to the Welfare Building of the Billet Preparation Yard, saw Snow in the locker room and asked him why he was assigned to the $7^3/8$ inch bars for three consecutive days. Daniels testified that Snow quickly became angry, accused him of lying, swore at him and hit him in the mouth, causing it to bleed. The two locked in a brief struggle and then, when they broke apart, Snow swung at Daniels with a scarfing torch, swearing that he would kill him. This attack was broken up by other employees. Shortly after the two had finished changing their clothes, Snow suggested that they go to see Foreman Wrenn. Both men left the Welfare Room and went towards the Foreman's office in an adjacent building. When they arrived there, however, Snow refused to enter the office and made remarks which he said were designed to get Daniels to fight him. Daniels, nevertheless, turned away to go to work. As soon as his back was turned, Daniels states, a piece of tie plate— apparently thrown by Snow—struck the wall just above his head. Daniels turned around and saw Snow running toward him. A scuffle ensued, during which Snow attempted to get hold of the tie plate again, and Daniels tried to prevent him from reaching it. Finally Snow broke free, picked up the tie plate and hit Daniels on the head and shoulders with it several times. The men were separated by other employees. Daniels then went to the Foreman's office, to the clinic for medical attention and to the Plant Police Department where he voluntarily made out a statement as to what happened. Following this he went home and on the following day entered the hospital where he remained for several weeks.

Conflicting Statement

This account of the affair, of course, is based on the testimony of Daniels and two of the employees who helped break up the fight in the locker room. In his written statement to the Plant Police and in his testimony at his discharge hearing, Snow accused Daniels of pulling a knife on him twice—once in the locker room and once outside of the Foreman's office—and alleged that all he was doing was trying to protect himself. Snow was not available for cross examination on these statements, however, and under the circumstances his written statements cannot be given weight equal to the oral testimony of Daniels and his supporting witnesses. It may be noted that these witnesses denied that Daniels had a knife in his hand at any time during the altercation in the locker room.

The Umpire must rule on the basis of the evidence before him. He cannot find in the record of this case any credible evidence that Daniels was at fault or was in any way responsible for the fight. Doubtless, he did question Snow about his favorable work schedule. The Umpire sees nothing wrong in his doing so. He was a Shop Steward; other employees had complained to him about Snow's preferential treatment; there was good reason to clear the matter up; and before complaining to the Foreman, it seems only natural and proper that Daniels should have asked Snow for his version. So far as the evidence reveals, Daniels said nothing provocatory. When Snow became angry, Daniels seems to have tried to quiet him down. It was Snow who lost control of himself, hit Daniels and swung on him with the scarfing torch. Daniels apparently tried only to prevent Snow from hitting him again by pinning his arms to his side until other employees broke them apart.

As to the second fight outside of the Foreman's office, the Umpire's conclusion is the same. After refusing to go into the office, Snow had insulted Daniels and stated that he wanted to fight. Daniels, nevertheless, was turning away to reenter the building when Snow threw the steel tie plate at his head and then rushed at him. The Umpire does not see what Daniels could have done under the circumstances but grapple with Snow and try to prevent him from picking up the tie plate again.

Conclusion

The Umpire concludes, therefore, that Daniels was not at fault in this affair and that he did nothing more than reasonably defend himself against an unprovoked and dangerous attack. He understands and approves of the general rule that equal penalties should be imposed on both participants in a fight. In most such cases, there is blame on both sides, and it cannot be said with certainty that one was the aggressor and the other did nothing more than defend himself and attempt to avoid injury. In the present case, however, the evidence before the Umpire strongly supports the conclusion that Snow was the aggressor and that Daniels was not to blame. Under the circumstances, the Umpire cannot hold that Daniels deserved a penalty.

It may be noted that as a result of this fight, both Daniels and Snow were tried before the City Court of the City of Lackawanna on charges of third degree assault. Snow was convicted and given a suspended sentence. The charge against Daniels was dismissed for insufficient evidence. The Company has submitted a transcript of the testimony given at this trial, suggesting the presence of inconsistencies between the statements of certain witnesses at the trial and the statements of the same witnesses before the Umpire. In the opinion of the Umpire, what inconsistencies exist are minor, and are insufficient to cast doubt on the general credibility of the testimony before him or to disturb the conclusions which he has drawn from that testimony.

The evidence indicates that Daniels was in the hospital for several weeks after Snow's attack. The period of his disability apparently ended on April 22, 1955. The Umpire will direct accordingly, that Daniels shall be reinstated with back pay to April 23, 1955.

Decision

It is held that just cause did not exist for the discharge of the grievant, James W. Daniels. He shall be reinstated to his job, with back pay to April 23, 1955.

Questions for Discussion

On what basis does Arbitrator Seward absolve grievant of responsibility for fighting?

What is the rationale of the general rule regarding responsibility for fighting?

Does Arbitrator Seward's decision suggest that he was bound by the findings in the criminal court case on the same incidents?

Why did Arbitrator Seward restrict back pay to April 23 when the incidents occurred on February 14?

Compare the style, form, and substance of this opinion and award with the other decisions included in this Part.

Jones & Laughlin Steel Corporation

Arbitrator Whitley P. McCoy
December 30, 1957
29 LA 644

DISCIPLINE: UNION OFFICERS

At a hearing held in New Orleans, Louisiana, on December 16, 1957, Grievance No. 5, protesting the three-day suspensions imposed on Frank G. Stritzinger, Harry McIntee, and Alex M. LeBlanc, were submitted to arbitration. Stritzinger is President of the Local, McIntee is Vice President, and LeBlanc is Chairman of the Grievance Committee. The penalties were imposed on them because, with practically the entire working force, they participated in a work stoppage lasting a day and a half.

Facts of Case

As background it may be stated that the work stoppage occurred as the result of an incident the preceding week when a foreman addressed abusive and threatening language to the Chairman of the Grievance Committee when the latter attempted to discuss with him a complaint concerning that foreman working. The abuse and threat were overheard by other employees, word of it spread, and considerable indignation was aroused. A grievance was filed concerning the matter the following day. The Plant Manager stated on the witness stand that he investigated, that the foreman admitted his wrong-doing, and that he apologized and stated it would not happen again. He also testified that no discipline had been administered to the foreman, and that he had not apologized to the Chairman of the Grievance Committee.

It was testified for the Union that the employees were "worked up," demanding action, and that on Monday, May 27, 1957, they gathered at lunch time in the driveway outside the Plant Gate, where Stritzinger, McIntee, and LeBlanc reported to them that the Plant Manager had said such a thing would not happen again. The men booed them down, showing dissatisfaction with the report. One of them shouted, "If you can't handle it, we'll show you how to handle it." Stritzinger told them that the Plant Manager was fair, and they should give him time. At the end of the lunch period the men went back to work.

The following morning, Tuesday, May 28, the men were still stirred up. Even a couple of non-Union men approached LeBlanc and asked if he was "going to take it lying down." There was talk of a walk-out at lunch time, and when that time arrived the three officers saw the men walking out the Gate. They went to the Gate, and were the last to leave.

Stritzinger immediately made efforts to contact a Staff Representative of the International Union, who phoned the Plant Manager about 2 P.M., and arranged to meet with him the next day. Following the meeting the next day, the Staff Representative and the three officers addressed the men gathered outside the Plant, persuaded them to return to work the following morning, and they did so. During the day and a half of the strike no picket line was set up, and no one was prevented from entering or leaving the Plant. A few non-Union men worked, but many did not.

The Company offered no evidence that Stritzinger, McIntee, or LeBlanc had instigated, encouraged, or led the walkout, or had done anything to prolong it, or had taken any active part in it. No effort was made to rebut the evidence of the Union that the three officers had sought to prevent it and had made efforts to end it—that they had been unwilling participants in it. On the contraty, the Plant Manager was quite frank in testifying as to why he had selected these three alone for penalties. He stated:

> "I picked those three because I knew they were fully aware of the grievance procedure, so felt they were no less guilty than the others of participating in the work stoppage. I did not find they were more guilty than the others . . . I did not know, and made no effort to find out whether they had tried to avert the strike."

Union Officers' Responsibility

Thus this case raises squarely the question whether the Company may select for penalty three out of 180 participants in a strike, merely because they are officers of the Union and therefore familiar with the contract, and without showing any other basis for such selection. The Contract of 1955, under which this incident arose, is conclusive of that question. Section V expressly provides that:

> "The right of the Corporation to discipline an employee for a violation of this Agreement shall be limited to the failure of such employee to discharge his responsibilities as an employee and may not in any way be based upon the failure of such employee to discharge his responsibilities as a representative or officer of the Union."

It is clear from this Contract provision that the fact that the three grievants were officers and representatives of the Union must be left out of consideration, and their cases considered as if they were merely employees and nothing more. So the further question arises, whether when 180 employees are all guilty of the same offense and same grade and degree of that offense, three may be selected for punishment and the rest be allowed to go unpunished.

I had thought that question had been answered in the negative so many times, and so unanimously, in arbitration cases, that it would never arise again. It is as well settled a principle as any I know, that discrimination in the imposition of penalties is inconsistent with "just cause." Section VIII of the 1955 Agreement expressly provides for reinstatement with full back pay where "the employee has been discharged or suspended unjustly." It is well settled that an employer may single out for penalties the *leaders* of a strike, or those who committed specific acts distinguishing them from others, but that unless there is a reasonable basis for distinction all must be treated alike.

Even without a contract provision such as that quoted above, it is generally held that the mere holding of office in the Union is not, standing alone, such a reasonable basis for distinction though a number of arbitrators, including the writer, have held it a proper element for consideration where specific acts of leadership are proved. *See Stockham Pipe Fittings Co.*, 4 LA 744. It is true that some arbitrators have used *language* indicating a broader holding, but the actual holdings, on the facts of the cases, have been more limited. I have found only one case which squarely decides (apart from obiter dicta and innuendo) that the mere holding of Union office affords a reasonable basis for distinguishing. That is *International Harvester Co. and Farm Equipment Workers*, 14 LA 986. Even that case may be distinguished on its facts, for the arbitrator there was giving effect to a long-standing practice of the Company which had theretofore been acquiesced in by the Union. But more important, the arbitrator who decided that case about seven years ago has apparently changed his mind and rejected the theory that Union office forms a basis for distinction. This appears in his decision rendered November 29, 1957, in *Bethlehem Steel Company and United Steelworkers*, Decision No. 381.* The two employees involved there were a Shop Steward and a former President of the Union who still exercised leadership. In setting the penalties aside, Arbitrator Ralph T. Seward said:

> "The Umpire has previously held—and he here repeats—that the Company need not penalize *all* employees who are guilty of an offense if it is to penalize *any* of them. But he also holds that if the Company is to select some employees for discipline and let others off scot-free (or if it is to impose heavy penalties on some and lighter penalties on others) it must—if it is to meet the standard of "just cause"—show that its reasons for making such distinctions were sound and just."

The Company relies heavily on a decision of Arbitrator Sidney L. Cahn, dated April 10, 1953, in *Jones and Laughlin and United Steelworkers*, J & L Case No. 9-308, where five employees were discharged for participation in a work stoppage and no other participants suffered discipline. The discharges were sustained without regard to the fact that the grievants were guilty of nothing more than others unpunished were guilty of. But that decision was expressly based upon a most unusual contract provision, reading:

---

*29 LA 635.

". . . in a case arising out of a strike or work stoppage involving a group of employees and in which the Corporation imposed discipline on part but not all of such employees, the Board shall have discretion, if it finds that *the employees disciplined are less guilty* than other employees . . . to modify the penalties." (emphasis supplied)

This contract provision clearly limited the arbitrator's power to cases where the employees disciplined were *less guilty* and the arbitrator was bound thereby. The case is no authority for the Company's position here, for no such unusual provision appears in the Agreement before me.

But even if the Agreement between these parties contained such a provision, the position of the Company would be no stronger on the facts of this case. According to the undisputed evidence in this case the three grievants were less guilty than others unpenalized. They cautioned patience, were booed for their pains, argued against striking, were the last to leave the Plant, were unwilling participants, and made successful efforts to end the strike. The evidence as to these matters was not contradicted.

Upon the facts of the case, and the controlling contract provisions, the grievance must be sustained.

Award

Grievance No. 5 is sustained, and the disciplinary suspensions of Frank G. Stritzinger, Harry McIntee, and Alex M. LeBlanc are set aside, and full compensation for pay lost is awarded as provided in the Agreement.

Questions for Discussion

On what basis does Arbitrator McCoy reject the argument that union officials have a higher duty than other employees?

Why does Arbitrator McCoy distinguish this case from those involving decisions by arbitrators Seward and Cahn?

How does Arbitrator McCoy's decision compare with contemporary arbitration decisions on the issue of selective discipline?

What evidence would be required to justify more severe discipline for selected participants in a strike in violation of a collective bargaining agreement under Arbitrator McCoy's rationale?

Compare the style, form, and substance of this opinion and award with the other decisions included in this Part.

Brooklyn Eagle, Inc.

Arbitrator W. Willard Wirtz
February 2, 1959
32 LA 156

DISCONTINUANCE OF BUSINESS

Opinion

These issues are before the Arbitrator:

1. Are former employees in the Editorial and Commercial departments of the Brooklyn Eagle, Inc., as listed in Guild Exhibits 1 and 2, entitled to severance indemnity under the provisions of Section 10 of the Agreement of November 30, 1952, between The Brooklyn Eagle, Inc., a New York Corporation, and the Newspaper Guild of New York, a local of the American Newspaper Guild?

2. Are these employees, as listed in Guild Exhibits 1 and 2, entitled to vacation pay under the provisions of Section 11 of the November 30, 1952 agreement?

3. Are these employees, as listed in Guild Exhibits 1 and 2, entitled to payment under the "notice of dismissal" provisions of Section 9(e) of the November 30, 1952 Agreement?

4. Is Brooklyn Eagle, Inc., entitled to payment to it by the Newspaper Guild of New York of money damages for losses resulting from a strike of the Editorial and Commercial department employees on January 28, 1955?

These issues have been submitted to arbitration under the provision in Section 21(b) of the November 30, 1952 Agreement (referred to after this as "the Agreement"):

> "(b) Any dispute, claim, grievance or difference arising out of or relating to this agreement which the Guild and the Publisher have not been able after reasonable effort to settle, shall be submitted to arbitration, upon notice of either party to the other, under the labor arbitration rules then obtaining of the American Arbitration Association. . . ."

The steps by which this matter has proceeded to arbitration, and the resolution of certain issues regarding the arbitrability of Issues No. 1, No. 2, and No. 3, as listed above, are set out in *Potoker v. Brooklyn Eagle, Inc.* 2 N.Y.2d 553, 141 N.E.2d 841, 28 LA 344 (1957), *affirming*, 286 App. Div. 733, 146 N.Y. Supp. 2d 616, (First Dept.,

1955), *cert. den.*, 355 U.S. 883, 29 LA 434 (1957). Although the Newspaper Guild of New York originally protested the arbitrability of Issue No. 4, as set out above, this objection was withdrawn by the Guild at the outset of the arbitration hearing. (R. 6–7)

Facts of Case

There is no substantial dispute about the facts from which this controversy developed.

The Agreement was a renewal of previous agreements between the parties. It provided in Section 27 as follows with respect to its duration:

> "This agreement shall, unless changed by mutual consent, be in effect from its date for a period of two years. . . .
>
> "Not more than 90 days and not less than 60 days prior to the expiration of this agreement, either party may give to the other party notice of desire to change the terms thereof. In the event of such notice, negotiations shall be immediately entered into and proceed with all due diligence. If an agreement has not been reached by the date upon which this agreement expires, status quo conditions shall be maintained during negotiations unless and until such negotiations are terminated by either party. . . ."

On September 1, 1954, the Guild served notice, in accordance with the terms of Section 27, of its desire to modify the Agreement. The Guild's proposals for revision of the contract terms included proposed wage increases. Bargaining between the parties on these contract demands followed. No agreement was reached by November 29, 1954. The bargaining continued, but no settlement could be arrived at, and at midnight on January 28, 1955—after previous notice to the Publisher—the employees in the Editorial and Commercial departments went out on strike. Publication of *The Brooklyn Eagle* ended with the January 28, 1955 issue.

The parties continued, but without accomplishment, to bargain about contract renewal terms. On March 8, the Guild negotiating committee declined to meet with the Publisher's negotiating representatives on the ground that the negotiations were getting nowhere. On March 16, the Publisher advised the Guild by letter as follows:

> "At midnight on January 28, 1955, the members of *The Brooklyn Eagle* Unit went on strike. This action effectively changed the "status quo" conditions then obtaining and, we are advised, terminated the "status quo" term referred to in Section 27 of the collective bargaining agreement of November 30, 1952.
>
> "Nevertheless, we continued negotiations, earnestly and in good faith in the hope that a new agreement might be reached. Negotiation developments, climaxed by the refusal of your negotiating committee to meet

in joint session with our committee on March 8, 1955, lead us to the conclusion that an insoluble impasse has been reached and that you have terminated negotiations.

"We agree that further negotiations will be futile, and we elect to, and hereby do, terminate them forthwith.

"The agreement of November 30, 1952, and the 'status quo' term referred to in Section 27 thereof, are at a complete end.

"The consequences of the strike have destroyed *The Brooklyn Eagle* and we do not intend ever to resume publication of the newspaper."

The Guild's demand for payments under various sections of the Agreement, and then for arbitration of these issues, followed. The Publisher's claim for damages for the strike in the amount of $2,000,000 and for arbitration of this claim if the Guild disputed it was made in a letter of December 3, 1957 from the Publisher to the Guild, with a copy to the American Arbitration Association.

These two sets of claims require separate rulings by the Arbitrator. They are interwoven, however, by virtue of the fact that the Publisher relies strongly (but by no means exclusively) on the strike as a defense against the Guild's payment demands. The significance of the strike must accordingly be considered in ruling upon the Guild's claims, as well as in connection with the Publisher's claim.

It is to be noted that at the time this controversy was submitted to arbitration there was also dispute between the parties regarding the Publisher's liability to certain employees represented by the Guild for overtime and holiday payments which had become due, but had not been paid, prior to January 29, 1955; and the relief sought before the Arbitrator included overtime and holiday pay items. (R. 3) This dispute was resolved by the parties in the course of the arbitration proceedings, the Publisher conceding liability with respect to these items to the extent identified in Guild Exhibit 1. (R. 24, 39–41) These matters are accordingly covered in the accompanying Award but are not discussed further in this Opinion.

Although the original claim for relief included additional reference to "sick leave and any and all other moneys due the employees," (R. 3) the Guild specifically withdrew, at the arbitration hearing, any claims other than those relating to severance indemnity, vacation pay, notice-of-dismissal payment, overtime and holiday payments. (R. 173)

Issue No. 1—Severance Indemnity

The Guild's claim here is based on the provisions in Section 10 (Severance Indemnity) of the Agreement:

"Except in cases of dismissal for dishonesty, repeated drunkenness after warning, gross neglect of duty or gross insubordination, each employee dismissed shall be paid Severance Indemnity at the rate of one (1) week's pay for each six (6) months of continuous employment, provided that the maximum payment shall be fifty (50) weeks' pay.

"Severance Indemnity will be paid in a lump sum on the basis of average weekly salary (exclusive of bonuses and payments for special work) for the twenty-six (26) weeks for which he was last paid previous to dismissal.

"Severance Indemnity of employees in the classified advertising department shall be calculated on a minimum basis of average weekly compensation over the one (1) year period preceding dismissal and, for that purpose, past practice regarding commissions paid during sick leave shall be continued.

"To qualify an employee must have been in continuous employment on the *Brooklyn Eagle* or on the *Brooklyn Eagle* and the *Times-Union*.

"In event of death of an employee, the Publisher agrees that the legal representative of the estate of the deceased shall be paid a sum equivalent to that which the deceased would have been paid had he been discharged under the terms of this contract, less any legal costs or expenses caused the Publisher in making said payment. The Publisher's said obligation hereunder, in regard to any deceased employee, shall be reduced by the amount of any sum paid to the beneficiary named by such employee under any policy of life insurance upon his life maintained by the Publisher at its own cost and expense.

"In case of bona fide retirement from regular, gainful employment because of physical or mental breakdown certified by a competent physician, the Publisher will pay the severance indemnity according to the above schedule except that the Publisher may make the payment weekly as the salary would become due instead of in a lump sum.

"Any employee reaching the age of sixty-five (65) years or more who then is and for twenty-five (25) years prior thereto has been continuously in the employ of the Publisher may voluntarily terminate his employment and, in the event of such termination, shall be paid an amount equal to the severance indemnity which he would have been entitled to receive hereunder if his employment then had been terminated by dismissal, in weekly installments equal to his weekly salary at the time his employment terminated."

The claim covers all persons in this bargaining unit who were employees as of January 28, 1955. The list of such persons has been drawn up as Guild Exhibits 1 and 2 and is stipulated to as being correct. (R. 1098–1101)

The Guild's position is that the employees' periods of continuous employment should be considered as having continued up to and including the last day they worked (January 28, 1955) preceding the strike. These employees were subsequently, and as of March 16, 1955, "dismissed," the Union contends, within the meaning of Section 10 and are accordingly entitled to severance indemnity according to the schedule established by that Section.

The Publisher's position is that any and all severance indemnity rights and obligations under Section 10 expired with the termination of the contract period (as extended pursuant to Section 27), particularly in view of the January 28 strike.

There are, in effect, two forms of the issue which is presented here. In its broader form the question is whether the severance indemnity rights of the claimant employees were such that they survived the expiration of the contract period. The second question, which remains only if the first is answered affirmatively, is whether the January 28 strike ended any right to severance pay the claimants might otherwise have had. These two questions are not entirely severable. The necessity of their separate analysis has been recognized by both parties, however, in the presentations in this case.

The answer to the first of these questions is compelled both by the form of Section 10 and by realization of the nature of the bargain expressed by it.

Section 10 provided for payment to "each employee dismissed," without any suggestion of a limitation upon the time within which such dismissal was to occur. The specific listing of certain exceptions to the general rule ("in cases of dismissal for dishonesty, repeated drunkenness after warning, gross neglect of duty or gross insubordination") denied an intention that there should be another exception. The Section created a right going beyond cases of dismissal to include instances of death or physical or mental breakdown. The provision in the last paragraph of Section 10 that after age 65 employees with 25 years' service would receive these severance indemnity payments even in the event of voluntary retirement reflected clearly the parties' recognition of the rights created here as being "earned rights."

What was agreed here was that by each six months of continuous service each covered employee built up an equity which would be his to use if he was dismissed by the Publisher (except in the specific instances enumerated in the first paragraph of the section). The services the employee performed during the cumulative six month periods were his part of the bargain. The Publisher's reciprocal commitment was to make the stipulated payments in the event of dismissal. The employee claimants in the present case had fulfilled completely their part of this bargain. To hold that the termination of the contract period terminated the Publisher's obligation to make this agreed upon deferred payment for services already rendered would be to deny a payment which had been fully earned, and to let one party escape liability where the other party had fully performed his reciprocal obligation.

The holding by the New York Court of Appeals in Potoker that the vitality of the arbitration clause in this Agreement survived the expiration of the contract period has no controlling effect on the interpretation of Section 10, for the question in both instances is what the parties agreed to in the paticular contract provision. Yet it is even clearer here than there, because the claim here is for previously earned payments, that the right arising under the contract cannot be assumed to have been intended by the parties to expire with the termination of the contract period. The fact that the event of dismissal which made the payments due came after the termination date does not affect the matter. This is often the case where agreements involve deferred payment arrangements.

History of Clause

Nothing in past practice or in the "legislative history" of Section 10 bears materially on the question of the parties' intention regarding the point at issue. There was no "past practice," this issue never having risen before. The Guild's unsuccessful attempt in the past to get the Publisher to "fund" the severance indemnity plan involved no question of whether the right to these payments was firm, but only the seeking of assurance of the availability of funds to cover the payments by having a particular fund earmarked for this purpose. The existence of a contract right to payment for services already performed is no less firm by virtue of an agreement to pay it from general rather than earmarked funds. The Guild's proposal (rejected by the Publisher) in 1945 and 1946 that the contract be reworded to require severance payments upon "termination for any reason whatsoever" (Publisher's Exhibits D, V and W) was clearly, from the record, directed at the treatment of instances of dismissal "for cause" and had nothing to do with the question of dismissals after the termination of the contract period. The Publisher's reliance on statements made in 1948 by New York delegates to the American Newspaper Guild convention (Publisher's Exhibit WW; "Severance pay must be vested in the employee, so that past earned severance pay credits cannot be jeopardized by contract expiration") and in 1947 by a Union witness in a wage arbitration proceeding (R. 1126–29) greatly exaggerates any significance which could be responsibly attached in interpreting a contract to statements of uncertain meaning made several years before the contract was entered into by others than the contracting parties. The footnote which appeared for a number of years in the Publisher's annual financial statements ("The Company is contingently liable, in an indeterminate amount, for severance pay which may be due employees in the event of termination of their employment by the Company." *See* R. 1064(ff)) offers at least as much support for the Guild's position in the present case as for the Publisher's.

The most that could be said of any of these items would be that they reflect an awareness at times past that there might sometime arise the very question which has now arisen. Yet nothing in this fragmentary record could be reasonably relied upon to establish one or the other presently disputed readings of Section 10. Some of these items would buttress one conclusion or the other regarding the application of the Section to a case such as the present one, but they offer no foundation for either conclusion.

It would be more to the point, if it were appropriate to seek out the parties' intent beyond its expression in the words of Section 10 itself, to recognize how sharply and with what certainty they would have rejected some of the necessary implications of the interpretation urged here by the Publisher. This position would mean that under such a clause the employer could, in his discretion, control and even defeat the realization of the earned and agreed upon severance benefits by waiting to make dismissals until a contract expired. It would mean, as a practical matter, that this is exactly what would be done in any case where an employer might decide to go out of business.

Such an interpretation would mean, too, that in any negotiation regarding the renewal of a collective bargaining agreement containing a severance payment provision one of the pressures on the union would be that unless agreement on new contract terms was reached part of the price would be the complete loss of the value of the severance payment rights of all employees based on their years of work already performed. These rights are plainly subject to modification, even elimination, in any new collective bargaining negotiation. But this would be by the action of the representatives of the employees who own them. The idea that having earned them, and owned them, the employees' bargaining position in a new contract negotiation would start again from nothing is not important here from the standpoint of its being inequitable. What is relevant is that this is clearly not the way these obligations and rights would be viewed by the parties. They would view them as obligations and rights covering services already performed, as established by bilateral agreement. It would violate such a view completely to suggest that the rights already earned would be wholly destructible at the end of any contract period by a unilateral determination of the employer that he was no longer willing or inclined to make payment on them.

The conclusion which has been reached regarding the nature of the Section 10 right is based on the language of this section and the circumstances of this case. It is relevant, however, that the considerations relied upon here have led to similar conclusions by courts and arbitrators in analogous cases.

Court Rulings

The New Jersey Supreme Court has held recently on facts indistinguishable from those in the present case (except for the fact of the strike, to be considered separately below) that employees dismissed after the termination of a collective bargaining agreement are entitled to the payments they had "earned" under the severance indemnity provisions of the agreement as of the date of contract expiration. *Owens v. Press Publishing Co.*, 20 N.J. 537, 120 A.2d 442 (1956). The Court affirmed there the decision below (34 N.J. Super 203, 111 A.2d 796 (1955)) that such payment rights "are 'earned and accrued,' 'only the time of payment' being 'postponed to the time when [the employees] were discharged, . . .,' the refusal of which would constitute a 'forfeiture' of 'earned and accrued' rights." The Supreme Court rejected in this situation "the employer's point . . . that the 'rights created and arising under a collective bargaining agreement do not extend beyond the term of the contract. . . .' " Severance pay, the Court said, is "in a real sense . . . remuneration for the service rendered during the period covered by the agreement." Regarding the specific point in issue, the Court concluded:

> "In short, the separation pay here stipulated was not conditioned upon the employee's discharge from service within the term of the collective bargaining agreement. Such qualification of the allowance would run counter to the letter and the manifest reason and spirit of the contract; it would plainly disserve the mutual interests the parties had in view, reasonably deducible from the contract taken as a whole.
> "Of course, the right to such pay can 'arise' only during the subsistence of the contract so providing, and not after its termination; but once the right thus comes into being it will survive the termination of the agreement. Discharge from service during the term of the contract is not a condition *sine qua non* to the enforcement of the accrued right." (20 N.J. at 548)

This was a unanimous decision, with Heher, J., speaking for a court which included Chief Justice Vanderbilt and Justices Oliphant, Wachenfeld, Burling, Jacobs and Brennan.

The Publisher rejects Owens as being "clearly wrong" and as being contrary to the law of New York, which is identified as being that "severance indemnity and notice of dismissal pay are liquidated damages for a dismissal." (Publisher's Brief, p. 46.) Yet it is relevant (although clearly not controlling in the present proceeding) that the Appellate Division commented in Potoker, regarding the very contract involved here:

> "However, the Guild contends that severance pay as contemplated in the contract was earned and accrued contemporaneously with the rendition of services over the years during which the contract provision for severance pay was operative and that the time for payment of such benefits was deferred; consequently, it contends that this issue survives the termination of the contract. The argument thus advanced is a tenable one and the pattern and course of the parties' conduct might be influential in determining the issue. If the Guild can sustain its contention in this regard, the accrued benefits under the severance pay provisions do not perish with the agreement, survive its terminatiion, and severance pay becomes payable on expiration of employment regardless of the date of termination of the contract." (146 N.Y. Supp.(2d) at pp. 619–20)

In *Montefalcone v. Banco Di Napoli Trust Co. of New York*, the court referred to severance pay as constituting "compensation earned, the amount of which was measured by the extent of previous service." 268 App. Div. 636 (1st Dept., 1945).

Other courts have identified, in a variety of situations, the earned and compensatory character of severance payments. *In re Public Ledger, Inc.*, 161 F.2d 762, 20 LRRM 2012 (C.A. 3. 1947) (severance pay is "a claim within the terms of the hiring," and becomes a "due debt"); *Hercules Powder Co. v. Brookfield*, 189 Va. 531. 53 S.E.2d 804, 24 LRRM 2250 (1949) (recognizing the expressed contract right of the employer to discontinue a severance payment plan, but holding him obligated for severance payments "already earned as of the date of its discontinuance.") These cases present different questions from the one at issue here. They illustrate, nevertheless, the now quite generally recognized interpretation of contractual severance pay provisions as being for services rendered.

So far as a review of the cases cited by the Publisher discloses, most of the judicial decisions denying claimed severance indemnity benefits in no way question this general proposition, turning rather on such facts as the claimants' having been dismissed for "gross misconduct" (*Talberth v. Guy Gannett Publishing Co.*, 149 Me. 286, 100 A.2d 726, 33 LRRM 2266 (1953), or his having "resigned" (*Fiance v. United Jewish Appeal of Greater New York*, 204 Misc. 19, 122 N.Y.S.2d 254, 32 LRRM 2761 (1953). The only cases suggesting a different rationale are those in which severance payments are analyzed as being in the nature of "liquidated damages" to cover the loss and costs to an employee incident to his being put out of a job. These decisions rest in part on the significance attributed to the fact that the severance payments are computed (i) on the basis of employee service periods antedating the establishment of the contractual severance indemnity plan, and (ii) on the basis of the employee's rate of pay just prior to dismissal. These facts conflict, a few courts have suggested, with the theory that the severance payments are for services previously rendered during the contractual period. *Cf. Ackerson v. Western Union Telegraph Co.*, 234 Minn. 271, 48 N.W.2d 338, 28 LRRM 89 (1951) (holding that receipt of severance payments is therefore not a bar to receiving unemployment compensation benefits); *In re Port Publishing Co.*, 231 N.C. 395, 57 S.E.2d 366 (1950) (denying a claim in an insolvency proceeding that a statutory lien for wages covered contractually established severance payments); *see Wanhope v. Press Co., Inc.*, 256 App. Div. 433, 435, 4 LRRM 821, (1939), *aff'd* 281 N.Y. 607, 4 LRRM 919 (1939) (the Appellate Division, Third Department, referring in passing to severance pay—which had been made and was not in issue—as "the liquidated damage" for dismissal).

It may be seriously questioned whether there is any real conflict between the "liquidated damages for dismissal" and "deferred payment for services previously rendered" rationales of severance pay. It is even more doubtful whether this analytical distinction would control any court's treatment of the specific issue presented in the present case. In *Owens*, where this issue has received its most direct and fullest judicial consideration, the New Jersey Court of Appeals, recognizing what would seem to be the simplest realities of the matter, accepted such payments as being *both* "a form of compensation for the termination of the employment relation" (20 N.J. at 545) and "remuneration for the service rendered during the period covered by the agreement." (*id.* at 546). It is relevant that in virtually all of the cited cases referring to severance payments as being in the nature of liquidated damages for dismissal there was some issue involved other than the right to receive such payments. In no case, so far as has been discovered, has the right to severance payments been judicially denied where the eligibility terms in the contract (i.e., dismissal not for cause, etc.) had been satisfied.

Arbitration Cases

A review of arbitration cases involving severance payment claims reveals a substantial uniformity of similar treatment. The parties have not, however, relied to any material extent on the body of rulings and they are therefore not developed further here.

The precedents and analogous rulings referred to so far bear on the issue in the present case from the standpoint of the evolving recognition of the nature of severance payment rights as being essentially for services rendered. Some of these cases (particularly *Owens*), but not all of them, have also involved the particular question of the effect upon such rights of the fact of the termination of the contract. A broader review of the decided cases, directed at this point and including but not limited to severance payment cases, discloses that in a variety of situations courts and arbitrators have identified the nature of the employment relationship under collective bargaining as being such that certain rights earned and obligations incurred during the period of a particular agreement survive the contract period and are binding and enforceable even though the event which triggers them occurs after the termination date of the agreement.

Botany Mills v. Textile Workers Union, 50 N.J. Super. 18, 30 LA 479 (App. Div. 1958), involved, for example, claims to vacation pay in a situation where the agreement had a termination date of March 15, 1956, its terms conditioned entitlement to vacation benefits on the employees being "in the employ of the employer on each April 15," and the Company had gone out of business and all employees had been laid off in December, 1955. Arbitrator David L. Cole had upheld the Union's claim for vacation payments, despite the fact of contract termination before the due date, on the ground that the employees were entitled to such payments "as part of their compensation." (27 LA 1 (1956)) This award was attacked, in a proceeding in the New Jersey courts, on the ground that since the vacation rights had not "'accrued' or (become) legally enforceable until after the contract was terminated" the arbitrator lacked authority to issue such an order. The Appellate Division of the Superior Court dismissed the company's petition, noting that the circumstances of collective bargaining are such that "rights to which employees are entitled under a collective bargaining agreement may not actually fructify in enjoyment until after the expiration of a given contract period with reference to which they may be regarded as having been earned." (50 N.J. Super. at p. 29) Vacation and severance benefits were referred to by the Court as "apt examples" of this, being "in the nature of deferred compensation, in lieu of wages, earned in part each week the employee works, and payable at some later time." (*id*. at p. 30)

Here again, independent reference to arbitration rulings in analogous cases reveals a pattern substantially similar to that developing in the courts.

So far as can be determined, the developing case law is virtually uniform in its recognition of payment rights arising under a collective bargaining agreement and measured by service already performed as being enforceable even where the event upon which their enforceability depends occurs after the termination of the agreement. Potoker and other cases involving the continuing vitality of the collective bargaining arbitration clauses suggest an even broader, or perhaps an additional, area of applicability of this same concept. This is at least in part a reflection of what is involved in the New Jersey Appellate Court's reference in *Botany Mills* to the fact that "While collective bargaining agreements are normally made for fixed periods of time, they generally contemplate renewals and a subsisting contractual relationship between the employer and the union of indefinite duration." (50 N.J. Super. at p. 29)

This perhaps unduly extended review of the decisions in analogous cases has been undertaken responsively to the approach of the parties in their development of the present case, and to insure so far as this is possible against the overlooking of elements here which may have occurred to others charged with decisional responsibility in analogous circumstances. It is recognized by both parties (*see* particularly Publisher's Brief, pp. 46–47), however, that the question at issue here "is not determined by a rule of law but by the agreement of the parties . . . . The question is what they agreed." The decision here is not based on the cases, or any of them, which have been referred to in this summary, but on the determination of the application of the parties' agreement as embodied in Section 10 to the issue which is presented here.

The decision on this first point is that by Section 10 the Publisher and the Guild agreed to the establishment of severance indemnity obligations and rights which did not expire with the termination of the contract period but were rather deferred payments for services already rendered, enforceable in the event of dismissals made after the contract termination date—unless the fact of the January 28 strike requires a different result.

Effect of Strike

The question of whether the claimant employees lost the rights they would otherwise have had under Section 10 by virtue of their going out on strike is presented here in what are substantially two forms: (i) under the Publisher's broad claim that the motivation and circumstances of this strike were so outrageous that the strikers cannot properly be recognized as having standing to pursue the severance indemnity claims; and (ii) as a more specific question of whether the strike was in violation of Section 27 of the Agreement so that the alleged violation of that clause destroyed any basis for subsequent claims under Section 10.

The considerations involved in evaluating this strike claim, presented here as a defense by the Publisher against the Guild's severance indemnity claims, are virtually identical with those involved in passing upon the Publisher's counter-claim for strike damages. They may accordingly be best discussed with both of these forms of the question in mind.

So far as the broader claim, going beyond the specific question of whether this strike was in violation of Section 27, is concerned, the necessary conclusion from the record is that this was essentially only a strike for higher wages—not basically different from other typical economic strikes except in the fact that this particular battle of economic strength ended in the disaster which is the over-hanging threat in every strike situation.

No one could be insensitive to the tragedy of what happened here. A century-old newspaper went out of existence. The valiant fifteen-year effort of a dedicated newspaperman and his sons to revive a dying newspaper was defeated. Over six hundred employees and their families were put to a crises in their lives. The borough of Brooklyn was left, probably forever, without a major newspaper of its own.

Economic Factors

It is equally clear that the root cause of this tragedy lay neither in the motivations nor in the tactics of the employees or their union, but in the harsh fact that the *Eagle* has out-lived its economic usefulness.

The most sympathetic attention to the depressing chronicle of the last fifteen years of the *Eagle* compels the conclusion that it was the victim of inexorable economic pressures—of which the wage demands of its employees represented only one part. It had gone through bankruptcy in 1940. In each succeeding year it had been necessary to impose increasingly spartan economies, to cut one feature and service after another, to feed its fires with its own substance. The Publisher's description of the advertising preferences of most Brooklyn merchants, the reading preferences of most Brooklyn residents, and the financial advantages of the other New York metropolitan papers, makes poignantly clear the central fact that the time had come when the *Eagle* could no longer meet its competition. The Schroth family was willing, for reasons beyond financial profit, to fight the inevitable. The employees of the paper were not.

To feel strongly that the diminishing number of papers in this country is a danger sign for democracy, to resent the forces which cause this, even to confess economic nostalgia—none of this is warrant for charging the employees of a particular newspaper with a responsibility to continue working for it at wages they consider inadequate and less than they can get elsewhere. The claims that the Guild's 1954 wage demand was "outrageous" does not consist with the facts that the demand was for the scale being paid by the other metropolitan newspapers, that this comparison had been held valid in three previous arbitration cases, that the Publisher was paying all of his employees in the craft bargaining units the "New York rates," and that the Guild offered to arbitrate the issues which were in dispute. The "strike" on January 28 was not the result of one decision, but of the conflict of two: the employees' decision that they would not continue to work for the wages they had been getting, and the employer's decision that he could pay no more. If some of the picketing tactics used by the Guild during the strike were "ruthless" (particularly in the refusal to permit the moving of the *Eagle* to its new building), they were nevertheless within the bounds of the law and of the practices of bargaining.

The epitaph of the *Brooklyn Eagle* will have to be that it died not at the hand of the Newspaper Guild of New York but rather because it had become an economic anachronism.

Contract's Strike Provisions

This has been said here only in response to the position pressed so strongly by the Publisher. It has nothing to do with the issue of contract interpretation which must control this case—for this is a matter of what the parties had agreed to, and of evaluating the effect of the strike action in terms of this agreement. Nor does the Publisher's "strike" defense rest essentially on these broad considerations. Its position with respect to the effect of the strike is based rather on this sentence in Section 27 of the Agreement:

> "If an agreement has not been reached by the date upon which this agreement expires, status quo conditions shall be maintained during negotiations unless and until such negotiations are terminated by either party."

The January 28 strike was, the Publisher insists, a violation by the Guild of its agreement that "status quo conditions shall be maintained during negotiations." By their action in violation of the agreement, the Publisher contends, the Guild employees lost any right to make a subsequent claim under it.

The words of the Agreement do not permit this interpretation.

The key question is what is meant in Section 27 by "status quo conditions." Yet this phrase can have only one meaning. What was agreed was that the conditions which were established in the Agreement, governing the relationship between the parties, were to continue during the negotiation period following the termination date of the Agreement.

The Publisher's position is that the "status quo" clause in Section 27 was, in effect, a no-strike clause. But it could have this effect only if one of the "conditions" in the Agreement had been that the employees were under agreement not to strike.

The Agreement was not silent on this matter. It specified carefully, in fact, the parties' intention and agreement about the employees' obligations on this point. Section 21 (b) provided that:

> "Any dispute, claim, grievance or difference arising out of or relating to this agreement which the Guild and the Publisher have not been able after reasonable effort to settle, shall be submitted to arbitration . . . ."

It was then further provided in Section 21 (b) that:

> "The parties further agree that there shall be no suspension of work over an issue which is in dispute and is in process of arbitration. . . ."

This is followed immediately by the provision in Section 21(c) that:

> "Renewal of this agreement shall [not] be subject to arbitration hereunder."

What is said here is (i) that the parties agreed that there would be no suspension of work over an issue which was in process of arbitration, and (ii) that renewal of the Agreement was not subject to arbitration under the Agreement. This language does not permit an interpretation that there was a no-strike commitment with respect to negotiations incident to renewal of the Agreement. It compels the contrary conclusion: that the parties deliberately decided to limit the no-strike commitment to cases where they had agreed to arbitration as an alternative to settlement by economic force, and that disputes regarding renewal of the Agreement were not to come within the arbitration-and-therefore-no-strike area. Their deliberate attention to this point precludes any possibility of implying here a no-strike commitment going beyond what is expressed.

What the parties agreed to in Section 27 was simply that the terms and conditions of their relationship under the 1952–54 agreement ("status quo conditions") should continue in effect even after the expiration date of that contract if negotiations had not produced a new agreement by that time; with the provision for a cut-off of this extension "by either party" if it decided to terminate negotiations. The Union could not have struck during this extended period "over an issue . . . in dispute and . . . process of arbitration"—but that was not this case. There is no basis in this clause for the argument that the no-strike commitment was broader during this extension period than by the express contract conditions which constituted the "status quo" for this period. Section 27 was designed by the parties simply as a bridge between the old contract and what it was expected would be a new one—an extension of the old terms until they were renewed or changed by negotiation.

Although this conclusion is required by the words of the Agreement themselves, it may be noted, more broadly, that the Publisher's construction of Section 27 would require the assumption that the parties had agreed that there would be no resort to economic force in the very situation—the negotiation of a new contract—where resort to such force is the recognized process of collective bargaining; this despite the fact that in Section 21 they had limited the no-strike clause to instances of issues being arbitrated and then had provided expressly that renewal of the agreement shall not be subject to arbitration.

The Publisher presses strongly the argument that while Section 27 requires maintenance of "status quo conditions" during negotiations and until they are terminated by either party, the Union struck while negotiations were still going on and at a time when termination of such negotiations would (at least arguably) have been an unfair labor practice under the federal Labor Management Relation Act. The necessary answer to this contention, at the level of relatively refined logic at which the argument is propounded, is included in what has been said above: this strike, not being in violation of the terms and conditions of the Agreement (i.e., the no-strike clause in Section 21), was in no way inconsistent with the Section 27 provision which extended these terms and conditions into the negotiation period. It would not be inconsistent with this technical analysis to suggest, also, the likelihood that a strike was exactly what the parties had in mind in their use of the phrase "until such negotiations are terminated by either party." To consider the implications of the logic the Publisher relies on here is to realize that it would lead, among other things, to the startling conclusion that what these parties agreed was that there could be a strike only if there were to be no further negotiations—which would require attributing to them a complete disregard of collective bargaining realities.

What is clearest of all here is that if these parties had desired and intended to write into their agreement a no-strike clause prohibiting the Union from striking to get a new contract, or requiring it to wait through some specified period before striking, they could and would have found plain language to do so. There would be no warrant for divining such an extraordinary rule from the language of Section 27, particularly when the parties had in fact written their no-strike agreement (in Section 21) in entirely different terms.

It would be necessary to consider, if a broader basis of decision on this point were required, the implications of the fact that at no time during the strike or for many months thereafter did the Publisher ever contend that it was illegal or in violation of the Agreement; nor was there resort during the strike to the legal remedies which would have been available to stop it if this had been the fact. The postponement of this claim does not in itself destroy the basis for it. But where the question is whether the parties intended Section 27 to bar a strike during the contract renegotiation period, the complete absence of any assertion to this effect when such a strike occurred is strong testament that the parties did not themselves feel that they had included such a covenant in their agreement.

The Publisher relies, in support of this claim, on various judicial and arbitral decisions recognizing and upholding the breach of a no-strike clause as a defense against certain claims for payment by the union or the employees involved in the strike and as a basis for the awarding of compensatory damages to the employer. (Publisher's Brief, pp. 49–50, 51–63.) It is enough to note that a review of the cited cases reveals that in all of them there was a clear no-strike clause in the contract which had unquestionably been violated. This was true in the case involving the proceeding instituted against the *Eagle* by its employees represented by Typographical Union No. 6 and incident to the same suspension of operations which is involved in the present case. New York Typographical Union No. 6 and The Brooklyn Eagle, Inc., 26 LA 111 (1956) (Publisher's Submittal Document A). These cases have no material relevance here—where the question is whether there was in fact a no-strike commitment and where the persuasive evidence requires the conclusion that there was not.

The necessary conclusion is that the strike of January 28, 1955, was not in violation of the Agreement. It was an economic strike for higher wages in a new contract and had no effect upon the strikers' continuing status as employees of the Publisher. That status was terminated when the employees were dismissed by the Publisher on March 16, 1955, and they became entitled as of that date to the payments guaranteed them by Section 10 for services they had already rendered.

Issue No. 2—Vacation Pay

Payment is claimed on behalf of each employee listed in Guild Exhibit 1, who worked from October 1, 1954 to January 28, 1955, in the amount of one-third of the annual vacation payment provided for in Section 11 of the Agreement.

Section 11 provides, in its entirety, as follows:

"(a) In each calendar year during which this agreement is in effect, beginning with the year 1951, the employee shall be granted vacations with pay as follows: One (1) week to all employees who have been continuously employed for six months or more but less than one year; two (2) weeks to all employees who have been continuously employed for one year or more but less that five years; three (3) weeks to all employees who have been continuously employed for five years or more but less than fifteen years; and four (4) weeks to all employees who have been continuously employed for fifteen years or more; provided, however, that no new employee shall be entitled to any vacation in any calendar year unless his employment began prior to March 30th of that year or to a vacation of two weeks unless his employment began prior to September 30th of the previous year, and any employee who shall have been granted one week's vacation after six (6) months of continued service shall not thereafter be entitled to any further vacation until he shall have completed eighteen (18) months of continuous employment.

"(b) Vacation credit shall begin with the day of employment. Wherever possible the full vacation shall be taken in the period of May 1st to September 30th. In the case of employees entitled to three (3) weeks vacation, it shall be the established practice of the Publisher to allow these three (3) weeks to be taken consecutively provided that, in the Publisher's judgment, it does not interfere with the smooth operation of the paper; the fourth week of vacation, when earned, need not be consecutive with the other three. Vacations cannot accumulate from year to year and shall not be retroactive.

"(c) An employee who resigns from his job between January 1st and May 1st shall be entitled to one (1) week's accrued vacation pay.

"(d) Vacation pay of employees in the classified advertising department shall be calculated on a minimum basis of average weekly compensation over the preceding one year period and, for that purpose, past practice regarding commissions paid during sick leave shall be continued."

It is the Guild's contention that the claimant employees had earned, by these four months of service, a one-third part of their vacation benefits and that payment of these partial benefits became due upon the employees' dismissal by the Publisher on March 16, 1955.

The Publisher's position is that since the vacation period provided for in Section 11 (May 1st to September 30th) "had not yet arrived when the Guild members went out on strike, no right to vacation pay ever came into existence." (Publisher's Brief, p. 67)

The controlling question here again is whether these parties did by this particular provision (Section 11) in their contract express an agreement under which vacation benefits should be considered payable where the employment relationship came to an end—this particular end—

prior to the event or date which would normally make such payments come due. The issue is not essentially one of law, nor of the denomination of the rights involved here as "accrued" or "contingent" or "vested." The question is solely that of how to apply the parties' agreement, most consistently with their intent, to a situation they did not refer to specifically.

The vacation plan established in Section 11 is based on a schedule of dates designed to coincide with the customs of vacation practice rather than with the anniversary dates of the agreement. The parties assumed, in accordance with the customary collective bargaining expectation, that the 1952–54 Agreement would be succeeded by renewal agreement, just as there had been an uninterrupted succession of contracts for many years. So the time provisions of the vacation plan were built around the central fact that most vacations are taken in the summer months. Setting a vacation period of May 1st to September 30th, with qualifying service periods (six months for one week's vacation, five years for two weeks, etc.) extending back from the vacation period, the parties made no attempt to tie the vacation clause calendar and the contract calendar together. Vacations taken in 1953 were measured by service performed in 1952 and previous years, under earlier agreements. Similarly, if a new agreement had been reached in late 1954 or early 1955, and the operations of the *Eagle* had continued, the 1955 vacation payments would have been measured by the services performed, for the most part, under the 1952–54 Agreement.

It is accordingly even clearer here than with respect to the interpretation of Section 10, that the parties' agreement in no way reflected any assumption that the obligation and rights which were created were tied to or confined to the contract period itself. The necessary implications, required by the terms of the Agreement, are strongly to the contrary. The parties did not, in the 1952–54 Agreement, specifically contemplate or cover the possibility that there would not be a successor agreement, or that the question which is presented now, would arise. But everything they did which bordered on this question confirms the conclusion that the effectuation of the October 1954 to January 1955 services of the claimant employees as a sufficient and complete basis for their right to receive one-third of their vacation payment according to the schedule in Section 11(a).

Judicial decisions and arbitration awards have divided sharply on the general question of whether vacation obligations and rights survive the expiration of a collective bargaining relationship and the termination of employment by virtue of the employer's going out of business. Review of a substantial number of such cases reveals that some of them turn on the differing analysis of vacation rights as being based, inherently and conceptually, on a theory of deferred payment for services rendered on the one hand, or, on the other, on the theory that the purpose of a vacation is to refresh the employee for future service. It is perhaps a sufficient summarization of this body of decisional precedent to suggest: (i) that the substantially larger number of arbitrators, but not all of them, have accepted the "payment for past services" rationale; (ii) that a slightly larger number of courts (including New York; see *Wanhope v. Press Co., Inc.*, 256 App. Div. 433, 4 LRRM 821 (1939), *aff'd*, 281 N.Y. 607, 4 LRRM 919 (1939) have proceeded on the "refresher" theory, (iii) that there is a marked trend in both groups of cases toward reliance on the "payment for past services" analysis. This trend has been concident with the development of the graduated vacation benefit practice, it being recognized that the measuring of vacation periods (one, two, three and now often four weeks) by the length of the individual employee's service is reflected much more clearly in the "payment for past services" rationale.

This accumulating case law reflects clearly, at the same time, the fact that this is essentially not a conceptual question of the inherent nature of vacation benefits but a question rather of the expressed intention of the parties to the particular contract.

What is controlling in the present case is the clear and consistent indication in the terms of Section 11 that the Publisher and the Guild had adopted for themselves the principle that vacation benefits were to be treated as payments for services rendered.

They agreed in Section 11(a), in accordance with the common practice, that the amount of each employee's vacation benefit was to be measured by the length of his service.

Their agreement omitted any provision, common in many contracts and the basis of a number of the decisions rejecting the "accrual theory," that the employee must be on the employment rolls as of the start of the vacation period in order to be eligible for vacation benefits. (*But see*, holding that even such a provision does not defeat the vacation benefit claims in a case like the present one, *Botany Mills v. Textile Workers Union*, 27 LA 1 (1956), *cf. same*, 50 N.J. Super. 18, 30 LA 479 (1958).)

The first sentence of Subsection (b) of Section 11 makes each day of continuous employment with the Company part of his "vacation credit."

It is perhaps most clearly indicative of the parties' intended treatment of this matter that in Section 11(c) they provided specifically for the payment of one week's "accrued vacation pay" to any employee who resigned from his job between January 1st and May 1st. Acceptance of the Publisher's argument that Subsection (c) represented the parties' *limitation* upon the application of the earned payment principle would

produce the clearly rnintended and inequitable result that an employee
who resigned voluntarily during this period would get his vacation pay
but an employee dismissed by the employer would not. Subsection (c)
must be recognized rather as an unusually clear illustration and reflection
of the fact that the Publisher and the Guild had adopted in their agreement the principle that an employee's vacation benefits were to be
considered as deferred payments for services rendered.

The necessary conclusion is that effectuation of the expressed intention of Section 11 requires that the claimant employees receive one-
third of their vacation pay, according to the schedule in Section 11(a),
as compensation for their services rendered between October 1, 1954
and January 28, 1955.

This conclusion is reached with recognition of the Publisher's contention that only services after the start of the calendar year (January 1,
1955) would be entitled to consideration in ruling on this point. This
contention is unsupportable under the terms of Section 11 and the practice which had been followed in administering it.

Insofar as the January 29 strike is relied on as a defense to the
vacation pay claim this defense is rejected for the reasons stated in the
discussion of Issue No. 1, above.

The Guild also claims payment for one or more employees for
vacation benefits carried over from the 1954 vacation period. This claim
is denied on the basis of the provision in Section 11(b) that "vacations
cannot accumulate from year to year and shall not be retroactive."

Issue No. 3—Notice-of-Dismissal Pay

The Guild contends that claimant employees are also entitled to
payments under the provisions of Section 9(e) of the Agreement:

> "The following periods of notice, where reasonably possible, in ad-
> vance of dismissal shall be given to employees, except in cases of dismissal
> for dishonesty, repeated drunkenness after warning, gross neglect of duty
> of gross insubordination:
>
> | | |
> |---|---|
> | Over 3 years' service .... | 3 weeks' notice |
> | 1 to 3 years' service .... | 2 weeks' notice |
> | 90 days' to 1 year's service .... | 1 week's notice |
> | Under 90 days' service .... | no notice" |

The Guild maintains that Section 9(e) establishes a "wage requirement," citing a single precedent of at best dubious applicability (*in re
Public Ledger*, 161 F.(2nd) 762 (C.A. 3, 1947). This might be arguable
under different factual circumstances. The claim has not been sufficiently supported here, however, nor would it appear that the facts of

the present case could be brought within the parties' contemplation as expressed in Section 9.

Issue No. 4—Strike Damages

The Publisher claims damages in the amount of $2,000,000 for the Guild's alleged breach of the no-strike agreement the Publisher contends was incorporated in Section 27 of the Agreement. A computation of damages actually suffered to the extent of $2,931,423.74 has been presented in these proceedings, based on an evaluation of the machinery and equipment of the *Eagle* at $2,000,000, its good will at $800,000, and certain expenditures in connection with the attempted move of the paper to new quarters at $386,103.55 with recognized offsets of $159,679.81.

Insofar as there is any question about the Arbitrator's jurisdiction to rule upon this claim, and to award damages in the event of a determination of a contract breach, it is concluded that he does have such jurisdiction.

To the extent that a question has been raised regarding that timeliness of this claim, it is ruled that whatever basis there might be for the claim would not properly be considered destroyed by the timing of its presentation.

This claim is denied, however, on the ground that no violation of Section 27 has been established. It was not a no-strike provision. Its effect was solely to continue in effect the terms and conditions established by the parties in the Agreement. These terms and conditions did not include a no-strike agreement except with respect to disputes "in process of arbitration," as provided in Section 21—which Section also provided expressly that "Renewal of this agreement shall not be subject to arbitration hereunder."

The considerations pertinent to this issue have been developed in detail above, in connection with the Publisher's reliance on the strike as a defense against the Guild's severance indemnity and vacation pay claims. What has been said there is equally applicable here and nothing would be added by its repetition. These considerations require the conclusion that the January 28 strike was not in violation of the Agreement.

Regarding the Form and Coverage of the Award

Guild Exhibit 1 is a statement of the Guild claims, identifying the claim made on behalf of each employee for each of the disputed payment items. This statement was prepared originally by the Guild but was then checked in detail with representatives of the Publisher. It has been stipulated that this statement sets forth accurately the employees entitled to receive payment if the Guild's claims are upheld, as well as the amounts of such payments. (R. 24–28, 1098–1101) The award upholding the Guild's severance indemnity, vacation pay, overtime and holiday pay claims may appropriately, therefore, be put in a form incorporating by reference the schedules in Guild Exhibit 1.

Guild Exhibit 2 lists twelve employees who were on maternity leave, military leave or other leaves of absence on January 29, 1955. (*And see* R. 47–50, 157–59, 190–93, 1100.) So far as appears from the record, these employees are entitled to severance indemnity payments based on the periods of their continuous employment by the Publisher, as well as to pro-rata vacation pay for periods, if any, during which they worked following September 30, 1954. The details of these individual cases have not, however, been set out. Nor have the parties presented to the Arbitrator their respective positions regarding the possible effect of various provisions of the Agreement (particularly Section 20, as well as Sections 10 and 11) on the question of the eligibility of these employees to receive severance and vacation payments. The claims of these employees are accordingly referred back to the parties for disposition in accordance with the principles adopted in this Opinion and the accompanying Award.

Award

Re *Severance Indemnity*: Claimant employees, as identified in Guild Exhibit 1, are entitled to severance indemnity payments in the amounts set forth in said Exhibit.

Re *Vacation Pay*: Claimant employees, as indentified in Guild Exhibit 1, are entitled to vacation pay in the amounts set forth in said Exhibit. Additional claims for payments for vacations which one or more employees could have taken but failed to take prior to January 1, 1955 are denied.

Re *Severance Indemnity and Vacation Pay in the case of employees who were on leaves of absence as of January, 28, 1955*: The claims of such employees, identified in Guild Exhibit 2, are referred back to the parties for disposition in accordance with the terms of the accompanying Opinion.

Re *"Notice of Dismissal" payments*: All claims to payments based on Section 9(e) of the Agreement of November 30, 1952 are denied.

Re *Strike Damages*: The claim of the Publisher for money damages for an alleged violation of Section 27 of the Agreement of November 30, 1952 is denied.

Questions for Discussion

Is the decision based upon the contract, external law, or a combination of both sources?

Is it accurate to describe successive collective agreements between the same parties as one continuing agreement subject to periodic modification? How does the adoption of this theory of the collective agreement affect the interpretation of the agreement?

What are other examples of "earned rights" or "deferred payments" under a collective agreement? How can an agreement provide for termination of such rights upon expiration?

Compare the style, form, and substance of this opinion and award with the other decisions included in this Part.

Westinghouse Electric Corporation

Arbitrator Carl A. Warns, Jr.
May 16, 1962
38 LA 1064

RADIO NOTICE

Preliminary Statement

On Sunday, December 11 and Monday, December 12, 1960, a severe blizzard struck the state of New Jersey and the surrounding areas. Over 20 inches of snow fell during the storm which was considered to be the third deepest snowfall in the state's history. This storm was followed by sub-freezing temperatures and gusty winds. In Edison Township where the plant is located, "virtually all business and social affairs in the Township" (Union Exhibit #1) were halted. All roads and highways throughout the area were clogged with snow. Evidence indicates that a true "state of emergency" existed on Monday, December 12. Only "one or two" of the Company's total work force reported for work on Monday, December 12. On Tuesday, many of the roads still were not open, and work continued to remove the snow from the remaining roads and to dig out the residents who were calling the Edison Township police for help. (Union Exhibit #3) However, on Tuesday, the Plant attempted to operate. Less than 60 percent of the work force reported for work and many of these employees were as much as two or three hours late. On Tuesday, the assembled work force was able to produce only a total of 44 television sets as compared to a normal production of more than 2000. The Company concluded that based on reports from the state police and municipal officials, sufficiently large number of absentees could be expected on Wednesday, December 14, 1960. Management decided to close the Plant around noon December 13 and reopen it on Thursday, December 15. The Local Union President was notified of this decision as well as supervision who were instructed to inform their employees who were at work that the next day Wednesday, December 14, would be an off day. The record indicates that the employees in the Plant on the 13th were also advised over the Plant's public address system at 11:50 A. M. by Management as follows:

> "Because there is every indication that the majority of employees will still have difficulty getting to work tomorrow, all manufacturing operations will be suspended tomorrow. Hourly employees should not report to work tomorrow. Employees in those activities that will be needed will be contacted by their supervisors. Normal operations will resume at 7:00 A.M. Thursday. Any change will be announced over Station WCTC tomorrow evening." (Co. Exhibit 3)

Telephone operators and plant guards were also given this announcement. Additionally, the Company purchased radio broadcast time for spot announcements advising employees of the plant closing. Station WCTU in New Brunswick and WOR in New York City were used. Six announcements were aired over WCTC, a station which serves a radius of approximately 50 miles from the plant. At various times on December 13 and 14 the following radio announcement was made over Station WCTC:

> "The Westinghouse Television-Radio Division Plant in Edison, N.J., has announced that 11 (first and second shift) manufacturing operations will be suspended tomorrow (today)—Wednesday. Hourly employees are not to report to work except at the specific request of their supervisor." (Co. Exh. 4)

It is the position of the Company that Station WCTC is the principal broadcasting station for the area (Tr. 86). The same announcement was made by radio Station WOR in New York City immediately prior to the

6 P.M. news on December 13. The grievants reported to the Plant gates for work on Wednesday, December 14, 1960, contending that they were not notified of the decision of Management to close the plant on that day. This is the basis of this grievance. In brief, it is the position of the Union that the Company violated the collective agreement by not paying 4 hours report-in pay to those employees who reported for work at their regular starting time and were sent home. The Union admits that an emergency existed on Monday, December 12, but contends that there was no emergency involved on Wednesday, December 14, the day in question. To the Union, any other conclusion "would mean the Company could argue where an emergency originally occurred that was beyond its control, everything that followed would be beyond the control of the Company and the emergency would exist indefinitely." (Union's brief, page 4.) The Union goes on to argue that the Company had sufficient time and knowledge to notify employees who were not at work on Tuesday, December 14, 1960. The Union states that more than 18 hours were available for supervisors to advise the absent employees by either telephone or telegraph. The Union emphasizes that each supervisor knows his employees, knows where they live, is aware that the majority of these employees have telephones, and yet no effort was made as is customary, to attempt personal contact. Instead, in the Union's view, the Company used a narrow and inadequate method of communication, a small radio station (WCTC) serving only a small area and yet utilized only one announcement on the stronger radio station WOR. The Union asks that all of the grievants be paid their reporting pay. The Company on the other hand, asserts that under the provisions of Section 8, Paragraph 4 of the National Agreement, it is not obligated to pay reporting pay to the employees who are the grievants in this dispute. The Company asserts that the combination of circumstances that existed created an emergency situation which continued through Wednesday, December 14; therefore, in the Company's view, the provisions of Paragraph 4 do not apply as provided in the exclusion clause. The Company argues further that even if the arbitrator should ultimately determine that no emergency existed on December 14, he should find that the hourly employees were properly advised of the shutdown in accordance with the provisions of Paragraph 4. The Company claims that the list of grievants is suspect, it is replete with inconsistencies, and offers no proof whatsoever that any of the employees named therein reported for work on December 14 at the regular starting time of their shift. In brief, it is the Company's position that it acted in a logical, prudent and reasonable manner under all of the circumstances surrounding this case. The Company emphasizes that any evaluation of a charge that the Com-

pany has violated the contract must be made in the context of the circumstances at the time Management's decision was made, and not from the vantage point of an after-the-fact review. The Company asks that the grievance be denied.

Contract Provision Involved

"SECTION VIII-WAGES (National Agreement)
"4. Four Hours of Work
"Hourly employees who report to work at the regular starting time of their shift and have not been advised at least ten (10) hours beforehand not to report, and those who report to work at other times at Management's request, will be guaranteed four (4) hours work at their guaranteed rate of pay for the job on which they work, whichever is higher. If work is not provided during some or all of such four (4) hours, the employee will be paid at his daywork rate for such period. If the employee has qualified for overtime in accordance with the overtime provisions of this Agreement, overtime rates based on the provisions of this Agreement (Section X-Overtime) will be paid for hours not worked.
"NOTE: The foregoing provisions will not apply in the case of an emergency such as fire, flood, power failure, or work stoppage by employees in the plant."

Opinion of the Arbitrator

All provisions in labor agreements have practical purposes behind them—to the extent that an arbitrator understands these practical purposes, to that extent his evaluation of whether the Company has breached a provision in question is meaningful and realistic. I suppose that practically all labor agreements have a provision similar to Paragraph 4 of Section VIII of the Agreement. I am sure that everyone will agree that such a provision is intended by economic sanction to force a company to intelligently schedule work and provide it in accordance with its schedule unless reasonable notices is given to the employees not to work. Most clauses of this type are interpreted to mean that if the company is unable to provide work in accordance with its predetermined schedule or to inform employees of its inability to fulfill normal production requirements because of an emergency, there is no duty to pay call-in pay. In other words, the whole idea behind call-in provisions is to impress upon the Company its responsibility to prevent an employee reporting for work when scheduled, and then finding no work available when the Company had adequate opportunity to notify him not to report. Beyond this generalization, each contract clause, and each set of facts must be evaluated separately in the context of the broad purposes of call-in provisions. As to the grievance before me, I suppose that it could be argued analytically that "work was available" on Wednesday, December 14, in the sense that the Company had adequate power, necessary equipment, and adequate materials with which to do the work. Regardless of what might be true in other plants, the record before me indicates that on many jobs, perhaps on most of them, the jobs are all interrelated and many are interdependent (Tr. 79). Practically, then, in this plant, work is not available unless a sufficient number of employees report to make it worth while for Management in its best judgment, to operate the plant. The Union did not controvert the evidence that when less than 60 percent of the work force showed up for work on Tuesday, December 13, only 44 sets were produced as compared to a normal production of more than 2000. What we have then before us is that on Monday, December 12 a "state of emergency" existed with only one or two employees reporting for work. Tuesday, we had approximately 60 percent of the work force with practically no production accomplished, and a reasonable belief on that date by the Company that on the following day, the 14th, absenteeism would still continue at a high rate. Under these facts, we can truly say that the blizzard of December 11 and 12, an "act of God" over which Company had no control projected itself into Tuesday, December 13 to the extent that it was not feasible to operate the plant, with all indications suggesting that the same would be true on Wednesday, the day in question. This is not to say I believe the failure to work on Wednesday was an "emergency" which prevented the Company from notifying the employees not to work. The Union introduced evidence that other plants in the area on Wednesday did work as a matter of fact, and presumably they had sufficient work force to get out production. But the size of other plants, the nature of their operations and other relevant considerations must be weighed before a true relationship can be drawn between what other plants did in the area and what Westinghouse did. Although I do not conclude, as I stated, that the circumstances precluded the Company from attempting to notify employees not to work on Wednesday, the blizzard and its consequences are relevant considerations to be weighed in determining whether the employees are entitled to their call-in pay. Inherent in Paragraph 4 of Section VIII is the obligation on the part of the Company to notify employees not to work if work will not be available. This obligation is not imposed on the Company if the special facts indicate that the Company was unable to do so because of an "emergency." Here, Management did attempt to notify the employees and as a matter of fact most of them did not report for work on Wednesday. The employees in the plant were advised not to report the following day by means of a plant wide broadcast announcement. In regard to the remaining 500 hourly employees, the record reveals that the Company utilized what had been the usual means of mass communication—the radio stations. Again, we must be realistic. If Employee Jones is to be furloughed on a particular day when he is scheduled to work, then it is only reasonable to expect his supervisor to attempt to contact him personally. But where, as here, we are speaking in terms of 500 employees, with approximately 18 hours in which to effectuate the notice, then the use of local radio stations becomes feasible, especially when such method of communication has been utilized in the past. It is only reasonable to assume, that along with some of the hourly employees some of the supervision and clerical help were also absent. To make 500 telephone calls, or to send several hundred telegrams would require that all of the supervisors, with some clerical help, be at the plant where the employees' names, telephone numbers, and addresses are located, and to make such calls from the plant. As stated previously, I doubt seriously as a practical matter, such a method of personal communication would have been more effective than the use of a radio and instructions to the guards and telephone operators to inform any employees to call in that they would be furloughed on Wednesday. Some consideration must be given to the point that of the approximately 500 employees to whom the radio announcements were addressed, approximately 450 received the communication. In brief, although the Company acted reasonably in deciding not to operate on Wednesday, I interpret Paragraph 4 of Section VIII as requiring the Company to notify the employees of the fact that work would not be provided on Wednesday. The Company did meet its obligation to notify the employees by utilizing a means of communication that was customary to them. Where 500 employees are to be notified not to work within an 18 hour period with busy telephone lines, road conditions which would undoubtedly delay the delivery of telegrams, along with the very serious question of whether administratively, such contact could be made by adequate supervision calling and sending telegrams from the plant where the records are located, the use of a radio station serving the area along with a back-up announcement from a still stronger station, is reasonable. To summarize, Paragraph 4 of Section VIII is intended to force the Company by means of a financial penalty to notify employees, previously scheduled to work that they are to be furloughed, unless an emergency, beyond the Company's control, makes notification or the providing of work impractical. I will not speculate on what the decision would have been had the Company not attempted to notify the employees in this case; the decision must be rendered in the context of what in fact happened. On that basis, as I have previously stated, the Company acted reasonably under all the circumstances, did not violate established past practice, or any provisions of the contract. The Dash decision, concerning the same snow storm, between Minneapolis-Honeywell Regulator Company, and another local of the same union involved somewhat different facts. Essentially, Umpire Dash concluded that the use of radio communications in notifying employees not to work was contrary to past practice under similar circumstances in the past. In the case before me, the evidence supports the conclusion that notifying employees by radio was reasonable under the circumstances and consistent with past practice. It is not completely clear what the facts were under the Israel Ben Scheiber decision between the same parties, but it appears that in that case, the Company rested on the assumption that since an emergency existed, notification was not necessary. The arbitrator held the Company liable for the report-in pay when the second shift was concelled. A consideration that impressed the arbitrator was that employees who called in to inquire whether the second shift would work, were informed that they should report for work. There was no attempt made to call them back and tell them not to work or to communicate in any way with the employees who had not called in. What the arbitrator decided was that a company which relies on the emergency "exception" of the call-in provision with no attempt at notification if time permits, does so at his own risk if the arbitrator concludes that no emergency in fact existed. It is apparent then that the two cases cited by the Union are sufficiently different in fact as to be distinguishable from the grievance under consideration here.

Award

Grievance No. 8335 is denied.

Questions for Discussion

What role does the emergency exception play in Arbitrator Warns' conclusion that employees who reported to work on Wednesday were not entitled to reporting pay?

How did Arbitrator Warns distinguish between the notification in this case and other cases cited by the union?

Under what circumstances would notification to employees be necessary or unnecessary when the collective bargaining agreement includes an emergency exception?

In this case what is the effect of past practice?

Compare the style, form, and substance of this opinion and award with the other decisions included in this Part.

National Annealing Box Company

Arbitrator Edwin R. Teple
August 4, 1965
45 LA 196

EXCESSIVE ABSENCES

The Issue

The primary question presented is whether the grievant, X—, was discharged for proper cause. There is also a question concerning the procedural regularity of the Company's action.

Background

The grievant was discharged by a notice dated November 16, 1964 (Company Ex. 1) which reads as follows:

> "We find it necessary to terminate your employment effective November 16, 1964. This is in line with our letter to you dated January 9, 1964 copy of which is attached."

The grievant had been discharged previously, on August 9, 1963, for the same reason, i.e., absenteeism which the Company considered excessive and without adequate explanation. After rather extensive negotiations the Union prevailed upon the Company to give the grievant one more chance and pursuant to these good services, the grievant was reinstated without back pay on January 13, 1964. The letter of January 9, referred to in the final notice of termination, was addressed to the grievant in connection with this reinstatement and advised him as follows (Union Ex. 1; Company Ex. 2):

> "Please be advised that due to negotiations between Union Local No. 2617 United Steelworkers Representatives and National Annealing Box Company Representatives it has been agreed that you shall be allowed to return to work at National Annealing Box Company on Monday, January 13, 1964 on the day shift under the following conditions:
> "1. No retroactive pay will be involved for time August 9, 1963 to January 13, 1964.

"2. You shall return as Utility Class 2 instead of Stress Relief Furnace Operator. Pay rate is the same for each classification.

"3. You are to change your conduct and not continue or in the future start to conduct yourself in the manner which culminated in your removal from the seniority list on August 9, 1963.

"4. Your date of seniority will remain April 15, 1956.

"5. Should you fail to do as stated in No. 3 you will be discharged without further ado.

"Your return on January 13, 1964 as indicated will be construed as acceptance on your part to above conditions."

No written grievance was filed after the grievant's final discharge, as contemplated by Section 8(b) of the Agreement (Joint Ex. 1), but this apparently resulted from the fact that the Company failed to impose a preliminary suspension as provided in Section 10 of the Agreement. A meeting was held between the Company and the Union after the discharge notice was received by the grievant and apparently the matter was discussed at some length. The Company, however, refused to change its action and the Union gave oral notice that the matter would be appealed to arbitration. It is apparent that the parties have departed somewhat from the normal grievance procedure outlined in Section 8, and no question has been raised concerning the manner in which the grievance was presented or its timeliness.

The grievant was hired on April 14, 1956. It is clear from the record that he has had a problem about regular attendance at work almost from the beginning. The first disciplinary action resulting from excessive absenteeism occurred in 1957. Since 1958 he has been variously employed by the Company as a welder (third class), sandblaster, radiographer (third class), furnace operater, utility man (Class II), and finally as a gardener.

So far as the record shows, there is no complaint concerning the quality of the grievant's work. His entire difficulty seems to stem from his inability to attend work regularly. Although illness was given as the reason for many of his absences over the years, the matter is complicated by the fact that his chief difficulty did not stem from injury or the kind of illness that is normally accepted without question. The grievant had been under treatment for an ulcer from time to time, but his inability to work seemed to stem largely, if not entirely, from a "nervous condition" which apparently affected his stomach and resulted in general agitation.

Between June 13 and August 6, 1957, the grievant was absent 16 days and was suspended by the Company and warned that future absence without good cause would result in more serious disciplinary action (Company Ex. 4). In 1958 the grievant was absent 16 days between January 3 and March 27, at which time he was laid off. After being recalled to work he was absent for 10 days between August 25 and October 21, at which time he was laid off again. Most of these absences were for reported illness.

Between January 6 and April 14, 1960, the grievant was absent a total of 14 days, part of this time being for reported illness. On April 19, after three absences without explanation, the grievant was again warned about the possible consequences of his inability to report for work regularly (Company Ex. 3). Between May 7 and July 5 of the same year the grievant was absent a total of 16 days, a substantial part of this time being for reported illness. At this point a 3-day suspension was imposed and the grievant was warned that discharge would result if his absences from work continued. When he was absent again from July 13 to July 20, 1960, a 5-day suspension was imposed (Company Ex. 3).

The next two years were substantially better. In 1961 the grievant was absent only five days for reported illness and one day without explanation. In 1962 he was absent ten days for reported illness and two days without explanation.

In 1963, however, the earlier pattern reappeared. Between February 11 and July 19 of that year the grievant was absent a total of 23 days for reported illness. After his vacation late in July he was absent five days without explanation. On August 6 the following letter was addressed to the grievant (Company Ex. 5):

> "The Company is considering you as A.W.O.L. inasmuch as no report was received on August 5, 1963 as to the reason for your absence.
> "You have been observed recently and were apparently in good health at that time.
> "Should your absence continue for three (3) more days A.W.O.L., it will be considered that you have resigned from employment here."

On August 9 the Company addressed a second letter to the grievant (Company Ex. 6), which concluded as follows:

> "Inasmuch as we have received no answer from you we are informing you by this letter that if no answer is received from you by 3:30 P.M. this date we shall consider you as having resigned from employment here and shall immediately remove your name from our employee record."

When the grievant failed to call the Company as requested he was discharged.

After his reinstatement in January, 1964 the grievant was absent for reported illness on only 4 days, June 29 to July 2, but he was absent without explanation on September 29 and then he called on November 3 that he could not report for work because of illness. When this absence continued without further explanation, the Company asked the shop clerk to call at the grievant's home on November 10. The grievant was not at home when this employee arrived, but his wife explained that he had gone to the doctor's office. The grievant reportedly called his wife while the shop clerk was there to say that the doctor's office was closed and he was coming home. The shop clerk reported that he waited approximately 25 minutes but did not see the grievant.

The following day the assistant superintendent went to the grievant's home about 10:00 A.M. and found the grievant in bed, apparently asleep. On November 12, which was payday, someone else came to the plant with a note from the grievant requesting his paycheck. This messenger reportedly advised the shop clerk that the grievant planned to see his doctor that afternoon.

On Monday, November 16, the grievant did not report for work and failed to call in. It was at this point that the Company determined that discharge action would be taken. The grievant's wife called the Company late that afternoon and reported that she was trying to arrange an appointment for the grievant with a specialist in Wheeling, West Virginia. She was reportedly advised of the action the Company had already taken.

The following day, November 17, the Union presented a "disability certificate" of the same date (Union Ex. 2) which consisted of a printed form filled in by Dr. Emil Sposato indicating that the grievant had been under this doctor's professional care from November 3 to November 17 and was totally incapacitated during this time. The statement also indicated that the patent was not recovered but was awaiting "specialist care in Wheeling, W. Va. Clinic." The grievant, however, acknowledged that he had not visited Dr. Sposato's office until November 14. On November 20 the Company received a statement from Dr. Sposato which listed November 14 as the date of treatment (Union Ex. 6).

Subsequently, on the first of December, the grievant reported for work, apparently with a doctor's certificate indicating that he had recovered. The Company reportedly was not satisfied concerning the nature of his illness and the next day the grievant brought in a statement from Dr. Super. Representatives of the Company and the Union went to Dr. Super's office on December 7, with the grievant's permission, and this doctor indicated that he had last treated the grievant on July 3, 1964.

Under date of December 10, Dr. Sposato addressed the following letter to the Company (Union Ex. 3):

> "Mr. X—came to my office on Nov. 14, 1964 complaining of nervousness, abdominal pain and cramps. He was visibly upset. He stated he had been treated for ulcers. Patient stated that he had been unable to work for several weeks. It was apparent that Mr. X—needed psychiatric help and he was referred to Dr. Stephen Ward in Wheeling, W. Va.
>
> "He returned to work as suggested by Dr. Ward."

The specialist in Wheeling made the following report under date of February 1, 1965 (Union Ex. 5):

> "I first saw the above-named on 11/30/64. He was referred by Dr. Emil Sposato, his family physician, in Washington, Pennsylvania. At that time he told me he had been unable to work for just about four weeks because of bad nerves. It is my opinion that Mr. Rogers was suffering from symptoms of anxiety and depression during this time. I put him on some medication at that time and I have seen him several times since then.
>
> "At the time I first saw him, I thought that his symptoms could be helped a great deal by returning to work and urged him to return to work as soon as possible.
>
> "During the past several months, Mr. Rogers has improved significantly and now there is no question about his ability to return to work."

In general the Company testified that no other employee had a record of absences as bad as the grievant. The Union pointed out, however, that one employee who came to mind had been on sick leave for a year.

The Union testified that its representative went to Dr. Super's office to find out whether the grievant had been under the doctor's care. It was learned that the grievant had not been treated on the date which he had reported, but his wife had called Dr. Super's office. Dr. Super had suggested that the grievant see another local doctor but the grievant preferred not to see the particular doctor suggested.

The grievant received sick pay under the Company's group health plan starting on November 14, the date when he first saw doctor Sposato (Company Ex. 7).

Company's Position

In general, the Company takes the position that the greivant's absences have been largely unexplained to the Company's satisfaction and that his absenteeism was therefore unjustified. The Company's action was free of discrimination, it is argued, and the grievant's long record of absenteeism constitutes justifiable cause for discharge.

The Company stresses the fact that with reference to the period from November 3 to November 14, there is no evidence that the grievant was examined or treated by a doctor and therefore the record contains no medical evidence that he was ill or had a justifiable excuse for his absence from work during this period.

The Company also refers to its minutes of the union-management cooperation, meeting held on September 23, 1964, which reflect the Company's position that if absence due to sickness extends through a week-end, the employee is expected to report again on Monday (Company

Ex. 8). The minute itself states that the Union and the Company had agreed to this (although the Union questioned this at the hearing), and the Company testified that these minutes had been posted on the plant bulletin board. The grievant's failure to report his continued illness on Monday morning, November 16, the Company contends, gives further cause for the discharge action.

The Company argues that this grievance has been treated by both parties as an exceptional case requiring exceptional treatment under the Agreement. In this connection it is pointed out that the grievant was finally reinstated after his previous discharge in 1963, but only in conjunction with certain conditions which were outlined in the letter of January 9, 1964. The Company feels that both parties have waived the provisions of the basic agreement with respect to the grievance procedure and accepted the special procedure which was, followed in this case.

Union's Position

The Union contends that the grievant was discharged improperly and without sufficient cause.

In the first place, the Union argues that the grievant was peremptorily discharged without the preliminary suspension required by Section 10 of the Agreement. This circumstance, the Union insists, places the Company in a position of having violated the Agreement and furnishes a basis for sustaining the grievance.

The Union also argues that the grievant's loss of five months of work after discharge in 1963, and his reinstatment in 1964 without back pay, were ample punishment for the long list of unexplained absences during the earlier years. The discharge action in November, 1964, the Union suggests, is a second punishment for the same offense.

The Union also contends that the grievant was in fact ill during the period of his absence early in November but that he is now physically and mentally able and ready to continue his employment with the Company.

Finally, the Union refers to the decision of the referee upholding the grievant's claim for unemployment compensation on the ground that the grievant's discharge was not due to willful misconduct in connection with his work within the meaning of the Pennsylvania law and that he was therefore eligible for benefits (Union Ex. 8).

Decision

The Arbitrator has always treated discharge cases with the greatest of care and with an appreciation of the importance which both sides attach to such matters. While it is the employer's duty to maintain an efficient working force which can be depended upon to report for work and accomplish the production at hand, the importance of a job to the individual employee must also be fully recognized. The particular factors in each case must be carefully weighed.

There can be little doubt, however, that the employer may be justified in imposing the penalty of discharge, after appropriate warning, where an employee has a record of excessive absences from work even though such absences may be due to illness. *Ohio Packing Co.*, 30 LA 1021; *Pacific Telephone & Telegraph Co.*, 32 LA 178 (where the employee's absences were reportedly due to migraine headaches and upset stomach); *Westinghouse Electric Corp.*, 38 LA 187 (in which it was noted that there was no assurance that the grievant's attendance would become more regular); *General Electric Co.*, 39 LA 979; *Keystone Steel & Wire Co.*, 43 LA 703; *Minnesota Mining & Mfg. Co.*, 41 LA 1257. It was variously reasoned in these cases that an employee may be dismissed for legitimate non-disciplinary reasons, including his inability to conform to minimum requirements of reasonably regular attendance, and that the employer has the right to expect an employee to be available with reasonable regularity to perform the work within his classification, regardless of the merits of his illness.

In cases of absence due to illness where discharge was not upheld, it has frequently been stressed that the conditions causing the grievant's absences had been corrected or eliminated. *General Electric Co.*, 32 LA 637 (where reinstatement with one-half of the earnings lost was awarded but it was also stated that discharge would be warranted if the grievant missed more than 20 work days per year in the future); *Union Carbide Chemical Co.*, 35 LA 469; *Western Electric Co.*, 38 LA 233 (where the employee's last absence was due to surgery after the employer had warned her to take steps to correct the most recent condition causing her sickness); *TWA*, 44 LA 280.

Considering the evidence in the record of this case and the nature of this grievant's difficulty, it is impossible to find with any assurance that the cause of his absences has either been cured or eliminated. His specialist recommended that a return to work would be beneficial, but he was working at the onset of the nervous condition which apparently caused his absence last November. Although there is no indication that the ulcer to which he referred was the direct cause of his series of absences, it was acknowledged that he was still receiving periodic checkups for this condition. His local physicians apparently were unable to effect a cure of the tension which the grievant said made it impossible for him to work when these spells hit him.

Neither the Union nor the Company can be blamed for the grievant's failure to seek prompt medical attention or to cope with the anxieties which apparently beset him. It seems evident that the grievant had not received medical attention when many of his earlier absences occurred, and on the last occasion, after he had been absent for an entire week, the grievant still had not consulted his own doctor. When his wife called his former doctor for him, the grievant admittedly declined to consult the doctor to whom she was referred. The reasons for his refusal are not clear. Although he led others to believe that he was trying to obtain medical advice, he did not actually see Dr. Sposato until November 14. With such a record, the grievant has only himself to blame.

It cannot be said that the grievant did not receive fair warning. He was warned on numerous occasions and received progressively longer suspensions for the very reason which caused his final discharge. On several of these occasions he was told that continued irregular attendance would result in the termination of his employment. To climax this long record, the grievant was discharged in 1963 when his former tendencies reoccurred, and was reinstated in January, 1964 upon his plea, through his Union representatives, for one more chance.

Under the circumstances shown, it cannot be said that the Company's action was entirely without justification when, in November, it seemed apparent that the grievant was slipping back into his former ways. It is understandable that the Company's confidence was shaken by the unconfirmed excuses which were given on behalf of the grievant prior to the date of the discharge action. Matters were not helped by a doctor's statement which initially indicated total disability to work from the beginning of the grievant's absence when a subsequent statement from this doctor acknowledged that he had not seen the grievant until November 14.

Under the circumstances, with due regard for the seriousness of the Company's action, it cannot properly be found that the decision to discharge the grievant was without just or proper cause.

The referee in the unemployment compensation proceedings merely determined that the record before him failed to indicate that the claimant had intentionally and deliberately committed acts of misconduct detrimental to the best interest of the employer. Wilfull misconduct, he ruled, was necessary in order to disqualify a claimant for unemployment benefits under the terms of the Pennsylvania law. The referee acknowledged that his determination did not affect the employer's right to discharge the employee.

The Company's failure to invoke the preliminary suspension contemplated by Section 10 of this Agreement, under the particular circumstances of this case, cannot be considered determinative of the basic issue here presented. In view of the long history of similar conduct and the basis on which the grievant was finally reinstated after his discharge in 1963, it is not apparent that any useful purpose would have been served if the prescribed procedure had in fact been followed. The Company's failure to impose the preliminary suspension did not deprive the grievant of his chance to be heard. It is clear that the matter was explored at some length after the Company's action on November 16, but the Company refused to change its position. The Company's failure in this respect eliminated its right to raise any question concerning the timeliness of the grievance or the failure of the aggrieved to reduce his complaint to writing. In the Arbitrator's opinion it should have no greater effect than this in this instance.

Award

For the reasons given, this grievance is denied.

Questions for Discussion

On what basis does Arbitrator Teple conclude that absences for illness can be the justification for discharge?

How does Arbitrator Teple's decision reflecting progressive discipline differ from a nondisciplinary termination?

What tests could an arbitrator apply to a claim that a grievant is cured in a case involving a nondisciplinary termination for excessive illness absences?

What problems are presented to an arbitrator by conflicting medical testimony on a grievant's physical condition?

Compare the style, form, and substance of this opinion and award with the other decisions included in this Part.

Enterprise Wire Company

Arbitrator Carroll R. Daugherty
March 28, 1966
46 LA 359

TESTS FOR 'JUST CAUSE'

Factual Background

On October 8, 1965, the Company communicated to grievant X—an employment termination notice, signed by the plant manager and by the assistant plant superintendent and giving as the reasons for X—'s dismissal unsatisfactory work, including absenteeism, plus insubordination or refusal to work as directed.

The aggrieved employee had been hired on April 13, 1965, and had been trained as a wire rod cleaner in the Cleaning Department, second shift. The Company received coils of wire rod from its suppliers, and said coils vary in diameter and metallurgical composition. Before the coils reach the cleaner employee, they are welded together at the ends in sets of three to form a "pin" and are tagged for identification as to diameter and composition. The cleaner's job is to clean the pins in an acid tank, preserve their identities, and respectively to re-tag them after they have been so pickled and as they are left suspended from a sort of beam called a "yoke." The tag is a rectangular piece of cardboard with spaces to be filled in as to size and other characteristics of the wire rod in the pin and as to the identity of the wire-drawing machine to which the pin is to go. At the top of the tag is a reinforced hole through which a fine, flexible wire is placed by the cleaner, fastened to a strand of rod in the pin, and wound or twisted to prevent detachment.

Failure properly to tag each pin results in production delays, cost increases, and customer dissatisfaction (when orders for wire are not filled according to specifications). Alleged continued failure to tag some of his pins properly—either through allegedly not tagging some pins at all or through allegedly not marking the machine number on some of them—was the immediate cause of X—'s discharge.

Other material facts are set forth below under *Findings and Opinion* in respect to the issue of "just cause."

Contract Provisions

The provisions of the Parties' controlling Agreement cited by the Company read as follows:

ARTICLE IV
Hours of Work and Overtime

Section 10. Absence From Work. Any employee absent from work for any cause is required to report at once to the Superintendent and arrange his next scheduled work shift. Any employee unable to report on his regularly scheduled shift shall notify his foreman or the Superintendent at least two hours prior to the start of the shift. Any employee failing to report as described above will, on the second offence, be given disciplinary layoff of one shift. Repetition of this practice without proper cause will be considered basis for discharge.

ARTICLE VII
Management

The Union hereby recognizes that the management of the plant and the direction of the working forces, including, but not limited to the right to direct, plan and control plant operations, to establish and change working schedules, to hire, transfer, suspend, discharge or otherwise discipline employees for cause, to promulgate, administer and enforce plant rules, to relieve employees because of lack of work or for other legitimate reasons, to introduce new or improved methods or facilities and to manage its properties, is vested exclusively in the Company. It is understood that the aforesaid rights of management shall not be exercised in a manner inconsistent with the other provisions of this Agreement.

Any rights not specifically abridged, qualified or limited by this Agreement are reserved exclusively to the Company

ARTICLE VIII
Discipline

Section 1. Proper Cause. No employee shall be discharged or otherwise disciplined except for proper cause.

Section 2. Discharge or Discipline Grievance. Any case of discharge or other discipline may be taken up through the grievance procedure, but any such grievance must be presented within three working days after the disciplinary action occurs.

Section 3. Notice to Union. The Union shall be notified within one working day of any disciplinary action taken against any employee covered by this Agreement.

The Union contends that the Company's disciplinary action violated the Agreement but cites no provisions thereof alleged to have been breached.

Arbitrator's Findings and Opinion

Article VII, quoted above, affirms the Company's right to discipline for "cause"; and Article VIII, Section 1, requires "proper cause" for discipline, including discharge. No provision in the Agreement defines these terms; that is, no contractual criteria exist for determining from the facts of any disciplinary case, including this one, whether or not the Company had just cause for its decision. Therefore it is necessary for the Arbitrator to supply and apply his own just cause standards. Same are set forth in detail as an Appendix to this decision. In what follows, the Arbitrator makes findings of fact from the evidence of record in respect to each criterion.

Question No. 1: The record establishes that the Company gives to each employee a copy of a booklet labeled "Introduction to Enterprise Wire Co." Pertinent portions thereof are reproduced just below:

PLANT INFORMATION AND RULES

In order to have our plant operate at maximum efficiency and insure the safety of the individual and plant property, it is necessary for all workers to abide by certain rules and regulations. We believe this will provide for our mutual protection and benefit. Rules cover the following areas: instructional, standard practice, and disciplinary.

GENERAL INFORMATION AND RULES

Absenteeism: Employees are required to notify or call their foreman or superintendent when, for any reason, they are unable to be present or anticipate a late arrival. (Shop employees are referred to Article IV, Section 10 of the union contract.)

ADMINISTRATION OF DISCIPLINE

The welfare of the company as a whole must be considered first, because it represents the total welfare of the entire group. Rules and regulations are established for the guidance and protection of all employees. Employees should be familiar with the rules and govern themselves accordingly. Failure to do so will result in disciplinary action, including suspension and discharge.

Disciplinary action may be in the form of verbal reprimand or written notice type. Our written notice type is based upon three notices within a twelve month period. The first warning notice is issued as a serious warning when verbal reprimand has failed. The second written warning notice carries a time off penalty related to the seriousness of the offense. The third notice requires suspension or discharge.

Disciplinary action will be taken in the following instances:

16. Insubordination, inability or refusal to perform assigned duties.
18. Unsatisfactory performance of duties assigned to the employee.

From the above the Arbitrator must find that X— had been put on notice in respect to (1) the necessity for notifying the Company about impending absence or tardiness; (2) the necessity for satisfactory compliance with job requirements and supervisory directions when actually at work; and (3) the possible disciplinary consequences of failing to fulfill said requirements.

In addition to the above finding, which is general in nature, the evidence of record supports the firm conclusion that X— had been put on much more specific notice in respect to absenteeism, absence notification and work performance: (1) On June 16, 1965, X—'s foreman spoke to him about his absences and placed in his personnel file a written memorandum (not a formal warning notice) summarizing said interview. (2) On July 27, 1965, a formal written warning notice was issued to X— (and placed in his file) and a one-day suspension was imposed for his having been absent on two preceding days and for his not having notified the Company thereon. Said notice also promised further discipline for repetition of the offense. (3) On September 13, 1965, X— received a second such notice and one-day suspension for the same offense. He was also then put on a three-month probation. "Further action" was promised for his next "warning for any Reason." (4) During the first week in October, 1965, X— received four oral communications from three management persons—his two immediate foremen (who divided supervision of X—'s shift) and the assistant plant superintendent—in respect to his alleged failure to tag some of his cleaned pins or properly to mark some of the pins he did tag. Neither of the foremen explicitly warned him that continued dereliction of tagging duty would lead to discipline; but on the evening before the discharge the assistant superintendent told X— that if he (the assistant superintendent) found the next morning that X—'s pins were not identified, the assistant superintendent would have to discharge him.

From all of the above, the Arbitrator must find that the answer to Question No. 1 is clearly and strongly "Yes."

Question No. 2: The record contains no evidence, nor indeed does the Union contend, that the Company's rules and warning against absenteeism, against failure to notify the Company or same, and against tagging laxity were and are not reasonably related to Company efficiency and X—'s work capability. The answer to the second criterion must also be a strong "Yes."

Question Nos. 3 and 4: On this Question the weight of the evidence of record warrants the following conclusions: (1) As to absenteeism and failure to notify: (a) The offense is of such a nature that, given X—'s records thereon, a prior further investigation into the fact was unnecessary. (b) But there was no explicit testimony about whether or not the Company asked X— to explain or excuse his lapses in this area. (2) As to X—'s alleged tagging failures: (a) This offense was of a different sort. At the hearing there was no controversion of the Company's evidence that on the three mornings preceding the date of X—'s discharge some of the pins that he had cleaned the prior evenings either lacked tags entirely or, if tagged, lacked wire-drawing-machine identification. Then, given the Company-conceded possibility that X— *might* have tagged all his cleaned pins properly those evenings and some one else or some post-shift occurrence *might* have caused the tickets to be removed or lost after X— went home, the Company would be on firmer ground here if it had taken the pains to question material handlers and other employees who conceivably might have been involved in order to remove as much doubt in this area as possible. On the other hand, if some of the tags that X— did attach on those evenings did not bear machine numbers, no further inquiry into this portion of his alleged offense was needed. (c) X—, at the times he was spoken to by management, had ample opportunity to try to justify or explain his tagging deficiencies if same existed. The Company cannot be held to have been seriously remiss in this field of its investigation. The Company is not shown actively to have solicited from X— any justification for his alleged sins of omission; but the Company may not rightly be found *to have denied* him such opportunity. (d) A relatively detached management official, higher than X—'s foreman, made the determining inquiries.

On balance, the Arbitrator holds that the answer to these two Questions is a moderate "Yes."

Question No. 5: Of all the seven questions, the fifth is the crucial one here. This statement is grounded on two facts of record: (1) The evidence on this Question is in direct conflict. At the hearing the Company witnesses testified forthrightly that on the mornings of that October week, after X— had left the preceding nights, some of his cleaned pins lacked tags entirely or, if tagged, lacked machine numbers. They also testified that, although X— at first denied any tagging failures whatever, he later (twice) admitted having tagged only "most" of his pins. On the other hand, X— himself at the hearing just as forthrightly testified that he had tagged all his pins, and only two tags lacked machine numbers because some one came to take them immediately to the right machine, thus obviating any need for so identifying them. He also denied ever conceding to the Company that he had tagged only "most" of his pins. (2) No management person checked on X—'s tagging at the ends of his shifts that week. His foreman spot-checked his tagging those evenings and found same entirely satisfactory; but his checking ended; and no further checking was done until the next mornings. Thus the record is blank on what happened from 10 P.M. until the morning checks.

This Arbitrator has no means for resolving the conflicts in testimony or for filling in the blank area in facts. His function here is to determine whether the Company's decision-maker or "judge" (the plant manager) had reasonable, non-arbitrary grounds for accepting the word and conclusions of his managerial subordinates rather than any denials X— may have made.

On this issue the Arbitrator finds as follows: He has no proper basis for ruling that the Company's decision that X— was guilty of the alleged tagging offense was so unreasonable or arbitrary as to have constituted an abuse of managerial discretion. The record contains no probative evidence that either the Company or some fellow employee was trying to "frame" X—. The Company's evidence on the tagging matter must be ruled to have been sufficiently substantial to support its decision.

In respect to the absenteeism question, the Company must be held to have had amply substantial evidence of X—'s failures.

Given all the above, the answer to Question No. 5 must be a fairly strong "Yes."

Question No. 6: The record contains no evidence of probative value that would support a finding of Company discrimination against X— in the action it took. The answer to this Question is "Yes."

Question No. 7: This Question is a twofold one. In the light of the Notes set forth in the Appendix hereto, as applied to the facts of record here, the answer to Question 7(a) must be "Yes." The Arbitrator has held that the Company properly found X— guilty of violating its reasonable rule on absenteeism and its reasonable shop rules Nos. 16 and 18. Such violations in the context of this case constituted a serious offense. The Company may not be found to have been unreasonable or arbitrary in deciding on discharge rather than on some lesser penalty.

As to Question No. 7(b), the Union makes two contentions: (1) X—'s record on absenteeism has no bearing on his discharge, for he had already been penalized for same. (2) The Company violated the contractual provision that three warning notices for the same offense are necessary before discharge can be imposed.

The Arbitrator is forced to reject both these contentions. As to (1), the reasons will be evident from the Appendix Notes to Question No. 7. As to (2), the following should be noted: (a) There is nothing in the Agreement about the necessity for three warning notices for the same offense before discharge. The Company's own discipline rules (previously quoted) were unilaterally issued and are not a part of the Agreement because not referred to there. (b) Even if same were in the Agreement, (i) they can not be interpreted in the manner contended for, because there is no statement that the three notices have to be for the same sort of offense; and (ii) nothing therein would prevent the Company from discharging an employee for a truly serious first offense.

The Arbitrator finds that the Company's decision here was not unreasonably related to X—'s record.

Then the answer to the whole of Question No. 7 must be held to be "Yes."

The Arbitrator has found that all seven Questions merit affirmative answers. Accordingly, he must now rule that there is no proper basis for sustaining X—'s grievance.

Award

The grievance is denied.

* * *

TESTS APPLICABLE FOR LEARNING WHETHER EMPLOYER HAD JUST AND PROPER CAUSE FOR DISCIPLINING AN EMPLOYEE

Few if any union-management agreements contain a definition of "just cause." Nevertheless, over the years the opinions of arbitrators in innumerable discipline cases have developed a sort of "common law" definition thereof. This definition consists of a set of guidelines or criteria that are to be applied to the facts of any one case, and said criteria are set forth below in the form of questions.

A "no" answer to any one or more of the following questions normally signifies that just and proper cause did not exist. In other words, such "no" means that the employer's disciplinary decision contained one or more elements of arbitrary, capricious, unreasonable, or discriminatory action to such an extent that said decision constituted an abuse of managerial discretion warranting the arbitrator to substitute his judgment for that of the employer.

The answers to the questions in any particular case are to be found in the evidence presented to the arbitrator at the hearing thereon. Frequently, of course, the facts are such that the guidelines cannot be applied with precision. Moreover, occasionally, in some particular case an arbitrator may find one or more "no" answers so weak and the other, "yes" answers so strong that he may properly, without any "political" or spineless intent to "split the difference" between the opposing positions of the parties, find that the correct decision is to "chastise" both the company and the disciplined employee by decreasing but not nullifying the degree of discipline imposed by the company—e.g., by reinstating a discharged employee without back pay.

It should be clearly understood also that the criteria set forth below are to be applied to the employer's conduct in making his disciplinary decision *before* same has been processed through the grievance procedure to arbitration. Any question as to whether the employer has properly fulfilled the contractual requirements of said procedure is entirely separate from the question of whether he fulfilled the "common law" requirements of just cause before the discipline was "grieved."

Sometimes, although very rarely, a union-management agreement contains a provision limiting the scope of the arbitrator's inquiry into the question of just cause. For example, one such provision seen by this arbitrator says that "the only question the arbitrator is to determine shall be whether the employee is or is not guilty of the act or acts resulting in his discharge." Under the latter contractual statement an arbitrator might well have to confine his attention to Question No. 5 below—or at most to Questions Nos. 3, 4, and 5. But absent any such restriction in an agreement, a consideration of the evidence on all seven Questions (and their accompanying Notes) is not only proper but necessary.

The Questions

1. Did the company give to the employee forewarning or foreknowledge of the possible or probable disciplinary consequences of the employee's conduct?

Note 1: Said forewarning or foreknowledge may properly have been given orally by management or in writing through the medium of typed or printed sheets or books of shop rules and of penalties for violation thereof.

Note 2: There must have been actual oral or written communication of the rules and penalties to the employee.

Note 3: A finding of lack of such communication does not in all cases require a "no" answer to Question No. 1. This is because certain offenses such as insubordination, coming to work intoxicated, drinking intoxicating beverages on the job, or theft of the property of the company or of fellow employees are so serious that any employee in the industrial society may properly be expected to know already that such conduct is offensive and heavily punishable.

Note 4: Absent any contractual prohibition or restriction, the company has the right unilaterally to promulgate reasonable rules and give reasonable orders; and same need not have been negotiated with the union.

2. Was the company's rule or managerial order reasonably related to (a) the orderly, efficient, and safe operation of the company's business and (b) the performance that the company might properly expect of the employee?

Note: If an employee believes that said rule or order is unreasonable, he must nevertheless obey same (in which case he may file a grievance thereover) unless he sincerely feels that to obey the rule or order would seriously and immediately jeopardize his personal safety and/or integrity. Given a firm finding to the latter effect, the employee may properly be said to have had justification for his disobedience.

3. Did the company, before administering discipline to an employee, make an effort to discover whether the employee did in fact violate or disobey a rule or order of management?

Note 1: This is the employee's "day in court" principle. An employee has the right to know with reasonable precision the offense with which he is being charged and to defend his behavior.

Note 2: The company's investigation must normally be made *before* its disciplinary decision is made. If the company fails to do so, its failure may not normally be excused on the ground that the employee will get his day in court through the grievance procedure after the exaction of discipline. By that time there has usually been too much hardening of positions. In a very real sense the company is obligated to conduct itself like a trial court.

Note 3: There may of course be circumstances under which management must react immediately to the employee's behavior. In such cases the normally proper action is to suspend the employee pending investigation, with the understanding that (a) the final disciplinary decision will be made after the investigation and (b) if the employee is found innocent after the investigation, he will be restored to his job with full pay for time lost.

Note 4: The company's investigation should include an inquiry into possible justification for the employee's alleged rule violation.

4. Was the company's investigation conducted fairly and objectively?

Note 1: At said investigation the management official may be both "prosecutor" and "judge," but he may not also be a witness against the employee.

Note 2: It is essential for some higher, detached management official to assume and conscientiously perform the judicial role, giving the commonly accepted meaning to that term in his attitude and conduct.

Note 3: In some disputes between an employee and a management person there are not witnesses to an incident other than the two immediate participants. In such cases it is particularly important that the management "judge" question the management participant rigorously and thoroughly, just as an actual third party would.

5. At the investigation did the "judge" obtain substantial evidence or proof that the employee was guilty as charged?

Note 1: It is not required that the evidence be conclusive or "beyond all reasonable doubt." But the evidence must be truly substantial and not flimsy.

Note 2: The management "judge" should actively search out witnesses and evidence, not just passively take what participants or "volunteer" witnesses tell him.

Note 3: When the testimony of opposing witnesses at the arbitration hearing is irreconcilably in conflict, an arbitrator seldom has any means for resolving the contradictions. His task is then to determine whether the management "judge" originally had reasonable grounds for believing the evidence presented to him by his own people.

6. Has the company applied its rules, orders, and penalties evenhandedly and without discrimination to all employees?

Note 1: A "no" answer to this question requires a finding of discrimination and warrants negation or modification of the discipline imposed.

Note 2: If the company has been lax in enforcing its rules and orders and decides henceforth to apply them rigorously, the company may avoid a finding of discrimination by telling all employees beforehand of its intent to enforce hereafter all rules as written.

7. Was the degree of discipline administered by the company in a particular case reasonably related to (a) the seriousness of the employee's proven offense and (b) the record of the employee in his service with the company?

Note 1: A trivial proven offense does not merit harsh discipline unless the employee has properly been found guilty of the same or other offenses a number of times in the past. (There is no rule as to what number of previous offenses constitutes a "good," a "fair," or a "bad" record. Reasonable judgment thereon must be used.)

Note 2: An employee's record of previous offenses may never be used to discover whether he was guilty of the immediate or latest one. The only proper use of his record is to help determine the severity of discipline once he has properly been found guilty of the immediate offense.

Note 3: Given the same proven offense for two or more employees, their respective records provide the only proper basis for "discriminating" among them in the administration of discipline for said offense. Thus, if employee A's record is significantly better than those of employees B, C, and D, the company may properly give A a lighter punishment than it gives the others for the same offense; and this does not constitute true discrimination.

Note 4: Suppose that the record of the arbitration hearing established firm "Yes" answers to all the first six questions. Suppose further that the proven offense of the accused employee was a serious one, such as drunkenness on the job; but the employee's record had been previously unblemished over a long, continuous period of employment with the company. Should the company be held arbitrary and unreasonable if it decided to discharge such an employee? The answer depends of course on all the circumstances. But, as one of the country's oldest arbitration agencies, the National Railroad Adjustment Board, has pointed out repeatedly in innumerable decisions on discharge cases, leniency is the prerogative of the employer rather than of the arbitrator; and the latter is not supposed to substitute his judgment in this area for that of the company unless there is compelling evidence that the company abused its discretion. This is the rule, even though an arbitrator, if he had been the original "trial judge," might have imposed a lesser penalty. Actually the arbitrator may be said in an important sense to act as an appellate tribunal whose function is to discover whether the decision of the trial tribunal (the employer) was within the bounds of reasonableness above set forth.—In general, the penalty of dismissal for a really serious first offense does not in itself warrant a finding of company unreasonableness.

Questions for Discussion

Where should arbitrators look for definitions of language found in collective bargaining agreements?

What is the basis of Arbitrator Daugherty's just-cause test?

Which elements of Arbitrator Daugherty's just-cause test are usually found in the decisions of other arbitrators?

Why does Arbitrator Daugherty regard Question Five as "the crucial one"?

Compare the style, form, and substance of this opinion and award with the other decisions included in this Part.

H. C. Capwell Company

Arbitrator David E. Feller
February 22, 1969
(unpublished decision)

Opinion and Award

On one view of the facts, this case resembles the hoary hypothetical involving Lady Eldon and the "French" lace. Lady Eldon, when traveling on the Continent, purchased what she believed to be French lace. On returning to England she hid it, hoping to avoid the payment of duty. The lace was discovered by a customs agent. But the "French" lace turned out to be English, and not subject to duty. The question of whether, under those circumstances, Lady Eldon could be found guilty of an attempt to smuggle is a matter still debated by legal scholars.[1] The latest I have read on the subject concludes that she could be found guilty, although a contrary result would follow if the hypothetical were changed so that the lace was in fact French but the failure to actually violate the anti-smuggling law resulted from the fact the duty on French lace had been removed, although Lady Eldon did not know it. In the latter case she did what she attempted to do, bring in French lace; she did not succeed in smuggling because she was mistaken as to the law.

In this case, the grievant, Charles R. Michael, was discharged for insubordination. The insubordination consisted of his refusal on November 8, 1968, to accept an assignment. He plainly did so refuse, relying upon grounds, the Company urges, which were invalid. It turns out, however, that unknown at the time to the supervisor who gave the order which the grievant refused to obey and, at least arguably, also unknown at that time to the grievant, the order was an invalid one which the grievant had a right to disobey. The question is: Was he discharged "for cause?"

This is what happened, as related by the Company's witness. Charles R. Michael, the grievant, is 63 years old. He was hired by the Company in 1962 as a cabinet maker. He works in the cabinet shop, with another cabinet maker, Hans Thomsen. New furniture when received from the manufacturer is first "stripped," i.e., removed from its carton, in a room

---

[1]The controversy is reviewed at length in Paulsen and Kadish, CRIMINAL LAW AND ITS PROCESSES 480–86 (1962).

adjacent to the cabinet shop. It is then pushed into the cabinet shop, where legs are put on and any other work necessary is performed. From the cabinet shop it then moves to a third room, the finishing room, where it is given a final finish. In addition to processing new furniture, the cabinet makers also repair and make adjustments to furniture which the store has an obligation to repair. Some is brought to the service shop. In other cases, a cabinet maker goes to the customer's home on what is called a "service call." Mr. Michael did all of his work in the shop. The other cabinet maker, Hans Thomsen, did the service calls and also worked in the shop.

In recent times Mr. Michael's performance on the job has not been entirely satisfactory. He was reprimanded in February, 1968 because he was involved in some heated arguments with Thomsen. Again, in June, 1968 he was reprimanded for not doing his work; the furniture was piling up in the shop and not getting out on time. From time to time Michael required help from the "stripper" who normally worked in the adjacent room, in moving furniture around the furniture shop and in putting legs on it. Michael had claimed to have received a back injury and had pending a number of workmen's compensation claims arising from the injury which the Company was contesting.

As a result of dissatisfaction with Mr. Michael's work, his immediate supervisor prepared and submitted to the personnel office on November 7, 1968, a "corrective interview" form. The standard procedure at Capwell's when an employee's performance is deficient is for his immediate supervisor to make out such a form, which then is given to the personnel department to review. If the form is satisfactory, in the sense that it is complete and indicates as specifically as possible the problems created by the employee, it is approved by the personnel office and sent back to the supervisor, who then gives it to the employee. Then the employee is sent to personnel to discuss the problem. The form contains a statement, to be signed by the employee, which expresses his understanding that his job performance is not in conformance with the Capwell's standard and that failure to improve substantially within a specified period, usually thirty days, will result in dismissal.

As stated, this form was prepared by Mr. Michael's immediate supervisor on November 7th. As prepared it specified a two-week warning period. The form was then sent to the personnel office for approval. The interview, however, was never given. On November 8, in the late afternoon, Michael's supervisor called Michael and Thomsen together and informed them that beginning on the following Monday, Michael would be assigned to service calls and Thomsen would work full time in the shop. According to the supervisor he had decided that because of Michael's unsatisfactory performance in the shop, which caused the work to back up, it would be better to switch assignments. Michael, on receiving this news, first said that he would not go on service calls. According to the Company's testimony, the reason specified at the time was that he could not stand to work with women looking over his shoulder. The conversation continued for some time. The supervisor became irritated and finally asked Michael point blank whether he was refusing to obey the order to go out on service calls the following Monday. Michael replied that he was. It is agreed that at some point during the course of the conversation Michael also said that he did not want to talk with the supervisor anymore and wanted to talk to his business agent.

After this episode, the supervisor then called the personnel office and described what had happened. He was told to send Michael up to the office. Michael first said that he would not go. Then he was informed that his supervisor, who normally delivered the week's pay in cash to him on Friday afternoon, had sent the pay over to the personnel office and it was necessary to go there to get it. Michael went.

When Michael arrived at the personnel office, his discharge papers had already been prepared. He was again asked whether he would go on service calls the following Monday. He again said that he would not do so. This time, however, according to the testimony of the personnel superintendent, he said that he could not do so because it would require climbing stairs, which hurt his back. He was then told that the Company had no choice but to discharge him and the personnel superintendent attempted to give him the prepared paper which Capwell's customarily delivers to employees who are discharged. He refused to accept it. Again, it is agreed that he requested an opportunity to talk to his business agent.

Capwell's normal procedure is not to discharge without first going through the procedure of a corrective interview and giving the employee an opportunity to rectify whatever problems there are in his work. This normal procedure is applied even in cases of insubordination if the particular instance of insubordination is the first instance of that kind of conduct, as it was in this case. The personnel superintendent testified that no such opportunity for corrective action by the employee was given in this case because the insubordination was combined with the other deficiencies which were to have formed the basis of the corrective interview. Principle among these were "laziness," and "untruthfulness." The personnel superintendent testified that she made the recommendation that Michael be discharged, although she had no personal knowledge as to either of these items. She was convinced of their accuracy, however, because she did have available to her at the time of her final meeting with Michael the written reports of his supervisor and a medical report prepared by a doctor retained by the Company in connection with the workmen's compensation claims which had been filed by Mr. Michael, which indicated to her that there was nothing wrong with Mr. Michael's back, although she was not enough of an expert to fully evaluate the doctor's report. On the basis of the report, however, she was convinced that the deficiencies in his production were not because of any back trouble which he may have had, and that his statement to her that he could not go out on service calls because of his back was untruthful.

The foregoing is a statement of the case as related by the Company's witnesses on direct and cross examination. The Union has quite a different version. I do not find it necessary to resolve the conflict between the two because there is one fact, so far not mentioned, which I believe is dispositive of the case. The agreement between the Union and the Company is a very short and simple one. One of its provisions, however, is quite specific. An employee who furnishes his own automobile in connection with the Company's business is to be compensated for the use of such automobile at the rate of not less than 10¢ per mile and is to be furnished public liability and property damage insurance covering the employee owner of the car while such employee is engaged in work for the employer. The agreement further provides that no employee can be required to use his car in connection with the employer's business if the employee does not desire to do so. Going out on service calls requires use of the employee's car. Capwell's does not provide an automobile for that purpose. Mr. Michael, does not and did not, on November 8, 1968, desire to use his own car. Indeed, he testified that his back condition was such that driving any period of time was very difficult for him. Although he testified before me that he had stated to his supervisor, when informed of his assignment to service calls, that he did not want to use his car, this testimony was sharply denied by the supervisor, and on at least this issue I find that the supervisor's testimony was the more credible. But, in any case, it is clear that under the contract, Mr. Michael could not be required to go out on service calls unless Capwell's was prepared, as it was not, to provide him with an automobile. It is equally clear that the supervisor who directed Mr. Michael to take that assignment on the following Monday was unaware of this provision of the agreement and did not offer to provide an automobile or the other matters required by the contract at the time he directed Michael to take that assignment.

It is clear, therefore, that Mr. Michael had a perfect right under the agreement to refuse to accept the assignment. I find, however, that neither he nor his supervisor knew at the time that he had such right.

The question, then, even if I accept the Company's testimony in all respects, is whether he was properly discharged for refusing to obey an order which he had a right to refuse, even though neither he nor his supervisor knew at the time that he had such a right.

I believe that the discharge, under these circumstances, was improper. There is much doctrine, which I believe to be sound, that an employee who is given an order which he believes to be improper is obliged to obey that order, and make his complaint known through the grievance procedure. In a case in which an employee is told to do certain work immediately, and in which he refuses to do so, it is entirely proper to say that he can be disciplined for insubordination if he refuses the order, even though on a later examination it might be found that the order was improper.[2] But this was not such a case. Mr. Michael was not told to go out that Friday afternoon on service calls, or even to begin his working day on Monday on service calls. To the contrary, he was informed that on Monday, after he reported to work, he would be expected to go out on the calls. He was discharged on Friday not because he had failed to work as directed but because he had said that he would not do so. The question therefore is whether he was properly discharged for his refusal, in advance, to agree to do that which, under the agreement, he had a right to refuse.

If I had any doubt on that matter, it would be resolved by the fact, admitted by the Company, that in the conversations with his supervisor, and again with the personnel superintendent, Mr. Michael had said that he wanted to talk to his business agent, and did not want to discuss the question of service calls any further until he had an opportunity to do so. Indeed, he was maneuvered into the discussion in the personnel office after he said he wanted to see his business agent only by the device of sending his pay there so that he would be induced to appear.

I, of course, do not know what would have happened if Mr. Michael had been given the opportunity to discuss the matter with the business agent, or even to reflect on his position, before reporting to work on Monday. Perhaps he would have decided that the contractually specified reimbursement of ten cents per mile, plus insurance coverage was sufficient inducement to go on service calls; perhaps he would have persisted in his refusal but asserted a contractually justified ground; perhaps the Company would have decided that, no car being available, it should

---

[2]Even in such cases, however, the usual discipline is less than discharge. *See, e.g., Goslin-Birmingham Mfg. Co.*, 38 LA 251; *Massachusetts Electric Co.*, 40 LA 997; *Greater Louisville Industries*, 40 LA 1343; *Bemis Brothers Bag Co.*, 44 LA 1139; *Bowser, Inc.*, 28 LA 486; *Hill Packing Co.*, 30 LA 548, and other cases cited in BNA, Labor Arbitration Cumulative Digest and Index, § 118.658.

not violate the agreement by insisting that he nevertheless use his own car on service calls. None of this is determinable because he was pressed for a "yes" or "no" answer on Friday and then discharged for the "no" answer.

If there were no possible grounds for that "no" answer the Company might have been justified in not waiting until Monday. But where there *were* grounds for that answer, whether known to Mr. Michael at the time or not, the Company was not entitled to discharge him for it. Mr. Michael may have intended to refuse a lawful order, just as Lady Eldon intended to smuggle in dutiable French lace. But, like Lady Eldon, he didn't. Accordingly, he was not discharged for cause.

As to his other alleged deficiencies, it is clear from the Company's testimony that it is its usual practice to give the employee a thirty-day warning and not to discharge him until he has had an opportunity to correct the indicated deficiencies (unless, of course, there is a violation of Company rules during that period). The grievant was not given that warning, or a period in which to correct his deficiencies because he was peremptorily discharged on November 8, 1968. Accordingly, he is entitled to be reinstated with back pay but this should not in any way prejudice any further proceedings in accordance with the agreement and the Company's established policies based on these other claimed deficiencies.

The Union also urges that I direct that "this incident should be removed from his personnel record." This I cannot do. The incident occurred. The discharge was invalid for the reasons stated. If it should figure in any subsequent personnel action, I assume that full account will also be taken of the limited findings I have made herein.

Award

The grievant, Charles R. Michael, should be reinstated by the Company with such back pay as will make him whole for the net loss suffered as a result of his discharge on November 8, 1968 taking into account any net moneys he may have earned in other employment and any unemployment compensation he may have received with respect to the period between his discharge and the date on which the Company offers him re-employment.

Questions for Discussion

What is the doctrine of progressive discipline? Was it applied in this case?

Was the employee's right to discuss the grievance with his business agent based upon the contract? Have arbitrators found such a right apart from the express language of the contract?

Does the decision prevent the company from disciplining grievant in the future for failure to properly perform his job?

Compare the style, form, and substance of this opinion and award with the other decisions included in this Part.

City of Birmingham, Michigan

Arbitrator Theodore J. St. Antoine (chairman)
October 9, 1970
55 LA 671

NEW PROVISIONS

Opinion, Findings, and Conclusions

This arbitration has been conducted pursuant to Act No. 312, Michigan Public Acts of 1969, and upon the initiation of the City of Birmingham (hereinafter "the City") following negotiations with the Birmingham Firefighters Association (hereinafter "the Association" or "the Union") for a new labor agreement to replace the one which expired on June 30, 1970. The statutory conditions precedent to arbitration, collective bargaining and mediation, have been fulfilled.

The Association is the collective bargaining representative, under Michigan law, of all employees in the Fire Department of the City of Birmingham, excluding the Fire Chief, Assistant Chief, Fire Marshal, and parttime and temporary employees, if any. The bargaining unit includes approximately 30 firefighters, six lieutenants, and three captains, or a total of about 40 employees.

In the course of the hearing on August 25, 1970, the parties agreed to withdraw certain items from arbitration; agreed, upon the recommendation of the Chairman of the Arbitration Panel, to the entry of a consent award covering (1) salaries, (2) holiday pay, (3) vacations, and (4) insurance contributions; and submitted for determination by the Arbitration Panel the Association's requests for (1) an agency shop and (2) binding arbitration as the last step in the grievance procedure.

Item 1—Agency Shop

Under an "agency shop," as traditionally defined, any employee in the bargaining unit who is not a member of the union must, as a condition of continued employment, pay to the union an amount equal to the customary initiation fee and periodic dues demanded of members. The Association contends that fees from all members of the bargaining unit are necessary to meet the increasing costs of collective bargaining (including, presumably, ths costs of arbitration under Public Act 312), and that any uncertainty about the legal status of the agency shop should not be a basis for denying it. The City argues, to the contrary, that the agency shop would be both unnecessary and undesirable in Birmingham. The City's position is that an agency shop clause is legally questionable in Michigan at this time; that the City is agreeable to a "checkoff" of the dues of those employees authorizing it; that only about two employees in the bargaining unit are not currently members of the Association; that few municipalities now have an agency shop; and that the City does not believe in coercion by contract in any form.

Section 9 of Public Act 312 provides that an arbitration panel in a dispute like that before us shall base its order upon a number of specified factors, including the following:

"(a) The lawful authority of the employer . . .
"(c) The interests and welfare of the public . . .
"(d) Comparison of the . . . conditions of employment of the employees involved in the arbitration proceeding with the . . . conditions of employment of other employees . . .
"(i) In public employment in comparable communities.
"(ii) In private employment in comparable communities."

The Michigan Employment Relations Commission, in a divided decision, has sustained the validity of the agency shop under the Public Employment Relations Act. Oakland County Sheriff's Dep't, 3 Mich. Emp. Rel. Comm. 1(a)(1968). Just over two months ago, however, the Court of Appeals held that an agency shop provision would violate the PERA if the required payment was "greater than or less than" a "nonmember's proportionate share of the cost of negotiating and administering the contract involved." *Smigel v. Southgate Community School District*, 74 LRRM 3080, GERR No. 363, G-1 (Mich. App. Aug. 3, 1970). Since we have no basis for determining a nonmember's proportionate cost of administering the contract to be executed between the City and the Association, any agency shop clause we might order would be of dubious legality under the Southgate decision.

The Arbitration Panel has not been supplied detailed information on the extent of the agency shop in public exmployee contracts in Michigan communities comparable to Birmingham. Independent research into a few police and firefighter contracts suggests that most *negotiated* agreements do not contain an agency shop clause. We note, however, that on April 24, 1970, an arbitration panel ordered the inclusion of an agency shop in the contract of the City of Southgate and the Southgate Firefighters Association. In *private* employment in the United States, the union shop, the agency shop, or some other form of union security arrangement is found, after many years of bargaining, in only about two-thirds of all collective bargaining agreements.

Despite its long history, union security continues to provoke strong feelings among many persons who find forced union adherence offensive. We can assume the sincerity of the City's opposition to "coercion by contract." At the same time, we do not think the Association has demonstrated any marked need for the special protections of union security. It already enjoys the voluntary allegiance of almost every member of the bargaining unit. In light of all these circumstances, therefore, we do not consider it appropriate to order the inclusion of an agency shop in the City-Association agreement at this time.

Item 2—Binding Arbitration

The City strongly opposes binding arbitration as the terminal step in the grievance procedure. At the present time, the Association has the right to carry a grievance unresolved at the City Manager level to the City Commission for final determination. The Commission is a three-man elective body responsive to the entire citizenry, and the City is jealous of the Commission's prerogatives. During the period of the last contract, the Association actually had no need to pursue a grievance beyond the City Manager, the City argues, as the police have recently demonstrated; they took a case to the Commission and won.

The Association insists that binding arbitration is necessary because otherwise the City, an interested party, remains the interpreter of its own contract and the judge of its own cause. Firefighter agreements in such comparable communities as Pontiac, Madison Heights, and Royal Oak contain arbitration clauses. Moreover, it is argued that the previous lack of appeals to the City Commission does not prove there is no need for arbitration. Perhaps the Association felt that the City Manager's ruling was likely to be as good as the Commission's. But in any event, the Association contends, the right to resort to an impartial outsider is so important that it should be available even if it does not have to be utilized.

We essentially agree with the Association's position. Binding arbitration by a disinterested third party has become accepted as the capstone of the American system for resolving grievances in the work place. Approximately 95 percent of the major labor agreements in private industry in this country provide for grievance arbitration. More pertinents for our purposes, arbitration provisions appear in three of the five Firefighter contracts agreed upon for '70–'71 in the "Woodward Corridor" cities, and in four of the eight agreed upon for '70–'71 in cities having between 25,000 and 50,000 population, all of which are comparable to Birmingham. Binding grievance arbitration was also included in the award of an arbitration panel issued on March 26, 1970, dealing with the City of Marquette and the Marquette Police.

However well intentioned, the City Commissioner is no substitute for arbitration as the final step in the grievance process. Quite properly, it is the responsibility of the Commission to look out for the best interests of the City as such, but in a dispute between the City and the Association this will inevitably tend to impair the capacity of the Commission to deal with the parties evenhandedly. At best, a determination by the Commission is likely to be eyed with suspicion by the employees. It will thus lack the acceptability and finality that should characterize an arbitral award.

The Arbitration Panel will therefore order inclusion of a provision for final and binding arbitration as the last step of the grievance procedure spelled out in the City-Association agreement. Generally, we shall follow the approach suggested by the Association, except that we shall delete the present City Commission step as unnecessary. Obviously, the parties can retain that step by mutual agreement, if they wish.

Consent Award and Award

For the foregoing reasons, the Panel of Arbitration makes the following awards:

1. The base salary of the employees covered by the City-Association agreement shall be increased $1,000 to $11,300, retroactive to and including July 4, 1970, with all other increments to be applied in accordance with past practice in the employees' schedule.

2. Unit men shall receive one additional day of holiday pay, from two and one-half days to three and one-half days, with a corresponding adjustment for day men.

3. (a) The employees' vacation schedule shall be as follows:

More than 1 year but less than 5 years' seniority prior to January 1 of any vacation year—5 work days

Five or more years' seniority but less than 10 years' seniority prior to January 1 of any vacation year—6 work days

10 or more years' seniority but less than 20 years' seniority prior to January 1 of any vacation year—8 work days

20 or more years' seniority prior to January 1 of any vacation year—10 work days.

(b) Employees shall not be permitted to take more than five work days vacation from and including June 1 through and including August 31 in any vacation year.

4. The City will increase its insurance contribution by $1.10 per pay period.

5. There shall be no agency shop provision in the City-Association agreement.

6. The present Step 6 of the grievance procedure, providing for referral to the City Commission, shall be deleted, and in its place shall be substituted the following (or such other arbitration provision as the parties may mutually agree upon):

Step 6. In the event the grievance is not satisfactorily settled in Step 5, the Union may, within thirty (30) days after date of the decision at Step 5, submit the grievance to final and binding arbitration to be conducted by the American Arbitration Association in accordance with its rules.

7. The Panel reserves jurisdiction to settle any dispute which may arise concerning the interpretation or implementation of this decision.

Questions for Discussion

What are the opposing factors, e.g., legislative or judicial, which distinguish interest arbitration from arbitration of rights?

How does Arbitrator St. Antoine's agency shop decision illustrate the application of external law in the public sector as distinguished from the private sector?

What weight does Arbitrator St. Antoine give to provisions found in other public sector contracts in deciding the "binding arbitration" issue?

Why does the decision differentiate between a consent award and award?

Compare the style, form, and substance of this opinion and award with the other decisions included in this Part.

Glass Containers Corporation

Arbitrator Harry J. Dworkin
November 26, 1971
57 LA 997

SEX DISCRIMINATION

The Issue

[The issue is:—]

Is the company in violation of Article 37, of the current GBBA Agreement, as well as the local call-in procedure at the Marienville Plant, in failing to call out a senior, female employee to perform available work on the sealer-stitcher machine?

Preliminary Statement and Background

The grievance is filed on behalf of a female, senior member of the Carton Assembler classification, assigned to the extra board. The grievant alleges that her contractual rights were disregarded in that a male, probationary employee was called out on June 17 and 18, 1971, and assigned work of Carton-Assembler, specifically on the Sealer-Stitcher machine. The grievant is regularly classified as Utility Worker, with two years of service. She claims that she was a qualified employee, capable of operating the Sealer-Stitcher machine, and that she was improperly denied available work opportunity solely by reason of her sex.

The company maintains an extra board complement for each shift. Employees assigned to the extra board are subject to call-out on the basis of seniority and qualifications. Such work is balanced out among members of the extra board, as nearly as practicable.

The company denied the grievance claiming that traditionally, the job of Carton-Assembler (Sealer-Stitcher) had been performed by males only. This was due largely to the job requirements, including lifting of heavy pallets, cartons of cardboard, and related duties that were considered onerous. The company considered that female employees were generally not qualified to operate the Sealer-Stitcher, unless through job experience they had demonstrated that they were physically capable of performing the duties required. As stated in its Step 3 Answer:

> We have never denied the request of a female employee, by seniority, to be placed in a vacancy traditionally performed by men, provided of course, the employee can perform all the physical aspects of the job.

The union maintains that the company has improperly discriminated against the grievant by reason of her sex, in violation of the contract:

ARTICLE 37
Fair Employment Practice and
Equal Opportunities

The Company and Union will comply with all laws preventing discrimination against any employee because of race, color, creed, national origin, age or sex.

Position of Union

The union maintains that the grievant was a two-year service employee assigned to the extra board, on the second shift; that she was qualified to work as Carton-Assembler, and that she should have been assigned the work on the Sealer-Stitcher for the two days in question, in preference to a junior, probationary employee. By reason of the grievant's prior experience as Utility Worker, she was qualified to operate the Sealer-Stitcher, and required merely direction as distinguished from job training. The machine is automatic; the operator is simply required to shape the broken down cartons and place each unit onto the machine for stitching, in accordance with a specified pattern. The machine is considered a simple operation. Its operation need only be demonstrated to an otherwise qualified employee, so as to enable him to perform the job. The union maintains that the stitching operation is simple, and does not require extensive training in order to adequately perform. The operator positions the carton onto a metal frame or post, and then maneuvers it about so as to effect the prescribed stitching pattern. When the carton is in its proper position, the operator activates the pedal.

The union acknowledges that prior to the current GBBA agreement, and inclusion of the fair employment practice provision, it was accepted practice to by-pass female employees on the extra board, for certain jobs. Some jobs were traditionally denied to female employees due to weight restrictions that were recognized in the contract. These restrictions were eliminated during the 1971 contract negotiations. Under the present agreement, there are no "male" or "female" jobs as such, and no distinction is recognized either in law or under the contract. The right to perform available work is dependent upon ability, qualifications, and seniority, irrespective of the factor of sex.

Employees have customarily been called in to work on the Sealer-Stitcher from the extra board, and have performed such operations without any additional training or experience. In fact, employees are called in on all available jobs from the extra board solely on the basis of their seniority and ability. The prior practice of by-passing senior, female employees on the extra board, and to call-in a male employee, was changed by the current contract, as well as applicable federal law. It is therefore the position of the union that the grievant, a member of the extra board, was entitled to be called-out for work on the Sealer-Stitcher, in preference to a probationary, male employee, and that the grievant is therefore entitled to be reimbursed for her lost earnings.

Position of Company

The company denies that any contract violation occurred. Its action was warranted by the established past practice, and lack of the grievant's qualifications. The company points to the numerous duties and responsibilities incidental to the operation of the Sealer-Stitcher, as set forth in the applicable, negotiated job descriptions. Under the factor of "Experience," the job "requires less than two months to become proficient and to gain required knowledge of materials and procedures." The job of Carton-Assembler is considered a "benchmark" job; the job encumbent may be assigned either to Carton-Assembly work, or to operate the Sealer-Stitcher. The job qualifications require two months of experience in order to become proficient as a Carton-Assembler and the operation of the Sealer-Stitcher.

The company states that since the filing of the instant grievance, available work in this job classification has been offered to female members on the extra board. In fact, on the day following the instant grievance, the grievant was assigned work on this job for two days, after which she voluntarily gave it up. Thus, the company admits that prior to June 17, 1971, it was customary practice to call in male employees from the extra board for work on the Sealer-Stitcher machine, and to by-pass female employees. The company reasons that in the event the union or employees had objected to this procedure, they were obligated to register a protest. Inasmuch as female employees had traditionally been by-passed for work on this job, the union must be deemed estopped from protesting after the fact, and is subject to the charge of laches. The company represents that had either the union, or grievant previously requested that she be considered for such job, she would have been accorded consideration, as the company did subsequent to the instant grievance.

As regard the grievant's qualifications, she had no prior training on this particular job. She was not qualified to perform the job as set forth in the job description. A number of analogous situations are cited by the company where it consistently by-passes female employees on the extra board as regard various job classifications that are generally considered unacceptable to female employees due to working conditions. This procedure has been followed without any protest having been registered by the union, and in fact, with the union's acquiescence.

In light of the foregoing circumstances, the company urges that there is no justification to support the charge of discrimination. The company states that each time a female employee requested a trial on the semi-automatic Sealer-Stitcher, she was given the opportunity in accordance with her seniority. The job has traditionally been performed by males due to the inherent duties of the job, including lifting of wooden pallets and stacks of cardboard. It is highly questionable that the grievant was qualified to operate the Sealer-Stitcher, inasmuch as she had had no prior training in its operation:

> The aggrieved employee could not have operated the sealer-stitcher machine on the dates in question since she had no prior operating experience.

The company reasons further as follows:

> Management is not discriminating against its female employees regarding its call-in procedure to operate the carton assembly machines. We have previously honored requests from females to operate the carton assembly machines and did so in the case of the aggrieved once we were aware she desired this type of assignment. All that was required was the female employee to request to be placed on the carton assembly machine and demonstrate she was capable of performing all the duties of the job, including the lifting of the cardboard stacks and wooden pallets. Experience has shown that females do not care to perform those duties which require repeated heavy lifting.

Opinion of Arbitrator

The company had previously operated pursuant to a long-standing practice of by-passing female employees for available work, as regard certain jobs that involved duties considered unsuitable for female workers. This practice was sanctioned by contract. The prior labor agreement included weight lifting restrictions which precluded the assignment of female employees to jobs that required repetitive lifting of weights exceeding 30 pounds. Inasmuch as the Carton-Assembler job, including the operation of the Sealer-Stitcher, involved work that exceeded the weight lifting restrictions set forth in the prior contract, and due to other characteristics of the job, female employees were by-passed in filling such jobs.

As conceded by the parties, discrimination in filling jobs on the basis of sex has been invalidated both by contract and federal law. The current, GBBA agreement contains no weight lifting restrictions applicable to female employees. In addition, Article 37 mandates that the company shall avoid discrimination against any employee because of sex. Accordingly, female employees are considered on an equal footing as regard available jobs, irrespective of the job characteristics or other circumstances. Male and female employees have equal claim to any work opportunity, subject only to their being eligible and qualified.

As a basic proposition, the company is obligated to adhere to the contractual requirements that prohibit discrimination in employment by reason of sex. The employer is subject to liability and the obligation to make restitution for resultant loss in earnings for failure to call in a female employee from the extra board to a job which she is qualified to perform, and in accordance with her seniority. This obligation currently is in force, notwithstanding a long-standing and mutually recognized practice of by-passing female employees on certain jobs. In light of the contract language, and by virtue of applicable, federal laws, management can no longer countenance a practice that excludes female employees from jobs which they are qualified to perform. Although continuation of the pre-existing practice may not indicate a willful violation, particularly where the procedure was with the approval of the union, nevertheless, where an indication of discrimination in filling available jobs is demonstrated, appropriate relief is required.

A preponderance of the evidence here presented, establishes that the grievant, who held the regular job classification of Utility Worker, and was a senior employee assigned to the extra board, had sufficient knowledge, background, experience and qualifications to enable her to operate the Sealer-Stitcher, with normal direction, as distinguished from job training. As stated by the union in its presentation, an experienced employee on the extra board need only be subject to a demonstration of the machine operation by the foreman in order to perform the job in a satisfactory manner. In the instant case, the evidence convinces the arbitrator that the sole reason for by-passing the grievant for the available work was that she was a female employee. The determination was not made on the basis that she lacked the necessary qualifications. As is clearly apparent, exclusively "male" or "female" jobs are no longer recognized, either in law or contract.

As a matter of practice, employees have been called in from the extra board on all available jobs on the basis of their seniority and general ability, without exclusion due to lack of experience in the operation of the Sealer-Stitcher. Since female employees are no longer "protected" from such duties as lifting pallets, heavy cartons, and similar "onerous" work, the grievant was entitled to be offered the job that was available on the two days in question. While it is here evident that female employees almost consistently avoid accepting work on the Sealer-Stitcher machine, this circumstance does not suspend the operation of the contract, including the obligation to avoid by-passing female employees in assignment of jobs. The company would be protected in the event a female employee assigned to the job fails to demonstrate her ability to perform the duties in a satisfactory manner. In such event the company would be authorized to take corrective action.

Although, as the company asserts, a finding in favor of the grievant would constitute the overruling of an established call-in procedure and practice, this result is required by the agreement of the parties, in which they have eliminated the practice of by-passing female employees, which result also finds sanction in the federal law. The arbitrator is therefore constrained to comply with the contract requirements and hold that under the facts here presented, the company was in violation of Article 37 of the contract in failing to call in the grievant, who was a senior employee assigned to the extra board, and qualified to perform the work of Sealer-Stitcher.

Award

1. The evidence establishes that the grievant was a senior employee, regularly classified as Utility Worker, assigned to the extra board;

2. The grievant was qualified to perform the work of Carton-Assembler available on June 17 and 18, 1971; the company was in violation of Article 37, of the contract in by-passing the grievant by reason of her sex;

3. The arbitrator finds that the job of Carton-Assembler has traditionally been performed by male employees at the Marienville Plant; the job involves duties that include repetitive weight lifting of stacks of cardboard and wooden pallets in excess of 30 pounds together with other duties that are considered onerous and objectionable; however, such conditions inherent in the job would not justify a failure to adhere to the contract requirements;

4. Inasmuch as the grievant is deemed qualified to perform the available work, and since she was by-passed by reason of her sex, and prior call-in procedure, which were eliminated from the current contract, the grievant is entitled to be reimbursed for her lost earnings.

Questions for Discussion

What is the effect of incorporating external law by reference in the collective bargaining agreement?

How does Arbitrator Dworkin apply external law in his decision?

Does Arbitrator Dworkin's decision foreclose a Title VII discrimination action by the grievant in federal court?

Why does Arbitrator Dworkin reject the evidence of an established past practice?

Compare the style, form, and substance of this opinion and award with the other decisions included in this Part.

Great Lakes Steel Corporation

Arbitrator Richard Mittenthal
May 14, 1973
60 LA 860

'HATE' LITERATURE

Subject

[The Subject is:—] Discharge—Bringing Newspapers onto Company Property

Statement of the Grievance

"I, S—, badge 32328, deny the charges as stated in the conversion letter to a discharge dated March 3, 1972 and ask to be reinstated to my job and reimbursed for all loss in earnings and the violation notice rescinded and stricken from my record."

—filed by S— March 8, 1972

Contract Provisions Involved

Sections 3 and 8 of the August 1, 1971 Agreement.

Grievance Data	*Date*
Case Heard:	Sept. 12, 1972
Transcript Received:	Oct. 2, 1972
Company Brief:	Oct. 27, 1972
Union Brief:	Dec. 13, 1972
Award Issued:	May 14, 1973

Statement of the Award

The grievance is denied.

Background

Management discharged S— in March 1971 for bringing "literature onto Company property in direct violation of Company notice" and for his "prior record of misconduct." The Union insists that the discharge was not for "proper cause." It seeks S—'s reinstatement with back pay.

A newspaper, entitled "Great Lakes Steal," initially appeared in the plant in January 1971. It was distributed to employees about once a month for more than a year. It was the product of a group of anonymous workers who felt they were being abused by the Company and badly represented by the Union. Its articles were highly derogatory of both parties. For example, the headline in Volume I, Issue 2 read, "Great Lakes Tries Legal Murder." The accompanying article alleged that "Plant Protection and one Millwright foreman . . . tried to MURDER [a man] with homicidal negligence. . . ." and an inside headline in Volume I, Issue 10 read, "Company 'Medicine' Kills." The accompanying article claimed that another employee had "died of Great Lakes Steel's 'Company Policies', policies of neglect, callousness and insufficient facilities," that "when the Company killed [him], it killed all the rest of us too," and that Management thus "proved it can and will do it to any one of us at any time." Other issues of the paper attacked Union officers as being racist, dishonest, undemocratic, and so on.

Two employees were apprehended in March 1971 distributing copies of "Great Lakes Steal" in the plant. They were suspended for five days. A hearing was held on the suspensions. The Union argued that the employees were unaware that there was anything wrong in distributing this newspaper and that the discipline was hence unjustified. Management reduced the suspensions to four days and decided to notify all employees that this kind of behavior would not be tolerated. It posted the following notice on March 8, 1971:

"1. No employee is permitted to distribute literature in any working area of the plants or during working hours without express authorization from Labor Relations.

"2. *No employee is permitted to bring in or distribute, at any time on Company property, literature which is libelous, defamatory, scurrilous, abusive or insulting or any literature which would tend to disrupt order, discipline or production within the plants.*

"ANY EMPLOYEE WHO BRINGS IN OR DISTRIBUTES LITERATURE IN VIOLATION OF THIS POLICY IS SUBJECT TO DISCIPLINE UP TO AND INCLUDING DISCHARGE."

The events which led to this dispute occurred the afternoon of February 24, 1972. Lieutenant Sword, a Plant Protection officer, received an anonymous phone call at 1:00 P.M. He was told that an employee named S— would be driving "an old Dodge" onto the Island and that S— "had some copper in that car that belonged to us." He was given the license number of S—'s car, KYH 576. He promptly called Staff Investigator Gatherum and they decided to search the car when it came on the Island. They went to the "compound area" with Sergeant Samfilippo. They stationed themselves there and observed all cars entering the parking lot. They saw an old Dodge with license number KYH 576 at about 2:45 P.M. They followed the Dodge into the parking lot. As the driver of the Dodge parked, they drove up behind him.

There is some dispute as to what happened next. According to the Company's witnesses, S— locked his car and was standing by the trunk when Lieutenant Sword approached him. Sword called S— by name and requested that he open the trunk. S— asked who they were. Sword identified himself and Investigator Gatherum, neither of whom were wearing a uniform. S— then opened the trunk. There were several pieces of copper inside, none of which had any rubber insulation.[1] Sword next requested that he let them look inside the car. S— tried to open the passenger door with a key but was unable to do so. He walked around to the driver's side, unlocked the door, reached across to the passenger side, and unlocked that door as well. Sword looked inside and found ten to twelve pieces of copper on the floor in front of the rear seat. They too were without insulation. Sword inquired where he got this copper. S— replied that it didn't come from the Company, that he and another man had picked it up elsewhere.

Sword noticed a black coat lying on the rear seat. He lifted the coat up and discovered a pile of "Great Lakes Steal" newspapers, the February 1972 edition. He confiscated them. At this point, Gatherum

---

[1] Without the insulation, there was no way to identify the copper as being the property of the Company or of anyone else.

took the top copy from the pile of papers and asked S— where he got them. S— said, "From a man" (according to Sword) or "From a man downtown" (according to Gatherum). Gatherum again asked, "Where?," apparently seeking a more specific answer. S— pointed to the "Who We Are" box[2] in the newspaper and replied, "There." Gatherum asked, "What is the man's name?" S— did not respond and would not say anything further. Sword informed S— he was in trouble. When S— requested a Union representative, he was told he wasn't working and he could go to the Union hall. The Plant Protection officers later counted the papers taken from S—'s car and the count came to 115.

S—'s account of these events is quite different. He drove into the parking lot, parked, and started toward the plant with his lantern and galoshes. He states that he did not lock the car doors and that he had already traveled 20 feet toward the plant when he was stopped. He sought a Union representative before opening the trunk. He swore at the Plant Protection men because he didn't think they had any right to search his car. His copper was obtained when working for a contractor who cleaned new houses and when foraging in an abandoned scrap yard near the Company plant. He claims Plant Protection never asked him where he obtained the copper. He was, however, questioned about where he got the papers. He replied that he didn't know how the papers got in his car. When the question was repeated, he simply pointed to the "Who We Are" box and told the officers, "If they could read, they could see where it came from." He denies having distributed "Great Lakes Steal" within the plant or outside the plant and contends he has never worked with any individuals who produced the paper.

Management concluded from the reports of the Plant Protection officers that S— was in violation of the rule set forth in the March 8, 1971 notice, that he knowingly brought abusive literature onto Company property. S— has a history of misconduct. He was suspended seven times in the five-year period preceding February 1972.[3] Six of those suspensions were for absenteeism—two days in August 1969, two days in October 1969, two days in June 1970, two days in September 1970, four days in March 1971. The seventh suspension was for sleeping in the locker room and consequently reporting late to his assigned job. He was given two days off in August 1971 because of this offense.

---

[2]The "Who We Are" box read: "This paper is published by and for workers at Great Lakes Steel. It is the first step in organizing the defense of workers' rights against the attacks of the Companies, the Government, and the Union."

[3]I have ignored an eighth suspension in January 1972 because that disciplinary action was protested by Grievance 1111-M which apparently is still pending.

Management suspended S— again on February 24, 1972, on account of the newspapers found in his car. It converted the suspension to discharge in early March for the following reasons:

"You brought literature onto Company property in direct violation of Company notice dated March 8, 1971
"You falsified material facts at your five-day suspension hearing.
"Your prior record of misconduct."

Discussion and Findings

I. The Union attacks the rule forbidding employees "to bring in or distribute, at any time on Company property, literature which is libelous, defamatory, scurrilous, abusive or insulting . . ." on two grounds. First, it contends that this Company rule "abridges employees' freedom of speech and press." Second, it urges that the language of the rule is "ambiguous" and should therefore be "strictly construed against the Company."

As for the first claim, the First Amendment to the United States Constitution provides that "Congress shall make no law . . . abridging the freedom of speech, or of the press." The rule in dispute, however, is not a Congressional act. Nor does it involve any kind of governmental action. That rule does not prohibit the publication of "Great Lakes Steal" or its distribution off of Company property. Hence, the publishers of this newspaper are still perfectly free to print and circulate their views. Their freedom has been limited only insofar as the papers may no longer be brought onto the Company's premises or distributed there. And the Company, as I shall explain later in this opinion, had perfectly sound reasons for establishing this prohibition.

In any event, freedom of speech does not encompass the right to publish or utter libels and slanders. The Company's rule is directed against the kind of deliberately false and vicious literature which is beyond the reach of constitutional protection. This principle was well-expressed in a recent United States Supreme Court decision:

". . . the use of the known lie as a tool is at once at odds with the premises of democratic government and with the orderly manner in which economic, social, or political change is to be effected. Calculated falsehood falls into that class of utterances which 'are no essential part of any exposition of ideas, and are of such slight social value as a step to truth that any benefit that may be derived from them is clearly outweighed by the social interest in order and morality. . . .' *Chaplinsky v. New Hampshire*, 315 U.S. 568, 572. Hence, the knowingly false statement and the false statement made with reckless disregard of the truth, do not enjoy constitutional protection."[4]

The Union's constitutional argument, for these reasons, is without merit.

As for the second claim, the union believes that portion of the rule prohibiting "bring[ing] in" literature is unclear. It asserts that the quoted words imply that "something must be brought into the plant, not simply on[to] Company property." It maintains that this ambiguity should be "strictly construed against the Company," that the rule hence should bar only bringing literature into the plant, and that S— committed no such offense.

There is no real ambiguity here. The rule states, "No employee is permitted to *bring in* or *distribute*, at any time *on Company property*, literature which . . ." (Emphasis added). The distribution of hate literature anywhere on "Company property" is forbidden. An employee surely could not avoid disciplinary action for this offense by arguing that he was free to distribute such literature in the parking lots. For the parking lots, like the plants, are "Company property." Because this reading is plainly correct as to "distribut[ion]" of literature, it should be correct for "bring[ing] in" literature as well. The words "Company property" must be interpreted the same for both offenses. Besides, when an employee chooses to use the Company's parking facilities and drives onto a lot, he subjects himself to the Company's rules and regulations. He certainly can be disciplined for misconduct (e.g., theft) in the parking lots. Therefore, the rule is broad enough on its face to prohibit employees "bring[ing] in" literature to any part of the Company premises, including the parking lots. The Union argument is not persuasive.

II. The Union next contends that the rule is inapplicable to the facts of this case. It states that the "Great Lakes Steal" newspaper "does not pose a threat to the Company so as to prevent its circulation." Its position thus appears to be that this paper is not "libelous, defamatory, scurrilous, abusive or insulting . . . ." It points to the sharp criticism of management contained in different issues of the Local Union paper and emphasizes that Management made no attempt to suppress the circulation of that publication. It believes the "Great Lakes Steal" paper should have been treated no differently.

This argument is not borne out by the evidence. The "Great Lakes Steal" papers were highly critical of both the Company and the Union. That criticism, however, went beyond all reasonable bounds. It accused the Company of "legal murder," "homicidal negligence," and a willing-

---

[4]*See Garrison v. Louisiana*, 379 U.S. 64, 75 (1964).

ness to kill "any one of us [employees] at any time." It charged the Company with viewing employees as if they were "animals." It claimed the Company was engaging in a "reign of terror." It referred to one Department Superintendent as a "little Hitler." And its characterization of the Union was equally extreme. It alleged that District and Local Union officials were "Company men," were "cheating" employees, were engaged in "racist policies," were part of a "conspiracy . . . to abolish democracy," and so on. These are merely illustrations of the vicious and defamatory material which is found on practically every page of these papers.

Most of these allegations in "Great Lakes Steal" are sheer nonsense. They are false statements made with a reckless disregard of the truth. Their effect would be to foster mistrust and discord in the plant and thereby disrupt the normal working relationship between employees and supervision and between employees and their Union representatives. The papers were, to a large extent, pure and simple hate literature. They sought to inflame the workers against both Management and the Union officers. They obviously posed a threat to order and discipline in the plant. Given these circumstances, Management was well within its rights in applying the rule to any employee who "bring[s] in" or "distribute[s]" this paper. The "Great Lakes Steal" was, as the rule states, "libelous, defamatory, scurrilous, abusive or insulting," the kind of literature "which would tend to disrupt order, discipline or production within the plants."[5]

S— contends that the rule is inapplicable to him because he did not knowingly "bring in" any "Great Lakes Steal" papers in his car on February 24, 1972. He insists, "I don't know how the papers got in the car." He urges therefore that he is not guilty of the rule violation for which he has been charged.

This is essentially a question of credibility. When Plant Protection officers looked inside S—'s car and lifted his coat off the rear seat, they discovered 115 copies of the February 1972 issue of "Great Lakes Steal." S— saw the papers also but said nothing to the officers. He did not express surprise; he did not promptly assert that he hadn't placed those papers in his car. The officers then asked him where he got the papers. They testified that S— answered, "From a man" (according to Lieutenant Sword) or "From a man downtown" (according to Investigator Gatherum) or "From Downtown" (according to Sergeant Samfilippo). S— claims he simply said he didn't know how the papers got in his car. His testimony,

---

[5]The Local Union papers are in no way comparable to the "Great Lakes Steal" papers.

however, was not credible on this point.[6] His supposed answer was not even responsive to the officers' question. It appears to me that he did tell the officers that he obtained the papers from someone else. Because he did obtain a large number of papers in this fashion, a fair presumption is that he was assisting in the distribution of this issue of "Great Lakes Steal." I find that he knowingly brought these papers onto the Company parking lot in violation of the Company rule. At no point in this proceeding did S— claim that he had been unaware of the rule.

Therefore, S—'s misconduct plainly called for disciplinary action.

III. The Union stresses that S—'s offense was "innocuous" and that "possession" of this kind of literature is far less serious than "distribution." It argues that the discharge penalty was "arbitrary, capricious and unreasonable" under the circumstances of this case.

As I have already explained, "bring[ing] in" or "distribut[ing]" hate literature on the Company premises is a serious offense. These actions promote mistrust and discord in the plant, disrupt normal work relationships, and undermine efficient operation. They are harmful to the best interests of employees and managers alike. This is no "innocuous" matter. And although "bring[ing] in" and "distribut[ing]" are different offenses, they may on occasion be closely related. Here, S— did not just bring a few papers onto the Company premises. He brought 115 copies with him. He obviously was part of the distribution network for the February 1972 issue of the paper. His actions were merely the step before the actual hand-to-hand distribution of the paper. Management properly regarded this as a most serious form of misconduct.

S—'s offense must be viewed in light of his prior disciplinary record. In the two and one-half years before his discharge, he received seven disciplinary suspensions. Six of them were for excessive absenteeism and the seventh was for sleeping in the locker room and consequently reporting late to his assigned job. He was suspended a total of 21 days for these offenses. He was given numerous written warnings as well.

In view of the extremely serious nature of his misconduct in February 1972, his lack of truthfulness with respect to this incident, his bad disciplinary record, and his failure to respond to corrective discipline, I find that S—'s discharge was for "proper cause." The discharge

---

[6]There are numerous contradictions and improbabilities in his testimony. For example, on direct examination, he insisted that the officers told him at the outset that "they had reason to believe that I had something in my car that belonged to Great Lakes Steel." But, on cross-examination, he flatly denied that the officers made any such statement. Also on direct examination, he insisted the officers did not ask him where he'd obtained the copper wiring found in his car. But, on cross-examination, he admitted that he had been asked this question and that he had told the officers the copper did not come from Great Lakes Steel.

was not "arbitrary, capricious and unreasonable." There is no sound basis in the record for modifying the discharge penalty.

Award

The grievance is denied.

Questions for Discussion

On what basis does Arbitrator Mittenthal find the company rule concerning literature was enforceable?

Why does Arbitrator Mittenthal conclude that the rule concerning literature was applicable to the newspaper, "Great Lakes Steal?"

How does Arbitrator Mittenthal resolve the question of credibility?

What is the significance of the grievant's work record in the determination of the appropriateness of the discipline imposed by the company?

Compare the style, form, and substance of this opinion and award with the other decisions included in this Part.

Armstrong Cork Company

Arbitrator Jean T. McKelvey
September 3, 1974
63 LA 517

BUMPING

The Issues

At the outset of the hearing the parties agreed to the submission of the following issues:

1. Is the grievance of C— arbitrable?
2. If so, from what job was C— displaced? Was C—'s displacement proper under the contract dated August 7, 1972–August 7, 1974? If not, to what remedy is he entitled?
3. Did the Union violate the contract by proceeding to arbitration today? If so, what shall be the remedy?

Despite the sequence of the issues set forth above, it is clear that Issues #1 and 3 deal with arbitrability, while Issue #2 concerns the merits of C—'s grievance which can be reached only if the Arbitrator finds that his grievance is arbitrable.

Relevant Contract Clauses

SECTION XIII—SENIORITY:
13.1 Seniority in Layoff and Rehire

Seniority is determined by length of last continuous service with the Company. All other things being approximately equal, including ability, skill and efficiency, length of continuous service on each successive job shall govern selections for promotions and demotions to positions in the bargaining unit. When employees in other departments are thus given consideration, it shall be on the basis of similarity of job or experience.

In case of layoffs, and rehiring of employees whose seniority has not been broken, length of continuous service on the job, or in the department, in that order, shall be the controlling factor where ability and skill are approximately equal (except in the case of jobs where time required to learn in the job description is not over three months—in which case only length of continuous service in the department will be considered).

. . .

SECTION IX—ARBITRATION:
9.1 Arbitration Procedure

Any and all differences with respect to the meaning and application of the provisions of this agreement which shall not have been satisfactorily settled through the grievance procedure set forth in Section VIII above, shall be submitted to an arbitrator at the request of either party. The notice of intention to arbitrate the matter must be given in writing by either party to the other within twenty (20) calendar days from the date of the Company's written answer following the Fourth Step of the grievance procedure set forth in Section VIII above. Either party may request the Federal Mediation and Conciliation Service to submit the names of five persons qualified to act as arbitrators. Representatives of the Union and the Company shall have the right to completely reject the first list of arbitrators submitted by the Federal Mediation and Concilation Service and ask for a second list. However, on either the first list if rejected or on the second list the representatives of the Union and the Company shall each have the choice of rejecting the names of two different persons of these five persons, and the remaining person shall be selected as the arbitrator, who shall submit to both parties a written opinion explaining his award. The scope of arbitration shall be limited to the specific subject matter submitted to the arbitrator. The arbitrator shall not be empowered to amend or to add to, or to eliminate any of the provisions of this Agreement. The decision of the arbitrator shall be final and binding upon the parties. The cost of the arbitrator and his incidental expenses shall be borne equally by the Company and the Union.

Background

In March 1973 the Company decided to phase out its industrial felt business which would necessitate a number of layoffs and transfers, especially in the Converting Department. It so informed the Union. Thereafter the parties met on a number of occasions in an effort to reach a mutual agreement on modifying Section 13.1 of their contract to deal with these anticipated problems. Several Memorandums of Understanding were signed by the then Plant Manager and the Business Agent on November 27, 1973, but these were rejected by the membership of the Union. Subsequently, on December 7, 1973, the principal agents signed a Memorandum of Understanding calling for the elimination of job seniority and the substitution therefor of departmental seniority for all the jobs in the Converting Department, but this agreement was likewise rejected by the membership. As a result of these rejections the Company told the Union that it intended to adhere to the contract provisions and to apply job seniority, except in those cases where the time required to learn the job was less than three months in which case only length of continuous service in the department would be considered. Accordingly, on December 12, 1973, the Company notified the Union of the names of 28 employees who were to be laid off. Some 20 employees in the nine Converting Department jobs which required three months or less to learn were asked to indicate their job preferences, following which they were assigned to these jobs in accordance with their departmental seniority.

One of the men displaced from a three months-or-less learning period job was Charles James, a 19-year employee who had held the job of industrial trucker for seven years. James lost his job to another employee whose own job had been eliminated, but whose departmental seniority was higher than that of James. In accordance with his expressed preferences James was assigned to the job of accopac helper.

On December 14, 1973 James filed a grievance protesting his transfer which was ultimately processed to arbitration. On August 12, 1974 the Arbitrator, Professor John Windmuller, rejected the Union's contention that under these circumstances Article 13.1 required the Company to assign higher priority to job seniority than to departmental seniority. After reviewing the efforts of the parties to modify the existing contract language and analyzing the interrelationships between the first two paragraphs and among the various sentences in Section 13.1, Professor Windmuller concluded that the parenthetical words in the second paragraph of Section 13.1 carved out an exception to the use of job seniority in layoff and transfer situations. This exception covered jobs requiring three months or less to learn "where departmental seniority would prevail and job seniority would not." Accordingly, he denied the grievance.

Meanwhile, on January 8, 1974, another employee in the Converting Department, C—, who had also been displaced from his job, filed a grievance protesting the impropriety of his transfer. It is this grievance which is at issue in the present proceeding and which raises a threshold issue of arbitrability.

The Issue of Arbitrability

The Company contends that C—'s grievance is non-arbitrable under the doctrine of res judicata (the matter has already been decided). It alleges that because of the similarity of the facts presented by the two grievances, Professor Windmuller's award in the James case is dispositive of the instant matter as well. According to the Company, C—'s job from which he was displaced was that of Pallet Nailer which the Job Classification sheet shows as requiring a learning period of a week to one month, thereby placing it well within the parenthetical exception set forth in Section 13.1, paragraph 2. Like James also, C— was transferred to the job of Accopac Finisher in accordance with his departmental seniority and his ranking of job preferences on December 11, 1973. Additionally the Company argues that in advancing the C— grievance to arbitration the Union has violated Section 9.1 of the contract, Arbitration Procedure, particularly the sentence reading: "The decision of the arbitrator shall be final and binding upon the parties." As remedy it requests that the Union be ordered to pay all the costs of the present arbitration, including the fees of the Company's attorneys.

The Union argues that the grievance is arbitrable because, although superficially similar, C—'s grievance is completely different from that of James. What C— is alleging, according to the Union, is that he was displaced from the job of 2d Class Carpenter, not that of Pallet Nailer. Since the job of 2d Class Carpenter requires a learning period of one and one-half to three years, the Union contends that in C—'s case the Company had no contractual right to ignore his job seniority. The issue in the instant case, according to the Union, concerns a dispute over which job C— was occupying when he was displaced, a matter neither presented, nor present, in the James grievance. Additionally, the Union contends that each case must be decided on its own merits since no rule of stare decisis is set forth in the contract.

Opinion on Issues #1 and #3

After hearing the issue on the merits, while reserving judgment on the issue of arbitrability, I find that the C— grievance is arbitrable because it poses a factual question, that of deciding what job S— held before he was displaced. This question was not present, nor even lurking, in the James arbitration which dealt solely with a question of contract interpretation. Although the Union here argued that the parties are not bound by any rule of stare decisis, it indicated at the hearing that while it disagreed with Professor Windmuller's decision, it was prepared to accept his interpretation of Section 13.1. What is at issue here, however, is the application of this interpretation to the facts of the C— grievance. Thus, if the job from which C— was displaced were that of Pallet Nailer for which the learning period is three months or less, then the result would be the same as in the James' case. On the other hand, if C—'s job had been that of 2d Class Carpenter, a different conclusion would follow. The Company's threshold argument that C—'s grievance is non-arbitrable essentially begs the question because it is premised on the assumption that the factual question has already been resolved. It is not until the second issue on the merits can be reached that the factual question can be answered.

My conclusion that the C— grievance is arbitrable also disposes of the third issue in the submission. By proceeding to arbitration on a dispute over facts, the Union did not violate the arbitration provisions of the agreement.

The Issues on the Merits

As stated above, the question here is: From what job was C— displaced?

According to the Company, C's job at the time of his displacement was that of Pallet Nailer, a position he was awarded on May 1, 1972 after he was the successful bidder for a posted job opening as Pallet Nailer.

From time to time thereafter C— worked as a 2d Class Carpenter on those occasions when the regular incumbent was sick or on vacation, or when a second shift operation was scheduled. Effective July 17, 1972 the Company considered that C— was qualified to do occasional work as a carpenter and authorized payment of the interim rate for this classification when he was performing 2d Class Carpenter work. Effective April 23, 1973 the Company authorized payment of the maximum rate for the 2d Class Carpenter classification when C— was assigned to the job. Both authorization sheets, which are Company records, bore the notation that C—'s regular job was 203-34—the Pallet Nailer classification.

To show the infrequency of these assignments, the Company produced its own records indicating that in the 101 weeks between May 1, 1972 and December 1973, C— worked six full weeks as a vacation fill-in and five full weeks when a second shift was added for a total of 11 weeks. In addition he occasionally filled in on days when the regular incumbent was absent.

In the six months preceding the phase-out, C— worked a total of three weeks as a 2d Class Carpenter; namely, the week of October 1, 1973 on the second shift, and the weeks of November 19 and December 17 as a vacation replacement for the regular incumbent.

From these records the Company concluded that although C— possessed the skills of a 2d Class Carpenter, the fact that he was upgraded on occasion, did not mean that his regular job assignment was that of a 2d Class Carpenter. His regular job, which he performed 85 percent of the time, was that of Pallet Nailer, the classification he carried on the Company's records and which had not been changed at the time of his displacement. Only if a vacancy had occurred in the 2d Class Carpenter classification to which C— might have been promoted by virtue of the bidding procedure could he have rightfully claimed this as his regular job. Hence the Company maintains that since his regular job was one which required a learning period of three months or less, his departmental seniority, not his job seniority, governed his displacement rights.

The Union argued that because C— was working as a 2d Class Carpenter during the week immediately preceding his transfer, this must be construed as his regular job. And since the learning period for a 2d Class Carpenter exceeds three months, he did not, according to the Union, fall within the exception set forth in Section 13.1 of the contract. Instead he should have been retained on this job and not been bumped by an employee with greater departmental but lesser job seniority who had only bid into the pallet shop in September 1973.

The Union also noted that although C— had ranked his choice of open jobs on a "Potential Layoff Preference" sheet, he had done so only under protest and only after he had been told that his failure to fill it out might foreclose him from exercising any bumping rights and leave him jobless.

Since C— had had both greater job seniority as a Pallet Nailer and more experience as a 2d Class Carpenter than did the employee who bumped him, the Union contended that he was the most qualified employee on the job and hence the most logical choice for retention in his former job. Moreover, his experience as a 2d Class Carpenter and the fact that he was paid the maximum rate for the job when he was upgraded meant that his regular job was that of 2d Class Carpenter which should have given him protection against being bumped by an employee with lesser job seniority and experience. As a remedy the Union asked that C— be returned to the Pallet Shop and paid the difference in earning between his former and his present job. It also asked that he receive the 2d Class Carpenter's maximum rate for all occasions on which those who displaced him were upgraded to the higher classification.

Opinion

It is easy to understand why C— feels himself aggrieved. As he perceives the situation, he was treated unfairly when he was displaced by employees with lesser job seniority and little, if any, experience in working in a higher classification. His written grievance expresses his sense of injustice:

> As of December 25, 1973 I have been working for one year, 8 months in the Pallet Shop. I was a Class 5 Leader and Saw Man in the Pallet Shop when the Company transferred me to Accopac 3 shifts, therefore losing $20 or $30 bonus a week. I have been replaced by a man who has only 3 months experience on same job and no experience on the saw or pallet shop leader. Why should someone with 3 months on the job replace me when I have 20 months—plus two men who are working on the nailing job that have had very little, if any, experience. In other words, I got bumped by three men. I find myself in the same position I was in 15 years ago when I started with the Company (Jt. Ex. 2).

Yet a sense of injustice is not necessarily proof of a contract violation. Moreover, the design of a perfectly fair seniority system eludes the skills of well-intentioned negotiators on both sides of the bargaining table. This can be clearly seen in the earnest, but unsuccessful, efforts of the parties to this case to work out mutually a more equitable system of seniority preferences to meet the predictable displacements resulting from the phase-out. The failure of these efforts left the parties with the unenviable task of applying the possibly ambiguous language of Section 13.1 to the reallocation of the work force. Whatever these ambiguities, they have now been clarified by the award of Professor Windmuller in the James case. Job seniority prevails over departmental seniority "except in the case of jobs where time required to learn in the job description is not over three months—in which case only length of continuous service in the department will be considered."

This brings us to the basic question at issue in this proceeding. What was C—'s regular job? If it were that of 2d Class Carpenter, as the Union contends, then he should have been protected against displacement because the learning period exceeds three months. If it were that of Pallet Nailer he could be bumped by someone with greater departmental seniority because the learning period in this classification does not exceed three months.

In my opinion C—'s regular job from which he was displaced was that of Pallet Nailer. I base this conclusion on the following reasons:

1. As the Company stated, C— spent between 85 percent to 90 percent of his time in the Pallet Nailer's job during the period from May 1, 1972 to December 1973 or a total of [90] out of 101 weeks, excluding hours or days on which he filled in during the regular incumbent's absence. This was confirmed by the Company's records and by C— himself under cross examination.

2. During the six months preceding the phase-out C— worked only a total of three weeks as a 2d Class Carpenter. Although he was working as a vacation replacement in the Carpenter classification during the week of December 17, immediately preceding his displacement, this could not in itself serve to change his regular job classification. Like the other ten weeks this represented a temporary upgrading from his regular job.

3. In order to be classified as a regular 2d Class Carpenter, C— would have had to obtain this job through the vacancy bidding procedures set forth in the contract. No proof that such a vacancy existed during this period was offered by the Union, nor did it attempt to show that C— had submitted a bid for a 2d Class Carpenter's job. The fact that he was qualified to perform this work is conceded by the Company. But incidents of upgrading on a temporary and infrequent basis do not serve to convert such a temporary assignment to a regular job.

4. The basis of C—'s written grievance was that he had been bumped out of his Pallet Nailer's job by an employee with only three months experience as a Pallet Nailer. More significant, perhaps, is the fact that the remedy the Union is seeking is that C— be returned to his Pallet Nailer's job, and made whole for the difference in earnings, including any that his replacement made at those times when he was upgraded to 2d Class Carpenter. It should be noted that the Union is not asking that C— be made a 2d Class Carpenter, for no such opening exists at present, but only that he be returned to a job, that of Pallet Nailer, which would afford him the opportunity, on occasion, to be upgraded temporarily to the job of 2d Class Carpenter.

Inasmuch as all of the evidence and testimony leads me to conclude that the job from which C— was displaced was that of Pallet Nailer, and since both sides agree that the Job Classification Sheet shows the learning period for this job to be one week to one month, the Pallet Nailer job clearly falls within the parenthetical exception set forth in the second paragraph of Section 13.1 which mandates the use of departmental rather than job seniority as the controlling consideration in case of layoffs. The Union concedes that the employee who bumped C— had greater departmental seniority. Hence C—'s displacement was proper under the contract.

Now, therefore, as the duly designated Arbitrator, I hereby make the following

Award

1. The C— grievance is arbitrable.
2. The job from which C— was displaced was that of Pallet Nailer. His displacement was proper under the contract dated August 7, 1972– August 7, 1974.
3. The Union did not violate the contract by processing this case to arbitration.

Questions for Discussion

Is the substantive arbitrability of an issue ordinarily a question for the arbitrator to decide?

Would the arbitrator have had the authority to determine the dispute if the parties had failed to agree upon the issues submitted to arbitration?

Would the result have been different if C— had worked as a 2d class carpenter fifty percent of the time, including the three months prior to layoff?

Compare the style, form, and substance of this opinion and award with the other decisions included in this Part.

Arnold Bakers, Inc.

Arbitrator Eva Robins
April 26, 1978
70 LA 1144

FOUR-DAY SCHEDULE

In their agreement to arbitrate, a memorandum agreement dated December 29, 1977, signed for the Company and the Union by appropriate officials, they described the issue as follows:

> 3. The Union and Company agree to arbitrate the issue of scheduling of four and five day week within a holiday week in the Maintenance Department. (Joint Ex. 2)

At the hearing the parties were unable to agree on the issue to be heard, the Union claiming it to be the limited issue described above, the Company proposing that the issue include the question of the Union's right to "advise" its employees not to work more than four days during Christmas 1977 week. While the Arbitrator believes that the circumstances of the dispute are relevant to the issue before her, she believes the statement of the issue as in Joint Exhibit 2 is the question which the Award is required to answer. But since the circumstances are of significance, and the Union and Company referred to them at the hearing, the Arbitrator considers it her obligation to indicate clearly in this opinion their impact on her decision.

A hearing was held by the Arbitrator on March 3, 1978, at the Rye Hilton Hotel in Port Chester, New York, at which the parties were afforded opportunity to present evidence, testimony and argument in support of their contentions. The parties' briefs were postmarked March 24, 1978 and received by the Arbitrator, one on March 27 and one on March 29. The hearing was considered closed as of March 29, 1978.

The employees involved in this dispute are employed in the Maintenance Department, as a department servicing the bakery plant. Maintenance operates around the clock, on three shifts. There are over 70 employees in that department. The events which occurred prior to Christmas Week, 1977, are described by various witnesses as follows:

> The Company prepared a schedule for Christmas Week, 1977, showing that the Bakery would be closed on Christmas Day, as contractually required. The schedule it fashioned was prepared in accordance with the master schedules, recognizing regular days off. For employees for whom

the day on which Christmas fell would have been a normal work day, the schedule showed them as working four days and off on the holiday. For employees for whom the day on which Christmas fell would have been a day off, the schedule showed them as working five days, and off on the holiday.

The Union and some Union officials questioned the schedule, and a meeting was held with management people. The Union testimony confirms that the Union President, Mr. Osorio, demanded that *all* employees work four days, or all work five days. While Mr. Osorio argued that this constituted unequal treatment, he also confirms that it is not unusual for some employees to work five days per week and others six, to cover for employees who are ill, on vacation, etc.

The Company, after the first meeting, advised the Union that all employees would work four days, except the handful of employees who were scheduled as vacation relief and therefore scheduled for five days. The Union then advised the Company that no employees would work overtime that week, and it appears very clear, from Mr. Osorio's own testimony, as well as that of other Union and Company witnesses, that he and others told the employees they were not required to work a fifth day and not required to work overtime—that all employees were to be "treated equally." Thus, it is clear from Mr. Harrison's testimony that he told employees if the Company scheduled four days, to work four days, and "just four days." Mr. Harrison refused to answer a question as to Union constitution or by-law authority to assess a penalty against a union member, but Mr. Osorio confirms such authority.

Mr. Osorio's testimony is that he advised every employee in the maintenance department that the employee had the right to refuse to work five days, but denies "forcing" anyone to refuse. He told them they could not be forced to work overtime.

The Company witness claims Mr. Osorio stated he would prevent people from working the fifth day. While no employee said to management that he did not want to work overtime (or the fifth day of work), none did. One employee, Marselo Flores, scheduled to work four hours of overtime on Christmas day, to complete a job on which he had been working, came to work but worked only two hours and left. The Union denies the Company's statement that Union officials persuaded him to leave, but the Union acknowledges that Mr. Flores came to the Union office to "apologize" for working.

The Company claims the Union had not cited any contract provision it claimed was violated. Obviously, the Union claim is that there is a 37½ hour guaranteed work week. At the hearing, the Union cited many contract provisions which it claims had been violated by the Company. The Company asserts that most of those provisions are not relevant to the dispute. It, too, cites certain provisions of the agreement as supportive of its position. Some of the provisions referred to by the parties will be quoted below; others merely will be listed and described. *All* have been reviewed by the Arbitrator.

ARTICLE III, §1.

It is understood and agreed that all employees will give their best efforts in the interests of the Company. It is understood and agreed that the Union shall in no way attempt to interfere with the management of the business of the Company . . . . (Company reference)

ARTICLE V—Wages

§8. Job openings posted for five (5) working days. Union considers this a reference to a five-day work week. (Union reference)

§12(a) . . . . Extra time and one-half is to be paid for all hours worked over thirty (30) hours in a holiday week. Thus in a holiday week an employee who works only the hours worked by his whole crew is paid thirty-seven and one-half (37½) hours at his regular hourly rate for the first thirty (30) hours, plus straight time for the number of hours worked on the holiday, plus additional time and one-half for each hour worked over the thirty (30) hours. (Referenced by Company and Union)

§13(f) An employee who works thirty (30) or more hours during a holiday week . . . . (Referenced by Union)

§14(b) and (b)(iii): In order to qualify for said double pay (for 7th day work), the employee must work every scheduled work day of a work week . . . . and (i) . . . .; or (ii) . . . .; or (iii) work five (5) days . . . . (Referenced by Union)

ARTICLE VI—Work Week

§1. It is understood and agreed that a *normal work week* shall consist of thirty-seven and one-half (37½) working hours . . . . (Referenced by Company and Union. Emphasis supplied).

§2. . . . . No employees shall be scheduled to work more than 47½ hours in any work week: 5 days of 9½ hours. Extra day limited to only 6 times per year, *excluding Holiday weeks*. (Referenced by Company and Union. Emphasis supplied).

§4. The Union agrees that the management may require an employee to carry out any work assignment . . . during a thirty-seven and one-half (37½) hour week regardless of the employee's regular job classifications. . . . (Referenced by Union)

§5(a) The Company agrees to post by noon Wednesday preceding the work week the working schedule of all shifts in convenient places. The regular work week and *holiday week schedule changes* shall be discussed with the Union. Such shift schedules will not be changed on less than twenty-four (24) hours notice. *The addition of reasonable overtime shall not be considered a change of schedule.* (References by Company. Emphasis supplied).

§5(b) (Changes in holiday schedule after holiday week begins:—notice provision—referenced by Company)

§7. The normal work week shall consist of five (5) days . . . . (Referenced by Union)

ARTICLE VII

§4(b) (Reference by Union to language re 5 consecutive days.)

ARTICLE IX—Vacations

§4 (Week's vacation pay defined as 37½ hours pay) (Referenced by Union)

ARTICLE XIII—Layoff

§2(b) (Reference to options to be considered in case of business problems—mention of 37½ hour week). (Referenced by Union)

Also, disability benefits, not in contract, based on percentage of 5-day pay rate, according to Union statement. Supporting evidence not supplied.

It is Union's claim that the contract provisions refer only to a 37½ hour week of five days and that this constitutes a guaranteed work week, which applies whether or not the week contains a holiday. All of the contract references to 37½ hours or five days are treated by the Union as confirming its claim that the Company has guaranteed a five day week to the employees. The Union considers the sole question before the Arbitrator is whether the Company has the right to schedule four and five day work weeks in a week in which a holiday occurs. It lists in its brief, questions which it claims are *not* before the Arbitrator.

The Company asserts that there is no guarantee of a five-day, 37½ hour work week. Article VI, Section 1, refers to a normal or regular work week, but references in Article V (13)(f) and elsewhere make it clear that the hours of a holiday week are 30 hours and four days, with eligibility for 7½ hours of "free time" during that week.

The Company further contends that the presence of a provision for 37½ hours, five days in a *normal* work week, and the absence of such a provision for a *holiday* work week, makes it plain that the parties had not so agreed.

The Company argues and offers evidence to support its claim that production needs dictate the scheduling during a holiday week. Thus, in previous Christmas and New Year holiday weeks, some employees worked four days and some worked five, without protest by the Union. In other holiday weeks, some employees worked five days and some six. The Company asserts an accepted practice that not all employees are scheduled the same in a holiday week, the needs of the operation determining the schedule in this regard. The Company points out that if *all* employees had been placed on five days, with the production end shut down, at least fifty of the maintenance men would have come in on Christmas day with no work to perform. It asserts a clear right to schedule some employees for the fifth day as overtime, without the Union engaging in a concerted action to prevent employees from working on the fifth day.

Discussion and Findings

It should be made clear, at the outset, that the many contract provisions cited by the Union as supporting a claim of a guaranteed work week of 37½ hours in five days in a holiday week have absolutely no relationship to that issue. The Arbitrator has read carefully all of the cited sections. They do not apply.

The evidence offered by the Union at the hearing (aside from argument as to the existence of a guaranteed five-day, 37½ hour holiday work week), dealt solely with testimony of Union officials attempting to prove they or others had not interfered with the business of the Company, had not ordered the employees not to work the fifth day or overtime. Thus, Mr. Osorio's testimony is that he "reminded" employees they had a right to refuse the fifth day of work. Mr. Parelli recalls Mr. Osorio saying "I would advise you not to work five days but it is up to you." Mr. Harrison recalls statements being made to employees that if the Company scheduled for four days, to work "four days and just four days." Mr. Varbaro said he told employees it was "up to them."

With the Union testimony largely limited to questions of what was said to the employees and by whom, and to the effort to prove no Union responsibility for the failure of a single employee to work a fifth day in Christmas week, it appears to the Arbitrator that the Union cannot now claim, as it did in its brief, that the Arbitrator cannot consider the impact of those actions on the matter before her. If she is not to consider it, it is difficult to understand why it was presented. While the Arbitrator has stated above that the limited question in Joint Exhibit 2 also serves to limit the scope of her *award*, she cannot in her opinion disregard the circumstances in which the dispute arose.

There is no doubt in the Arbitrator's mind, from the testimony and demeanor of the witnesses, that the Union officials and the maintenance representative discouraged the employees who were on schedule to work five days in Christmas Week, the fifth day as overtime. The Arbitrator considers that whether the Union officials told them not to work more than four days, or ordered, "advised," suggested or told the employees it was "optional with them," is really immaterial. What *is* material is that the Union did not tell the employees what is by now well known in labor-management relations: that employees should be directed to work as properly instructed and scheduled, and grieve if they thought the schedule violated the agreement. It is plain that employees who had good reason for not working the fifth day would not have been required to do so. And it is also a reasonable inference that employees who might have wanted to work the fifth day in the holiday week were deterred from doing so by the "advice" given them by union officials. As the Union's President acknowledges, the Company has the right to prepare schedules. It also has the right to direct the work force and to expect that the contractual grievance procedure will be utilized if the Union or employees believe the scheduling to be in error. If the Company has made a mistake, it can be held to account through the grievance procedure. The application of self-help, the Union's "advice" to the employees that they were not obliged to work a fifth overtime day in that work week, was improper under the contract.

On the claim of a guaranteed 37½ hour, five-day work week in a holiday week, the Union makes conflicting claims: (1) It argues that the language of the agreement supports that claim; and (2) It argues that overtime is voluntary and thus need not be worked and that work on the fifth day was not obligatory. If, in fact, there was a guaranteed work week of 37½ hours, five days, applicable to holiday weeks, then work on the fifth day could hardly be voluntary.

The Arbitrator does not find that there is a guaranteed 37½ hour, five-day work week for holiday weeks. The contract reference to thirty hours in a holiday week (as to pay provisions) and other references to holiday weeks to distinguish them from normal or regular weeks, appear to the Arbitrator clearly to indicate that the parties differentiated in the treatment of normal and holiday weeks. Further, the practice in the past was clearly the same as that attempted by the Company here, and there is no evidence before the Arbitrator of any attempt to grieve or even question the Company's interpretations in the past.

Absent a guaranteed work week of five days, the Company had the clear right to schedule employees for whom the holiday was a scheduled work day (i.e., those who were scheduled to be off on two other days) for four work days that week, with the holiday off. The Company also had the right to schedule employees for whom the holiday was not a scheduled work day (i.e., those who were scheduled to be off on one other day and on the holiday) for five days of work. After the Union opposed the schedule, wanting all employees to be on four days or on five days, the Company had the right to place all on four days and to schedule some for overtime work on the fifth day. It had the right to do so without Union pressure on the employees and without interference with the scheduling. The Union's appropriate remedy, if it thought it had a claim of contract violation, was through the grievance procedure.

Award

The Company did not violate the collective bargaining agreement by scheduling employees in the Maintenance Department for four-day and five-day work weeks in Christmas Week, 1977. For the reason given in the opinion attached hereto, the Union's grievance is denied.

Questions for Discussion

Was past practice an important factor in the decision?

Are there circumstances under which the union would have had the right to advise employees not to work on the holiday?

How could the contract have been changed to provide for a guaranteed 37½ hour work week, including holiday weeks?

Compare the style, form, and substance of this opinion and award with the other decisions included in this Part.

Part VI

Selected Training Materials

Each is given a bag of tools,
A shapeless mass and a book of rules;
And each must make, ere life is flown,
A stumblingblock or a stepping stone.

R. L. Sharpe

Report of ABA Subcommittee on Qualifications and Training of Arbitrators

A. Background of Survey

The Labor Relations Law Letter for January 1978, reported in some detail on the arithmetical responses to a survey taken during the previous year by the subcommittee on qualifications of law arbitrators. The purpose of the present report is to present an analysis of the survey with particular emphasis upon the narrative responses supplied by those participating in the survey. The thoughful nature of many of the comments appended to the questionnaires both supplement and complement the arithmetical print-out.

The value of any survey, of course, is greatly dependent upon two basic factors: first, the quality, particularly fairness and objectivity, of the questions themselves and the areas of the field to which they pertain and second, the cross-section of participants in the survey. In a tripartite field such as labor arbitration it is essential that there be participation by representatives of employers, and in particular, by arbitrators themselves. The first of these factors will be treated in the form of a brief historical view of the genesis of the survey and the manner in which the questions were prepared and selected. The second factor will be considered in connection with the responses to the first three questions, which identify the degree of participation and the type of representation of those responding to the questionnaire.

B. History of Survey

The concept of conducting a survey of this type is believed to have had its origin at the August 1974 meeting of the Committee on Arbitration and the Law of Collective Bargaining Agreements at the annual convention of the Association in Honolulu, Hawaii. A preliminary draft of the questionnaire was prepared in the first half of 1975 and copies were distributed to members of the subcommittee for comments and suggestions. A second draft was prepared later that year and submitted to each member of the Committee on Labor Arbitration and the Law of Collective Bargaining Agreements. Over 50 percent of the questionnaires were returned, and the results were surprising. At the annual meeting in Atlanta, Georgia in 1976, the Council decided to submit a review of the original survey to all of the members of the Section and to a group of nonlawyers involved in the arbitration process.

In December 1976, a revised survey was submitted to the 7,000 members of the Section. Again, over one-half (3,573) of the membership participated in the survey.

C. Introduction to Survey Results

Many of the returned questionnaires contained written, narrative comments in the "Optional Comment" sections following each of the questions. To obtain some insight into these comments, all of the questionnaires were carefully reviewed, recorded, catalogued, and summarized. The following summary represents the results of this process:

Approximately 38 percent of the questionnaires contained narrative comments. The number of responses (expressed in percentages to questions) is noted at the beginning of a question's analysis and summary. The percentages set forth in brackets relate to those who elected to add comments to that question—not to the total number of questionnaires returned. In many instances, the number of responses represented a very small percentage of the total number of questionnaires.

In addition, there was considerable overlap in the written responses. Answers to one question were often more appropriate to other questions, and therefore, some correlation was necessary to achieve the true emphasis of the narrative responses.

The report includes the text of each question, the number of responses in each category (multiple responses were common), and an analysis of narrative responses.

D. Analysis of Responses to Individual Questions

1. I have been active in the field of Labor Relations Law for:
    a. From 0 to 1 year 196
    b. From 2 to 5 years 971
    c. From 6 to 10 years 746
    d. More than 10 years 1,641

The number of optional comments received amounted to approximately 2 percent of the number of questionnaires returned.

Two-thirds of those responding have been involved in the field more than six years and almost one-half possess more than 10 years such experience.

Approximately 40 noted that they had been active in the field of labor relations for more than 25 years, of which 12 reported 40 to 50 years experience in the field. Twenty of the comments were only germane to the role played in the process: these were evaluated in analyzing the written responses to question No. 2.

2 My role in the process is:
   a. Union representative 716
   b. Management representative 2,379
   c. Arbitrator 157
   d. Other 278

The number of written responses to this question amounted to 12 percent of the total questionnaires returned. This was more than twice the response to any of the other questions except No. 18.

Of those responding the ratio is more than three to one management oriented. However, responses from each category frequently contained a narrative comment to the effect that fidelity to the client did not impinge upon the ability to respond effectively in another capacity. Also, as pointed out below, respondents construed the word "representative" in "a" and "b" to exclude lawyers. Finally there were many [9 percent[1]] who checked both "a" and "b".

The narrative responses of those who checked "other" disclosed a wide variety of professional occupations. The largest group [18 percent] were employed in a legal or judicial capacity by the federal or a state government. Of these, approximately one-half were with the National Labor Relations Board at various levels. Another sizable group [10 percent] were in the academic field (labor law) either on a full-time [six percent] or part-time four percent basis. All in all, virtually the entire panoply of labor law and labor relations was represented by the narrative responses. As demonstrated by the checked categories, however, the vast bulk of those who returned questionnaires were in the mainstream of the tri-partite pattern.

Approximately 9 percent of those offering comments apparently distinguished between acting as a "respresentative" and as a lawyer.

---

[1]This percentage, as all percentages appearing in the individual question summaries, represents that percent of the total participants responding to this particular question, unless otherwise indicated.

They did not check "a" or "b" but listed themselves as "union attorney" [6 percent] or "management attorney" [3 percent]. If projected from the sample to the entire survey, this would somewhat ameliorate the rather pronounced management orientation of the statistical responses. As thus revised, it is still a 3 to 1 ratio, however.

Of those identifying themselves as union or management 9 percent also indicated they had previously represented the other side. Most of these had crossed over from union to management. Along the same line, 7 percent of those responding in narrative form stated that they currently represent both union and management clients. A small number of arbitrators reported a similar type of part-time practice, and a small number of the dual practitioners stated they do not represent both sides in the same industry.

It is encouraging to note that only a small portion [2 percent] of those who appended comments stated they were not active in the field of labor relations law. This, plus the very high percentage of questionnaires that were returned [50 percent], attests to the soundness of the survey results.

3. I have participated in:
    a. No labor arbitration hearings 392
    b. 1 to 10 labor arbitration hearings 862
    c. 10 to 100 labor arbitration hearings 1,541
    d. More than 100 labor arbitration hearings 764

The number of written responses to this question amounted to approximately one percent of questionnaires returned.

Here again there is a considerable disparity; with only 20 percent of those responding having participated in as many as 100 labor arbitration hearings.

4. Labor arbitrators should have a law degree from an accredited law school:
    a. I strongly agree 747
    b. I believe this would be desirable 1,980
    c. I do not think this is relevant 659
    d. I strongly disagree 103

The number of written responses to this question amounted to approximately five percent of the total questionnaires reviewed.

Most of those who commented stated that a law degree was not necessary in all cases; i.e., not for factual cases, but was often necessary for contract interpretation or specialized cases. Twenty percent indicated that other backgrounds were also acceptable and that law school graduates were not the only persons who possessed qualities that made good labor arbitrators.

Some respondents said that arbitrators should be trained in such areas as evidence and industrial relations; objectivity was also mentioned in these series of responses. These qualities were also as important as a law degree in evaluating the arbitrator according to 6 percent of the respondents. Others (3 percent) stated that a general knowledge of evidentiary rules was a desirable quality in an arbitrator; however, the arbitrator should not necessarily be too legalistic in applying them.

5. Admission to the practice of law should be a prerequisite for labor arbitrators:
   a. I strongly agree   547
   b. I believe this would be desirable 1,676
   c. I do not think this is relevant 1,028
   d. I strongly disagree   273

The number of written responses to this question amounted to approximately one percent of the total questionnaires reviewed.

Almost two-fifths (39 percent) of those responding by written comment stated that a legal education or a working knowledge of the law in the area of a given dispute was necessary, but a specific license to practice was not a prerequisite. And 18 percent stated that it depended on the case in question.

Eight percent stated that experience and common sense were the most important qualities for an arbitrator. While 10 percent said that many of the best arbitrators were not attorneys.

6. Labor arbitrators should be required to pass a certification examination which tests their knowledge of arbitration procedure and/or substantive law of collective bargaining agreements:
   a. I strongly agree 1,318
   b. I believe this would be desirable 1,506
   c. I do not think this is relevant   528
   d. I strongly disagree   177

The number of written responses to this question amounted to approximately 2 percent of the total questionnaires reviewed.

There was a real consensus regarding this question; most respondents concluded that specific training was desirable, but a certification examination was not necessary.

Seventeen percent stated that although it might be desirable to have such an examination, they were doubtful that certification was practical and that the examination's value depended partially on the nature of the examination. Eight percent said that it would be desirable if the person had no law school training. Others (7 percent) responded that the parties should be free to select arbitrators and should satisfy themselves as to the arbitrator's qualifications.

Five percent stated a certification examination would be desirable, but that the person's failure to take the test should not prevent that individual from becoming an arbitrator; the failure would only prevent some type of official recognition or approval.

Ten percent stated that "newcomers" should take a certification examination.

7. Any individual acceptable to representative adversaries, regardless of any other qualifications should be recognized as a qualified arbitrator:
    a. I strongly agree 636
    b. I tend to agree 1,223
    c. I tend to disagree 1,031
    d. I strongly disagree 775

The number of written responses to this question amounted to approximately four percent of the total questionnaires reviewed.

About one-half (46 percent) of those responding to this question by written comment stated that parties have the right to choose their own arbitrator as qualified to handle their particular problem, but that the arbitrator should only be considered "qualified" for that case and not necessarily for all others; an exception was when third party interests were involved.

Fifteen percent noted that uninformed people make poor choices which can damage the entire collective bargaining system—particularly when the public interest is involved. Some participants (7 percent) expressed the view that without knowledge as to the arbitrator's qualifications by the selecting parties, clear standards must be established.

Four percent stated that absolute control of the arbitral process by the parties could lead to abuse of due process and individual rights because adversaries could act in collusion with each other to the detriment of the aggrieved party.

8. Any individual who continues to represent management or unions should *not* be regarded as a qualified arbitrator:

    a. I strongly agree 744
    b. I tend to agree 799
    c. I tend to disagree 1,231
    d. I strongly disagree 775

The number of written responses to this question amounted to approximately four percent of the total questionnaires reviewed.

Most people responding (43 percent) stated that a person's advocacy did not destroy acceptability, provided that there was full disclosure and that the parties had the right to make the selection.

One quarter of the total respondents stated that attorneys in private practice could perform objectively, and that it was only necessary that the arbitrator make a fair decision based on the facts. Some respondents (2 percent) stated it was appropriate to select known advocates if the parties concurred, but that they should be excluded from the panels submitted by AAA and FMCS. While other (3 percent) stated, in contrast, that such a person should be allowed to sit on panels, but not as a sole arbitrator.

9. There ought to be significant differences in the type of qualifications required of arbitrators as between the private and public sectors:
    a. I strongly agree 259
    b. I tend to agree 717
    c. I tend to disagree 1,642
    d. I strongly disagree 856

The number of written responses to this question amounted to approximately two percent of the total questionnaires reviewed.

Thirty-five percent of those who provided written responses to this question stated that to the degree public sector disputes differed from private ones, qualifications should vary according to the respective needs.

10. There ought to be significant differences in the type of qualifications required of arbitrators as between arbitration of "rights" (grievance arbitration under an existing collective bargaining agreement) and arbitration of "interests" (arbitration to establish the terms and conditions of a new collective bargaining agreement).
    a. I strongly agree 472
    b. I tend to agree 1,056
    c. I tend to disagree 1,379
    d. I strongly disagree 598

The number of written responses to this question amounted to approximately two percent of the total questionnaires reviewed.

Most respondents (27 percent) stated that experience and knowledge of the areas of economics and finance were essential to all disputes, but particularly, to interest disputes. Seventeen percent stated that the qualifications for either field (economics and finance) should include knowledge of the area of the dispute and this would entail a general understanding of what was involved in a given situation. Eighteen percent of the respondents said that arbitrators should be qualified to handle both interests and rights disputes.

11. Acceptable sources for new arbitrators include: (Check as many as you deem appropriate.)
    a. Experienced labor lawyers who have represented either union or companies 3,244
    b. Experienced lawyers not specialized in labor law 1,137
    c. Union officials 497
    d. Retired union officials 1,343
    e. Management officials 532
    f. Retired management officials 1,428
    g. Law professors 2,760
    h. Economics professors 1,355
    i. Industrial relations professors 2,535
    j. Business school professors 1,225
    k. Retired government lawyers or hearing officers with experience in some field of labor law 2,723
    l. Retired government lawyers or hearing officers without experience in labor law 612
    m. Retired government officials experienced in labor relations 2,056
    n. Retired government officials not experienced in labor relations 152
    o. Clergymen 189
    p. Retired judges 1,905

The number of written responses to this question amounted to approximately five percent of the total questionnaires reviewed.

Twenty-two percent stated that knowledge and experience in labor law (particularly evidence and appreciation for substantive labor relations principles) and arbitration procedures (mechanics and substance) were strongly recommended.

12. If an experienced arbitrator were to use an assistant or trainee, I would:
    a. Be willing to utilize the experienced arbitrator with knowledge that the assistant or attorney would assist only in research 1,652
    b. Be willing to utilize the experienced arbitrator with knowledge that the assistant or trainee would assist in opinion drafting 1,404
    c. Be willing to utilize the experienced arbitrator with knowledge that the assistant or trainee would assist in opinion drafting provided that the name of the assistant or trainee appeared on the award along with that of the experienced arbitrator 798
    d. Be willing to utilize the experienced arbitrator with knowledge that the assistant or trainee could be assigned as a hearing officer for all or part of the proceeding, provided the experienced arbitrator supervised the writing of the award and issued it in his own name 440
    e. Be *un*willing to utilize the experienced arbitrator for fear that the assistant or trainee might play too large a part in deciding the issue submitted 293

The number of written responses to this question amounted to approximately two percent of the total questionnaires reviewed.

Twenty-nine percent of the participants felt that arbitrators should determine the responsibilities of the assistant and should accept full responsibility for the award issued; there should be no "rubberstamping" of the assistant's opinion.

13. Labor arbitrators should serve an apprenticeship with an established arbitrator:
    a. I strongly agree 411
    b. I believe this would be desirable 1,941
    c. I do not believe that this would be worthwhile 948
    d. I strongly disagree 173

A large number of the written responses (41 percent) stated that an apprenticeship program would be a valuable experience getting approach, adding to the person's credibility, but that it should not be required of everyone, particularly those with experience.

Thirteen percent stated that it would be worthwhile for those with no experience in either labor law or arbitration to engage in such a program.

14. The ABA should participate in programs for the development of arbitrators:
    a. I strongly agree 1,842
    b. I tend to agree 1,366
    c. I tend to disagree 241
    d. I strongly disagree 71

Most of those responding (2 percent of the total questionnaires reviewed) stated that this type of program should be administered by another group, such as NAA, AAA, or FMCS (or jointly with these groups).

One-quarter noted that although the ABA should participate in such programs, the ABA should not dominate them because the programs should not favor attorneys.

15. The ABA should actively encourage the development and training of arbitrators:
    a. I strongly agree 2,223
    b. I tend to agree 1,138
    c. I tend to disagree 128
    d. I strongly disagree 38

The largest number (47 percent) of this very small response (less than 1 percent of the total number of questionnaires reviewed) stated that other groups such as NAA, AAA or FMCS would be better suited and equipped to handle such a program.

16. The ABA should develop a policy statement with regard to the qualifications of labor arbitrators:
    a. I strongly agree 1,640
    b. I tend to agree 1,277
    c. I tend to disagree 419
    d. I strongly disagree 171

One-fifth of the respondents stated that the matter should be left to the NAA, AAA or FMCS or state labor boards.

Thirteen percent stated that the selecting parties should decide qualifications.

17. The ABA should, through periodic polling of the Labor Law
    Section or by some other method, attempt to certify arbitrators
    as "qualified" or "not qualified":
    a. I agree 1,114
    b. I believe this would be desirable 949
    c. I believe this would be desirable if limited to
       new arbitrators 213
    d. I do not believe this would be worth-
       while 750
    e. I strongly disagree 445

There was very little continuity to the written responses (five percent
of the total number of questionnaires reviewed) to this question.

Sixteen percent stated that it was not a proper function of the ABA,
since arbitrators were not all lawyers.

Others (12 percent) suggested that before deciding this question,
a criterion should be developed.

18. The ABA should take a position that qualification of an ar-
    bitrator to interpret and apply the terms of a collective bar-
    gaining agreement does not constitute qualification to interpret
    and apply federal or other statutes:
    a. I strongly agree 1,038
    b. I tend to agree 1,079
    c. I tend to disagree 794
    d. I strongly disagree 484

The answers to this question were quite varied and accounted for
the greatest number of written "optional" responses to any of the survey's
questions (10 percent of the total of questionnaires reviewed). There
were some trends in favor of not excluding the possibility of an arbitrator
interpreting statutes. Of the responses to this question, a majority were
apparently in favor of not excluding the possibility of an arbitrator interpreting federal and state laws that could impact an arbitral issue;
however, a majority also indicated that this conclusion was built upon
the foundation that there was a "fundamental" disagreement between
the language of the agreement and the relevant statute.

A large number of participants (28 percent) stated that it was often
necessary to construe statutes in order to decide a dispute regarding a
contract (especially in OSHA and EEOC cases); therefore, arbitrators
should be chosen with care in order that they be qualified and competent
to handle such cases.

Proposal for ABA Labor Arbitrator Development Program

A Growing Problem: The Need for More and Better Arbitrators

Approximately ninety-five percent of the collective bargaining agreements in the Country provide for arbitration as the peaceful means for settling disputes. During the past several years, there has been a growing need for increasing the number of acceptable arbitrators in the field of labor-management relations. As the number of disputes increases, this need has accelerated because of the advancing age of established arbitrators, many of whom received their training during World War II and the Korean War under various governmental arbitration boards. Those who have entered the field since then have generally acquired their skills on the job with little or no professional guidance.[1] Despite the substantial entry in the work force of minorities and women in the past 20 years, the number of arbitrators drawn from these ranks is minute. Further, the sudden rise in the use of arbitration in the public sector involving municipal and state employees has placed an unprecedented strain on the ever-shrinking group of established arbitrators.

At the same time, as reflected by the 1977 Survey on Qualifications and Training of Arbitrators,[2] the members of the Section of Labor Relations Law of the American Bar Association are concerned about the qualifications of labor arbitrators in terms of selection criteria as well as "their knowledge of arbitration procedure and/or substantive law of collective bargaining agreements."

A handful of uncoordinated and isolated programs for the training of arbitrators previously offered on an *ad hoc* basis have had only limited

---

[1]This is particularly true of arbitrators who, like judges, cannot readily seek advice on matters which they are presumed knowledgeable to decide.

[2]This Survey was conducted by the Section's Committee on Labor Arbitration and the Law of Collective Bargaining Agreements.

success either in having their "graduates" selected as arbitrators or in providing a sufficient quantity of graduates—especially in the areas of greatest need. With few exceptions, neither appointing agencies nor users have systematically participated in screening the candidates. The training has been entirely academic and generally without provisions for actual experience. The key flaw has been the failure to insure that the program participants would be given an opportunity to enter the mainstream of the disputes resolution field. What is genuinely needed is the development of a comprehensive program that would: (1) serve as the basic training course for qualified persons seeking to become labor arbitrators; (2) provide mechanisms through which these individuals, once trained, would be able to use their newly-acquired skills; and (3) result in publication of a manual providing detailed curriculum materials and program planning guides so that local regional organizations can conduct similar labor arbitrator development programs and thus help to increase the availability of qualified arbitrators for the resolution of labor-management disputes.

A Summary of the Proposal to Answer the Problem

The American Bar Association Section of Labor Relations Law is in a unique position to conduct a prototype arbitrator development program which recognizes these considerations because its membership includes the entire spectrum of advocates and neutrals involved in the labor arbitration process. Under the Section's auspices, this program, while retaining a strong academic component through the participation of Columbia University School of Law and its Dean Michael Sovern, would involve representative participation of all parties involved in the arbitration process across neutral, union and industry lines. This program would provide trainees with the opportunity to observe several actual hearings and write mock awards for professional review. It would guarantee the trainees who complete the program the assignment, as the arbitrator of record, in two actual cases under advance commitments from management and unions obtained through attorneys of the Section. These awards would be published by the Bureau of National Affairs in its Labor Arbitration Reports series and would be submitted to the various other services for publication. Trainees who complete the program would be assured listing on the rosters of the American Arbitration Association and the Federal Mediation and Conciliation Service. A "how-to-do-it" manual to guide the presentation of the pilot program would be developed and published under the direction of the ABA.

Because of their significant participation in the work force, qualified minorities and women would be actively sought out for selection as trainees in order to provide for the introduction of qualified persons from these areas into the system. Consideration would also be given to finding qualified trainees in geographic areas where there is a known shortage of labor arbitrators.

Program Participants

Many leading organizations interested in labor arbitration have affirmatively indicated their willingness to actively participate in the program. They include: The Federal Mediation and Conciliation Service, the American Arbitration Association, Columbia University School of Law, members of the National Academy of Arbitrators, the Bureau of National Affairs, and various labor organizations and employers.

Administration of the Program

The entire program would be directed and monitored by the Labor Relations Law Section's Committee on Labor Arbitration and the Law of Collective Bargaining Agreements. The Subcommittee on the Development and Training of Labor Arbitrators would be assigned general administrative reponsibility, with primary supervision maintained by the academic and administrative directors.

The academic phases of the program would be administered by the Columbia University School of Law which would be responsible for the employment of the Academic Director and faculty. It would make arrangements for necessary physical facilities and the housing of trainees while in residence. Michael I. Sovern, Dean of the Faculty of Law, would serve as Director of the program. Lewis B. Kaden, Associate Professor of Law, would serve as Academic Director of the program.

Assignments to arbitration cases for initial observation as well as actual decision would be administered by the American Arbitration Association and the Federal Mediation and Conciliation Service as appropriate under collective bargaining agreements.

The Pilot Program

Phase One: The pilot program would include approximately 15 trainees. Candidates on a nationwide basis would be nominated by the AAA and the FMCS on the basis of labor relations experience, education and potential for development as qualified and acceptable arbitrators.

Experience as an arbitrator would not be required; nor would the program be limited to attorneys or those with legal training. A special effort would be made in the selection process to insure that consideration is given to qualified women and minorities. The Federal Mediation and Conciliation Service and the American Arbitration Association would each submit a preliminary list of 50 candidates. From the initial list of 100, the Subcommittee on Development and Training of Labor Arbitrators of the Committee on Labor Arbitration and the Law of Collective Bargaining Agreements of the Section of Labor Relations Law of the American Bar Association (ABA) would recommend 30 candidates to the program's Director. He would then select the 15 trainees to be enrolled in the program after reviewing the recommendations of the Subcommittee.

Phase Two: The formal development program would include academic training as well as field observation experience. The program would be structured as follows:

(a) First week of academic training, June–July, 1978, in New York. This part of the course curriculum would introduce the trainees to the substantive and procedural aspects of arbitration. Appendix B lists many of the subjects to be covered during the academic part of the program. The faculty will include leading labor arbitrators and other individuals with expertise in labor arbitration.

(b) Field observation of five actual arbitration proceedings between September, 1978 and June, 1979, in the trainees' own regional areas to give them exposure to various approaches used by different arbitrators. During this period, each trainee would be required to prepare mock awards for two of these hearings. These awards would be critiqued by the arbitrator of record and two faculty members of the program.

(c) Second week of academic training, June–July, 1979, in New York. This period would build upon both the first week's academic training and the trainees' intervening field observation experiences.

Completion of Phase Two is expected to be by August 1, 1979, to enable the next phase of case assignments to begin right after the Labor Day holiday the following month.

Phase Three: This portion would provide each trainee, following completion of Phase Two, with the assignment as the arbitrator *of record* in two actual cases designated by the participating labor organizations and employers who have agreed to utilize the trainees in the one-year period following their completion of the program. Awards would be submitted to the various services for publication. The BNA has agreed to publish these awards in its Labor Arbitration Reports service which is distributed nationally, thus giving substantial exposure to the work product of the newly trained arbitrators.

Phase Four: This part of the project involves the preparation of a manual on how to set up and run the model program in any area of the Country. It would contain complete information on the methods for selecting and screening potential arbitrator trainees including the criteria utilized. Also included would be the complete curriculum in a "lesson plan" type arrangement for utilization by the faculty presenting the program elsewhere. This manual would be prepared under the direction of the Co-Chairman of the ABA Committee on Labor Arbitration and the Law of Collective Bargaining Agreements. It will be printed and made available to other groups who wish to run the program.

Program Funding

The total cost of the program is realistically estimated at approximately $60,000 for all four phases. A budget breakdown of this amount is attached as Exhibit A. The Section of Labor Relations Law has already committed $5,000 of its own revenues from the current administrative year as seed money to start the program. It is anticipated that the additional funds will be obtained from sources interested in supporting this worthwhile effort.

Anticipated Results of the Program

This program would serve as a model for the training of additional acceptable labor arbitrators and could be conducted by other state and local bar associations, academic institutions and other groups throughout the Country. The structure and method employed in the program and the results achieved would be published and made available for study to labor organizations, employers and educational institutions to assist in the development of additional programs. While this prototype would involve residence and travel costs, due to its national scope, the how-to-do-it manual would describe adaptations such as an extended evening program and include the text of the academic training. It is expected that the prototype would result, over the next few years, in a substantial increase in the number of acceptable labor arbitrators, thus improving the quality of adjudication and reducing delays in the time necessary to hear and decide disputes. This result will contribute significantly to peaceful, constructive labor-management relations to the benefit of the nation's economy.

Appendix A

Budget for the Labor Arbitrator Development Program

I. Academic Phase (Weeks 1 and 2)
  A. Student Costs

1. Meals and lodging for 15 students at Columbia University; 2 weeks	$6,075.00	
2. Travel to N.Y. twice with average fare $181.33 for 15 students	5,440.00 *	
3. Ground transportation; to and from airport at home and in N.Y. including taxi and tips	720.00	$12,235.00

  B. Faculty Costs

1. Meals and lodging for out-of-state faculty members at Columbia University; 2 weeks	1,700.00	
2. Travel to N.Y. of special faculty members; average fare $181.33	$3,626.60 *	
3. Ground transportation; to and from airport at home and in N.Y. including taxi and tips	480.00	
4. Teaching Honoraria		
a. Course instruction by faculty members	7,000.00	
b. Review of participants' 30 mock awards by faculty members	6,000.00	$18,806.60

  C. Administration Costs

1. Director's fees	$2,500.00	
2. Staff time, course materials, coffee break and miscellaneous expenses	4,250.00	$ 6,750.00

II. Field Observation of Arbitration Hearings

---

*Air fares are projected at current average rates used for ABA meetings.

Administrative expenses (telephone and mail in scheduling attendance)		5,000.00

III. Scheduling Cases as Arbitrator of Record

Administrative expenses (telephone, mail, and miscellaneous)		3,000.00
IV. Development of Program Manual		10,000.00
TOTAL DIRECT COSTS		$55,791.60
Indirect Costs (ABA Administrative Charges at 9.8%)		5,467.58
TOTAL BUDGET		$61,259.18

Appendix B

Academic Portion of the Labor Arbitrator Development Program

A. History and Development
  1. General history
  2. Legal history

B. The Arbitration Role
  1. Disputes of rights; Disputes of interest
  2. Public sector; Private sector
  3. The Arbitrator
    a. Qualifications
    b. Responsibilities
    c. Ethics
    d. Selection
  4. Arbitration Clauses
    a. Grievance procedure
    b. Final step
    c. Contract language
  5. Authority
    a. Contract
    b. Statute
    c. Review

C. Appointing Agencies
D. Appointment

1. Initial Contract
    a. Procedural determination
    b. Submission agreement
    c. Prehearing brief
    d. Notice

E. Preparation
    1. Prehearing conference

F. Hearing
    1. Facilities
    2. Transcript
    3. Who goes first?
    4. Oath and affirmation
    5. Opening statements
    6. Documents
    7. Witnesses
        a. Examination
        b. Cross-Examination
    8. Summaries
    9. Post-hearing briefs

G. Panel Participation

H. Contract Interpretation

I. Custom, past practice, precedent

J. Past arbitration cases on point

K. Opinion and Award

L. The Arbitrator's "Bench" Decisional Duties

M. Arbitrator's High Intensity Areas
    1. Discharge and discipline cases.
    2. Job evaluation: Work standards, i.e., problems
    3. Public sector—disputes of interest
    4. Permanent arbitrator selection
    5. Wildcat strikes
    6. Incentive systems
    7. Seniority
    8. Jurisdictional questions
    9. Overtime distribution
    10. Strikes and arbitration procedures
    11. Recesses and adjournment

N. Maintaining up-to-date awareness
    1. Arbitration awards
    2. Court decision
    3. NLRB action
    4. Negotiations

O. Conferences and Seminars

Voluntary Labor Arbitration Rules of the American Arbitration Association

As amended and in effect
April 1, 1983

1. *Agreement of Parties*—The parties shall be deemed to have made these Rules a part of their arbitration agreement whenever, in a collective bargaining agreement or submission they have provided for arbitration by the American Arbitration Association (hereinafter AAA) or under its Rules. These Rules shall apply in the form obtaining at the time the arbitration is initiated.

2. *Name of Tribunal*—Any Tribunal constituted by the parties under these Rules shall be called the Voluntary Labor Arbitration Tribunal.

3. *Administrator*—When parties agree to arbitrate under these Rules and an arbitration is instituted thereunder, they thereby authorize the AAA to administer the arbitration. The authority and obligations of the Administrator are as provided in the agreement of the parties and in these Rules.

4. *Delegation of Duties*—The duties of the AAA may be carried out through such representatives or committees as the AAA may direct.

5. *National Panel of Labor Arbitrators*—The AAA shall establish and maintain a National Panel of Labor Arbitrators and shall appoint arbitrators therefrom, as hereinafter provided.

6. *Office of Tribunal*—The general office of the Labor Arbitration Tribunal is the headquarters of the AAA, which may, however, assign the administration of an arbitration to any of its Regional Offices.

7. *Initiation under an Arbitration Clause in a Collective Bargaining Agreement*—Arbitration under an arbitration clause in a collective bar-

483

gaining agreement under these Rules may be initiated by either party in the following manner:

(a) By giving written notice to the other party of intention to arbitrate (Demand), which notice shall contain a statement setting forth the nature of the dispute and the remedy sought, and

(b) By filing at any Regional Office of the AAA three copies of said notice, together with a copy of the collective bargaining agreement, or such parts thereof as relate to the dispute, including the arbitration provisions. After the Arbitrator is appointed, no new or different claim may be submitted except with the consent of the Arbitrator and all other parties.

8. *Answer*—The party upon whom the Demand for Arbitration is made may file an answering statement with the AAA within seven days after notice from the AAA, simultaneously sending a copy to the other party. If no answer is filed within the stated time, it will be assumed that the claim is denied. Failure to file an answer shall not operate to delay the arbitration.

9. *Initiation under a Submission*—Parties to any collective bargaining agreement may initiate an arbitration under these Rules by filing at any Regional Office of the AAA two copies of a written agreement to arbitrate under these Rules (Submission), signed by the parties and setting forth the nature of the dispute and the remedy sought.

10. *Fixing of Locale*—The parties may mutually agree upon the locale where the arbitration is to be held. If the locale is not designated in the collective bargaining agreement or Submission, and if there is a dispute as to the appropriate locale, the AAA shall have the power to determine the locale and its decision shall be binding.

11. *Qualifications of Arbitrator*—No person shall serve as a neutral Arbitrator in any arbitration in which he or she has any financial personal interest in the result of the arbitration, unless the parties, in writing, waive such disqualification.

12. *Appointment from Panel*—If the parties have not appointed an Arbitrator and have not provided any other method of appointment, the Arbitrator shall be appointed in the following manner: Immediately after the filing of the Demand or Submission, the AAA shall submit simultaneously to each party an identical list of names of persons chosen from the Labor Panel. Each party shall have seven days from the mailing

date in which to cross off any names to which it objects, number the remaining names indicating the order of preference, and return the list to the AAA. If a party does not return the list within the time specified, all persons named therein shall be deemed acceptable. From among the persons who have been approved on both lists, and in accordance with the designated order of mutual preference, the AAA shall invite the acceptance of an Arbitrator to serve. If the parties fail to agree upon any of the persons named or if those named decline or are unable to act, or if for any other reason the appointment cannot be made from the submitted lists, the Administrator shall have the power to make the appointment from other members of the Panel without the submission of any additional lists.

13. *Direct Appointment by Parties*—If the agreement of the parties names an Arbitrator or specifies a method of appointing an Arbitrator, that designation or method shall be followed. The notice of appointment, with the name and address of such Arbitrator, shall be filed with the AAA by the appointing party.

If the agreement specifies a period of time within which an Arbitrator shall be appointed and any party fails to make such appointment within that period, the AAA may make the appointment.

If no period of time is specified in the agreement, the AAA shall notify the parties to make the appointment and if within seven days thereafter such Arbitrator has not been so appointed, the AAA shall make the appointment.

14. *Appointment of Neutral Arbitrator by Party-Appointed Arbitrators*—If the parties have appointed their Arbitrators, or if either or both of them have been appointed as provided in Section 13, and have authorized such Arbitrators to appoint a neutral Arbitrator within a specified time and no appointment is made within such time or any agreed extension thereof, the AAA may appoint a neutral Arbitrator, who shall act as Chairman.

If no period of time is specified for appointment of the neutral Arbitrator and the parties do not make the appointment within seven days from the date of the appointment of the last party-appointed Arbitrator, the AAA shall appoint such neutral Arbitrator, who shall act as Chairman.

If the parties have agreed that the Arbitrator shall appoint the neutral Arbitrator from the Panel, the AAA shall furnish to the party-appointed Arbitrators, in the manner prescribed in Section 12, a list selected from the Panel, and the appointment of the neutral Arbitrator shall be made as prescribed in such Section.

15. *Number of Arbitrators*—If the arbitration agreement does not specify the number of Arbitrators, the dispute shall be heard and determined by one Arbitrator, unless the parties otherwise agree.

16. *Notice to Arbitrator of Appointment*—Notice of the appointment of the neutral Arbitrator shall be mailed to the Arbitrator by the AAA and the signed acceptance of the Arbitrator shall be filed with the AAA prior to the opening of the first hearing.

17. *Disclosure by Arbitrator of Disqualification*—Prior to accepting the appointment, the prospective neutral Arbitrator shall disclose any circumstances likely to create a presumption of bias or which the Arbitrator believes might disqualify him or her as an impartial Arbitrator. Upon receipt of such information, the AAA shall immediately disclose it to the parties. If either party declines to waive the presumptive disqualification, the vacancy thus created shall be filled in accordance with the applicable provisions of these Rules.

18. *Vacancies*—If any Arbitrator should resign, die, withdraw, refuse, or be unable or disqualified to perform the duties of office, the AAA shall, on proof satisfactory to it, declare the office vacant. Vacancies shall be filled in the same manner as that governing the making of the original appointment, and the matter shall be reheard by the new Arbitrator.

19. *Time and Place of Hearing*—The Arbitrator shall fix the time and place for each hearing. At least five days prior thereto, the AAA shall mail notice of the time and place of hearing to each party, unless the parties otherwise agree.

20. *Representation by Counsel*—Any party may be represented at the hearing by counsel or by other authorized representative.

21. *Stenographic Record*—Any party may request a stenographic record by making arrangements for same through the AAA. If such transcript is agreed by the parties to be, or in appropriate cases determined by the Arbitrator to be, the official record of the proceeding, it must be made available to the Arbitrator and to the other party for inspection, at a time and place determined by the Arbitrator. The total

cost of such a record shall be shared equally by those parties that order copies.

22. *Attendance at Hearings*—Persons having a direct interest in the arbitration are entitled to attend hearings. The Arbitrator shall have the power to require the retirement of any witness or witnesses during the testimony of other witnesses. It shall be discretionary with the Arbitrator to determine the propriety of the attendance of any other persons.

23. *Adjournments*—The Arbitrator for good cause shown may adjourn the hearing upon the request of a party or upon his or her own initiative, and shall adjourn when all the parties agree thereto.

24. *Oaths*—Before proceeding with the first hearing, each Arbitrator may take an Oath of Office, and if required by law, shall do so. The Arbitrator may require witnesses to testify under oath administered by any duly qualified person, and if required by law or requested by either party, shall do so.

25. *Majority Decision*—Whenever there is more than one Arbitrator, all decisions of the Arbitrators shall be by majority vote. The award shall also be made by majority vote unless the concurrence of all is expressly required.

26. *Order to Proceedings*—A hearing shall be opened by the filing of the Oath of the Arbitrator, where required, and by the recording of the place, time, and date of hearing, the presence of the Arbitrator and parties, and counsel, if any, and the receipt by the Arbitrator of the Demand and answer, if any, of the Submission.

Exhibits, when offered by either party, may be received in evidence by the Arbitrator. The names and addresses of all witnesses and exhibits in order received shall be made a part of the record.

The Arbitrator may vary the normal procedure under which the initiating party first presents its claim, but in any case shall afford full and equal opportunity to all parties for presentation of relevant proofs.

27. *Arbitration in the Absence of a Party*—Unless the law provides to the contrary, the arbitration may proceed in the absence of any party who, after due notice, fails to be present or fails to obtain an adjournment. An award shall not be made solely on the default of a party. The Arbitrator shall require the other party to submit such evidence as may be required for the making of an award.

28. *Evidence*—The parties may offer such evidence as they desire and shall produce such additional evidence as the Arbitrator may deem necessary to an understanding and determination of the dispute. An Arbitrator authorized by law to subpoena witnesses and documents may do so independently or upon the request of any party. The Arbitrator shall be the judge of the relevancy and materiality of the evidence offered and conformity to legal rules of evidence shall not be necessary. All evidence shall be taken in the presence of all of the Arbitrators and all of the parties except where any of the parties is absent in default or has waived its right to be present.

29. *Evidence by Affidavit and Filing of Documents*—The Arbitrator may receive and consider the evidence of witnesses by affidavit, giving it only such weight as seems proper after consideration of any objections made to its admission.

All documents not filed with the Arbitrator at the hearing, but which are arranged at the hearing or subsequently by agreement of the parties to be submitted, shall be filed with the AAA for transmmission to the Arbitrator. All parties shall be afforded opportunity to examine such documents.

30. *Inspection*—Whenever the Arbitrator deems it necessary, he or she may make an inspection in connection with the subject matter of the dispute after written notice to the parties who may, if they so desire, be present at such inspection.

31. *Closing of Hearings*—The Arbitrator shall inquire of all parties whether they have any further proofs to offer or witnesses to be heard. Upon receiving negative replies, the Arbitrator shall declare the hearings closed and a minute thereof shall be recorded. If briefs or other documents are to be filed, the hearings shall be declared closed as of the final date set by the Arbitrator for filing with the AAA. The time limit within which the Arbitrator is required to make an award shall commence to run, in the absence of other agreements by the parties, upon the closing of the hearings.

32. *Reopening of Hearings*—The hearings may be reopened by the Arbitrator at will or on the motion of either party, for good cause shown, at any time before the award is made, but if the reopening of the hearings would prevent the making of the award within the specific time agreed upon by the parties in the contract out of which the controversy has arisen, the matter may not be reopened, unless both parties agree upon

the extension of such time limit. When no specific date is fixed in the contract, the Arbitrator may reopen the hearings, and the Arbitrator shall have 30 days from the closing of the reopened hearings within which to make an award.

33. *Waiver of Rules*—Any party who proceeds with the arbitration after knowledge that any provision or requirement of these Rules has not been complied with, and who fails to state an objection thereto in writing, shall be deemed to have waived the right to object.

34. *Waiver of Oral Hearings*—The parties may provide, by written agreement, for the waiver of oral hearings. If the parties are unable to agree as to the procedure, the AAA shall specify a fair and equitable procedure.

35. *Extensions of Time*—The parties may modify any period of time by mutual agreement. The AAA for good cause may extend any period of time established by these Rules, except the time for making the award. The AAA shall notify the parties of any such extension of time and its reason therefor.

36. *Serving of Notices*—Each party to a Submission or other agreement which provides for arbitration under these Rules shall be deemed to have consented and shall consent that any papers, notices, or process necessary or proper for the initiation or continuation of an arbitration under these Rules and for any court action in connection therewith or the entry of judgment on an award made thereunder, may be served upon such party (a) by mail addressed to such party or its attorney at the last known address, or (b) by personal service, within or without the state wherein the arbitration is to be held.

37. *Time of Award*—The award shall be rendered promptly by the Arbitrator and, unless otherwise agreed by the parties or specified by the law, not later than 30 days from the date of closing the hearings, or if oral hearings have been waived, then from the date of transmitting the final statements and proofs to the Arbitrator.

38. *Form of Award*—The award shall be in writing and shall be signed either by the neutral Arbitrator or by a concurring majority if there be more than one Arbitrator. The parties shall advise the AAA whenever they do not require the Arbitrator to accompany the award with an opinion.

39. *Award upon Settlement*—If the parties settle their dispute during the course of the arbitration, the Arbitrator, upon their request, may set forth the terms of the agreed settlement in an award.

40. *Delivery of Award to Parties*—Parties shall accept as legal delivery of the award the placing of the award or a true copy thereof in the mail by the AAA, addressed to such party at its last known address or to its attorney, or personal service of the award, or the filing of the award in any manner which may be prescribed by law.

41. *Release of Documents for Judicial Proceedings*—The AAA shall, upon the written request of a party, furnish to such party, at its expense, certified facsimiles of any papers in the AAA's possession that may be required in judicial proceedings relating to the arbitration.

42. *Judicial Proceedings*—The AAA is not a necessary party in judicial proceedings relating to the arbitration.

43. *Administrative Fee*—As a not-for-profit organization, the AAA shall prescribe an administrative fee schedule to compensate it for the cost of providing administrative services. The schedule in effect at the time of filing shall be applicable.

44. *Expenses*—The expense of witnesses for either side shall be paid by the party producing such witnesses.

Expenses of the arbitration, other than the cost of the stenographic record, including required traveling and other expenses of the Arbitrator and of AAA representatives, and the expenses of any witnesses or the cost of any proofs produced at the direct request of the Arbitrator, shall be borne equally by the parties unless they agree otherwise, or unless the Arbitrator in the award assesses such expenses or any part thereof against any specified party or parties.

45. *Communication with Arbitrator*—There shall be no communication between the parties and a neutral Arbitrator other than at oral hearings. Any other oral or written communications from the parties to the Arbitrator shall be directed to the AAA for transmittal to the Arbitrator.

46. *Interpretation and Application of Rules*—The Arbitrator shall interpret and apply these Rules insofar as they relate to the Arbitrator's powers and duties. When there is more than one Arbitrator and a difference arises among them concerning the meaning or application of any

such Rules, it shall be decided by majority vote. If that is unobtainable, either Arbitrator or party may refer the question to the AAA for final decision. All other Rules shall be interpreted and applied by the AAA.

Administrative Fee Schedule

Initial Administrative Fee—The initial administrative fee is $75.00 for each party, due and payable at the time of filing. No refund of the initial fee is made when a matter is withdrawn or settled after the filing of the Demand for Arbitration.

Additional Hearings—A fee of $50.00 is payable by each party for each second and subsequent hearing which is either clerked by the AAA or held in a hearing room provided by the AAA.

Postponement Fee—A fee of $40.00 is payable by a party causing postponement of any scheduled hearing.

Expedited Labor Arbitration Rules of the American Arbitration Association

As amended and in effect
April 1, 1983

1. *Agreement of Parties*—These Rules shall apply whenever the parties have agreed to arbitrate under them, in the form obtaining at the time the arbitration is initiated.

2. *Appointment of Neutral Arbitrator*—The AAA shall appoint a single neutral Arbitrator from its Panel of Labor Arbitrators, who shall hear and determine the case promptly.

3. *Initiation of Expedited Arbitration Proceeding*—Cases may be initiated by joint submission in writing, or in accordance with a collective bargaining agreement.

4. *Qualifications of Neutral Arbitrator*—No person shall serve as a neutral Arbitrator in any arbitration in which that person has any financial or personal interest in the result of the arbitration. Prior to accepting an appointment, the prospective Arbitrator shall disclose any circumstances likely to prevent a prompt hearing or to create a presumption of bias. Upon receipt of such information, the AAA shall immediately replace that Arbitrator or communicate the information to the parties.

5. *Vacancy*—The AAA is authorized to substitute another Arbitrator if a vacancy occurs or if an appointed Arbitrator is unable to serve promptly.

6. *Time and Place of Hearing*—The AAA shall fix a mutually convenient time and place of the hearing, notice of which must be given at least 24 hours in advance. Such notice may be given orally.

7. *Representation by Counsel*—Any party may be represented at the hearing by counsel or other representative.

8. *Attendance at Hearings*—Persons having a direct interest in the arbitration are entitled to attend hearings. The Arbitrator may require the retirement of any witness during the testimony of other witnesses. The Arbitrator shall determine whether any other person may attend the hearing.

9. *Adjournments*—Hearings shall be adjourned by the Arbitrator only for good cause, and an appropriate fee will be charged by the AAA against the party causing the adjournment.

10. *Oaths*—Before proceeding with the first hearing, the Arbitrators shall take an oath of office. The Arbitrator may require witnesses to testify under oath.

11. *No Stenographic Record*—There shall be no stenographic record of the proceedings.

12. *Proceedings*—The hearing shall be conducted by the Arbitrator in whatever manner will most expeditiously permit full presentation of the evidence and arguments of the parties. The Arbitrator shall make an appropriate minute of the proceedings. Normally, the hearings shall be completed within one day. In unusual circumstances and for good cause shown, the Arbitrator may schedule an additional hearing, within five days.

13. *Arbitration in the Absence of a Party*—The arbitration may proceed in the absence of any party who, after due notice, fails to be present. An award shall not be made solely on the default of a party. The Arbitrator shall require the attending party to submit supporting evidence.

14. *Evidence*—The Arbitrator shall be the sole judge of the relevancy and materiality of the evidence offered.

15. *Evidence by Affidavit and Filing of Documents*—The Arbitrator may receive and consider evidence in the form of an affidavit, but shall give appropriate weight to any objections made. All documents to be considered by the Arbitrator shall be filed at the hearing. There shall be no post hearing briefs.

16. *Close of Hearings*—The Arbitrator shall ask whether parties have any further proofs to offer or witnesses to be heard. Upon receiving negative replies, the Arbitrator shall declare and note the hearing closed.

17. *Waiver of Rules*—Any party who proceeds with the arbitration after knowledge that any provision or requirement of these Rules has not been compiled with and who fails to state objections thereto in writing shall be deemed to have waived the right to object.

18. *Serving of Notices*—Any papers or process necessary or proper for the initiation or continuation of an arbitration under these Rules and for any court action in connection therewith or for the entry of judgment on an award made thereunder, may be served upon such party (a) by mail addressed to such party or its attorney at its last known address, or (b) by personal service, or (c) as otherwise provided in these Rules.

19. *Time of Award*—The award shall be rendered promptly by the Arbitrator and, unless otherwise agreed by the parties, not later than five business days from the date of the closing of the hearing.

20. *Form of Award*—The award shall be in writing and shall be signed by the Arbitrator. If the Arbitrator determines that an opinion is necessary, it shall be in summary form.

21. *Delivery of Award to Parties*—Parties shall accept as legal delivery of the award the placing of the award or a true copy thereof in the mail by the AAA, addressed to such party at its last known address or to its attorney, or personal service of the award, or the filing of the award in any manner which may be prescribed by law.

22. *Expenses*—The expenses of witnesses for either side shall be paid by the party producing such witnesses.

23. *Interpretation and Application of Rules*—The Arbitrator shall interpret and apply these Rules insofar as they relate to the Arbitrator's powers and duties. All other Rules shall be interpreted and applied by the AAA, as Administrator.

Administrative Fee Schedule

Initial Administrative Fee—The initial administrative fee is $75.00 for each party, due and payable at the time of filing. No refund of the initial fee is made when a matter is withdrawn or settled after the filing of the Demand for Arbitration.

Additional Hearings—A fee of $50.00 is payable by each party for each second and subsequent hearing which is either clerked by the AAA or held in a hearing room provided by the AAA.

Postponement Fee—A fee of $40.00 is payable by a party causing a postponement of any scheduled hearing.

Arbitration Rules of the Federal Mediation and Conciliation Service

Part 1404—Arbitration Services

Subpart A—Arbitration Policy; Administration of Roster

Subpart B—Roster of Arbitrators; Admission and Retention

Subpart C—Procedures for Arbitration Services

AUTHORITY: Sec. 202, 61 Stat. 153, as amended; 29 U.S.C. 172, and interpret or apply sec. 3, 80 Stat. 250, sec. 203, 61 Stat. 153; 5 U.S.C. 552, 29 U.S.C. 173.

SOURCE: 44 FR 13008, Mar. 9, 1979, unless otherwise noted.

Subpart A—Arbitration Policy; Administration of Roster

§ 1404.1 *Scope and authority.*

This chapter is issued by the Federal Mediation and Conciliation Service (FMCS) under Title II of the Labor Management Relations Act of 1947 (Pub. L. 80-101) as amended in 1959 (Pub. L. 86-257) and 1974 (Pub. L. 93-360). The chapter applies to all arbitrators listed on the FMCS Roster of Arbitrators, to all applicants for listing on the Roster, and to all persons or parties seeking to obtain from FMCS either names or panels of names of arbitrators listed on the Roster in connection with disputes which are to be submitted to arbitration or fact-finding.

§ 1404.2 *Policy.*

The labor policy of the United States is designed to promote the settlement of issues between employers and represented employees through the processes of collective bargaining and voluntary arbitration. This policy encourages the use of voluntary arbitration to resolve disputes over the interpretation or application of collective bargaining agreements. Voluntary arbitration and fact-finding in disputes and disagreements over establishment or modification of contract terms are important features of constructive labor-management relations, as alternatives to economic strife in the settlement of labor disputes.

§ 1404.3 *Administrative responsibilities.*

(a) *Director.* The Director of FMCS has ultimate responsibility for all aspects of FMCS arbitration activities and is the final agency authority on all questions concerning the Roster or FMCS arbitration procedures.

(b) *Office of Arbitration Services.* The Office of Arbitration Services (OAS) maintains a Roster of Arbitrators (the "Roster"); administers Subpart C of these regulations (Procedures for Arbitration Services); assists, promotes, and cooperates in the establishment of programs for training and developing new arbitrators; collects information and statistics concerning the arbitration function, and performs other tasks in connection with the function that may be assigned by the Director.

(c) *Arbitrator Review Board.* The Arbitrator Review Board (the "Board") shall consist of a presiding officer and such members and alternate members as the Director may appoint, and who shall serve at the Director's pleasure and may be removed at any time. The Board shall be composed entirely of full-time officers or employees of the Federal Government. The Board shall establish its own procedures for carrying out its duties.

(1) *Duties of the Board.* The Board shall:

(i) Review the qualifications of all applicants for listing on the Roster, interpreting and applying the criteria set forth in § 1404.5;

(ii) Review the status of all persons whose continued eligibility for listing on the Roster has been questioned under § 1404.5;

(iii) Make recommendations to the Director regarding acceptance or rejection of applicants for listing on the Roster, or regarding withdrawal of listing on the Roster for any of the reasons set forth herein.

Subpart B—Roster of Arbitrators; Admission and Retention

§ 1404.4   *Roster and Status of Members.*

(a) *The Roster.* The FMCS shall maintain a Roster of labor arbitrators consisting of persons who meet the criteria for listing contained in § 1404.5 and whose names have not been removed from the Roster in accordance with § 1404.5(d).

(b) *Adherence to Standards and Requirements.* Persons listed on the Roster shall comply with the FMCS rules and regulations pertaining to arbitration and with such guidelines and procedures as may be issued by OAS pursuant to Subpart C of this part. Arbitrators are also expected to conform to the ethical standards and procedures set forth in the Code of Professional Responsibility for Arbitrators of Labor Management Disputes, as approved by the Joint Steering Committee of the National Academy of Arbitrators.

(c) *Status of Arbitrators.* Persons who are listed on the Roster and are selected or appointed to hear arbitration matters or to serve as factfinders do not become employees of the Federal Government by virtue of their selection or appointment. Following selection or appointment, the arbitrator's relationship is solely with the parties to the dispute, except that arbitrators are subject to certain reporting requirements and to standards of conduct as set forth in this part.

(d) *Role of FMCS.* FMCS has no power to:

(1) Compel parties to arbitrate or agree to arbitration;

(2) Enforce an agreement to arbitrate;

(3) Compel parties to agree to a particular arbitrator;

(4) Influence, alter or set aside decisions of arbitrators listed on the Roster:

(5) Compel, deny or modify payment of compensation to an arbitrator.

(e) *Nominations and Panels.* On request of the parties to an agreement to arbitrate or engage in fact-finding, or where arbitration or fact-finding may be provided for by statute, OAS will provide names or panels of names without charge. Procedures for obtaining these services are contained in Subpart C of this part. Neither the submission of a nomination or panel nor the appointment of an arbitrator constitutes a determination by FMCS that an agreement to arbitrate or enter fact-finding proceedings exists; nor does such action constitute a ruling that the matter in controversy is arbitrable under any agreement.

(f) *Rights of persons listed on the Roster.* No person shall have any right to be listed or to remain listed on the Roster. FMCS retains the authority and responsibility to assure that the needs of the parties using its facilities are served. To accomplish this purpose it may establish procedures for the preparation of arbitrators or fact-finders which include consideration of such factors as background and experience, availability, acceptability, geographical location and the expressed preferences of the parties.

§ 1404.5 *Listing on the Roster; Criteria for listing and retention.*

Persons seeking to be listed on the Roster must complete and submit an application form which may be obtained from the Office of Arbitration Services. Upon receipt of an executed form, OAS will review the application, assure that it is complete, make such inquiries as are necessary, and submit the application to the Arbitrator Review Board. The Board will review the completed applications under the criteria set forth in paragraphs (a), (b) and (c) of this section, and will forward to the Director its recommendation on each applicant. The Director makes all final decisions as to whether an applicant may be listed. Each applicant shall be notified in writing of the Director's decision and the reasons therefore.

(a) *General Criteria.* Applicants for the Roster will be listed on the Roster upon a determination that they:

(1) Are experienced, competent and acceptable in decision-making roles in the resolution of labor relations disputes; or

(2) Have extensive experience in relevant positions in collective bargaining; and

(3) Are capable of conducting an orderly hearing, can analyze testimony and exhibits and can prepare clear and concise findings and awards within reasonable time limits.

(b) *Proof of Qualification.* The qualifications listed in paragraph (a) of this section are preferably demonstrated by the submission of actual arbitration awards prepared by the applicant while serving as an impartial arbitrator chosen by the parties to disputes. Equivalent experience acquired in training, internship or other development programs, or experience such as that acquired as a hearing officer or judge in labor relations controversies may also be considered by the Board.

(c) *Advocacy*—(1) *Definition.* An advocate is a person who represents employers, labor organizations, or individuals as an employee, attorney or consultant, in matters of labor relations, including but not limited to the subjects of union representation and recognition matters, collective bargaining arbitration, unfair labor practices, equal employment opportunity and other areas generally recognized as constituting labor relations. The definition includes representatives of employers or employees in individual cases or controversies involving workmen's compensation, occupational health or safety, minimum wage or other labor standards matters. The definition of advocate also includes a person who is directly associated with an advocate in a business or professional relationship as, for example, partners or employees of a law firm.

(2) *Eligibility.* Except in the case of persons listed on the Roster before November 17, 1976, no person who is an advocate, as defined above, may be listed. No person who was listed on the Roster at any time who was not an advocate when listed or who did not divulge advocacy at the time of listing may continue to be listed after becoming an advocate or after the fact of advocacy is revealed.

(d) *Duration of listing, retention.* Initial listing may be for a period not to exceed three years, and may be renewed thereafter for periods not to exceed two years, provided upon review that the listing is not canceled by the Director as set forth below. Notice of cancellation may be given to the member whenever the member:

(1) No longer meets the criteria for admission;

(2) Has been repeatedly and flagrantly delinquent in submitting awards;

(3) Has refused to make reasonable and periodic reports to FMCS, as required in Subpart C of this part, concerning activities pertaining to arbitration;

(4) Has been the subject of complaints by parties who use FMCS facilities and the Director, after appropriate inquiry, concludes that just cause for cancellation has been shown.

(5) Is determined by the Director to be unacceptable to the parties who use FMCS arbitration facilities; the Director may base a determination of unacceptability on FMCS records showing the number of times the arbitrator's name has been proposed to the parties and the number of times it has been selected.

No listing may be canceled without at least sixty days notice of the reasons for the proposed removal, unless the Director determines that the FMCS or the parties will be harmed by continued listing. In such cases an arbitrator's listing may be suspended without notice or delay pending final determination in accordance with these procedures. The member shall in either case have an opportunity to submit a written response showing why the listing should not be cancelled. The Director may, at his discretion, appoint a hearing officer to conduct an inquiry into the facts of any proposed cancellation and to make recommendations to the Director.

§ 1404.6 *Freedom of choice.*

Nothing contained herein should be construed to limit the rights of parties who use FMCS arbitration facilities jointly to select any arbitrator or arbitration procedure acceptable to them.

Subpart C—Procedures for Arbitration Services

§ 1404.10 *Procedures for requesting arbitration panels.*

The Office of Arbitration Services has been delegated the responsibility for administering all requests for arbitration services under these regulations.

(a) The Service will refer a panel of arbitrators to the parties upon request. The Service prefers to act upon a joint request which should be addressed to the Federal Mediation and Conciliation Service, Washington, D.C. 20427, Attention: Office of Arbitration Services. In the event that the request is made by only one party, the Service will submit a panel; however, any submission of a panel should not be construed as anything more than compliance with a request and does not necessarily reflect the contractual requirements of the parties.

(b) The parties are urged to use the Request for Arbitration Panel form (R-43) which has been prepared by the Service and is available in quantity at all FMCS regional offices and field stations or upon request to the Office of Arbitration Services, 2100 K Street, Washington, D.C. 20427. The form R-43 is reproduced herein for purposes of identification.

(c) A brief statement of the issues in dispute should accompany the request to enable the Service to submit the names of arbitrators qualified for the issues involved. The request should also include a current copy of the arbitration section of the collective bargaining agreement or stipulation to arbitrate.

(d) If form R-43 is not utilized, the parties may request a panel by letter which must include the names, addresses, and phone numbers of the parties, the location of the contemplated hearing, the issue in dispute, the number of names desired on the panel, the industry involved and any special qualifications of the panel or special requirement desired.

§ 1404.11   *Arbitrability.*

Where either party claims that a dispute is not subject to arbitration, the Service will not decide the merit of such claim.

§ 1404.12   *Nominations of arbitrators.*

(a) When the parties have been unable to agree on an arbitrator, the Service will submit to the parties on request the names of seven arbitrators unless the applicable collective bargaining agreement provides for a different number, or unless the parties themselves request a different number. Together with the submission of a panel of arbitrators, the Service will furnish a biographical sketch for each member of the panel. This sketch states the background, qualifications, experience, and per diem fee established by the arbitrator. It states the existence, if any, of other fees such as cancellation, postponement, rescheduling or administrative fees.

(b) When a panel is submitted, an FMCS control case number is assigned. All future communication between the parties and the Service should refer to the case number.

(c) The Service considers many factors when selecting names for inclusion on a panel, but the agreed-upon wishes of the parties are paramount. Special qualifications of arbitrators experienced in certain issues or industries, or possessing certain backgrounds, may be identified for purposes of submitting panels to accommodate the parties. The Service may also consider such things as general acceptability, geographical location, general experience, availability, size of fee, and the need to expose new arbitrators to the selection process in preparing

[6732-01-C]

FMCS Form R-43
Sep. 1975

FEDERAL MEDIATION AND CONCILIATION SERVICE
WASHINGTON, D.C. 20427

Form Approved
OMB No.   23 R007

REQUEST FOR ARBITRATION PANEL

To Director, Arbitration Services
    Federal Mediation and Conciliation Service
    Washington, D.C. 20427

Date _____

1.   (For Company)

Name of Company	_____
Name and Address of Representative to Receive Panel	_____ (NAME)
	_____ (STREET)
	_____ (CITY, STATE, ZIP)
Telephone (include area code)	_____

2.   (For Union)

Name of Union and Local No.	_____
Name and Address of Representative to Receive Panel	_____ (NAME)
	_____ (STREET)
	_____ (CITY, STATE, ZIP)
Telephone (include area code)	_____

3. Site of Dispute _____
   (CITY, STATE, ZIP)

4. Type of Issue _____
   (DISCHARGE, HOLIDAY PAY, SICK LEAVE, ETC.)

5. A panel of seven (7) names is usually provided; if you desire a different number, please indicate _____

6. Type of Industry

   ☐ Manufacturing   ☐ Federal Government   ☐ Public Utilities, Communications, Transportation (including trucking)

   ☐ Construction   ☐ State Government

   ☐ Mining, Agriculture and Finance   ☐ Local Government   ☐ Retail, Wholesale and Service Industries

   ☐ Other (Specify) _____

7. Special Requirements _____
   (SPECIAL ARBITRATOR QUALIFICATIONS, TIME LIMITATIONS ON HEARING OR DECISION, GEOGRAPHICAL RESTRICTIONS, ETC)

8. Signatures

   _____
   (COMPANY)

   _____
   (UNION)

Although the FMCS prefers to act upon a joint request of the parties, a submission will be made based on the request of a single party. However, any submission of a panel should not be construed as anything more than compliance with a request and does not reflect on the substance or arbitrability of the issue in dispute.

Additional forms may be obtained from the Federal Mediation and Conciliation Service or any FMCS Regional Office. See list on reverse of Copy No. 3.

To be retained by party filing request

panels. The Service has no obligation to put an individual on any given panel, or on a minimum number of panels in any fixed period, such as a month or a year.

(1) It at any time both parties request for valid reason, that a name or names be omitted from a panel, such name or names will be omitted, unless they are excessive in number.

(2) If at any time both parties request that a name or names be included on a panel, such name or names will be included.

(3) If only one party requests that a name or names be omitted from a panel, or that specific individuals be added to the panel, such request shall not be honored.

(4) If the issue described in the request appears to require special technical experience or qualifications, arbitrators who possess such qualifications will, where possible, be included on the panel submitted to the parties.

(5) In almost all cases, an arbitrator is chosen from one panel. However, if either party requests another panel, the Service shall comply with the request providing that an additional panel is permissible under the terms of the agreement or the other party so agrees. Requests for more than two panels must be accompanied by a statement of explanation and will be considered on a case-by-case basis.

§ 1404.13   *Selection and appointment of arbitrators.*

(a) The parties should notify the OAS of their selection of an arbitrator. The arbitrator, upon notification by the parties, shall notify the OAS of his selection and willingness to serve. Upon notification of the parties' selection of an arbitrator, the Service will make a formal appointment of the arbitrator.

(b) Where the contract is silent on the manner of selecting arbitrators, the parties may wish to consider one of the following methods for selection of an arbitrator from a panel:

(1) Each party alternately strikes a name from the submitted panel until one remains.

(2) Each party advises the Service of its order of preference by numbering each name on the panel and submitting the numbered list in writing to OAS. The name on the panel that has the lowest accumulated numerical number will be appointed.

(3) Informal agreement of the parties by whatever method they choose.

(c) The Service will, on joint or unilateral request of the parties, submit a panel or, when the applicable collective bargaining agreement authorizes, will make a direct appointment of an arbitrator. Submission of a panel or name signifies nothing more than compliance with a request and in no way constitutes a determination by the Service that the parties are obligated to arbitrate the dispute in question. Resolution of disputes as to the propriety of such a submission or appointment rests solely with the parties.

(d) The arbitrator, upon notification of appointment, is required to communicate with the parties immediately to arrange for preliminary matters, such as date and place of hearing.

§ 1404.14   *Conduct of hearings.*

All proceedings conducted by the arbitrator shall be in conformity with the contractual obligations of the parties. The arbitrator is also expected to conduct all proceedings in conformity with § 1404.4(b). The conduct of the arbitration proceeding is under the arbitrator's jurisdiction and control and the arbitrator's decision is to be based upon the evidence and testimony presented at the hearing or otherwise incorporated in the record of the proceeding. The arbitrator may, unless prohibited by law, proceed in the absence of any party who, after due notice, fails to be present or to obtain a postponement. An award rendered in an *ex parte* proceeding of this nature must be based upon evidence presented to the arbitrator.

§ 1404.15   *Decision and award.*

(a) Arbitrators are encouraged to render awards not later than 60 days from the date of the closing of the record as determined by the arbitrator, unless otherwise agreed upon by the parties or specified by law. A failure to render timely awards reflects upon the performance of an arbitrator and may lead to his removal from the FMCS roster.

(b) The parties should inform the OAS whenever a decision is unduly delayed. The arbitrator shall notify the OAS if and when the arbitrator (1) cannot schedule, hear and determine issues promptly, or (2) learns a dispute has been settled by the parties prior to the decision.

(c) After an award has been submitted to the parties, the arbitrator is required to submit a Fee and Award Statement, form R-19 showing a breakdown of the fee and expense charges so that the Service may be in a position to review conformance with stated charges under § 1404.12(a). Filing the Statement within 15 days after rendering an award is required of all arbitrators. The Statements are not used for the purpose of compelling payment of fees.

(d) The Service encourages the publication of arbitration awards. However, the Service expects arbitrators it has nominated or appointed not to give publicity to awards they issue if objected to by one of the parties.

[44 FR 13008, Mar. 9, 1979, as amended at 47 FR 9823, Mar. 8, 1982]

§ 1404.16   *Fees and charges of arbitrators.*

(a) No administrative or filing fee is charged by the Service. The current policy of the Service permits each of its nominees or appointees to charge a per diem fee and other predetermined fees for services, the amount of which has been certified in advance to the Service. Each arbitrator's maximum per diem fee and the existence of other predetermined fees, if any, are set forth on a biographical sketch which is sent to the parties when panels are submitted and are the controlling fees. The arbitrator shall not change any fee or add charges without giving at least 30 days advance notice to the Service.

(b) In cases involving unusual amounts of time and expenses relative to pre-hearing and post-hearing administration of a particular case, an administrative charge may be made by the arbitrator.

(c) All charges other than those specified by § 1404.16(a) shall be divulged to and agreement obtained by the arbitrator with the parties immediately after appointment.

(d) The Service requests that it be notified of any arbitrator's deviation from the policies expressed herein. However, the Service will not attempt to resolve any fee dispute.

§ 1404.17   *Reports and biographical sketches.*

(a) Arbitrators listed on the Roster shall execute and return all documents, forms and reports required by the Service. They shall also keep the Service informed of changes of address, telephone number, availability, and of any business or other connection or relationship which involves labor-management relations, or which creates or gives the appearance of advocacy as defined in § 1404.4(c)(1).

(b) The Service may require each arbitrator listed on the Roster to prepare at the time of initial listing, and to revise, biographical information in accordance with a format to be provided by the Service at the time of initial listing or biennial review. Arbitrators may also request revision of biographical information at other times to reflect changes in fees, the existence of additional charges, address, experience and background, or other relevant data. The Service reserves the right to decide and approve the format and content of biographical sketches.

Code of Professional Responsibility for Arbitrators of Labor-Management Disputes

of the
National Academy of Arbitrators
American Arbitration Association
Federal Mediation and Conciliation Service

Foreword

This "Code of Professional Responsibility for Arbitrators of Labor-Management Disputes" supersedes the "Code of Ethics and Procedural Standards of Labor-Management Arbitration," approved in 1951 by a Committee of the American Arbitration Association, by the National Academy of Arbitrators, and by representatives of the Federal Mediation and Conciliation Service.

Revision of the 1951 Code was initiated officially by the same three groups in October, 1972. The Joint Steering Committee named below was designated to draft a proposal.

Reasons for Code revision should be noted briefly. Ethical considerations and procedural standards are sufficiently intertwined to warrant combining the subject matter of Parts I and II of the 1951 Code under the caption of "Professional Responsibility." It has seemed advisable to eliminate admonitions to the parties (Part III of the 1951 Code) except as they appear incidentally in connection with matters primarily involving responsibilities of arbitrators. Substantial growth of third party participation in dispute resolution in the public sector requires consideration. It appears that arbitration of new contract terms may become more significant. Finally, during the interval of more than two decades, new problems have emerged as private sector grievance arbitration has matured and has become more diversified.

JOINT STEERING COMMITTEE

. . .

November 30, 1974

Preamble

Background

Voluntary arbitration rests upon the mutual desire of management and labor in each collective bargaining relationship to develop procedures for dispute settlement which meet their own particular needs and obligations. No two voluntary systems, therefore, are likely to be identical in practice. Words used to describe arbitrators (Arbitrator, Umpire, Impartial Chairman, Chairman of Arbitration Board, etc.) may suggest typical approaches but actual differences within any general type of arrangement may be as great as distinctions often made among the several types.

Some arbitration and related procedures, however, are not the product of voluntary agreement. These procedures, primarily but not exclusively applicable in the public sector, sometimes utilize other third party titles (Fact-Finder, Impasse Panel, Board of Inquiry, etc.). These procedures range all the way from arbitration prescribed by statute to arrangements substantially indistinguishable from voluntary procedures.

The standards of professional responsibility set forth in this Code are deisgned to guide the impartial third partly serving in these diverse labor-management relationships.

Scope of Code

This Code is a privately developed set of standards of professional behavior. It applies to voluntary arbitration of labor-management grievance disputes and of disputes concerning new or revised contract terms. Both "ad hoc" and "permanent" varieties of voluntary arbitration, private and public sector, are included. To the extent relevant in any specific case, it also applies to advisory arbitration, impasse resolution panels, arbitration prescribed by statutes, fact-finding, and other special procedures.

The word "arbitrator," as used hereinafter in the Code, is intended to apply to any impartial person, irrespective of specific title, who serves in a labor-management dispute procedure in which there is conferred authority to decide issues or to make formal recommendations.

The Code is not designed to apply to mediation or conciliation, as distinguished from arbitration, nor to other procedures in which the third party is not authorized in advance to make decisions or recommendations. It does not apply to partisan representatives or tripartite boards. It does not apply to commercial arbitration or to other uses of arbitration outside the labor-management dispute area.

Format of Code

Bold Face type, sometimes including explanatory material, is used to set forth general principles. *Italics* are used for amplification of general principles. Ordinary type is used primarily for illustrative or explanatory comment.

Application of Code

Faithful adherence by an arbitrator to this Code is basic to professional responsibility.

The National Academy of Arbitrators will expect its members to be governed in their professional conduct by this Code and stands ready, through its Committee on Ethics and Grievances, to advise its members as to the Code's interpretation. The American Arbitration Association and the Federal Mediation and Conciliation Service will apply the Code to the arbitrators on their rosters in cases handled under their respective appointment or referral procedures. Other arbitrators and administrative agencies may, of course, voluntarily adopt the Code and be governed by it.

In interpreting the Code and applying it to charges of professional misconduct, under existing or revised procedures of the National Academy of Arbitrators and of the administrative agencies, it should be recognized that while some of its standards express ethical principles basic to the arbitration profession, others rest less on ethics than on considerations of good practice. Experience has shown the difficulty of drawing rigid lines of distinction between ethics and good practice and this Code does not attempt to do so. Rather, it leaves the gravity of alleged misconduct and the extent to which ethical standards have been violated to be assessed in the light of the facts and circumstances of each particular case.

1. Arbitrator's Qualifications and Responsibilities to the Profession

A. General Qualifications

1. Essential personal qualifications of an arbitrator include honesty, integrity, impartiality and general competence in labor relations matters.

An arbitrator must demonstrate ability to exercise these personal qualities faithfully and with good judgment, both in procedural matters and in substantive decisions.

    a. Selection by mutual agreement of the parties or direct designation by an administrative agency are the effective methods of appraisal of this combination of an individual's potential and performance, rather than the fact of placement on a roster of an administrative agency or membership in a professional association of arbitrators.

2. An arbitrator must be as ready to rule for one party as for the other on each issue, either in a single case or in a group of cases. Compromise by an arbitrator for the sake of attempting to achieve personal acceptability is unprofessional.

B. *Qualifications for Special Cases*

1. An arbitrator must decline appointment, withdraw, or request technical assistance when he or she decides that a case is beyond his or her competence.

    a. An arbitrator may be qualified generally but not for specialized assignments. Some types of incentive, work standard, job evaluation, welfare program, pension, or insurance cases may require specialized knowledge, experience or competence. Arbitration of contract terms also may require distinctive background and experience.

    b. Effective appraisal by an administrative agency or by an arbitrator of the need for special qualifications requires that both parties make known the special nature of the case prior to appointment of the arbitrator.

C. *Responsibilities to the Profession*

1. An arbitrator must uphold the dignity and integrity of the office and endeavor to provide effective service to the parties.

    a. To this end, an arbitrator should keep current with principles, practices and developments that are relevant to his or her own field of arbitration practice.

2. An experienced arbitrator should cooperate in the training of new arbitrators.

3. An arbitrator must not advertise or solicit arbitration assignments.

a. It is a matter or personal preference whether an arbitrator includes "Labor Arbitrator" or similar notation on letterheads, cards, or announcements. *It is inappropriate, however, to include memberships or offices held in professional societies or listings on rosters of administrative agencies.*

b. *Information provided for published biographical sketches, as well as that supplied to administrative agencies, must be accurate.* Such information may include membership in professional organizations (including reference to significant offices held), and list-ings on rosters of administrative agencies.

2. Responsibilities to the Parties

A. *Recognition of Diversity in Arbitration Arrangements*

1. An arbitrator should conscientiously endeavor to understand and observe, to the extent consistent with professional responsibility, the significant principles governing each arbitration system in which he or she serves.

a. Recognition of special features of a particular arbitration arrangement can be essential with respect to procedural matters and may influence other aspects of the arbitration process.

2. Such understanding does not relieve an arbitrator from a corollary responsibility to seek to discern and refuse to lend approval or consent to any collusive attempt by the parties to use arbitration for an improper purpose.

B. *Required Disclosures*

1. Before accepting an appointment, an arbitrator must disclose directly or through the administrative agency involved, any current or past managerial, representational, or consultative relationship with any company or union involved in a proceeding in which he or she is being considered for appointment or has been tentatively designated to serve. Disclosure must also be made of any pertinent pecuniary interest.

a. The duty to disclose includes membership on a Board of Directors, full-time or part-time service as a representative or advocate, consultation work for a fee, current stock or bond ownership (other than mutual fund shares or appropriate trust arrangements) or any other pertinent form of managerial, financial or immediate family interest in the company or union involved.

2. When an arbitrator is serving concurrently as an advocate for or representative of other companies or unions in labor relations matters, or has done so in recent years, he or she must disclose such activities before accepting appointment as an arbitrator.

An arbitrator must disclose such activities to an administrative agency if he or she is on that agency's active roster or seeks placement on a roster. Such disclosure then satisfies this requirement for cases handled under that agency's referral.

a. It is not necessary to disclose names of clients or other specific details. It is necessary to indicate the general nature of the labor relations advocacy or representational work involved, whether for companies or unions or both, and a reasonable approximation of the extent of such activity.

b. *An arbitrator on an administrative agency's roster has a continuing obligation to notify the agency of any significant changes pertinent to this requirement.*

c. When an administrative agency is not involved, an arbitrator must make such disclosure directly unless he or she is certain that both parties to the case are fully aware of such activities.

3. An arbitrator must not permit personal relationships to affect decision-making.

Prior to acceptance of an appointment, an arbitrator must disclose to the parties or to the administrative agency involved any close personal relationship or other circumstance, in addition to those specifically mentioned earlier in this section, which might reasonably raise a question as to the arbitrator's impartiality.

a. Arbitrators establish personal relationships with many company and union representatives, with fellow arbitrators, and with fellow members of various professional associations. There should be no attempt to be secretive about such friendships or acquaintances but disclosure is not necessary unless some feature of a particular relationship might reasonably appear to impair impartiality.

4. If the circumstances requiring disclosure are not known to the arbitrator prior to acceptance of appointment, disclosure must be made when such circumstances become known to the arbitrator.

5. The burden of disclosure rests on the arbitrator. After appropriate disclosure, the arbitrator may serve if both parties so desire. If the arbitrator believes or perceives that there is a

clear conflict of interest, he or she should withdraw, irrespective of the expressed desires of the parties.

C. *Privacy of Arbitration*

1. All significant aspects of an arbitration proceeding must be treated by the arbitrator as confidential unless this requirement is waived by both parties or disclosure is required or permitted by law.

a. Attendance at hearings by persons not representing the parties or invited by either or both of them should be permitted only when the parties agree or when an applicable law requires or permits. Occasionally, special circumstances may require that an arbitrator rule on such matters as attendance and degree of participation of counsel selected by a grievant.

b. *Discussion of a case at any time by an arbitrator with persons not involved directly should be limited to situations where advance approval or consent of both parties is obtained or where the identity of the parties and details of the case are sufficiently obscured to eliminate any realistic probability of identification.*

A commonly recognized exception is discussion of a problem in a case with a fellow arbitrator. *Any such discussion does not relieve the arbitrator who is acting in the case from sole responsibility for the decision and the discussion must be considered as confidential.*

Discussion of aspects of a case in a classroom without prior specific approval of the parties is not a violation provided the arbitrator is satisfied that there is no breach of essential confidentiality.

c. *It is a violation of professional responsibility for an arbitrator to make public an award without the consent of the parties.*

An arbitrator may request but not press the parties for consent to publish an opinion. Such a request should normally not be made until after the award has been issued to the parties.

d. It is not improper for an arbitrator to donate arbitration files to a library of a college, university or similar institution without prior consent of all the parties involved. When the circumstances permit, there should be deleted from such donations any cases concerning which one or both of the parties have expressed a desire for privacy. As an additional safeguard, an arbitrator may also decide to withhold recent cases or indicate to the donee a time interval before such cases can be made generally available.

e. *Applicable laws, regulations, or practices of the parties may permit or even require exceptions to the above noted principles of privacy.*

D. Personal Relationships with the Parties

1. An arbitrator must make every reasonable effort to conform to arrangements required by an administrative agency or mutually desired by the parties regarding communications and personal relationships with the parties.

a. *Only an "arm's-length" relationship may be acceptable to the parties in some arbitration arrangements or may be required by the rules of an administrative agency. The arbitrator should then have no contact of consequence with representatives of either party while handling a case without the other party's presence or consent.*

b. *In other situations, both parties may want communications and personal relationships to be less formal. It is then appropriate for the arbitrator to respond accordingly.*

E. Jurisdiction

1. An arbitrator must observe faithfully both the limitations and inclusions of the jurisdiction conferred by an agreement or other submission under which he or she serves.

2. A direct settlement by the parties of some or all issues in a case, at any stage of the proceedings, must be accepted by the arbitrator as relieving him or her of further jurisdiction over such issues.

F. Mediation by an Arbitrator

1. When the parties wish at the outset to give an arbitrator authority both to mediate and to decide or submit recommendations regarding residual issues, if any, they should so advise the arbitrator prior to appointment. If the appointment is accepted, the arbitrator must perform a mediation role consistent with the circumstances of the case.

a. Direct appointments, also, may require a dual role as mediator and arbitrator of residual issues. This is most likely to occur in some public sector cases.

2. When a request to mediate is first made after appointment, the arbitrator may either accept or decline a mediation role.

a. *Once arbitration has been invoked, either party normally has a right to insist that the process be continued to decision.*

b. *If one party requests that the arbitrator mediate and the other party objects, the arbitrator should decline the request.*

c. *An arbitrator is not precluded from making a suggestion that he or she mediate. To avoid the possibility of improper pressure, the arbitrator should not so suggest unless it can be discerned that both parties are likely to be receptive. In any event, the arbitrator's suggestion should not be pursued unless both parties readily agree.*

G. Reliance by an Arbitrator on Other Arbitration Awards or on Independent Research

1. An arbitrator must assume full personal responsibility for the decision in each case decided.

a. *The extent, if any, to which an arbitrator properly may rely on precedent, on guidance of other awards, or on independent research is dependent primarily on the policies of the parties on these matters, as expressed in the contract, or other agreement, or at the hearing.*

b. When the mutual desires of the parties are not known or when the parties express differing opinions or policies, the arbitrator may exercise discretion as to these matters, consistent with acceptance of full personal responsibility for the award.

H. Use of Assistants

1. An arbitrator must not delegate any decision-making function to another person without consent of the parties.

a. *Without prior consent of the parties, an arbitrator may use the services of an assistant for research, clerical duties, or preliminary drafting under the direction of the arbitrator, which does not involve the delegation of any decision-making function.*

b. *If an arbitrator is unable, because of time limitations or other reasons, to handle all decision-making aspects of a case, it is not a violation of professional responsibility to suggest to the parties an allocation of responsibility between the arbitrator and an assistant or associate. The arbitrator must not exert pressure on the parties to accept such a suggestion.*

I. Consent Awards

1. Prior to issuance of an award, the parties may jointly request the arbitrator to include in the award certain agreements between them, concerning some or all of the issues. If the arbitrator believes that a suggested award is proper, fair, sound, and lawful, it is consistent with professional responsibility to adopt it.

   a. *Before complying with such a request, an arbitrator must be certain that he or she understands the suggested settlement adequately in order to be able to appraise its terms. If it appears that pertinent facts or circumstances may not have been disclosed, the arbitrator should take the initiative to assure that all significant aspects of the case are fully understood. To this end, the arbitrator may request additional specific information and may question witnesses at a hearing.*

J. Avoidance of Delay

1. It is a basic professional responsibility of an arbitrator to plan his or her work schedule so that present and future commitments will be fulfilled in a timely manner.

   a. *When planning is upset for reasons beyond the control of the arbitrator, he or she, nevertheless, should exert every reasonable effort to fulfill all commitments. If this is not possible, prompt notice at the arbitrator's initiative should be given to all parties affected. Such notices should include reasonably accurate estimates of any additional time required. To the extent possible, priority should be given to cases in process so that other parties may make alternative arbitration arrangements.*

2. An arbitrator must cooperate with the parties and with any administrative agency involved in avoiding delays.

   a. *An arbitrator on the active roster of an administrative agency must take the initiative in advising the agency of any scheduling difficulties that he or she can foresee.*

   b. *Requests for services, whether received directly or through an administrative agency, should be declined if the arbitrator is unable to schedule a hearing as soon as the parties wish. If the parties, nevertheless, jointly desire to obtain the services of the arbitrator and the arbitrator agrees, arrangements should be made by agreement that the arbitrator confidently expects to fulfill.*

c. *An arbitrator may properly seek to persuade the parties to alter or eliminate arbitration procedures or tactics that cause unnecessary delay.*

3. Once the case record has been closed, an arbitrator must adhere to the time limits for an award, as stipulated in the labor agreement or as provided by regulation of an administrative agency or as otherwise agreed.

a. *If an appropriate award cannot be rendered within the required time, it is incumbent on the arbitrator to seek an extension of time from the parties.*

b. If the parties have agreed upon abnormally short time limits for an award after a case is closed, the arbitrator should be so advised by the parties or by the administrative agency involved, prior to acceptance of appointment.

K. *Fees and Expenses*

1. An arbitrator occupies a position of trust in respect to the parties and the administrative agencies. In charging for services and expenses, the arbitrator must be governed by the same high standards of honor and integrity that apply to all other phases of his or her work.

An arbitrator must endeavor to keep total charges for services and expenses reasonable and consistent with the nature of the case or cases decided.

Prior to appointment, the parties should be aware of or be able readily to determine all significant aspects of an arbitrator's bases for charges for fees and expenses.

a. *Services Not Primarily Chargeable on a Per Diem Basis*

By agreement with the parties, the financial aspects of many "permanent" arbitration assignments, of some interest disputes, and of some "ad hoc" grievance assignments do not include a per diem fee for services as a primary part of the total understanding. *In such situations, the arbitrator must adhere faithfully to all agreed-upon arrangements governing fees and expenses.*

b. *Per Diem Basis for Charges for Services*

(1) *When an arbitrator's charges for services are determined primarily by a stipulated per diem fee, the arbitrator should establish in advance his or her bases for application of such per diem fee and for determination of reimbursable expenses.*

Practices established by an arbitrator should include the basis for charges, if any, for:

(a) hearing time, including the application of the stipulated basic per diem hearing fee to hearing days of varying lengths;

(b) study time;

(c) necessary travel time when not included in charges for hearing time;

(d) postponement or cancellation of hearings by the parties and the circumstances in which such charges will normally be assessed or waived;

(e) office overhead expenses (secretarial, telephone, postage, etc.);

(f) the work of paid assistants or associates.

(2) *Each arbitrator should be guided by the following general principles:*

(a) *Per diem charges for a hearing should not be in excess of actual time spent or allocated for the hearing.*

(b) *Per diem charges for study time should not be in excess of actual time spent.*

(c) *Any fixed ratio of study days to hearing days, not agreed to specifically by the parties, is inconsistent with the per diem method of charges for services.*

(d) *Charges for expenses must not be in excess of actual expenses normally reimbursable and incurred in connection with the case or cases involved.*

(e) *When time or expense are involved for two or more sets of parties on the same day or trip, such time or expense charges should be appropriately prorated.*

(f) *An arbitrator may stipulate in advance a minimum charge for a hearing without violation of (a) or (e) above.*

(3) *An arbitrator on the active roster of an administrative agency must file with the agency his or her individual bases for determination of fees and expenses if the agency so requires. Thereafter, it is the responsibility of each such arbitrator to advise the agency promptly of any change in any basis for charges.*

Such filing may be in the form of answers to a questionnaire devised by an agency or by any other method adopted by or approved by an agency.

Having supplied an administrative agency with the information noted above, an arbitrator's professional responsibility of disclosure under this Code with respect to fees and expenses has been satisfied for cases referred by that agency.

(4) *If an administrative agency promulgates specific standards with respect to any of these matters which are in addition to or more*

restrictive than an individual arbitrator's standards, an arbitrator on its active roster must observe the agency standards for cases handled under the auspices of that agency, or decline to serve.

(5) *When an arbitrator is contacted directly by the parties for a case or cases, the arbitrator has a professional responsibility to respond to questions by submitting his or her bases for charges for fees and expenses.*

(6) *When it is known to the arbitrator that one or both of the parties cannot afford normal charges, it is consistent with professional responsibility to charge lesser amounts to both parties or to one of the parties if the other party is made aware of the difference and agrees.*

(7) *If an arbitrator concludes that the total of charges derived from his or her normal basis of calculation is not compatible with the case decided, it is consistent with professional responsibility to charge lesser amounts to both parties.*

2. An arbitrator must maintain adequate records to support charges for services and expenses and must make an accounting to the parties or to an involved administrative agency on request.

3. Responsibilities to Administrative Agencies

A. *General Responsibilities*

1. An arbitrator must be candid, accurate, and fully responsive to an administrative agency concerning his or her qualifications, availability, and all other pertinent matters.

2. An arbitrator must observe policies and rules of an administrative agency in cases referred by that agency.

3. An arbitrator must not seek to influence an administrative agency by any improper means, including gifts or other inducements to agency personnel.

a. It is not improper for a person seeking placement on a roster to request references from individuals have knowledge of the applicant's experience and qualifications.

b. Arbitrators should recognize that the primary responsibility of an administrative agency is to serve the parties.

4. Prehearing Conduct

1. All prehearing matters must be handled in a manner that fosters complete impartiality by the arbitrator.

a. The primary purpose of prehearing discussions involving the arbitrator is to obtain agreement on procedural matters so that the hearing can proceed without unnecessary obstacles. If differences of opinion should arise during such discussions and, particularly, if such differences appear to impinge on substantive matters, the circumstances will suggest whether the matter can be resolved informally or may require a prehearing conference or, more rarely, a formal preliminary hearing. When an administrative agency handles some or all aspects of the arrangements prior to a hearing, the arbitrator will become involved only if differences of some substance arise.

b. *Copies of any prehearing correspondence between the arbitrator and either party must be made available to both parties.*

5. Hearing Conduct

A. *General Principles*

1. An arbitrator must provide a fair and adequate hearing which assures that both parties have sufficient opportunity to present their respective evidence and argument.

a. *Within the limits of this responsibility, an arbitrator should conform to the various types of hearing procedures desired by the parties.*

b. An arbitrator may: encourage stipulations of fact; restate the substance of issues or arguments to promote or verify understanding; question the parties' representatives or witnesses, when necessary or advisable, to obtain additional pertinent information; and request that the parties submit additional evidence, either at the hearing or by subsequent filing.

c. *An arbitrator should not intrude into a party's presentation so as to prevent that party from putting forward its case fairly and adequately.*

B. *Transcripts or Recordings*

1. Mutual agreement of the parties as to use or non-use of a transcript must be respected by the arbitrator.

a. *A transcript is the official record of a hearing only when both parties agree to a transcript or an applicable law or regulation so provides.*

b. An arbitrator may seek to persuade the parties to avoid use of a transcript, or to use a transcript if the nature of the case appears to require one. *However, if an arbitrator intends to make his or her appointment to a case contingent on mutual agreement to a transcript, that requirement must be made known to both parties prior to appointment.*

c. If the parties do not agree to a transcript, an arbitrator may permit one party to take a transcript at its own cost. The arbitrator may also make appropriate arrangements under which the other party may have access to a copy, if a copy is provided to the arbitrator.

d. Without prior approval, an arbitrator may seek to use his or her own tape recorder to supplement note taking. The arbitrator should not insist on such a tape recording if either or both parties object.

C. *Ex Parte Hearings*

1. **In determining whether to conduct an ex parte hearing, an arbitrator must consider relevant legal, contractual, and other pertinent circumstances.**

2. **An arbitrator must be certain, before proceeding ex parte, that the party refusing or failing to attend the hearing has been given adequate notice of the time, place, and purposes of the hearing.**

D. *Plant Visits*

1. **An arbitrator should comply with a request of any party that he or she visit a work area pertinent to the dispute prior to, during, or after a hearing. An arbitrator may also initiate such a request.**

a. *Procedures for such visits should be agreed to by the parties in consultation with the arbitrator.*

E. *Bench Decisions or Expedited Awards*

1. **When an arbitrator understands, prior to acceptance of appointment, that a bench decision is expected at the conclusion of the hearing, the arbitrator must comply with the understanding unless both parties agree otherwise.**

a. *If notice of the parties' desire for a bench decision is not given prior to the arbitrator's acceptance of the case, issuance of such a bench decision is discretionary.*

b. *When only one party makes the request and the other objects, the arbitrator should not render a bench decision except under most unusual circumstances.*

2. When an arbitrator understands, prior to acceptance of appointment, that a concise written award is expected within a stated time period after the hearing, the arbitrator must comply with the understanding unless both parties agree otherwise.

6. Post Hearing Conduct

A. *Post Hearing Briefs and Submissions*

1. An arbitrator must comply with mutual agreements in respect to the filing or nonfiling of post hearing briefs or submissions.

a. An arbitrator, in his or her discretion, may either suggest the filing of post hearing briefs or other submissions or suggest that none be filed.

b. When the parties disagree as to the need for briefs, an arbitrator may permit filing but may determine a reasonable time limitation.

2. An arbitrator must not consider a post hearing brief or submission that has not been provided to the other party.

B. *Disclosure of Terms of Award*

1. An arbitrator must not disclose a prospective award to either party prior to its simultaneous issuance to both parties or explore possible alternative awards unilaterally with one party, unless both parties so agree.

a. Partisan members of tripartite boards may know prospective terms of an award in advance of its issuance. Similar situations may exist in other less formal arrangements mutually agreed to by the parties. In any such situation, the arbitrator should determine and observe the mutually desired degree of confidentiality.

C. *Awards and Opinions*

1. The award should be definite, certain, and as concise as possible.

    a. When an opinion is required, factors to be considered by an arbitrator include: desirability of brevity, consistent with the nature of the case and any expressed desires of the parties; need to use a style and form that is understandable to responsible representatives of the parties, to the grievant and supervisors, and to others in the collective bargaining relationship; necessity of meeting the significant issues; forthrightness to an extent not harmful to the relationship of the parties; and avoidance of gratuitous advice or discourse not essential to disposition of the issues.

D. *Clarification or Interpretation of Awards*

    1. No clarification or interpretation of an award is permissible without the consent of both parties.
    2. Under agreements which permit or require clarification or interpretation of an award, an arbitrator must afford both parties an opportunity to be heard.

E. *Enforcement of Award*

    1. The arbitrator's responsibility does not extend to the enforcement of an award.
    2. In view of the professional and confidential nature of the arbitration relationship, an arbitrator should not voluntarily participate in legal enforcement proceedings.

Suggested Reading

Aaron, Benjamin, et al. *The Future of Labor Arbitration in America*. New York: American Arbitration Association, 1976.

Coulson, Robert. *Labor Arbitration*. 2d ed. New York: American Arbitration Association, 1978.

Cox, Archibald. "Reflections Upon Labor Arbitration." 72 *Harvard Law Review* 1482 (1959).

——*Dispute Resolution Training*. Edited by Charlotte Gold and Ruth E. Lyons. New York: American Arbitration Association, 1978.

Elkouri, Frank, and Edna Elkouri. *How Arbitration Works*. 3d ed. Washington: BNA Books, 1973.

Fairweather, Owen. *Practice and Procedure in Labor Arbitration*. 2d ed. Washington: BNA Books, 1983.

Fleming, R. W. *The Labor Arbitration Process*. Urbana: University of Illinois Press, 1965.

Hill, Marvin, and Anthony V. Sinicropi. *Evidence in Arbitration*. Washington: BNA Books, 1980.

Kagel, Sam. *Anatomy of a Labor Arbitration*. Washington: BNA Books, 1961.

Meltzer, Bernard D. "Ruminations About Ideology, Law and Labor Arbitration." 34 *University of Chicago Law Review* 545 (1967).

Prasow, Peter, and Edward Peters. *Arbitration and Collective Bargaining*. New York: McGraw-Hill, 1970.

Proceedings of the Annual Meetings of the National Academy of Arbitrators. Washington: BNA Books, 1948–

Schulman, Harry. "Reason, Contract and Law in Labor Relations." 68 *Harvard Law Review* 999 (1955).

Teple, Edwin R., and Robert B. Moberly. *Arbitration and Conflict Resolution*. Washington: BNA Books, 1979.

Updegraff, Clarence M. *Arbitration and Labor Relations*. 3d ed. Washington: BNA Books, 1970.

Zack, Arnold M., and Richard I. Bloch. *Labor Agreement in Negotiation and Arbitration*. Washington: BNA Books, 1983.

Index

Wingspread Conference,
     Second   245
Wirtz, W. Willard   369–392
Wisconsin arbitration statute   95
Witnesses
  affidavits from   89–91, 488, 493
  credibility of, sample case   197–
     216
  sequestration of   63
  subpoena of   80, 187
  swearing of   58–59, 82, 487,
     493

Work assignments   313–324, 335–
     340
Work week   453–459
Workers' compensation, waiver
     of   330–335

XYZ

Zack, Arnold   111–134, 217–227,
     232, 234–236
Zimny, Max   185n, 193–196